# NCLEX-RN®
# Content Review Guide

SIXTH EDITION

KAPLAN NURSING

Judy Hyland, MSN, RN

*Executive Director of Nursing*

Barbara Arnoldussen, MBA, RN

Judith A. Burckhardt, PhD, RN

Barbara Dobish, MSN, RN

Cindy Finesilver, MSN, RN

Pamela Gardner, MSN, RN

Barbara J. Irwin, MSN, RN

Ellen Mahoney, CS, DNS, RN

Marlene Redemske, MSN, MA, RN

# Table Of Contents

# Introduction

Welcome! By using Kaplan Nursing resources, you've taken an important step toward passing the National Council Licensure Examination for Registered Nurses (NCLEX-RN®* examination).

Our many years of experience indicate that your success on the NCLEX-RN® examination is keyed to two specific factors: your educational background and your preparation for the exam. It is the amount and intensity of study you devote that will earn you the greatest benefit from the resources. The best results come to those who actively participate in exam preparation. We will show you how the NCLEX-RN® examination works, what you do and don't need to know, and the smartest way to take the NCLEX-RN® examination. We provide you with data to help you analyze your practice performance and determine where you need to make improvements. We will give you all the help, advice, and encouragement we can, but only you can do the work. Get to know all the benefits that Kaplan Nursing has to offer so you can make the most of your study time.

After you complete your resources and take the NCLEX-RN® examination, please tell us how you did. Kaplan's Research and Curriculum Development Team works hard to ensure that our course materials employ the most effective and innovative teaching methods. In order to evolve and improve, we need your help. Please take a few moments to share your thoughts on how the materials helped you. Thank you in advance for choosing Kaplan for your studies.

KAPLAN
750 Third Avenue,
New York, NY 10017
Attn: NCLEX Curriculum

customer.care@kaplan.com (kaptest.com)
integrated.support@kaplan.com (nursing.kaplan.com)

Our best wishes for an interesting and satisfying nursing career.

*NCLEX is a trademark of N.C.S.B.N., Inc.

Chapter 1

# THE NCLEX–RN® EXAMINATION

**Section**

Have you talked to graduate nurses about their experiences taking the NCLEX-RN® exam? They probably told you that the test wasn't like any nursing test they had ever taken. How can that be? The NCLEX-RN® exam is primarily multiple-choice test questions, and as a nursing student you are used to taking multiple-choice tests. In fact, you've taken so many tests by the time you graduate from nursing school that you probably believe there can't be any surprises on a nursing test. Yet there is one more surprise waiting for you, and it is called the NCLEX-RN® exam.

The NCLEX-RN® exam is similar to other standardized exams in some ways, yet different in others:

- The NCLEX-RN® exam is written by nurse specialists who are experts in a content area of nursing.
- All content is selected to allow the beginning practitioner to prove minimum competency on all areas of the test plan.
- NCLEX-RN® questions are written at 4 different levels based on Bloom's Taxonomy for the Cognitive Domain: knowledge, understanding, application, and analysis.
- Minimum competency questions are the passing level questions. They are asked at the application level, not the knowledge level. All the responses to a question are similar in length and subject matter and are grammatically correct.
- All test items have been extensively tested. National Council knows that the questions are valid; all correct responses are documented in two different sources.

What does this mean for you?

- National Council defines what is minimum-competency, entry-level nursing.
- Questions and answers are written in such a way that you will not be able to predict or recognize the correct answer.
- National Council is knowledgeable about the strategies regarding length of answers, grammar, etc. They make sure you can't use these strategies to select correct answers. English majors have no advantage!
- The answer choices have been extensively tested. The people who write the test questions make the incorrect answer choices look attractive to the unwary test-taker.

## ▶ WHAT BEHAVIORS DOES THE NCLEX-RN® EXAMINATION TEST?

The NCLEX-RN® exam does not want to test your body of nursing knowledge; it assumes you have a body of knowledge because you have graduated from nursing school. Likewise, it does not want to test your understanding of the material; it assumes you understand the nursing knowledge you learned in nursing school. So what does this exam test?

The NCLEX-RN® exam primarily tests your nursing judgment and discretion. It tests your ability to think critically and solve problems. The test writers recognize that as a beginning practitioner you will be managing LPNs/LVNs and nursing assistants to provide care to a group of clients. As the leader of the nursing team, you are expected to make safe and competent judgments about client care.

## ▶ CRITICAL THINKING AND CLINICAL JUDGMENT

What does the term critical thinking mean? Critical thinking is problem solving that involves thinking creatively.

Using clinical judgment, you successfully solve problems every day in the clinical area. You are probably comfortable with this concept when actually caring for clients. Although you've had lots of practice critically thinking in the clinical area, you may have had less practice thinking critically and using clinical judgment on test questions. Why is that?

During nursing school, you take exams developed by nursing faculty to test a specific body of content. Many of these questions are at the knowledge level. This involves recognition and recall of ideas or material that you read in your nursing textbooks and discussed in class. This is the most basic level of testing.

In nursing school, you are also given test questions written at the comprehension level. These questions require you to understand the meaning of the material. If you are answering minimum competency questions on the NCLEX-RN® exam, you will not see many comprehension-level questions. The test writers assume you know and understand the facts you learned in nursing school.

Minimum competency questions on the NCLEX-RN® exam are written at the application and/or analysis level. Remember, the exam tests your ability to make safe judgments about client care. Your ability to solve problems is not tested with knowledge- or comprehension-level questions. Application involves taking the facts that you know and using them to make a nursing judgment. You must be able to answer questions at the application level to prove your competence on the NCLEX-RN® exam.

## ▶ STRATEGIES THAT DON'T WORK ON THE NCLEX-RN® EXAMINATION

Whether you realize it or not, you developed a set of strategies in nursing school to answer teacher-generated test questions that are written at the knowledge/comprehension level. These strategies include:

- "Cramming" hundreds of facts about disease processes and nursing care
- Recognizing and recalling facts, rather than understanding the pathophysiology and the needs of a client with an illness
- Knowing who wrote the question and what is important to that faculty
- Predicting answers based on what you remember
- Selecting the response that is a different length compared with the other choices
- Selecting the answer choice that is grammatically correct
- When in doubt, choosing answer choice C

## ▶ CRITICAL THINKING AND CLINICAL JUDGMENT ON THE NCLEX-RN® EXAMINATION

- The NCLEX-RN® exam is not a test about recognizing facts.
- You must be able to correctly identify what the question is asking.
- Only focus on background information that is necessary to answer the question.

Remember, the NCLEX-RN® exam tests your ability to think critically. Critical thinking for the nurse involves:

- Observation
- Deciding what is important
- Looking for patterns and relationships
- Identifying the problem
- Transferring knowledge from one situation to another
- Applying knowledge
- Discriminating between possible choices and/or courses of action
- Evaluating according to established criteria

## ▶ FACTS ABOUT THE NCLEX-RN® EXAMINATION

### The Purpose of the Exam
- To determine if you are a safe and competent nurse
- To safeguard the public
- To test for minimum competency to practice nursing

### Test Content

- Based on the knowledge and activities of an entry-level nurse
- Written by nursing faculty and clinical specialists
- Majority of questions are self-contained, multiple-choice questions with four possible answer choices
- Some questions may ask you to select all answers that apply, fill in the blank, listen to an audio item, or answer questions that include graphics
- Some questions may ask you to use the mouse to identify a location on a graphic, drag and drop answers from an unordered answer column to an ordered answer column, or click on an exhibit tab
- Based on integrated nursing content—not on the medical model of medical, surgical, obstetrics, pediatrics, and psychiatric nursing
- Includes 15 experimental questions being tested for future exams; these questions do not count

### Administration of the CAT

- The CAT (Computer Adaptive Test) is adapted to your knowledge, skills, and ability level.
- The question sequence is determined interactively.
- The computer selects questions based on the item difficulty and the test plan.
- You individually schedule a date and time to take the exam at a testing center.
- You sit at an individual computer station.

### Taking the Exam

- Computer knowledge is not required to take this exam.
- You use a mouse to highlight and lock in your answer.
- You receive instructions and a practice exercise before beginning the exam.
- Any necessary background information appears on the screen with the question.
- The computer selects a first question on or around the passing level.
- The next question is selected by the computer on the basis of your response to the first question. If you receive a question that is similar to a question already answered, do not assume that you answered the first question incorrectly. Select the BEST answer to every question.
- If your answer is correct, the next question requires a higher level of critical thinking.
- If your answer is incorrect, the next question requires a lower level of critical thinking.
- Questions are selected to precisely measure your ability in each area of the test plan.

## Timing

- There is no time limit for each individual question.
- You will answer a minimum of 75 questions to a maximum of 265 questions.
- The maximum time for the exam is 6 hours, including the practice exercise and all breaks.
- A pop-up window appears reminding you to take a break after 2 hours and 3.5 hours of testing. The time continues to run during all breaks.

The exam will end:

- When the computer has determined your ability, or
- When a maximum of 6 hours of testing is reached, or
- When a maximum of 265 questions have been answered.

## Scoring

- It is a pass/fail exam.
- You are required to choose an answer before the computer will provide your next question. Take your best educated guess if you have to.
- The 15 experimental questions are not counted.

## Concerns

- You can't change answers once you select NEXT. Questions are selected by the computer according to the accuracy of your previous responses.
- You can't scroll back.
- You can't skip a question. You must answer the question to go on.

## Advantages

- Testing is available year-round, 15 hours a day, 6 days a week, in 6-hour time slots.
- Results are released by the individual State (Province or Territory) Board; length of time before you receive results will vary by State (Province or Territory) Board.
- If you fail, your state will determine when you can re-test.

## ▶ WHAT THE NCLEX-RN® EXAMINATION TESTS: CLIENT NEEDS

- Safe and Effective Care
    Management of Care (17–23%)
    Safety and Infection Control (9–15%)
- Health Promotion and Maintenance (6–12%)
- Psychosocial Integrity (6–12%)
- Physiological Integrity
    Basic Care and Comfort (6–12%)
    Pharmacological and Parenteral Therapies (12–18%)
    Reduction of Risk Potential (9–15%)
    Physiological Adaptation (11–17%)

## ▶ REGISTRATION

Registration information is available from your State (Province or Territory) Board of Nursing or your nursing school senior advisor. To obtain the address and phone number of an individual State Board of Nursing, contact:

National Council of State Boards of Nursing
111 E. Wacker Drive
Suite 2900
Chicago, IL 60601-4277
www.ncsbn.org

# Chapter 2

## KAPLAN'S REVIEW FOR THE NCLEX-RN® EXAMINATION

### Sections

1. Kaplan's NCLEX-RN® Course Materials

2. How to Use Kaplan's NCLEX-RN® Online Study Center Resources

3. Kaplan's RN Decision Tree

4. Guide for Test-Takers Repeating the NCLEX-RN® Examination

This chapter is for students enrolled in a Kaplan NCLEX-RN® Review Course.

If you are interested in the Kaplan NCLEX-RN® Course, start at kaptest.com

# KAPLAN'S NCLEX-RN® COURSE MATERIALS

You have chosen the best course to prepare for the NCLEX-RN® exam. It is important that you take advantage of all the resources found in Kaplan's Review Course to ensure your success on the exam.

Familiarize yourself with all of the material so you can prepare a study plan that fits into your schedule. Access to online study center resources start after payment has been received and for 3 months after your class begins. Since most students test within 8 weeks of graduation, Kaplan has designed a schedule that continues for 8 weeks after class ends.

## ▶ MATERIALS FOR KAPLAN'S NCLEX-RN® REVIEW COURSE

(Available 24 hours a day, 7 days a week during your enrollment period)

### Phase One: Content Review

Orientation to Kaplan's NCLEX-RN® Review Course
- Learn about Kaplan's NCLEX-RN® Review Course
- Explains how to use online assets

Pathway to Success Videos
- Learn how to think your way through the types of questions you will see on the NCLEX-RN® exam
- Establish a way to approach application- and analysis-level questions

Kaplan's Strategy Seminar for the NCLEX-RN® Examination
- Learn what you need to know about the NCLEX-RN® exam

Diagnostic Exam
- 180-question online exam that evaluates your strengths and weaknesses
- Indicates areas of the NCLEX-RN® test plan in which you will need concentrated study

NCLEX-RN® Content Review Guide
- Review frequently tested, minimum-competency nursing content
- Read content sections before class or study session

Video Review of Content
- Guided review of essential nursing content for success on the NCLEX-RN® exam
- Review the content as often as required

### Phase Two: Learn How to Answer High-Level Critical Thinking Questions

RN Decision Tree
- Kaplan's critical thinking framework based on clinical nursing judgment
- Enables candidates to correctly answer application/analysis questions utilizing critical thinking

### Class Lessons

- Learn how to apply your nursing knowledge to answer questions similar to those on the actual exam
- Discuss critical thinking and clinical judgment specific to the NCLEX-RN® exam
- Review exam-style questions using Kaplan's RN Decision Tree to ensure success on the NCLEX-RN® examination

### Review of Questions

- Guided review of questions using Kaplan's RN Decision Tree; includes explanations of correct and incorrect responses
- Master critical thinking by repeating and/or reviewing the questions at your own pace

### NCLEX-RN® Practice Test

- 60-Question Test (60 questions is the minimum for a computer decision. Remember: 15 of the first 75 are pretest, non-scored items.)
- Designed using the NCSBN test plan

### Roadmap to Success

- Understand the importance of self regulation
- Review selected questions from the RN Practice Test
- Develop your study plan

## *Phase Three: Practice*

### The Question Trainers

- 1,000+ practice questions divided into 7 tests
- Provides practice with exam-style questions
- Review the explanations for correct and incorrect answers
- Includes alternate question types

### Qbank

- 2000+  exam-style questions
- Create customized practice tests
-  4 sample tests (one with all alternate format style questions)
- Receive immediate on-screen feedback
- Review detailed explanations of correct and incorrect answers

### Readiness Test

- 180 Application and Analysis Level Question Test
- Complete 1 week before your scheduled NCLEX Examination
- Review and remediate every question

# HOW TO USE KAPLAN'S NCLEX-RN® ONLINE STUDY CENTER RESOURCES

Whether you take the Kaplan NCLEX-RN® Review Live, Live Online, or On Demand, Kaplan's NCLEX-RN® course offers many resources to ensure your success on the exam. These resources include the *NCLEX-RN® Content Review Guide*, review of exam-style questions, and the online study center. To make the best use of your NCLEX-RN® course, follow these steps and keep track of what you have accomplished.

This is the recommended study plan for utilizing the Kaplan NCLEX-RN® Prep resources. These resources are designed to give you plenty of realistic practice for success on test day. As you begin your preparation, please keep in mind that preparing for the NCLEX-RN® is a marathon, not a sprint! It is important to not rush your studies, but also not to procrastinate.

While you are utilizing the Kaplan NCLEX-RN® Prep resources, it is important that you follow these steps: analyze, review/remediate, think, study, and then continue practicing. Thoughtful review is the key to your NCLEX-RN® success.

## ▶ PHASE ONE: PRIOR TO YOUR KAPLAN NCLEX REVIEW COURSE

Phase one of the course is designed to help you establish and review the essential nursing knowledge content. This content provides the base for you to move to the higher-level critical thinking questions.

As you are completing tests, look at your **Analysis** page to see how you performed on each test. Aim for a score of 65 percent or higher *(Institutional students: your school may require higher.)* Use the test analyses to identify the client need categories where you scored the lowest. Use the **Test Reflection Worksheet** as you ask yourself the following, and assess how you are thinking:

1. Did I change any answers? Which way: correct to incorrect, or incorrect to correct?
2. Did I take enough time on each question or did I take too much time on each question?
3. Did I lose concentration, and if so, is there a pattern? Did I need to take a break?

**Review/remediate** all questions. Ask yourself the following:

1. Did I not know the content of the question?
2. For questions I answered incorrectly, why did the author of this question choose one answer, and why did I choose another?

Use the **Essential Nursing Content/Review of Content Videos** and your *NCLEX-RN® Content Review Guide* eBook to fill in any knowledge gaps, working from your content need area of greatest weakness toward your area of greatest strength.

Remember the goal of this phase: build and review <u>essential</u> nursing content.

## ▶ PHASE TWO: DECISION TREE, KAPLAN NCLEX REVIEW COURSE

Kaplan's review course consists of 7 three-hour sessions led by one of our expert nurse educators. Your review will concentrate on helping you answer passing-level NCLEX questions utilizing the Decision Tree and your clinical judgment skills in order to ensure success on test day.

While the structure of the lectures is not content focused, you will receive high-yield content tips while reviewing NCLEX-style questions in class.

In the second to last session (7/8) you will complete the **RN Practice Test.** Part of Session Eight is designed to review some of these questions with you.

Remember the goal of this phase: learn and review the Decision Tree process to answer high-level critical thinking questions. These questions are the passing-level questions of the NCLEX-RN® examination.

## ▶ PHASE THREE: AFTER ATTENDING THE KAPLAN NCLEX REVIEW COURSE

The goal of phase three is practice, practice, practice. The key to your practice is to take the time to review, remediate, and think about how you performed on the test you completed. Identify patterns that you need to change to become more successful on the next test.

Continue to look at your **Analysis** page to see how you performed on each of these tests and **continue to review/remediate** <u>all</u> questions. For Question Trainers 4 and 5, aim for scores of 65 percent or higher. For Question Trainers 6, 7, and the Qbank, aim for scores of 60 percent or higher *(Institutional students: your school may require higher on any of these resources.)*

Use the **Test Reflection Worksheet** and ask yourself:

1. Did I use the Decision Tree?
2. Am I seeing improvement as I progress from test to test?
3. Am I assessing <u>how I am thinking</u>?
4. Did I take a break at the best time for me?

Continue to use the **Online Content Lectures/***Review of Content Videos* and your *NCLEX-RN ® Content Review Guide* eBook to fill in any knowledge gaps, working from your content need area of greatest weakness toward your area of greatest strength.

**You should complete all Question Trainers, Qbank questions, and review/remediate all questions before you take the NCLEX.**

The day before your test, rest your mind and exercise your body. You are embarking upon the final step towards beginning your exciting new career as a nurse!

**Additional Resources**

The **Orientation, Decision Tree,** and **Review Class Questions/***Review of Questions* videos revisit information covered in the Review Course. Additional guidance on formulating your study plan leading up to your NCLEX test date can be found in Chapter 2 of the *NCLEX-RN® Content Review Guide* eBook. You can email NCLEX-Expert@kaplan.com for specific questions on the Decision Tree or using critical thinking to answer the question correctly.

# ▶ STUDY SCHEDULE

Designing your study schedule is a process that only you can do. Consideration of your work, family, and personal time mixed with your study time can only be determined by you. We provide you with a process of creating the schedule, but you have to prioritize your time and fill in the calendar.

Plan a test date that allows you adequate time to complete all of Kaplan's questions prior to testing. Stick closely to your schedule. Delaying test dates can negatively affect your outcome on the NCLEX-RN® exam. (See research at https://www.ncsbn.org/delaystudy2006.pdf)

Not completing all the recommended requirements also may affect your outcome.

**How to create your study plan:** (This process is also in session eight of the class videos)

**Timing for Kaplan NCLEX-RN® Resources**

| RESOURCE | APPROXIMATE TIME TO COMPLETE | APPROXIMATE TIME TO REVIEW |
|---|---|---|
| **Phase 1** | | |
| Diagnostic Test | 3 hours | 9 hours |
| Trainer 1 | 1.5 hours | 4.5 hours |
| Trainer 2 | 1.5 hours | 4.5 hours |
| Trainer 3 | 2 hours | 6 hours |
| Content Videos | 30 hours | |
| *RN Content Review Guide* | Determine how long it will take **you** to read this resource | |
| **Phase 2** | | |
| Sessions 1–6 and 8 | 21 hours | |
| Session 7 NCLEX-RN® Practice Test | 1.2 hours | 3.6 hours |
| **Phase 3** | | |
| Trainer 4 | 3 hours | 9 hours |
| Trainer 5 | 3 hours | 9 hours |
| Trainer 6 | 4 hours | 12 hours |
| Trainer 7 | 6 hours | 18 hours |
| 26–75q Qbank tests | 1.5 hrs each (39 hrs) | 4.5 hrs each (117 hrs) |
| Readiness Test | 3 hours | 9 hours |
| Total | | approximately: 319 hours |
| Do NOT study the 24 hours before your test. Let your mind rest! | | |

**FIRST METHOD:** Use this to choose your date based on how much time **you** require to prepare. This is the method we recommend.

1. How many days a week can you study? *Example: 5 days a week*
2. How many hours a day can you focus on studying? *Example: 6 hours a day*
3. Multiply your answer from #1 by #2. *Example: 5 x 6 = 30 hours/ week*
4. Divide the total number of hours from the study guide by the numbers of hours you have a week. *Example: 260/30 = 8.7 weeks needed to prepare*
5. Set your date that many weeks from now. *Example: 8 weeks from now*

**SECOND METHOD:** If you have a date picked out, use this method to determine how many hours a week you have to prepare.

1. How many weeks from today until your test date?
   - *Example: My test is in 5 weeks.*
2. Divide the total hours needed for preparation by the number of weeks you have until your test date.
   - *Example: 260/5 weeks = 52 hours/week*

- Ask yourself, can you study 52 hours a week?
- If not, consider moving your test date.

3. Divide the hours per week you got in step 2 by the number of days a week you have available to study.
   - *Example: I can study 5 days a week.*
   - 52 hours a week/ 5 days = 10.4 hours a day
   - Ask yourself, can you study 10.4 hours a day?
   - If not, consider moving your test date.

4. Calendar Example: Put in your time just like a class.
   *Example: studying 6 hours a day for 6 days a week.*

| Sun | Mon | Tues | Wed | Thur | Fri | Sat |
|-----|-----|------|-----|------|-----|-----|
| Off | 9–12<br>1–4 | 9–12<br>1–4 | 9–12<br>1–5 | 9–12<br>1–4 | 9–12<br>1–4 | 10–1<br>2–5 |

5. Your study plan will look different from everyone else's because you have different work and family needs and study preferences. Use your critical thinking to achieve the best study plan for you.

## ▶ REVIEWING QUESTIONS

Use the **Test Reflection Worksheet to help you review and remediate each test and every question.** Make sure to review the rationales to all the questions answered. Review the questions you answered correctly to reinforce successful critical thinking. Review the questions you missed to learn from your mistakes. To identify why you missed questions, ask yourself these questions:

1. **Did you miss the question because you did not know the content?**

   If so, look up the content immediately. Focus on understanding the concepts and principles rather than trying to memorize content.

2. **Did you miss the question because you did not correctly identify the topic of the question?**

   You know you have misidentified the topic if you are reading the rationale and it is about a topic you did not consider. Look carefully at the stem of the question and the answers to determine the topic. Refer to the Decision Tree.

3. **Did you miss the question even though you correctly identified the topic?**

   Use all the steps of the Decision Tree. Many times students will choose the second best answer because they did not recognize the patterns found in the answer choices. Another reason students answer questions incorrectly is because they do not thoughtfully consider each answer choice. Slow down and THINK!

## ▶ MONEY-BACK GUARANTEE

If you are a kaptest.com student and graduate of an NLN or CCNE-accredited nursing program taking the exam for the first time within 6 months of graduation, and you do not pass the NCLEX-RN® exam, you are entitled to either a 100% tuition refund or a free 3-month continuation of your enrollment. If you are an Institutional Program student, check the school policy.

You must meet the following eligibility criteria:

- Take the Kaplan Diagnostic and Readiness Tests from your online account.
- Attend all class sessions: Live, Live Online, or On Demand. Up to 2 live Classroom sessions can be made up online.
- Answer all questions on the 7 Question Trainer tests.

To qualify for the 100% tuition refund, you must not access the Online Study Center resources after the date of your NCLEX-RN® exam. The money-back guarantee applies ONLY to the original 3- month enrollment, and does not apply to any enrollment renewal. You must call 1-800-KAP-TEST within 20 days of the date of your NCLEX-RN® exam for instructions.

# KAPLAN'S RN DECISION TREE

The RN Decision Tree is Kaplan Nursing's critical thinking framework to answer application/analysis nursing test questions. Your Kaplan instructor will teach you how to use the Decision Tree and will use it when reviewing test questions. Open your book to these pages when you practice answering questions or print the Decision Tree Poster. Consistently use the Decision Tree to be successful on the NCLEX-RN® exam.

## Step 1: Can you identify the topic of the question?

**No**

Trap: NCLEX-RN® "hides" the topic of the question.

**Yes**

Read answer choices for clues.
Identify the topic of the question.
Proceed to **Step 2.**

Proceed to **Step 2.**

## Step 2: Are the answers assessments or implementations?

A mix of assessments and implementations?

Trap: Is validation required?

Are answers all assessment or implementation?

Read stem to determine if you should assess or implement.

Proceed to **Step 3.**

**Select correct answer.**

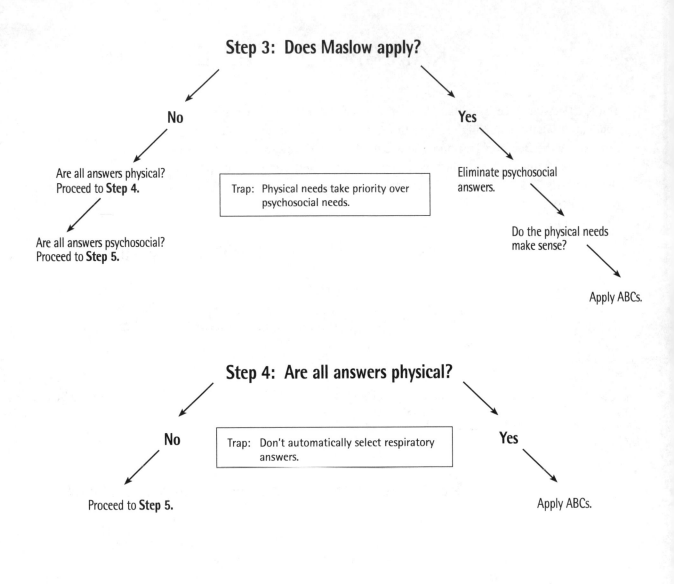

## Step 3: Does Maslow apply?

**No**

Are all answers physical?
Proceed to **Step 4.**

Are all answers psychosocial?
Proceed to **Step 5.**

Trap:  Physical needs take priority over
psychosocial needs.

**Yes**

Eliminate psychosocial
answers.

Do the physical needs
make sense?

Apply ABCs.

## Step 4:  Are all answers physical?

**No**

Trap:  Don't automatically select respiratory
answers.

**Yes**

Proceed to **Step 5.**

Apply ABCs.

## Step 5:  What is the outcome of each of the remaining answers?

Trap:  Don't select answers that "sound" right.

Determine outcome of each answer.  Is it desired?

**Select correct answer.**

# GUIDE FOR TEST-TAKERS REPEATING THE NCLEX-RN® EXAMINATION

Some people may never have to read this section, but it's a certainty that others will. The most important advice we can give to repeat test-takers is: don't despair. There is hope. We can get you through the NCLEX-RN® exam. Contact nclex-expert@kaplan.com to assist you if you purchased the Kaplan Review Course to begin the next path to success.

## You Are Not Alone

Think about that awful day when your envelope arrived. You just couldn't believe it. You had to tell family, friends, your supervisor, and coworkers that you didn't pass. When this happens, each unsuccessful candidate feels like they are the only person that failed the exam.

## Should You Test Again?

Absolutely! You completed your nursing education to become an RN. The initial response of many unsuccessful candidates is to declare, "I'm never going back! That was the worst experience of my life! What do I do now?" When you first received your results, you went through a period of grieving—the same stages that you learned about in nursing school. Three to four weeks later, you find that you want to begin preparing to retake the exam.

## How to Interpret Unsuccessful Test Results

Most unsuccessful candidates on the NCLEX-RN® exam will usually say, "I almost passed." Some of you did almost pass, and some of you weren't very close. If you fail the exam, you will receive a Candidate Performance Report from National Council. In this report, you will be told how many questions you answered on the exam. The more questions you answered, the closer you came to passing. The only way you will continue to get questions after you answer the first 75 is if you are answering questions close to the level of difficulty needed to pass the exam. If you answered questions far below the level needed to pass, your exam will end.

Figure 1 shows a representation of what happens when a candidate fails in 75 questions. This student does not come close to passing. In 75 questions, this student demonstrates an inability to consistently answer questions correctly at or above the level of difficulty needed to pass the exam. This usually indicates a lack of nursing knowledge, considerable difficulties with taking a standardized test, or a deficiency in critical thinking skills.

**Figure 1**

Figure 2 shows what happens when a candidate takes all 265 questions and fails. This candidate "almost passed." If the last question is below the level of difficulty needed to pass, the candidate fails.

**Figure 2**

If the last question is above the level of difficulty needed to pass, the candidate passes. If you took a test longer than 75 questions and failed, you were probably familiar with most of the content you saw on the exam, but you may have had difficulty using critical thinking skills or taking a standardized test.

The information contained on the Candidate Performance Report helps you identify your strengths and weaknesses on this particular NCLEX–RN® exam. This knowledge will help you identify where to concentrate your study when you prepare to retake the exam.

▶ ## COMMON PROBLEMS WITH THE NCLEX-RN®

**I saw nursing topics that were not familiar to me.**

Review the Candidate Performance Report and identify the client need areas where you were "below passing." Review your Kaplan test results and identify client need areas where your scores were below the benchmark score. If you purchased the Kaplan Preparation Course, review content using the content videos and review your *NCLEX-RN® Content Review Guide,* beginning with your weakest content areas and progressing to your stronger areas.

**I saw medications that were not familiar to me.**

It is difficult to memorize individual medications. Organize your study of medications based on the classification system. The pharmacology section in your *NCLEX-RN® Content Review Guide* is organized according to medication classifications. You will need to know the generic names of medications in each classification. As you read topics in your guide, if a medication is mentioned, look it up so you understand the context in which it is being used.

**I prepared for the exam just like I prepared for tests in nursing school.**

The purpose of the NCLEX-RN® exam is to test critical thinking and clinical judgment needed to safely care for clients in all health care settings. Passing-level questions on NCLEX-RN® are written at the application and analysis level. If you prepare for NCLEX-RN® by answering knowledge and comprehension questions, you are not using the type of thinking required. The Decision Tree, taught in the Kaplan Course, has been designed to act as a framework or guide to approach application and analysis level questions.

**I memorized facts without understanding the principles of client care.**

If you memorize facts about a disease process, that may not help you answer the questions on NCLEX-RN®. NCLEX-RN® tests the candidate's ability to prioritize, provide safe and effective nursing care, and evaluate the client's response to care. Understanding, not memorization, allows you to approach, analyze, and determine the best clinical judgment for each question.

**I was not sure about the type of questions I would see on NCLEX-RN®.**

Go to www.ncsbn.org and review the candidate information about the alternate-format item questions and the test plan for the exam. When you take Kaplan nursing tests, the questions are written at the level of difficulty needed to pass NCLEX-RN®. The NCLEX-RN® exam is testing your ability to critically think in complex client care situations.

**I did not understand Computer Adaptive Testing (CAT).**

Review the candidate information on www.ncsbn.org about Computer Adaptive Testing. When taking the NCLEX-RN® exam, the next question depends on only 2 things: first, whether you answered the previous question correctly or incorrectly, and second, the area of the test plan from which the next question must come to maintain the percentages in each area.

**I thought I would complete the exam with the minimum amount of questions.**

It is possible to pass or fail the test with the minimum or maximum amount of questions or anywhere in between the minimum or maximum number. The computer will continue to give you questions as long as you are around the passing line. You need to prepare to take the maximum number of questions. It's better to be prepared for longer and end up short, than the reverse. If you are getting questions, you are still in the game—stay focused!

**I began to lose my concentration when the computer continued to give me questions.**

If you lose your concentration, you need to recognize what's happening and regain your ability to concentrate. Take a mental break while sitting at the computer or leave the computer station for a short time. The Kaplan Course uses longer tests that allow you to get in mental shape. Follow the guidelines given for each test.

**I had difficulty identifying what the questions were asking.**

Take your time and read the question and answers. Do not try to answer a question without identifying the topic. Remember, you cannot answer the question until you are clear about what you are being asked.

**I did not carefully consider each answer choice.**

NCLEX questions are written so that you may like more than one answer. It is important to consider each answer choice before selecting an answer.

**I did not eliminate answers when I considered the answer choices.**

Eliminate answers you know are incorrect. If you are not sure about an answer, keep it in for consideration.

**I am not good at selecting answers that require me to establish priorities of care.**

When you are answering questions, think about answers that provide for client safety or reduce the risk of injury. Is gathering more data or implementation the best and most important action for the nurse to take? Do Maslow's hierarchy or the ABCs apply?

I answered the questions based on my "real world" experiences.

The NCLEX-RN® exam is based on "ivory-tower nursing." When you answer a question, think about what the author of a nursing text book would do. Do not consider what you do at work or what you see others doing.

When I thought 2 answer choices seemed correct, I did not know how to choose the correct one.

Read the question and then each answer choice. Think about priorities: client safety, Maslow, and the ABCs. There is only one best answer. If you can do only one thing and walk away, what will the outcome be for your client?

I began to believe I would not pass.

When you feel this coming on, you need to take a break and do some positive thinking. As long as the computer is still asking you questions, you are still in the running. Tell yourself you are doing okay. Repeat positive thinking statements. Refocus your brain on each question.

## *Evaluate Your CAT Experience*

Some students attribute their failure to the CAT experience. Comments we have heard include:

*"I didn't like answering questions on the computer."*

*"I found the background noise distracting."*

*"I looked up every time the door opened."*

*"I should have taken a snack. I got so hungry!"*

*"After two and a half hours I didn't care what I answered. I just wanted the computer to shut off!"*

*"I didn't expect to be there for four hours!"*

*"I should have rescheduled my test, but I just wanted to get it over with!"*

Do any of these comments sound familiar? It is important for you to take charge of your CAT experience. Here's how:

- Choose a familiar testing site.
- Select the time of day that you test your best. (Are you a morning or afternoon person?)
- Accept the earplugs when offered.
- Take a snack and a drink for your break.
- Take a break if you become distracted or fatigued during the test.
- Contact the proctors at the test site if something bothers you during the test.
- Plan on testing for six hours. If you get out early, it's a pleasant surprise.
- Say to yourself every day, "I will be successful."

After determining why you failed, the next step is to establish a plan of action for your next test. Remember, you should prepare differently this time.

Consider the following when setting up your new plan of study:

### You've Seen the Test

You may wish that you didn't have to walk back into the testing center again, but if you want to be a registered professional nurse, you must go back. But this time you have an advantage over a first time test taker: you've seen the test! You know exactly what you are preparing for, so there are no unknowns. The computer will remember what questions you took before, and you will not be given any of the same questions. But the content of the question, the style of the question, and the kinds of answer choices will not change. You will not be surprised this time.

### Study Both Content and Test Questions

By the time you retest, you will be out of nursing school for 3–6 months or longer. Remember that old saying, "What you are not learning, you are forgetting"? Because this exam is based on nursing as it is practiced in the United States and Canada, you must remember all you can about nursing theory and use sound clinical judgment to select the correct answers. You must study content that is integrated and organized like the NCLEX-RN® exam.

You must also master exam-style test questions. It is essential that you be able to correctly identify what each question is asking. You will not predict answers. You will think about each and every answer choice to decide if it answers the reworded question. To master test questions, you must practice answering them. We recommend you answer and review hundreds of exam-style test questions, especially at the application level of difficulty. The Kaplan Course provides all the high-level critical thinking question you will need to prepare.

### Know All of the Words and their Meanings

Some students who have to learn a great deal of material in a short period of time have trouble learning the extensive vocabulary of the discipline. For example, difficulty with terminology is a problem for even strong students who study history. They enjoy the concepts, but find it hard to memorize all of the names and dates that allow them to do well on history tests. If you are a student who has trouble memorizing terms, you may find it useful to review a list of the terminology you must know to pass the NCLEX-RN® exam.

### Practice Test-Taking Strategies

There is no substitute for mastering critical thinking and essential nursing content. But combining this knowledge with test-taking strategies, will help you select a greater number of correct answers. For many students, the strategies mean the difference between a passing test and a failing test. Using strategies effectively can also determine whether you take a short test (75 questions) or a longer test (up to 265 questions).

## *Test-Taking Strategies That Don't Work on the NCLEX-RN® Examination*

Whether you realize it or not, you developed a set of test-taking strategies in nursing school to answer teacher-generated test questions that are written at the knowledge/comprehension level of difficulty. These strategies include:

- "Cramming" hundreds of facts about disease processes and nursing care
- Recognizing and recalling facts rather than understanding the pathophysiology and the needs of a client with an illness
- Knowing who wrote the question and what is important to that instructor
- Predicting answers based on what you remember or who wrote the test question
- Selecting the response that is a different length compared to the other choices
- Selecting the answer choice that is grammatically correct
- When in doubt, choosing answer choice C

These strategies will not work because the NCLEX-RN® exam tests your ability to make safe, competent decisions.

## *Successful Test-Takers of the NCLEX-RN® Examination:*

- Have a good understanding of nursing content
- Have the ability to tackle each test question with a lot of confidence because they assume that they can figure out the right answer
- Don't give up if they are unsure of the answer; they are not afraid to think about the question and the possible choices in order to select the correct answer
- Possess the know-how to correctly identify the question
- Stay focused on the question
- Can pace themselves for a long test, and take a break when they need one

## *Unsuccessful Test-Takers of the NCLEX-RN® Examination:*

- Assume that they either know or don't know the answer to the question
- Memorize facts to answer questions by recall or recognition
- Read the question, read the answers, read the question, and pick an answer
- Choose answer choices based on a hunch or a feeling instead of thinking critically
- Answer questions based on personal experience rather than nursing theory
- Give up too soon because they aren't willing to think hard about questions and answers
- Don't stay focused on the question
- Push through questions without taking a break when they need one

Work to become a successful test-taker!

## ▶ PREPARE TO RETAKE THE NCLEX-RN® EXAMINATION

(Some resources are only available in the Kaplan NCLEX-RN® Review Course)

1.  **Evaluate your content knowledge.**

    Compare your individualized results from the Kaplan Diagnostic Test (course only) with the Candidate Performance Report you received from the National Council of State Boards of Nursing. What similarities are there in the two results? What differences are there? In which areas did you do well? In which areas do you need more study?

2.  **Think about your strong and weak areas.**

    You will note that both the Kaplan Diagnostic Test (course only) results and the National Council's Diagnostic Profile are organized according to the Categories of Client Needs. It is important that you have a comprehensive understanding of the concept of Client Needs.

3.  **Plan a study schedule.**

    Plan your study time to include all nursing content, but emphasize areas identified as weaknesses on the Kaplan Diagnostic exam (course only) and on your Candidate Performance Report from the National Council. Preparation for retaking the NCLEX-RN® exam should include a minimum of 4–6 weeks of concentrated study. Establish specific daily goals and reward yourself when you accomplish them. Don't let yourself fall behind.

4.  **Begin studying.**

    At first you may find it difficult to review the nursing content. You may find yourself saying, "I know this already." You may find yourself remembering the questions that were on your NCLEX-RN® exam. Forget them! You will not see any of the same questions when you retest. Focus your energy on understanding the nursing content.

5.  **Read the *NCLEX-RN® Content Review Guide*.**

    Begin with your areas of weakness and work toward your areas of strength. If you don't understand a word or have a question about a topic, look it up in your nursing school textbooks. Include these notes in your *NCLEX-RN® Content Review Guide*.

6.  **Watch the Essential Nursing Content Videos (course only).**

    Watch the essential nursing content video in the areas identified as weaknesses on your Candidate Performance Report. Take notes in the *NCLEX-RN® Content Review Guide* as you watch the content videos.

7.  **Review the Decision Tree. (Interested in the course? Start at kaptest.com.)**

    Kaplan developed the Decision Tree (course only) to provide you with the critical thinking framework and clinical judgment required to successfully answer passing level questions on the NCLEX-RN® exam. Make the commitment to use the Decision Tree when practicing questions in preparation for the NCLEX-RN® exam and when taking the actual exam.

8.  **Review Kaplan's Path to Success Videos. (course only)**

These ideas/practices are not a substitute for knowledge of nursing content, but will provide you with tools to utilize your nursing knowledge and answer application/analysis-level questions correctly.

9. **Review the recorded class lessons.** (course only; for some students this will be available after your in-class course)

The questions reviewed in these lessons are exam-style and of varying levels of difficulty. The discussion of the explanations to the questions does three things: first, it gives you the correct answer; second, it reviews the knowledge and thought processes that lead to the correct answer; third, it points out the wrong thinking behind the incorrect answer choices. If you have difficulty with a question, stop the recording and ask yourself why you missed the question. Did the question concern nursing knowledge you didn't know? Did you misread the question? Did you make an assumption or base your answer on what you have seen in the "real world" instead of "ivory tower nursing"? Was it a test-taking problem?

If there is content that you don't understand or don't remember, look it up.

10. **After you finish, go back and review your notes.**

Do you have a complete understanding of the content areas? If not, more study is needed.

11. **Practice with the Question Trainers.** (course only)

If your evaluation of your previous testing experience identified problems with the computer format of the exam, now is the time to work out any difficulties you experienced when taking the "real thing." Use these 7 practice tests to evaluate your knowledge of nursing content, practice your critical thinking skills, and become comfortable with the testing format.

12. **Practice with the Qbank.** (course only)

Build your confidence by using the Decision Tree to answer Qbank questions. You determine the content and select the number of questions contained in each test (at least 75 questions). Build your Qbank test from all 8 client need areas. This will enable you to consistently review essential nursing content. To make the most of your Qbank experience, only answer questions using "testing mode." Typically, students who use "tutor mode" answer more questions correctly because they view explanations prior to selecting answers. This does not, however, give you accurate feedback about how you are answering questions.

13. **Be Confident!**

Don't schedule to retake the NCLEX-RN® exam until you have allowed yourself sufficient time to prepare. Then, walk into the exam knowing that you are prepared and ready to pass. Take charge of your environment. Arrange the computer keyboard and light for comfort. Approach the exam like a marathon and ration your energy and effort. Be prepared to answer all 265 questions. If you lose your concentration, raise your hand and take a short break. Comprehensive preparation and a positive attitude are the ingredients for success on the NCLEX-RN® exam.

# Chapter 3

## PHYSIOLOGICAL INTEGRITY: PHARMACOLOGICAL AND PARENTERAL THERAPIES

| Sections | Concepts Covered |
|---|---|
| 1. Blood Component Therapy | Perfusion |
| 2. Intravenous Therapy | Fluid Balance |
| 3. Medications | Client Education: Providing |
| 4. Adverse Effects of Medications | Anaphylaxis |

# BLOOD COMPONENT THERAPY

**BLOOD COMPONENT THERAPY** *Section 1*

**A.** Procedure

1. Equipment

   a. Blood or blood products (see Table 1)

   b. Tubing with filter

   c. 19-gauge needle for venous access

| Table 1  BLOOD COMPONENTS | | |
|---|---|---|
| **PRODUCT** | **ADVERSE REACTIONS** | **NURSING CONSIDERATIONS** |
| Packed red blood cells | Reactions less common than with whole blood | Companion solution–0.9% NaCl Monitor client during transfusion Give over 2–4 h<br>Use standard blood filter<br>Mix cells every 20–30 minutes (squeeze bag)<br>Give over 2–4 h |
| Platelets | Some febrile reactions | Companion solution–0.9% NaCl<br>Nonwettable filter<br>Give as quickly as possible, 4 units/hour |
| Plasma | Circulatory overload risk | Administer with straight line set<br>Give as quickly as possible (coagulation factors become unstable) |
| Albumin | Possible circulatory overload | Use administration set provided<br>25% albumin–give at 1 mL/min<br>Give as quickly as possible if client in shock |
| Prothrombin | Hepatitis risk greater than with whole blood<br>Allergic/febrile reactions | Use straight line set |
| Factor VIII | Allergic and febrile reactions | Use component drip set or syringe |

2. Ask client about allergies or previous blood reactions

3. Type and cross-match blood—ensures that the donor's blood and recipient's blood are compatible (see Table 2)

| Table 2  BLOOD GROUP COMPATIBILITY | | |
| --- | --- | --- |
| **BLOOD GROUP** | **CAN ACT AS DONOR** | **CAN RECEIVE BLOOD FROM** |
| **O** | O, A, B, AB | O |
| **A** | A, AB | O, A |
| **B** | B, AB | O, B |
| **AB** | AB | O, A, B, AB |

4. Check blood for bubbles, dark color, or cloudiness

5. Check by two nurses

   a. Health care provider's order

   b. Client's identity

   c. Hospital ID band name and number

   d. Blood component tag name and number

   e. Blood type and Rh

6. Check baseline vital signs, including temperature

7. Start with normal saline (0.9% NaCl)

8. Run blood slowly for first 15 minutes

9. Stay with client for first 15–30 minutes after blood starts into the client

10. Recheck vital signs 15 minutes after infusion started

11. If no untoward effects, increase rate; should be infused in 2 hours for each unit (depending on client's cardiovascular status) (see Table 3)

12. Obtain vital signs every hour until completed, then hourly for 3 hours

13. For elderly check vital signs every 15 minutes throughout transfusion

14. For elderly infuse each unit over 3–4 hours

15. Ask client to report itching or flank pain over kidneys

16. Change entire IV line for each unit of blood.

17. If transfusion reaction suspected

   a. Stop blood or blood product

   b. Restart normal saline

   c. Save blood container and tubing and return to blood bank

   d. Draw blood sample for plasma, hemoglobin, culture, retyping

   e. Collect urine sample and send to lab for hemoglobin determination

   f. Monitor voiding for hematuria

**B.** Autologous transfusion

1. Preoperative donation collected 4–6 weeks before surgery

2. Iron supplements may be ordered

Per unit of blood, change whole IV line

3. Benefits
    a. Prevention of viral infection from donated blood
    b. Used for clients with history of transfusion reactions
    c. Rare blood type
4. Contraindications ✱ *for autologous donation*
    a. Acute infection
    b. Chronic disease
    c. Hemoglobin less than 11 g/L, hematocrit less than 33%
    d. Cerebrovascular disease
    e. Cardiovascular disease

| TYPE OF REACTION | CAUSE | SYMPTOMS | NURSING CONSIDERATIONS |
|---|---|---|---|
| Allergic reaction Hypersensitivity | Hypersensitivity to antibodies in donor's blood | Occurs immediately or within 24 hours<br>Mild—urticaria, itching, flushing<br>Anaphylaxis—hypotension, dyspnea, decreased oxygen saturation, flushing | Prevention—premedicate with antihistamines<br>Stop the blood<br>Restart the 0.9% NaCl<br>Notify the health care provider Supportive care: diphenhydramine, oxygen, corticosteroids |
| Acute intravascular hemolytic reaction | Incompatibility | Occurs within minutes to 24 hours<br>Nausea, chills, vomiting, pain in lower back, hypotension, increase in pulse rate, decrease in urinary output, hematuria | Stop the blood<br>Supportive care: oxygen, diphenhydramine, airway management |
| Febrile nonhemolytic reaction (most common) | Antibodies to donor platelets or leukocytes | Occurs in minutes to hours<br>Fever, chills, nausea, headache, flushing, tachycardia, palpitations | Stop the blood<br>Supportive care<br>Antipyretics (avoid aspirin in thrombocytopenic clients)<br>Seen with clients after multiple transfusions |
| Sepsis | Contaminated blood products | Occurs within minutes to less than 24 hours<br>Tachycardia, hypotension, high fever, chills, shock | Stop the blood<br>Obtain blood culture<br>Antibiotics, IV fluids, vasopressors, steroids |
| Circulatory overload | Large volume over short time | Occurs within minutes to hours—dyspnea, crackles, increased respiratory rate, tachycardia | Monitor clients at high-risk (elderly, heart disease, children)<br>Slow or discontinue transfusion |

Table 3  BLOOD TRANSFUSION REACTIONS

## ▶ PARENTERAL FLUIDS

A. Definition of terms

1. Tonicity—concentration of a substance dissolved in water

2. ECF—extracellular fluid

3. Isotonic fluids—same concentration as ECF

4. Hypertonic solution—solute concentration greater than that of ECF

5. Hypotonic solution—solute concentration less than that of ECF

6. Intake refers to all possible avenues of intake, e.g., oral fluids, food, IV fluids, gavage feedings, irrigations

7. Output refers to all possible avenues of output, e.g., insensible losses, urine, diarrhea, vomitus, sweat, blood, and any drainage

B. Types (see Table 1)

| Table 1   INTRAVENOUS FLUIDS | | |
|---|---|---|
| **TYPE OF FLUID** | **IV FLUID** | **NURSING CONSIDERATIONS FOR IVS** |
| Isotonic | 0.9% NaCl<br>Lactated Ringer's<br>5% dextrose in water (is isotonic but becomes hypotonic when glucose metabolized) | Main purpose—to maintain or restore fluid and electrolyte balance<br><br>Secondary purpose—to provide a route for medication, nutrition, and blood components<br><br>    Type, amount, and sterility of fluid must be carefully checked<br><br>Macrodrip—delivers 10, 12, or 15 drops per milliliter; should be used if rapid administration is needed |
| Hypotonic | 0.45% NaCl | Microdrip—delivers 60 drops per milliliter; should be used when fluid volume needs to be smaller or more controlled, e.g., clients with compromised renal or cardiac status, clients on "keep-open" rates, pediatric clients |
| Hypertonic | 10–15% dextrose in water 3% NaCl<br>Sodium bicarbonate 5% | Maintain sterile technique<br><br>Monitor rate of flow<br><br>Assess for infiltration—cool skin, swelling, pain<br><br>Assess for phlebitis—redness, pain, heat, swelling<br><br>Change tubing every 72 hours, bag every 24 hours or according to agency policy |

**C.** Administration

1. Calculate IV flow rate (see Table 2)

| Table 2  CALCULATIONS FOR IV RATE |
|---|
| 1) Milliliters per hour: |

$$\frac{\text{Total solution}}{\text{hours to run}} = \text{ml/h}$$

*Example:* 1,000 ml in 8 hours

$$\frac{1,000}{8} = 125\text{ml/h}$$

2) Drops per minute:

$$\frac{\text{Total volume} \times \text{drop factor}}{\text{time in minutes}} = \text{gtts/min}$$

*Example:* 1,000 ml in 8 hours, with a drop factor of 15

$$\frac{1,000 \times 15}{8 \times 60} =$$

$$\frac{1,000 \times 1}{8 \times 4} =$$

$$\frac{250}{8} =$$

31.25 or 31 gtts/min

*Change normal IV tubing q 96 hours (4 days)*

2. Nursing care

a. Change continuous use standard tubing every 96 hours unless contaminated—if contaminated change immediately

b. Intermittent use tubing is changed every 24 hours unless contaminated—if contaminated change immediately

c. Change fluid container every 24 hours

## ▶ PERIPHERAL IV

**A.** Location

1. Condition of vein

2. Type of fluid/med to be infused

3. Duration of therapy

4. Client's age, size, status

5. Skill of nurse

6. Non-dominant side for client

7. Type of catheter

**B.** Insertion of catheter

1. Explain procedure, check ID

2. Have all equipment at the bedside and prepared

3. Apply appropriate PPE

4. Distend veins by applying tourniquet 4–6" above site, apply warmth or have client open and close fist, or hang arm over side of bed to help dilate vein

5. Clean site with alcohol swab; start at center and work outward

6. Repeat cleaning with povidone-iodine

7. Hold skin taut to stabilize vein

8. Insert catheter bevel up at 10–30°, (direct method—thrust catheter through skin and vein in one smooth motion: (indirect method—first pierce skin, then vessel)

9. Lessen the angle and advance catheter; watch for flashback of blood

10. Once you see blood return, advance catheter 1/4" and then remove tourniquet

11. Withdraw needle from catheter, advance catheter up to hub

12. Secure catheter

13. Attach IV tubing

14. Begin IV infusion

15. Check for infiltration or hematoma

C. Complications

   1. Circulatory overload

      a. Assessment

         1) Crackles

         2) Dyspnea

         3) Confusion

         4) Seizures

      b. Nursing care

         1) Reduce IV rate

         2) Assess VS

         3) Assess lab values

         4) Notify HCP

   2. Infiltration (extravasation if tissue-damaging medication is used)

      a. Assessment

         1) Edema

         2) Pain

         3) Coolness in area

         4) Significant decrease in flow rate

         5) Apply tourniquet above infusion site; if infusion continues to drip, it is infiltrated

      b. Nursing care

         1) Discontinue IV

         2) Apply warm compresses to infiltrated site

         3) Apply sterile dressing

         4) Elevate arm

         5) Start IV at new site proximal to infiltrated site if same extremity used; may use different vein distal to infiltrated site (basilic or cephalic)

3. Phlebitis
   a. Assessment
      1) Reddened, warm area around insertion site or on path of vein
      2) Tenderness
      3) Swelling
   b. Nursing care
      1) Discontinue IV
      2) Apply warm, moist compresses
      3) Restart IV at new site

4. Thrombophlebitis (inflammation of the vein with clot formation)
   a. Assessment
      1) Pain
      2) Swelling
      3) Redness and warmth around insertion site or along path of vein
      4) Fever
      5) Leukocytosis
   b. Nursing care
      1) Discontinue IV
      2) Apply warm compress
      3) Elevate the extremity
      4) Restart the IV in the opposite extremity

5. Hematoma
   a. Assessment
      1) Ecchymosis
      2) Immediate swelling at site
      3) Leakage of blood at site
   b. Nursing care
      1) Discontinue IV
      2) Apply pressure with sterile dressing
      3) Apply cool compresses (or ice bag) intermittently for 24 h to site, followed by warm compresses
      4) Restart IV in opposite extremity

6. Clotting
   a. Assessment
      1) Decreased IV flow rate
      2) Back flow of blood into IV tubing
   b. Nursing care
      1) Discontinue IV
      2) Do *not* irrigate or milk the tubing
      3) Do *not* increase the IV flow rate or hang the solution higher
      4) Do *not* aspirate clot from the cannula

# ▶ CENTRAL VENOUS ACCESS DEVICES

Four types: peripherally inserted central catheter (PICC), tunneled central catheter, non-tunneled (percutaneous) central catheter, implanted port

**A.** Peripherally inserted central catheter (PICC)

1. Venipuncture performed above or below anticubital fossa into basilic, cephalic, or axillary veins of dominant arm (encourages blood flow and reduces risk of dependent edema)

2. Tip of catheter is in superior vena cava or brachiocephelic veins

3. May stay in place several days to months

4. Potential complications

   a. Malposition

   b. Pneumothorax

   c. Dysrhythmias

   d. Nerve or tendon damage

   e. Respiratory distress

   f. Catheter embolism

   g. Thrombophlebitis

5. Nursing care

   a. Change dressing 2–3 times a week and when wet or nonocclusive

   b. Flush with normal saline alone or with normal saline followed by heparinized saline according to agency policy

   c. Do not take blood pressure or draw blood from extremity with PICC line

**B.** Tunneled central catheter

1. Increases in size (2 gauges, 2.5 cm in length) 2 hours after insertion, becomes softer

2. Long-term use—can remain in place for years

3. Catheter is cuffed and can be single- to double-lumen

4. Venipuncture 2–3 finger breadths above antecubital fossa or 1 finger breadth below anticubital fossa into cephalic, basilic, or median cubital vein

5. Inserted surgically in subclavian vein, advanced to superior vena cava

6. Examples: Hickman, Groshong, Permacath

7. Complications

   a. Thrombosis

   b. Phlebitis

   c. Air embolism

   d. Infection

   e. Bleeding

   f. Vascular perforation

8. Nursing care
   a. Change dressing 2–3 times a week and when wet or nonocclusive
   b. Flush with normal saline alone or with normal saline followed by heparinized saline according to agency policy
   c. Anchor catheter securely
   d. Avoid chemotherapy or parenteral nutrition
C. Non-tunneled percutaneous central catheters
   1. Inserted through subclavian vein
   2. Triple-lumen central catheter—distal lumen (16-gauge) used to infuse or draw blood samples, middle lumen (18-gauge) used for PN infusion, proximal port (18-gauge) used to infuse or draw blood and administer medications
   3. Used for short term IV therapy
   4. Insertion
      a. Placed supine in head-low position (dilates vessel and prevents air embolism)
      b. Client turns head away from site during procedure
      c. While catheter is being inserted, client performs Valsalva maneuver
      d. Antibiotic ointment and transparent dressing applied using sterile technique
      e. Verify position of tip catheter by x-ray
      f. Each lumen secured with Leur-Lok cap and labeled to indicate location (proximal, middle, distal)
   5. Nursing care
      a. Site of catheter is used for less than 6 weeks
      b. Flush each lumen with normal saline alone or with normal saline followed by heparinized saline according to agency policy; flush after insertion, after infusions, after specimen withdrawal, or when disconnected
      c. Never use force to flush catheter; if resistance met, notify health care provider
      d. Dressing changes 2–3 times a week and PRN; place in low- Fowler's position; nurse and client wear masks; alcohol and then iodine swabs used to clean site
      e. Change IV tubing every 72 to 96 hours according to agency policy.

**D.** Implanted ports

1. Used for long-term therapy
2. Examples: Port-a-Cath, Hickman
3. Surgically placed
4. Allows client increased movement and decreased care
5. Tip of the catheter is under the skin
6. Access requires non-coring needle through the skin into the port
7. Complications:
   a. Embolism
   b. Clotted access
   c. Sepsis
8. Nursing Care:
   a. Cleanse skin prior to access
   b. Never use force to flush the port

## ▶ HOW TO LEARN MEDICATIONS

The best way to learn medication information is to use the classification and subclassification systems which group and organize the medications.

**Step 1:** The *Content Review Guide* is organized by the most common classifications and subclassifications of medications.

**Step 2:** Identify the medications included in the classification and subclassification. Identify suffixes for the classification and subclassification. NCLEX-RN® will identify the generic name of the medication.

**Step 3:** Identify the action or effect of the classification or subclassification.

**Step 4:** Based on the action of the classification or subclassification, identify the therapeutic use for the medications.

**Step 5:** Based on the action of the classification or subclassification, identify common precautions or contraindications for use of that classification.

**Step 6:** Side/Adverse effects are more intense effects of the action of the medications included in the classification or subclassification. Knowledge about management of adverse effects is critical when answering questions on NCLEX-RN®. Identify common side effects then identify medications that have unique side effects

**Step 7:** Adverse reactions include potentially dangerous consequences related to the action of the medications in the classification or subclassification. The health care provider should be notified when adverse reactions occur.

**Step 8:** How do you evaluate the effect of the medications in the classification or subclassification? Is it a therapeutic or desired effect? Is it a nontherapeutic or undesired effect?

**Step 9:** Identify what the client needs to know to take the medication safely.

**Step 10:** Identify what the nurse needs to know to give the medication safely.

## ▶ PHARMACOLOGY CALCULATIONS

- Rounding rules:
  1. Follow the rounding directions given in the question.
  2. If no directions are given, do not round.
  3. Consider the value asked for, you cannot divide a drop.
- If the answer is fraction of 1 use the placeholder 0. Not having the place holder is unsafe. Example: .3 is unsafe and incorrect, 0.3 is the safe and correct way to express 3 tenths.

- If the answer is a whole number using a trailing zero after the decimal is unsafe. For example 5.0 mg is unsafe and incorrect whereas 5 mg is the safe ans correct way to express 5.

Pharmacology Conversions

| EMERGENCY MEDICATION FOR SHOCK, CARDIAC ARREST, AND ANAPHYLAXIS | | |
|---|---|---|
| MEDICATION | ADVERSE EFFECTS | NURSING CONSIDERATIONS |
| Norepinephrine | Headache<br>Palpitations<br>Nervousness<br>Epigastric distress<br>Angina, hypertension **tissue necrosis with extravasation** | Vasoconstrictor to increase blood pressure and cardiac output<br>Reflex bradycardia may occur with rise in BP<br>Client should be attended at all times<br>Monitor urinary output<br>Infuse with dextrose solution, not saline<br>Monitor blood pressure<br>Protect medication from light |
| Dopamine | Increased ocular pressure<br>Ectopic beats<br>Nausea<br>Tachycardia, chest pain, dysrhythmias | Low-dose–dilates renal and coronary arteries<br>High-dose–vasoconstrictor, increases myocardial oxygen consumption<br>Headache is an early symptom of drug excess<br>Monitor blood pressure, peripheral pulses, urinary output<br>Use infusion pump |
| Epinephrine | Nervousness<br>Restlessness<br>Dizziness<br>Local necrosis of skin | Stimulates alpha and beta adrenergic receptors<br>Monitor BP<br>Carefully aspirate syringe before IM and subcutaneous doses; inadvertent<br>IV administration can be harmful<br>Always check strength:<br>1:100 only for inhalation, 1:1,000 for parenteral administration (SC or IM)<br>Ensure adequate hydration |
| Isoproterenol | Headache<br>Palpitations<br>Tachycardia<br>Changes in BP<br>Angina, bronchial asthma<br>Pulmonary edema | Stimulates beta 1 and beta 2 adrenergic receptors<br>Used for heart block, ventricular arrhythmias, and bradycardia<br>Bronchodilator used for asthma and bronchospasms<br>Don't give at hs–interrupts sleep patterns<br>Monitor BP, pulse |

| EMERGENCY MEDICATION FOR SHOCK, CARDIAC ARREST, AND ANAPHYLAXIS *(CONTINUED)* | | |
|---|---|---|
| **MEDICATION** | **ADVERSE EFFECTS** | **NURSING CONSIDERATIONS** |
| Phenylephrine | Palpations <br> Tachycardia <br> Hypertension <br> Dysrhythmia <br> Angina <br> Tissue necrosis with extravasation | Potent alpha 1 agonist <br> Used to treat hypotension |
| Dobutamine hydrocholoride | Hypertension <br> PVCs <br> Asthmatic episodes <br> Headache | Stimulates beta 1 receptors <br> Incompatible with alkaline solutions (sodium bicarbonate) <br> Administer through central venous catheter or large peripheral vein using an infusion pump <br> Don't infuse through line with other meds (incompatible) <br> Monitor EKG, BP, I and O, serum potassium |
| Milrinone | Dysrhythmia <br> Thrombocytopenia <br> Jaundice | Positive inotropic agent <br> Smooth muscle relaxant used to treat severe heart failure |
| Sodium nitroprusside | Hypotension <br> Increased intracranial pressure | Dilates cardiac veins and arteries <br> Decreases preload and afterload <br> Increases myocardial perfusion <br> Keep medication in dark after fixed <br> Use infusion pump |
| Diphenhydramine HCl | Drowsiness <br> Confusion <br> Insomnia <br> Headache <br> Vertigo <br> Photosensitivity | Blocks effects of histamine on bronchioles, GI tract, and blood vessels |
| **Actions** | Varies with med | |
| **Indications** | Hypovolemic shock <br> Cardiac arrest <br> Anaphylaxis | |
| **Adverse effects** | Serious rebound effect may occur <br> Balance between underdosing and overdosing | |
| **Nursing considerations** | Monitor vital signs <br> Measure urine output <br> Assess for extravasation <br> Observe extremities for color and perfusion | |

| ADRENOCORTICAL MEDICATIONS: GLUCOCORTICOID | | |
|---|---|---|
| **MEDICATION** | **ADVERSE EFFECTS** | **NURSING CONSIDERATIONS** |
| Cortisone acetate<br>Hydrocortisone<br>Dexamethasone<br>Methylprednisolone<br>Prednisone<br>Beclomethasone<br>Betamethasone<br>Budesonide | Increases susceptibility to infection<br>May mask symptoms of infection<br>Edema, changes in appetite<br>Euphoria, insomnia<br>Delayed wound healing<br>Hypokalemia, hypocalcemia<br>Hyperglycemia<br>Osteoporosis, fractures<br>Peptic ulcer, gastric hemorrhage<br>Psychosis | Prevents/suppresses cell-mediated immune reactors<br>Used for adrenal insufficiency<br>Overdosage produces Cushing's syndrome<br>Abrupt withdrawal of drug may cause headache, nausea and vomiting, and papilledema (Addisonian crisis)<br>Give single dose before 9 A.M.<br>Give multiple doses at evenly spaced intervals<br>Infection may produce few symptoms due to anti-inflammatory action<br>Stress (surgery, illness, psychic) may lead to increased need for steroids<br>Nightmares are often the first indication of the onset of steroid psychosis<br>Check weight, BP, electrolytes, I and O<br>Used cautiously with history of TB (may reactivate disease)<br>May decrease effects of oral hypoglycemics, insulin, diuretics, $K^+$ supplements<br>Assess children for growth retardation<br>Protect from pathological fractures<br>Administer with antacids. Do not stop abruptly<br>Methylprednisolone also used for arthritis, asthma, allergic reactions, cerebral edema<br>Dexamethasone also used for allergic disorders, cerebral edema, asthma attack, shock |
| **Action** | Stimulates formation of glucose (gluconeogenesis) and decreases use of glucose by body cells; increases formation and storage of fat in muscle tissue; alters normal immune response | |
| **Indications** | Addison's disease, Crohn's disease, COPD, lupus erythematosus, leukemias, lymphomas, myelomas, head trauma, tumors to prevent/treat cerebral edema | |
| **Adverse effects** | Psychoses, depression, weight gain, hypokalemia, hypocalcemia, stunted growth in children, petechiae, buffalo hump | |

| ADRENOCORTICAL MEDICATIONS: GLUCOCORTICOID *(CONTINUED)* | | |
|---|---|---|
| **MEDICATION** | **ADVERSE EFFECTS** | **NURSING CONSIDERATIONS** |
| **Nursing considerations** | Monitor fluid and electrolyte balance<br>Don't discontinue abruptly<br>Monitor for signs of infection | |
| **Herbal interactions** | Cascara, senna, celery seed, juniper may decrease serum potassium; when taken with corticosteroids may increase hypoglycemia<br>Ginseng taken with corticosteroids may cause insomnia<br>Echinacea may counteract effects of corticosteroids<br>Licorice potentiates effect of corticosteroids | |

| ADRENOCORTICAL MEDICATIONS: MINERALOCORTICOID | | |
|---|---|---|
| **MEDICATION** | **ADVERSE EFFECTS** | **NURSING CONSIDERATIONS** |
| Fludrocortisone acetate | Hypertension, edema due to sodium retention<br>Muscle weakness and dysrhythmia due to hypokalemia | Give PO dose with food<br>Check BP, electrolytes, I and O, weight<br>Give low-sodium, high-protein, high-potassium diet<br>May decrease effects of oral hypoglycemics, insulin, diuretics, $K^+$ supplements |
| **Action** | Increases sodium reabsorption, potassium and hydrogen excretion in the distal convoluted tubules of the nephron | |
| **Indications** | Adrenal insufficiency | |
| **Adverse effects** | Sodium and water retention<br>Hypokalemia | |
| **Nursing considerations** | Monitor BP and serum electrolytes<br>Daily weight, report sudden weight gain to health care provider<br>Used with cortisone or hydrocortisone in adrenal insufficiency | |

| ANTACID MEDICATIONS | | |
|---|---|---|
| **MEDICATION** | **ADVERSE EFFECTS** | **NURSING CONSIDERATIONS** |
| Aluminum hydroxide gel<br><br>Calcium carbonate<br><br>Aluminum hydroxide and magnesium trisilicate | Constipation that may lead to impaction, phosphate depletion | Monitor bowel pattern<br><br>Compounds contains sodium; check if client is on sodium-restricted diet<br><br>Aluminum and magnesium antacid compounds interfere with tetracycline absorption<br><br>Encourage fluids<br><br>Monitor for signs of phosphate deficiency—malaise, weakness, tremors, bone pain<br><br>Shake well<br><br>Careful use advised for kidney dysfunction |
| Magnesium hydroxide | Excessive dose can produce nausea, vomiting, and diarrhea | Store at room temperature with tight lid to prevent absorption of $CO_2$<br>Prolonged and frequent use of cathartic dose can lead to dependence<br><br>Administer with caution to clients with renal disease |
| Aluminum hydroxide and magnesium hydroxide | Slight laxative effect | Encourage fluid intake<br><br>Administer with caution to clients with renal disease |
| **Action** | Neutralizes gastric acids; raises gastric pH; inactivates pepsin | |
| **Indications** | Peptic ulcer<br>Indigestion<br>Reflux esophagitis<br>Prevent stress ulcers | |
| **Adverse effects** | Constipation, diarrhea<br>Acid rebound between doses<br>Acid/Base Imbalance | |
| **Nursing considerations** | Use medications with sodium content cautiously for clients with cardiac and renal disease<br><br>Absorption of tetracyclines, quinolones, phenothiazides, iron preparations, isoniazid reduced when given with antacids<br><br>Effectiveness of oral contraceptives and salicylates may decrease when given with antacids | |

| ANTIANXIETY MEDICATIONS | | |
|---|---|---|
| MEDICATION | ADVERSE EFFECTS | NURSING CONSIDERATIONS |
| Benzodiazepine Derivatives | | |
| Chlordiazepoxide<br>Diazepam | Lethargy, hangover<br>Respiratory depression<br>Hypotension | CNS depressant<br>Use–anxiety, sedation, alcohol withdrawal, seizures<br>May result in toxic build-up in the elderly<br>Potential for physiological addiction/overdose<br>Can develop tolerance and cross-tolerance<br>Cigarette smoking increases clearance of drug<br>Alcohol increases CNS depression |
| Alprazolam<br>Lorazepam<br>Oxazepam | Drowsiness, light-headedness, hypotension, hepatic dysfunction<br>Increased salivation<br>Orthostatic hypotension<br>Memory impairment and confusion | CNS depressant<br>Safer for elderly<br>Don't combine with alcohol or other depressants<br>Check renal and hepatic function<br>Don't discontinue abruptly (true for all antianxiety medications)<br>Teach addictive potential |
| Midazolam | Retrograde amnesia<br>Euphoria<br>Hypotension<br>Dysrhythmia<br>Cardiac arrest<br>Respiratory depression | CNS depressant<br>Use–preoperative sedation, conscious sedation for endoscopic procedures and diagnostic tests |
| Anxiolytics: Nonbenzodiazepine | | |
| Buspirone | Light-headedness<br>Confusion<br>Hypotension, palpitations | Little sedation<br>Requires approximately 3 weeks to be effective<br>Cannot be given as a PRN medication<br>Particularly useful for generalized anxiety disorder (GAD)<br>No abuse potential<br>Used for clients with previous addiction<br>Avoid alcohol and grapefruit juice<br>Monitor for worsening depression or suicidal tendencies |
| Hydroxyzine | Drowsiness, ataxia<br>Leukopenia, hypotension | Produces no dependence, tolerance, or intoxication<br>Can be used for anxiety relief for indefinite periods |

| ANTIANXIETY MEDICATIONS *(CONTINUED)* | | |
|---|---|---|
| **MEDICATION** | **ADVERSE EFFECTS** | **NURSING CONSIDERATIONS** |
| Herbals | | |
| Kava | Impaired thinking, judgment, motor reflexes, vision, decreased plasma proteins, thrombocytopenia, leukocytopenia, dyspnea, and pulmonary hypertension | Similar activity to benzodiazepines <br><br> Suppresses emotional excitability and produces mild euphoria <br><br> Do not take with CNS depressants <br><br> Should not be taken by women who are pregnant or lactating or by children under the age of 12 |
| Melatonin | Sedation, confusion, headache, and tachycardia | Influences sleep-wake cycles (levels are high during sleep) <br><br> Used for prevention and treatment of "jet lag" and insomnia <br><br> Use cautiously if given with benzodiazepines and CNS depressants <br><br> Contraindicated in hepatic insufficiency, history of cerebrovascular disease, depression, and neurologic disorders |
| **Action** | Affects neurotransmitters | |
| **Indications** | Anxiety disorders, insomnia, petit mal seizures, panic attacks, acute manic episodes | |
| **Adverse effects** | Sedation <br><br> Depression, confusion <br><br> Anger, hostility <br><br> Headache <br><br> Dry mouth, constipation <br><br> Bradycardia <br><br> Elevations in LDH, AST, ALT <br><br> Urinary retention | |
| **Nursing considerations** | Monitor liver function <br><br> Monitor for therapeutic blood levels <br><br> Avoid alcohol <br><br> Caution when performing tasks requiring alertness (e.g., driving car) <br><br> Benzodiazepines are also used as muscles relaxants, sedatives, hypnotics, anticonvulsants | |

| ANTICHOLINERGIC MEDICATIONS | | |
|---|---|---|
| **MEDICATION** | **ADVERSE EFFECTS** | **NURSING CONSIDERATIONS** |
| Propantheline bromide | Decreased gastric motility<br>Decreased effect of vagus nerve | Used for urinary incontinence and peptic ulcer disease<br>Give 30 minutes ac<br>Give hs dose at least 2 h after last meal<br>Monitor vital signs, I and O |
| Belladonna | Dry mouth, vertigo | Action peaks in 2 hours |
| Atropine sulfate | Tachycardia<br>Headache, blurred vision<br>Insomnia, dry mouth<br>Dizziness<br>Urinary retention<br>Angina, mydriasis | Used for bradycardia<br>When given PO give 30 minutes before meals<br>Check for history of glaucoma, asthma, hypertension Monitor I and O, orientation<br>When given in non-emergency situations make certain client voids before taking drug<br>Educate client to expect dry mouth, increased respiration and heart rate<br>Client should avoid heat (perspiration is decreased)<br>Antidote-physostigmine salicylate |
| Iproproprium<br>Tiotropium<br>Iprotropium plus albuterol | Dry mouth<br>Irritation of pharynx | Used for bronchospasm and long-term treatment of asthma<br>Iproproprium administered as aerosol or in nebulizer<br>Tiotropium administered in powder form by HandiHaler |
| Benztropine<br>Trihexyphenydil | Urinary retention<br>Blurred vision<br>Dry mouth<br>Constipation | Used for Parkinson's Disease<br>Increase fluids, bulk foods and exercise<br>Taper before discontinuation<br>Orthostatic hypotension precautions |
| Scopolamine | Urinary retention<br>Blurred vision<br>Dry mouth<br>Constipation<br>Confusion and sedation | Used for motion sickness<br>Contraindicated in acute angle glaucoma |
| **Actions** | Competes with acetylcholine at receptor sites in autonomic nervous system; causes relaxation of ciliary muscles (cycloplegia) and dilation of pupil (mydriasis); causes bronchodilation and decreases bronchial secretions; decreases mobility and GI secretions | |
| **Indications** | Atropine—bradycardia, mydriasis for ophthalmic exam, preoperatively to dry secretions<br>Scopolamine—motion sickness, vertigo, mydriasis for ophthalmic exam, preoperative to dry secretions | |

| ANTICHOLINERGIC MEDICATIONS (CONTINUED) | | |
|---|---|---|
| MEDICATION | ADVERSE EFFECTS | NURSING CONSIDERATIONS |
| **Adverse effects** | Blurred vision<br>Dry mouth<br>Urinary retention<br>Changes in heart rate | |
| **Nursing considerations** | Monitor for urinary retention<br>Contraindicated for clients with glaucoma | |

| ANTICOAGULANT MEDICATIONS | | |
|---|---|---|
| MEDICATION | ADVERSE EFFECTS | NURSING CONSIDERATIONS |
| **Action: Inhibits synthesis of clotting factors** | | |
| Heparin | Can produce hemorrhage from any body site (10%)<br>Tissue irritation/pain at injection site<br>Anemia<br>Thrombocytopenia<br>Fever<br>Dose dependant on aPTT | Monitor therapeutic partial thromboplastin time (PTT) at 1.5–2.5 times the control without signs of hemorrhage<br>Lower limit of normal 20–25 sec; upper limit of normal 32–39 sec<br>For IV administration: use infusion pump, peak 5 minutes, duration 2–6 hours<br>For injection: give deep SQ; never IM (danger of hematoma), onset 20–60 minutes, duration 8–12 hours<br>**Antidote: protamine sulfate within 30 minutes**<br>Can be allergenic |
| Low-molecular weight heparin<br>Enoxaparin | Bleeding<br>  Minimal widespread affect<br>  Fixed dose | Less allergenic than heparin<br>Must be given deep SQ, never IV or IM<br>Does not require lab test monitoring |
| Warfarin | Hemorrhage<br>Diarrhea<br>Rash<br>Fever | Monitor therapeutic prothombin time (PT) at 1.5–2.5 times the control, or monitor international normalized ratio (INR)<br>Normal PT 9.5–12 sec; normal INR 2.0–3.5<br>Onset: 12–24 hours, peak 1.5–3 days, duration: 3–5 days<br>**Antidotes: vitamin K, whole blood, plasma**<br>Teach measures to avoid venous stasis<br>Emphasize importance of regular lab testing<br>Client should avoid foods high in vitamin K: many green vegetables, pork, rice, yogurt, cheeses, fish, milk |
| Dabigatran | Directly inhibits thrombin | thrombin Used to treat atrial fibrillation Increased risk bleeding age greater than 75, kidney disease, gastrointestinal bleeding, use of NSAIDs |
| **Action: inhibits activity of clotting** | | |
| **Action** | Heparin blocks conversion of fibrinogen to fibrin<br>Warfarin interferes with liver synthesis of vitamin K–dependent clotting factors | |

| ANTICOAGULANT MEDICATIONS *(CONTINUED)* | | |
|---|---|---|
| MEDICATION | ADVERSE EFFECTS | NURSING CONSIDERATIONS |
| **Indications** | For heparin: prophylaxis and treatment of thromboembolic disorders; in very low doses (10–100 units) to maintain patency of IV catheters (heparin flush) | |
| | For warfarin: management of pulmonary emboli, venous thromboembolism, MI, atrial dysrhythmias, post cardiac valve replacement | |
| | For dipyridamole: as an adjunct to warfarin in postop cardiac valve replacement, as an adjunct to aspirin to reduce the risk of repeat stroke or TIAs | |
| **Adverse effects** | Nausea | |
| | Alopecia | |
| | Urticaria | |
| | Hemorrhage | |
| | Bleeding/heparin-induced thrombocytopetria (HIT) | |
| **Nursing considerations** | Check for signs of hemorrhage: bleeding gums, nosebleed, unusual bleeding, black/tarry stools, hematuria, fall in hematocrit or blood pressure, guaiac-positive stools | |
| | Client should avoid IM injections, ASA-containing products, and NSAIDs | |
| | Client should wear medical information tag | |
| | Instruct client to use soft toothbrush, electric razor, to report bleeding gums, petechiae or bruising, epistaxis, black tarry stools | |
| | Monitor platelet counts and signs and symptoms of thrombosis during heparin therapy; if HIT suspected, heparin discontinued and non-heparin anticoagulant given | |
| **Herbal interactions** | Garlic, ginger, ginkgo may increase bleeding when taken with warfarin | |
| | Large doses of anise may interfere with anticoagulants | |
| | Ginseng and alfalfa my decrease anticoagulant activity | |
| | Black haw increases action of anticoagulant | |
| | Chamomile may interfere with anticoagulants | |
| **Vitamin interaction** | Vitamin C may slightly prolong PT | |
| | Vitamin E will increase warfarin's effect | |

| ANTICONVULSANT MEDICATIONS | | |
|---|---|---|
| MEDICATION | ADVERSE EFFECTS | NURSING CONSIDERATIONS |
| Clonazepam | Drowsiness<br>Dizziness<br>Confusion<br>Respiratory depression | Benzodiazepine<br>Do not discontinue suddenly<br>Avoid activities that require alertness |
| Diazepam | Drowsiness, ataxia<br>Hypotension<br>Tachycardia<br>Respiratory depression | IV push doses shouldn't exceed 2 mg/minute<br>Monitor vital signs–resuscitation equipment available if given IV<br>Alcohol increases CNS depression<br>After long-term use, withdrawal leads to symptoms such as vomiting, sweating, cramps, tremors, and possibly convulsions |

| ANTICONVULSANT MEDICATIONS *(CONTINUED)* | | |
|---|---|---|
| **MEDICATION** | **ADVERSE EFFECTS** | **NURSING CONSIDERATIONS** |
| Fosphenytoin | Drowsiness<br>Dizziness<br>Confusion<br>Leukopenia<br>Anemia | Used for tonic–clonic seizures, status epilepticus<br>Highly protein-bound<br>Contact healthcare provider if rash develops |
| Levetiracetam | Dizziness<br>Suicidal ideation | Avoid alcohol<br>Avoid driving and activities that require alertness |
| Phenytoin sodium | Drowsiness, ataxia<br>Nystagmus<br>Blurred vision<br>Hirsutism<br>Lethargy<br>GI upset<br>Gingival hypertrophy | Give oral medication with at least 1/2 glass of water, or with meals to minimize GI irritation<br>Inform client that red-brown or pink discoloration of sweat and urine may occur<br>IV administration may lead to cardiac arrest—have resuscitation equipment at hand<br>Never mix with any other drug or dextrose IV<br>Instruct in oral hygiene<br>Increase vitamin D intake and exposure to sunlight may be necessary with long-term use<br>Alcohol increases serum levels<br>Increased risk toxicity older adults |
| Phenobarbital | Drowsiness, rash<br>GI upset<br>Initially constricts pupils<br>Respiratory depression<br>Ataxia | Monitor vital signs—resuscitation equipment should be available if given IV<br>Drowsiness diminishes after initial weeks of therapy<br>Don't take alcohol or perform hazardous activities<br>Nystagmus may indicate early toxicity<br>Sudden discontinuation may lead to withdrawal<br>Tolerance and dependence result from long-term use<br>Folic acid supplements are indicated for long-term use<br>Decreased cognitive function older adults |

| ANTICONVULSANT MEDICATIONS *(CONTINUED)* | | |
| --- | --- | --- |
| MEDICATION | ADVERSE EFFECTS | NURSING CONSIDERATIONS |
| Primidone | Drowsiness<br>Ataxia, diplopia<br>Nausea and vomiting | Don't discontinue use abruptly<br>Full therapeutic response may take 2 weeks<br>Shake liquid suspension well<br>Take with food if experiencing GI distress<br>Decreased cognitive function older adults |
| Magnesium sulfate | Flushing<br>Sweating<br>Extreme thirst<br>Hypotension<br>Sedation, confusion | Monitor intake and output<br>Before each dose, knee jerks should be tested<br>Vital signs should be monitored often during parenteral administration<br>Used for pregnancy-induced hypertension |
| Valproic acid | Sedation<br>Tremor, ataxia<br>Nausea, vomiting<br>Prolonged bleeding time | Agent of choice in many seizure disorders of young children<br>Do not take with carbonated beverage<br>Take with food<br>Monitor platelets, bleeding time, and liver function tests |
| Carbamazepine | Myelosuppression<br>Dizziness, drowsiness<br>Ataxia<br>Diplopia, rash | Monitor intake and output<br>Supervise ambulation<br>Monitor CBC<br>Take with meals<br>Wear protective clothing due to photosensitivity<br>Multiple drug interactions |
| Ethosuximide | GI symptoms<br>Drowsiness<br>Ataxia, dizziness | Monitor for behavioral changes<br>Monitor weight weekly |
| Gabapentin | Increased appetite<br>Ataxia<br>Irritability<br>Dizziness<br>Fatigue | Monitor weight and behavioral changes.<br>Can also be used to treat postherpetic neuralgia |
| Lamotrigine | Diplopia<br>Headaches<br>Dizziness<br>Drowsiness<br>Ataxia<br>Nausea, vomiting<br>Life-threatening rash when given with valproic acid | Take divided doses with meals or just afterward to decrease adverse effects |

Chapter 3
PHYSIOLOGICAL INTEGRITY:
PHARMACOLOGICAL AND
PARENTERAL THERAPIES

| ANTICONVULSANT MEDICATIONS *(CONTINUED)* | | |
|---|---|---|
| **MEDICATION** | **ADVERSE EFFECTS** | **NURSING CONSIDERATIONS** |
| Topiramate | Ataxia<br>Confusion<br>Dizziness<br>Fatigue<br>Vision problems | Adjunct therapy for intractable partial seizures<br>Increased risk for renal calculi<br>Stop drug immediately if eye problems—could lead to permanent damage |
| **Action** | Decreases flow of calcium and sodium across neuronal membranes | |
| **Indications** | Partial seizures: phenobarbitol, carbamazepine, gabapentin<br>Generalized tonic-clonic seizures: phenobarbitol, carbamazepine<br>Absence seizures: ethosuximide<br>Status epilepticus: diazepam, phenytoin | |
| **Adverse effects** | Cardiovascular depression<br>Respiratory depression<br>Agranulocytosis<br>Aplastic anemia | |
| **Nursing considerations** | Tolerance develops with long-term use<br>Don't discontinue abruptly<br>Caution with use of medications that lower seizure threshold (MAO inhibitors)<br>Barbiturates and benzodiazepines also used as anticonvulsants<br>Increased risk adverse reactions older adults | |

| ANTIDEPRESSANT MEDICATIONS: HETEROCYCLICS | |
|---|---|
| **Examples** | Bupropion<br>Trazodone |
| **Actions** | Does not inhibit MAO; has some anticholinergic and sedative effects; alters effects of serotonin on CNS |
| **Indications** | Treatment of depression and smoking cessation |
| **Adverse effects** | Dry mouth<br>Nausea<br>Bupropion–insomnia and agitation<br>Trazodone–sedation, orthostatic hypotension |
| **Nursing considerations** | May require gradual reduction before stopping<br>Avoid use with alcohol, other CNS depressants for up to 1 week after end of therapy |

58    **KAPLAN) NURSING**

| ANTIDEPRESSANT MEDICATION: MONOAMINE OXIDASE (MAO) INHIBITORS | |
|---|---|
| **Examples** | Phenelzine sulfate, isocarboxazid, tranylcypromine |
| **Actions** | Interferes with monoamine oxidase, allowing for increased concentration of neurotransmitters (epinephrine, norepinephrine, serotonin) in synaptic space, causing stabilization of mood |
| **Indications** | Depression<br>Chronic pain syndromes |
| **Adverse effects** | Hypertensive crisis when taken with foods containing tyramine (aged cheese, bologna, pepperoni, salami, figs, bananas, raisins, beer, Chianti red wine) or OTC meds containing ephedrine, pseudoephedrine<br>Photosensitivity<br>Weight gain<br>Sexual dysfunction<br>Orthostatic hypotension |
| **Nursing considerations** | Not first-line drugs for depression<br>Should not be taken with SSRIs<br>Administer antihypertensive medications with caution<br>Avoid use of other CNS depressants, including alcohol<br>Discontinue 10 days before general anesthesia<br>Medications lower seizure threshold<br>Monitor for urinary retention |

| ANTIDEPRESSANT MEDICIATION: SELECTIVE SEROTONIN REUPTAKE INHIBITORS | |
|---|---|
| **Example** | SSRIs: fluoxetine, paroxetine, sertraline hydrochloride, citalopram<br>SNRIs: venlafaxine, duloxetine |
| **Actions** | Inhibits CNS neuronal uptake of serotonin; acts as stimulant counter-acting depression and increasing motivation |
| **Indications** | Depression<br>Obsessive-compulsive disorders<br>Obesity<br>Bulimia |
| **Adverse effects** | Headache, dizziness<br>Nervousness<br>Insomnia, drowsiness<br>Anxiety<br>Tremor<br>Dry mouth<br>GI upset<br>Taste changes<br>Sweating<br>Rash<br>URI<br>Painful menstruation<br>Sexual dysfunction<br>Weight gain |
| **Nursing considerations** | Take in A.M.<br>Takes 4 weeks for full effect<br>Monitor weight<br>Good mouth care<br>Do not administer with MAOIs–risk of serotonin syndrome<br>Monitor for thrombocytopenia, leukopenia, and anemia |

| ANTIDEPRESSANT MEDICATIONS: TRICYCLICS | |
|---|---|
| **Examples** | Amitriptyline<br>Imipramine |
| **Actions** | Inhibits presynaptic reuptake of neurotransmitters norepinephrine and serotonin; anticholinergic action at CNS and peripheral receptors |
| **Indications** | Depression<br>Obstructive sleep apnea |

| ANTIDEPRESSANT MEDICATIONS: TRICYCLICS *(CONTINUED)* | |
|---|---|
| **Adverse effects** | Sedation |
| | Anticholinergic effects (dry mouth, blurred vision) |
| | Confusion (especially in elderly) |
| | Photosensitivity |
| | Disturbed concentration |
| | Orthostatic hypotension |
| | Bone marrow depression |
| | Urinary retention |
| **Nursing considerations** | Therapeutic effect in 1–3 weeks; maximum response in 6–9 weeks |
| | May be administered in daily dose at night to promote sleep and decrease adverse effects during the day |
| | Orthostatic hypotension precautions |
| | Instruct client that adverse effects will decrease over time |
| | Sugarless lozenges for dry mouth |
| | Do not abruptly stop taking medication (headache, vertigo, nightmares, malaise, weight change) |
| | Avoid alcohol, sleep-inducing drugs, OTC drugs |
| | Avoid exposure to sunlight, wear sunscreen |
| | Older adults: strong anticholinergic and sedation effects |

| ANTIDEPRESSANT MEDICATION OVERVIEW | | |
|---|---|---|
| **MEDICATION** | **ADVERSE EFFECTS** | **NURSING CONSIDERATIONS** |
| **Monoamine oxidase inhibitors (MAOIs)**<br><br>Isocarboxazid<br><br>Tranylcypromine sulfate<br><br>Phenelzine sulfate | Postural hypotension<br><br>If foods with tyramine ingested, can have hypertensive crisis: headache, sweating, palpitations, stiff neck, intracranial hemorrhage<br><br>Potentiates alcohol and other medications | Inhibits monoamine oxidase enzyme, preventing destruction of norepinephrine, epinephrine, and serotonin<br><br>Avoid foods with tyramine—aged cheese, liver, yogurt, herring, yeast, beer, wine, sour cream, pickled products<br><br>Avoid caffeine, antihistamines, amphetamines<br><br>Takes 3–4 weeks to work<br><br>Avoid tricyclics until 3 weeks after stopping MAO inhibitors<br><br>Monitor vital signs<br><br>Sunblock required |
| **Tricyclics**<br><br>Amitriptyline hydrochloride<br><br>Imipramine<br><br>Desipramine hydrochloride<br><br>Doxepin<br><br>Nortriptyline | Sedation/drowsiness, especially with Elavil<br><br>Blurred vision, dry mouth, diaphoresis<br><br>Postural hypotension, palpitations<br><br>Nausea, vomiting<br><br>Constipation, urinary retention<br><br>Increased appetite | Increases brain amine levels<br><br>Suicide risk high after 10–14 days because of increased energy<br><br>Monitor vital signs<br><br>Sunblock required<br><br>Increase fluid intake<br><br>Take dose at bedtime (sedative effect)<br><br>Use sugarless candy or gum for dry mouth<br><br>Delay of 2–6 weeks before noticeable effects |

## ANTIDEPRESSANT MEDICATION OVERVIEW *(CONTINUED)*

| MEDICATION | ADVERSE EFFECTS | NURSING CONSIDERATIONS |
|---|---|---|
| **Selective serotonin reuptake inhibitors**<br>Fluoxetine<br>Paroxetine<br>Sertraline hydrochloride<br>Citalopram<br>**Serotonin-norepinephrine reuptake inhibitors**<br>Venlafaxine<br>Duloxetine | Palpitations, bradycardia<br>Nausea, vomiting, diarrhea or constipation, increased or constipation, increased or decreased appetite<br>Urinary retention<br>Nervousness, insomnia | Decreases neuronal uptake of serotonin<br>Take in AM to avoid insomnia<br>Takes at least 4 weeks to work<br>Can potentiate effect of digoxin, warfarin, and diazepam<br>Used for anorexia |
| **Heterocyclics/Atypical**<br>Bupropion<br>Trazodone | Dry mouth<br>Nausea | May require gradual reduction before stopping<br>Avoid use with alcohol, other CNS depressants for up to 1 week after end of therapy |
| **Herbals**<br>St. John's Wort | Dizziness, hypertension, allergic skin reaction, phototoxicity | Avoid use of St. John's wort and MAOI within 2 weeks of each other<br>Do not use alcohol<br>Contraindicated in pregnancy<br>Avoid exposure to sun and use sunscreen<br>Discontinue 1 to 2 weeks before surgery |
| **Herbal interactions** | St. John's wort—interacts with SSRIs; do not take within 2 weeks of MAOI<br>Ginseng may potentiate MAOIs<br>Avoid Ma huang or ephedra with MAOIs<br>Kava kava should not be combined with benzodiazepines or opioids due to increased sedation<br>Increase use of Brewer's yeast with MAOIs can increase blood pressure | |

## ANTIDIABETIC MEDICATIONS: INSULIN

| INSULIN TYPES | ONSET OF ACTION | PEAK ACTION | DURATION OF ACTION | TIME OF ADVERSE REACTION | CHARACTERISTICS |
|---|---|---|---|---|---|
| **Rapid–acting** | | | | | |
| Lispro | 15–30 min | 0.5–2.5 h | 3–6 h | Mid-morning: trembling, weakness | Client should eat within 5–15 min after injection; also used in insulin pumps |
| Aspart | 15–30 min | 1–3 h | 3–5 h | | |
| Glulisine | 10–15 min | 1–1.5 h | 3–5 h | | |
| **Short-acting**<br>Regular | 30–60 min | 1–5 h | 6–10 h | Mid-morning, midafternoon: weakness, fatigue | Clear solution; given 20–30 min before meal; can be alone or with other insulins |
| **Intermediate-acting**<br>Isophane (NPH)<br>Insulin detemir | 1–2 h | 6–14 h<br>12–24 h | 16 h<br>varies | Early evening: weakness, fatigue | White and cloudy solution; can be given after meals |

| ANTIDIABETIC MEDICATIONS: INSULIN *(CONTINUED)* | | | | | |
|---|---|---|---|---|---|
| INSULIN TYPES | ONSET OF ACTION | PEAK ACTION | DURATION OF ACTION | TIME OF ADVERSE REACTION | CHARACTERISTICS |
| **Very long-acting** Glargine (Lantus) | 3–4 h | Continuous (no peak) | 24 h | | Maintains blood glucose levels regardless of meals; cannot be mixed with other insulins; given at bedtime |
| **Action** | Reduces blood glucose levels by increasing glucose transport across cell membranes; enhances conversion of glucose to glycogen | | | | |
| **Indications** | Type 1 diabetes; type 2 diabetes not responding to oral hypoglycemic medications; gestational diabetes not responding to diet | | | | |
| **Adverse effects** | Hypoglycemia | | | | |
| **Nursing considerations** | Teach client to rotate sites to prevent lipohypertrophy, fibrofatty masses at injection sites; do not inject into these masses Only regular insulin can be given IV; all can be given SQ | | | | |
| **Herbal interactions** | Bee pollen, ginkgo biloba, glucosamine may increase blood glucose Basil, bay leaf, chromium, echinacea, garlic, ginseng may decrease blood glucose | | | | |

| ANTIDIABETIC MEDICATIONS: ORAL HYPERGLYCEMIC MEDICATIONS | | |
|---|---|---|
| MEDICATION | ADVERSE EFFECTS | NURSING CONSIDERATIONS |
| **Sulfonylureas** Glimepiride Glipizide Glyburide | GI symptoms and dermatologic reactions | Only used if some pancreas beta-cell function Stimulates release of insulin from pancreas Many drugs can potentiate or interfere with actions Take with food if GI upset occurs |
| **Biguanides** Metformin | Nausea Diarrhea Abdominal discomfort | No effect on pancreatic beta cells; decreases glucose production by liver Not given if renal impairment Can cause lactic acidosis Avoid alcohol Do not give with alpha-glucodiase inhibitors |
| **Alpha glucosidase inhibitors** Acarbose Miglitol | Abdominal discomfort Diarrhea Flatulence | Delays digestion of carbohydrates Must be taken immediately before a meal Can be taken alone or with other medications |

| ANTIDIABETIC MEDICATIONS: ORAL HYPERGLYCEMIC MEDICATIONS (CONTINUED) | | |
|---|---|---|
| MEDICATION | ADVERSE EFFECTS | NURSING CONSIDERATIONS |
| **Thiazolidinediones**<br>Rosiglitazone<br>Pioglitazone | Infection<br>Headache<br>Pain<br>Rare cases of liver failure | Decreases insulin resistance and inhibits gluconeogenesis<br>Regularly scheduled liver-function studies<br>Can cause resumption of ovulation in perimenopause |
| **Meglitinides**<br>Repaglinide | Hypoglycemia<br>GI disturbances<br>URIs<br>Back pain<br>Headache | Increases pancreatic insulin release<br>Medication should not be taken if meal skipped |
| **Gliptins**<br>Sitagliptin | Upper respiratory infections<br>Hypoglycemia | Enhances action of incretin hormones |
| **Incretin mimetics**<br>Exanatide | GI upset<br>Hypoglycemia<br>Pancreatitis | Interacts with many medications<br>Administer 1 hour before meals |
| **Indications** | Type 2 diabetes | |
| **Nursing considerations** | Monitor serum glucose levels<br>Avoid alcohol<br>Teaching for disease: dietary control, symptoms of hypoglycemia and hyperglycemia<br>Good skin care | |
| **Herbal interactions** | Bee pollen, ginkgo biloba, glucosamine may increase blood glucose<br>Basil, bay leaf, chromium, echinacea, garlic, ginseng may decrease blood glucose | |

| HYPOGLYCEMIA REVERSAL MEDICATION | | |
|---|---|---|
| MEDICATION | ADVERSE EFFECTS | NURSING CONSIDERATIONS |
| Glucagon | Nausea, vomiting | Given SQ or IM, onset is 8–10 min with duration of 12–27 min<br>Should be part of emergency supplies for diabetics<br>May repeat in 15 min if needed |
| **Action** | Hormone produced by alpha cells of the pancreas to simulate the liver to change glycogen to glucose | |
| **Indications** | Acute management of severe hypoglycemia | |

| HYPOGLYCEMIA REVERSAL MEDICATION *(CONTINUED)* | | |
|---|---|---|
| **MEDICATION** | **ADVERSE EFFECTS** | **NURSING CONSIDERATIONS** |
| **Adverse effects** | Hypotension<br>Bronchospasm<br>Dizziness | |
| **Nursing considerations** | May repeat in 15 minutes if needed<br>IV glucose must be given if client fails to respond<br>Arouse clients from coma as quickly as possible and give carbohydrates orally to prevent secondary hypoglycemic reactions | |

| ANTIDIARRHEAL MEDICATIONS | | |
|---|---|---|
| **MEDICATION** | **ADVERSE EFFECTS** | **NURSING CONSIDERATIONS** |
| Bismuth subsalicylate | Darkening of stools and tongue<br>Constipation | Give 2 h before or 3 h after other medications to prevent impaired absorption<br>Encourage fluids<br>Take after each loose stool until diarrhea controlled<br>Notify health care provider if diarrhea not controlled in 48 h Absorbs irritants and soothes intestinal muscle<br>Do not administer for more than 2 days in presence of fever or in clients less than 3 years of age<br>Monitor for salicylate toxicity<br>Use cautiously if already taking aspirin<br>Avoid use before x-rays (is radiopaque) |
| Diphenoxylate hydrochloride and atropine sulfate | Sedation<br>Dizziness<br>Tachycardia<br>Dry mouth<br>Paralytic ileus | Onset 45–60 min<br>Monitor fluid and electrolytes<br>Increases intestinal tone and decreases peristalsis<br>May potentiate action of barbiturates, depressants |
| Loperamide | Drowsiness<br>Constipation | Monitor children closely for CNS effects |
| Opium alkaloids | Narcotic dependence, nausea | Acts on smooth muscle to increase tone<br>Administer with glass of water<br>Discontinue as soon as stools are controlled |
| **Action** | Absorbs water, gas, toxins, irritants, and nutrients in bowel; slows peristalsis; increases tone of smooth muscles and sphincters | |
| **Indications** | Diarrhea | |
| **Adverse effects** | Constipation, fecal impaction<br>Anticholinergic effects | |
| **Nursing considerations** | Not used with abdominal pain of unknown origin<br>Monitor for urinary retention | |

## ANTIDYSRHYTHMIC MEDICATIONS

| MEDICATION | ADVERSE EFFECTS | NURSING CONSIDERATIONS |
|---|---|---|
| **CLASS IA**<br>Procainamide<br>Quinidine | Hypotension<br>Heart failure | Monitor blood pressure<br>Monitor for widening of the PR, QRS or QT intervals<br>Toxic adverse effects have limited use |
| **CLASS IB**<br>Lidocaine | CNS: slurred speech, confusion, drowsiness, confusion, seizures<br>Hypotension and bradycardia | Monitor for CNS adverse effects<br>Monitor BP and heart rate and cardiac rhythm |
| **CLASS IC**<br>Flecainide<br>Propafenone HCL | | |
| **CLASS II**<br>(**Beta-blockers**)<br>Propranolol<br>Esmolol hydrochloride | Bradycardia and hypotension<br>Bronchospasm<br>Increase in heart failure<br>Fatigue and sleep disturbances | Monitor apical heart rate, cardiac rhythm and blood pressure<br>Assess for shortness of breath and wheezing<br>Assess for fatigue, sleep disturbances<br>Assess apical heart rate for 1 minute before administration |
| **CLASS III**<br>Amiodarone hydrochloride<br>Ibutilide fumarate | Hypotension<br>Bradycardia and atrioventricular block<br>Muscle weakness, tremors<br>Photosensitivity and photophobia<br>Liver toxicity | Continuous monitoring of cardiac rhythm during IV administration<br>Monitor QT interval during IV administration<br>Monitor heart rate, blood pressure during initiation of therapy<br>Instruct client to wear sunglasses and sunscreen |
| **CLASS IV**<br>(**Calcium channel blocker**)<br>Verapamil<br>Diltiazem hydrochloride | Bradycardia<br>Hypotension<br>Dizziness and orthostatic hypotension<br>Heart failure | Monitor apical heart rate and blood pressure<br>Instruct clients about orthostatic precautions<br>Instruct clients to report signs of heart failure to health care provider |

## ANTIEMETIC MEDICATIONS

| MEDICATION | ADVERSE EFFECTS | NURSING CONSIDERATIONS |
|---|---|---|
| Trimethobenzamide HCl | Drowsiness<br>Headache | Give IM deep into upper outer quadrant of gluteal muscle to reduce pain and irritation |
| Prochlorperazine dimaleate | Drowsiness<br>Orthostatic hypotension<br>Diplopia, photosensitivity | Check CBC and liver function with prolonged use<br>Wear protective clothing when exposed to sunlight |

| ANTIEMETIC MEDICATIONS *(CONTINUED)* | | |
|---|---|---|
| **MEDICATION** | **ADVERSE EFFECTS** | **NURSING CONSIDERATIONS** |
| Ondansetron | Headache, sedation<br><br>Diarrhea, constipation<br><br>Transient elevations in liver enzymes | New class of antiemetics—serotonin receptor antagonist<br><br>Administer 30 min prior to chemotherapy |
| Metoclopramide | Restlessness, anxiety, drowsiness<br><br>Extrapyramidal symptoms<br><br>Dystonic reactions | Monitor BP<br><br>Avoid activities requiring mental alertness<br><br>Take before meals<br><br>Used with tube feeding to decrease residual and risk of aspiration<br><br>Administer 30 min prior to chemotherapy |
| Meclizine | Drowsiness, dry mouth<br><br>Blurred vision<br><br>Excitation, restlessness | Contraindicated with glaucoma<br><br>Avoid activities requiring mental alertness |
| Dimenhydrinate | Drowsiness<br><br>Palpitations, hypotension<br><br>Blurred vision | Avoid activities requiring mental alertness |
| Promethazine | Drowsiness<br><br>Dizziness<br><br>Constipation<br><br>Urinary retention<br><br>Dry mouth | If used for motion sickness, take 1/2 to 1 hour before traveling; avoid activities requiring alertness; avoid alcohol, other CNS depressants |
| Droperidol | Seizures<br><br>Arrhythmias<br><br>Hypotension<br><br>Tachycardia | Often used either IV or IM in ambulatory care settings; observe for extrapyramidal symptoms (dystonia, extended neck, flexed arms, tremor, restlessness, hyperactivity, anxiety), which can be reversed with anticholinergics |
| **Action** | Blocks effect of dopamine in chemoreceptor trigger zone; increases GI motility | |
| **Indications** | Nausea and vomiting caused by surgery, chemotherapy, radiation sickness, uremia | |
| **Adverse effects** | Drowsiness, sedation<br><br>Anticholinergic effects | |
| **Nursing considerations** | When used for viral infections may cause Reye's syndrome in clients less than 21 years old Phenothiazine medications are also used as antiemetics | |
| **Herbals** | Ginger—used to treat minor heartburn, nausea, vomiting; may increase risk of bleeding if take with anticoagulants, antiplatelets, thrombolytic medication; instruct to stop medication if easily bruised or other signs of bleeding noted, report to health care provider; not approved for morning sickness during pregnancy | |

## ANTIFUNGAL MEDICATIONS

| MEDICATION | ADVERSE EFFECTS | NURSING CONSIDERATIONS |
|---|---|---|
| Amphotericin B | IV: nicknamed "amphoterrible"<br>GI upset<br>Hypokalemia-induced muscle pain<br>CNS disturbances in vision, hearing<br>Peripheral neuritis<br>Seizures<br>Hematological, renal, cardiac, hepatic abnormalities<br>Skin irritation and thrombosis if IV infiltrates | Refrigerate medication and protect from sunlight<br>Monitor vital signs; report febrile reaction or any change in function, especially nervous system dysfunction<br>Check for hypokalemia<br>Meticulous care and observation of injection site |
| Nystatin | Mild GI distress<br>Hypersensitivity | Discontinue if redness, swelling, irritation occurs<br>Instruct client in good oral, vaginal, skin hygiene |
| Flucanozal | Nausea, vomiting<br>Diarrhea<br>Elevated liver enzymes | Drug excreted unchanged by kidneys; dosage reduced if creatine clearance is altered due to renal failure<br>Administer after hemodialysis |
| Metronidazole | Headaches, vaginitis, nausea, flu-like symptoms (systemic use) | Reduce dosage hepatic disease<br>Monitor CBC, LFTs, cultures<br>Give tablet with food or milk |
| **Action** | Impairs cell membrane of fungus, causing increased permeability | |
| **Indications** | Systemic fungal infections (e.g., candidiasis, oral thrush, histoplasmosis) | |
| **Adverse effects** | Hepatotoxicity<br>Thrombocytopenia<br>Leukopenia<br>Pruritus | |
| **Nursing considerations** | Administer with food to decrease GI upset<br>Small, frequent meals<br>Check hepatic function<br>Teach client to take full course of medication, may be prescribed for prolonged period | |

| ANTIGOUT MEDICATIONS | | |
|---|---|---|
| **MEDICATION** | **ADVERSE EFFECTS** | **NURSING CONSIDERATIONS** |
| Colchicine | GI upset<br>Agranulocytosis<br>Peripheral neuritis | Anti-inflammatory<br>Give with meals<br>Check CBC, I and O<br>For acute gout in combination with NSAIDs |
| Probenecid | Nausea, constipation<br>Skin rash | For chronic gout<br>Reduces uric acid<br>Check BUN, renal function tests<br>Encourage fluids<br>Give with milk, food, antacids<br>Alkaline urine helps prevent renal stones |
| Allopurinol | GI upset<br>Headache, dizziness, drowsiness | Blocks formation of uric acid<br>Encourage fluids<br>Check I and O<br>Check CBC and renal function tests<br>Give with meals<br>Alkaline urine helps prevent renal stones<br>Avoid ASA because it inactivates drug |
| **Action** | Decreases production and reabsorption of uric acid | |
| **Indications** | Gout<br>Uric acid stone formation | |
| **Adverse effects** | Aplastic anemia<br>Agranulocytosis<br>Renal calculi<br>GI irritation | |
| **Nursing considerations** | Monitor for renal calculi | |

| ANTIHISTAMINE MEDICATIONS | | |
|---|---|---|
| MEDICATION | ADVERSE EFFECTS | NURSING CONSIDERATIONS |
| Chlorpheniramine maleate | Drowsiness, dry mouth | Most effective if taken before onset of symptoms |
| Diphenhydramine HCl | Drowsiness<br>Nausea, dry mouth<br>Photosensitivity | Don't combine with alcoholic beverages<br>Give with food<br>Use sunscreen<br>Older adults: greater risk of confusion and sedation |
| Promethazine HCl | Agranulocytosis<br>Drowsiness, dry mouth<br>Photosensitivity | Give with food<br>Use sunscreen |
| Loratadine<br>Cetirizine<br>Fexofenadine | Drowsiness | Reduce dose or give every other day for clients with renal or hepatic dysfunction |
| **Action** | Blocks the effects of histamine at peripheral $H_1$ receptor sites; anticholinergic, antipruritic effects | |
| **Indications** | Allergic rhinitis<br>Allergic reactions<br>Chronic idiopathic urticaria | |
| **Adverse effects** | Depression<br>Nightmares<br>Sedation<br>Dry mouth<br>GI upset<br>Bronchospasm<br>Alopecia | |
| **Nursing considerations** | Administer with food<br>Good mouth care, sugarless lozenges for dry mouth<br>Good skin care<br>Use caution when performing tasks requiring alertness (e.g., driving car)<br>Avoid alcohol | |

## ANTI-INFECTIVE: AMINOGLYCOSIDES MEDICATIONS

| | |
|---|---|
| **Examples** | Gentamicin<br>Tobramycin<br>Amikacin |
| **Actions** | Bacteriocidal<br>Inhibits protein synthesis of many Gram-negative bacteria |
| **Indications** | Treatment of severe systemic infections of CNS, respiratory, GI, urinary tract, bone, skin, soft tissues, acute pelvic inflammatory disease (PID), tuberculosis (streptomycin) |
| **Adverse effects** | Ototoxicity, Nephrotoxicity<br>Anorexia, nausea, vomiting, diarrhea |
| **Nursing considerations** | Check eighth cranial nerve function (hearing)<br>Check renal function (BUN, creatinine)<br>Usually prescribed for 7–10 days<br>Encourage fluids<br>Small, frequent meals |

## ANTI-INFECTIVE: CEPHALOSPORIN MEDICATIONS

| | |
|---|---|
| **Example** | Multiple preparations:<br>1st generation example: cephalexin<br>2nd generation example: cefoxitin sodium<br>3rd generation example: ceftriaxone sodium<br>4th generation example: cefepime HCL<br>5th generation example: fosamil |
| **Actions** | Bacteriocidal<br>Inhibits synthesis of bacterial cell wall |
| **Indications** | Pharyngitis<br>Tonsillitis<br>Otitis media<br>Upper and lower respiratory tract infections<br>Dermatological infections<br>Gonorrhea<br>Septicemia<br>Meningitis<br>Perioperative prophylaxis<br>Urinary tract infections |

| ANTI-INFECTIVE: CEPHALOSPORIN MEDICATIONS *(CONTINUED)* | |
|---|---|
| **Adverse effects** | Abdominal pain, nausea, vomiting, diarrhea |
| | Increased risk bleeding |
| | Hypoprothrombinemia |
| | Rash |
| | Superinfections |
| | Thrombophlebitis (IV), abscess formation (IM, IV) |
| **Nursing considerations** | Take with food |
| | Administer liquid form to children, don't crush tablets |
| | Have vitamin K available for hypoprothrombinemia |
| | Avoid alcohol while taking medication and for 3 days after finishing course of medication |
| | Cross allergy with penicillins (cephalosporins should not be given to clients with a severe penicillin allergy) |
| | Monitor renal and hepatic function |
| | Monitor for Thrombophlebitis |

| ANTI-INFECTIVE: FLUOROQUINOLONES MEDICATION | |
|---|---|
| **Examples** | Ciprofloxacin |
| | Levofloxacin |
| **Actions** | Bactericidal; interferes with DNA replication in Gram-negative bacteria |
| **Indications** | Treatment of infection caused *by E. coli* and other bacteria, chronic bacterial prostatitis, acute sinusitis, postexposure inhalation anthrax |
| **Adverse effects** | Headache |
| | Nausea |
| | Diarrhea |
| | Elevated BUN, AST, ALT, serum creatinine, alkaline phosphatase |
| | Decreased WBC and hematocrit |
| | Rash |
| | Photosensitivity |
| | Achilles tendon rupture |
| **Nursing considerations** | Culture and sensitivity before starting therapy |
| | Take 1 h before or 2 h after meals with glass of water |
| | Encourage fluids |
| | If needed administer antacids 2 h after medication |
| | Take full course of therapy |

## ANTI-INFECTIVE: GLYCOPEPTIDE MEDICATIONS

| | |
|---|---|
| **Example** | Vancomycin |
| **Action** | Bacteriocidal<br>Binds to bacterial cell wall, stopping its synthesis |
| **Indications** | Treatment of resistant staph infections, pseudomembranous entero-colitis due to c. *difficile* infection |
| **Adverse effects** | Thrombophlebitis<br>Abscess formation<br>Nephrotoxicity<br>Ototoxicity |
| **Nursing considerations** | Monitor renal function and hearing<br>Poor absorption orally; administer IV: peak 5 minutes, duration 12–24 hours<br>Avoid extravasation during therapy; it may cause necrosis<br>Give antihistamine if "red man syndrome": decreased blood pressure, flushing of face and neck<br>Contact health care provider if signs of superinfection: sore throat, fever, fatigue |

## ANTI-INFECTIVE: LINCOSAMIDE MEDICATIONS

| | |
|---|---|
| **Example** | Clindamycin HCl Phosphate |
| **Action** | Both bacteriostatic and bactericidal, it suppresses protein synthesis by preventing peptide bond formation |
| **Indications** | Staph, strep, and other infections |
| **Adverse effects** | Diarrhea<br>Rash<br>Liver toxicity |
| **Nursing considerations** | Administer oral med with a full glass of water to prevent esophageal ulcers<br>Monitor for persistent vomiting, diarrhea, fever, or abdominal pain and cramping, superinfectious |

## ANTIBIOTICS/ANTI-INFECTIVE: MACROLIDE MEDICATIONS

| | |
|---|---|
| **Examples** | Erythromycin<br>AzIthromycin |
| **Actions** | Bacteriostatic; bactericidal; binds to cell membrane and causes changes in protein function |
| **Indications** | Acute infections<br>Acne and skin infections<br>Upper respiratory tract infections<br>Prophylaxis before dental procedures for clients allergic to PCN with valvular heart disease |

| ANTIBIOTICS/ANTI-INFECTIVE: MACROLIDE MEDICATIONS *(CONTINUED)* | |
|---|---|
| **Adverse effects** | Abdominal cramps, diarrhea |
| | Confusion, uncontrollable emotions |
| | Hepatotoxicity |
| | Superinfections |
| **Nursing considerations** | Take oral med 1 h before or 2–3 h after meals with full glass of water |
| | Take around the clock to maximize effectiveness |
| | Monitor liver function |
| | Take full course of therapy |

| ANTI-INFECTIVE: PENICILLIN MEDICATIONS | |
|---|---|
| **Examples** | Amoxicillin |
| | Ampicillin |
| | Methicillin |
| | Nafcillin |
| | Penicillin G |
| | Penicillin V |
| **Actions** | Bactericidal; inhibit synthesis of cell wall of sensitive organisms |
| **Indications** | Effective against gram positive organisms |
| | Moderate to severe infections |
| | Syphilis |
| | Gonococcal infections |
| | Lyme disease |
| **Adverse effects** | Glossitis, stomatitis |
| | Gastritis |
| | Diarrhea |
| | Superinfections |
| | Hypersensitivity reactions |
| **Nursing considerations** | Culture and sensitivity before treatment |
| | Monitor serum electrolytes and cardiac status if given IV |
| | Monitor and rotate injection sites |
| | Good mouth care |
| | Yogurt or buttermilk if diarrhea develops |
| | Instruct client to take missed drugs as soon as possible; do not double dose |

| ANTI–INFECTIVE: SULFONAMIDE MEDICATIONS ||
|---|---|
| **Example** | Sulfasalazine |
| | Trimethoprim/Sulfamethoxazole |
| **Actions** | Bacteriostatic; competitively antagonize paraminobenzoic acid, essential component of folic acid synthesis, causing cell death |
| **Indications** | Ulcerative colitis, Crohn's disease |
| | Otitis media |
| | Conjunctivitis |
| | Meningitis |
| | Toxoplasmosis |
| | UTIs |
| | Rheumatoid arthritis |
| **Adverse effects** | Peripheral neuropathy |
| | Crystalluria, proteinuria |
| | Photosensitivity |
| | GI upset |
| | Stomatitis |
| | Hypersensitvity reaction |
| **Nursing considerations** | Culture and sensitivity before therapy |
| | Take with a full glass of water |
| | Take around the clock |
| | Encourage fluid intake (8 glasses of water/day) |
| | Protect from exposure to light (sunscreen, protective clothing) |
| | Good mouth care |

| ANTI-INFECTIVE: TETRACYCLINE MEDICATIONS | |
|---|---|
| **Examples** | Doxycycline<br>Minocycline HCL<br>Tetracycline HCl |
| **Actions** | Bacteriostatic; inhibits protein synthesis of susceptible bacteria |
| **Indications** | Treatment of syphilis, chlamydia, gonorrhea, malaria prophylaxis, chronic periodontitis, acne; treatment of anthrax (doxycycline); as part of combination therapy to eliminate *H. pylori* infections; drug of choice for stage 1 Lyme disease (tetracycline HCl) |
| **Adverse effects** | Discoloration and inadequate calcification of primary teeth of fetus if taken during pregnancy<br>Glossitis<br>Dysphagia<br>Diarrhea<br>Phototoxic reactions<br>Rash<br>Superinfections |
| **Nursing considerations** | Take 1 h before or 2–3 h after meals<br>Do not take with antacids, milk, iron preparations (give 3 h after medication)<br>Note expiration date (becomes highly nephrotoxic)<br>Protect from sunlight<br>Monitor renal function<br>Topical applications may stain clothing<br>Use contraceptive method in addition to oral contraceptives |

| ANTI-INFECTIVE MEDICATIONS: VANCOMYCIN | |
|---|---|
| **Examples** | Vancomycin |
| **Action** | Bacteriocidal<br>Binds to bacterial cell wall, stopping its synthesis |
| **Indications** | Treatment of resistant staph infections, pseudomembranous enterocolitis due to c. difficile infection |
| **Adverse effects** | Thrombophlebitis<br>Abscess formation<br>Nephrotoxicity<br>Ototoxicity |
| **Nursing considerations** | Monitor renal function and hearing<br>Poor absorption orally; administer IV: peak 5 minutes, duration 12–24 hours<br>Avoid extravasation during therapy; it may cause necrosis<br>Give antihistamine if "red man syndrome": decreased blood pressure, flushing of face and neck<br>Contact health care provider if signs of superinfection: sore throat, fever, fatigue |

| ANTI-INFECTIVE MEDICATION OVERVIEW | | |
|---|---|---|
| **MEDICATION** | **ADVERSE EFFECTS** | **NURSING CONSIDERATIONS** |
| **Penicillins**<br>Amoxicillin<br>Ampicillin<br>Methicillin<br>Penicillin G<br>Penicillin V | Skin rashes, diarrhea<br>Allergic reactions<br>Renal, hepatic, hematological abnormalities<br>Nausea, vomiting | Obtain C and S before first dose<br>Take careful history of penicillin reaction<br>Observe for 20 minutes post IM injection<br>Give 1–2 h ac or 2–3 h pc to reduce gastric acid destruction of drug<br>Monitor for loose, foul-smelling stool and change in tongue<br>Teach to continue medication for entire time prescribed, even if symptoms resolve<br>Check for hypersensitivity to other drugs, especially cephalosporins |
| **Sulfonamides**<br>Sulfisoxazole | Headache,<br>GI disturbances<br>Allergic rash<br>Urinary crystallization | Monitor I and 0, force fluids<br>Maintain alkaline urine<br>Bicarbonate may be indicated to elevate pH<br>Avoid vitamin C, which acidifies urine |
| Sulfasalazine | Nausea, vomiting<br>Skin eruption<br>Agranulocytosis | Advise client to avoid exposure to sunlight<br>Maintain fluid intake at 3,000 mL/day to avoid crystal formation |
| Trimethoprim/ Sulfamethoxazole | Hypersensitivity reaction<br>Blood dyscrasias<br>Rash | Obtain C and S before first dose<br>IV solution must be given slowly over 60–90 minutes<br>Never administer IM<br>Encourage fluids to 3,000/day |
| **Tetracylines**<br>Tetracycline | Photosensitivity<br>GI upset, renal, hepatic, hematological abnormalities<br>Dental discoloration of deciduous ("baby") teeth, enamel hypoplasia | Give between meals<br>If GI symptoms occur, administer with food EXCEPT milk products or other foods high in calcium (interferes with absorption)<br>Assess for change in bowel habits, perineal rash, black "hairy" tongue<br>Good oral hygiene<br>Avoid during tooth and early development periods (fourth month prenatal to 8 years of age)<br>Monitor I and 0<br>Caution client to avoid sun exposure<br>Decomposes to toxic substance with age and exposure to light |
| Doxycycline | Photosensitivity | Check client's tongue for *Monilia* infection |
| **Aminogylcosides**<br>Gentamicin | Ototoxicity cranial nerve VIII<br>Nephrotoxicity | Check creatinine and BUN<br>Check peak—2 h after med given<br>Check trough—at time of dose/prior to med<br>Monitor for symptoms of bacterial overgrowth, photosensitivity<br>Teach to immediately report tinnitus, vertigo, nystagmus, ataxia<br>Monitor I and 0<br>Audiograms if given long-term |

| ANTI-INFECTIVE MEDICATION OVERVIEW *(CONTINUED)* | | |
|---|---|---|
| **MEDICATION** | **ADVERSE EFFECTS** | **NURSING CONSIDERATIONS** |
| Neomycin sulfate | Hypersensitivity reactions | Ophthalmic—remove infective exudate around eyes before administration of ointment |
| **Fluoroquinolones**<br>Ciprofloxacin | Seizures<br>GI upset<br>Rash | Contraindicated in children less than 18 years of age<br>Give 2 hours pc or 2 hours before an antacid or iron preparation<br>Avoid caffeine<br>Encourage fluids |
| **Macrolides**<br>Azithromycin<br>Erythromycin | Pain at injection site<br>Nausea, diarrhea | Can be used in clients with compromised renal function because excretion is primarily through the bile |
| **Cephalosporins** | Diarrhea, nausea<br>Dizziness, abdominal pain<br>Eosinophilia, superinfections<br>Allergic reactions | Can cause false-positive Coombs' test (which will complicate transfusion cross-matching procedure)<br>Cross-sensitivity with penicillins<br>Take careful history of penicillin reactions |
| **Glycopeptides**<br>Vancomycin | Liver damage | Poor absorption orally, but IV peak 5 minutes, duration 12–24 hours<br>Avoid extravasation during therapy—may cause necrosis<br>Give antihistamine if "red man syndrome": decreased blood pressure, flushing of face and neck<br>Contact health care provider if signs of superinfection: sore throat, fever, fatigue |
| **Lincosamides**<br>Clindamycin HCl phosphate | Nausea<br>Vaginitis<br>Colitis may occur 2–9 days or several weeks after starting meds | Administer oral med with a full glass of water to prevent esophageal ulcers<br>Monitor for persistent vomiting, diarrhea, fever, or abdominal pain and cramping |

| ANTI-INFECTIVE MEDICATIONS: TOPICAL | | |
|---|---|---|
| **MEDICATION** | **ADVERSE EFFECTS** | **NURSING CONSIDERATIONS** |
| Bacitracin ointment | Nephrotoxicity<br>Ototoxicity | Overgrowth of nonsusceptible organisms can occur |
| Neosporin cream | Nephrotoxicity<br>Ototoxicity | Allergic dermatitis may occur |
| Povidone-iodine solution | Irritation | Don't use around eyes<br>May stain skin<br>Don't use full-strength on mucous membranes |
| Silver sulfadiazine cream | Neutropenia<br>Burning | Use cautiously if sensitive to sulfonamides |

| ANTI-INFECTIVE MEDICATIONS: TOPICAL *(CONTINUED)* | | |
|---|---|---|
| MEDICATION | ADVERSE EFFECTS | NURSING CONSIDERATIONS |
| Tolna flake cream | Irritation | Use small amount of medication<br>Use medication for duration prescribed |
| Nystatin cream | Contact dermatitis | Do not use occlusive dressings |

| ANTIHYPERTENSIVE MEDICATIONS: ANGIOTENSIN II RECEPTOR ANTAGONISTS (ACE RECEPTOR BLOCKERS/ARBS) | |
|---|---|
| **Examples** | Candesartan<br>Eprosartan<br>Irbesartan<br>Losartan<br>Valsartan |
| **Indications** | Hypertension<br>Heart failure<br>Diabetic neuropathy<br>Myocardial infarction<br>Stroke prevention |
| **Adverse effects** | Angioedema<br>Renal failure<br>Orthostatic hypotension |
| **Nursing considerations** | Instruct client about position changes<br>Monitor for edema<br>Instruct client to notify health care provider if edema occurs |

| ANTIHYPERTENSIVE MEDICATIONS: ACE INHIBITORS (ANGIOTENSIN–CONVERTING ENZYME) | |
|---|---|
| **Example** | Captopril<br>Enalapril<br>Lisinopril<br>Benazepril<br>Fosinopril<br>Quinapril<br>Ramipril |
| **Actions** | Blocks ACE in lungs from converting angiotensin I to angiotensin II (powerful vasoconstrictor); causes decreased BP, decreased aldosterone secretion, sodium and fluid loss |
| **Indications** | Hypertension<br>CHF |

| ANTIHYPERTENSIVE MEDICATIONS: ACE INHIBITORS (ANGIOTENSIN–CONVERTING ENZYME) *(CONTINUED)* | |
|---|---|
| **Adverse effects** | Gastric irritation, peptic ulcer, orthostatic hypotension |
| | Tachycardia |
| | Myocardial infarction |
| | Proteinuria |
| | Rash, pruritis |
| | Persistent dry nonproductive cough |
| | Peripheral edema |
| **Nursing considerations** | Decreased absorption if taken with food—give 1 h ac or 2 h pc |
| | Small, frequent meals |
| | Frequent mouth care |
| | Change position slowly |
| | Can be used with thiazide diuretics |

| ANTIHYPERTENSIVE MEDICATIONS: ALPHA–1 ADRENERGIC BLOCKERS | |
|---|---|
| **Examples** | Doxazosin |
| | Prazosin |
| | Terazosin |
| **Actions** | Selective blockade of alpha-1 adrenergic receptors in peripheral blood vessels |
| **Indications** | Hypertension |
| | Benign prostatic hypertrophy |
| | Pheochromocytoma |
| | Raynaud's disease |
| **Adverse effects** | Orthostatic hypotension |
| | Reflex tachycardia |
| | Nasal congestion |
| | Impotence |
| **Nursing considerations** | Administer first dose at bedtime to avoid fainting |
| | Change positions slowly to prevent orthostatic hypotension |
| | Monitor BP, weight, BUN/creatinine, edema |

| ANTIHYPERTENSIVE MEDICATIONS: BETA-ADRENERGIC BLOCKERS | |
| --- | --- |
| **Examples** | Atenolol |
| | Nadolol |
| | Propranolol |
| | Metoprolol |
| | Acebutolol |
| | Carvedilol |
| | Pindolol |
| **Actions** | Blocks beta-adrenergic receptors in heart; decreases excitability of heart; reduces cardiac workload and oxygen consumption; decreases release of renin; lowers blood pressure by reducing CNS stimuli |
| **Indications** | Hypertension (used with diuretics) |
| | Angina |
| | Supraventricular tachycardia |
| | Prevent recurrent MI |
| | Migraine headache (propranolol) |
| | Stage fright (propranolol) |
| | Heart failure |
| **Adverse effects** | Gastric pain |
| | Bradycardia/tachycardia |
| | Acute severe heart failure |
| | Cardiac dysrhythmias |
| | Impotence |
| | Decreased exercise tolerance |
| | Nightmares, depression |
| | Dizziness |
| | Bronchospasm (nonselective beta blockers) |
| **Nursing considerations** | Do not discontinue abruptly, taper gradually over 2 weeks |
| | Take with meals |
| | Provide rest periods |
| | For diabetic clients, blocks normal signs of hypoglycemia (sweating, tachycardia); monitor blood glucose |
| | Medications have antianginal and antiarrhythmic actions |

| ANTIHYPERTENSIVE MEDICATIONS: CALCIUM–CHANNEL BLOCKERS | |
| --- | --- |
| **Examples** | Nifedipine |
| | Verapamil |
| | Diltiazem |
| | Amlodipine |
| | Felodipine |
| **Actions** | Inhibits movement of calcium ions across membrane of cardiac and arterial muscle cells; results in slowed impulse conduction, depression of myocardial contractility, dilation of coronary arteries; decreases cardiac workload and energy consumption, increases oxygenation of myocardial cells |

| ANTIHYPERTENSIVE MEDICATIONS: CALCIUM-CHANNEL BLOCKERS *(CONTINUED)* | |
| --- | --- |
| **Indications** | Angina<br>Hypertension<br>Dysrhythmias<br>Interstitial cystitis<br>Migraines |
| **Adverse effects** | Dizziness<br>Headache<br>Nervousness<br>Peripheral edema<br>Angina<br>Bradycardia<br>AV block<br>Flushing, rash<br>Impotence |
| **Nursing considerations** | Monitor vital signs<br>Do not chew or divide sustained-release tablets<br>Medications also have antianginal actions<br>Contraindicated in heart block<br>Contact health care provider if blood pressure less than 90/60 Instruct client to avoid grapefruit juice (verapamil)<br>Monitor for signs of heart failure |

| ANTIHYPERTENSIVE MEDICATIONS: CENTRALLY ACTING ALPHA-ADRENERGICS | |
| --- | --- |
| **Examples** | Clonidine<br>Methyldopa |
| **Actions** | Stimulates alpha receptors in medulla, causing reduction in sympathetic action in heart; decreases rate and force of contraction, decreasing cardiac output |
| **Indications** | Hypertension |
| **Adverse effects** | Drowsiness, sedation<br>Orthostatic hypotension<br>CHF |
| **Nursing considerations** | Don't discontinue abruptly<br>Monitor for fluid retention<br>Older adults: potential for orthostatic hypotension and CNS adverse effects |

| ANTIHYPERTENSIVE MEDICATIONS: DIRECT–ACTING VASODILATORS | |
|---|---|
| **Examples** | Hydralazine<br>Minoxidil |
| **Actions** | Relaxes smooth muscle of blood vessels, lowering peripheral resistance |
| **Indications** | Hypertension |
| **Adverse effects** | Same as centrally acting alpha adrenergics |
| **Nursing considerations** | Same as centrally acting alpha adrenergics |

| ANTIHYPERTENSIVE MEDICATIONS OVERVIEW | | |
|---|---|---|
| **MEDICATION** | **ADVERSE EFFECTS** | **NURSING CONSIDERATIONS** |
| Methyldopa | Drowsiness, dizziness, bradycardia, hemolytic anemia, fever, orthostatic hypotension | Monitor CBC<br>Monitor liver function<br>Take at hs to minimize daytime drowsiness<br>Change position slowly |
| Clonidine | Drowsiness, dizziness<br>Dry mouth, headache<br>Dermatitis<br>Severe rebound hypertension | Don't discontinue abruptly<br>Apply patch to nonhairy area (upper outer arm, anterior chest) |
| Atenolol | Bradycardia<br>Hypotension<br>Bronchospasm | Once-a-day dose increases compliance<br>Check apical pulse; if less than 60 bpm hold drug and call health care provider<br>Don't discontinue abruptly<br>Masks signs of shock and hypoglycemia |
| Metoprolol | Bradycardia, hypotension, heart failure, depression | Give with meals<br>Teach client to check pulse before each dose; take apical pulse before administration<br>Withhold if pulse less than 60 bpm |
| Nadolol | Bradycardia, hypotension, heart failure | Teach client to check pulse before each dose; check apical pulse before administering<br>Withhold if pulse less than 60 bpm<br>Don't discontinue abruptly |
| Hydralazine | Headache, palpitations, edema, tachycardia, lupus erythematosus-like syndrome | Give with meals<br>Observe mental status<br>Check for weight gain, edema |
| Minoxidil | Tachycardia, angina pectoris, edema, increase in body hair | Teach client to check pulse; check apical pulse before administration<br>Monitor I and 0, weight |

### ANTIHYPERTENSIVE MEDICATIONS OVERVIEW (CONTINUED)

| MEDICATION | ADVERSE EFFECTS | NURSING CONSIDERATIONS |
|---|---|---|
| Captopril<br><br>Enalapril<br><br>Lisinopril | Dizziness<br><br>Orthostatic hypotension | Report swelling of face, lightheadedness<br><br>ACE-inhibitor medication |
| Propranolol | Weakness<br><br>Hypotension<br><br>Bronchospasm<br><br>Bradycardia<br><br>Depression | Beta blocker: blocks sympathetic impulses to heart<br><br>Client takes pulse at home before each dose<br><br>Dosage should be reduced gradually before discontinued |
| Nifedipine<br><br>Verapamil<br><br>Diltiazem | Hypotension<br><br>Dizziness<br><br>GI distress<br><br>Liver dysfunction<br><br>Jitteriness | Calcium-channel blocker: reduces workload of left ventricle<br><br>Coronary vasodilator; monitor blood pressure during dosage adjustments<br><br>Assist with ambulation at start of therapy |
| **Herbal interaction** | Ma-huang (ephedra) decreases effect of antihypertensive drugs<br><br>Ephedra increases hypertension when taken with beta blockers<br><br>Black cohosh increases hypotensive effects of antihypertensives<br><br>Goldenseal counteracts effects of antihypertensives | |

### ANTILIPEMIC MEDICATIONS

| MEDICATION | ADVERSE EFFECTS | NURSING CONSIDERATIONS |
|---|---|---|
| **Bile acid sequestrants**<br><br>Cholestyramine<br><br>Colestipol<br><br>HMG-COA reductase inhibitors<br><br>Folic acid derivatives<br><br>Nicotinic acid | Constipation<br><br>Rash<br><br>Fat-soluble vitamin deficiency<br><br>Abdominal pain and bloating | Increases loss of bile acid in feces; decreases cholesterol<br><br>Sprinkle powder on noncarbonated beverage or wet food, let stand 2 min, then stir slowly<br><br>Administer 1 h before or 4–6 h after other medication to avoid blocking absorption<br><br>Instruct client to report constipation immediately |
| **HMG-CoA reductase inhibitors (statins)**<br><br>Lovostatin<br><br>Pravastatin<br><br>Simvastatin<br><br>Atorvastatin<br><br>Fluvastatin<br><br>Rosuvastatin | Myopathy<br><br>Increased liver enzyme levels | Decreases LDL cholesterol levels; causes peripheral vasodilation<br><br>Take with food; absorption is reduced by 30% on an empty stomach; avoid alcohol<br><br>Contact health care provider if unexplained muscle pain, especially with fever or malaise<br><br>Take at night<br><br>Give with caution with ↓ liver function |

## ANTILIPEMIC MEDICATIONS *(CONTINUED)*

| MEDICATION | ADVERSE EFFECTS | NURSING CONSIDERATIONS |
|---|---|---|
| **Nicotinic acid**<br>Niacin | Flushing<br>Hyperglycemia<br>Gout<br>Upper GI distress<br>Liver damage | Decreases total cholesterol, LDL, triglycerides, increases HDL<br>Flushing will occur several hours after med is taken, will decrease over 2 wk<br>Also used for pellagra and peripheral vascular disease<br>Avoid alcohol |
| Folic acid derivatives<br>Fenofibrate Gemfibrozil | Abdominal pain<br>Increased risk gallbladder disease<br>Myalgia and swollen joints | Decreases total cholesterol, VLDL, and triglycerides<br>Administer before meals<br>Instruct clients to notify health care provider if muscle pain occurs |
| **Action** | Inhibits cholesterol and triglyceride synthesis; decreases serum cholesterol and LDLs | |
| **Indications** | Elevated total and LDL cholesterol<br>Primary hypercholesterolemia<br>Reduce incidence of cardiovascular disease | |
| **Adverse effects** | Varies with medication | |
| **Nursing considerations** | Medication should be used with dietary measures, physical activity, and cessation of tobacco use<br>Lipids should be monitored every 6 wk until normal, then every 4–6 mo | |
| **Herbals used to lower cholesterol** | Flax or flax seed—decreases the absorption of other medications<br>Garlic—increases the effects of anticoagulants; increases the hypoglycemic effects of insulin<br>Green tea—produces a stimulant effect with the tea contains caffeine<br>Soy | |

## ANTINEOPLASTIC MEDICATIONS: ANTIMETABOLITES

| | |
|---|---|
| **Examples** | Cytarabine<br>Fluorouracil<br>Pemetrexed<br>Mercaptopurine<br>Methotrexate |
| **Actions** | Closely resembles normal metabolites, "counterfeits" fool cells; cell division halted |
| **Indications** | Acute lymphatic leukemia<br>Rheumatoid arthritis<br>Psoriasis<br>Cancer of colon, breast, stomach, pancreas<br>Sickle cell anemia |

| ANTINEOPLASTIC MEDICATIONS: ANTIMETABOLITES *(CONTINUED)* | |
|---|---|
| **Adverse effects** | Nausea, vomiting<br>Diarrhea<br>Stomatitis and oral ulceration<br>Hepatic dysfunction<br>Bone marrow suppression<br>Renal dysfunction<br>Alopecia |
| **Nursing considerations** | Monitor hematopoietic function<br>Good mouth care<br>Small frequent feedings<br>Counsel about body image changes (alopecia); provide wig<br>Good skin care<br>Photosensitivity precautions<br>Infection control precautions |

| ANTINEOPLASTIC MEDICATIONS: ANTIBIOTICS | |
|---|---|
| **Examples** | Bleomycin<br>Dactinomycin<br>Doxorubicin |
| **Actions** | Interferes with DNA and RNA synthesis |
| **Indications** | Hodgkin's disease<br>Non-Hodgkin's lymphoma<br>Leukemia<br>Many cancers |
| **Adverse effects** | Bone marrow depression<br>Nausea, vomiting<br>Alopecia<br>Stomatitis<br>Heart failure<br>Septic shock |
| **Nursing considerations** | Monitor closely for septicemic reactions<br>Monitor for manifestations of extravasation at injection site (severe pain or burning that lasts minutes to hours, redness after injection is completed, ulceration after 48 hours) |

| ANTINEOPLASTIC MEDICATIONS: CYTOXIC MEDICATIONS | |
|---|---|
| **Examples** | Busulfan<br>Chlorambucil<br>Cisplatin platinol-AQ<br>Cyclophosphamide |
| **Actions** | Interferes with rapidly reproducing cell DNA |
| **Indications** | Leukemia<br>Multiple myeloma |
| **Adverse effects** | Bone marrow suppression<br>Nausea, vomiting<br>Stomatitis<br>Alopecia<br>Gonadal suppression<br>Renal toxicity (cisplatin)<br>Ototoxicity |
| **Nursing considerations** | Used with other chemotherapeutic medications<br>Check hematopoietic function weekly<br>Encourage fluids (10–12 glasses/day) |

| ANTINEOPLASTIC MEDICATIONS: HORMONAL MEDICATIONS | |
|---|---|
| **Examples** | Tamoxifen<br>Anastrozole Letrozole<br>Leuprolide Degarelix<br>Testolactone Testosterone |
| **Actions** | Tamoxifen–antiestrogen (competes with estrogen to bind at estrogen receptor sites on malignant cells)<br>Leuprolide–progestin (causes tumor cell regression by unknown mechanism)<br>Testolactone–androgen (used for palliation in advanced breast cancer) |
| **Indications** | Breast cancer |
| **Adverse effects** | Hypercalcemia<br>Jaundice<br>Increased appetite<br>Masculinization or feminization<br>Sodium and fluid retention<br>Nausea, vomiting<br>Hot flashes<br>Vaginal dryness |
| **Nursing considerations** | Baseline and periodic gyn exams recommended<br>Not given IVLK<br>Discuss pregnancy prevention |

| ANTINEOPLASTIC MEDICATIONS: TOPOISOMERASE ||
|---|---|
| **Examples** | Irinotecan<br>Topotecan |
| **Actions** | Binds to enzyme that breaks the DNA strands |
| **Indications** | Ovary, lung, colon, and rectal cancers |
| **Adverse effects** | Bone marrow suppression<br>Diarrhea<br>Nausea, vomiting<br>Hepatotoxicity |

| ANTINEOPLASTIC MEDICATIONS: VINCA ALKALOIDS ||
|---|---|
| **Examples** | Vinblastine<br>Vincristine |
| **Actions** | Interferes with cell division |
| **Indications** | Hodgkin's disease<br>Lymphoma<br>Cancers |
| **Adverse effects** | Bone marrow suppression (mild with VCR)<br>Neuropathies (VCR)<br>Stomatitis |
| **Nursing considerations** | Same as antitumor antibiotics |

| ANTINEOPLASTIC MEDICATION: NURSING IMPLICATIONS FOR ADVERSE EFFECTS ||
|---|---|
| Bone marrow suppression | Monitor bleeding: bleeding gums, bruising, petechiae, guaiac stools, urine and emesis<br>Avoid IM injections and rectal temperatures<br>Apply pressure to venipuncture sites |
| Nausea, vomiting | Monitor intake and output ratios, appetite and nutritional intake<br>Prophylactic antiemetics may be used<br>Smaller, more frequent meals |
| Altered immunologic response | Prevent infection by handwashing<br>Timely reporting of alterations in vital signs or symptoms indicating possible infection |
| Impaired oral mucous membrane; stomatis | Oral hygiene measures |
| Fatigue | Encourage rest and discuss measures to conserve energy<br>Use relaxation techniques, mental imagery |

| ANTIPARKINSON MEDICATIONS | | |
|---|---|---|
| **MEDICATION** | **ADVERSE EFFECTS** | **NURSING CONSIDERATIONS** |
| Trihexyphenidyl | Dry mouth<br><br>Blurred vision<br><br>Constipation, urinary hesitancy<br><br>Decreased mental acuity, difficulty concentrating, confusion, hallucination | Acts by blocking acetylcholine at cerebral synaptic sites<br><br>Intraocular pressure should be monitored<br><br>Supervise ambulation<br><br>Causes nausea if given before meals<br><br>Suck on hard candy for dry mouth |
| Levodopa | Nausea and vomiting, anorexia<br><br>Postural hypotension<br><br>Mental changes: confusion, agitation, mood alterations<br><br>Cardiac arrhythmias<br><br>Twitching | Precursor of dopamine<br><br>Thought to restore dopamine levels in extrapyramidal centers<br><br>Administered in large prolonged doses<br><br>Contraindicated in glaucoma, hemolytic anemia<br><br>Give with food<br><br>Monitor for postural hypotension<br><br>Avoid OTC meds and foods that contain vitamin $B_6$ (pyridoxine); reverses effects |
| Bromocriptine mesylate<br>Pergolide | Dizziness, headache, hypotension<br><br>Tinnitus<br><br>Nausea, abdominal cramps<br><br>Pleural effusion<br><br>Orthostatic hypotension | Give with meals<br><br>May lead to early postpartum conception<br><br>Monitor cardiac, hepatic, renal, hematopoietic function |
| Carbidopa–Levodopa | Hemolytic anemia<br><br>Dystonic movements, ataxia<br><br>Orthostatic hypotension<br><br>Dysrhythmias<br><br>GI upset, dry mouth | Stimulates dopamine receptors<br><br>Don't use with MAO inhibitors<br><br>Advise to change positions slowly<br><br>Take with food |
| Amantadine | CNS disturbances, hyperexcitability<br><br>Insomnia, vertigo, ataxia<br><br>Slurred speech, convulsions | Enhances effect of L-Dopa<br><br>Contraindicated in epilepsy, arteriosclerosis<br><br>Antiviral |
| **Action** | Levodopa–precursor to dopamine that is converted to dopamine in the brain<br><br>Bromocriptine–stimulates postsynaptic dopamine receptors | |
| **Indications** | Parkinson's disease | |

| ANTIPARKINSON MEDICATIONS *(CONTINUED)* | | |
|---|---|---|
| MEDICATION | ADVERSE EFFECTS | NURSING CONSIDERATIONS |
| **Adverse effects** | Dizziness<br>Ataxia<br>Confusion<br>Psychosis<br>Hemolytic anemia | |
| **Nursing considerations** | Monitor for urinary retention<br>Large doses of pyridoxine (vitamin $B_6$) decrease or reverse effects of medication<br>Avoid use of other CNS depressants (alcohol, narcotics, sedatives)<br>Anticholinergics, dopamine agonists, MAO inhibitors, catechol-*O*-methyltransferase (COMT) inhibitors, and antidepressants may also be used | |

| ANTIPLATELET MEDICATIONS | | |
|---|---|---|
| MEDICATION | ADVERSE EFFECTS | NURSING CONSIDERATIONS |
| Adenosine diphosphate receptor antagonists<br>Ticlodipine<br>Clopidrogrel | Thrombocytopenic purpura<br>GI upset | Prevents platelet aggregation<br>Higher risk of hemorrhage with ticlopidine |
| Dipyridamole<br>Dipyridamole plus aspirin | Headache<br>Dizziness<br>EKG changes<br>Hypertension, hypotension | Administer 1 h ac or with meals<br>Monitor BP<br>Check for signs of bleeding |
| Glycoprotein IIb and IIIa receptor antagonists<br>Eptifibatide<br>Abciximab | GI, retroperitoneal, and urogenital bleeding | Does not increase risk of fatal hemorrhage or hemorrhagic stroke |
| Asprin | Short-term use—GI bleeding, heartburn, occasional nausea<br>Prolonged high dosage—salicylism: metabolic acidosis, respiratory alkalosis, dehydration, fluid and electrolyte imbalance, tinnitus | Observe for bleeding gums, bloody or black stools, bruises<br>Give with milk, water, or food, or use enteric-coated tablets to minimize gastric distress<br>Contraindications—GI disorders, severe anemia, vitamin K deficiency<br>Anti-inflammatory, analgesic, antipyretic |
| **Action** | Interferes with platelet aggregation | |
| **Indications** | Venous thrombosis<br>Pulmonary embolism<br>CVA and acute coronary prevention<br>Post-cardiac surgery; post-percutaneous coronary interventions<br>Acute coronary syndrome | |

| ANTIPLATELET MEDICATIONS *(CONTINUED)* | | |
|---|---|---|
| MEDICATION | ADVERSE EFFECTS | NURSING CONSIDERATIONS |
| **Adverse effects** | Hemorrhage, bleeding<br>Thrombocytopenia<br>Hematuria<br>Hemoptysis | |
| **Nursing considerations** | Teach client to check for signs of bleeding<br>Inform health care provider or dentist before procedures<br>Older adults at higher risk for ototoxicity<br>Instruct client to contact health care provider before taking any over-the-counter medications<br>Instruct client to avoid gingko, garlic and ginger herbal preparations | |
| **Gerontologic considerations** | Dipyridamole causes orthostatic hypotention in older adults<br>Ticlopidine–greater risk of toxicity with older adults | |

| ANTIPSYCHOTIC MEDICATIONS | | |
|---|---|---|
| MEDICATION | ADVERSE EFFECTS | NURSING CONSIDERATIONS |
| **High potency (traditional)**<br>Haloperidol<br>Haloperidol decanoate<br>Fluphenazine<br>Fluphenazine decanoate | Low sedative effect<br>Low incidence of hypotension<br>High incidence of extrapyramidal adverse effects | Used in large doses for assaultive clients<br>Used with elderly (risk of falling reduced)<br>Decanoate: long-acting form given every 2–4 wk; IM into deep muscle Z-track |
| **Medium potency (traditional)**<br>Perphenazine | Orthostatic hypotension<br>Dry mouth<br>Constipation | Can help control severe vomiting<br>Medication is available PO, IM, and IV |
| **Low potency (traditional)**<br>Chlorpromazine | High sedative effect<br>High incidence of hypotension<br>Irreversible retinitis pigmentosus at 800 mg/day | Educate client about increased sensitivity to sun (as with other phenothiazines)<br>No tolerance or potential for abuse |
| **Atypical** | | |
| Risperidone | Moderate orthostatic hypotension<br>Moderate sedation<br>Significant weight gain<br>Doses over 6 mg can cause tardive dyskinesia | Chosen as first-line antipsychotic due to mild EPS and very low anticholinergic adverse effects |
| Quetiapine | Moderate orthostatic hypotension<br>Moderate sedation<br>Very low risk of tardive dyskinesia and neuroleptic malignant syndrome | Chosen as first-line antipsychotic due to mild EPS and very low anticholinergic adverse effects |

| ANTIPSYCHOTIC MEDICATIONS *(CONTINUED)* | | |
|---|---|---|
| **MEDICATION** | **ADVERSE EFFECTS** | **NURSING CONSIDERATIONS** |
| Ziprasidone<br>Aripiprazole<br>Clozapine<br>Olanzapine | ECG changes—QT prolongation | Effective with depressive symptoms of schizophrenia<br>Low propensity for weight gain |
| **Indications** | Acute and chronic psychosis | |
| **Adverse effects** | Akathisia (motor restlessness)<br>Dyskinesia (abnormal voluntary movements)<br>Dystonias (abnormal muscle tone producing spasms of tongue, face, neck)<br>Parkinson syndrome (shuffling gait, rigid muscles, excessive salivation, tremors, mask-like face, motor retardation)<br>Tardive dyskinesia (involuntary movements of mouth, tongue, trunk, extremities; chewing motions, sucking, tongue thrusting)<br>Photosensitivity<br>Orthostatic hypotension<br>Neuroleptic malignant syndrome | |
| **Nursing considerations** | Lowers seizure threshold<br>May slow growth rate in children<br>Monitor for urinary retention and decreased GI motility<br>Avoid alcohol<br>May cause hypotension if taken with antihypertensives, nitrates<br>Phenothiazines also used | |

| ANTIPSYCHOTIC MEDICATION ADVERSE EFFECTS | | |
|---|---|---|
| **MEDICATION** | **ADVERSE EFFECTS** | **NURSING CONSIDERATIONS** |
| Extrapyramidal | Pseudoparkinsonism<br><br>Dystonia (muscle spasm)<br><br>Acute dystonic reaction<br><br>Early signs: tightening of jaw, stiff neck, swollen tongue<br><br>Late signs: swollen airway, oculogyric crisis<br><br>Akathisia (inability to sit or stand still, foot tap, pace)<br><br>Tardive dyskinesia (abnormal, involuntary movements); may be irreversible | Pharmacologic management of Parkinsonian adverse effects: benztropine or trihexyphenidyl<br><br>Recognize early symptoms of acute dystonic reaction<br><br>Notify health care provider for IM diphenhydramine protocol |
| Anticholinergic | Blurred vision<br><br>Dry mouth<br><br>Nasal congestion<br><br>Constipation<br><br>Acute urinary retention | Educate client that some anticholinergic adverse effects often diminish over time<br><br>Maintain adequate fluid intake and monitor<br><br>I and O |
| Sedative | Sleepiness<br><br>Possible danger if driving or operating machinery | Monitor sedative effects and maintain client safety |
| Hypotensive | Orthostatic hypotension is common | Frequent monitoring of BP and advise client to rise slowly |
| Other | Phototoxicity | Educate client regarding need for sunscreen |
| Neuroleptic malignant syndrome | Rigidity<br><br>Fever<br><br>Sweating<br><br>Autonomic dysfunction (dysrhythmias, fluctuations in BP)<br><br>Confusion<br><br>Seizures, coma | Immediately withdraw antipsychotics<br><br>Control hyperthermia<br><br>Hydration<br><br>Dantroline (muscle relaxant) used for rigidity and severe reactions<br><br>Bromocriptine (dopamine receptor antogonist) used for CNS toxicity and mild reactions |
| Atropine psychosis | Skin hot to touch without fever–"red as a beet" (flushed face)<br><br>Dehydration–"dry as a bone"<br><br>Altered mental status–"mad as a hatter" | Reduce or discontinue medication<br><br>Hydration<br><br>Stay with client while confused for safety |

| ANTIPSYCHOTIC: DEGREE OF ADVERSE EFFECTS | |
|---|---|
| **Action** | Blocks postsynaptic dopamine receptors in brain |
| **Indications** | Psychotic disorders |
| | Severe nausea and vomiting |
| **Adverse effects** | Drowsiness |
| | Pseudoparkinsonism |
| | Dystonia |
| | Akathisia |
| | Tardive dyskinesia |
| | Neuroleptic malignant syndrome |
| | Dysrhythmias |
| | Photophobia |
| | Blurred vision |
| | Photosensitivity |
| | Lactation |
| | Discolors urine pink to red-brown |
| **Nursing considerations** | May cause false-positive pregnancy tests |
| | Dilute oral concentrate with water, saline, 7-Up, homogenized milk, carbonated orange drink, fruit juices (pineapple, orange, apricot, prune, V-8, tomato, grapefruit); use 60 mL for each 5 mL of medication |
| | Do not mix with beverages that contain caffeine (coffee, tea, cola) or apple juice; incompatible |
| | Monitor vital signs |
| | Takes 4–6 weeks to achieve steady plasma levels |
| | Monitor bowel function |
| | Monitor elderly for dehydration (sedation and decreased thirst sensation) |
| | Avoid activities requiring mental alertness |
| | Avoid exposure to sun |
| | Maintain fluid intake |
| | May have anticholinergic and antihistamine actions |

| ANTIPSYCHOTIC: DEGREE OF ADVERSE EFFECTS | | | | |
|---|---|---|---|---|
| **MEDICATION** | **EXTRAPYRAMIDAL** | **ANTICHOLINERGIC** | **SEDATIVE** | **HYPOTENSIVE** |
| Chlorpromazine | ↑ | ↑↑ | ↑↑↑ | ↑↑↑ |
| Thioridazine | ↑ | ↑↑↑ | ↑↑↑ | ↑↑ |
| Trifluoperazine | ↑↑↑ | ↑ | ↑ | ↑ |
| Fluphenazine | ↑↑↑ | ↑ | ↑ | ↑ |
| Perphenazine | ↑↑↑ | ↑ | ↑↑ | ↑ |
| Haloperidol | ↑↑↑ | ↑ | ↑ | ↑ |
| Thiothixene | ↑↑ | ↑ | ↑ | ↑↑ |
| KEY: ↑ mild; ↑↑ moderate; ↑↑↑ severe | | | | |

| ANTIPYRETIC MEDICATIONS | | |
|---|---|---|
| MEDICATION | ADVERSE EFFECTS | NURSING CONSIDERATIONS |
| Acetaminophen | Overdosage may be fatal<br><br>GI adverse effects are not common | Do not exceed recommended dose |
| Asprin | Short-term use—GI bleeding, heartburn, occasional nausea<br><br>Prolonged high dosage—salicylism: metabolic acidosis, respiratory alkalosis, dehydration, fluid and electrolyte imbalance, tinnitus | Observe for bleeding gums, bloody or black stools, bruises<br><br>Give with milk, water, or food, or use enteric-coated tablets to minimize gastric distress<br><br>Contraindications—GI disorders, severe anemia, vitamin K deficiency<br><br>Anti-inflammatory, analgesic, antipyretic |
| **Action** | Antiprostaglandin activity in hypothalamus reduces fever; causes peripheral vasodilation; anti-inflammatory actions | |
| **Indications** | Fever | |
| **Adverse effects** | GI irritation<br><br>Occult bleeding<br><br>Tinnitus<br><br>Dizziness<br><br>Confusion<br><br>Liver dysfunction (acetaminophen) | |
| **Nursing considerations** | Aspirin contraindicated for client less than 21 years old due to risk of Reye's syndrome<br><br>Aspirin contraindicated for clients with bleeding disorders due to anticlotting activity<br><br>NSAIDS are also used for fever | |

| ANTIPYRETIC MEDICATIONS | | |
|---|---|---|
| MEDICATION | ADVERSE EFFECTS | NURSING CONSIDER-ATIONS |
| Acetaminophen | Overdosage may be fatal<br><br>GI adverse effects are not common | Do not exceed recommended dose |
| Salicylates | Short-term use—GI bleeding, heartburn, occasional nausea<br><br>Prolonged high dosage—salicylism: metabolic acidosis, respiratory alkalosis, dehydration, fluid and electrolyte imbalance, tinnitus | Observe for bleeding gums, bloody or black stools, bruises<br><br>Give with milk, water, or food, or use enteric-coated tablets to minimize gastric distress<br><br>Contraindications—GI disorders, severe anemia, vitamin K deficiency<br><br>Anti-inflammatory, analgesic, antipyretic |

| ANTIPYRETIC MEDICATIONS *(CONTINUED)* | | |
|---|---|---|
| **MEDICATION** | **ADVERSE EFFECTS** | **NURSING CONSIDER-ATIONS** |
| **Action** | Antiprostaglandin activity in hypothalamus reduces fever; causes peripheral vasodilation; anti-inflammatory actions | |
| **Indications** | Fever | |
| **Adverse effects** | GI irritation<br>Occult bleeding<br>Tinnitus<br>Dizziness<br>Confusion<br>Liver dysfunction (acetaminophen) | |
| **Nursing consid-erations** | Aspirin contraindicated for client less than 21 years old due to risk of Reye's syndrome<br>Aspirin contraindicated for clients with bleeding disorders due to anticlotting activity<br>NSAIDS are also used for fever | |

| ANTITHYROID MEDICATIONS | | |
|---|---|---|
| **MEDICATION** | **ADVERSE EFFECTS** | **NURSING CONSIDERATIONS** |
| Methimazole<br>Propylthiouracil | Leukopenia,<br>fever,<br>rash,<br>sore throat, jaundice | Inhibits synthesis of thyroid hormone by thyroid gland<br>Check CBC and hepatic function<br>Give with meals<br>Report fever, sore throat to health care provider |
| Lugol's iodine solution<br>Potassium iodide | Nausea, vomiting, metallic taste<br>Rash | Iodine preparation<br>Used 2 weeks prior to surgery; decreases vascularity, decreases hormone release<br>Only effective for a short period<br>Give after meals<br>Dilute in water, milk, or fruit juice<br>Stains teeth<br>Give through straw |
| Radioactive iodine ($^{131}$I) | Feeling of fullness in neck<br>Metallic taste<br>Leukemia | Destroys thyroid tissue<br>Contraindicated for women of childbearing age<br>Fast overnight before administration<br>Urine, saliva, vomit radioactive 3 days<br>Use full radiation precautions<br>Encourage fluids |

| ANTITHYROID MEDICATIONS *(CONTINUED)* | | |
|---|---|---|
| **MEDICATION** | **ADVERSE EFFECTS** | **NURSING CONSIDERATIONS** |
| **Action** | Antithyroid agents—inhibits oxidation of iodine<br><br>Iodines—reduces vascularity of thyroid gland; increases amount of inactive (bound) hormone; inhibits release of thyroid hormones into circulation | |
| **Indications** | Hyperthyroidism<br>Thyrotoxic crisis | |
| **Adverse effects** | Nausea, vomiting<br>Diarrhea<br>Rashes<br>Thrombocytopenia<br>Leukopenia | |
| **Nursing considerations** | Changes in vital signs or weight and appearance may indicate adverse reactions, which should lead to evaluation of continued medication use | |

| THYROID REPLACEMENT MEDICATIONS | | |
|---|---|---|
| **MEDICATION** | **ADVERSE EFFECTS** | **NURSING CONSIDERATIONS** |
| Levothyroxine | Nervousness, tremors<br>Insomnia<br>Tachycardia, palpitations<br>Dysrhythmias, angina | Tell client to report chest pain, palpitations, sweating, nervousness, shortness of breath to health care provider |
| Liothyronine sodium | Excessive dosages produce symptoms of hyperthyroidism | Take at same time each day<br>Take in AM<br>Monitor pulse and BP |
| **Action** | Increases metabolic rate of body | |
| **Indications** | Hypothyroidism | |
| **Adverse effects** | Nervousness<br>Tachycardia<br>Weight loss | |
| **Nursing considerations** | Obtain history of client's medications<br>Enhances action of oral anticoagulants, antidepressants<br>Decreases action of insulin, digitalis<br>Obtain baseline vital signs<br>Monitor weight<br>Avoid OTC drugs | |

| ANTITUBERCULOTIC MEDICATION | | |
|---|---|---|
| MEDICATION | ADVERSE EFFECTS | NURSING CONSIDERATIONS |
| First-line medications | | |
| Isoniazid | Hepatitis<br>Peripheral neuritis<br>Rash<br>Fever | Pyridoxine (B6 ): 10–50 mg as prophylaxis for neuritis; 50–100 mg as treatment<br>Teach signs of hepatitis<br>Check liver function tests<br>Alcohol increases risk of hepatic complications<br>Therapeutic effects can be expected after 2–3 weeks of therapy<br>Monitor for resolution of symptoms (fever, night sweats, weight loss); hypotension (orthostatic) may occur initially, then resolve; caution client to change position slowly<br>Give before meals<br>Do not combine with phenytoin, causes phenytoin toxicity |
| Ethambutol | Optic neuritis | Use cautiously with renal disease<br>Check visual acuity |
| Rifampin | Hepatitis<br>Fever | Orange urine, tears, saliva<br>Check liver function tests<br>Can take with food |
| Streptomycin | Nephrotoxicity<br>VIII nerve damage | Check creatinine and BUN<br>Audiograms if given long-term |
| Second-line medications | | |
| Para-amino- salicyclic acid | GI disturbances<br>Hepatotoxicity | Check for ongoing GI adverse effects |
| Pyrazinamide | Hyperuricemia<br>Anemia<br>Anorexia | Check liver function tests, uric acid, and hematopoietic studies |
| **Action** | Inhibits cell wall and protein synthesis of *Mycobacterium tuberculosis* | |
| **Indications** | Tuberculosis<br>INH—used to prevent disease in person exposed to organism | |

| ANTITUBERCULOTIC MEDICATION *(CONTINUED)* | | |
|---|---|---|
| MEDICATION | ADVERSE EFFECTS | NURSING CONSIDERATIONS |
| **Adverse effects** | Hepatitis<br>Optic neuritis<br>Seizures<br>Peripheral neuritis | |
| **Nursing considerations** | Used in combination (2 medications or more)<br>Monitor for liver damage and hepatitis<br>With active TB, the client should cover mouth and nose when coughing, confine used tissues to plastic bags, and wear a mask with crowds until three sputum cultures are negative (no longer infectious)<br>In inpatient settings, client is placed under airborne precautions and workers wear a N95 or high-efficiency particulate air (HEPA) respirator until the client is no longer infectious | |

| ANTITUSSIVE/EXPECTORANT MEDICATIONS | | |
|---|---|---|
| MEDICATION | ADVERSE EFFECTS | NURSING CONSIDERATIONS |
| Dextromethorphan hydrobromide | Drowsiness<br>Dizziness | Antitussive<br>Onset occurs within 30 min, lasts 3–6 h<br>Monitor cough type and frequency |
| Guaifenesin | Dizziness<br>Headache<br>Nausea, vomiting | Expectorant<br>Monitor cough type and frequency<br>Take with glass of water |
| **Action** | Antitussives—suppresses cough reflex by inhibiting cough center in medulla<br>Expectorants—decreases viscosity of bronchial secretions | |
| **Indications** | Coughs due to URI and/or COPD | |
| **Adverse effects** | Respiratory depression<br>Hypotension<br>Bradycardia<br>Anticholinergic effects<br>Photosensitivity | |
| **Nursing considerations** | Elderly clients may need reduced dosages<br>Avoid alcohol | |

| ANTIVIRAL MEDICATIONS | | |
|---|---|---|
| MEDICATION | ADVERSE EFFECTS | NURSING CONSIDERATIONS |
| Acyclovir | Headaches, dizziness<br><br>Seizures<br><br>Diarrhea | Used for herpes simplex and herpes zoster<br><br>Given PO, IV, topically<br><br>Does not prevent transmission of disease<br><br>Slows progression of symptoms<br><br>Encourage fluids<br><br>Check liver and renal function tests |
| Ribavarin | Worsening of pulmonary status, bacterial pneumonia<br><br>Hypotension, cardiac arrest | Used for severe lower respiratory tract infections in infants and children<br><br>Must use special aerosol-generating device for administration<br><br>Can precipitate<br><br>Contraindicated in females who may become pregnant during treatment |
| Zidovudine | Anemia<br><br>Headache<br><br>Anorexia, diarrhea, nausea, GI pain<br><br>Paresthesias, dizziness<br><br>Insomnia<br><br>Agranulocytosis | Used for HIV infection<br><br>Teach clients to strictly comply with dosage schedule |
| Zalcitabine | Oral ulcers<br><br>Peripheral neuropathy, headache<br><br>Vomiting, diarrhea<br><br>CHF, cardiomyopathy | Used in combination with zidovudine for advanced HIV |
| Didanosine | Headache<br><br>Rhinitis, cough<br><br>Diarrhea, nausea, vomiting<br><br>Pancreatitis, granulocytopenia<br><br>Peripheral neuropathy<br><br>Seizures<br><br>Hemorrhage | Used for HIV infection<br><br>Monitor liver and renal function studies<br><br>Note baseline vital signs and weight<br><br>Take on empty stomach<br><br>Chew or crush tablets |
| Famciclovir | Fatigue, fever<br><br>Nausea, vomiting, diarrhea, constipation<br><br>Headache, sinusitis | Used for acute herpes zoster (shingles)<br><br>Obtain baseline CBC and renal function studies<br><br>Remind clients they are contagious when lesions are open and draining |

| ANTIVIRAL MEDICATIONS *(CONTINUED)* | | |
|---|---|---|
| MEDICATION | ADVERSE EFFECTS | NURSING CONSIDERATIONS |
| Ganciclovir | Fever<br>Rash<br>Leukemia<br>Seizures<br>GI hemorrhage<br>MI, stroke | Used for retinitis caused by cytomegalovirus<br>Check level of consciousness<br>Monitor CBC, I and O<br>Report any dizziness, confusions, seizures immediately<br>Need regular eye exams |
| Amantadine | Dizziness<br>Nervousness<br>Insomnia<br>Orthostatic hypotension | Used for prophylaxis and treatment of influenza A<br>Orthostatic hypotension precautions<br>Instruct clients to avoid hazardous activities |
| Oseltamivir<br>Zanamivir | Nausea, vomiting<br>Cough and throat irritation | Used for the treatment of Types A and B influenza<br>Best effect if given within 2 days of infection<br>Instruct clients that medication will reduce flu-symptom duration |
| **Action** | Inhibits DNA or RNA replication in virus | |
| **Indications** | Recurrent HSV 1 and 2 in immunocompromised clients<br>Encephalitis<br>Herpes zoster<br>HIV infections | |
| **Adverse effects** | Vertigo<br>Depression<br>Headache<br>Hematuria | |
| **Nursing considerations** | Encourage fluids<br>Small, frequent feedings<br>Good skin care<br>Wear glove when applying topically<br>Not a cure, but relieves symptoms | |

| ATTENTION–DEFICIT HYPERACTIVITY DISORDER MEDICATIONS | | |
|---|---|---|
| **MEDICATION** | **ADVERSE EFFECTS** | **NURSING CONSIDERATIONS** |
| Methylphenidate | Nervousness, palpitations<br>Insomnia<br>Tachycardia<br>Weight loss, growth suppression | May precipitate Tourette's syndrome<br>Monitor CBC, platelet count<br>Has paradoxical calming effect in ADD<br>Monitor height/weight in children<br>Monitor BP<br>Avoid drinks with caffeine<br>Give at least 6 h before bedtime<br>Give pc |
| Dextroamphetamine sulfate | Insomnia<br>Tachycardia, palpitations | Controlled substance<br>May alter insulin needs<br>Give in AM to prevent insomnia<br>Don't use with MAO inhibitor (possible hypertensive crisis) |
| **Action** | Increases level of catecholamines in cerebral cortex and reticular activating system | |
| **Indications** | Attention-deficit hyperactivity disorder (ADHD)<br>Narcolepsy | |
| **Adverse effects** | Restlessness<br>Insomnia<br>Tremors<br>Tachycardia<br>Seizures | |
| **Nursing considerations** | Monitor growth rate in children | |

| BIPOLAR DISORDER MEDICATIONS | | |
|---|---|---|
| MEDICATION | ADVERSE EFFECTS | NURSING CONSIDERATIONS |
| Lithium | Dizziness<br>Headache<br>Impaired vision<br>Fine hand tremors<br>Reversible leukocytosis | Use for control of manic episodes in the syndrome of manic-depressive psychosis; mood stabilizer<br>Blood levels must be monitored frequently<br>GI symptoms can be reduced if taken with meals<br>Therapeutic effects preceded by lag of 1–2 weeks<br>Signs of intoxication–vomiting, diarrhea, drowsiness, muscular weakness, ataxia<br>Dosage is usually halved during depressive stages of illness<br>Normal blood target level = 1–1.5 mEq/L<br>Check serum levels 2–3 times weekly when started and monthly while on maintenance; serum levels should be drawn in AM prior to dose<br>Should have fluid intake of 2,500–3,000 mL/day and adequate salt intake |
| Carbamazepine | Dizziness, vertigo<br>Drowsiness<br>Ataxia<br>CHF<br>Aplastic anemia, thrombocytopenia | Mood stablizer used with bipolar disorder<br>Traditionally used for seizures and trigeminal neuralgia<br>Obtain baseline urinalysis, BUN, liver function tests, CBC<br>Shake oral suspension well before measuring dose<br>When giving by NG tube, mix with equal volume of water, 0.9% NaCl or $D_5$ W, then flush with 100 mL after dose<br>Take with food<br>Drowsiness usually disappears in 3–4 days |

| BIPOLAR DISORDER MEDICATIONS *(CONTINUED)* | | |
|---|---|---|
| **MEDICATION** | **ADVERSE EFFECTS** | **NURSING CONSIDERATIONS** |
| Divalproex sodium | Sedation<br>Pancreatitis<br>Indigestion<br>Thrombocytopenia<br>Toxic hepatitis | Mood stablizers used with bipolar disorder<br>Traditionally used for seizures<br>Monitor liver function tests, platelet count before starting med and periodically after med<br>Teach client symptoms of liver dysfunction (e.g., malaise, fever, lethargy)<br>Monitor blood levels<br>Take with food or milk<br>Avoid hazardous activities |
| **Action** | Reduces amount of catecholamines released into synapse and increases reuptake of norepinephrine and serotonin from synaptic space; competes with $Na^+$ and $K^+$ transport in nerve and muscle cells | |
| **Indications** | Manic episodes | |
| **Adverse effects** | GI upset<br>Tremors<br>Polydipsia, polyuria | |
| **Nursing considerations** | Monitor serum levels carefully<br>Severe toxicity: exaggerated reflexes, seizures, coma, death | |

| BONE-RESORPTION INHIBITOR (BISPHOSPHONATE) MEDICATIONS | | |
|---|---|---|
| **MEDICATION** | **ADVERSE EFFECTS** | **NURSING CONSIDERATIONS** |
| Alendronate<br>Risedronate<br>Ibandronate | Esophagitis<br>Arthralgia<br>Nausea, diarrhea | Prevention and treatment of postmenopausal osteoporosis, Paget's disease, glucocorticoid-induced osteoporosis<br>Instruct clients to take medication in the morning with 6–8 ounces of water before eating and to remain in upright position for 30 minutes<br>Bone density tests may be monitored |

| BRONCHODILATORS/LEUKOTRIENE-RECEPTOR BLOCKER MEDICATIONS | | |
|---|---|---|
| **MEDICATION** | **ADVERSE EFFECTS** | **NURSING CONSIDERATIONS** |
| Aminophylline | Nervousness<br>Nausea<br>Dizziness<br>Tachycardia<br>Seizures | IM injection causes intense pain<br>Coffee, tea, cola increase risk of adverse reactions<br>Monitor blood levels<br>IV–incompatible with multiple medications |
| Terbutaline sulfate | Nervousness, tremor<br>Headache<br>Tachycardia<br>Palpitations<br>Fatigue | Short-acting beta agonist most useful when about to enter environment or begin activity likely to induce asthma attack<br>Pulse and blood pressure should be checked before each dose |
| Ipratropium bromide<br>Tiotropium | Nervousness<br>Tremor<br>Dry mouth<br>Palpitations | Cholinergic antagonist<br>Don't mix in nebulizer with cromolyn sodium<br>Not for acute treatment<br>Teach use of metered dose inhaler: inhale, hold breath, exhale slowly |
| Albuterol | Tremors<br>Headache<br>Hyperactivity<br>Tachycardia | Short-acting beta agonist most useful when about to enter environment or begin activity likely to induce asthma attack<br>Monitor for toxicity if using tablets and aerosol<br>Teach how to correctly use inhaler |
| Epinephrine | Cerebral hemorrhage<br>Hypertension<br>Tachycardia | When administered IV monitor BP, heart rate, EKG<br>If used with steroid inhaler, use bronchodilator first, then wait 5 minutes before using steroid inhaler (opens airway for maximum effectiveness) |
| Salmeterol | Headache<br>Pharyngitis<br>Nervousness<br>Tremors | Dry powder preparation<br>Not for acute bronchospasm or exacerbations |
| Montelukast sodium<br>Zafirlukast<br>Zileuton | Headache<br>GI distress | Used for prophylactic and maintenance therapy of asthma<br>Liver tests may be monitored<br>Interacts with theophylline |

| CARBONIC ANHYDRASE INHIBITOR MEDICATIONS | | |
|---|---|---|
| MEDICATION | ADVERSE EFFECTS | NURSING CONSIDERATIONS |
| Acetazolamide | Lethargy, depression<br>Anorexia, weakness<br>Decreased K$^+$ level, confusion | Used for glaucoma<br>Assess client's mental status before repeating dose |
| **Action** | Decreases production of aqueous humor in ciliary body | |
| **Indications** | Open-angle glaucoma | |
| **Adverse effects** | Blurred vision<br>Lacrimation<br>Pulmonary edema | |
| **Nursing considerations** | Monitor client for systemic effects | |

| CARDIAC GLYCOSIDE MEDICATION | | |
|---|---|---|
| MEDICATION | ADVERSE EFFECTS | NURSING CONSIDERATIONS |
| Digoxin | Anorexia<br>Nausea<br>Bradycardia<br>Visual disturbances<br>Confusion<br>Abdominal pain | Administer with caution to elderly or clients with renal insufficiency<br>Monitor renal function and electrolytes<br>Instruct clients to eat high-potassium foods<br>Take apical pulse for 1 full minute before administering<br>Notify health care provider if AP less than 60 (adult), less than 90–110 (infants and young children), less than 70 (older children)<br>Rapid digitalization–0.5 to 0.75 mg po, then 0.125 mg - 0.375mg cautiously until adequate effect is noted<br>Gradual digitalization–0.25 to 0.5 mg may increase dosage every 2 weeks until desired clinical effect achieved<br>Digoxin immune fab (Digibind)–used for treatment of life-threatening toxicity<br>Maintenance dose 0.125–0.5 mg IV or PO (average is 0.25 mg)<br>Teach client to check pulse rate and discuss adverse effects<br>Low K$^+$ increases risk of digitalis toxicity<br>Serum therapeutic blood levels 0.5–2 nanograms/mL<br>Toxic blood levels θ 2 nanograms/mL |
| **Action** | Increases force of myocardial contraction and slows heart rate by stimulating the vagus nerve and blocking the AV node | |
| **Indications** | Heart failure, Dysrhythmias | |
| **Adverse effects** | Tachycardia, bradycardia, heart block<br>Anorexia, nausea, vomiting<br>Halos around dark objects, blurred vision, halo vision<br>Dysrhythmias, heart block | |

| CARDIAC GLYCOSIDE MEDICATION *(CONTINUED)* | | |
|---|---|---|
| MEDICATION | ADVERSE EFFECTS | NURSING CONSIDERATIONS |
| **Nursing considerations** | Instruct client to eat high potassium foods<br>Monitor for digitalis toxicity<br>Risk of digitalis toxicity increases if client is hypokalemic | |
| **Herbal interactions** | Licorice can potentiate action of digoxin by promoting potassium loss<br>Hawthorn may increase effects of digoxin<br>Ginseng may falsely elevate digoxin levels<br>Ma-huang (ephedra) increases risk of digitalis toxicity | |

| CYTOPROTECTIVE MEDICATIONS | | |
|---|---|---|
| MEDICATION | ADVERSE EFFECTS | NURSING CONSIDERATIONS |
| Sucralfate | Constipation<br>Dizziness | Take medication 1 hour ac<br>Should not be taken with antacids or $H_2$ blockers |
| **Action** | Adheres to and protects ulcer's surface by forming a barrier | |
| **Indications** | Duodenal ulcer | |
| **Adverse effects** | Constipation<br>Vertigo<br>Flatulence | |
| **Nursing considerations** | Action lasts up to 6 h<br>Give 2 hours before or after most medications to prevent decreased absorption | |

| DISEASE–MODIFYING ANTIRHEUMATIC MEDICATIONS(DMARDS) | | |
|---|---|---|
| **MEDICATION** | **ADVERSE EFFECTS** | **NURSING CONSIDERATIONS** |
| **Nonbiologic DMARDs**<br><br>Methotrexate<br><br>Hydroxychloroquine sulfate<br><br>Sulfasalazine<br><br>Cyclosporine | GI track irritation<br>Hematuria<br>Leukopenia<br>Thrombocytopenia<br>Respiratory involvement | Assess hepatic<br>Notify HCP if dry non-productive cough noted or renal function<br>Assess severe skin reactions<br>Assess for opportunistic infections |
| **Biologic DMARDs**<br><br>Entanercept<br><br>Infliximab<br><br>Adalimumab<br><br>Anakinra<br><br>Rituximab<br><br>Abatacept | Leukopenia<br>Neutropenia<br>Thrombocytopenia<br>Intestinal obstruction<br>Fatigue | Assess for infusion related reactions (fever chills, dyspnea, chest discomfort)<br>Assess for CNS adverse reactions<br>Assessfor lymphoma and infection<br>Assess for opportunistic infections |
| **Action** | Non-biologic DMARDs:<br><br>Interfere with immune system<br><br>Indirect and nonspecific effect<br><br>Biologic DMARDs:<br><br>Interfere with immune system (tumor necrosis factor, interleukins, T- or B-cell lymphocytes) | |
| **Indications** | Rheumatoid arthritis<br><br>Psoriasis<br><br>Inflammatory bowel disease | |
| **Adverse effects** | Stomatitis<br><br>Liver toxicity<br><br>Bleeding<br><br>Anemia<br><br>Infections<br><br>Hypersensitivity<br><br>Kidney failure | |
| **Nursing considerations** | Precautions: infections, bleeding disorders<br><br>Monitor liver function tests<br><br>Monitor BUN and creatinine<br><br>Monitor for signs of infection<br><br>Monitor response to medication<br><br>Teach client about risk of live vaccines<br><br>Teach client to avoid alcohol<br><br>Teach client about risk of infection | |

| DIURETIC MEDICATIONS | | |
|---|---|---|
| MEDICATION | ADVERSE EFFECTS | NURSING CONSIDERATIONS |
| **Thiazide diuretics**<br><br>Hydrochlorothiazide<br><br>Chlorothiazide | Hypokalemia<br><br>Hyperglycemia<br><br>Blurred vision<br><br>Loss of $Na^+$<br><br>Dry mouth<br><br>Hypotension | Monitor electrolytes, especially potassium<br><br>I and O<br><br>Monitor BUN and creatinine<br><br>Don't give at hs<br><br>Weigh client daily<br><br>Encourage potassium-containing foods |
| **Potassium sparing**<br><br>Spironlactone | Hyperkalemia<br><br>Hyponatremia<br><br>Hepatic and renal damage<br><br>Tinnitus<br><br>Rash | Used with other diuretics<br><br>Give with meals<br><br>Avoid salt substitutes containing potassium<br><br>Monitor I and O |
| **Loop diuretics**<br><br>Furosemide<br><br>Ethacrynic acid | Hypotension<br><br>Hypokalemia<br><br>Hyperglycemia<br><br>GI upset<br><br>Weakness | Monitor BP, pulse rate, I and O<br><br>Monitor potassium<br><br>Give IV dose over 1–2 minutes, causes diuresis in 5–10 min<br><br>After PO dose diuresis in about 30 min<br><br>Weigh client daily<br><br>Don't give at hs<br><br>Encourage potassium-containing foods |
| Ethacrynic acid<br>  bumetanide | Potassium depletion<br><br>Electrolyte imbalance<br><br>Hypovolemia<br><br>Ototoxicity | Supervise ambulation<br><br>Monitor blood pressure and pulse<br><br>Observe for signs of electrolyte imbalance |
| **Osmotic diuretic**<br><br>Mannitol | Dry mouth<br><br>Thirst | I and O must be measured<br><br>Monitor vital signs<br><br>Monitor for electrolyte imbalance |
| **Other**<br><br>Chlorthalidone | Dizziness<br><br>Aplastic anemia<br><br>Orthostatic hypotension | Acts like a thiazide diuretic<br><br>Acts in 2–3 h, peak 2–6 h, lasts 2–3 days<br><br>Administer in AM<br><br>Monitor output, weight, BP, electrolytes<br><br>Increase $K^+$ in diet<br><br>Monitor glucose levels in diabetic clients<br><br>Change position slowly |

| DIURETIC MEDICATIONS *(CONTINUED)* | | |
|---|---|---|
| MEDICATION | ADVERSE EFFECTS | NURSING CONSIDERATIONS |
| **Action** | Thiazides—inhibits reabsorption of sodium and chloride in distal renal tubule<br><br>Loop—inhibits reabsorption of sodium and chloride in loop of Henle and distal renal tubules<br><br>Potassium-sparing—blocks effect of aldosterone on renal tubules, causing loss of sodium and water and retention of potassium<br><br>Osmotic—pulls fluid from tissues due to hypertonic effect | |
| **Indications** | Heart failure<br>Hypertension<br>Renal diseases<br>Diabetes insipidus<br>Reduction of osteoporosis in postmenopausal women | |
| **Adverse effects** | Dizziness, vertigo<br>Dry mouth<br>Orthostatic hypotension<br>Leukopenia<br>Polyuria, nocturia<br>Photosensitivity<br>Impotence<br>Hypokalemia (except for potassium-sparing)<br>Hyponatremia | |
| **Nursing considerations** | Take with food or milk<br>Take in A.M.<br>Monitor weight and electrolytes<br>Protect skin from the sun<br>Diet high in potassium for loop and thiazide diuretics<br>Limit potassium intake for potassium-sparing diuretics<br>Used as first-line drugs for hypertension | |
| **Herbal interactions** | Licorice can promote potassium loss, causing hypokalemia<br>Aloe can decrease serum potassium level, causing hypokalemia<br>Gingko may increase blood pressure when taken with thiazide diuretics | |

| ELECTROLYTES AND REPLACEMENT SOLUTIONS | | |
|---|---|---|
| MEDICATION | ADVERSE EFFECTS | NURSING CONSIDERATIONS |
| Calcium carbonate<br>Calcium chloride | Dysrhythmias<br>Constipation | Foods containing oxalic acid (rhubarb, spinach), phytic acid (bran, whole cereals), and phosphorus (milk, dairy products) interfere with absorption<br>Monitor EKG<br>Take 1–1.5 h pc if GI upset occurs |
| Magnesium chloride | Weak or absent deep tendon reflexes<br>Hypotension<br>Respiratory paralysis | Respirations should be greater than 16/min before medication given IV<br>Test knee-jerk and patellar reflexes before each dose<br>Monitor I and O |
| Potassium chloride<br>Potassium gluconate | Dysrhythmias, cardiac arrest<br>Adominal pain<br>Respiratory paralysis | Monitor EKG and serum electrolytes<br>Take with or after meals with full glass of water or fruit juice |
| Sodium chloride | Pulmonary edema | Monitor serum electrolytes |

## ELECTROLYTES/ELECTROLYTE MODIFIER MEDICATIONS

| | |
|---|---|
| **Action** | Alkalinizing agents—release bicarbonate ions in stomach and secrete bicarbonate ions in kidneys |
| | Calcium salts—provide calcium for bones, teeth, nerve transmission, muscle contraction, normal blood coagulation, cell membrane strength |
| | Hypocalcemic medications—decrease blood levels of calcium |
| | Hypophosphatemic agents—bind phosphates in GI tract lowering blood levels; neutralize gastric acid, inactivate pepsin |
| | Magnesium salts—provide magnesium for nerve conduction and muscle activity and activate enzyme reactions in carbohydrate metabolism |
| | Phosphates—provide body with phosphorus needed for bone, muscle tissue, metabolism of carbohydrates, fats, proteins, and normal CNS function |
| | Potassium exchange resins—exchange $Na^+$ for $K^+$ in intestines, lowering $K^+$ levels |
| | Potassium salts—provide potassium needed for cell growth and normal functioning of cardiac, skeletal, and smooth muscle |
| | Replacement solution—provide water and $Na^+$ to maintain acid-base and water balance, maintain osmotic pressure |
| | Urinary acidifiers—secrete $H^+$ ions in kidneys, making urine acidic |
| | Urinary alkalinizers—convert to sodium bicarbonate, making the urine alkaline |
| **Indications** | Fluid and electrolyte imbalances |
| | Renal calculi |
| | Peptic ulcers |
| | Osteoporosis |
| | Metabolic acidosis or alkalosis |
| **Adverse effects** | See individual medications |
| **Nursing considerations** | Monitor clients with CHF, hypertension, renal disease |

## GENITOURINARY MEDICATIONS

| MEDICATION | ADVERSE EFFECTS | NURSING CONSIDERATIONS |
|---|---|---|
| Nitrofurantoin | Diarrhea<br>Nausea, vomiting<br>Asthma attacks | Anti-infective<br>Check CBC<br>Give with food or milk<br>Avoid acidic foods (cranberry juice, prunes, plums) which increase drug action<br>Check I and O<br>Monitor pulmonary status |
| Phenazopyridine | Headache<br>Vertigo | Urinary tract analgesic, spasmolytic<br>Inform client that urine will be bright orange<br>Take with meals |

| GENITOURINARY MEDICATIONS *(CONTINUED)* | | |
|---|---|---|
| MEDICATION | ADVERSE EFFECTS | NURSING CONSIDERATIONS |
| **Anticholinergics**<br>Oxybutynin<br>Hyoscyamine<br>Propantheline<br>Darifenacin<br>Solifenacin<br>Tolterodine | Drowsiness<br>Blurred vision<br>Dry mouth<br>Constipation<br>Urinary retention | Used to reduce bladder spasms and treat urinary incontinence<br>Increase fluids and fiber in diet<br>Oxybutynin–older adults require higher dose and have greater incidence of adverse effects |
| **Anti-impotence**<br>Sildenafil<br>Vardenafil<br>Tadalafil | Headache<br>Flushing<br>Hypotension<br>Priapism | Treatment of erectile dysfunction<br>Take 1 hour before sexual activity<br>Never use with nitrates–could have fatal hypotension<br>Do not take with alpha blockers, e.g., doxazosin–risk of hypotension<br>Do not drink grapefruit juice |
| **Testosterone inhibitors**<br>Finasteride | Decreased libido<br>Impotence<br>Breast tenderness | Treatment of benign prostatic hyperplasia (BPH), male hair loss<br>Pregnant women should avoid contact with crushed drug or client's semen–may adversely affect male fetus |

| GI ULCER MEDICATIONS | | |
|---|---|---|
| MEDICATION | ADVERSE EFFECTS | NURSING CONSIDERATIONS |
| **H2-antagonists**<br>Cimetidine<br>Ranitidine<br>Famotidine<br>Nizatidine | Diarrhea<br>Confusion and dizziness (esp. in elderly with large doses)<br>Headache | Bedtime dose suppresses nocturnal acid production<br>Compliance may increase with single-dose regimen<br>Avoid antacids within 1 hour of dose<br>Dysrhythmias<br>Cimetidine–greater incidence of confusion and agitation with older adults |
| **Antisecretory**<br>Omeprazole<br>Lansoprazole<br>Rabeprazole<br>Esomeprazole<br>Pantoprazole | Dizziness<br>Diarrhea | Bedtime dose suppresses nocturnal acid production<br>Do not crush sustained-release capsule; contents may be sprinkled on food or instilled with fluid in NG tube |

| GI ULCER MEDICATIONS *(CONTINUED)* | | |
|---|---|---|
| MEDICATION | ADVERSE EFFECTS | NURSING CONSIDERATIONS |
| **Prostaglandin analogs** <br> Misoprostol | Abdominal pain <br> Diarrhea (13%) <br> Miscarriage | Notify health care provider if diarrhea more than 1 week or severe abdominal pain or black, tarry stools |
| **Nursing considerations** | Other medications may be prescribed, included antacids (time administration to avoid canceling med effect) and antimicrobials to eradicate *H. pylori* infections <br> Client should avoid smoking, alcohol, ASA, and caffeine, all of which increase stomach acid | |

| EYE MEDICATIONS: MIOTIC | | |
|---|---|---|
| MEDICATION | ADVERSE EFFECTS | NURSING CONSIDERATIONS |
| Pilocarpine | Painful eye muscle spasm, blurred or poor vision in dim lights <br> Photophobia, cataracts, or floaters | Teach to apply pressure on lacrimal sac for 1 min following instillation <br> Used for glaucoma <br> Caution client to avoid sunlight and night driving |
| Carachol | Headache <br> If absorbed systemically, can cause sweating, abdominal cramps, and decreased blood pressure | Cholinergic (ophthalmic) <br> Similar to acetylcholine in action <br> Produces pupillary miosis during ocular surgery |
| **Action** | Causes contraction of sphincter muscles of iris, resulting in miosis | |
| **Indications** | Pupillary miosis in ocular surgery <br> Primary open-angle glaucoma | |
| **Adverse effects** | Headache <br> Hypotension <br> Bronchoconstriction | |
| **Nursing considerations** | Teach how to instill eye drops correctly <br> Apply light pressure on lacrimal sac for 1 minute after medication instilled <br> Avoid hazardous activities until temporary blurring disappears <br> Transient brow pain and myopia are common initially, disappear within 10–14 days | |

## EYE MEDICATIONS: MYDRIATIC AND CYCLOPLEGIC

| MEDICATION | ADVERSE EFFECTS | NURSING CONSIDERATIONS |
|---|---|---|
| Atropine sulfate | Blurred vision, photophobia<br>Flushing, tachycardia<br>Dry mouth | Contraindicated with narrow-angle glaucoma<br>Suck on hard candy for dry mouth |
| Cyclopentolate | Photophobia, blurred vision<br>Seizures<br>Tachycardia | Contraindicated in narrow-angle glaucoma<br>Burns when instilled |
| **Action** | Anticholinergic action leaves the pupil under unopposed adrenergic influence, causing it to dilate | |
| **Indications** | Diagnostic procedures<br>Acute iritis, uveitis | |
| **Adverse effects** | Headache<br>Tachycardia<br>Blurred vision<br>Photophobia<br>Dry mouth | |
| **Nursing considerations** | Mydriatics cause pupil dilation; cycloplegics paralyze the iris sphincter<br>Watch for signs of glaucoma (increased intraocular pressure, headache, progressive blurring of vision)<br>Apply light pressure on lacrimal sac for 1 minute after instilling medication<br>Avoid hazardous activities until blurring of vision subsides<br>Wear dark glasses | |

| EYE MEDICATIONS: OVERVIEW | | |
|---|---|---|
| **MEDICATION** | **ADVERSE EFFECTS** | **NURSING CONSIDERATIONS** |
| Methylcellulose | Eye irritation if excess is allowed to dry on eyelids | Lubricant<br>Use eyewash to rinse eyelids of "sandy" sensation felt after administration |
| Polyvinyl alcohol | Blurred vision<br><br>Burning | Artificial tears<br>Applied to contact lenses before insertion |
| Tetrahydrozoline | Cardiac irregularities<br>Pupillary dilation, increased intraocular pressure<br>Transient stinging | Used for ocular congestion, irritation, allergic conditions<br>Rebound congestion may occur with frequent or prolonged use<br>Apply light pressure on lacrimal sac for 1 min instillation |
| Timolol maleate<br>Levobunolol | Eye irritation<br><br>Hypotension | Beta-blocking agent<br>Reduces intraocular pressure in management of glaucoma<br>Apply light pressure on lacrimal sac for 1 min following instillation<br>Monitor BP and pulse |
| Proparacaine HCl<br>Tetracaine HCl, cocaine | Corneal abrasion | Topical anesthetic<br>Remind client not to touch or rub eyes while anesthetized<br>Patch the eye to prevent corneal abrasion |
| Prednisolone acetate | Corneal abrasion | Topical steroid<br>Steroid use predisposes client to local infection |
| Gentamicin<br>Tobramycin | Eye irritation; itching, redness | Anti-infective agent<br>Clean exudate from eyes before use |
| Idoxuridine | Eye irritation<br>Itching lids | Topical antiviral agent<br>Educate client about possible adverse effects |
| Dipivefrin HCl | Increase in heart rate and blood pressure | Adrenergic<br>Monitor vital signs because of systemic absorption |
| Flurbiprofen | Platelet aggregation disorder | Nonsteroidal anti-inflammatory medications<br>Monitor client for eye hemorrhage<br>Client should not continue wearing contact lens |
| **Nursing considerations** | Place pressure on tear ducts for one minute<br>Wash hands before and after installation<br>Do not touch tip of dropper to eye or body | |

| HEAVY METAL ANTAGONIST MEDICATIONS | | |
|---|---|---|
| **MEDICATION** | **ADVERSE EFFECTS** | **NURSING CONSIDERATIONS** |
| Deferoxamine mesylate | Pain and induration at injection site<br>Urticaria<br>Hypotension<br>Generalized erythema | Used for acute iron intoxication, chronic iron overload |
| Dimercaprol | Hypertension<br>Tachycardia<br>Nausea, vomiting<br>Headache | Used for treatment of arsenic, gold, and mercury poisoning; acute lead poisoning when used with edetate calcium disodium<br>Administered as initial dose because of its improved efficiency in removing lead from brain tissue |
| Edetate calcium disodium (EDTA) | | Used for acute and chronic lead poisoning, lead encephalopathy<br>Renal tubular necrosis<br>Multiple deep IM doses or IV<br>Very painful—local anesthetic procaine is injected with the drug (drawn into syringe last, after which the syringe is maintained with needle held slightly down so that it is administered first); rotate sites; provide emotional support and play therapy as outlet for frustration<br>Ensure adequate hydration and monitor I and O and kidney function—CaNa$_2$ EDTA and lead are toxic to kidneys<br>Seizure precautions—initial rapid mobilization of lead may cause an increase in brain lead levels, exacerbating symptoms |
| **Action** | Forms stable complexes with metals | |
| **Indications** | Poisoning (gold, arsenic)<br>Acute lead encephalopathy | |
| **Adverse effects** | Tachycardia<br>Burning sensation in lips, mouth, throat<br>Abdominal pain | |
| **Nursing considerations** | Monitor I and O, BUN, EKG<br>Encourage fluids | |

| IMMUNOSUPPRESSANT MEDICATIONS | | |
|---|---|---|
| **MEDICATION** | **ADVERSE EFFECTS** | **NURSING CONSIDERATIONS** |
| Cyclosporine | Nephrotoxicity<br>Headache<br>Seizures<br>Hypertension<br>Gingival hyperplasia<br>Leukopenia<br>Thrombocytopenia<br>Infections<br>Tremor | Take once daily in AM<br>Measure dosage carefully in oral syringe<br>Mix with whole milk, chocolate milk, fruit juice<br>Always used with adrenal corticosteroids<br>Monitor BUN, serum creatinine, liver function tests<br>To prevent thrush, swish and swallow nystatin QID<br>Use mechanical contraceptives, not oral contraceptives |
| **Action** | Prevents production of T cells and their response to interleukin-2; recognizes antigens foreign to body | |
| **Indications** | Prevent rejection for transplanted organs | |
| **Adverse effects** | Nausea, vomiting<br>Diarrhea<br>Hepatotoxicity<br>Nephrotoxicity<br>Infection<br>Myocardial fibrosis | |
| **Nursing considerations** | Monitor carefully for infections | |

| IMMUNOMODULATOR MEDICATIONS | |
|---|---|
| **MEDICATION** | **ADVERSE EFFECTS** |
| Beta interferons | "Flu-like" symptoms<br>Liver dysfunction<br>Bone marrow depression<br>Injection site reactions<br>Photosensitivity<br>Central nervous system infection (natalizumab) |
| Interferon beta-1a<br>Interferon beta-1b | |
| Glatiramer acetate<br>Natalizumab | |
| **Action** | Modify the immune response<br>Decrease the movement of leukocytes into the central nervous system neurons |
| **Indications** | Multiple sclerosis |

## IMMUNOMODULATOR MEDICATIONS *(CONTINUED)*

| MEDICATION | ADVERSE EFFECTS |
|---|---|
| **Adverse effects** | "Flu-like" symptoms<br>Liver dysfunction<br>Bone marrow depression<br>Injection site reactions<br>Photosensitivity<br>Central nervous system infection (natalizumab) |
| **Nursing considerations** | Monitor liver function tests<br>Monitor complete blood count<br>Subcutaneous injection: rotate injection sites, apply ice, and then use warm compresses, analgesics for discomfort<br>Photosensitivity precautions |

## IRON PREPARATION MEDICATION

| MEDICATION | ADVERSE EFFECTS | NURSING CONSIDERATIONS |
|---|---|---|
| Ferrous sulfate | Nausea<br>Constipation<br>Black stools | Food decreases absorption but may be necessary to reduce GI effects<br>Monitor Hgb, Hct<br>Dilute liquid preparations in juice, but not milk or antacids<br>Use straw for liquid to avoid staining teeth |
| Iron dextran | Nausea<br>Constipation<br>Black stools | IM injections cause pain and skin staining; use the Z-track technique to put med deep into buttock; IV administration is preferred |
| **Action** | Iron salts increase availability of iron for hemoglobin | |
| **Indications** | Iron-deficiency anemia | |
| **Adverse effects** | Constipation, diarrhea<br>Dark stools<br>Tooth enamel stains<br>Seizures<br>Flushing, hypotension<br>Tachycardia | |
| **Nursing considerations** | Take iron salts on empty stomach (absorption is reduced by one-third when taken with food)<br>Absorption of iron decreased when administered with tetracyclines, antacids, coffee, tea, milk, eggs (bind to iron)<br>Concurrent use of iron decreases effectiveness of tetracyclines and quinolone antibiotics<br>Vitamin C increases absorption of iron salts<br>Vitamin E delays therapeutic responses to iron salts | |

| LAXATIVES AND STOOL SOFTENER MEDICATIONS | | |
|---|---|---|
| **MEDICATION** | **ADVERSE EFFECTS** | **NURSING CONSIDERATIONS** |
| Cascara | Anorexia, nausea, abdominal cramps, hypokalemia, calcium deficiency | Avoid exposure to sunlight<br>Should be taken with full glass of water<br>Relieves constipation and softens stool in about 8 hours |
| Bisacodyl | Mild cramps, rash, nausea, diarrhea | Stimulant<br>Tablets should not be taken with milk or antacids (causes dissolution of enteric coating and loss of cathartic action)<br>Can cause gastric irritation<br>Effects in 6–12 hours |
| Phenolphthalein | Urticaria, rash, electrolyte imbalance<br>Allergic reactions, skin eruption | Caution clients against prolonged use<br>Will turn alkaline urine a pink-red color |
| Mineral oil | Pruritus ani, anorexia, nausea | Lubricant<br>Administer in upright position<br>Prolonged use can cause fat-soluble vitamin malabsorption |
| Docusate | Few adverse effects<br>Abdominal cramps | Stool softener<br>Contraindicated in atonic bowel, nausea, vomiting, GI pain<br>Effects in 1–3 days |
| Milk of Magnesia (Magnesium hydroxide) | Hypermagnesemia, dehydration | Saline agent<br>Na$^+$ salts can exacerbate heart failure |
| Psyllium hydrophilic mucilloid | Obstruction of GI tract | Take with a full glass of water; do not take dry<br>Report abdominal distention or unusual amount of flatulence |
| Polyethylene glycol and electrolytes | Nausea and bloating | Large-volume product—allow time to consume it safely |
| **Action** | Bulk-forming—absorbs water into stool mass, making stool bulky, thus stimulating peristalsis<br>Lubricants—coat surface of stool and soften fecal mass, allowing for easier passage<br>Osmotic agents and saline laxatives—draw water from plasma by osmosis, increasing bulk of fecal mass, thus promoting peristalsis<br>Stimulants—stimulate peristalsis when they come in contact with intestinal mucosa<br>Stool softeners—soften fecal mass | |
| **Indications** | Constipation<br>Preparation for procedures or surgery | |

| LAXATIVES AND STOOL SOFTENER MEDICATIONS *(CONTINUED)* | | |
|---|---|---|
| **MEDICATION** | **ADVERSE EFFECTS** | **NURSING CONSIDERATIONS** |
| **Adverse effects** | Diarrhea<br>Dependence | |
| **Nursing considerations** | Contraindicated for clients with abdominal pain, nausea and vomiting, fever (acute abdomen)<br>Chronic use may cause hypokalemia | |

| MINERALS | | |
|---|---|---|
| **MEDICATION** | **ADVERSE EFFECTS** | **NURSING CONSIDERATIONS** |
| Calcium | Cardiac dysrhythmias<br>Constipation<br>Hypercalcemia<br>Renal calculi | Give 1 h before meals<br>Give 1/3 dose at bedtime<br>Monitor for urinary stones |
| Vitamin D (Ergocalciferol) | Seizures<br>Impaired renal function<br>Hypercalcemia<br>Renal calculi | Treatment of vitamin D deficiency, rickets, psoriasis, rheumatoid arthritis<br>Check electrolytes<br>Restrict use of antacids containing Mg |
| Sodium fluoride | Bad taste<br>Staining of teeth<br>Nausea, vomiting | Observe for synovitis |
| Potassium | Nausea, vomiting<br>Cramps, diarrhea | Prevention and treatment of hypokalemia<br>Report hyperkalemia: lethargy, confusion, fainting, decreased urine output<br>Report continued hypocalcemia: fatigue, weakness, polyuria, polydipsia, cardiac changes |

| MUSCULOSKELETAL MEDICATIONS | | |
|---|---|---|
| MEDICATION | ADVERSE EFFECTS | NURSING CONSIDERATIONS |
| Edrophonium | Seizures<br>Hypotension<br>Diarrhea<br>Bronchospasm<br>Respiratory paralysis | Diagnostic test for myasthenia gravis<br>Increased muscular strength within 30–60 seconds confirms diagnosis, lasts 4–5 minutes<br>Monitor respirations closely<br>Have atropine 0.5 mg injection available |
| Neostigmine | Nausea, vomiting<br>Abdominal cramps<br>Respiratory depression<br>Bronchoconstriction<br>Hypotension<br>Bradycardia | Monitor vital signs frequently<br>Have atropine injection available<br>Observe for improvement in strength, vision, ptosis 45 min after each dose<br>Schedule dose before periods of fatigue (e.g., ac)<br>Take with milk or food<br>Potentiates action of morphine<br>Diagnostic test for myasthenia gravis |
| Pyridostigmine bromide | Seizures<br>Bradycardia<br>Hypotension<br>Bronchoconstriction | Monitor vital signs frequently<br>Have atropine injection available<br>Take extended-release tablets same time each day at least 6 h apart<br>Drug of choice for myasthenia gravis to improve muscle strength |
| Alendronate sodium | Vitamin D deficiency<br>Osteomalacia | Prevents and treats osteoporosis<br>Longer-lasting treatment for Paget's disease<br>Take in A.M. at least 30 min before other medication, food, water, or other liquids<br>Should sit up for 30 min after taking medication<br>Use sunscreen and wear protective clothing |
| Glucosamine | Nausea, heartburn, diarrhea | Antirheumatic<br>Contraindicated with shellfish allergy, pregnancy, and lactation<br>May worsen glycemic control<br>Must be taken on regular basis to be effective |

| MUSCULOSKELETAL MEDICATIONS *(CONTINUED)* | | |
|---|---|---|
| **MEDICATION** | **ADVERSE EFFECTS** | **NURSING CONSIDERATIONS** |
| **Action** | Inhibits destruction of acetylcholine released from parasympathetic and somatic efferent nerves | |
| **Indications** | Myasthenia gravis Postoperative and postpartum functional urinary retention | |
| **Adverse effects** | Bronchoconstriction Diarrhea Respiratory paralysis Muscle cramps | |
| **Nursing considerations** | Give with milk or food Administer exactly as ordered and on time Doses vary with client's activity level Monitor vital signs, especially respirations | |

| NITRATES/ANTIANGINAL MEDICATIONS | | |
|---|---|---|
| **MEDICATION** | **ADVERSE EFFECTS** | **NURSING CONSIDERATIONS** |
| Nitroglycerin | Flushing Hypotension Headache Tachycardia Dizziness Blurred vision | Renew supply every 3 months Avoid alcoholic beverages Sublingual dose may be repeated every 5 minutes for 3 doses Protect drug from light Should wet tablet with saliva and place under tongue |
| Isosorbide | Headache Orthostatic hypotension | Change position slowly Take between meals Don't discontinue abruptly |
| **Action** | Relaxes vascular smooth muscle; decreases venous return; decreases arterial blood pressure; reduces myocardial oxygen consumption | |
| **Indications** | Angina Perioperative hypertension CHF associated with MI Raynaud's disease (topical) | |

| NITRATES/ANTIANGINAL MEDICATIONS *(CONTINUED)* | | |
|---|---|---|
| MEDICATION | ADVERSE EFFECTS | NURSING CONSIDERATIONS |
| **Adverse effects** | Hypotension<br>Tachycardia<br>Headache<br>Dizziness<br>Syncope<br>Rash | |
| **Nursing considerations** | Take sublingual tablets under tongue or in buccal pouch; tablet may sting<br><br>Check expiration date on bottle<br><br>Discard unused med after 6 months<br><br>Take sustained-release tablets with water, don't chew them<br><br>Administer topically over 6 × 6 inch area using applicator, cover with plastic wrap, rotate sites<br><br>Administer transdermal to skin free of hair; do not apply to distal extremities; remove before defibrillation or cardioversion<br><br>Administer transmucosal tablets between lip and gum above the incisors or between cheek and gum; do not swallow or chew<br><br>Administer translingual spray into oral mucosa; do not inhale<br><br>Withdraw medication gradually over 4–6 wks<br><br>Provide rest periods<br><br>Teach to take medication when chest pain anticipated<br><br>May take q 5 min × 3 doses<br><br>Beta-adrenergic blockers and calcium-channel blockers also used for angina | |

| NONSTEROIDAL ANTI-INFLAMMATORY MEDICATIONS (NSAIDs) | | |
|---|---|---|
| MEDICATION | ADVERSE EFFECTS | NURSING CONSIDERATIONS |
| Ibuprofen | GI upset—nausea, vomiting, diarrhea, constipation<br>Skin eruption, dizziness, headache, fluid retention | Use cautiously with aspirin allergy<br>Give with milk |
| Indomethacin | Peptic ulcer, ulcerative colitis<br>Headache, dizziness<br>Bone marrow depression | Observe for bleeding tendencies<br>Monitor I and O |
| Naproxen | Headache, dizziness, epigastric distress<br>Myocardial infaction | Administer with food<br>Optimal therapeutic response is seen after 2 weeks of treatment<br>Use cautiously in client with history of aspirin allergy |

| NONSTEROIDAL ANTI-INFLAMMATORY MEDICATIONS (NSAIDs) *(CONTINUED)* | | |
|---|---|---|
| **MEDICATION** | **ADVERSE EFFECTS** | **NURSING CONSIDERATIONS** |
| Celecoxib | Fatigue<br><br>Anxiety, depression, nervousness<br><br>Nausea, vomiting, anorexia<br><br>Dry mouth, constipation | COX-2 inhibitor<br><br>Increasing doses do not appear to increase effectiveness<br><br>Do not take if allergic to sulfonamides, ASA, or NSAIDs |
| Ketorolac | Peptic ulcer disease<br><br>GI bleeding, prolonged bleeding<br><br>Renal impairment | Dosage is decreased in clients greater than 65 years or with impaired renal function<br><br>Duration of treatment is less than 5 days |
| **Actions** | NSAIDs inhibit prostaglandins<br><br>COX-2 inhibitors block the enzyme responsible for inflammation without blocking the COX-1 enzyme<br><br>ASA has antiplatelet activity | |
| **Indications** | Pain, fever, arthritis, dysmenorrhea<br><br>ASA: transient ischemic attacks, prophylaxis of MI, ischemic stroke, angina<br><br>Ibuprofen: gout, dental pain, musculoskeletal disorders | |
| **Adverse effects** | Headache<br><br>Eye changes<br><br>Dizziness<br><br>Somnolence<br><br>GI disturbances<br><br>Constipation<br><br>Bleeding<br><br>Rash | |
| **Nursing considerations** | Take with food or after meals<br><br>Periodic ophthalmologic exam<br><br>Monitor liver and renal function<br><br>Avoid OTC drugs; may contain similar medications<br><br>Also have analgesic and antipyretic actions<br><br>Post-op clients with adequate pain relief have fewer complications and a shorter recovery<br><br>Pain is the fifth vital sign and needs to be assessed with others | |

| OPIOD ANALGESIC MEDICATIONS | | |
|---|---|---|
| MEDICATION | ADVERSE EFFECTS | NURSING CONSIDERATIONS |
| Morphine sulfate | Dizziness, weakness<br><br>Sedation or paradoxic excitement<br><br>Nausea, flushing, and sweating<br><br>Respiratory depression, decreased cough reflex<br><br>Constipation, miosis, hypotension | Give in smallest effective dose<br><br>Observe for development of dependence<br><br>Encourage respiratory exercises<br><br>Use cautiously to prevent respiratory depression<br><br>Monitor vital signs<br><br>Monitor I and O, bowel patterns<br><br>Used for cardiac clients—reduces preload and afterload pressures, decreasing cardiac workload |
| Codeine | Same as morphine<br><br>High dose may cause restlessness and excitement<br><br>Constipation | Less potent and less dependence potential compared with morphine |
| Methadone | Same as morphine | Observe for dependence, respiratory depression<br><br>Encourage fluids and high-bulk foods |
| Hydromorphone | Sedation, hypotension<br><br>Urine retention | Keep narcotic antagonist (naloxone) available<br><br>Monitor bowel function |
| Oxycodone and acetaminophen<br><br>Oxycodone and aspirin | Lightheadedness, dizziness, sedation, nausea<br><br>Constipation, pruritus<br><br>Increased risk bleeding (oxycodone and aspirin) | Administer with milk after meals<br><br>Commonly prescribed as oxycodone/acetaminophen or asprin, an acetaminophen and oxycodone combination |
| Hydrocodone/ Acetaminophen | Confusion<br><br>Sedation<br><br>Hypotension<br><br>Constipation | Use with extreme caution with MAO inhibitors<br><br>Additive CNS depression with alcohol, antihistamines, and sedative/hypnotics |

| OPIOD ANALGESIC MEDICATIONS *(CONTINUED)* | | |
|---|---|---|
| **MEDICATION** | **ADVERSE EFFECTS** | **NURSING CONSIDERATIONS** |
| **Action** | Produces analgesia, euphoria, sedation; acts on CNS receptor cells | |
| **Indications** | Moderate-to-severe pain<br>Chronic pain<br>Preoperative medication | |
| **Adverse effects** | Dizziness<br>Sedation<br>Respiratory depression<br>Cardiac arrest<br>Hypotension | |
| **Nursing considerations** | Provide narcotic antagonist if needed<br>   Turn, cough, deep breathe<br>     Safety precautions (side rails, assist when walking)<br>     Avoid alcohol, antihistamines, sedative, tranquilizers, OTC drugs<br>     Avoid activities requiring mental alertness | |

| PAGET'S DISEASE MEDICATIONS | | |
|---|---|---|
| **MEDICATION** | **ADVERSE EFFECTS** | **NURSING CONSIDERATIONS** |
| Calcitonin | Nausea, vomiting, flushing of face<br>Increased urinary frequency | Retards bone resorption<br>Decreases release of calcium from bone<br>Relieves pain<br>Observe for symptoms of tetany<br>Give at hs |
| Etidronate disodium | Diarrhea | Prevents rapid bone turnover<br>Don't give with food, milk, or antacids (reduces absorption)<br>Monitor renal function |
| Mithramycin | GI upset<br>Bone marrow depression<br>Facial flushing | Cytotoxic<br>Antibiotic<br>Monitor BUN, liver, and renal function tests, platelet count and PT<br>Check for signs of infection or bleeding |
| **Action** | Inhibits osteocytic activity | |
| **Indications** | Paget's disease | |
| **Adverse effects** | Decreased serum calcium<br>Facial flushing | |
| **Nursing considerations** | Monitor serum calcium levels<br>Facial flushing and warmth last 1 hour | |

## THROMBOLYTIC MEDICATIONS

| MEDICATION | ADVERSE EFFECTS | NURSING CONSIDERATIONS (SPECIFIC) |
|---|---|---|
| Reteplase<br>Alteplase<br>Tissue plasminogen activator | Bleeding | Tissue plasminogen activator is a naturally occurring enzyme<br>Low allergenic risk but high cost |
| Anistreplase<br>Streptokinase | Bleeding | Because streptokinase is made from a bacterium, client can have an allergic reaction. Not used if client had recent *Streptococcus* infection or received Streptase in past year |
| **Action** | Reteplase and Alteplase break down plasminogen into plasmin, which dissolves the fibrin network of a clot<br>Anistreplase and Streptokinase bind with plasminogen to form a complex that digests fibrin | |
| **Indications** | MIs within the first 6 hours after symptoms, limited arterial thrombosis, thrombotic strokes, occluded shunts | |
| **Nursing considerations (general)** | Check for signs of bleeding; minimize number of punctures for inserting IVs; avoid IM injections; apply pressure at least twice as long as usual after any puncture | |

## VITAMINS

| MEDICATION | ADVERSE EFFECTS | NURSING CONSIDERATIONS |
|---|---|---|
| Cyanocobalamin (Vitamin $B_{12}$) | Anaphylaxis<br>Urticaria | Treatment of vitamin $B_{12}$ deficiency, pernicious anemia, hemorrhage, renal and hepatic diseases<br>Monitor reticulocyte count, iron, and folate levels<br>Don't mix with other solutions in syringe<br>Monitor $K^+$ levels<br>Clients with pernicious anemia need monthly injections |
| Folic acid | Bronchospasm<br>Malaise | Treatment of anemia, liver disease, alcoholism, intestinal obstruction, pregnancy<br>Don't mix with other meds in syringe |
| **Action** | Coenzymes that speed up metabolic processes | |
| **Indications** | Vitamin deficiencies | |
| **Adverse effects** | Some vitamins are toxic at high levels | |
| **Nursing considerations** | Avoid exceeding RDA (recommended daily allowance) | |

| WOMEN'S HEALTH MEDICATIONS | | |
|---|---|---|
| MEDICATION | ADVERSE EFFECTS | NURSING CONSIDERATIONS |
| **Contraceptives, systemic**<br>Example: Ethinyl Estradiol/norgestrel | Headache<br>Dizziness<br>Nausea<br>Breakthrough bleeding, spotting | Used to prevent pregnancy<br>Use condoms against sexually transmitted diseases<br>Take pill at same time every day<br>No smoking |
| **Contraceptives, systemic**<br>Levonorgestrel | Breakthrough bleeding, spotting | Prevention of pregnancy for 5 years as a contraceptive implant; emergency contraceptive in oral form when given within 72 hours of unprotected intercourse |
| **Estrogens**<br>Estradiol<br>Estrogens conjugated | Nausea<br>Gynecomastia<br>Contact lens intolerance | Treatment of menopausal symptoms, some cancers<br>Prevention of osteoporosis<br>Client should contact health care provider if breast lumps, vaginal bleeding, edema, jaundice, dark urine, clay-colored stools, dyspnea, blurred vision, numbness or stiffness in leg, chest pain |
| **Progestins**<br>Medroxyprogestrone acetate | Nausea<br>Contact lens intolerance | Management of abnormal uterine bleeding; prevent endometrial changes of estrogen replacement therapy, some cancers |
| **Actions** | Female hormones | |
| **Indications** | Contraceptives<br>Treatment of menopausal symptoms<br>Prevention of osteoporosis | |
| **Adverse effects** | Nausea<br>Breakthrough bleeding<br>Headache | |
| **Nursing considerations** | Client should know when to take medication and what to do for skipped doses<br>Client should know when to contact prescribing health care provider | |
| Herbal | Black cohosh—relieves hot flashes; may increase hypotensive effect of antihypertensives; do not take for more than 6 months | |

| MEDICATION INTERACTIONS WITH GRAPEFRUIT JUICE (INCREASED SERUM DRUG LEVELS) | |
| --- | --- |
| Calcium channel blockers: amlodipine, diltiazem, felodipine, nicardipine, nifedipine, nimodipine, nisoldipine, verapamil | |
| Statins<br>Caffeine | Carbamazepine<br>Buspirone<br>Midazolam |
| SSRIs: fluoxetine, fluvoxamine, sertraline<br>Dextromethorphan<br>Sirolimus | Sildenafil<br>Praziquantel<br>Tacrolimus |

| MEN'S HEALTH MEDICATIONS | | |
|---|---|---|
| **MEDICATION** | **ADVERSE EFFECTS** | **NURSING CONSIDERATIONS** |
| **Alpha$_1$–adrenergic blockers** | | |
| Terazosin | Dizziness | Used to decrease urinary urgency, hesitancy, nocturia in prostatic hyperplasia |
| | Headache | |
| | Weakness | Caution to change position slowly |
| | Nasal congestion | Avoid alcohol, CNS depressant, hot showers due to orthostatic hypotension |
| | Orthostatic hypotension | |
| | | Requires titration |
| | | Administer at bedtime due to risk orthostatic hypotension |
| | | Effects may not be noted for 4 weeks |
| Tamsulosin | Dizziness | Used to decrease urinary urgency, hesitancy, nocturia in prostatic hyperplasia |
| | Headache | |
| | | Caution to change position slowly |
| | | Administer 30 min. after same meal each day |
| **5–alpha–reductase inhibitor** | | |
| Finasteride | Decreased libido | Used to treat benign prostatic hyperplasia by slowing prostatic growth |
| | Impotence | |
| | | May decrease serum PSA levels |
| | | 6–12 months therapy required to determine if medication effective |
| | | May cause harm to male fetus. Pregnant women should not be exposed to semen of partner taking finasteride or they should not handle crushed medication |
| | | Monitor liver function tests |
| Dutasteride | Decreased libido | Used to treat benign prostatic hyperplasia by slowing prostatic growth |
| | Impotence | |
| | | May cause harm to male fetus. Pregnant women should not be exposed to semen of partner taking finasteride or they should not handle crushed medication |
| | | Monitor liver function |
| **Anti-impotence** | Headache | Enhances blood flow to the corpus cavernosum to ensure erection to allow sexual intercourse |
| Sildenafil | Flushing | |
| Vardenafil | Dyspepsia | Should not take with nitrates in any form due to dramatic decrease in blood pressure |
| Tadalafil | Nasal congestion | |
| | Mild visual disturbance | Usually taken 1 hour before sexual activity (sildenafil, vardenafil) |
| | | Tadalafil has longer duration of action (up to 36 hours) |
| | | Should not take more than one time per day |
| | | Notify health care provider if erection lasts longer than 4 hours |
| Saw palmetto | Urinary antiseptic used to treat PBH; may cause false-negative PSA test result | |

| HERBAL SUPPLEMENTS | | |
|---|---|---|
| SUPPLEMENT | ADVERSE EFFECTS/ CONTRAINDICATIONS | NURSING CONSIDERATIONS |
| Immune System | | |
| **Echinacea**<br><br>Immunostimulant, anti-inflammatory, antiviral, antibacterial<br><br>Used to prevent and treat colds, flu, wound healing, urinary tract infections | Immune suppression, tingling sensation and/ or unpleasant taste on tongue, nausea, vomiting, allergic reactions | Decreases effectiveness of immunosuppressants<br><br>Contraindicated in autoimmune diseases<br><br>Avoid if allergic to ragweed, members of daisy family of plants |
| **Garlic**<br><br>Antimicrobial, antilipidemic, antithrombotic, antitumor, anti-inflammatory<br><br>Used to reduce cholesterol, prevent atherosclerosis, cancer, stroke, and MI; decrease blood pressure prevent and treat colds and flu | Flatulence, heartburn, halitosis, irritation of mouth, esophagus, stomach, allergic reaction<br><br>Contraindicated with peptic ulcer, reflux | May potentiate anticoagulant and antiplatelets, antihyperlipidemics, antihypertensives, antidiabetic medications, and herbs with these effects<br><br>May decrease efficacy of cyclosporine, hormonal contraceptives<br><br>Avoid if allergic to members of the lily family of plants |
| **Ginseng**<br><br>Stimulant and tonic to immune and nervous systems<br><br>Used to increase stamina, as aphrodisiac, adjunct chemotherapy and radiation therapy | Headache, insomnia, nervousness, palpitations, excitation, diarrhea, vaginal bleeding<br><br>May cause headache, tremors, irritability, manic episodes if combined with MAOIs or caffeine | May falsely elevate digoxin levels; observe for signs usually associated with high digoxin levels<br><br>May antagonize Coumadin<br><br>Potentiates antidiabetic medications, steroids, estrogens<br><br>Caution with cardiovascular disease, hypotension, hypertension, steroid therapy |
| Female Reproductive System | | |
| **Evening Primrose Oil**<br><br>Anti-inflammatory, sedative, astringent<br><br>Used for premenstrual and menopausal problems, rheumatoid arthritis, elevated serum cholesterol, hypertension, eczema, diabetic neuropathy | Headache, rash, nausea, seizures, inflammation<br><br>Contraindicated for clients with epilepsy, schizophrenia | May potentiate antiplatelet and anticoagulant meds<br><br>Increases risk for seizures when taken with phenothiazines, antidepressants |
| Musculoskeletal System | | |
| **Chondroitin**<br><br>Collagen synthesis<br><br>Used for arthritis for cartilage synthesis (with glucosamine) | Dyspepsia, nausea | May potentiate effects of anticoagulants |
| **Glucosamine**<br><br>Collagen synthesis<br><br>Used for arthritis for cartilage synthesis (with chondroitin) | Dyspepsia, nausea | May impede insulin secretion or increase resistance |

| HERBAL SUPPLEMENTS *(CONTINUED)* | | |
|---|---|---|
| **SUPPLEMENT** | **ADVERSE EFFECTS/ CONTRAINDICATIONS** | **NURSING CONSIDERATIONS** |
| *Neurological System* | | |
| **Capsicum/Cayenne Pepper** <br><br> Analgesia, improves blood circulation <br><br> Used for arthritis, bowel disorders, nerve pain, PAD, chronic laryngitis, personal self-defense spray | GI discomfort, burning pain in eyes, nose, mouth, blepharospasm and swelling in eyes, skin tissue irritation, cough, bronchospasm <br><br> Avoid if allergic to ragweed or to chili pepper | May decrease effectiveness of antihypertensives, increases risk of cough with ACE inhibitors <br><br> May potentiate antiplatelet and anticoagulant meds and herbs <br><br> May cause hypertensive crisis with MAOIs <br><br> Increases theophylline absorption |
| **Feverfew** <br><br> Analgesic, antipyretic <br><br> Used for migraine prophylaxis, fever, menstrual problems, arthritis | Mouth ulcers, heartburn, indigestion, dizziness, tachycardia, allergic reactions | Potentiates antiplatelet and anticoagulant meds <br><br> Do not stop abruptly—causes moderate to severe pain with joint and muscle stiffness <br><br> Caution if allergic to daisy family of plants |
| *Gastrointestinal System* | | |
| **Flaxseed** <br><br> Laxative, anticholesteremic <br><br> Used for constipation, decrease cholesterol, prevent atherosclerosis, colon disorders | Diarrhea, flatulence, nausea <br><br> Contraindicated if client has strictures or acute GI inflammation | May decrease absorption of oral meds—do not take within 2 hrs <br><br> Immature flax seeds can be very toxic <br><br> Increase fluids to minimize flatulence |
| **Ginger** <br><br> Antiemetic, antioxidant, digestive aid, anti-inflammatory <br><br> Used for nausea, vomiting, indigestion, gas, lack of appetite | Minor heartburn, dermatitis <br><br> Contraindicated with gallstones | May potentiate antiplatelet and anticoagulant meds, antidiabetic meds, herbs that increase bleeding times |
| **Licorice** <br><br> Demulcent (soothes), expectorant, anti-inflammatory <br><br> Used for coughs, colds, stomach pains, ulcers | Hypokalemia, headache, edema, lethargy, hypertension, heart failure (with overdose), cardiac arrest <br><br> Contraindicated in renal or liver disease, heart disease, hypertension; caution with hormonal contraceptives | Decreases effect of spironolactone <br><br> Avoid use with digoxin, loop diuretics, corticosteroids |
| *Genitourinary System* | | |
| **Saw Palmetto** <br><br> Mild diuretic, urinary antiseptic <br><br> Used for BPH, increasing sexual vigor, cystitis | Constipation, diarrhea, nausea, decreased libido, back pain | May interact with hormonal medications such as HRT and oral contraceptives <br><br> May cause a false negative PSA test result |
| *Psychiatric* | | |
| **Chamomile** <br><br> Sedative/hypnotic, anti-inflammatory, antispasmodic, anti-infective <br><br> Used for stress, anxiety, insomnia, GI disorders | Allergic reactions, contact dermatitis, vomiting, depression | May potentiate sedatives and anticoagulants <br><br> Avoid if allergic to ragweed, members of daisy family of plants |
| **Kava** <br><br> Anti-anxiety, sedative/hypnotic, muscle relaxant <br><br> Used for anxiety, insomnia, seizure disorders | Hepatotoxicity, psychological dependence, mild euphoria, fatigue, sedation, suicidal thoughts, visual problems, scaly skin reaction <br><br> Contraindicated in Parkinson's, history of stroke, endogenous depression | May potentiate sedative effects of other sedating medications (benzodiazepines, barbiturates), anticonvulsants, and herbs (chamomile, valerian) |

| HERBAL SUPPLEMENTS *(CONTINUED)* | | |
|---|---|---|
| **SUPPLEMENT** | **ADVERSE EFFECTS/ CONTRAINDICATIONS** | **NURSING CONSIDERATIONS** |
| **Melatonin**<br><br>Hormone from pineal gland<br><br>Used for insomnia, jet lag | Headache, confusion, sedation, tachycardia | Potentiates CNS depressants<br><br>May decrease effectiveness of immunosuppressants, nifedipine |
| **St. John's Wort**<br><br>Antidepressant, sedative effects, antiviral, antimicrobial<br><br>Used for mild to moderate depression, sleep disorders, skin and wound healing | Photosensitivity, fatigue, allergic reactions, dry mouth, dizziness, restlessness, nausea<br><br>Contraindicated for major depression, transplant recipients, clients taking SSRIs (increases risk of serotonin syndrome), MAOIs (increases risk of hypertensive crisis), hormonal contraceptives | Usually decreases effectiveness of (digoxin, antineoplastics, antiviral AIDS drugs, anti-rejection drugs, theophylline, warfarin, hormonal contraceptives<br><br>May potentiate drugs and herbs with sedative effects<br><br>Should avoid tyramine in diet, OTC medications |
| **Valerian**<br><br>Sedative/hypnotic, antispasmodic<br><br>Used for insomnia, restlessness, anxiety | Headache, blurred vision, nausea, excitability<br><br>Contraindicated in liver disease may be hepatotoxic | May potentiate other CNS depressant medications, antihistamines, and sedating herbs |
| **Cardiovascular System** | | |
| **Gingko**<br><br>Enhances cerebral and peripheral blood circulation; antidepressive<br><br>Used for dementia, short-term memory loss, vertigo, PADs, depression, sexual dysfunction (including from SSRIs) | Headache, GI upset, contact dermatitis, dizziness | May potentiate antiplatelet and anticoagulant meds, ASA, NSAIDS, and herbs, which increase bleeding time<br><br>May potentiate MAOIs<br><br>May decrease effectiveness of anticonvulsants |
| **Hawthorn**<br><br>Antianginal, antiarrhythmic, vasodilator, antihypertensive, antilipidemic<br><br>Used for mild to moderate heart failure, hypertension, cholesterol reduction | Nausea, fatigue, sweating | May potentiate or interfere with wide range of cardiovascular medications used for CHF, angina, arrhythmias, hypertension, vasodilation<br><br>Potentiates digoxin<br><br>Potentiates CNS depressants<br><br>Avoid if allergic to members of the rose family of plants |
| **Respiratory System** | | |
| **Eucalyptus**<br><br>Decongestant, anti-inflammatory, antimicrobial, antifungal<br><br>Used for coughs, bronchitis, nasal congestion, sore muscles, wounds | Nausea, vomiting, epigastric burning, dizziness, muscle weakness, seizures<br><br>Contraindicated with liver disease, inflammation of intestinal tract | Potentiates antidiabetic medications and possibly other herbs that cause hypoglycemia<br><br>May increase metabolism of any drugs metabolized in liver |

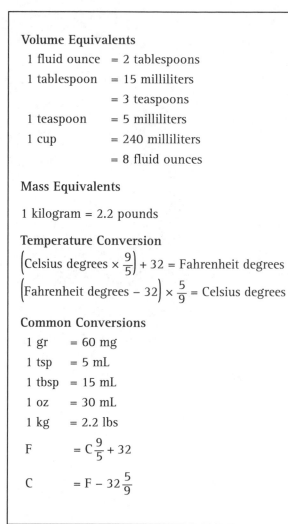

**Volume Equivalents**

| | |
|---|---|
| 1 fluid ounce | = 2 tablespoons |
| 1 tablespoon | = 15 milliliters |
| | = 3 teaspoons |
| 1 teaspoon | = 5 milliliters |
| 1 cup | = 240 milliliters |
| | = 8 fluid ounces |

**Mass Equivalents**

1 kilogram = 2.2 pounds

**Temperature Conversion**

$$\left(\text{Celsius degrees} \times \frac{9}{5}\right) + 32 = \text{Fahrenheit degrees}$$

$$\left(\text{Fahrenheit degrees} - 32\right) \times \frac{5}{9} = \text{Celsius degrees}$$

**Common Conversions**

| | |
|---|---|
| 1 gr | = 60 mg |
| 1 tsp | = 5 mL |
| 1 tbsp | = 15 mL |
| 1 oz | = 30 mL |
| 1 kg | = 2.2 lbs |
| F | $= C\dfrac{9}{5} + 32$ |
| C | $= F - 32\dfrac{5}{9}$ |

A. Assessment
   1. Hives, rash
   2. Difficulty breathing
   3. Decreased BP, increased pulse, increased respirations
   4. Dilated pupils
   5. Diaphoresis
   6. "Panicked" feeling
B. Nursing considerations
   1. Epinephrine 0.3 ml of 1:1,000 solution IM
   2. Massage site to speed absorption
   3. May repeat dose in 15–20 min
   4. Wear Medic-Alert identification
   5. Carry emergency epinephrine

## ▶ DELAYED ALLERGIC REACTION

A. Assessment
   1. Rash, hives
   2. Swollen joints
B. Nursing considerations
   1. Discontinue medication
   2. Notify health care provider
   3. Skin care
   4. Comfort measures
   5. Antihistamines, topical
   6. Corticosteriods

## ▶ DERMATOLOGICAL REACTIONS

A. Assessment
   1. Hives, rashes, lesions
   2. Exfoliative dermatitis (rash, fever, enlarged lymph nodes, enlarged liver)
   3. Erythema multiform excudativum (Stevens-Johnson syndrome—dark red papules that don't itch or hurt)
B. Nursing considerations
   1. Frequent skin care
   2. Avoid rubbing, tight clothing, harsh soaps, perfumed lotions
   3. Antihistamines
   4. Topical corticosteroids

# ▶ STOMATITIS

A. Assessment
   1. Swollen gums (gingivitis)
   2. Swollen, red tongue (glossitis)
   3. Difficulty swallowing
   4. Bad breath
   5. Pain in mouth and throat
B. Nursing considerations
   1. Frequent mouth care with nonirritating (nonalcoholic) solution
   2. Frequent, small feedings
   3. Antifungal meds
   4. Local anesthetics

# ▶ SUPERINFECTIONS

A. Assessment
   1. Fever
   2. Diarrhea
   3. Black hairy tongue
   4. Glossitis
   5. Mucous membrane lesions
   6. Vaginal itching and discharge
B. Nursing considerations
   1. Frequent mouth care
   2. Good skin care
   3. Small, frequent feedings
   4. Antifungal meds

# ▶ BONE MARROW DEPRESSION

A. Assessment
   1. Fever
   2. Chills
   3. Sore throat
   4. Weakness
   5. Back pain
   6. Dark urine
   7. Anemia (low Hct)
   8. Thrombocytopenia (low platelet count)
   9. Leukopenia (low WBC)
B. Nursing considerations
   1. Monitor CBC
   2. Rest

3. Protection from infections

4. Avoid activities that may cause injury

## ▶ LIVER IMPAIRMENT

A. Assessment

1. Fever

2. Malaise

3. Nausea, vomiting

4. Jaundice

5. Light stools, dark urine

6. Abdominal pain

7. Elevated AST, ALT

8. Elevated bilirubin

9. Altered PTT

B. Nursing considerations

1. Small, frequent feedings

2. Good skin care

3. Comfort measures

4. Cool environment

5. Rest

## ▶ RENAL IMPAIRMENT

A. Assessment

1. Elevated BUN, creatinine

2. Decreased Hct

3. Altered electrolytes ($K^+$, $Na^+$)

4. Fatigue

5. Edema

6. Irritability

7. Skin care

B. Nursing considerations

1. Diet and fluid restrictions

2. Good skin care

3. Electrolyte replacement

4. Rest

5. Dialysis

## ▶ OCULAR IMPAIRMENT

A. Assessment

1. Blurred vision

2. Color vision changes

3. Blindness

**B.** Nursing considerations

1. Monitor vision carefully

2. Monitor lighting and exposure to light

## ▶ AUDITORY IMPAIRMENT

**A.** Assessment

1. Dizziness

2. Ringing in ears

3. Loss of balance

4. Loss of hearing

**B.** Nursing considerations

1. Monitor hearing ability

2. Safety measures to prevent injury (falls)

## ▶ CNS IMPAIRMENT

**A.** Assessment

1. Confusion, delirium

2. Insomnia

3. Drowsiness

4. Hallucinations

**B.** Nursing considerations

1. Safety measures to prevent injury

2. Avoid activities that require alertness (driving a car)

3. Orient to surroundings

## ▶ ANTICHOLINERGIC EFFECTS

**A.** Assessment

1. Dry mouth

2. Altered taste perception

3. Dysphagia

4. Heartburn

5. Urinary retention

6. Impotence

7. Blurred vision

8. Nasal congestion

**B.** Nursing considerations

1. Sugarless lozenges

2. Good mouth care

3. Void before taking medication

4. Safety measures for vision changes

# ▶ PARKINSON-LIKE EFFECTS

**A.** Assessments

1. Akinesia
2. Tremors
3. Drooling
4. Changes in gait
5. Rigidity
6. Akathisia (extreme restlessness)
7. Dyskinesia (spasms)

**B.** Nursing considerations

1. Anticholinergic meds
2. Antiparkinson meds
3. Safety measures for gait changes

# Chapter 4

# PHYSIOLOGICAL INTEGRITY: REDUCTION OF RISK POTENTIAL

| **Sections** | **Concepts Covered** |
|---|---|
| 1. Sensory and Perceptual Alterations | Sensory Perception, Client Education: Providing |
| 2. Alterations in Body Systems | Metabolism, Client Education: Providing |
| 3. Perioperative Care | Gas Exchange, Comfort, Client Education: Providing |
| 4. Diagnostic Tests | Blood Tests |
| 5. Therapeutic Procedures | Therapeutic Techniques, Client Education: Providing |

# SENSORY AND PERCEPTUAL ALTERATIONS

## ▶ IMPAIRED VISION

**A.** Assessment

1. Redness, burning, pain in eyes
2. Edema
3. Increased lacrimation and exudate
4. Headache, squinting
5. Nausea and vomiting
6. Altered growth and development
7. Visual disturbances
8. Altered visual function tests (see Table 1)

| Table 1 VISUAL FUNCTION TESTS | | |
|---|---|---|
| **TEST** | **PROCEDURE** | **CLIENT PREPARATION** |
| Tonometry—measures intraocular pressure | Cornea is anesthetized<br>Tonometer registers degree of indentation on cornea when pressure is applied<br>Pressure increased in glaucoma | Client will be recumbent<br>Remove contact lenses<br>Advise not to squint, cough, or hold breath during procedure |
| Visual fields— measurement of range of vision (perimetry) | Client is seated a measured distance from chart of concentric circles<br>Client asked to fix eyes on a point on a chart at center of circle<br>Client instructed to indicate when he/she first sees pointer; this point is recorded as a point in field of vision<br>This procedure is repeated around 360° of a circle<br>Normal visual fields for each eye are approximately a 50° angle superiorly, 90° laterally, 70° inferiorly, and 60° medially | None |
| Snellen test—test of visual acuity | Client stands 20 feet from chart of letters<br>One eye is covered at a time<br>Client reads chart to smallest letter visible<br>Test results indicate comparison of distance at which this client reads to what normal eye sees at 20 feet | None |

**B.** Diagnose

    1. Disorders of accommodation (see Table 2)

    2. Burns of the eye (see Table 3)

    3. Eye trauma (see Table 4)

    4. Eye infections/inflammation (see Table 5)

| Table 2 DISORDERS OF ACCOMMODATION | |
|---|---|
| TYPES | NURSING CONSIDERATIONS |
| Myopia (nearsightedness)—light rays refract at a point in front of the retina | Corrective lenses |
| Hyperopia (farsightedness)—light rays refract behind the retina | Corrective lenses |
| Presbyopia with aging | Commonly occurs after age 35 Corrective lenses |
| Astigmatism—uneven curvature of cornea causing blurring of vision | Corrective lenses |

| Table 3 BURNS OF THE EYE | |
|---|---|
| TYPES | NURSING CONSIDERATIONS |
| **Chemical** Acids, cleansers, insecticides | Eye irrigation with copious amounts of water for 15–20 minutes |
| **Radiation** Sun, lightening, eclipses | Prevention—use of eye shields |
| **Thermal** Hot metals, liquids, other occupational hazards | Use of goggles to protect the cornea; patching; analgesics |

| Table 4 EYE TRAUMA | |
|---|---|
| TYPES | NURSING CONSIDERATIONS |
| Nonpenetrating—abrasions | Eye patch for 24 hours |
| Nonpenetrating—contusions | Cold compresses, analgesics |
| Penetrating—pointed or sharp objects | Cover with patch; refer to surgeon |

**C.** Plan/Implementation

    1. Prevent eye injuries

        a. Provide safe toys

        b. Use eye protectors when working with chemicals, tools

        c. Use eye protectors during sports

        d. Protect eyes from ultraviolet light

2.  Care of the blind client
    a.  Enhance communication
        1)  Address client by name
        2)  Always introduce self
        3)  State reason for being there
        4)  Inform client when leaving the room

| Table 5   EYE INFECTION/INFLAMMATION | | |
|---|---|---|
| TYPE OF INFECTION | CAUSE | NURSING CONSIDERATIONS |
| Conjunctivitis (pinkeye) | Bacteria<br>Virus<br>Allergies | Warm, moist compresses<br>Topical antibiotics<br>Hydrocortisone ophthalmic ointment |
| Stye | *Staphylococcal* organism | Warm compresses<br>Antibiotics<br>Incision and drainage |
| Chalazion (inflammatory cyst) | Duct obstruction | Incision and drainage |
| Keratitis (inflammation of cornea) | Virus<br>Spread of systemic disease | Antibiotics<br>Hot compresses<br>Steroids, except with herpes simplex |
| Uveitis (inflammation of iris, ciliary body, choroid) | Local or systemic infection | Warm compresses<br>Dark glasses<br>Antibiotics, analgesics, sedatives |

    b.  Provide sense of safety and security
        1)  Explain all procedures in detail
        2)  Keep furniture arrangement consistent
        3)  Provide hand rail
        4)  Doors should never be half open
        5)  Have client follow attendant when walking by lightly touching attendant's elbow (1/2 step ahead)
        6)  Instruct client in use of lightweight walking stick when walking alone
    c.  Foster sense of independence
        1)  Provide assistance only when needed
        2)  Identify food and location on plate or tray
        3)  Encourage recreational and leisure time activities
3.  Care of artificial eye
    a.  Remove daily for cleansing
    b.  Cleanse with mild detergent and water
    c.  Dry and store in water or contact-lens soaking solution
    d.  Remove before general surgery

e. Insertion method

1) Raise upper lid and slip eye beneath it

2) Release lid

3) Support lower lid and draw it over the lower edge of eye

f. Removal method

1) Draw lower lid downward

2) Slip eye forward over lower lid and remove

4. Instill eye drops

D. Evaluation

1. Has client safety been maintained?

2. Is the client able to instill eye drops using correct technique?

## ▶ RETINOPATHY OF PREMATURITY (ROP)

A. Assessment

1. Demarcation line forms (separates avascular retina anteriorly with vascularized retina posteriorly)

2. Ridge forms

3. Retinal detachment

B. Diagnose

1. Cause of blindness in premature infants

2. High concentrations of oxygen cause the premature infant's retinal vessels to constrict, causing blindness

3. Sometimes occurs when oxygen concentrations are greater than 40%, and when used for longer than 48 to 72 hours in infants

C. Plan/Implementation

1. Ensure that all infants born before 36 weeks or less than 2,000 g at birth have eye exam by experts

2. Use minimum amount of oxygen

3. Monitor $pO_2$ continuously

4. Maintain $SaO_2$ level within normal limits (range 95–100 mm Hg)

5. Administer vitamin E as ordered—thought to affect tissue response to oxygen (therapy is controversial)

6. Decrease environmental stimuli and continuous direct lighting

D. Evaluation

1. Have complications of oxygen administration been avoided in the premature infant?

2. Has the infant's eyesight been maintained?

## ▶ STRABISMUS

A. Assessment

1. Visible deviation of eye

2. Diplopia

3. Child tilts head or squints to focus

**B.** Diagnose

  1. Eyes do not function as a unit

  2. Imbalance of the extraocular muscles

**C.** Plan/Implementation

  1. Nonsurgical intervention begins no later than age 6

  2. Occlusion of unaffected eye to strengthen weaker eye

  3. Corrective lenses combined with other therapy to improve acuity

  4. Orthoptic exercises designed to strengthen eye muscles

  5. Surgery on rectus muscles of eye

**D.** Evaluation

  1. Has normal vision been restored?

  2. Is child compliant with exercise regime?

# ▶ DETACHED RETINA

**A.** Assessment

  1. Flashes of light

  2. Blurred or "sooty" vision, "floaters"

  3. Sensation of particles moving in line of vision

  4. Delineated areas of vision blank

  5. A feeling of a curtain coming up or down

  6. Loss of vision

  7. Confusion, apprehension

**B.** Diagnose

  1. Separation of the retina from the choroid

  2. Cause

     a. Trauma

     b. Aging process

     c. Diabetes

     d. Tumors

**C.** Plan/Implementation

  1. Bedrest—do not bend forward, avoid excessive movements

  2. Affected eye or both eyes may be patched to decrease movement of eye (as ordered by health care provider)

  3. Specific positioning—area of detachment should be in the dependent position

  4. Take precautions to avoid bumping head, moving eyes rapidly, or rapidly jerking the head

  5. Surgery to reattach retina to choroid; gas or air bubble used to apply pressure to retina

  6. No hair-washing for 1 week

  7. Administer sedatives and tranquilizers

  8. Avoid strenuous activity for 3 months

9. Care of client undergoing eye surgery
   a. Preoperative care
      1) Assess visual acuity
      2) Prepare periorbital area
      3) Orient to surroundings
      4) Preoperative teaching—prepare for postoperative course
      5) Teach postop need to avoid straining at stool, stooping
   b. Postoperative care
      1) Observe for complications—hemorrhage, sharp pain, infection
      2) Avoid sneezing, coughing, straining at stool, bending down
      3) Protect from injury; restrict activity
      4) Keep signal bell within reach
      5) Administer medications as ordered: antiemetics for nausea/vomiting, sedatives for restlessness
      6) Eye shield worn for protective purposes
      7) Discharge teaching—avoid stooping or straining at stool; use proper body mechanics

**D.** Evaluation
   1. Has normal vision been restored?
   2. Have complications been prevented?

▶ **CATARACTS**

**A.** Assessment
   1. Objects appear distorted and blurred; decreased color perception
   2. Annoying glare; double vision
   3. Pupil changes from black to gray to milky white

**B.** Diagnose
   1. Partial or total opacity of the normally transparent crystalline lens
   2. Cause
      a. Congenital
      b. Trauma
      c. Aging process
      d. Associated with diabetes mellitus, intraocular surgery
      e. Drugs—steroid therapy
      f. Exposure to radioactivity

**C.** Plan/Implementation
   1. Surgical management—laser surgery
      a. Extracapsular extraction—cut through the anterior capsule to expose the opaque lens material, most common procedure
      b. Intracapsular extraction—removal of entire lens and capsule; easier for health care provider to do; places client at greater risk for retinal detachment and loss of structure for intraocular lens implant
      c. Lens implantation

    d. Observe for postoperative complications

        1) Hemorrhage indicated by sudden sharp pain

        2) Increased intraocular pressure

        3) Infection—yellow or green drainage

        4) Slipped suture(s)

        5) If lens implant—pupil should remain constricted; if aphakic (without lens) pupil remains dilated

    e. Avoid straining; no heavy lifting

    f. Bend from the knees to pick things up

    g. Instruct in instillation of eye drops to affected eye, use of night shields

    h. Usually suggest to sleep on unaffected side (decreases pain and swelling when elevated)

    i. Protect eye from bright lights and water

    j. Adjustments needed in perception if aphakic

    k. Report increased pain, change in vision, increased floaters

**D.** Evaluation

    1. Has vision been restored?

    2. Have complications been prevented?

## ▶ GLAUCOMA

**A.** Assessment

    1. Cloudy, blurry vision or loss of vision

    2. Artificial lights appear to have rainbows or halos around them

    3. Decreased peripheral vision

    4. Pain, headache

    5. Nausea, vomiting

**B.** Diagnose

    1. Abnormal increase in intraocular pressure leading to visual disability and blindness; obstruction of outflow of aqueous humor

    2. Types

        a. Angle-closure (closed-angle) glaucoma—sudden onset, emergency

        b. Open-angle (primary glaucoma)—blockage of aqueous humor flow

    3. Causes

        a. Closed-angle glaucoma—associated with emotional disturbances, allergy, and vasomotor disturbances

        b. Open-angle glaucoma—associated with trauma, tumor, hemorrhage, iritis, and aging

    4. Potential nursing diagnosis

        a. Disturbed sensory perception

**C.** Plan/Implementation

    1. Medications: prostaglandin agonists, adrenergic agonists, beta-adrenergic blockers, cholinergic agonists, carbonic anhydrase inhibitors

    2. Surgery—laser trabeculoplasty

3. Avoid tight clothing (e.g., collars)

4. Reduce external stimuli

5. Avoid heavy lifting, straining at stool

6. Avoid use of mydriatics (e.g., Atropine)

7. Educate public to five danger signs of glaucoma

    a. Brow arching

    b. Halos around lights

    c. Blurry vision

    d. Diminished peripheral vision

    e. Headache or eye pain

**D.** Evaluation

1. Has vision been restored?

2. Have complications been prevented?

## ▶ HEARING LOSS

**A.** Conductive loss

1. Assessment

    a. Pain, fever, headache

    b. Discharge

    c. Altered growth and development

    d. Personality changes, e.g., irritability, depression, suspiciousness, withdrawal

2. Analysis

    a. Disorder in auditory canal, eardrum, or ossicles

    b. Causes

        1) Infection

        2) Inflammation

        3) Foreign body

        4) Trauma

        5) Ear wax

    c. Complications—meningitis resulting from initial infection

    d. Diagnostics

        1) Audiogram—quantitative (degree of loss)

        2) Tuning fork—qualitative (type of loss)

3. Plan/Implementation

    a. Heat

    b. Antibiotics

    c. Hearing aid

    d. Ear irrigations

        1) Tilt head toward side of affected ear; gently direct stream of fluid against sides of canal

        2) After procedure, instruct client to lie on affected side to facilitate drainage

        3) Contraindicated if there is evidence of swelling or tenderness

    e.  Ear drops

        1)  Position the affected ear uppermost

        2)  Pull outer ear upward and backward for adult (3 years of age and older)

        3)  Pull outer ear downward and backward for child (under 3 years of age)

        4)  Place drops so they run down the wall of ear canal

        5)  Have client lie on unaffected ear to encourage absorption

    f.  Surgery

        1)  Preoperative care

            a)  Baseline hearing assessment

            b)  Assessment of preoperative symptoms

            c)  Preparation depends on nature of incision

            d)  Encourage client to wash hair prior to surgery

            e)  Teaching—expect postoperative hearing loss; discuss need for special position of operative ear as ordered

        2)  Postoperative care

            a)  Reinforce dressing, don't change

            b)  Avoid noseblowing, sneezing, and coughing

            c)  Observe for possible complications

                i)  Facial nerve damage—may be transient

               ii)  Infection

             iii)  Vertigo, tinnitus

            d)  Do not apply any pressure if surgery is on internal ear-notify health care provider immediately

            e)  Administer medications

            f)  Provide for client safety

            g)  Position on unaffected side (decreases swelling and pain of surgical site)

        3)  Discharge teaching—avoid getting water in ear, flying, drafts, crowds, people with respiratory infections

  4.  Evaluation

    a.  Have complications been prevented?

    b.  Have efforts been made to minimize hearing loss?

**B.**  Perceptive (sensorineural) loss

  1.  Assessment

    a.  Pain, fever, headache

    b.  Discharge

    c.  Altered growth and development

    d.  Personality changes, e.g., irritability, depression, suspiciousness, withdrawal

  2.  Analysis

    a.  Due to disorder of the organ of Corti or the auditory nerve

      b. Causes

          1) Congenital—maternal exposure to communicable disease

          2) Infection, drug toxicity

          3) Trauma

          4) Labyrinth dysfunction—Ménière's disease

      c. Complications

          1) Vertigo

          2) Tinnitus

          3) Vomiting

3. Plan/Implementation

      a. Care of the deaf/hard of hearing client

          1) Enhance communication

              a) Position self directly in front of client

              b) Well-lit, quiet room

              c) Get client's attention

              d) Move close to better ear, if appropriate

              e) Speak clearly and slowly; do not shout

              f) Keep hands and other objects away from mouth when speaking

              g) Have client repeat statements

              h) Use appropriate hand motions

              i) Write messages down if client able to read

          2) Health teaching

              a) Provide health care resources

              b) Encourages use of visual cues

              c) Advise that auditory cues (such as smoke alarms) may not be feasible

      b. Surgery

4. Evaluation

      a. Has hearing loss been reversed/minimized?

      b. Has client adjusted to change in hearing?

## ▶ ACUTE OTITIS MEDIA

**A.** Assessment

1. Fever, chills

2. Headache

3. Ringing in ears

4. Deafness

5. Sharp pain

6. Head rolling, crying, ear-tugging (child)

7. Nausea, vomiting

8. Red, bulging, tympanic membrane

B. Diagnose

   1. Definition—infection of middle ear

   2. Cause—pathogenic organisms, (i.e., bacteria and viruses)

   3. Complications

      a. Chronic otitis media—children more susceptible because of short eustachian tube

      b. Residual deafness

      c. Perforation of tympanic membrane

      d. Cholesteatoma growth

      e. Mastoiditis or meningitis

C. Plan/Implementation

   1. Administer medication as ordered

      a. Antibiotics—organism-specific

      b. Antihistamines for allergies

      c. Nasal decongestants

   2. Report persistent symptoms to health care provider

   3. Ventilatory tubes—inserted in eustachian tube for continuous ventilation

   4. Myringotomy—tympanic membrane incision to relieve pressure and release purulent fluid; no water can be allowed to enter the ear

   5. Tympanoplasty—surgical reconstruction of ossicles and tympanic membrane

   6. Bedrest if temperature is elevated

   7. Position on side of involved ear to promote drainage

D. Evaluation

   1. Has permanent hearing loss been prevented?

   2. Have complications been prevented?

## ▶ MÉNIÈRE'S DISEASE

A. Assessment

   1. Nausea and vomiting

   2. Incapacitating vertigo, tinnitus

   3. Feeling of pressure/fullness in the ear

   4. Fluctuating, progressive decreased hearing on involved side

   5. Nystagmus, headache

B. Diagnose

   1. Dilation of the membrane of the labyrinth

   2. Recurrent attacks of vertigo with sensorineural hearing loss

   3. Attacks recur several times a week; periods of remission may last several years

   4. Diagnostic tests—Weber and Rinne test, CT

   5. Complication—hearing loss

C. Plan/Implementation
  1. Drug therapy
     a. Antihistamines in acute phase (epinephrine, diphenhydramine)
     b. Antiemetics (e.g., prochlorperazine)
     c. Antivertigo medications (e.g., meclizine, diazepam)
     d. Diuretics (e.g., hydrochlorothiazide, triamterene)
  2. Bedrest during acute phase
  3. Provide protection when ambulatory
  4. Low-sodium diet (2,000 mg/day); avoid caffeine, nicotine, alcohol
  5. Decompression of endolymphatic sac with Teflon shunt (method of choice)
  6. Total labyrinthectomy—last resort due to possible complication of Bell's palsy
  7. Client education
     a. Need to slow down body movements—jerking or sudden movements may precipitate attack
     b. Need to lie down when an attack occurs
     c. If driving, pull over and stop car
  8. Occupational counseling—if occupation involves operating machinery
D. Evaluation
  1. Does client use strategies to prevent injury secondary to dizziness, vertigo?
  2. Does client demonstrate knowledge of medications?

# ► CRANIAL NERVE DISORDERS

**A.** Assessment (see Table 6)

**B.** Diagnose (see Table 6)

**C.** Plan/Implementation (see Table 6)

**D.** Evaluate

    1. Has client adjusted to altered body image?

| Table 6   CRANIAL NERVE DISORDERS | | | |
|---|---|---|---|
| | **TRIGEMINAL NEURALGIA (TIC DOULOUREUX)** | **BELL'S PALSY (FACIAL PARALYSIS)** | **ACOUSTIC NEUROMA** |
| **Assessment** | Stabbing or burning facial pain—excruciating, unpredictable, paroxysmal<br><br>Twitching, grimacing of facial muscles | Inability to close eye<br><br>Decreased corneal reflex<br><br>Increased lacrimation<br><br>Speech difficulty<br><br>Loss of taste<br><br>Distortion of one side of face | Deafness—partial, initially<br><br>Dizziness |
| **Analysis** | Type of neuralgia involving one or more branches of the fifth cranial nerve<br><br>Causes—infections of sinuses, teeth, mouth, or irritation of nerve from pressure | Peripheral involvement of the seventh cranial nerve<br><br>Predisposing factors—vascular ischemia, viral disease, edema, inflammatory reactions | Benign tumor of the eighth cranial nerve |
| **Nursing considerations** | Identify and avoid stimuli that exacerbate the attacks<br><br>Administer medications—carbamazepine and analgesics<br><br>Treatment—carbamazepine, alcohol injection to nerve, resection of the nerve, microvascular decompression<br><br>Avoid rubbing eye<br><br>Chew on opposite side of mouth | Protect head from cold or drafts<br><br>Administer analgesics<br><br>Assist with electric stimulation<br><br>Teach isometric exercises for facial muscles (blow and suck from a straw); massage, warm packs<br><br>Provide emotional support for altered body image<br><br>Prevent corneal abrasions (artificial tears)<br><br>Treatment—electrical stimulation, analgesics, steroid therapy, antiviral medications<br><br>Recovery takes 3–5 weeks | Pre- and postoperative care for posterior fossa craniotomy<br><br>Comfort measures—assist with turning of head and neck<br><br>Treatment—surgical excision of tumor |

# ► GUILLAN-BARRÉ SYNDROME

**A.** Assessment

    1. Paresthesias, pain often occurring in glove-and-stocking distribution; pain

    2. Motor losses symmetrical, usually beginning in lower extremities, then extend upward to include trunk, upper extremities, cranial nerves, and vasomotor function; deep tendon reflexes disappear; respiratory muscle compromise

    3. Excessive or inadequate autonomic dysfunction

        a. Hypotension, tachycardia

        b. Vasomotor flushing

        c. Paralytic ileus

        d. Profuse sweating

    4. Plateau period—progresses to peak severity between 2–4 weeks; average 10 days

    5. Recovery period—several months to a year; 10% residual disability

**B.** Diagnose

    1. Progressive inflammatory autoimmune response occurring in peripheral nervous system, resulting in compression of nerve roots and peripheral nerves; demyelination occurs and slows or alters nerve conduction

    2. Possible causes

        a. Infective, viral

        b. Autoimmune response

        c. May follow immunizations

    3. Course

        a. Acute, rapidly ascending sensory and motor deficit that may stop at any level of the CNS

        b. Protracted, develops slowly, regresses slowly

        c. Prolonged course with phases of deterioration and partial remission

**C.** Plan/Implementation

    1. Intervention is symptomatic

    2. Steroids in acute phase

    3. Plasmapheresis, IV immunoglobulins, adrenocorticotropic hormone, corticosteroids

    4. Mechanical ventilation, elevate head of bed, suctioning

    5. Prevent hazards of immobility

    6. Maintain adequate nutrition, hydration

    7. Physical therapy, range of motion

    8. Pain-reducing measures

    9. Eye care

   10. Prevention of complications—URI, aspiration, constipation, urinary retention

   11. Psychosocial support to deal with fear, anxiety, and altered body image

**D.** Evaluation

    1. Has client recovered without major complications?

    2. Has client comfort been maintained?

# ▶ MENINGITIS

**A.** Assessment

1. Headache, fever, photophobia

2. Signs of meningeal irritation

   a. Nuchal rigidity—stiff neck

   b. Kernig's sign—when hip flexed to 90°, complete extension of the knee is restricted and painful

   c. Brudzinski's sign—attempts to flex the neck will produce flexion at knee and thigh

   d. Opisthotonic position—extensor rigidity with legs hyperextended and forming an arc with the trunk

3. Changes in level of consciousness

4. Seizures

5. Symptoms in infants

   a. Refuse feedings, vomiting, diarrhea

   b. Bulging fontanelles

   c. Vacant stare, high-pitched cry

**B.** Diagnose

1. Causes

   a. Infection (viral, bacterial, fungal)

   b. Neurosurgical procedures, basilar-skull fractures

   c. Otitis media, mastoiditis

**C.** Plan/Implementation

1. IV antibiotic therapy—penicillin, cephalosporin, vancomycin

2. Monitor ABG, arterial pressures, body weight, serum electrolytes, urine volume, specific gravity, osmolality

3. Droplet precautions for *Haemophilus influenzae* type b and *Neisseria meningitidis*

4. Prevention

   a. Vaccine 65+ years old with chronic diseases; revaccination in 5 years

   b. Hib vaccine for infants

**D.** Evaluation

1. Is client able to maintain optimal neurological function?

2. Have complications been prevented?

# ▶ MIGRAINE HEADACHE

**A.** Assessment

1. Prodromal—depression, irritability, feeling cold, food cravings, anorexia, change in activity level, increased urination

2. Aura—light flashes and bright spots, numbness and tingling (lips, face, hands), mild confusion, drowsiness, dizziness, diploplia

3.  Headache—throbbing (often unilateral), photophobia, nausea, vomiting, 4 to 72 hours

4.  Recovery—pain gradually subsides, muscle aches in neck and scalp, sleep for extended period

**B.** Diagnose

1.  Episodic events or acute attacks

2.  Seen more often in women before menses

3.  Familial disorders due to inherited vascular response to different chemicals

4.  Precipitating factors—stress, menstrual cycles, bright lights, depression, sleep deprivation, fatigue, foods containing tyramine, monosodium glutamate, nitrites, or milk products (aged cheese, processed foods)

**C.** Plan/Implementation

1.  Prevention and treatment

    a.  Medications

        1)  Beta blockers

        2)  Triptan preparations—activate serotonin receptors

        3)  Acetaminophen, NSAIDS

        4)  Topiramate

        5)  Ergotamines—dihydroergotamine; take at beginning of headache

    b.  Modify trigger factors

2.  Implementation

    a.  Avoid triggers

    b.  Comfort measures

    c.  Quiet dark environment

    d.  Elevate head of bed 30°

3.  Complementary/Alternate therapy

    a.  Riboflavin (vitamin $B_2$) supplement

        1)  400 mg daily may reduce the number and duration but not the severity of the headaches

        2)  Take as an individual supplement

    b.  Massage, meditation, relaxation techniques

## ▶ HUNTINGTON'S DISEASE

**A.** Assessment

1.  Depression and temper outbursts

2.  Choreiform movements

    a.  Slight to severe restlessness

    b.  Facial grimacing

    c.  Arm movements

    d.  Irregular leg movements

    e.  Twisting, turning, struggling

    f.  Tongue movements

    g.  Person is in constant motion by end of diseased progression

3. Personality changes
   a. Irritabilty
   b. Paranoia, demanding, memory loss, decreased intellectual function
   c. Dementia
   d. Psychosis seen at end stage

**B.** Diagnose
   1. Rare, familial, progressive, degenerative disease that is passed from generation to generation (dominant inheritance)

**C.** Plan/Implementation
   1. Drug therapy—intended to reduce movement and subdue behavior changes
      a. Chlordiazepoxidehydrochloride
      b. Haloperidol
      c. Chlorpromazine
   2. Supportive, symptomatic
   3. Genetic counseling for all family members

**D.** Evaluation
   1. Has family undergone genetic counseling?
   2. Has client comfort been maintained?

# ALTERATIONS IN BODY SYSTEMS Section 2

## ► ALTERATIONS IN GLUCOSE METABOLISM

**A.** Assessment

1. Polyuria, polydipsia, polyphagia    *Diabetes*
2. Weight change

**B.** Diagnose

1. Diabetes mellitus is a genetically heterogeneous group of disorders that is characterized by glucose intolerance
2. Types (see Table 1)

| Table 1 ALTERATIONS IN GLUCOSE METABOLISM | |
|---|---|
| **TYPE** | **NURSING CONSIDERATIONS** |
| Type 1 diabetes | Acute onset before age 30 |
| | Insulin-producing pancreatic beta cells destroyed by autoimmune process |
| | Requires insulin injection |
| | Ketosis prone |
| Type 2 diabetes | Usually older than 30 and obese |
| | Decreased sensitivity to insulin (insulin resistance) or decreased insulin production |
| | Ketosis rare |
| | Treated with diet and exercise |
| | Supplemented with oral hypoglycemic medications |
| Others: Gestational diabetes Impaired fasting glucose | Onset during pregnancy, second or third trimester |
| | High-risk pregnancy |
| | Fasting plasma glucose of greater than or equal to 100 mg/dL (5.6 mmol/L) and less than 126 mg/dL (7mmol/L); risk factor for future diabetes risk |

3. Risk factors for type 2 diabetes
   a. Parents or siblings with diabetes
   b. Obesity (20% or more above ideal body weight)
   c. African American, Hispanic, Native American, or Asian American
   d. Older than 45 years
   e. Previously impaired fasting glucose
   f. Hypertension
   g. HDL cholesterol levels less than or equal to 35 mg/dL; triglyceride levels greater than or equal to 250 mg/dL
   h. History of gestational diabetes or delivery of baby greater than 9 lb

*Ketones
↑ Fat breakdown
↑ metabolism*

4. Diagnostic tests

   a. Blood glucose monitoring—presence of sugar in the urine is a sign of diabetes and calls for an immediate blood glucose test; normal range in fasting blood is 60–110 mg/dL(3.3–6.1 mmol/L)

   b. Urine ketones indicate that diabetic control has deteriorated; body has started to break down stored fat for energy

   c. Glycosylated hemoglobin (HbA1c)—blood sample can be taken without fasting; normal 4–6%

   d. Special considerations—medications, illness, and stress will affect testing

**C.** Plan/Implementation

1. Nutrition management

   a. Provide all essential food constituents—lower lipid levels if elevated

   b. Achieve and maintain ideal weight

   c. Meet energy needs

   d. Achieve normal-range glucose levels

   e. Methods

      1) Food exchange—foods on list in specified amounts contain equal number of calories and grams of protein, fat, and carbohydrate (see Table 2)

      2) Carbohydrate counting

      3) Food guide pyramid

      4) Glycemic index

| Table 2  DIABETIC EXCHANGE LIST ||
| --- | --- |
| **EXCHANGE** | **EXAMPLE** |
| Bread/starch | 1 slice of bread<br>1/2 cup pasta |
| Vegetable | 1 cup raw leafy vegetables<br>1/2 cup cooked vegetables |
| Milk | 1 cup yogurt<br>2 oz processed cheese |
| Meat, poultry, eggs, fish | 2–3 oz cooked meat, fish, poultry<br>2 eggs |
| Fruit | 1/2 cup cooked fruit<br>1 medium apple |
| Fat | 1 tsp mayonnaise |
| Free items | Mustard, pickle, herbs |

2. Insulin management

   a. Insulin lowers blood glucose by facilitating uptake and the use of glucose by muscle and fat cells; decreases the release of glucose from the liver

   b. Mixing insulins—draw up regular insulin first

   c. Site selection—abdomen, posterior arms, anterior thighs, hips; rotate sites

   d. Self-injection—use disposable syringe once and discard into hard plastic container with tight-fitting top

   e. "Sick day rules"

     1) Take insulin or oral agent as ordered

     2) Check blood glucose and urine ketones every 3–4 hours

     3) Report altered levels to health care provider

     4) If unable to follow normal meal plan, substitute soft foods (soup, custard, gelatin) 6–8 times per day

     5) If vomiting, diarrhea, or fever, report to health care provider and take liquids (cola, broth, Gatorade) every 0.5–1 hour

3. Oral hypoglycemic medications—improve both tissue responsiveness to insulin and/or the ability of the pancreatic cells to secrete insulin

4. Self-monitoring of blood glucose (SMBG)

   a. Check client's eyesight to make sure he/she can see directions and read results

   b. Calibrate monitor as instructed by manufacturer

   c. Check expiration date on test strips

   d. If taking insulin, check 2–4 times daily

   e. If not receiving insulin, check 2–3 times per week

   f. Keep log book of results

   g. Testing should be done at peak action time of medication

5. Skin and foot care

   a. Inspect feet daily (use mirror if client is elderly or has decreased joint mobility)

   b. Wear well-fitting shoes; break in new shoes slowly (wear 1–2 hours initially with gradual increase in time)

   c. Don't walk barefoot or use heating pad on feet

   d. Cut toenails straight across without rounding corners

6. Exercise

   a. Use proper foot care

   b. Don't exercise in extreme temperatures

   c. Don't exercise when control of diabetes is poor

7. Complications

   a. Hypoglycemia (insulin reaction) (see Table 3)

   b. Hyperglycemia (diabetic ketoacidosis) (see Table 3)

   c. HHNKS (hyperglycemic hyperosmolar nonketotic syndrome; see Table 3)

   d. Diabetic retinopathy

   e. Coronary artery disease

   f. Cerebrovascular disease

| Table 3  GLUCOSE IMBALANCES | | | |
|---|---|---|---|
| | HYPOGLYCEMIA (INSULIN REACTION) | HYPERGLYCEMIA (DIABETIC KETOACIDOSIS) | HHNKS (HYPERGLYCEMIA HYPEROSMOLAR NONKETOTIC SYNDROME) |
| Assessment | Blood sugar less than 50–60 mg/dL (2.8–3.3 mmol/L)<br><br>Irritability, confusion, tremors, blurring of vision, coma, seizures<br><br>Hypotension, tachycardia<br><br>Skin cool and clammy, diaphoresis | Blood sugar 300–800 mg/dL (16.7–44.4 mmol/L)<br><br>Headache, drowsiness, weakness stupor, coma<br><br>Hypotension, tachycardia<br><br>Skin warm and dry, dry mucous membranes, elevated temperature<br><br>Polyuria progressing to oliguria, polydipsia, polyphagia<br><br>Kussmaul's respirations (rapid and deep)<br><br>Fruity odor to breath | Glucose levels greater than 800 mg/dL (44.4 mmol/L)<br><br>Occurs in adults greater than 50 year old<br><br>Occurs in Type 2 (NIDDM) diabetics<br><br>Ketosis and acidosis do not occur<br><br>Hypotension<br><br>Dry mucous membranes, poor skin turgor<br><br>Tachycardia<br><br>Alteration in sense of awareness, seizures, hemiparesis |
| Plan/Implementation | Liquids containing sugar if conscious; skim milk is ideal if tolerated<br><br>Dextrose 50% IV if unconscious, glucagon 1 mg IM, SQ<br><br>Follow with additional carbohydrate in 15 minutes<br><br>Determine and treat cause<br><br>Client education | Major complication is fluid volume deficit<br><br>1 L of 0.9% NaCl per hour during first 2–3 hrs followed by 0.45% NaCl 200–500 ml/h; then $D_5W$ or $D_5$ 1/2 NS<br><br>Regular IV insulin 5 units/h<br><br>Potassium replacement<br><br>EKG q 2–4 h<br><br>Check $K^+$ q 2–4 h<br><br>Assess level of consciousness, urine output, temperature hourly<br><br>Assess vital signs q 15 minutes until stable<br><br>Assess CVP q 30 minutes<br><br>Check blood glucose levels hourly | Normal saline or 0.45% NaCl<br><br>Regular insulin<br><br>Potassium as soon as urine output is satisfactory<br><br>Determine and treat cause<br><br>Client education<br><br>Exercise regimen |
| Cause | Too much insulin or oral hypoglycemia agent<br><br>Inadequate food<br><br>Excessive physical activity | Decreased or missed insulin<br><br>Illness or infection<br><br>Untreated diabetes | Acute illness<br><br>Medications (thiazides)<br><br>Treatments (dialysis) |

## ▶ ALTERATIONS IN PROTEIN METABOLISM

**A.** Assessment (see Table 4)

**B.** Diagnose—potential nursing diagnoses

    1. Nutrition: less than body requirements, altered

    2. Knowledge deficit regarding dietary restrictions

**C.** Plan/Implementation (see Table 4)

**D.** Evaluation

    1. Have complications been prevented?

    2. Are parents knowledgeable about nutritional need of infant?

| Table 4   ALTERATIONS IN PROTEIN METABOLISM | | |
|---|---|---|
| **DISORDER** | **ASSESSMENT** | **NURSING CONSIDERATIONS** |
| Phenylketonuria (PKU)—inborn error of phenylalanine utilization | High blood phenylalanine that leads to intellectual delay | Specially prepared milk substitutes for infants (Lofenalac)<br>Low-protein diet for children (no meat, dairy products, eggs, NutraSweet) |
| Gout—inborn error of purine metabolism | High uric acid level that leads to progressive joint deterioration | Low-purine diet (no fish or organ meats) |
| Celiac disease–(sprue) inborn error of wheat and rye metabolism | Intestinal malabsorption that leads to malnutrition<br>Diarrhea<br>Failure to thrive | Gluten-free diet (no wheat, oats, rye, barley) |
| Renal failure | Increased protein and albumin losses in urine that leads to protein deficiency | High-calorie, low-protein diet, as allowed by kidney function |
| Protein allergy | Diarrhea that leads to malnutrition and water loss | Change dietary protein source |

*Handwritten note: If ↑PKU, must treat with diet of ↓protein*

## ▶ ALTERATIONS IN FAT METABOLISM

**A.** Assessment (see Table 5)

**B.** Diagnose—potential nursing diagnoses

1. Nutrition: less than body requirements, altered

2. Knowledge deficit regarding dietary restriction

**C.** Plan/Implementation (see Table 5)

**D.** Evaluation

1. Have client's nutritional needs been met?

2. Is client knowledgeable about dietary modifications?

| Table 5   ALTERATIONS IN FAT METABOLISM | | |
|---|---|---|
| **DISORDER** | **ASSESSMENT** | **NURSING CONSIDERATIONS** |
| Hepatobiliary disease | Decreased bile leads to fat malabsorption | Low-fat, high-protein diet<br>Vitamins |
| Cystic fibrosis | Absence of pancreatic enzymes leads to malabsorption of fat (and fat-soluble vitamins), weight loss<br>Infection and lung disease lead to increased need for calories and protein | Pancreatic enzyme replacement (cotazym pancreas) before or with meals<br>High-protein diet<br>High-calorie diet in advanced stages |
| Atherosclerosis (thickening and hardening of the arteries) | Associated with high blood cholesterol and triglyceride levels<br>Risk factors—diet, high blood pressure, diabetes, stress, sedentary lifestyle, and smoking | Low-saturated fat diet<br>Cholesterol-lowering medications given before meals |

## ▶ INFECTIONS OF THE GI TRACT

**A.** Assessment

1. Headache

2. Abdominal discomfort, anorexia

3. Watery diarrhea, nausea, vomiting

4. Low-grade fever

**B.** Diagnose

1. Acute illness caused by ingested food contaminated by toxins or parasites

2. Types (see Table 6)

| Table 6  COMMON INFECTIONS OF THE GASTROINTESTINAL TRACT | | |
|---|---|---|
| PARASITE OR BACTERIUM | SOURCE | NURSING CONSIDERATIONS |
| Enterotoxigenic *E. coli* | Undercooked beef | Causes rapid, severe dehydration; cook beef until meat no longer pink and juices run clear |
| *Salmonella* | Poultry, eggs | Causes gastroenteritis, systemic infection |
| *Campylobacter* | Poultry, beef, pork | Cook and store food at appropriate temperatures |
| *Giardia lamblia* | Protozoan, contaminated water | Treated with metronidazole, good personal hygiene |
| *Shigella* | Fecal contamination | Affects pediatric population, antimicrobial therapy |

**C.** Plan/Implementation

1. Prevention

   a. Good sanitation

   b. Good hygiene measures, e.g., handwashing

   c. Proper food preparation, e.g., thorough cooking; heat canned foods 10–20 minutes and inspect cans for gas bubbles

2. Nursing considerations

   a. Maintain fluid and electrolytes

   b. Monitor vital signs

   c. Medications: antibiotics, antispasmodics, antiemetics

   d. Teach importance of good handwashing and cleaning of utensils when preparing food

**D.** Evaluation

1. Have client's symptoms resolved?

2. Are the stool cultures negative?

## ▶ HIATAL HERNIA

**A.** Assessment

1. Heartburn

2. Regurgitation

3. Dyspepsia

B. Diagnose

   1. Opening in diaphragm through which the esophagus passes becomes enlarged, part of the upper stomach comes up into the lower portion of the thorax

C. Plan/Implementation

   1. Administer medications

      a. $H_2$ receptor blockers (e.g., cimetadine, ranitidine)

      b. Antacids (e.g., aluminum hydroxide, magnesium hydroxide)

      c. Cytoprotective medications (e.g., sucralfate)

      d. Proton pump inhibitors (pantoprazole)

   2. Surgery to tighten cardiac sphincter (fundoplication)

   3. Small, frequent feedings

   4. Do not lie down for at least 1 hour after meals; elevate head of bed 4–8 inches when sleeping

   5. Do not eat before going to bed to prevent reflux of food

D. Evaluation

   1. Has client comfort been maintained?

   2. Is client knowledgeable about ways to prevent symptoms?

# ▶ PYLORIC STENOSIS

A. Assessment

   1. Vomiting (projectile in infants)

   2. Epigastric fullness

   3. Irritability (in infants)

   4. Infant always hungry

   5. Infant fails to gain weight

   6. Palpable olive-shaped tumor in epigastrium (infants)

   7. Peristaltic waves

B. Diagnose

   1. In adults, narrowing or obstruction of the pyloric sphincter caused by scarring from healing ulcers; in infants, obstruction caused by hypertrophy and hyperplasia of pylorus

   2. Inflammation and edema can reduce the size of the opening until there is complete obstruction

   3. Infants usually don't show symptoms until the second to fourth week after birth; then regurgitation develops into projectile vomiting; most frequently seen in male, white, full-term infants

   4. Obstruction in adults usually caused by peptic ulcer

   5. Surgical intervention

      a. Pyloromyotomy (infants)—incision through circular muscles of the pylorus

      b. Vagotomy and antrectomy—removal of gastrin-secreting portion of the stomach and severing of vagus nerves

      c. Vagotomy and pyloroplasty or gastroenterostomy—establishes gastric drainage, involves severing of vagus nerves

**C.** Plan/Implementation

    1. Preoperative

        a. Prevent regurgitation and vomiting

            1) IV fluids

            2) Check skin turgor, fontanelles, urinary output

            3) Measure vomitus

            4) Correct fluid and electrolyte abnormalities—alkalosis, hypokalemia

            5) Gastric decompression with NG tube

            6) Monitor for complications—alkalosis, hypokalemia, dehydration, and shock

            7) Support parents

                a) Allow verbalization of parents' anxieties

                b) Instruct parents on expected progress and behavior

    2. Postoperative

        a. Keep incision site clean and dry

        b. Provide parenteral fluids at ordered rate

        c. Monitor warmth

        d. Small, frequent feedings of glucose water or electrolyte solution 4–6 hours postoperatively

        e. If clear fluids retained start formula 24 hours postop

        f. Teach parents to fold diaper so it doesn't touch incision

**D.** Evaluation

    1. Has client's fluid and electrolyte balance been maintained?

    2. Have complications been prevented?

## ▶ GASTRITIS

**A.** Assessment

    1. Uncomfortable feeling in abdomen

    2. Headache

    3. Anorexia, nausea, vomiting (possibly bloody)

    4. Hiccupping

**B.** Diagnose

    1. Inflammation of stomach that may be acute or chronic

**C.** Plan/Implementation

    1. NPO slowly progressing to bland diet

    2. Antacids often relieve pain

    3. Referral to appropriate agency if alcohol abuse is verified

**D.** Evaluation

    1. Has client comfort been maintained?

    2. Have proper referrals been made?

# ▶ GI ULCER

**A.** Assessment (see Table 7)

**B.** Diagnose

1. Excavation formed in the mucosal wall, caused by erosion that may extend to muscle layers or through the muscle to the peritoneum (see Figure 1)

2. *H. pylori* frequently present

3. Familial tendency

| Table 7   DUODENAL VERSUS GASTRIC ULCER | | |
|---|---|---|
| | **CHRONIC DUODENAL ULCER** | **CHRONIC GASTRIC ULCER** |
| Age | 30–60 years | 50 years and older |
| Sex | Male-female ratio: 3:1 | Male-female ratio: 1:1 |
| Risk factors | Blood group type O, COPD, chronic renal failure, alcohol, smoking, cirrhosis, stress | Gastritis, alcohol, smoking, NSAIDs, stress |
| Gastric secretion | Hypersecretion | Normal to hyposecretion |
| Pain | 2–3 hours after meal; nighttime, often in early sleeping hours<br><br>Food intake relieves pain | 1/2 to 1 hour after meal or when fasting<br><br>Relieved by vomiting<br><br>Ingestion of food does not help |
| Vomiting | Rare | Frequent |
| Hemorrhage | Less likely | More likely |
| Malignancy | Rare | Occasionally |

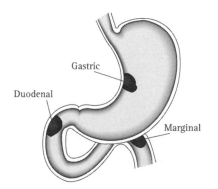

**Figure 1.  Sites for Ulcers**

**C.** Plan/Implementation

1. Avoid oversecretion and hypermotility in the gastrointestinal tract

2. Dietary modification

   a. Eat 3 meals per day; small frequent feedings not necessary if taking antacids or histamine blocker

   b. Avoid extremes in temperature

    c. Avoid coffee, alcohol, and caffeinated beverages

    d. Avoid milk and cream

3. Reduce stress

4. Stop smoking—inhibits ulcer repair

5. Medications

    a. Antacids (e.g., magnesium and aluminum hydroxide); administer 1 hour before or after meals

    b. Histamine receptor site antagonist (e.g., cimetidine, ranitidine); take with meals

    c. Anticholinergics (e.g., propantheline); give 30 minutes before meals

    d. Cytoprotective medications (e.g., sucralfate); give 1 hour before meals

    e. Proton pump inhibitors (e.g., omeprazole)

6. Surgical intervention (see Figure 2: Common Surgeries for Ulcers)

    a. Diagnostic workup—upper-GI series, endoscopy, CT scan

    b. Gastrectomy—removal of stomach and attachment to upper portion of duodenum

    c. Vagotomy—cutting the vagus nerve (decreases HCl secretion)

    d. Billroth I—partial removal (distal one-third to one-half) of stomach, anastomosis with duodenum

    e. Billroth II—removal of distal segment of stomach and antrum, anastomosis with jejunum

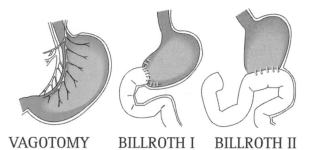

VAGOTOMY    BILLROTH I    BILLROTH II

**Figure 2. Common Surgeries for Ulcers**

7. Postoperative

    a. Assess vital signs

    b. Inspect dressings

    c. Provide gastric decompression as ordered

    d. Vitamin $B_{12}$ via parenteral route (required for life); iron supplements

    e. Encourage deep breathing

    f. Observe for peristalsis

        1) Levin tube—single-lumen tube at low suction

        2) Salem sump—double-lumen for drainage

            a) Prevent irritation to nostril

            b) Lubricate tube around nares with water-soluble jelly

            c) Control excessive nasal secretions

            d) Observe nasogastric drainage for volume and blood

3) Listen for bowel sounds

4) Record passage of flatus or stool

g. Teach preventive measures for "dumping syndrome" (rapid passage of food from stomach causing diaphoresis, diarrhea, hypotension)

1) Restrict fluids with meals, drink 1 hour ac or 1 hour pc

2) Eat in semi-recumbent position

3) Lie down 20–30 minutes after eating

4) Eat smaller, frequent meals

5) Complex carbohydrates, avoid simple sugars

6) Antispasmotics

**D.** Evaluation

1. Have client's nutritional needs been met?

2. Is client knowledgeable about measures to prevent complications postoperatively?

# ▶ ESOPHAGEAL ATRESIA AND TRACHEOESOPHAGEAL FISTULA

**A.** Assessment

1. Excessive saliva, drooling

2. Stomach distention

3. Choking, coughing, sneezing

4. Cyanosis

**B.** Diagnose

1. Failure of esophagus to develop as a continuous tube (see Figure 3)

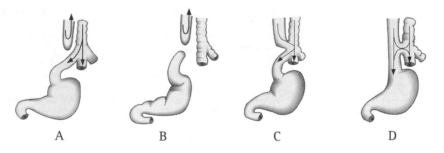

A       B       C       D

**Figure 3. Tracheoesophageal Fistula**

2. Often occurs with anomalies of heart or the genitourinary or musculoskeletal system

**C.** Plan/Implementation

1. Surgical repair

a. Preoperative

1) Position supine or prone with head of bed elevated on incline plane at least 30 degrees

2) IV fluids and antibiotics through umbilical artery catheter

3) Maintain patent airway

    b. Postoperative

       1) Care for incision site—observe for inflammation

       2) Prevent pulmonary complications—suction and position

       3) IV fluids and antibiotics

       4) PN until gastrostomy or oral feedings tolerated

**D.** Evaluation

    1. Has defect been repaired?

    2. Have infant's nutritional needs been met?

## ▶ CROHN'S DISEASE (REGIONAL ENTERITIS, ILEITIS, OR ENTEROCOLITIS) ULCERATIVE COLITIS

**A.** Assessment (see Table 8)

**B.** Diagnose

    1. Crohn's disease—inflammatory condition of any area of large or small intestine, usually ileum and ascending colon

    2. Ulcerative colitis—inflammatory condition of the colon characterized by eroded areas of the mucous membrane and tissues beneath it

| Table 8  CROHN'S DISEASE VERSUS ULCERATIVE COLITIS | | |
|---|---|---|
| | **CROHN'S DISEASE REGIONAL ENTERITIS** | **ULCERATIVE COLITIS** |
| **Assessment** | | |
| Usual age of onset | 20–30 and 50–80 years | Young adult to middle age (30–50) |
| Fatty stool (steatorrhea) | Frequent | Absent |
| Malignancy results | Rare | 10–15% |
| Rectal bleeding | Occasional: mucus, pus, fat in stool | Common; blood, pus, mucus in stool |
| Abdominal pain | After meals | Predefecation |
| Diarrhea | Diarrhea rare; 5–6 unformed stools per day | 10–20 liquid stools per day; often bloody |
| Nutritional deficit, weight loss, anemia, dehydration | Common | Common |
| Fever | Present | Present |
| Anal abscess | Common | Common |
| Fistula and anorectal fissure fistula | Common | Rare |
| **Diagnose** | | |
| Level of involvement | Ileum, right colon | Rectum, left colon |
| Inflammation | Noncontinuous segment | Continuous segment |

| Table 8 CROHN'S DISEASE VERSUS ULCERATIVE COLITIS *(CONTINUED)* | | |
|---|---|---|
| | **CROHN'S DISEASE REGIONAL ENTERITIS** | **ULCERATIVE COLITIS** |
| Course of disease | Prolonged, variable | Remissions and relapses |
| | Complications–bowel abscess, fistula formation, intestinal obstruction | Complications–hemorrhage, abscess formation, arthritis, uveitis |
| Nursing considerations | High-protein, high-calorie, low-fat, and low-fiber diet | |
| | May require PN to rest bowel | |
| | Analgesics, anticholinergics, sulfonamides (Gantrisin), corticosteriods, antidiarrheals, and antiperistaltics | |
| | Maintain fluid/electrolyte balance | |
| | Monitor electrolytes | |
| | Promote rest, relieve anxiety | |
| | Ileostomy in severe cases | |

**C.** Plan/Implementation

1. Diet—high-protein, high-calorie, low-fat, and fiber; PN used for bowel rest

2. Medications—analgesics, anticholinergics, antibiotics, corticosteroids to reduce inflammation; immune modulators, salicylate-containing compounds

3. Maintain fluid, electrolyte balance; provide PN if bowel rest is needed

4. Ileostomy

**D.** Evaluation

1. Is client able to care for ileostomy?

2. Did client adjust to the change in body image?

# ▶ APPENDICITIS

**A.** Assessment

1. Periumbilical abdominal pain shifts to right lower quadrant at McBurney's point (located between umbilicus and the right iliac crest)

2. Anorexia, nausea, vomiting

3. Localized tenderness

4. Muscle guarding

5. Low-grade fever

**B.** Diagnose

1. Highest incidence 11–30 years of age

2. Differential CBC count; WBC 15,000 to 20,000 cells/mm$^3$

**C.** Plan/Implementation

1. No heating pads, enemas, or laxatives preop

2. Maintain NPO status until blood laboratory reports received, IV fluids to prevent dehydration

3. No analgesics until cause of pain is determined

4. Ice bag to abdomen to alleviate pain

5. Observe for signs and symptoms of peritonitis
6. Surgical removal of appendix (appendectomy)
   a. Normal postop care
   b. Fowler's position to relieve abdominal pain and ease breathing
7. Sudden cessation of pain—perforation emergency
8. Antibiotic therapy

**D.** Evaluation
1. Is client comfort maintained after surgery?
2. Is client able to resume normal activities?

### ▶ DIVERTICULAR DISEASE

**A.** Assessment
1. Cramping pain in left lower quadrant of abdomen relieved by passage of stool or flatus
2. Fever, increased WBC
3. Constipation alternating with diarrhea

**B.** Diagnose
1. Infection, inflammation, or obstruction of diverticula (sacs or pouches in the intestinal wall) cause the client to become symptomatic
2. Associated with deficiency in dietary fiber

**C.** Plan/Implementation
1. Uncomplicated
   a. Antispasmodics, anticholinergic (e.g., dicyclomine)
   b. Bulk laxatives
   c. High-fiber diet; avoid food with seeds
   d. Increase fluids
2. Acute
   a. Bedrest
   b. NPO progressing to oral fluids to semi-solids
   c. IV fluids
   d. NG tube
   e. Antibiotics
   f. Surgery—drain abscess, resect obstruction

**D.** Evaluation
1. Has client comfort been maintained?
2. Is client compliant with medication regimen?

### ▶ PERITONITIS

**A.** Assessment
1. Abdominal pain, possibly severe
2. Abdominal rigidity and distension, rebound tenderness
3. Nausea, vomiting
4. Ascites

5.  Increased temperature, leukocytosis

6.  Paralytic ileus

7.  Symptoms may be masked in elderly persons or those receiving corticosteroids

**B.** Diagnose

1.  Inflammation of part or all of the parietal and visceral surfaces of the abdominal cavity

2.  Causes

    a.  Ruptured appendix, ectopic pregnancy

    b.  Perforated ulcer, bowel, or bladder

    c.  Traumatic injury

    d.  Blood-borne organisms

**C.** Plan/Implementation

1.  Preoperative care

    a.  Monitor vital signs, I and O

    b.  Antibiotics and IV fluids

    c.  Gastric decompression; monitor NG drainage

    d.  NPO

    e.  Reestablish fluid/electrolyte balance, monitor serum electrolytes

    f.  Analgesics

2.  Postoperative care

    a.  NPO

    b.  NG tube

    c.  Semi-Fowler's position

    d.  IV fluids with electrolyte replacement

    e.  Antibiotics

    f.  PN

**D.** Evaluation

1.  Are the client's vital signs stable?

2.  Has the client's fluid and electrolyte balance been maintained?

# ▶ HIRSCHSPRUNG'S DISEASE

**A.** Assessment

1.  Newborn—failure to pass meconium, refusal to suck, abdominal distention

2.  Child—failure to gain weight, delayed growth, constipation alternating with diarrhea, foul-smelling stools, abdominal distension, visible peristalsis

**B.** Diagnose

1.  A ganglionic disease of the intestinal tract; inadequate motility causes mechanical obstruction of intestine

2.  Diagnostic tests—radiographic contrast studies

**C.** Plan/Implementation

1.  Help parents adjust to congenital defect in child

2.  Foster infant/parent bonding

3. Prepare for surgery

   a. Enemas

   b. Low-fiber, high-calorie, high-protein diet

   c. PN if needed

   d. Oral antibiotics

   e. Measure abdominal girth at level of umbilicus

4. Postoperative care

   a. Monitor fluid and electrolytes

   b. Maintain nutrition

   c. Let parents know colostomy is usually temporary, closed when child is 17–22 lb

**D.** Evaluation

1. Have the child and parents adjusted to the change in body image?

2. Are the parents knowledgeable about stoma care?

## ▶ INTUSSUSCEPTION

**A.** Assessment

1. Colicky abdominal pain

2. Causes child to scream and draw knees to abdomen

3. Vomiting

4. Currant jellylike stools containing blood and mucus

5. Tender, distended abdomen

6. May have palpable sausage-shaped mass in the upper right quadrant of the abdomen

7. Usual client is 3 months to 3 years old

**B.** Diagnose

1. Telescoping of one portion of the bowel into another (usually the ileum into the cecum and colon)

2. Results in intestinal obstruction, and blocked blood and lymph circulation

3. Diagnosis can often be made based on findings alone

**C.** Plan/Implementation

1. Non-surgical intervention

   a. Water-soluble contrast medium or air pressure to "push" the telescoped portion out

   b. Postprocedural care

     1) Assess vital signs

     2) Auscultate bowel sounds

     3) Observe for passage of water-soluble contrast medium

     4) Encourage parental rooming-in

2. Surgical intervention

   a. Manually reducing the telescoped portion of the bowel

   b. Removal of any damaged bowel portions

3. Preparation for surgery

   a. NPO

  b.  CBC and urinalysis

  c.  Sedation

  d.  Correct hypovolemia and electrolyte imbalances

  e.  Treat peritonitis, if present

  f.  Nasogastric suctioning (decompression) may be needed

  g.  Consent form signed

4.  Postoperative care

  a.  Assess vital signs

  b.  Inspect sutures and dressing

  c.  Auscultate for return of bowel sounds

  d.  Administer pain medications and antibiotics as ordered

  e.  Progress diet with return of bowel sounds

5.  Evaluation

  a.  Have the child and parents adjusted to the change in body image?

  b.  Are the parents knowledgeable about care?

# ▶ ABDOMINAL HERNIAS

**A.** Assessment

1.  Lump at site of hernia may disappear in reclining position and reappear on standing/coughing/lifting

2.  Strangulated hernia—severe abdominal pain, nausea and vomiting, distention, intestinal obstruction

**B.** Diagnose

1.  Protrusion of an organ through the wall of the cavity in which it is normally contained

2.  Types

  a.  Inguinal—protrusion of intestine through abdominal ring into inguinal canal

  b.  Femoral—protrusion of intestine into femoral canal

  c.  Umbilical—protrusion of intestine through umbilical ring

  d.  Ventral or incisional—protrusion through site of an old surgical incision

  e.  Reducible—the protruding structure can be replaced by manipulation into the abdominal cavity

  f.  Irreducible or incarcerated—the protruding structure cannot be replaced by manipulation

  g.  Strangulated—blood supply to the intestines is obstructed (emergency situation)

**C.** Plan/Implementation

1.  Preoperative care for herniorrhaphy

  a.  Assess respiratory system for potential causes of increased intra-abdominal pressure—may cause interference with postop healing

  b.  Surgery is postponed until respiratory conditions are controlled

  c.  Truss—pad placed under hernia, held in place with belt

2. Postoperative care

   a. Relieve urinary retention

   b. Turning and deep breathing, but avoid coughing

   c. Provide scrotal support

   d. Provide ice packs for swollen scrotum

   e. Advise no pulling, pushing, heavy lifting for 6–8 weeks

   f. Inform client that sexual function is not affected

   g. Instruct client that ecchymosis will fade in a few days

**D.** Evaluation

  1. Has normal bowel function been re-established?

  2. Has client comfort been maintained?

## ▶ MECKEL'S DIVERTICULUM

**A.** Assessment

  1. Symptoms seen by 2 years of age

  2. Painless rectal bleeding, abdominal pain

  3. Hematochezia (currant jelly–like stool)

  4. Signs and symptoms of appendicitis if diverticulum becomes inflamed from infection

**B.** Diagnose

  1. A congenital sac or pouch in the ileum

  2. Contains gastric or pancreatic tissue that secretes acid

  3. Most common GI malformation

**C.** Plan/Implementation

  1. Preoperative care

    a. IV fluids

    b. Observe for rectal bleeding

    c. Bedrest

  2. Postoperative care

    a. Surgical (if symptomatic)–removal of the diverticulum

    b. Prevent infection

    c. Maintain nutrition

**D.** Evaluation

  1. Has client comfort been maintained?

  2. Has the client's elimination been maintained?

## ▶ INTESTINAL OBSTRUCTION

**A.** Assessment

  1. Nausea, vomiting

  2. High-pitched bowel sounds above area of obstruction, decreased or absent bowel sounds below the area of obstruction

  3. Abdominal pain and distention, pain often described as "colicky"

  4. Obstipation (absence of stool and gas)

**B.** Diagnose

1. Mechanical obstruction—physical blockage of lumen of intestines, usually seen in the small intestine

   a. Hernia

   b. Tumors

   c. Adhesions

   d. Strictures due to radiation or congenital

   e. Intussusception (telescoping of bowel within itself)

   f. Volvulus (twisting of bowel)

2. Nonmechanical obstruction (paralytic ileus)—no mechanical blockage, absence of peristalsis

   a. Abdominal trauma/surgery

   b. Spinal injuries

   c. Peritonitis, acute appendicitis

   d. Wound dehiscence (breakdown)

**C.** Plan/Implementation

1. Intestinal decompression

   a. Insertion of a plastic or rubber tube into the stomach or intestine via the nose or mouth; the purpose may be diagnostic, preventive, or therapeutic; fluid or air may be removed

   b. Tubes

      1) Salem sump or Levin tubes (nasogastric)

      2) Miller-Abbot (intestinal)

      3) Cantor (intestinal)

2. NPO

3. Fluid/electrolyte replacement; monitor I and O and electrolyte levels

4. Assist with ADL

5. Good oral and skin care

6. Fowler's position to facilitate breathing

7. Bowel surgery

   a. Purpose—removal of diseased portion of bowel; creation of an outlet for passage of stool when there is an obstruction or need for "bowel rest"

   b. Types of surgeries

      1) Exploratory laparotomy; possible adhesion removal

      2) Resection and anastomosis—diseased portion of bowel is removed and remaining ends are joined together

      3) Abdominal perineal resection—abdominal incision through which the proximal end of the sigmoid colon is exteriorized through a permanent colostomy; the distal end of the sigmoid colon, rectum, and anus are removed through the perineal route

      4) Intestinal ostomies

**D.** Evaluation

1. Has intestinal obstruction been cleared?

2. Has normal bowel function returned?

## ▶ INTESTINAL OSTOMIES FOR FECAL DIVERSION

**A.** Assessment

1. Cancer of colon or rectum

2. Diverticulitis

3. Intestinal obstruction

**B.** Diagnose

1. Ostomy is opening into colon to allow passage of intestinal contents

2. Stoma is opening on abdomen where intestine is sutured to skin surface

3. Types (see Figure 4)

SINGLE-BARREL          DOUBLE-BARREL          LOOP
(usually permanent)    (usually temporary)    (can be temporary
                                               or permanent)

**Figure 4. Types of Colostomies**

4. Common intestinal ostomies (see Table 9)

5. Continent ileal reservoir (Koch pouch)—surgical creation of pouch of small intestine acts as an internal reservoir for fecal discharge, nipple value as outlet

**C.** Plan/Implementation

1. Preoperative care

   a. Psychological support and explanations

   b. Diet—high calorie, high protein, high carbohydrates, low-residue week before; NPO after midnight

   c. Place tube prior to surgery—NG or intestinal

   d. Activity—assist PRN, client will be weakened from extensive preparation procedures

   e. Elimination—laxatives, enemas evening before and morning of surgery

   f. Have enterostomal health care provider see client for optimum placement of stoma

   g. Medications—antibiotics (e.g., erythromycin) day before surgery

   h. Monitor for fluid/electrolyte imbalance

   i. Referral to enterostomal therapist and United Ostomy Association

2. Postoperative care

   a. NG or intestinal decompression until peristalsis returns; maintain NPO status

   b. Clear liquids progressing to solid, low-residue diet for first 6–8 weeks

c.  Monitor I and O and fluid/electrolyte balance

d.  Observe and record condition of stoma

   1)  First few days appears beefy-red and swollen

   2)  Gradually, swelling recedes and color is pink or red

   3)  Notify health care provider immediately if stoma is dark blue, "blackish," or purple—indicates insufficient blood supply

e.  Observe and record description of any drainage from stoma

   1)  Usually just mucus or serosanguineous for first 1–2 days

   2)  Begins to function 3–6 days postop

f.  Promote positive adjustment to ostomy

   1)  Encourage client to look at stoma

   2)  Encourage early participation in ostomy care

   3)  Reinforce positive aspects of colostomy

| Table 9  COMMON INTESTINAL OSTOMIES FOR FECAL DIVERSION | | | |
|---|---|---|---|
|  | **ILEOSTOMY** | **TRANSVERSE COLOSTOMY** | **DESCENDING OR SIGMOID COLOSTOMY** |
| **Part of intestine involved** | End of ileum, rest of large intestine removed | Transverse colon (usually temporary) | Descending or sigmoid colon (usually permanent) |
| **Ostomy returns** | Liquid, semiliquid, soft | Soft to fairly firm; softer toward ileum | Descending—fairly firm stool; sigmoid—solid stool |
| **Odor** | Slightly odorous | Very foul-smelling | Usually foul-smelling |
| **Drainage** | Highly corrosive because of enzymes | Irritating | Less irritating |
| **Appliance** | Open-ended pouch worn at all times (fecal material drained, then appliance reclosed) | Pouch worn continually | Varies; with regular irrigation, sometimes no appliance is worn; if firm stool, many use closed pouch; if liquid, open-ended pouch |
| **Nursing considerations** | If continent ileal reservoir (Koch pouch) made in surgery, no appliance worn; contents removed q 4–6 hours via catheter<br><br>Usually on low-residue diet; no meats, corn, nuts | Usually single-loop colostomy; inflamed bowel segment brought through abdominal wall; incision closed; opening made by cautery (painless) in loop for fecal drainage<br><br>Diet usually not restricted after first 6 weeks | Typical for colon cancers<br><br>Reinforce dressing postop<br><br>Diet usually not restricted after first 6 weeks |

3.  Skin care

   a.  Effect on skin depends on composition, quantity, consistency of drainage, medications, location of stoma, frequency in removal of appliance adhesive

   b.  Principles of skin protection (see Figure 5)

     1)  Pouch opening $\frac{1}{8}$ inch larger than stoma

     2)  Use skin barrier under all tapes (water, paste, powder)

     3)  Use skin barrier to protect skin immediately surrounding the stoma

     4)  Cleanse skin gently and pat dry; do not rub

5) Pouch applied by pressing adhesive area to skin for 30 seconds

6) Change appliance immediately when seal breaks or when $^1/_3$ or $^1/_4$ full

Stoma

Adhesive Ring

Skin Barrier

**Figure 5. Colostomy Appliance**

4. Colostomy irrigations for sigmoid colostomy

   a. Purpose—to stimulate emptying of colon of gas, mucus, feces at scheduled times to avoid need for appliance

   b. Usually begins 5–7 days postop

   c. When possible, should be sitting upright on toilet for procedure

   d. Performed after a meal, same time each day

   e. 500–1,500 mL of lukewarm water used for solution

   f. Special irrigating sleeve and cone are used

   g. Insert catheter 8 cm (3 inches)

   h. Hang irrigating container at shoulder height (18–20 inches above stoma)

   i. Clamp tubing if client reports cramps; allow client to rest before resuming procedure

   j. Water flows in over 5–10 minutes

   k. Allow 10–15 minutes for most of return

   l. Leave sleeve in place while client moves around for 30–45 minutes

   m. Clean with soap and water, pat dry

5. Care of continent ileal reservoir (Koch pouch)

   a. Postop—catheter inserted and attached to drainage bag, q3h instill 10–20 mL NS into pouch, drain by gravity, kept in place 2 weeks

   b. To drain—lubricate catheter, insert 5 cm (2 inches), drain into toilet, wash and dry stoma

   c. If resistance, inject 20 mL air or water using syringe through catheter

**D.** Evaluation

1. Has client accepted alteration in body image?

2. Is client able to care for colostomy at home?

# ▶ CIRRHOSIS

**A.** Assessment

1. Digestive disturbances
   a. Indigestion, dyspepsia
   b. Flatulence, constipation, diarrhea
   c. Anorexia, weight loss
   d. Nausea and vomiting
2. Circulatory
   a. Esophageal varices, hematemesis, hemorrhage
   b. Ascites
   c. Hemorrhoids
   d. Increased bleeding tendencies, anemia
   e. Edema in extremities
   f. Spider angiomas
3. Biliary
   a. Jaundice, pruritus
   b. Dark urine, clay-colored stools
   c. Increased abdominal girth
4. Compensated
   a. Vascular spiders
   b. Ankle edema
   c. Indigestion
   d. Flatulence
   e. Abdominal pain
   f. Enlarged liver
5. Decompensated
   a. Ascites
   b. Jaundice
   c. Weight loss
   d. Purpura
   e. Epistaxis

**B.** Diagnose

1. Replacement of normal liver tissue with widespread fibrosis and nodule formation
   a. Alcoholic cirrhosis—due to alcoholism and poor nutrition
   b. Biliary cirrhosis—result of chronic biliary obstruction and infection
   c. Postnecrotic cirrhosis—result of previous viral hepatitis
2. Complications
   a. Portal hypertension with esophageal varices due to elevated pressure throughout entire portal venous system
      1) Dilated tortuous veins usually found in the submucosa of the lower esophagus

2) Hemorrhage from rupture leading cause of death in clients with cirrhosis

  b. Peripheral edema and ascites

    1) Ascites—accumulation of serous fluid in peritoneal and abdominal cavity

    2) Associated with dehydration and hypokalemia

  c. Hepatic encephalopathy (coma)

    1) Occurs with liver disease

    2) Results from accumulation of ammonia and other toxic metabolites in the blood

    3) Change in level of consciousness

    4) Symptoms of impending coma—disorientation to time, place, person, asterixis (flapping tremor of hand when arm extended and hand help upward [dorsiflexed])

    5) Jaundice

  d. Hepatorenal syndrome

    1) Functional renal failure

    2) Azotemia, ascites

**C.** Plan/Implementation

  1. Shunts to relieve portal hypertension

  2. Provide appropriate nutrition

    a. Early stages—high-protein, high-carbohydrate diet, supplemented with vitamin B complex

    b. Advanced stages—fiber, protein, fat, and sodium restrictions, high-calorie diet, protein foods of high biologic value

    c. Small, frequent feedings

    d. Fluid restriction

    e. Avoid alcohol

  3. Monitor for bleeding, administer blood products

  4. Observe vital signs for shock

  5. Monitor abdominal girth, daily weights

  6. Maintain skin integrity

    a. Avoid strong soaps

    b. Alleviate dry, itching skin

    c. Frequent position changes

  7. Assess degree of jaundice

  8. Promote rest

  9. Promote adequate respiratory function

  10. Reduce exposure to infection

  11. Promote safety

    a. Electric razor

    b. Soft-bristle toothbrush

    c. Pressure to site after venipuncture

12. Reduce ascites

    a. Sodium, fluid restrictions

    b. Diuretics

13. Treatment of bleeding esophageal varices

    a. Balloon tamponade—Sengstaken-Blakemore tube (see Figure 6), Minnesota tube

        1) Gastric inflation balloon—inflated with 100–200 mL air

        2) Gastric aspiration—connect to suction

        3) Esophageal inflation balloon—pressure on esophageal and gastric balloons 25–40 mm Hg, measured by manometer q 2–4 h

        4) Esophageal aspiration

        5) Tubing irrigated hourly

        6) Deflate balloons sequentially, esophageal balloon first

        7) Complications—necrosis of nose, stomach mucosa, or esophagus; asphyxiation

    b. Endoscopic sclerotherapy—injection of sclerosing agent into the esophagus, causes varices to become fibrotic

    c. Administration of vasopressin or propranolol IV or interarterial temporarily lowers portal pressure by constriction of splenic artery, IV octreotide

    d. Room-temperature saline lavage

    e. Esophageal banding therapy—modified endoscope with rubber band passed into esophagus, varices are banded

    f. Transjugular intrahepatic postsystemic shunting (TIPS)

    g. Surgical bypass

14. Treatment of hepatic encephalopathy

    a. Administer medications: lactulose, Neomycin

    b. Bedrest

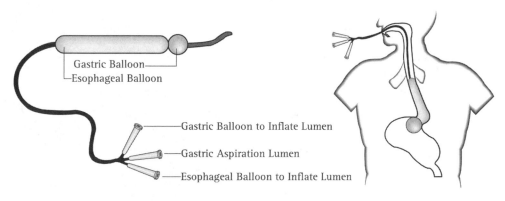

**Figure 6. Sengstaken–Blakemore Tube**

**D.** Evaluation

  1. Are client's vital signs stable?

  2. Has ascites been reduced?

# ▶ JAUNDICE

**A.** Assessment

1. Yellowish or greenish-yellow discoloration of skin and sclerae due to elevated bilirubin concentration in the blood

2. Dark-colored urine, clay-colored stools

3. Pruritus

**B.** Diagnose

1. Hemolytic—caused by destruction of great number of blood cells, leads to a high concentration of bilirubin that exceeds the liver's ability to excrete it

   a. Hemolytic transfusion reactions

   b. Hemolytic anemia

   c. Sickle-cell crisis

2. Intrahepatic—due to obstructed flow of bile through liver or biliary duct system

   a. Cirrhosis

   b. Hepatitis

3. Extrahepatic—due to obstructed flow of bile through liver or biliary duct system

   a. Cholelithiasis

   b. Tumors

   c. Adverse effect of medications—(e.g., phenothiazine, antithyroids, sulfonamides, tricyclic antidepressants, androgens, estrogens)

**C.** Plan/Implementation

1. Treat underlying cause

2. Relief of pruritus

   a. Medications: antihistamines

   b. Baking soda or alpha Keri baths

   c. Keep nails trimmed and clean; teach to rub with knuckles rather than nails

   d. Soft, old linen

   e. Moderate temperature (not too hot or cold)

**D.** Evaluation

1. Has cause of jaundice been identified and treated?

2. Has client's comfort been maintained?

# ▶ REYE'S SYNDROME (RS)

**A.** Assessment

1. Fever

2. Increased ICP

3. Decreased level of consciousness, coma

4. Decreased hepatic function

5. Diagnosed by liver biopsy

**B.** Diagnose

   1. Acute metabolic encephalopathy of childhood that causes hepatic dysfunction

   2. Causes

      a. Link between use of aspirin with viral illness

      b. Associated with viruses, especially URI, gastroenteritis

**C.** Plan/Implementation

   1. Neurological checks

   2. Maintain hydration and electrolytes with IV

   3. Endotracheal tube and respirator may be needed

   4. Monitor CVP or Swan-Ganz catheter

   5. Promote family support

**D.** Evaluation

   1. Has child recovered from Reye's syndrome with minimal or no neuropsychological deficit?

   2. Have needs of family been met during acute phase of client's hospitalization?

## ▶ CHOLECYSTITIS, CHOLELITHIASIS

**A.** Assessment

   1. Intolerance to fatty foods

   2. Indigestion

   3. Nausea, vomiting, flatulence, eructation

   4. Severe pain in upper right quadrant of abdomen radiating to back and right shoulder (biliary colic)

   5. Elevated temperature

   6. Leukocytosis

   7. Diaphoresis

   8. Dark urine, clay-colored stools

**B.** Diagnose

   1. Cholecystitis—inflammation of gallbladder

   2. Cholelithiasis—presence of stones in gallbladder

   3. Risk factors

      a. Obesity

      b. Sedentary lifestyle

      c. Women, especially multiparous

      d. Highest incidence 40+ years

      e. Pregnancy

      f. Familial tendency

      g. Hypothyroidism

      h. Increased serum cholesterol

**C.** Plan/Implementation

1. Rest

2. IV fluids

3. NG suction

4. Analgesics

5. Antibiotics

6. Low-fat liquids—powdered supplements high in protein, carbohydrates stirred into skim milk

7. Avoid fried foods, pork, cheese, alcohol

8. Laparoscopic laser cholecystectomy—removal of gallbladder by a laser through a laparoscope; laparoscope is attached to video camera and procedure is viewed through monitor; four small puncture holes made in abdomen

    a. Preoperative care

    1) NPO on day prior to outpatient (ambulatory) procedure

    b. Postoperative care

    1) Monitor for bleeding

    2) Resume normal activity in 1 week

    3) May need to be on low-fat diet for several weeks

9. Traditional cholecystectomy—removal of gallbladder through a high abdominal incision

    a. Preoperative care

    1) Nutritional supplements of glucose and protein hydrolysates to aid in would healing and prevent liver damage, if needed

    2) NG tube insertion before surgery

    b. Postoperative care

    1) Medicate for pain

    2) Monitor T-tube, if present—inserted to ensure drainage of bile from common bile duct until edema in area diminishes; keep T-tube drainage bag below level of gallbladder

    3) Maintain in semi-Fowler's position

    4) Observe for jaundice—yellow sclerae, stool that does not slowly progress from light to dark color after removal of T-tube

    5) Low-fat, high-carbohydrate, high-protein diet

**D.** Evaluation

1. Have postoperative complications been avoided?

2. Has client comfort been maintained?

## ▶ PANCREATITIS

**A.** Assessment

1. Abdominal pain, nausea, vomiting 24–48 hours after heavy meal or alcohol ingestion; pain relief with position change

2. Hypotension

   3. Acute renal failure

   4. Grey-blue discoloration in flank and around umbilicus

**B.** Diagnose

   1. Acute pancreatitis (acute inflammation of the pancreas) is brought about by digestion of the organ by the enzymes it produces, principally trypsin

   2. Chronic pancreatitis—progressive chronic fibrosis and inflammation of the pancreas, with obstruction of its ducts and destruction of its secreting cells

   3. History

      a. Alcoholism

      b. Bacterial or viral infection

      c. Trauma

      d. Complication of mumps

   4. Medications—thiazide diuretics, corticosteroids, oral contraceptives

**C.** Plan/Implementation

   1. NPO, gastric decompression

   2. Medications—antibiotics, opiods (meperidine avoided because of toxicity), histamine-blockers, proton pump inhibitors

   3. Maintain fluid/electrolyte imbalance

   4. Respiratory care—ABG, humidified oxygen, intubation, and ventilation

   5. Cough and deep breathe q2h

   6. Semi-Fowler's position or other position of comfort

   7. Monitor for shock and hyperglycemia

   8. PN

   9. Long-term treatment includes avoidance of alcohol and caffeine; low-fat, bland diet; small, frequent meals

**D.** Evaluation

   1. Is client knowledgeable about dietary restrictions?

   2. Has client comfort been maintained?

# ▶ SYSTEMIC LUPUS ERYTHEMATOSUS (SLE)

**A.** Assessment

   1. Musculoskeletal problems

      a. Polyarthralgia, arthritis, joint swelling

      b. Polymyositis—inflammation of skeletal muscle

   2. Dermatological problems

      a. Butterfly rash across bridge of nose and cheeks—characteristic facial sign

      b. Papular rash; erythematous, purpuric lesions

      c. Oral ulcers

      d. Alopecia

   3. Cardiopulmonary problems

      a. Pericarditis

      b. Pleural effusion

4. Renal problems
    a. Hematuria
    b. Proteinuria
    c. May end in renal failure
5. CNS problems
    a. Changes in behavior
    b. Psychosis
6. Vascular and lymphatic problems
    a. Papular, erythematous and purpuric lesions on fingertips, toes, forearms and hands
    b. Lymphadenopathy
    c. Raynaud's phenomenon–pain and color changes of extremities during exposure to cold

**B.** Diagnose
1. Chronic, systemic inflammatory disease of connective tissue that involves skin, joints, serous membranes, kidneys, hematologic system, CNS
2. Exaggerated production of autoantibodies
3. Diagnostic tests–rheumatoid factor (RF), antinuclear antibody (ANA), decreased C3 and C4 complement levels, increased immunoglobulin levels, increased anti-DNA levels, increased C-reactive protein levels
4. Potential nursing diagnosis
    a. Disturbed skin/tissue integrity
    b. Disturbed body image
    c. Fatigue

**C.** Plan/Implementation
1. Monitor for exacerbations–fever
2. Relieve pain and discomfort, NSAID therapy, acetaminophen
3. Antimalarial (e.g., hydroxychloroquine)
4. Protect skin from ultraviolet rays and sunlight because of photosensitivity, scaly and itchy rash
5. Corticosteroids for exacerbations
6. Immunosuppressive medications (cyclophosphamide, azathioprine)
7. Gamma globulins
8. Plasmapheresis
9. Education and support

**D.** Evaluation
1. Have complications been avoided?
2. Has client adjusted to living with a chronic disease?

▶ **DERMATOLOGICAL DISORDERS**

**A.** Assessment (see Table 10)

| Table 10 SELECTED SKIN DISORDERS | | |
|---|---|---|
| **DISORDER** | **ASSESSMENT** | **NURSING CONSIDERATIONS** |
| Impetigo | Reddish macule becomes honey-colored crusted vesicle, then crust; pruritus<br><br>Caused by *Staphylococcus*, *Streptococcus* | Skin isolation: careful handwashing; cover draining lesions; discourage touching lesions<br><br>Antibiotics—may be topical ointment and/or PO<br><br>Loosen scabs with Burow's solution compresses; remove gently<br><br>Restraints if necessary; mitts for infants to prevent secondary infection<br><br>Monitor for acute glomerulonephritis (complication of untreated impetigo) |
| Herpes simplex type I | Pruritic vesicular groupings on nose, lips, and oral mucous membranes<br><br>Chronically recurrent | Spread by direct contact, handwashing; bland, soft foods; mouth rinses with tetracycline- based preparations; avoid direct contact; administer antivirals (acyclovir, famciclovir and valacyclovir) |
| Herpes zoster | Vesicular eruption along nerve distribution<br><br>Pain, tenderness, and pruritus over affected region<br><br>Primarily seen on face, thorax, trunk | Caused by reactivation of chickenpox virus (varicella)<br><br>Analgesics; compresses, antivirals<br><br>Systemic corticosteroids to diminish severity<br><br>Prevent spread—contagious to anyone who has not had chickenpox or who is immunosuppressed<br><br>Antivirals: Famciclovir, valacyclovir |
| Scabies | Minute, reddened, itchy lesions<br><br>Linear burrowing of a mite at finger webs, wrists, elbows, ankles, penis | Reduce itching—topical antipruritic (calamine lotion/topical steroids), permethrin 5% cream or crotamiton 10%<br><br>Institute skin precautions to prevent spread<br><br>Scabicide—lindane or crotamiton lotion; apply lotion (not on face) to cool, dry skin (not after hot shower because of potential for increased absorption); leave lindane on for 8–12 hours, then shower off; crotamiton may be applied at bedtime for 2 or more consecutive nights; treat all family members (infants upon recommendation of health care provider)<br><br>Repeat in 10 days for eggs<br><br>Launder all clothing and linen after above treatment<br><br>The rash and itching may last for 2–3 weeks even though the mite has been destroyed; treat with antipruritic |
| Pediculosis (lice) | Scalp: white eggs (nits) on hair shafts, with itchy scalp<br><br>Body: macules and papules<br><br>Pubis: red macules | OTC pyrethrin, permethrin 1%, lindane<br><br>Kills both lice and nits with one application<br><br>May suggest to repeat in 7 d—depends on severity |

| Table 10 SELECTED SKIN DISORDERS *(CONTINUED)* | | |
|---|---|---|
| **DISORDER** | **ASSESSMENT** | **NURSING CONSIDERATIONS** |
| Tinea | Pedis (athlete's foot)—vesicular eruptions in interdigital webs<br><br>Capitis (ringworm)—breakage and loss of hair; scaly circumscribed red patches on scalp that spread in circular pattern; fluoresces green with Wood's lamp<br><br>Corporis (ringworm of body)—rings of red scaly areas that spread with central clearing | Antifungal—topical ointment, creams, lotions; PO griseofulvin for resistant cases or if fingernails/toenails are involved; other topical antifungals include butenafine, ciclopirox, econazole, ketoconazole, miconazole, terbinafine<br><br>Keep areas dry and clean<br><br>Frequent shampoos |
| Psoriasis | Chronic recurrent thick, itchy, erythematous papules/plaques covered with silvery white scales with symmetrical distribution<br><br>Commonly on the scalp, knees, sacrum, elbows, and behind ears<br><br>Elevated sedimentation rate with negative rheumatoid factor | Topical administration of coal-tar preparations—protect from direct sunlight for 24 h<br><br>Steroids followed by warm, moist dressings with occlusive outer wrapping (enhances penetration)<br><br>Tar preparations—may stain skin<br><br>Antimetabolites (e.g., methotrexate)—check liver function studies<br><br>Ultraviolet light (wear goggles to protect eyes)<br><br>Anthralin preparations—apply only to affected areas using tongue blade or gloves<br><br>Counseling to support/enhance self-image/self-esteem<br><br>Important for nurse to touch client to demonstrate acceptance |
| Acne vulgaris | Comedones (blackheads/whiteheads), papules, pustules, cysts occurring most often on the face, neck, shoulders, and back | Good hygiene and nutrition<br><br>PO tetracycline (advise sunscreen with SPF of 15; avoid sun exposure)<br><br>Antibacterial medications—azelaic acid, clindamycin, erythromycin<br><br>Isotretinoin—risk of elevated LFTs, dry skin and fetal damage<br><br>Drying preparations—Benoxyl/vitamin A may cause redness and peeling early in treatment and photosensitivity<br><br>Ultraviolet light and surgery<br><br>Monitor for secondary infection<br><br>Emotional support<br><br>Isotretinoin (contraindicated with pregnancy) |
| Eczema (Atropic dermatitis) | Children: rough, dry, erythematous skin lesions that progress to weeping and crusting; distributed on the cheeks, scalp, and extensor surfaces in infants and on flexor surfaces in children<br><br>Adults: hard, dry, flaking, scaling on face, upper chest, and antecubital and popliteal fossa | Onset usually in infancy around 2–3 mo; often outgrown by 2–3 y<br><br>May be precursor of adult asthma or hay fever<br><br>Elimination from diet of common offenders, especially milk, eggs, wheat, citrus fruits, and tomatoes<br><br>Eliminate clothing that is irritating (rough/wool) or that promotes sweating; cotton clothing is best<br><br>Avoid soap and prolonged or hot baths/showers, which tend to be drying; may use warm colloid baths<br><br>Lotions to affected areas<br><br>Keep fingernails short and clean; arm restraints/mittens may be necessary<br><br>Topical steroids<br><br>Antihistamines |

**B.** Diagnose—potential nursing diagnoses

1. Impaired tissue integrity

2. Acute or chronic pain

3. Risk for infection

4. Impaired social interaction

**C.** Plan/Implementation (see Table 10)

**D.** Evaluation

1. Has client comfort been maintained?

2. Has spread of infection been prevented?

# ▶ PREOPERATIVE CARE

**A.** Assessment

    1. Stress—vasovagal responses

**B.** Diagnose

    1. Fears (see Table 1)

| Table 1  FEARS OF SURGERY AT DIFFERENT DEVELOPMENTAL STAGES | | |
|---|---|---|
| **AGE GROUP** | **SPECIFIC FEARS** | **NURSING CONSIDERATIONS** |
| Toddler | Separation | Teach parents to expect regression, e.g., in toilet training and difficult separations |
| Preschooler | Mutilation | Allow child to play with models of equipment Encourage expression of feelings, e.g., anger |
| School-ager | Loss of control | Explain procedures in simple terms <br><br> Allow choices when possible |
| Adolescent | Loss of independence, being different from peers, e.g., alterations in body image | Involve adolescent in procedures and therapies <br><br> Expect resistance <br><br> Express understanding of concerns <br><br> Point out strengths |

**C.** Plan/Implementation

    1. Teaching (see Tables 2 and 3)

        a. Age-appropriate

            1) Toddler—simple directions

            2) Preschool and school-aged—allow to play with equipment

            3) Adolescent—expect resistance

        b. Family-oriented—have parents reinforce teaching

    2. Promote safe environment for hospitalized child

        a. Prevent or minimize the effects of separation on the child

            1) Encourage parental involvement in child's care, especially through rooming-in facilities

            2) Assign the same nurse to care for the child

            3) Provide objects that recreate familiar surroundings (e.g., toys from home)

| Table 2  AGE-APPROPRIATE PREPARATION FOR HEALTH-CARE PROCEDURES | | |
|---|---|---|
| AGE | SPECIAL NEEDS | TYPICAL FEARS |
| Newborn | Include parents<br>Mummy restraint | Loud noises<br>Sudden movements |
| 6–12 month | Model desired behavior | Strangers, heights |
| Toddler | Simple explanations<br>Use distractions<br>Allow choices | Separation from parents<br>Animals, strangers<br>Change in environments |
| Preschooler | Encourage understanding by<br>  playing with puppets, dolls<br>Demonstrate equipment<br>Talk at child's eye level | Separation from parents<br>Ghosts<br>Scary people |
| School-ager | Allow questions<br>Explain why<br>Allow to handle equipment | Dark, injury<br>Being alone<br>Death |
| Adolescent | Explain long-term benefit<br>Accept regression<br>Provide privacy | Social incompetence<br>War, accidents<br>Death |

3. Preparation for surgery

   a. Preoperative checklist

      1) Informed consent

      2) Lab tests, chest x-ray, EKG

      3) Skin prep

      4) Bowel prep

      5) IVs

      6) NPO

      7) Preop meds, sedation, antibiotics

      8) Removal of dentures, jewelry, nail polish

      9) Nutrition—may need PN or tube feedings preoperatively

4. Complementary/Alternative Therapies

   a. Supplements should not be taken near the time of surgery, may interact with anesthesia, may affect coagulation parameters

      1) Echinacea

      2) Garlic

      3) Ginkgo

      4) Ginseng

      5) Kava

      6) St. John's wort

   b. Eliminate all dietary supplements (other than multivitamins) at least 2–3 weeks before surgery

   c. May resume the supplements if health care provider advises

   d. What to expect postoperatively

      1) Discuss postoperative procedures—deep breathing, leg exercises, moving in bed, incentive spirometer (sustained maximal inspiration device), equipment to expect postoperatively

      2) Explain importance of reporting pain or discomfort after surgery

      3) Explain pain relieve interventions, e.g., changing position, medication

      4) Provide for growth and development needs of children

| Table 3   PREOPERATIVE TEACHING GUIDE |
| --- |
| **FACTORS FOR NURSE TO ASSESS BEFORE TEACHING** |
| History of illness |
| Rationale for surgery |
| Nature of surgery—curative or palliative, minor or major, extent of disfigurement, potential alterations, e.g., ostomies |
| Factors related to client's readiness for learning—age, mental status, pre-existing knowledge about condition, concerns about condition, family's reaction to need for surgery |
| **CONTENT AREAS TO COVER DURING TEACHING** |
| Elicit client's concerns, e.g., fears about anesthesia |
| Provide information to clear up misconceptions |
| Explain preoperative procedures, remove jewelry, nail polish |
| Lab tests |
| Skin preparation—cleansing, possibly shaving |
| Enemas if indicated, e.g., before intestinal surgery |
| Rationale for withholding food and fluids (NPO) |
| Preoperative medications, IV line |
| Teach postoperative procedures—deep breathing, leg exercises, moving in bed, incentive spirometer (sustained maximal inspiration device), equipment to expect postoperatively |
| Explain importance of reporting pain or discomfort after surgery |
| Explain what will be done to relieve pain, e.g., changing position, medication |
| Provide for growth and development needs of children |

**D.** Evaluation

   1. Is the preoperative check list complete?

   2. Is the client able to demonstrate postoperative exercises?

# ▶ INTRAOPERATIVE CARE

**A.** Assessment (see Table 4)

**B.** Diagnose (see Table 4)

| Table 4 ANESTHESIA | | |
|---|---|---|
| **MEDICATION** | **ADVERSE EFFECTS** | **NURSING CONSIDERATIONS** |
| General anesthesia via inhalation (Halothane) | Respiratory depression, circulatory depression <br> Delirium during induction and recovery <br> Nausea and vomiting, aspiration during induction, myocardial depression, hepatic toxicity | Check history of sensitization <br> Maintain airway <br> Protect and orient client <br> Monitor vital signs, labs <br> Prevent aspiration postop by elevating head of bed, turning head to side (unless contraindicated) |
| Nitrous oxide | Hypotension, postop nausea and vomiting | Monitor vital signs <br> Adequate oxygenation is essential, especially during emergence |
| IV thiopental sodium | Respiratory depression, low BP, laryngospasm <br> Poor muscle relaxation, hypotension, irritating to skin and subcutaneous tissue | Monitor vital signs, especially airway, breathing <br> Straps for operative table, proper positioning <br> Protect IV site, check for placement periodically |
| Spinal anesthesia <br> Saddle | Hypotension, headache | Monitor vital signs <br> Encourage oral fluids |
| Conduction blocks <br> Epidural <br> Caudal | Hypotension, respiratory depression | Headache not experienced <br> Monitor vital signs |
| Local anesthesia <br> Lidocaine hydrochloride | Excitability, toxic reactions such as respiratory difficulties, vasoconstriction if substance contains epinephrine | Monitor client <br> Do not use local anesthesia with epinephrine on fingers (circulation is less optimal) |
| Moderate sedation <br> Midazolam <br> Diazepam | Respiratory depression, apnea, hypotension, bradycardia | Never leave the client alone <br> Constantly monitor airway, level of consciousness, pulse oximetry, ECG <br> Vital signs every 15–30 minutes <br> Assess client's ability to maintain patent airway and respond to verbal commands |

**C.** Plan/Implementation

1. Monitor effects of anesthesia postinduction
2. Continuously monitor vital signs
3. Aseptic technique
4. Appropriate grounding devices
5. Fluid balance
6. Perform sponge/instrument count

**D.** Potential complications

1. Nausea and vomiting
2. Hypoxia

3. Hypothermia

4. Malignant hyperthermia—inherited muscle disorder chemically induced by anesthesia; stop surgery, treated with 100% oxygen, skeletal muscle relaxant, sodium bicarbonate

**E.** Evaluation

1. Are client's vital signs stable?

2. Has the client's fluid balance been maintained?

# ▶ POSTOPERATIVE CARE

**A.** Assessment

1. Anesthesia, immobility, and surgery can affect any system in the body

2. Full systems assessment required

**B.** Diagnose

1. Neuropsychosocial

   a. Stimulate client postanesthesia

   b. Monitor level of consciousness

2. Cardiovascular

   a. Monitor vital signs q 15 min × 4, q 30 min × 2, q 1 hour × 2, then as needed

   b. Monitor I and O

   c. Check potassium level

   d. Monitor CVP

3. Respiratory

   a. Check breath sounds

   b. Turn, cough, and deep breathe (unless contraindicated, e.g., brain, spinal, eye surgery)

   c. Assess pain level—use verbal or visual scale, offer pain medication

   d. Teach how to use incentive spirometer—hold mouthpiece in mouth, exhale normally, seal lips and inhale slowly and deeply, keep ballsor cylinder elevated 2–3 seconds, exhale and repeat

   e. Teach how to use client-controlled analgesia (PCA)

   f. Get out of bed as soon as possible

4. Gastrointestinal

   a. Check bowel sounds in 4 quadrants for 5 minutes (high-pitched tympany is abnormal)

   b. Keep NPO until bowel sounds are present

   c. Provide good mouth care while NPO

   d. Provide antiemetics for nausea and vomiting

   e. Check abdomen for distention

   f. Check for passage of flatus and stool

5. Genitourinary
   a. Monitor I and 0
   b. Encourage to void
   c. Notify health care provider if unable to void within 8 hours
   d. Catheterize if needed
6. Extremities
   a. Check pulses
   b. Assess color, edema, temperature
   c. Inform client not to cross legs
   d. Keep knee gatch flat
   e. Prohibit use of pillows behind knee
   f. Apply antiembolic stockings (TED hose) before getting out of bed
   g. Pneumatic compression devices (Venodynes)
   h. Assess for pain, swelling, and warmth in the distal extremity
7. Wounds
   a. Dressing
      1) Document amount and character of drainage
      2) Health care provider changes first postop dressing
      3) Use aseptic technique
      4) Note presence of drains
   b. Incision
      1) Assess site (e.g,. edematous, inflamed, excoriated)
      2) Assess drainage (e.g., serous, serosanguineous, purulent)
      3) Note type of sutures
      4) Note if edges of wound are well approximated
      5) Anticipate infection 3–5 days postop
      6) Debride wound, if needed, to reduce inflammation
      7) Change dressing frequently to prevent skin breakdown around site and minimize bacterial growth
8. Drains—prevent fluids from accumulating in tissues
9. GI tubes—check placement
   a. Upper GI tubes—used for gastric decompression
   b. Lower GI tubes—used to decompress bowel
10. Potential complications (see Table 5)

| Table 5  POTENTIAL COMPLICATIONS OF SURGERY | | |
|---|---|---|
| COMPLICATION | ASSESSMENT | NURSING CONSIDERATIONS |
| Hemorrhage | Decreased BP, increased pulse<br>Cold, clammy skin | Replace blood volume<br>Monitor vital signs |
| Shock | Decreased BP, increased pulse<br>Cold, clammy skin | Treat cause<br>Oxygen<br>IV fluids |

| Table 5 POTENTIAL COMPLICATIONS OF SURGERY (CONTINUED) | | |
|---|---|---|
| **COMPLICATION** | **ASSESSMENT** | **NURSING CONSIDERATIONS** |
| Atelectasis and pneumonia | Dyspnea, cyanosis, cough<br>Tachycardia<br>Elevated temperature<br>Pain on affected side | Experienced second day postop<br>Suctioning<br>Postural drainage<br>Antibiotics<br>Cough and turn |
| Embolism | Dyspnea, pain, hemoptysis<br>Restlessness<br>ABG—low $O_2$, high $CO_2$ | Experienced second day postop<br>Oxygen<br>Anticoagulants (heparin)<br>IV fluids |
| Venous Thromboembolism | Positive ultrasound | Experienced 6–14 days up to 1 year later<br>Anticoagulant therapy |
| Paralytic ileus | Absent bowel sounds, no flatus or stool | Nasogastric suction<br>IV fluids<br>Decompression tubes |
| Infection of wound | Elevated WBC and temperature<br>Positive cultures | Experienced 3–5 days postop<br>Antibiotics, aseptic technique<br>Good nutrition |
| Dehiscence | Disruption of surgical incision or wound | Experienced 5–6 days postop<br>Low Fowler's position, no coughing<br>NPO<br>Notify health care provider |
| Evisceration | Protrusion of wound contents | Experienced 5–6 days postop<br>Low Fowler's position, no coughing<br>NPO<br>Cover viscera with sterile saline dressing or wax paper (if at home)<br>Notify health care provider |
| Urinary retention | Unable to void after surgery<br>Bladder distension | Experienced 8–12 hours postop<br>Catheterize as needed |
| Urinary infection | Foul-smelling urine<br>Elevated WBC | Experienced 5–8 days postop<br>Antibiotics<br>Force fluids |
| Psychosis | Inappropriate affect | Therapeutic communication<br>Medication |

| | Table 1 LABORATORY TESTS | | |
|---|---|---|---|
| **TEST** | **PURPOSE/PREPARATION** | **CONVENTIONAL VALUES** | **SI;(INTERNATIONAL SYSTEM OF UNITS)** |
| Red blood cell count (RBC), erythrocytes | Determines actual number of cells in relation to volume | Adult man—4.6–6.2 million/mm$^3$<br>Adult woman—4.2–5.4 million/mm$^3$<br>Child—3.2–5.2 million/mm$^3$ | Adult man 4.6–6.2 x$10^{12}$/L<br>Adult woman 4.2–5.4 x $10^{12}$/L<br>Child 3.2–5.2 x $10^{12}$/L |
| White blood cell count (WBC), leukocytes | Establishes amount and maturity of white blood cell elements | Adult—4,500–11,000/mm$^3$<br>Child—5,000–13,000/mm$^3$ | Adult- 4.5– 11 x $10^9$ /L<br>Child- 5-13 x $10^9$/L |
| Hemoglobin | Determines the amount of hemoglobin/100 mL of blood | Man—13–18 g/dL<br>Woman—12–16 g/dL<br>Child (3–12 years)—11–12.5 g/dL | Man 130–180g/L<br><br>Woman 120–160 g/L<br>Child (3–12 years) 110–125 g/L |
| Hematocrit | Measures percentage of red blood cells per fluid volume of blood | Man—42–52%<br>Woman—35–47%<br>Child (3–12 years)—35–45% | Man 0.42–0.52<br><br>Woman 0.35–0.47<br><br>Child (3–12 yrs) 0.35–0.45 |
| Bleeding time | Measures duration of bleeding after standardized skin incision<br>Used for preoperative screening | 1.5–9.5 minutes | |
| Partial thromboplastin time (PTT) | Monitors effectiveness of heparin therapy<br>Detects coagulation disorders | Lower limit of normal: 20–25 sec<br>Upper limit of normal: 32–39 sec | |
| Platelet count (thrombocyte count) | Used to diagnose hemorrhagic diseases, thrombocytopenia | 150,000–450,000/mm$^3$ | 150–450 x $10^9$/L |
| Prothrombin time (PT) | Monitors effectiveness of warfarin therapy<br>Detects coagulation disorders | 9.5–12.0 seconds | |
| International normalized ratio (INR) | Monitors effectiveness of anticoagulation therapy | 1.0<br>2–3 for therapy in atrial fibrillation, deep venous thrombosis, and pulmonary embolism<br>2.5–3.5 for therapy in prosthetic heart valves | |
| Sedimentation rate (ESR) | Speed at which RBCs settle in well-mixed venous blood<br>Indicates inflammation | Man less than 50 yrs: less than 15 mm/h<br>Man greater than 50 yrs: less than 20 mm/h<br>Woman less than 50 yrs: less than 25 mm/h<br>Woman greater than 50 yrs: less than 30 mm/h | |
| Glucose tolerance test (GTT) | Measures ability of body to secrete insulin in response to hyperglycemia | Fasting—60–110 mg/dL<br>1 hour—190 mg/dL<br>2 hours—140 mg/dL<br>3 hours—125 mg/dL | Fasting 3.3–6.1 mmol/L<br>1 hour 10.5 mmol/L<br>2 hours 7.8 mmol/L<br>3 hours 6.9 mmol/L |

| | Table 1 LABORATORY TESTS *(CONTINUED)* | | |
|---|---|---|---|
| **TEST** | **PURPOSE/PREPARATION** | **CONVENTIONAL VALUES** | **SI;(INTERNATIONAL SYSTEM OF UNITS)** |
| Total cholesterol | Evaluates tendency for athlerosclerosis<br><br>Overnight fast | 150–200 mg/dL | 3.9–5.2 mmol/L |
| Low-density lipoproteins (LDL) | Determines whether elevated cholesterol levels are caused by increased LDL or HDL<br><br>Fast for 12–14 hours | Less than 160 mg/dL if no CAD and less than 2 risk factors<br><br>Less than 130 mg/dL if no CAD and 2 or more risk factors<br><br>Less than 100 mg/dL if CAD present | Less than 4.1 mmol/L<br><br>Less than 3.3 mmol/L<br><br>Less than 2.6 mmol/L |
| High-density lipoproteins (HDL) | Same as for LDLs, above | Men 35–70 mg/dL,<br>Women 35–85 mg/dL | Men 0.91–1.8 mmol/L<br>Women 0.91–2.2 mmol/L |
| Creatinine (CR) | Test of renal function<br><br>NPO 8 hours<br><br>List medications client is taking on lab slip | Adult—0.7–1.4 mg/dL<br>Child—0.4–1.2 mg/dl<br>Infant—0.3–0.6 mg/dL | Adult 62–124 µmol/L<br>Child 35–106 µmol/L<br>Infant 27–53 µmol/L |
| Alkaline phosphatase | Evaluates liver and bone function<br><br>NPO 8–12 hours<br><br>List medications client is taking on lab slip | Adult—50–120 units/L<br><br>Infant and adolescent up to 104 FU/L | Adult - 0.5-2 µkat/L |
| Creatine kinase (CK) | Used to diagnose acute MI<br><br>Detected in blood in 3–5 hours | MM bands present = skeletal muscle damage<br><br>MB bands present = heart muscle damage | |
| Serum albumin | Used to detect protein malnutrition | 3.5–5.5 g/dL | 35–55 g/L |
| BUN | Evaluate renal function | Values affected by protein intake, tissue breakdown, fluid volume changes<br><br>10–20 mg/dL | 3.6–7.1 mmol/L |
| Triglycerides | Detect risk for atherosclerosis | 100–200 mg/dL | 1.13–2.26 mmol/L |
| Alanine aminotransferase (ALT) | Increase liver disease, hepatitis | 10–40 units (males) | |
| Aspartate aminotransferase | Increase liver disease, hepatitis | 10–40 units (males) | |

▶ **ARTERIAL TESTS**

| Table 2 ARTERIAL DIAGNOSTIC TESTS | | | |
|---|---|---|---|
| TEST | PURPOSE | PREPARATION/TESTING | POST–TEST NURSING CARE |
| Oscillometry | Abnormal findings help to pinpoint the level of arterial occlusion | Alterations in pulse volume are measured by placing a pneumatic cuff around the extremity at different levels, attached to a monitor | None |
| Skin temperature studies | Coldness of one or both extremities at normal room temperature implies poor circulation | Palpate and compare skin warmth or coolness in opposing limbs<br><br>Use direct-reading skin temperature thermometer<br><br>Immerse one extremity in warm water, and observe for rise in skin temperature in the other extremity, which should normally follow because of reflex vasodilation<br><br>Place a hot water bottle on the client's abdomen and observe extremities for reflex rise in skin temperature | None |
| Angiography (arteriography) | Indicates abnormalities of blood flow due to arterial obstruction or narrowing | Contrast dye is injected into the arteries and x-ray films are taken of the vascular tree | Disadvantages include potential allergic reactions to radiopaque dye, potential irritation, or thrombosis of the injection site |
| Exercise tests for intermittent claudication | Claudication with exercise indicates inability of damaged arteries to increase the blood flow needed for increased tissue oxygenation | Client exercises until pain occurs; the length of time between start of exercise and the onset of pain is recorded | None |
| Lumbar sympathetic block | Decreased limb pain and increased temperature indicate sympathectomy could improve circulation to the extremities | Local anesthetic is injected into sympathetic ganglia, temporarily blocking the sympathetic vasomotor nerve fibers supplying an ischemic limb | Shock due to movement of blood from vital organs to peripheral vessels |

# ▶ VENOUS TESTS

| Table 3   VENOUS DIAGNOSTIC TESTS | | | |
|---|---|---|---|
| TEST | PURPOSE | PREPARATION/TESTING | POST–TEST NURSING CARE |
| Phlebography | Lack of filling of a vein is indicative of venous occlusion due to a thrombus | Thrombi are identified as radiolucent areas in opaque-filled veins | None |
| Venous pressure measurements | Significant only in early stages of thrombophlebitis before collateral veins develop | Venous occlusion in one leg causes venous pressure to be higher in other leg | None |
| Isotope studies | Helpful in diagnosing early formation of thrombi | Fibrinogen labeled with radioactive iodine molecules make up a clot along with naturally occurring fibrinogen<br><br>Radioactivity counts are increased over thrombi | None |
| Ultrasonic flow detection—Doppler studies | Indicates obstruction in blood flow in extremities | Electronic stethoscope that detects sound of blood flow | None |

# ▶ RESPIRATORY/CARDIAC TESTS

| Table 4   RESPIRATORY/CARDIAC TESTS | | | |
|---|---|---|---|
| TEST | PURPOSE | PREPARATION/TESTING | POST–TEST NURSING CARE |
| Pulmonary function | Detects impaired pulmonary function<br><br>Follows the course of pulmonary disease and evaluates treatment responses | Explain purpose<br><br>No smoking 4 hours before test<br><br>May withhold bronchodilator medications<br><br>Asked to breathe into machine | Observe for dyspnea |
| Arterial blood gases (ABGs) | Measurements of tissue oxygenation, carbon dioxide removal, and acid-base balance<br><br>$pO_2$—partial pressure oxygen<br><br>$pCO_2$—partial pressure carbon dioxide<br><br>Evaluates clients being mechanically ventilated or with cardiovascular disease | Perform Allen test—checks collateral circulation<br><br>Arterial blood is obtained in heparinized syringe<br><br>Unclotted blood is necessary<br><br>Air bubbles cannot be present in specimen<br><br>Results (see Table 5) | Apply pressure to site for 5 minutes to prevent hematoma (15 minutes if client is receiving anticoagulants)<br><br>Send specimen on ice and occlude needle to avoid air in syringe<br><br>Note on lab slip if client was breathing room air or oxygen (document liters)<br><br>Check arm for swelling, discoloration, pain, numbness, tingling |
| Lung scan (VQ scan) | Evaluates pulmonary perfusion when pulmonary infarction or space-occupying disorders are suspected | Perfusion scan—intravenous injection of iodinated radioactive dye<br><br>Significance—high level of radioactivity in areas of good perfusion; low levels of radioactivity in obstructed areas<br><br>Ventilation scan—radioactive gas inhaled, should be equal distribution of gas | None |

| | Table 4 RESPIRATORY/CARDIAC TESTS *(CONTINUED)* | | |
|---|---|---|---|
| **TEST** | **PURPOSE** | **PREPARATION/TESTING** | **POST-TEST NURSING CARE** |
| Sputum analysis | Identify cause of pulmonary infection<br>Identify abnormal lung cells | Encourage fluid intake night before test<br>Instruct client to rinse mouth with water<br>Do not brush teeth, eat, or use mouthwash before test<br>Use sterile container<br>Ultrasonic/heated nebulizer treatment 10–15 minutes prior aids in collection<br>Teach client how to expectorate<br>Collect early in the AM if possible | None |
| Bronchoscopy | Allows visualization of larynx, trachea, and mainstem bronchi<br>Possible to obtain tissue biopsy, apply medication, aspirate secretions for laboratory examination, aspirate a mucus plug causing airway obstruction, or remove aspirated foreign objects | Explain procedure<br>Maintain NPO for 6 hours before test<br>Inspect mouth for infection<br>Administer premedication—diazepam, midazolam, meperidine, atropine<br>Remove dentures<br>Prepare client for sore throat after procedure | Sit or lie on side, remain NPO until gag reflex returns<br>Observe for respiratory difficulties |
| Thoracentesis | Aspiration of fluid or air from pleural space<br>To obtain specimen for analysis, relieve lung compression, obtain lung tissue for biopsy, or instill medications into pleural space | Explain procedure<br>Take vital signs<br>Shave area around needle insertion site<br>Position client sitting with arms on pillows on over-bed table or lying on side in bed<br>Expect stinging sensation with injection of local anesthetic and feeling of pressure when needle inserted<br>No more than 1,000 mL fluid removed at one time | Auscultate breath sounds frequently<br>Monitor vital signs frequently<br>Check for leakage of fluid, location of puncture site, client tolerance<br>Sterile dressing after procedure |
| Chest x-ray | To identify abnormalities such as foreign bodies, fluid, infiltrates, tumors | Explain procedure<br>Remove all jewelry from neck and chest<br>Female clients of childbearing age wear a lead apron | None |
| Lung biopsy | Removal of lung tissue for culture or cytology | Explain procedure<br>Administer premedication—sedatives or analgesics<br>Have client hold breath in midexpiration<br>Performed with fluoroscopic monitoring<br>Position client as for thoracentesis | Monitor vital signs and breath sounds every 4 hours for 24 hours<br>Report signs of respiratory distress<br>Chest x-ray taken after procedure to check for complication of pneumothorax<br>Sterile dressing applied after procedure |
| Computed tomography (CT) | Provides three-dimensional assessment of the lungs and thorax | Noninvasive | If dye, assess reaction |

| Table 4 RESPIRATORY/CARDIAC TESTS *(CONTINUED)* | | | |
|---|---|---|---|
| **TEST** | **PURPOSE** | **PREPARATION/TESTING** | **POST–TEST NURSING CARE** |
| Magnetic resonance imaging (MRI) | Provides detailed pictures of body structures | Explain procedure<br><br>Assess the client for claustrophobia<br><br>Remove all metal jewelry and metal objects<br><br>Ask if client has metal implanted in body (pacemaker, clips) | None |
| Angiography | Evaluates specific areas of the arterial system | Explain procedure<br><br>Remove all jewelry<br><br>Client may experience nausea, flushing, warmth, salty taste with injection of dye | Assess for hematoma<br><br>Assess distal pulses<br><br>Compare skin temperature, color, sensation in both extremities<br><br>Check vital signs frequently<br><br>Notify health care provider if bleeding or change in vital signs occurs |
| Pulse oximetry | Measures oxygen saturation through the skin | Clean site using cotton ball with soap and water, then alcohol<br><br>Dry skin | Rotate site every 4 hours to prevent skin irritation |
| Stress test | Assess cardiovascular response to increased workload | Client walks on treadmill, pedals stationary bicycle, or climbs set of stairs<br><br>EKG monitored before, during, and after exercise testing | None |
| Ultrasound echocar-diogram | Noninvasive sound waves used to determine cardiac structures | None | None |
| Cardiac catheterization | Usually used with angiography<br><br>Introduction of catheter into chambers of heart to evaluate ventricular function and obtain chamber pressures | NPO 8–12 hours<br><br>Signed permit<br><br>Empty bladder<br><br>Check pulse<br><br>Explain that client may experience feeling of heat, palpitations, desire to cough when dye injected | Monitor vital signs q 15 min for 2 hours, then q 30 min for 1 hour, then q 1 hour for 3 hours<br><br>Check pulses, sensation, bleeding at insertion site q 30 min for 3 hours, then q 1 hour for 3 hours<br><br>Bedrest 6–8 hours with insertion site extremity straight |

| Table 5 ARTERIAL BLOOD GASES (ABG) | | | |
|---|---|---|---|
| **VALUE** | **NORMAL** | **ACIDOSIS** | **ALKALOSIS** |
| pH | 7.35–7.45 | Below 7.35 | Above 7.45 |
| $PaO_2$ | 85–95 mm Hg | | |
| $SaO_2$ | 95–99% | | |
| $PaCO_2$ | 35–45 mm Hg | Respiratory greater than 45 mm Hg | Respiratory less than 35mm Hg |
| $HCO_3$ | 22–26 mEq/L | Metabolic less than 22 mEq/L | Metabolic greater than 26 mEq/L |

▶ # NEUROLOGICAL TESTS

| Table 6  NEUROLOGICAL TESTS | | | |
|---|---|---|---|
| **TEST** | **PURPOSE** | **PREPARATION/TESTING** | **POST–TEST NURSING CARE** |
| Cerebral angiography | Indentifies aneurysms, vascular malformations, narrowed vessels | Informed consent<br><br>Explain procedure:<br><br>    Lie flat; dye injection into femoral artery by needle/catheter; fluoroscopy and radiologic films taken after injection<br><br>Well hydrated<br><br>Preprocedure sedation<br><br>Skin prep, chosen site shaved<br><br>Mark peripheral pulses<br><br>May experience feeling of warmth and metallic taste when dye injected | Neurological assessment every 15–30 minutes until vital signs are stable<br><br>Keep flat in bed 12–14 hours<br><br>Check puncture site every hour<br><br>Immobilize site for 6–8 hours<br><br>Assess distal pulses, color, and temperature<br><br>Observe symptons of complications, allergic response to dye, puncture site hematoma<br><br>Force fluids, accurate intake and output |
| Lumbar puncture (LP) | Insertion of needle into subarachnoid space to obtain specimen, relieve pressure, inject dye or medications | Explain procedure<br><br>Informed consent<br><br>Procedure done at bedside or in treatment room<br><br>Positioned in lateral recumbent fetal position at edge of bed | Neurological assessment every 15–30 minutes until stable<br><br>Position flat for several hours<br><br>Encourage PO fluid to 3,000 mL<br><br>Oral analgesics for headache<br><br>Observe sterile dressing at insertion site for bleeding or drainage |
| Electroencephalogram (EEG) | Records electrical activity of brain | Explain procedure<br><br>Procedure done by technician in a quiet room<br><br>Painless<br><br>Tranquilizer and stimulant medications withheld for 24–48 hours pre-EEG<br><br>Stimulants such as caffeine, cola, and tea, cigarettes withheld for 24 hours pre-EEG<br><br>May be asked to hyperventilate 3–4 minutes and watch bright, flashing light<br><br>Meals not withheld<br><br>Kept awake night before test | Help client remove paste from hair<br><br>Administer prescribed medication withheld before EEG<br><br>Observe for seizure activity in seizure-prone clients |
| Echoencephalography | Evaluates brain structure through sound waves | Explain procedure–hand-held transducer used to record sound waves | None |
| CT (computed tomography) | Detects hemorrhage, infarction, abscesses, tumors | Informed consent<br><br>Explain procedure<br><br>Painless<br><br>Immobile during exam<br><br>If contrast dye used, may experience flushed, warm face, and metallic taste during injection | Assess for allergic responses to contrast dye (e.g., rash, pruritus, urticaria)<br><br>Encourage PO fluids |

| Table 6 NEUROLOGICAL TESTS *(CONTINUED)* | | | |
|---|---|---|---|
| **TEST** | **PURPOSE** | **PREPARATION/TESTING** | **POST–TEST NURSING CARE** |
| Myelogram | Visualizes spinal column and subarachnoid space | Informed consent<br><br>Explain procedure<br><br>NPO for 4–6 hours before test<br><br>Obtain allergy history<br><br>Phenothiazines, CNS depressants, and stimulants withheld for 48 h prior to test<br><br>Table will be moved to various positions during test | Neurologic assessment every 2–4 hours<br><br>When metrizamide water-soluble dye used, head should be raised 30–45° for 3 hours<br><br>Oral analgesics for headache<br><br>Encourage PO fluids<br><br>Assess for distended bladder<br><br>Inspect injection site<br><br>Assess for allergic responses to contrast dye (e.g., rash, pruritus, urticaria) |
| PET (positron emission tomography) | Used to assess metabolic and physiological function of brain; diagnose stroke, brain tumor, epilepsy, Parkinson's disease, head injury | Client inhales or is injected with radioactive substance, then is scanned<br><br>Tell client may experience dizziness, headache<br><br>Teach relaxation exercises | None |

## ▶ LIVER FUNCTION TESTS

| Table 7 LIVER FUNCTION TESTS | | | |
|---|---|---|---|
| **TEST** | **PURPOSE** | **PREPARATION/TESTING** | **POST–TEST NURSING CARE** |
| Pigment studies | Parameters of hepatic ability to conjugate and excrete bilirubin<br><br>Abnormal in liver and gall bladder disorders, e.g., with jaundice<br><br>Direct bilirubin increases in obstruction | Fast 4 h<br><br>Normal<br><br>Serum bilirubin, direct 0.1–0.4 mg/dL (1.7–3.1 mcmol/L)<br><br>Serum bilirubin, total 0.3–1 mg/dL (5–17 mcmol/L)<br><br>Urine bilirubin, total 0 | Over 70% of the parenchyma of the liver may be damaged before liver function tests become abnormal |
| Protein studies Serum albumin | Proteins are produced by the liver<br><br>Levels may diminish in hepatic disease<br><br>Severely decreased serum albumin results in generalized edema | Normal<br><br>3.5–5.5 g/dL (35–55 g/L) | None |
| Coagulation studies Prothrombin time (PT)<br><br>Partial thromboplastin time (PTT) | May be prolonged in hepatic disease<br><br>In liver disease, PTT prolonged due to lack of vitamin K | Normal<br><br>PT 9.5–12.0 seconds<br><br>PTT<br><br>Lower limit of normal 20–25 seconds; upper limit of normal 32–39 seconds | Put specimen in ice<br><br>Apply pressure to site for 5 min (15 min if on anticoagulants) |
| Liver enzymes | With damaged liver cells, enzymes are released into bloodstream | Normal<br><br>AST 10–40 units (males)<br><br>ALT 10–40 units (males)<br><br>LDH 90–176 units/L | None |

| Table 7 LIVER FUNCTION TESTS *(CONTINUED)* | | | |
|---|---|---|---|
| **TEST** | **PURPOSE** | **PREPARATION/TESTING** | **POST–TEST NURSING CARE** |
| Blood ammonia (arterial) | Liver converts ammonia to urea<br><br>With liver disease, ammonia levels rise | Normal 15–45 mcg/dL (11–32 mcmol/L) | None |
| Abdominal X-ray | To determine gross liver size | None | None |
| Liver scan | To demonstrate size, shape of liver, visualize scar tissue, cysts, or tumors; use radiopaque dye | None | Question client about seafood (iodine) allergy before radiopaque dye administration; anaphylaxis common, aqueous-based dye available for hypersensitive individuals<br><br>Resume diet |
| Cholecystogram and cholangiography | For gallbladder and bile duct visualization; radiopaque material injected directly into biliary tree | Fat-free dinner evening before exam<br><br>Ingestion of dye in tablet form (Telepaque tablets—check history of allergies to iodine) evening before<br><br>NPO after dye ingestion<br><br>X-rays followed by ingestion of high-fat meal followed by further x-rays | Question client about seafood (iodine) allergy |
| Celiac axis arteriography | For liver and pancreas visualization; uses contrast media of organic iodine | None | Question client about seafood (iodine) allergy prior to radiopaque dye administration; anaphylaxis common |
| Splenoportogram (splenic portal venography) | To determine adequacy of portal blood flow; uses contrast media of organic iodine | None | Question client about seafood (iodine) allergy prior to radiopaque dye administration; anaphylaxis common |
| Liver biopsy | Sampling of tissue by needle aspiration | Administer vitamin K IM to decrease chance of hemorrhage<br><br>NPO morning of exam (6 h)<br><br>Sedative administration just before exam<br><br>Teach client that he will be asked to hold his breath for 5–10 seconds<br><br>Performed at bedside, supine position, lateral with upper arms elevated | Position on right side for 2–3 h with pillow under costal margin<br><br>Frequent vital signs to detect hemorrhage and shock; check clotting time, platelets, hematocrit<br><br>Expect mild local pain and mild pain radiating to right shoulder<br><br>Client reports of severe abdominal pain immediately—may be indication of perforation of bile duct and peritonitis<br><br>Avoid heavy lifting for 1 week |
| Bilirubin | Detect presence of bilirubin due to hemolytic or liver disease | Total bilirubin 0.3–1.0 mg/dL (5–17 mcmol/L)<br><br>Direct (conjugated) bilirubin 0.1–0.4 mg/dL (1.7–3.7 mcmol/L)<br><br>Indirect (unconjugated) bilirubin 0.2–0.6 mg/dL (3.4–11.2 mcmol/L) | None |

# ▶ GASTROINTESTINAL TESTS

| Table 8   GASTROINTESTINAL DIAGNOSTIC TESTS | | | |
|---|---|---|---|
| **TEST** | **PURPOSE** | **PREPARATION/TESTING** | **POST–TEST NURSING CARE** |
| Stomach/esophagus endoscopy | Visualization of esophagus and/or stomach by means of a lighted, flexible fiberoptic tube introduced through the mouth to the stomach to determine presence of ulcerations, tumors, or to obtain tissue or fluid samples | Verify that informed consent from client has been obtained<br><br>Maintain NPO before procedure (at least 8 h)<br><br>Teach client about numbness in throat due to local anesthetic applied to posterior pharynx by spray or gargle | Maintain NPO until gag reflex returns<br><br>Observe for vomiting of blood, respiratory distress<br><br>Inform client to expect sore throat for 3 to 4 days after procedure |
| Sigmoidoscopy/ Proctoscopy | Direct visualization of the sigmoid colon, rectum, and anal canal | Laxative night before exam and enema or suppository morning of procedure<br><br>NPO at midnight | Allow client to rest<br><br>Observe for hemorrhage, perforation<br><br>Encourage fluids |
| Colonoscopy | Direct visualization of the colon; used as a diagnostic aid; removes foreign bodies, polyps, or tissue for biopsy | Clear liquid diet 24–72 h before exam (per health care provider order)<br><br>Cathartic in evening for 2 days prior to exam<br><br>Enema on morning of exam<br><br>polyethelene glycol solution to cleanse bowel; clear liquid diet noon day before test | Allow to rest<br><br>Observe for passage of blood and abdominal pain, signs of perforation, hemorrhage, or respiratory distress Follow-up x-rays<br><br>Resume diet |
| Ammonia | Detect liver disorders | Normal 15–45 mcg/dL (11–32 mcmol/L)<br><br>Avoid smoking before test | None |
| Amylase | Diagnose pancreatitis and acute cholecystitis | Normal 6–160 Somogyi U/dL<br><br>Restrict food 1–2 hours before test<br><br>Avoid opiates 2 hours before test | None |
| Lipase | Diagnose acute and chronic pancreatitis, biliary obstruction, hepatitis, cirrhosis | Normal less than 200 U/mL<br><br>NPO 8–12 hrs before test<br><br>Avoid opiates 24 hrs prior to test | None |
| Gastric aspirate | Aspiration of gastric contents to evaluate for presence of abnormal constituents such as blood, abnormal bacteria, abnormal pH, or malignant cells | NPO before test<br><br>NG tube passed, stomach contents aspirated and sent for evaluation<br><br>Histamine is sometimes used to stimulate hydrochloric acid secretion<br><br>pH—measures acid/alkaline range; (4.5–7.5); normal gastric pH less than 4; generally overly acidic environment can lead to ulcerative activity<br><br>Guaiac—tests for presence of blood; normally, blood absent | Encourage fluids |
| Upper GI series Barium swallow | Ingestion of barium sulfate to determine patency and size of esophagus, size and condition of gastric walls, patency of pyloric valve, and rate of passage to small bowel | Maintain NPO after midnight<br><br>Inform client that stool will be light-colored after procedure | Encourage fluids<br><br>Laxatives to prevent constipation<br><br>Stool will be white from barium |

| Table 8  GASTROINTESTINAL DIAGNOSTIC TESTS *(CONTINUED)* | | | |
|---|---|---|---|
| **TEST** | **PURPOSE** | **PREPARATION/TESTING** | **POST–TEST NURSING CARE** |
| Lower GI series<br>  Barium enema | Instillation of barium (radiopaque substance) into colon via rectum for fluoroscopy x-rays to view tumors, polyps, strictures, ulcerations, inflammation, or obstructions of colon | Low-residue diet for 1–2 days<br><br>Clear liquid diet and laxative evening before test; cleansing enemas until clear morning of test | Cleansing enemas after exam to remove barium and prevent impaction<br><br>X-rays may be repeated after all barium is expelled |
| Paracentesis | Needle aspiration of fluid in abdominal cavity used for diagnostic examination of ascitic fluid and treatment of massive ascites resistant to other therapies | Done at bedside—client in semi-Fowler's position or sitting upright on edge of bed<br><br>Empty bladder prior to procedure to avoid accidental perforation | Check vital signs frequently for shock and/or infection<br><br>Report elevated temperature and/or abdominal pain to health care provider<br><br>Observe for sign of hypovolemic shock |

► # REPRODUCTIVE TESTS

| Table 9  REPRODUCTIVE TESTS AND PROCEDURES | | | |
|---|---|---|---|
| **TEST** | **PURPOSE** | **PREPARATION/TESTING** | **POST–TEST NURSING CARE** |
| Culdoscopy | Visualization of ovaries, fallopian tubes, uterus via lighted tube inserted into vagina and through cul-de-sac | Local anesthetic and/or light sedation<br><br>Knee-chest position during procedure | Position on abdomen after procedure<br><br>Observe for vaginal bleeding<br><br>Avoid douching and intercourse for 2 weeks |
| Colposcopy | Similar to pelvic exam | Performed between menstrual periods<br><br>Takes 20 minutes<br><br>Lithotomy position<br><br>Cervix is washed with dilute acetic acid | None |
| Laparoscopy | Visualization of pelvic cavity through an incision beneath the umbilicus to view structures | Carbon dioxide introduced to enhance visualization<br><br>General anesthesia<br><br>Foley catheter inserted for bladder decompression | Out of bed after procedure<br><br>Regular diet |
| Cultures and smears | Samples of tissues are taken to identify infectious processes or identify abnormal cells | No anesthetic needed<br><br>Chlamydia smear needs media preparation by laboratory | None |
| Cervical biopsy | Sample tissue taken to identify unusual cells | No anesthesia used<br><br>May have cramping sensation | Provide written instructions<br><br>Restrictions on intercourse, douching, and swimming for 3 days |

▶ **URINARY SYSTEM TESTS**

| Table 10 URINARY SYSTEM DIAGNOSTIC TESTS | | | |
|---|---|---|---|
| TEST | PURPOSE | PREPARATION/TESTING | POST–TEST NURSING CARE |
| Urinalysis | Detect kidney abnormalities | Advise client to save first am specimen<br><br>Overnight specimen is more concentrated pH 4.5–8<br><br>Specific gravity 1.010–1.030 | None |
| Urine culture and sensitivity | Identify bacteria in urine | Cleanse external meatus with povidone-iodine or soap and water before test<br><br>Obtain midstream specimen<br><br>Normal—less than 100,000 colonies/mL | None |
| Cystometrogram | Test of muscle tone | Prepare client for Foley catheter<br><br>Instillation of saline may cause feeling of pressure in bladder during test | Advise client to report any post-test symptoms |
| Creatinine clearance | Evaluate renal function | 24-hour urine collection<br><br>Blood drawn for creatinine level at end of urine collection<br><br>Normal—1.42–2.08 mL/min (males) | None |
| BUN | Evaluate renal function | Values affected by protein intake, tissue breakdown, fluid volume changes 10–20 mg/dL (3.6–7.1 mmol/L) | None |
| Cystoscopy | Direct visualization by cystoscope of bladder and urethra | Bowel preparation<br><br>Teach client to deep-breathe to decrease discomfort<br><br>NPO if general anesthesia used | Monitor character and volume of urine<br><br>Check for abdominal distention, urinary frequency, fever<br><br>Urine usually pink-tinged<br><br>Abdominal or pelvic pain indicates trauma<br><br>Provide antimicrobial prophylaxis |
| Cystourethrogram | X-ray study of bladder and urethra | Explain procedure to client: catheter inserted into urethra, radiopaque dye injected, client voids, x-rays taken during voiding | Advise client to report any symptoms |
| Intravenous pyelogram | Provides x-ray visualization of kidneys, ureters, and bladder | Bowel preparation<br>NPO after midnight<br>Check allergies to shellfish or iodine, chocolate, eggs, milk<br>Burning or reports of salty taste may occur during injection of radiopaque dye into vein<br>X-rays are taken at intervals after dye injection | Post procedure x-rays usually done<br><br>Client should be alert to signs of dye reaction: edema, itching, wheezing, dyspnea |
| Renal scan | Evaluation of kidneys | Radioactive isotope injected IV<br>Radioactivity measured by radioactivity counter<br>Fluids forced before procedure | None |

| | Table 10 URINARY SYSTEM DIAGNOSTIC TESTS *(CONTINUED)* | | |
|---|---|---|---|
| TEST | PURPOSE | PREPARATION/TESTING | POST–TEST NURSING CARE |
| Ultrasound | Images of renal structures obtained by sound waves | Noninvasive procedure<br><br>No preparation required<br><br>Full bladder required | None |
| Kidney biopsy | Kidney tissue obtained by needle aspiration for pathological evaluation | NPO 6–8 hours<br><br>X-ray taken prior to procedure<br><br>Skin is marked to indicate lower pole of kidney (fewer blood vessels)<br><br>Position: prone<br><br>Client instructed to hold breath during needle insertion | Pressure applied to site for 20 minutes<br><br>Keep on affected side for 30–60 minutes<br><br>Pressure dressing applied<br><br>Check vital signs q 15–15 min for 1 h<br><br>Client kept flat in bed<br><br>Bedrest for 6–8 hours<br><br>Intake 3,000/day<br><br>Observe for hematuria and site bleeding |
| Schilling test | Diagnoses vitamin $B_{12}$ deficiency (pernicious anemia) | Radioactive vitamin $B_{12}$ is administered to the client<br><br>Low value excreted in urine indicates pernicious anemia, (normal is greater than 10% of dose excreted in 24 hours) | Vitamin $B_{12}$ (cyancobalamin injection for life) |

▶ **CHEST PHYSIOTHERAPY**

A. Breathing exercises
1. Diaphragmatic or abdominal breathing
   a. Client positioned on back with knees bent
   b. Place hands on abdomen
2. Pursed lip breathing
   a. Breathe in through nose
   b. Purse lips and breathe out through mouth
   c. Exhalation should be twice as long as inspiration

B. Coughing techniques
1. Instruct client to lean slightly forward and take three slow, deep breaths though the nose, exhaling slowly through slightly parted or pursed lips
2. Client should then take another deep breath and cough several times during expiration
3. Client must be encouraged to cough from deep within the chest and avoid nonproductive coughing that wastes energy

C. Postural drainage—uses gravity to facilitate removal of bronchial secretions
1. Client is placed in a variety of positions to facilitate drainage into larger airways
2. Five positions used—head down, prone, right and left lateral, upright
3. Stay in each position 10–15 minutes
4. Breathe in slowly through nose; breathe out through pursed lips
5. Performed 2–4 times daily before meals and at hs
6. Secretions may be removed by coughing or suctioning

D. Percussion and vibration—usually performed during postural drainage to augment the effect of gravity drainage
1. Percussion—rhythmic striking of chest wall with cupped hands over areas where secretions are retained
2. Vibration—hand and arm muscles of person doing vibration are tensed, and a vibrating pressure is applied to the chest as the client exhales
3. Place towel over area
4. Percussion alternated with vibration, 5 min in each position

E. Incentive spirometer—used to maximize respiration and mobilize secretions
1. Client must inhale deeply and hold breath for 3–5 seconds to achieve effective lung expansion
2. Client must form seal around mouthpiece with lips
3. Sitting in semi-Fowler's position
4. Do 10 breaths/h while awake

# ► SUCTIONING

A. Procedure

1. Wear protective eyewear

2. Hyperoxygenate before, during, and after suctioning—100% oxygen for 3 minutes or 3 deep breaths

3. Explain procedure to client (potentially frightening procedure)

4. Semi-Fowler's position

5. Lubricate catheter with sterile saline and insert without applying suction

6. Advance catheter as far as possible or until client coughs; do not apply suction

7. Withdraw catheter 1–2 cm, apply suction and withdraw catheter with a rotating motion for no more than 10 seconds; wall suction set between 80–120 mm Hg

8. Repeat procedure after client has rested

9. Hyperoxygenate for 1–5 minutes after suctioning endotracheal tube or tracheostomy tube suctioned, then mouth is suctioned; provide mouth care

B. Complications

1. Hypoxia

2. Bronchospasm

3. Vagal stimulation

4. Tissue trauma

5. Cardiac dysrhythmias

6. Infection

# ► TRACHEOSTOMY CARE

A. Procedure

1. Perform every 8 hours and as needed

2. Explain procedure

3. Hyperoxygenate or deep breathe

4. Suction tracheostomy tube

5. Remove old dressings

6. Open sterile tracheostomy care kit

7. Put on sterile gloves

8. Remove inner cannula (permanent or disposable)

9. Clean with hydrogen peroxide if permanent inner cannula

10. Rinse with sterile water, dry

11. Reinsert into outer cannula

12. Clean stoma site with hydrogen peroxide and sterile water, then dry

13. Change ties or velcro tracheostomy tube holders as needed; old ties must remain in place until new ties are secured; tie on side of neck, allowing 2 fingers to be inserted under tie

14. Apply new sterile dressing; do not cut gauze pads

15. Document site of tracheostomy, type/quantity of secretions, client tolerance of procedure

16. Purpose of cuff—prevents aspiration of fluids; inflated during continuous mechanical ventilation, during and after eating, during and 1 hour after a tube feeding, when client is unable to handle oral secretions, when client may aspirate; check cuff pressure q 8 hours, maintain at less than 25 cm/$H_2O$

**B.** Complications

1. Airway obstruction

2. Trachial necrosis

3. Infection

# ▶ OXYGEN THERAPY

| Table 1  OXYGEN ADMINISTRATION | | |
|---|---|---|
| METHOD | OXYGEN DELIVERED | NURSING CONSIDERATIONS |
| Nasal cannula or prongs | 23–42% at 1–6 L/min | Assess patency of nostril<br>Apply water-soluble jelly to nostrils every 3–4 hours<br>Perform good mouth care |
| Face mask | 40–60% at 6–8 L/min (oxygen flow minimum 5 L) | Remove mask every 1–2 hours<br>Wash, dry, apply lotion to skin<br>Emotional support to decrease feeling of claustrophobia |
| Partial rebreather mask | 50–75% at 8–11 L/min | Adjust oxygen flow to keep reservoir bag two-thirds full during inspiration |
| Nonrebreather mask | 80–100% at 12 L/min | Adjust oxygen flow to keep bag two-thirds full |
| Venturi mask | 24–40% at 4–8 L/min | Provides high humidity and fixed concentrations<br>Keep tubing free of kinks |
| Tracheostomy collar or T-piece | 30–100% at 8–10 L/min | Assess for fine mist<br>Empty condensation from tubing<br>Keep water container full |
| Oxygen hood | 30–100% at 8–10 L/min | Used for infants and young children<br>Provides cooled humid air<br>Check $O_2$ concentration with $O_2$ analyzer every 4 hours<br>Refill humidity jar with sterile distilled water<br>Clean humidity jar daily<br>Cover client with light blanket and towel or cap for head<br>Change linen frequently<br>Monitor client's temperature frequently |

| Table 2  HAZARDS OF OXYGEN ADMINISTRATION | |
|---|---|
| COMPLICATION | NURSING CONSIDERATIONS |
| Infection | Change masks, tubing, mouthpieces daily |
| Drying and irritation of mucosa | Administer humidified oxygen |
| Respiratory depression ($CO_2$ narcosis) | Monitor respiratory rates frequently<br>Alternate between breathing room air and $O_2$ at prescribed intervals<br>Administer mixed $O_2$ (air and $O_2$) rather than pure $O_2$<br>Administer minimal concentrations necessary<br>Periodically inflate the lungs fully |
| Oxygen toxicity | Premature infants exposed to excessive amounts of $O_2$ for prolonged periods may develop retinopathy of prematurity (ROP); may result in irreversible blindness from vasoconstriction of the retinal blood vessels<br>Lungs of clients on respirators (children and adults) are most susceptible to pulmonary damage<br>Pulmonary damage includes atelectasis, exudation of protein fluid into alveoli, damage to and proliferation of pulmonary capillaries, and interstitial hemorrhage<br>Early symptoms include cough, nasal congestion, sore throat, reduced vital capacity, and substernal discomfort |
| Combustion | Be sure electrical plugs and equipment are properly grounded<br>Enforce no-smoking rules<br>Do not use oils on the client or on $O_2$ equipment |

## ▶ CHEST TUBES

**A.** Intrapleural drainage system with one or more chest catheters held in pleural space by suture to chest wall, attached to drainage system

**B.** Nursing care (see Figures 1 and 2)

1. Fill water-seal chamber with sterile water to the level specified by manufacturer

2. If suction is to be used, fill the suction control chamber with sterile water to the 20-cm level, or as ordered by the health care provider

3. Encourage the client to change position and cough and deep breathe frequently

4. The drainage system must be maintained below the level of insertion, without kinks in tubing

5. Chest tubes are clamped *only momentarily* to check for air leaks and to change the drainage apparatus

6. Observe for fluctuations of fluid in water-seal chamber; stops fluctuating when:

   a. Lung re-expands

   b. Tubing is obstructed

   c. Loop hangs below rest of tubing

**Figure 1  Chest Tubes**

**Figure 2  Pleur-evac**

**C.** Removal of the chest tube

1. Instruct the client to do the Valsalva maneuver (forcibly bear down while holding breath)

2. Chest tube is clamped and quickly removed by the health care provider

3. Occlusive dressing is applied to the site

**D.** Complications

1. Observe for constant bubbling in the water-seal chamber; this indicates air leak in the drainage system; report to health care provider

2. If the chest tube becomes dislodged, apply pressure over the insertion site with a dressing that is tented on one side to allow for the escape of air; immediately report to health care provider

3. If the tube becomes disconnected from the drainage system, cut the contaminated tip off of the tubing, insert a sterile connector, and reattach to the drainage system; otherwise immerse the end of the chest tube in 2 cm of sterile water until the system can be re-established; report to health care provider.

# ▶ CENTRAL VENOUS PRESSURE (CVP)

**A.** Purpose

1. Measurement of effective blood volume and efficiency of cardiac pumping

2. Indicates ability of right side of heart to manage a fluid load

3. Guide to fluid replacement

**B.** Equipment

1. Central line threaded into right atrium

2. Water manometer with three-way stopcock

3. IV fluids

**C.** Procedure (see Figure 3)

1. Client has catheter in jugular, subclavian, or antecubital vein

2. Attach manometer to a three-way stopcock that also connects IV to central catheter

3. Zero on manometer placed at the phlebostatic axis—line from fourth intercostal space at point where it joins the sternum and a line midway between the anterior and posterior surface of the chest at the outermost point of the sternum

4. Measured with client flat in bed or elevated up to 45°

5. Stopcock opened to the manometer, which allows for filling with IV fluid to level of 18–20 cm

6. Stopcock turned to allow for fluid in manometer to flow to client

7. Level of fluid fluctuates with respirations

8. When level stabilizes, reading is taken at highest level of fluctuation

9. Return stopcock to proper position and adjust IV flow rate

10. Normal reading: 4–12 mm Hg

    a. Elevated: greater than 12 mm hypervolemia or poor cardiac contractility

    b. Lowered: less than 4 mm hypovolemia

**Figure 3  Central Venous Pressure**

**D.** Potential complications

   1. Pneumothorax from catheter insertion

   2. Air embolism

   3. Infection at insertion site

**E.** Nursing care

   1. Dry, sterile dressing

   2. Change dressing, IV fluid bag, manometer, and tubing every 24 hours

   3. Instruct client to hold breath (Valsalva maneuver) when inserted and withdrawn or when tubing is changed to prevent air embolism

   4. Check and secure all connections

## ▶ EAR PROCEDURES

**A.** Ear irrigations

   1. Tilt head toward side of affected ear, gently direct stream of fluid against sides of canal

   2. After procedure, instruct client to lie on affected side to facilitate drainage

   3. Contraindicated if there is evidence of swelling or tenderness

B. Ear drops

  1. Position the affected ear uppermost

  2. Pull outer ear upward and backward for adult

  3. Pull outer ear downward and backward for child

  4. Place drops so they run down the wall of ear canal

  5. Have client lie on unaffected ear to encourage absorption

# ▶ EYE PROCEDURES

A. Eye irrigation

  1. Tilt head back and toward the side of affected area

  2. Allow irrigating fluid to flow from the inner to the outer canthus

  3. Use a small bulb syringe or eye dropper to dispense fluid

  4. Place small basin close to head to collect excess fluid and drainage

B. Eyedrop instillation

  1. Equipment must be sterile

    a. Wash hands, before instillation

    b. Do not allow dropper to touch eye

    c. Do not allow drops from eye to flow across nose into opposite eye

  2. Tilt head back and look up; pull lid down

  3. Place drops into center of lower conjunctival sac

    a. Instruct client not to squeeze eye

    b. Teach client to blink between drops

  4. To prevent systemic absorption, press the inner canthus near the bridge of the nose for 1–2 minutes

# ▶ NASOGASTRIC TUBES

A. Types

  1. Levin—single-lumen stomach tube used to remove stomach contents or provide tube feeding

  2. Salem sump—double-lumen stomach tube; most frequently used tube for decompression with suction

  3. Sengstaken-Blakemore—triple-lumen gastric tube with inflatable esophagus balloon, stomach ballon, gastric suction lumen used for treatment of bleeding esophageal varices

  4. Keofeed/Dobhoff—soft silicone rubber, medium-length tube used for long-term feedings; placement verified by x-ray; takes 24 hours to pass from stomach into intestines; lay on right side to facilitate passage

  5. Cantor—single-lumen tube with mercury-filled balloon and suction port

  6. Miller-Abbott—double-lumen tube with mercury-filled balloon and suction

  7. Harris—single-lumen tube with mercury-filled balloon and suction port

B. Insertion of Levin/Salem sump

  1. Measure distance from tip of nose to earlobe plus distance from earlobe to bottom of xiphoid process

2. Mark distance on tube with tape and lubricate end of tube with water-soluble jelly

3. Insert tube through the nose to the stomach

4. Offer sips of water and advance the tube gently; bend the head forward (closes the epiglottis, closing the trachea)

5. Observe for respiratory distress, an indication that tube is misplaced in the lungs; if in correctly, secure tube with hypoallergenic tape

C. Verify placement of tube initially and before administering feeding

1. X-ray is only sure way to verify placement

2. Aspirate gastric contents

3. Observe color–gastric aspirate usually cloudy and green but may also be off-white, tan, bloody, or brown

4. Measure pH of aspirate

   a. Gastric–usually less than or equal to 4

   b. Intestinal–usually greater than 4

   c. Respiratory–usually greater than 5.5

D. Nursing care of Levin/Salem pump

1. Check residual before intermittent feeding and q 4 hours with continuous feeding; hold feeding if more than 100 mL

2. Instill 15–30 mL saline or water according to agency policy

   a. Before and after each dose of medications and each tube feeding

   b. After checking residuals and pH

   c. Every 46 hours with continuous feedings

   d. When feeding is discontinued

3. Control rate of feeding–use enteral pump or count drops in gravity administration

4. Administer fluid at room temperature

5. Change bag every 24–72 hours

6. Elevate head of bed 30° while feeding is running and for 30 min after feeding

7. Check patency every 4 h; document drainage

8. Measure I and O

9. Good mouth care, lubricate tube around nares with water-soluble jelly

10. Hang the amount of fluid that will be infused in 4 hours

E. Irrigation of Levin/Salem sump

1. Verify placement of tube

2. Insert 30–50 mL syringe filled with normal saline into tube, inject slowly

3. If resistance felt, check to see if tube is kinked, have client change position

4. Pull back on plunger or bulb to withdraw solution; if irrigating solution not removed, record as input

5. Repeat if needed

**F.** Removal of Levin/Salem sump

1. Clamp tube, remove tape

2. Instruct client to exhale and remove tube with smooth, continuous pull

**G.** Insertion of intestinal tubes (Cantor, Miller-Abbott, Harris)

1. Mechanical passage into stomach; same as NG tube

2. Passage of tube along intestines is aided by gravity, weight of mercury, and peristalsis

3. After tube is in stomach, have client lie on right side, then on back (in Fowler's position), and then on left side to use gravity to position tube

4. Position of tube is ascertained by x-ray—do not tape tube to face, but coil loosely on bed

5. Position of tube and absence of telescoping of bowel from weight of tube is ascertained daily by x-ray

**H.** Nursing care of intestinal tubes

1. Measure drainage every shift

2. General care of client with NG tube

3. Report signs of return of peristalsis, e.g., bowel sounds, flatus

**I.** Removal of intestinal tubes

1. Clamp tube, remove tape

2. Deflate balloon or aspirate contents of intestine tube balloon

3. Instruct client to exhale

4. Remove 6 inches every 10 minutes until it reaches stomach, then remove completely with smooth continuous pull

## ▶ SURGICAL DRAINS

| Table 3 SURGICAL DRAINS | | |
|---|---|---|
| TYPE | DESCRIPTION | NURSING CONSIDERATIONS |
| Penrose | Simple latex drain | Note location<br>Usually not sutured in place, but layered in gauze dressing<br>Expect drainage on dressing |
| T tube | Used after gallbladder surgery<br>Placed in common bile duct to allow passage of bile | Monitor drainage<br>Fasten tubing to dressings<br>Keep below waist<br>May clamp for 1 hour before and after each meal<br>May be discharged with T tube in place<br>Remove 7–14 days<br>Teach client about care |

| Table 3  SURGICAL DRAINS *(CONTINUED)* | | |
|---|---|---|
| TYPE | DESCRIPTION | NURSING CONSIDERATIONS |
| Jackson-Pratt | Portable wound self-suction device with reservoir | Monitor amount and character of drainage<br><br>Notify health care provider if it suddenly increases or becomes bright red |
| Hemovac | Larger portable wound self-suction device with reservoir<br><br>Used after mastectomy | Monitor and record amount and character of drainage<br><br>Notify health care provider if it suddenly increases or becomes bright red<br><br>Empty when full or every 8 h<br><br>Remove plug (maintain sterility), empty contents, place on flat surface, cleanse opening and plug with alcohol sponge, compress evacuator completely to remove air, replace plug, check system for operation |

## ▶ ENEMAS

A. Types

1. Oil retention—softens feces

2. Soapsuds—irritates colon, causing reflux evacuation

3. Tap water—softens feces, stimulating evacuation, volume expander

B. Procedure—instillation of solution into rectum and sigmoid colon; promote defecation by stimulating peristalsis

1. Explain procedure to client

2. Position in Sims' position with right knee flexed

3. Use tepid solution

4. Hold irrigation set at 12–18 inches for high enema, 3 inches for low enema

5. Insert tube no more than 3–4 inches for adult, 2–3 inches for child, 1–1.5 inches for infant

6. Ask client to retain solution for 5–10 minutes

7. Do not administer in presence of abdominal pain, nausea, vomiting, or suspected appendicitis

## ▶ URINARY CATHETERS

A. Types of catheters (see Table 4)

B. Procedure for catheterization

1. Female

a. Explain procedure to client

b. Assemble equipment

c. Client should be placed in dorsal recumbent position or in Sims' position

    d. Drape client with sterile drapes using sterile technique

    e. Apply sterile gloves

    f. Lubricate catheter tip and place in sterile catheter tray

    g. Separate labia with thumb and forefinger and wipe from the meatus toward the rectum with sterile povidone-iodine swab and discard swab

    h. Insert catheter 2 to 3 inches into the urethra

    i. Insert catheter an additional inch after urine begins to flow to ensure balloon portion of catheter is in the bladder

    j. Inflate balloon

    k. Gently apply traction to the catheter

    l. Tape drainage tubing to client's thigh

  2. Male

    a. If uncircumcised, retract the foreskin to expose urinary meatus

    b. Cleanse glans and meatus with sterile povidone-iodine swabs in circular motion

    c. Hold penis perpendicular to the body; insert catheter into urethra 6–7 inches

    d. Replace the foreskin

| Table 4  URINARY CATHETERS | | |
|---|---|---|
| **TYPE** | **CHARACTERISTICS** | **COMMENTS** |
| Whistle-tip | Straight | For blood clot removal |
| Coude | Curved | For BPH to avoid prostate trauma |
| Robinson | Hollow—2 openings | For intermittent catheterizations |
| Filiform | Stiff | For urethral strictures |
| Foley | Double lumen with inflatable balloon toward tip | Indwelling for urinary drainage |
| Pezzer | Mushroom tip, otherwise like a Foley | Indwelling for urinary drainage |
| Malecot | Wing-shaped tip | Used as nephrostomy tube—anchored in renal pelvis through flank incision |
| Suprapubic | Placed in bladder via abdominal incision Dressing over site | Used in conjunction with urethral drainage |

    e. Inflate balloon

    f. Gently apply traction to the catheter until resistance is felt, indicating the catheter is at the base of the bladder

    g. Tape drainage tubing to client's thigh

**C.** Principles of drainage system care

  1. Catheter should not be disconnected from drainage system, except to perform ordered irrigations

2. Urine samples should be obtained from drainage port with a small-bore needle using sterile technique; clamp tubing below port

3. Drainage bags should not be elevated above level of cavity being drained (to prevent reflux)

4. Avoid kinks in tubing

5. Avoid removing more than 1000 mL at one time; if more urine in bladder clamp after 1000 mL, wait 15–30 min, then continue or follow facility policy.

6. Coil excess tubing on bed

**D.** Catheter irrigation

1. Purpose—prevent obstruction of flow and catheter or remove buildup of sediment in long-term use

2. Procedure—urethral catheter irrigation

   a. Closed urethral catheter irrigation

      1) Draw solution into syringe using sterile technique

      2) Clamp catheter below injection port

      3) Cleanse port with antiseptic swab

      4) Insert needle into injection port at 30° angle

      5) Slowly inject fluid

      6) Withdraw needle

      7) Remove clamp

      8) Solution drains into the bag

   b. Open urethral catheter irrigation

      1) Use sterile technique

      2) Cleanse around catheter; disconnect tubing

      3) Gently instill 30 mL of solution

      4) Allow fluid to drain by gravity into sterile basin

      5) If solution is easily instilled but does not return, have client turn to side; if still doesn't return, depress the syringe bulb to provide gentle suction

      6) Disinfect ends of catheter tubing and reconnect

**E.** Nursing care

1. Use aseptic technique on insertion

2. Do not disturb integrity of closed drainage system

3. Check for kinks

4. Perineal care with soap and water 2–3 times daily, then apply antimicrobial ointment to insertion site

5. Keep urine collection bag below the level of the urinary bladder

6. Secure to leg to prevent traction

7. Monitor I and O; minimum urinary drainage catheter output should be 30 mL/h

8. Monitor for signs and symptoms of infection (foul-smelling urine with pus, blood, or mucus streaks)

9. Adhere to special precautions for type of catheter used

    a. Ureterostomy tube—never irrigate

    b. Straight catheter—do not remove more than 1,000 mL at one time

    c. Nephrostomy tube—never clamp

10. Clamp indwelling catheters intermittently prior to removal

F. Intermittent self-catheterization

1. Used to treat neurogenic bladder caused by spinal cord injury, multiple sclerosis (MS), brain injury

    a. Caused by neurologic conditions: spinal cord injury, multiple sclerosis (MS), brain injury

2. Preparation

    a. Gather equipment

        1) Straight or curved-tip 12 or 14 Fr Tiemann catheter (most common for male clients)

        2) Clean container or plastic bag

        3) Water-soluble lubricant

        4) Washcloth with soap and water

        5) Container for urine

    b. Wash hands

    c. Wash catheter with warm water and soap, rinse, and dry completely

3. Insertion

    a. Clear perineum with soap and water

    b. Lubricate catheter with water-soluble lubricant

    c. Locate catheter insertion point

        1) Female: combination visualization and palpation

        2) Male: visualize penile meatus

    d. Insert catheter slowly until urine returns, then advance 1/2–1 inch

    e. Press down with abdominal muscles to promote complete emptying

    f. Once bladder is drained, remove gently

    g. Immediately rinse catheter with cool tap water to remove residue, dry thoroughly

    h. Wash hands

4. Client teaching

    a. Should be done every 4–6 hours

    b. Should be performed at consistent times daily

    c. Uses clean technique, not sterile technique

    d. Removes 350–400 ml each time

    e. Performed in a comfortable postition, sitting or standing

    f. Use catheter for 2–4 weeks and then discard

    g. Store catheter in sandwich-sized bag or clean container

    h. Never store catheter wet or in antiseptic solution

    i. Should drink 250 ml at 2-hour intervals or up to 2 L at regular intervals

# Chapter 5

## PHYSIOLOGICAL INTEGRITY: PHYSIOLOGICAL ADAPTATION

| Sections | Concepts Covered |
|---|---|
| 1. Medical Emergencies | Perfusion, Gas Exchange, Intracranial Regulation, Client Education: Providing |
| 2. Fluid and Electrolyte Imbalances | Fluid and Electrolyte Balance, Skin Integrity |
| 3. Alterations in Body Systems | Perfusion, Gas Exchange, Intracranial Regulation, Client Education: Providing |
| 4. Cancer | Cellular Regulation |

## ▶ UPPER AIRWAY OBSTRUCTION

**A.** Assessment

　1. Inability to breathe or speak

　2. Cyanosis

　3. Collapse

　4. Death can occur within 4–5 minutes

**B.** Diagnose—potential nursing diagnosis

　1. Airway clearance, ineffective

**C.** Planning/Implementation

　1. If conscious

　　a. Assess client's ability to speak and or cough

　　b. Give 5 back blows between shoulder blade with heel of hand (per American Red Cross)

　　c. Give 5 abdominal thrusts (Heimlich maneuver)

　　d. Alternate between 5 back blows and 5 thrusts until the blockage is dislodged

　2. If unconscious

　　a. Begin CPR

　　b. Remove object if it becomes visible

　3. Intubation (see Table 1 and Figure 1)

| Table 1  AIRWAY INTUBATION | |
| --- | --- |
| **METHOD** | **NURSING CONSIDERATIONS** |
| Endotracheal tube—tube passed through the nose or mouth into the trachea | Assess for bilateral breath sounds and bilateral chest excursion<br>Mark tube at level it touches mouth or nose<br>Secure with tape to stabilize<br>Encourage fluids to facilitate removal of secretions |
| Tracheostomy—surgical incision made into trachea via the throat; tube inserted through incision into the trachea | Cuff is used to prevent aspiration and to facilitate mechanical ventilation<br>Maintain cuff pressure at 14–20 mm Hg<br>Encourage fluids to facilitate removal of secretions<br>Sterile suctioning if necessary<br>Frequent oral hygiene<br>Indications for suctioning tracheostomy<br>　• Noisy respirations<br>　• Restlessness<br>　• Increased pulse<br>　• Increased respirations<br>　• Presence of mucus in airway |

**Figure 1    Endotracheal Tube**

4.  Tracheostomy (see Table 1 and Figure 2)

**Figure 2    Tracheostomy Tube**

5.  Suctioning

6.  Mechanical ventilation

    a.  Prepare client psychologically for use of ventilator

    b.  Monitor client's response to the ventilator

        1)  Assess vital signs at least q 4 hours

        2)  Listen to breath sounds (crackles, wheezes, equal breath sounds, decreased or absent breath sounds)

        3)  Assess need for suctioning

        4)  Respiratory monitoring

        5)  Evaluate ABGs, continuous pulse oximetry monitoring

        6)  Check for hypoxia (restlessness, cyanosis, anxiety, tachycardia, increased respiratory rate)

        7)  Check neurologic status

        8)  Check chest for bilateral expansion

    c.  Provide good oral hygiene at least twice each shift

    d.  Assess need for tracheal/oral/nasal suctioning q 2 hours and perform as necessary

    e.  Move endotracheal tube to opposite side of mouth q 24 hours to prevent ulcers

    f.  Monitor intake and output

    g.  Create alternative methods of communication with client (letter board, pencil and paper); provide access to call light

    h. Perform and document ventilator and equipment checks—care for client first, ventilator second

        1) Check ventilator settings as ordered by health care provider—tidal volume (TV), respiratory rate, $pO_2$ (fraction of inspired oxygen), mode of ventilation, sigh button/cycle (usually 1–3/h) (may cause lung damage from excessive pressure)

        2) Check that alarms are set (low pressure and low exhaled volume)

        3) Check temperature and level of water in humidification system

        4) Check PEEP (positive end-expiratory pressure) maintained at end of expiration to open collapsed alveoli and improve oxygenation

        5) Drain condensation from tubing away from client

        6) Verify that tracheostomy or endotracheal cuff is inflated to ensure tidal volume

    i. Observe for gastrointestinal distress (diarrhea, constipation, tarry stools)

    j. Document observations/procedures in medical record

  7. Oxygen administration

**D.** Evaluation

  1. Does respiratory rate return to normal?

  2. Is client able to speak?

# ▶ CARDIOPULMONARY ARREST

**A.** Assessment

  1. Breathless

  2. Pulseless

  3. Unconscious

**B.** Diagnose

  1. Failure to institute ventilation within 4–6 minutes will result in cerebral anoxia and brain damage

  2. Purpose—to re-establish $CO_2/O_2$ exchange and adequate circulation

**C.** Plan/Implementation

  1. Basic Life Support

    a. Recognition

        1) All ages: unresponsive

        2) Adults: no breathing or no normal breathing (i.e., only gasping)

        3) Children and infants: no breathing or only gasping

        4) No pulse palpated within 10 seconds (HCP only)

    b. Activate EMS system

    c. CPR sequence: C-A-B

    d. Compression rate: at least 100/minute

    e. Compression depth

       1) Adults: at least 2 inches (5 cm)

       2) Children: at least ½ anterior posterior diameter or about 2 inches (5 cm)

       3) Infants: at least ¼ anterior posterior diameter or about 1 ½ inches (4 cm)

    f. Chest wall recoil

       1) Allow complete recoil between compressions

       2) HCPs rotate compressors every 2 minutes

    g. Compression interruptions

       1) Minimize interruptions in chest compressions

       2) Attempt to limit interruptions to less than 10 seconds

    h. Airway

       1) Head tilt-chin lift

       2) HCP suspected trauma; jaw thrust

    i. Compression-to-ventilation ratio (until advance airway placed)

       1) Adult: 30:2; 1 or 2 rescuers

       2) Children and infants: 30:2 single rescuer; 15:2 2 HCP rescuers

    j. Ventilations when rescuer untrained or trained and not proficient: compressions only

    k. Ventilations with advanced airway (HCP)

       1) 1 breath every 6–8 seconds (8–10 breaths/minute)

       2) Asynchronous with chest compressions

       3) About 1 second per breath

       4) Visible chest rise

    l. Defibrillation

       1) Attach and use AED as soon as possible

       2) Minimize compressions before and after shock

       3) Resume CPR beginning with compressions immediately after each shock

  2. Continue CPR until one of the following occurs

    a. Victim responds

    b. Another qualified person takes over

    c. Victim is transferred to an emergency room

    d. Rescuer is physically unable to continue

**D.** Evaluation

  1. Has cardiac function been re-established?

  2. Has cerebral anoxia been prevented?

# ► CROUP SYNDROMES: ACUTE EPIGLOTTITIS, ACUTE LARYNGOTRACHEOBRONCHITIS

**A.** Assessment

1. Barklike cough, use of accessory muscles
2. Dyspnea, inspiratory stridor, cyanosis
3. Decrease in noisy respirations may indicate decompensation

**B.** Diagnose

1. Viral—infection in the area of the larynx
2. Medical emergency due to narrowed airway in children
3. Potential nursing diagnoses
   a. Risk for suffocation
   b. Anxiety

**C.** Plan/Implementation

1. Care at home
   a. Steamy shower
   b. Sudden exposure to cold air
   c. Sleep with cool humidified air
2. Hospitalization required
   a. Increasing respiratory distress
   b. Hypoxia or depressed sensorium
   c. High temperature (102°F)
3. Nursing care if hospitalized
   a. Maintain airway (keep tracheostomy set at bedside)
   b. Oxygen hood
   c. Monitor heart rate and respiration for early sign of hypoxia
   d. Oxygen with humidification
   e. IV fluids
   f. Medications—antipyretics, bronchodilators, nebulized epinephrine, steroids
   g. Position in infant seat or prop with pillow

**D.** Evaluation

1. Does the child have adequate respirations and airway clearance?
2. Is there a reduction in the child's anxiety?

# ► MYOCARDIAL INFARCTION (MI)

**A.** Assessment

1. Symptoms vary depending on whether pain, shock, or pulmonary edema dominates clinical picture
2. Chest pain—severe, crushing, prolonged; unrelieved by rest or nitroglycerin; often radiating to one or both arms, jaw, neck, and back (see Figure 3); women may present with atypical symptoms (fatigue, shortness of breath)

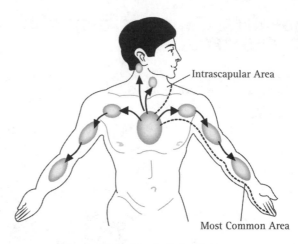

**Figure 3  Ischemic Pain Patterns**

3. Dyspnea

4. Nausea, vomiting, gastric discomfort, indigestion

5. Apprehension, restless, fear of death

6. Acute pulmonary edema, sense of suffocating

7. Cardiac arrest

8. Shock—systolic blood pressure below 80 mm Hg, gray facial color, lethargy, cold diaphoresis, peripheral cyanosis, tachycardia or bradycardia, weak pulse

9. Oliguria—urine output of less than 20 ml/hour

10. Low-grade fever—temperature rises to 100°–103°F (38°–39° C) within 24 hours and lasts 3 to 7 days

11. Dysrhythmias, heart block, asystole

12. WBC—leukocytosis within 2 days, disappears in 1 week

13. Erythrocyte sedimentation rate (ESR)—elevated

14. CK–MB—first enzyme tube to be elevated after MI; appears 3–6 hours; peaks 18–24 hours

15. LDH—appears 12–24 hours; peaks 48–72 hours; lasts 6–12 days

16. Troponin—peaks in 4–12 hours; remains elevated for up to 2–3 weeks

17. Myoglobin—begins to rise within 1 hour; peaks in 4–6 hours; returns to normal in less than 24 hours

18. Electrocardiogram—ST segment elevation, T wave inversion, Q wave formation

**B.** Diagnose

1. Formation of localized necrotic areas within the myocardium, usually following the sudden occlusion of a coronary artery and the abrupt decrease of blood and oxygen to the heart muscle

2. Causes

a. Complete or near complete occlusion of a coronary vessel (most common)

b. Decreased blood and oxygen supply to the heart muscle; vasospasm

    c. Hypertrophy of the heart muscle from CHF or hypertension

    d. Embolism to a coronary artery

  3. Potential nursing diagnoses

    a. Risk for decreased cardiac output

    b. Anxiety/fear

    c. Deficient knowledge

**C.** Plan/Implementation

  1. Provide thrombolytic therapy—streptokinase or tissue-type plasminogen activator (t-PA) to dissolve thrombus in coronary artery within 6 hours of onset

  2. Relieve client's and family's anxiety

  3. Bedrest to decrease stress on heart, allow to use bedside commode for bowel movement; semifowler's position

  4. Monitor vital signs, pain status, lung sounds, level of consciousness, ECG, oxygen saturation

  5. Monitor intake and output

    a. Intake—fluid intake 2,000 ml daily; too much may precipitate CHF, and too little may result in dehydration

    b. Output—Foley catheter, if necessary; oliguria indicates inadequate renal perfusion, concentrated urine indicates dehydration

  6. Carefully monitor IV infusion—vein should be kept open in case emergency IV drugs are necessary

  7. Administer medications: beta blockers (e.g., propranolol), morphine sulfate for pain (reduces preload, afterload pressures, and decreases anxiety), antidysrhythmics (e.g., lidocaine, verapamil, solalol, propafenone), anticoagulant medications (e.g., heparin, warfarin)

  8. Administer oxygen

  9. Prevent complications

    a. Dysrhythmias

    b. Shock

    c. Congestive heart failure

    d. Rupture of heart muscle

    e. Pulmonary embolism

    f. Recurrent MI

 10. Teaching

    a. Healing not complete for 6–8 weeks

    b. Modify lifestyle

      1) Stop smoking

      2) Reduce stress

      3) Decrease caffeine

      4) Modify intake of calories, sodium, and fat

    c. Maintain regular physical activity

    d. Medication schedule and adverse effects

**D.** Evaluation

1. Does client experience relief of pain and reduction in anxiety?
2. Does client institute lifestyle changes to decrease stress?
3. Does client comply with medication, diet, and activity recommendations?

## ▶ RHYTHM DISTURBANCES (DYSRHYTHMIAS)

**A.** Assessment

1. Dizziness, syncope
2. Chest pain, palpitations, abnormal heart sounds
3. Nausea, vomiting
4. Dyspnea
5. Abnormal pulse rate—increased, decreased, or irregular

**B.** Diagnose

1. Caused by interruption in normal conduction process
2. Can occur at any point in the normal conduction pathway
3. Types of dysrhythmias

   a. <u>Sinus dysrhythmias</u>—dysrhythmias originate in the sinoatrial node and are conducted along the normal conductive pathways

      1) *Tachycardia*—sympathetic nervous system increases the automaticity of the SA node

         a) Heart rate is increased above 100 beats per minute

         b) Causes—pain, exercise, hypoxia, pulmonary embolism, hemorrhage, hyperthyroidism, or fever

         c) Symptoms—dizziness, dyspnea, hypotension, palpitations

Rules for Sinus Tachycardia

         d) Treatment—treat underlying problem, beta blockers (metoprolol), calcium channel blockers (diltiazem), or cardio version

      2) *Bradycardia*—parasympathetic nervous system (vagal stimulation) causes automaticity of the SA node to be depressed

         a) Heart rate decreased to below 60 beats per minute

         b) Causes—myocardial infarction, the Valsalva maneuver, or vomiting, arteriosclerosis in the carotid sinus area, ischemia of SA node, hypothermia, hyperkalemia, or drugs such as digitalis and propranolol

c)  Symptoms—Pale, cool, hypotension, syncope, dyspnea, weakness

Rules for Sinus Bradycardia

d)  Treatment—Atropine or possible pacemaker

b.  <u>Atrial dysrhythmias</u>—abnormal electrical activity that results in stimulation outside the SA node but within the atria

1)  *Premature atrial contractions (PAC)*

a)  Ectopic focus within one of the atria fires prematurely

b)  Causes—Normal phenomenon in some individuals, but may be caused by emotional disturbances, fatigue, tobacco, or caffeine

c)  Symptoms—"sense of skipped beat"

Rules for Premature Atrial Contraction

d)  Treatment—treat the underlying cause

2)  *Atrial flutter*

a)  Arises from an ectopic focus in the atrial wall causing the atrium to contract 250–400 times per minute (AV node blocks most of the impulses, thereby protecting the ventricles from receiving every impulse)

b)  Causes—stress, hypoxia, drugs, or disorders such as chronic heart disease, hypertension

c)  Symptoms—chest discomfort, dyspnea, hypotension

Rules for Atrial Flutter

    d) Treatment—Vagal maneuvers, adenosine, cardioversion or ablation

  3) *Atrial fibrillation*

    a) Uncoordinated atrial electrical activation that causes a rapid, disorganized uncoordinated twitching of the atrial muscle. (Most common atrial dysrhythmia) (presents with a grossly irregular pulse rate)

    b) Causes—chronic lung disease, heart failure, and rheumatic heart disease, chronic hypertension

    c) Symptoms—stroke symptoms, hypotension, syncope, dyspnea

Rules for Fibrillation

    d) Treatment—address underlying cause, calcium channel blockers (diltiazem), beta blockers (metoprolol), digoxin, cardioversion, warfarin

 c. <u>Ventricular dysrhythmias</u>—occur when one or more ectopic foci arise within the ventricles

  1) *Premature ventricular contractions (PVCs)*

    a) One or more ectopic foci stimulate a premature ventricular response

    b) Causes—ischemia due to a myocardial infarction, infection, mechanical damage due to pump failure, deviations in concentrations of electrolytes (e.g., potassium, calcium), nicotine, coffee, tea, alcohol, drugs such as digitalis and reserpine, psychogenic factors (stress, anxiety, fatigue), and acute or chronic lung disease

    c) Symptoms—Angina, shortness of breath, "heart flip" feeling

Rules for Premature Ventricular Contractions

   d) Treatment—amiodarone, beta blockers (metoprolol), procainamide

2) *Ventricular tachycardia*

   a) Three or more PVCs occurring in a row at a rate exceeding 100 bpm (severe myocardial irritability)

   b) Causes—large MI, low ejection fraction, same as for PVCs

   c) Symptoms—hypotension, pulmonary edema, confusion, cardiac arrest

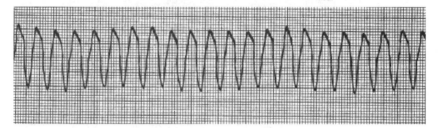

Rules for Ventricular Tachycardia

   d) Treatment—determine if monomorphic (procainamide, sotalol, amiodarone) or polymorphic (magnesium, isoproterenol), pulseless (CPR, defibrillation, epinephrine, amiodarone)

3) *Ventricular fibrillation*

   a) Several ectopic foci within the ventricles are discharged at a very rapid rate. Most serious of all dysrhythmias because of potential cardiac standstill

   b) Causes—acute myocardial infarction, hypertension, rheumatic or arteriosclerotic heart disturbances, or hypoxia

   c) Symptoms—unresponsive, pulseless, apneic

Rules for Ventricular Fibrillation

d) Treatment—CPR; Unless blood flow is restored (by CPR) and the dysrhythmia is interrupted (by defibrillation), death will result within 90 seconds to 5 minutes

d. <u>Heart block</u>—delay in the conduction of impulses within the atrioventricular system

1) *First-degree block*

a) AV junction conducts all impulses, but at a slower-than-normal rate

b) Causes—digitalis, calcium channel blockers, beta blockers, MI, and/or increased vagal tone.

c) Symptoms—asymptomatic

Rules for First-Degree Heart Block

d) Treatment—Address underlying cause

2) *Second-degree block (Type I and Type II)*

a) AV junction conducts only some impulses arising in the atria

b) Causes—infections, digitalis toxicity, coronary artery disease

c) Symptoms—May note hypotension, dyspnea, syncope

Rules for Classic Second-Degree Heart Block

d) Treatment—Atropine, pacemaker

3) *Third-degree heart block*

a) AV junction blocks all impulses to the ventricles, causing the atria and ventricles to dissociate and beat independently (each with its own pacemaker establishing a rate, ventricular rate is low, 20 to 40 beats per minute)

b) Causes—congenital defects, vascular insufficiency, fibrosis of the myocardial tissue, or myocardial infarction

c) Symptoms—shock symptoms, syncope

Rules for Third-Degree Heart Block

d) Treatment—Pacemaker, atropine dopamine, epinephrine. If not treated immediately, may lead to death

4. Diagnostic tests

a. EKG (see Figure 4)

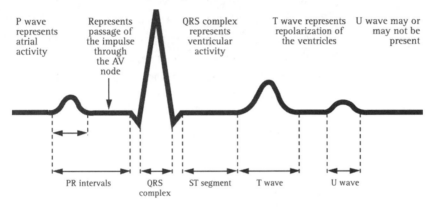

| P wave represents atrial activity | Represents passage of the impulse through the AV node | QRS complex represents ventricular activity | T wave represents repolarization of the ventricles | U wave may or may not be present |

PR intervals | QRS complex | ST segment | T wave | U wave

**Figure 4. Components of an EKG**

b. ABGs

c. Holter recorder

   1) 24-hour continuous EKG tracing

   2) Client keeps diary of activities

d. Cardiac catheterization and coronary angiography (see Reduction of Risk Potential)

e. Echocardiogram—noninvasive, sound waves used to examine cardiac structures

f. Stress testing—client walks on treadmill, pedals stationary bicycle, or climbs set of stairs, EKG monitored before, during, and after exercise testing

**C.** Plan/Implementation

1. Vital signs

2. Frequent assessment of cardiac monitor

3. Administer medication as needed/ordered

4. Evaluateneed of oxygen

5. Cardiac monitor identifies changes in rhythm and rate (see Figure 5)

**Figure 5. Components of an EKG**

a. Determine rate

   1) Each small box = 0.04 seconds

   2) 1,500 small boxes = 1 minute

   3) Each large box = 0.2 seconds (5 small boxes)

   4) 15 large boxes = 3 seconds

   5) EKG paper marked at 3-second intervals at top by vertical line

   6) If regular, count the number of 0.04–second intervals between two R waves, divide by 1,500

   7) If irregular, count the number of R-R intervals in 6 seconds, multiply by 10

b. Determine rhythm

   1) Presence or absence of P wave—SA node originated impulse

   2) Measure P-R interval—normal: 0.12–0.20 seconds (each small box = 0.04 seconds)

   3) Measure QRS duration—normal: 0.04–0.12 seconds

   4) Check P wave, QRS complex, ST segment, and T wave

| Table 2 DEFIBRILLATION VERSUS CARDIOVERSION | | |
|---|---|---|
| | **DEFIBRILLATION** | **CARDIOVERSION** |
| Indication | Emergency treatment of ventricular fibrillation | Elective procedure for dysrhythmias such as atrial fibrillation |
| Action | Completely depolarizes all myocardial cells so SA node can re-establish as pacemaker | Same |
| Nursing considerations | Start CPR before defibrillation<br><br>Plug in defibrillator and turn on<br><br>Turn on monitor and attach leads to client<br><br>Apply gel or paste to paddles (rub paddle surfaces together)<br><br>Select electric charge as ordered<br><br>Paddles placed over right sternal-border and over the apex of the heart<br><br>Person with paddles calls "all clear"<br><br>Push discharge button<br><br>Check monitor between shocks for rhythm<br><br>Don't stop to check pulse after shocks, continue CPR, intubate, start IV<br><br>Epinephrine given 1 mg IV push every 3–5 minutes<br><br>Sodium bicarbonate given to treat acidosis | Informed consent<br><br>Diazepam IV<br><br>Digoxin withheld for 48 hours prior to procedure<br><br>Synchronizer turned on, check at the R wave<br><br>Oxygen discontinued<br><br>Assess airway patency<br><br>Plug in defibrillator and turn on<br><br>Turn on oscilloscope and attach leads to client<br><br>Apply gel or paste (rub paddle surfaces together)<br><br>Voltage 25–360 joules<br><br>Paddles placed over right sternal border and over the apex of the heart<br><br>Person with paddles calls "all clear"<br><br>Push discharge button<br><br>Check monitor between shocks for rhythm<br><br>After procedure, assess vital signs every 15 minutes for 1 hour; every 30 minutes for 2 hours; then every 4 hours |

   c. Medications

     1) Antiarrhythmics (e.g., lidocaine, quinidine, procanimide)

     2) Antilipid medications (e.g., lovastatin, cholestyramine)

6. Defibrillation (see Table 2)

7. Pacemakers—apparatus used to initiate heartbeat when the SA node is seriously damaged and unable to act as a pacemaker (see Table 3)

| Table 3 PACEMAKERS | | | |
|---|---|---|---|
| TYPES | ACTION | COMPLICATIONS | NURSING CONSIDERATIONS |
| Demand (synchronous; noncompetitive) | Functions when heart rate goes below set rate | Dislodgement and migration of endocardial leads | Assess for infection, bleeding |
| Fixed rate (asynchronous; competitive) | Stimulates ventricle at preset constant rate | Wire breakage | Monitor heart rate and rhythm; for preset rate pacemakers, client's rate may vary 5 beats above or below set rate |
| Temporary | Used in emergency situations (after MI with heart block, cardiac arrest with bradycardia) | Cracking of insulation surrounding wires | Provide emotional support |
| | Inserted through peripheral vein, tip of catheter is placed at apex of right ventricle | Infection of sites surrounding either pacing wires or pulse generator | Check pulse daily, report any sudden increase or decrease in rate |
| Permanent | Lead is passed into right ventricle, or right atrium and right ventricle, and generator is implanted under skin below clavicle or in abdominal wall | Interference with pacemaker function by exposure to electromagnetic fields (old microwave ovens, MRI equipment, metal detectors at airports) | Carry ID card or wear identification |
| | | Perforation of myocardium or right ventricle | Request hand scanning at security check points at airports |
| | | Abrupt loss of pacing | Avoid situations involving electromagnetic fields |
| | | | Periodically check generator |
| | | | Take frequent rest periods at home and at work |
| | | | Wear loose clothing over area of pacemaker |
| | | | All electrical equipment used in vicinity of client should be properly grounded |
| | | | Immobilize extremity if temporary electrode pacemaker is used to prevent dislodgement |
| | | | Document model of pacemaker, date and time of insertion, location of pulse generator, stimulation threshold, pacer rate |
| | | | Place cell phone on side opposite generator |

D. Evaluation

1. Is client free from dysrhythmias as evidenced by stable vital signs?

2. Have complications been prevented?

## ▶ HEAD INJURY

A. Assessment

1. Skull fracture—Battle's sign (ecchymosis over mastoid bone), raccoon eyes (bilateral periorbital ecchymosis), rhinnorrhea, otorrhea

2. Concussion—transient mental confusion or loss of consciousness, headache, no residual neurological deficit, possible loss of memory surrounding event, long-term effects (lack of concentration, personality changes)

3. Contusion—varies from slight depression of consciousness to coma, with decorticate posturing (flexion and internal rotation of forearms and hands) or decerebrate posturing (extension of arms and legs, pronation of

arms, plantar flexion, opisthotonos), indicates deeper dysfunction, generalized cerebral edema

4. Laceration—penetrating trauma with bleeding

5. Hematoma

    a. Epidural—short period of unconsciousness, followed by lucid interval with ipsilateral pupillary dilation, weakness of contralateral extremities

    b. Subdural—decreased level of consciousness, ipsilateral pupillary dilation, contralateral weakness, personality changes

**B.** Diagnose

1. Skull is a closed vault with a volume ratio of three components: brain tissue, blood, and CSF; sudden increase in any of these can cause brain dysfunction

2. Ingestion of drugs and alcohol may delay manifestations of symptoms of damage

3. Generalized brain swelling occurs in response to injury

4. Diagnosed by x-ray, CT scan, lumbar puncture (LP), EEG, MRI

5. May be two points of impact of brain with skull

    a. Coup (direct impact)

    b. Contrecoup (rebound to skull wall opposite direct impact)

6. May cause twisting of brain stem

**C.** Plan/Implementation

1. Evaluate level of consciousness; check vital signs, pupil size, shape, equality, and reaction to light; check nose and ears for CSF leakage

2. Neurological assessment

3. Monitor level of consciousness, careful I and O

4. Seizure precautions, prophylactic anticonvulsants

5. Elevate the head of bed 30° to decrease intracranial pressure; monitor neurologic status after position change

6. Regulate hydration according to I and O, avoid overhydration

7. Prevent infection of open wound, keep dressing dry and intact

8. Manage increased intracranial pressure (ICP) and cerebral edema, administer glucocorticoids (e.g., dexamethasone), mannitol, furosemide

9. Hypothermia—to decrease metabolic demands

10. Barbiturate therapy—to decrease cerebral metabolic rate

11. Minimal procedures (e.g., suctioning, turning, positioning)

12. Prevent complications of immobility

**D.** Evaluation

1. Have complications been prevented?

2. Is client alert and oriented?

## ▶ CHEST TRAUMA

**A.** Assessment

1. Flail chest—affected side goes down with inspiration and up during expiration

2. Open pneumothorax

   a. Sucking sound on both inspiration and expiration

   b. Pain

   c. Hyperresonance

   d. Decreased respiratory excursion

   e. Diminished/absent breath sounds on affected side

   f. Weak, rapid pulse

   g. Anxiety, diaphoresis

   h. Altered ABGs

3. Pneumothorax

   a. Dyspnea, pleuritic pain

   b. Absent or restricted movement on affected side

   c. Decreased or absent breath sounds, cyanosis

   d. Cough and fever

   e. Hypotension

**B.** Diagnose

1. Flail chest—fracture of multiple adjacent ribs causing the chest wall to become unstable and respond paradoxically

2. Open pneumothorax—penetrating chest wound causing the intrapleural space to be open to atmospheric pressure and resulting in collapse of lung

3. Pneumothorax—collapse of lung due to air in the pleural space caused by surgery, disease, or trauma (see Figure 6)

   a. Spontaneous—without a known cause

   b. Tension—pressure builds up; shifting of heart and great vessels

   c. Hemothorax—blood in pleural space

**Figure 6. Pneumothorax and Hemothorax**

    4. Potential nursing diagnoses

        a. Ineffective breathing pattern

        b. Impaired gas exchange

        c. Anxiety

        d. Acute pain

**C.** Plan/Implementation

    1. Flail chest

        a. Monitor for shock

        b. Humidified $O_2$

        c. Pain management

        d. Monitor ABGs

        e. Encourage turning, deep breathing, and coughing

    2. Open pneumothorax

        a. Thoracentesis

        b. Chest tubes (see Reduction of Risk Potential)

**D.** Evaluation

    1. Has the client's breathing pattern returned to normal?

    2. Has the client's oxygenation been maintained?

## ▶ ABDOMINAL INJURIES

**A.** Assessment

    1. Penetrating—symptoms of hemorrhage

    2. Blunt—abdominal pain, rigidity, distension; nausea and vomiting; shock; ecchymosis (around umbilicus—Cullen's-sign; in either flank—Turner's sign) indicative of retroperitoneal bleeding; bruits indicate renal artery injury; resonance over spleen with client on left side (Balance's sign) indicates rupture of spleen; resonance over liver indicates pathology

    3. Diagnosis—X-ray, CT scan; exploratory laparotomy

**B.** Diagnose

    1. Penetrating—open wound resulting in hemorrhage if major blood vessels/ liver/spleen/pancreas/kidney are involved; increased risk of infection (peritonitis) from rupture of bowel

    2. Blunt—usually injury to solid organs (spleen, liver, pancreas)

**C.** Plan/Implementation

    1. Penetrating—NPO, NG tube, monitor drainage, bowel sounds; indwelling catheter, monitor output carefully, assess for hematuria

    2. Blunt—IV with large-bore needle in upper extremities; monitor CVP; check hematological values, ABGs, serum electrolytes, liver and kidney function, and clotting studies; cardiac monitor; indwelling catheter

**D.** Evaluation

    1. Has shock been prevented?

    2. Are client's vital signs stable?

# ▶ SHOCK

**A.** Assessment

1. Cool, clammy skin, cyanosis, decreased capillary refill
2. Restlessness, decreased alertness, anxiety
3. Weakness
4. Tachycardia, weak or absent pulse, decreased blood pressure
5. Metabolic acidosis
6. Oliguria, increased urine specific gravity
7. Respirations shallow, rapid
8. Increased muscle weakness

**B.** Diagnose

1. Sudden reduction of oxygen and nutrients; decreased blood volume causes a reduction in venous return, decreased cardiac output, and a decrease in arterial pressure

2. Types of shock

   a. Hypovolemic shock—loss of fluid from circulation

      1) Hemorrhagic shock (external or internal)

      2) Cutaneous shock, e.g., burns resulting in external fluid loss

      3) Diabetic ketoacidosis

      4) Gastrointestinal obstruction, e.g., vomiting and diarrhea

      5) Diabetes insipidus

      6) Excessive use of diuretics

      7) Internal sequestration, e.g., fractures, hemothorax, ascites

   b. Cardiogenic shock—decreased cardiac output

      1) Myocardial infarction

      2) Dysrhythmias

      3) Pump failure

   c. Distributive shock—inadequate vascular tone

      1) Neural-induced loss of vascular tone

         a) Anesthesia

         b) Pain

         c) Insulin shock

         d) Spinal cord injury

      2) Chemical-induced loss of vascular tone

         a) Toxic shock

         b) Anaphylaxis

         c) Capillary leak—burns, decreased serum protein levels

**C.** Plan/Implementation

1. Maintain adequate oxygenation
2. Increase tissue perfusion
3. Maintain systolic BP greater than 90 mm Hg
4. Treat acidosis

5.  Maintain patent airway

    a.  If necessary, ensure ventilation by Ambu bag or ventilator assistance

    b.  Provide supplemental oxygen to maintain adequate blood $pO_2$

6.  Indwelling catheter, hourly outputs

7.  Assess CVP

8.  Assess ABGs

9.  Treat acidosis

10. Keep warm (maintain body temperature)

11. Intravenous administration of blood or other appropriate fluids (plasma expanders, electrolyte solutions)

12. Large amounts of fluid may be pushed until systemic blood pressure, urine volume, and lactate levels return to a relatively normal level or central venous or pulmonary artery pressures, or both, become elevated

    a.  Crystalloids—normal saline, Ringer's lactate (isotonic)

    b.  Colloids—blood, packed red cells, plasma, plasma expanders e.g., hetastarch

13. Medications

    a.  Antibiotics—when shock is due to an infection (septic shock), antibiotic therapy should be instituted immediately; blood, urine, sputum, and drainage of any kind should be sent for culture and sensitivity (C and S); usually use combination of ampicillin, polymyxin, and cephalothin

    b.  Medications to vasoconstrict and improve myocardial contractility

    c.  Medications to maintain adequate urine output, e.g., mannitol, furosemide

    d.  Medications used to restore blood pressure, adrenergics/sympathomimetics (e.g., dobutamin hydrochloride)

    e.  Low-dose corticosteroids for septic shock

14. Infuse and assess large volumes of fluids

D.  Evaluation

    1.  Is client's systolic blood pressure maintained over 90 mm Hg?

    2.  Has the client's normal circulation been restored?

    3.  Is client's urinary output greater than 30 ml/hour?

## ▶ INCREASED INTRACRANIAL PRESSURE

A.  Assessment

    1.  Altered LOC—often earliest sign

    2.  Glasgow coma scale (see Table 4)

        a.  Level of consciousness

        b.  Score of 3–8 indicates severe head trauma; score of 15 indicates client is alert and oriented

| Table 4  GLASGOW COMA SCALE | | | | | | | | | | | | | | | | | | | |
|---|---|---|---|---|---|---|---|---|---|---|---|---|---|---|---|---|---|---|---|
| Eyes Open | Spontaneously | 4 | | | | | | | | | | | | | | | | | |
| | To speech | 3 | | | | | | | | | | | | | | | | | |
| | To pain | 2 | | | | | | | | | | | | | | | | | |
| | None | 1 | | | | | | | | | | | | | | | | | |
| Best Verbal Response | Oriented | 5 | | | | | | | | | | | | | | | | | |
| | Confused | 4 | | | | | | | | | | | | | | | | | |
| | Inappropriate words | 3 | | | | | | | | | | | | | | | | | |
| | Incomprehensible sounds | 2 | | | | | | | | | | | | | | | | | |
| | None | 1 | | | | | | | | | | | | | | | | | |
| Best Motor Response | Obeys commands | 6 | | | | | | | | | | | | | | | | | |
| | Localizes pain | 5 | | | | | | | | | | | | | | | | | |
| | Flexes to pain | 4 | | | | | | | | | | | | | | | | | |
| | Flexor posture | 3 | | | | | | | | | | | | | | | | | |
| | Extensor posture | 2 | | | | | | | | | | | | | | | | | |
| | No response | 1 | | | | | | | | | | | | | | | | | |

3. Confusion, restlessness (early signs)

4. Pupillary changes (early signs)

5. Vital signs changes—increased BP, decreased pulse (late changes)

**B.** Analysis

1. Diagnostic tests

   a. Neurological tests (e.g., lumbar puncture, EEG, myelogram)

2. Causes

   a. Cerebral edema

   b. Hemorrhage

   c. Space-occupying lesions

3. Complications

   a. Cerebral hypoxia

   b. Decreased cerebral perfusion

   c. Herniation—pupil constriction

**C.** Plan/Implementation

1. Monitor vital signs hourly—be alert for increased systolic pressure, widening pulse pressure, and bradycardia (Cushing's triad—very late sign)

2. Monitor pupillary reactions

3. Monitor muscle strength

4. Monitor verbal response and change in level of consciousness

5. Monitor Glasgow coma scale

6. Maintain respiratory function

7. Elevate head 30–45° to promote venous drainage from brain

8. Avoid neck flexion, head rotation, coughing, sneezing, and bending forward—support in cervical collar or neck rolls

9. Reduce environmental stimuli

10. Prevent the Valsalva maneuver, teach client to exhale while turning or moving in bed

11. Administer stool softeners (e.g., docusate)

12. Restrict fluids to 1,200–1,500 ml/day

13. Administer medications

    a. Osmotic diuretics—to reduce fluid volume (e.g., mannitol)

    b. Corticosteroid therapy—to reduce cerebral edema (e.g., dexamethazone)

    c. Antiseizure medications—(e.g., diazepam, phenytoin, phenobarbital)

**D.** Evaluation

1. Have complications of increased intracranial pressure been prevented?

2. Is the client alert and oriented?

# ▶ SEIZURES

**A.** Assessment (see Table 5)

1. Episodes of abnormal motor, sensory, autonomic, or psychic activity due to abnormal discharge from brain cells

**B.** Analysis

1. Causes

    a. Epilepsy

    b. Fever in child

    c. Head injury

    d. Hypertension

    e. CNS infection

    f. Brain tumor or metastasis

    g. Drug withdrawal

    h. Stroke

**C.** Plan/Implementation

1. During seizure

    a. Protect from injury

    b. Raise side rails or ease client to floor and protect client from injury

    c. Use padded side rails according to agency policy

    d. Loosen restrictive clothing

    e. Do not restrain

    f. Do not try to insert a bite block, padded tongue blade, or oral airway

    g. Protect nurse—client may be flailing arms

    h. Place client on side with head flexed

    i. Monitor onset, duration, pattern of seizure

    j. Administer medications for status epilepticus

| Table 5  SEIZURES | | |
|---|---|---|
| TYPE | AGE GROUP | ASSESSMENT |
| **Generalized seizures** Tonic-clonic | All | Aura Usually starts with tonic or stiffening phase, followed by clonic or jerking phase May have bowel/bladder incontinence; in postictal phase, sleeps, hard to arouse |
| Absence | Usually children | Staring spell, or staring spell with lip smacking, chewing |
| Myoclonic | Onset in children | Brief muscular contraction involving one or more limbs, trunk |
| Infantile spasms | Infants and children | Gross flexion, extension of limbs Treated with ACTH |
| Atonic seizures | Infants and children | Sudden loss of muscle tone and posture control, causing child to drop to floor |
| Tonic seizures | Infants and children | Stiffening of limbs |
| **Partial seizures** Seizures beginning locally | All | Jacksonian, or focal seizure, starting at one location, may spread |
| Sensory | All | Tingling, numbness of a body part; visual, olfactory, taste symptoms |
| Affective | All | Inappropriate fear, laughter, dreamy states, depersonalization |
| **Complex partial seizures** Temporal lobe/ psychomotor seizures | All | Aura complex Most commonly involves automatism—lip-smacking, picking at clothing, dreamy states, feelings of déja vu, hallucinations; may have antisocial, violent behavior, somatosensory reports, bizarre behavior |
| Partial seizures with secondary generalization | All | May spread from an original discharge site to other parts of the brain and become generalized |

2. After seizure

    a. Position on side to prevent aspiration, reduce environmental stimuli

    b. Provide oxygen and suction equipment, if needed

    c. Reorient as needed

    d. Provide description of seizure in record

        1) Circumstances surrounding seizure

        2) How seizure started (location of first tremors or stiffness)

        3) Type of body movements

        4) Areas of body involved

    5) Presence of automations (involuntary motor activities, e.g., lip smacking)

    6) Incontinence

    7) Duration of each phase

    8) Unconsciousness during seizure or paralysis after seizure

    9) Actions after seizures (e.g., confusion, sleep, speech)

3. To prevent seizures

  a. Administer anticonvulsant medications (e.g., phenytoin, phenobarbital)

    1) Don't discontinue abruptly

    2) Avoid alcohol

    3) Good oral hygiene

    4) Carry medical identification

  b. Avoid seizure triggers

    1) Alcoholic beverages

    2) Stress

    3) Caffeine

    4) Fever

    5) Hyperventilation

  c. Complementary/Alternative therapies

    1) Ketogenic diet to prevent seizures

      a) Diet high in fat and low in carbohydrates mimics effects of fasting and places the body in a constant state of ketosis

      b) Suppresses many types of seizures (tonic-clonic, absence, complex partial) and is effective when other methods of seizure control fail

**D.** Evaluation

1. Is client compliant with medication regimen?

2. Have injuries from seizure been prevented?

## ▶ STROKE

**A.** Assessment

1. Confusion/disorientation

2. Changes in vital signs and neurological signs

3. Change in level of consciousness, seizures

4. Aphasia

5. Hemiplegia

6. Bladder and/or bowel incontinence

7. Headache, vomiting

8. Hemianopsia—loss of half of visual field

9. Dysphagia—difficulty swallowing

10. Decreased sensation/neglect syndrome

11. Emotional lability

**B.** Diagnose

  1. Abrupt onset of neurological deficits resulting from interference with blood supply to the brain

  2. Causes

    a. Thrombosis

    b. Embolism

    c. Hemorrhage

  3. Risk factors

    a. Age

    b. Hypertension

    c. Transient ischemic attacks (TIAs)

    d. Diabetes mellitus

    e. Smoking

    f. Obesity

    g. Elevated blood lipids

    h. Oral contraceptives

    i. Atrial fibrillation

**C.** Plan/Implementation

  1. Immediate care

    a. Maintain patent airway

    b. Minimize activity

    c. Keep head of bed elevated 15–30° to prevent increased intracranial pressure

    d. Maintain proper body alignment

    e. Keep side rails in upright position

    f. Administer thrombolytics within 3 hours of onset of symptoms

  2. Intermediate care and rehabilitative needs

    a. Position for good body alignment and comfort

    b. Institute measures that facilitate swallowing

      1) Allow client to sit in upright position with head flexed slightly

      2) Instruct client to use tongue actively

      3) Administer liquids slowly, avoid milk-based products

      4) Place food on unaffected side of mouth

      5) Provide semisolid foods (easiest to swallow)

      6) Instruct to swallow while eating; maintain upright position for 30–45 minutes after eating

    c. Monitor elimination patterns

    d. Provide skin care

    e. Perform passive and/or active range-of-motion exercises

    f. Orient to person, time, and place

    g. Move affected extremities slowly and gently

    h. Teach use of supportive devices (e.g., commode, trapeze, cane)

i. Address communication needs—face client and speak clearly and slowly; give the client time to respond; use verbal and nonverbal communication

j. Do not approach from visually impaired side

k. Encourage use of affected side

**D.** Evaluation

1. Are client's vital signs stable?

2. Has client regained mobility?

3. Is client oriented?

# ► SPINAL CORD INJURY

**A.** Assessment

1. Loss of motor and sensory function below level of injury (see Table 6)

2. Spinal shock symptoms

   a. Flaccid paralysis of skeletal muscles

   b. Complete loss of all sensation

   c. Decreased pulses, bradycardia

   d. Suppression of somatic (pain, touch, temperature) and visceral reflexes

3. Postural hypotension

4. Circulatory problems—edema

5. Alteration in normal thermoregulation

**B.** Diagnose

1. Types of spinal cord injuries

   a. Concussion without direct trauma

   b. Penetrating wound or fracture dislocation

   c. Hemorrhage

   d. Laceration—damage related to level of cord affected

   e. Compression—often dural/epidural hematoma; if pressure on the cord is not relieved early, will cause ischemia, cord necrosis, and permanent damage

2. Categories of neurological deficit

   a. Complete—no voluntary motor activity or sensation below level of injury

   b. Incomplete—some voluntary motor activity or sensation below level of injury

   c. Paraplegia—thoracic vertebral injury or lower; lower extremity involvement

   d. Tetraplegia (quadriplegia)—cervical/vertebral injury; all 4 extremities involved

3. Causes

   a. Trauma due to accidents

      1) Car accidents, falls, sports, and industrial accidents

2) Occurs predominantly in young white males (ages 15–30)

3) May be related to substance abuse

b. Neoplasms

4. Diagnosis—neurological examination, x-rays, CT scan, MRI, myelography, digital rectal exam to determine extent of neurological deficit

**C.** Plan/Implementation

1. Prevention

a. Drive within the speed limit

b. Use seat belts in car

c. Wear helmets when riding motorcycles and bicycles

d. Don't drink and drive

2. Assessment (triage)

a. Airway, breathing, circulation (ABC)

b. Stabilization of vital signs

c. Head-to-toe assessment

3. Immobilize cervical spine

a. Skeletal traction—Gardner-Wells, Crutchfield, Vinke tongs, halo traction

b. Surgical stabilization—reduction and stabilization by fusion, wires, and plates

4. Administer steroid therapy and antispasmodics

5. Administer antispasmodics—baclofen, diazepam

6. Hyperbaric oxygen therapy

7. Move client by log-rolling technique; use turning frames

8. Provide good skin care

9. Provide emotional support

10. Ensure adequate nutrition

11. Reduce aggravating factors that cause spasticity

12. Bladder and bowel training, catheterization

13. Client and family education to cope with detailed care at home

14. Prevent complication of autonomic hyperreflexia (dysreflexia)

a. Usually caused by bladder or bowel distention; other causes: pain, tactile stimulation

b. Occurs in clients with spinal cord lesions at or above T6 after spinal shock has subsided

c. Symptoms—pounding headache, profuse sweating, especially of forehead, nasal congestion, piloerection (goose flesh), bradycardia, hypertension

d. Place client in sitting position

e. Catheterize or irrigate existing catheter to re-establish patency

f. Check rectum for fecal mass

g. Hydralazine may be given slowly IV

**D.** Evaluation

1. Is client able to regain optimal functioning?

2. Have complications been prevented?

| Table 6  SPINAL CORD INJURY | | |
|---|---|---|
| **LEVEL OF INJURY** | **FUNCTIONAL ABILITY** | **SELF–CARE CAPABILITY** |
| C3 and above | Inability to control muscles of breathing | Unable to care for self, life-sustaining ventilatory support essential |
| C4 | Movement of trapezius and sternocleidomastoid muscles, no upper extremity muscle function, minimal ventilatory capacity | Unable to care for self, may self-feed with powered devices (depending on respiratory function) |
| C5 | Neck movement, possible partial strength of shoulder and biceps | Can drive electric wheelchair, may be able to feed self with powered devices |
| C6 | Muscle function in C5 level; partial strength in pectoralis major | May self-propel a lightweight wheelchair, may feed self with devices, can write and care for self, can transfer from chair to bed |
| C7 | Muscle function in C6 level, no finger muscle power | Can dress lower extremities, minimal assistance needed, independence in wheelchair, can drive car with hand controls |
| C8 | Muscle function in C7 level, finger muscle power | Same as C7; in general, activities easier |
| T1-T4 | Good upper extremity muscle strength | Some independence from wheelchair, long leg braces for standing exercises |
| T5-L2 | Balance difficulties | Still requires wheelchair, limited ambulation with long-leg braces and crutches |
| L3-L5 | Trunk-pelvis muscle function intact | May use crutches or canes for ambulation |
| L5-S3 | Waddling gait | Ambulation |

# FLUID AND ELECTROLYTE IMBALANCES  *Section 2*

## ▶ FLUID VOLUME IMBALANCES

**A.** Assessment (see Table 1)

**B.** Diagnose (see Table 1)

**C.** Plan/Implementation (see Table 1)

| Table 1  FLUID VOLUME IMBALANCES | | |
|---|---|---|
| | **VOLUME DEFICIT** | **VOLUME OVERLOAD** |
| **Assessment** | Thirst (early sign)<br>Temperature increases<br>Rapid and weak pulse Respirations increase<br>Poor skin turgor—skin cool, moist<br>Hypotension<br>Emaciation, weight loss<br>Dry eye sockets, mouth and mucous membranes<br>Anxiety, apprehension, exhaustion<br>Urine specific gravity greater than 1.030<br>Decreased urine output<br>Increased hemoglobin, hematocrit, Na$^+$, serum osmolality<br>Headache, lethargy, confusion, disorientation, weight loss | No change in temperature<br>Pulse increases slightly and is bounding<br>Respirations increase, shortness of breath, dyspnea, rales (crackles)<br>Peripheral edema—bloated appearance, weight gain<br>Hypertension<br>May have muffled heart sounds<br>Jugular vein distention<br>Urine specific gravity less than 1.010<br>Apprehension<br>Increased venous pressure<br>Decreased hematocrit BUN, hemoglobin, Na$^+$, serum osmolality |
| **Diagnose** | Isotonic loss<br>Vomiting Diarrhea<br>GI suction<br>Sweating<br>Decreased intake<br>Hemorrhage<br>Third space shift | Isotonic gain, increase in the interstitial compartment, intravascular compartment, or both<br>CHF<br>Renal failure<br>    Cirrhosis of the liver<br>       Excessive ingestion of sodium<br>Excessive or too rapid intravenous infusion |
| **Plan/Implementation** | Force fluids<br>Provide isotonic IV fluids: lactated ringer's or 0.9% NaCl<br>I and O, hourly outputs<br>Daily weights (1 liter fluid = 1 kg or 2.2 lb)<br>Monitor vital signs<br>Check skin turgor<br>Assess urine specific gravity | Administer diuretics<br>Restrict fluids<br>Sodium-restricted diet (average daily diet—6–15 mg Na$^+$)<br>Daily weight<br>Assess breath sounds<br>Check feet/ankle/sacral region for edema<br>Semi-Fowler's position if dyspneic |

**D.** Evaluation

1. Has client's fluid and electrolyte balance been re-established?

2. Have complications been prevented?

## ▶ ADH DISORDERS

**A.** Assessment (see Table 2)

**B.** Analysis (see Table 2)

**C.** Plan/Implementation (see Table 2)

**D.** Evaluation

    1. Has the client's fluid and electrolyte balance been maintained?

    2. Is client knowledgeable about medications?

| Table 2  ADH DISORDERS | | |
|---|---|---|
| | **DIABETES INSIPIDUS (DECREASED ADH)** | **SIADH—SYNDROME OF INAPPROPRIATE ANTIDIURETIC HORMONE SECRETION (INCREASED ADH)** |
| **Assessment** | Excessive urine output<br>Chronic, severe dehydration<br>Excessive thirst<br>Anorexia, weight loss<br>Weakness<br>Constipation | Anorexia, nausea, vomiting<br>Lethargy<br>Headaches<br>Change in level of consciousness<br>Decreased deep tendon reflexes<br>Tachycardia<br>Increased circulating blood volume<br>Decreased urinary output |
| **Diagnose** | Head trauma<br>Brain tumor<br>Meningitis<br>Encephalitis<br>Deficiency of ADH<br>Diagnosis tests:<br>    Low urine specific gravity<br>    Urinary osmolality below plasma level<br>High serum sodium | Small cell carcinoma of lung<br>Pneumonia<br>Positive-pressure ventilation<br>Brain tumors<br>Head trauma<br>Stroke<br>Meningitis<br>Encephalitis<br>Feedback mechanism that regulates ADH does not function properly; ADH is released even when plasma hypo-osmolality is present<br>Diagnostic tests:<br>    Serum sodium decreased, plasma osmolality decreased<br>Increased urine specific gravity |
| **Nursing considerations** | Record intake and output<br>Monitor urine specific gravity, skin condition, weight, blood pressure, pulse, temperature<br>Administer vasopressin | Restrict water intake (500–600 ml/24 h)<br>Administer diuretics to promote excretion of water<br>Hypertonic saline (3% NaCl) IV<br>Administer demeclocycline<br>Weigh daily<br>I and O<br>Monitor serum Na$^+$ levels<br>Assess LOC |

# ▶ POTASSIUM IMBALANCES

**A.** Assessment (see Table 3)

**B.** Diagnose (see Table 3)

**C.** Plan/Implementation (see Table 3)

| Table 3   POTASSIUM IMBALANCES | | |
|---|---|---|
| | HYPOKALEMIA | HYPERKALEMIA |
| **Assessment** | less than 3.5 mEq/L (3.5 mmol/L)<br><br>Anorexia, nausea, and vomiting<br><br>Muscle weakness, paresthesias<br><br>Dysrhythmias, increased sensitivity to digitalis | greater than 5.0 mEq/L (5 mmol/L)<br><br>EKG changes, dysrhythmias, cardiac arrest<br><br>Muscle weakness<br><br>Paralysis<br><br>Nausea<br><br>Diarrhea |
| **Diagnose** | Potassium—main intracellular ion; involved in cardiac rhythm, nerve transmission<br><br>Normal level—3.5–5.0 mEq/L (3.5–5 mmol/L)<br><br>Causes—vomiting, gastric suction, diarrhea, diuretics and steroids, inadequate intake | Causes—renal failure, use of potassium supplements, burns, crushing injuries |
| **Plan/Implementation** | Administration of oral potassium supplements—dilute in juice to avoid gastric irritation<br><br>Increase dietary intake—raisins, bananas, apricots, oranges, beans, potatoes, carrots, celery<br><br>IV supplements—40 mEq/L usual concentration; cannot give concentration greater than 40 mEq/L into peripheral IV or without cardiac monitor<br><br>Increases risk of digoxin toxicity<br><br>    Protect from injury<br><br>       Assess renal function prior to administration | Restrict dietary potassium and potassium-containing medications<br><br>Sodium polystyrene sulfonate—cation exchange resin (causes diarrhea)<br><br>Orally—dilute to make more palatable<br><br>Rectally—give in conjunction with sorbitol to avoid fecal impaction<br><br>In emergency situation, calcium gluconate given IV, sodium bicarbonate given IV, regular insulin and dextrose<br><br>IV administration of regular insulin and dextrose shifts potassium into the cells<br><br>Peritoneal or hemodialysis<br><br>Diuretics |

**D.** Evaluation

1. Has client's fluid and electrolyte balance been re-established?

2. Have complications been prevented?

▶ **SODIUM IMBALANCES**

  **A.** Assessment (see Table 4)

  **B.** Diagnose (see Table 4)

  **C.** Plan/Implementation (see Table 4)

| Table 4  SODIUM IMBALANCES | | |
|---|---|---|
| | HYPONATREMIA | HYPERNATREMIA |
| Assessment | Less than 135 mEq/L (135 mmol/L) <br> Nausea <br> Muscle cramps <br> Increased intracranial pressure, confusion, muscular twitching, convulsions | greater than 145 mEq/L (145 mmol/L) <br> Elevated temperature <br> Weakness <br> Disorientation <br> Delusion and hallucinations <br> Thirst, dry swollen tongue, sticky mucous membranes <br> Postural hypotension with decreased ECF <br> Hypertension with normal or increased ECF <br> Tachycardia |
| Diagnose | Sodium—main extracellular ion; responsible for water balance <br> Normal—135–145 mEq/L (135–145 mmol/L) <br> Causes—vomiting, diuretics, excessive administration of dextrose and water IVs, prolonged low-sodium diet, excessive water intake | Causes—hypertonic tube feedings without water supplements, diarrhea, hyperventilation, diabetes insipidus, ingestion of OTC drugs such as Alka-Seltzer, inhaling large amounts of salt water (near-drowning), inadequate water ingestion |
| Plan/Implementation | Oral administration of sodium-rich foods—beef broth, tomato juice <br> IV lactated Ringer's or 0.9% NaCl <br> Water restriction (safer method) <br> I and O <br> Daily weight | IV administration of hypotonic solution—0.3% NaCl or 0.45% NaCl; 5% dextrose in water <br> Offer fluids at regular intervals <br> Decrease sodium in diet <br> Daily weight |

  **D.** Evaluation

     1. Has client's fluid and electrolyte balance been re-established?

     2. Have complications been prevented?

▶ **CALCIUM IMBALANCES**

  **A.** Assessment (see Table 5)

  **B.** Diagnose (see Table 5)

  **C.** Plan/Implementation (see Table 5)

  **D.** Evaluation

     1. Has client's fluid and electrolyte balance been re-established?

     2. Have complications been prevented?

| Table 5  CALCIUM IMBALANCES | | |
|---|---|---|
| | **HYPOCALCEMIA** | **HYPERCALCEMIA** |
| **Assessment** | Ionized serum calcium less than 4.5 mg/dL or total serum calcium less than 8.6 mg/dL (2.2 mmol/L) (total serum calcium levels used)<br><br>Nervous system becomes increasingly excitable<br><br>Tetany<br>　Trousseau's sign—inflate BP cuff on upper arm to 20 mm Hg above systolic pressure; carpal spasms within 2–5 minutes indicate tetany<br>　Chvostek's sign—tap facial nerve 2 cm anterior to the earlobe just below the zygomatic arch; twitching of facial muscles indicates tetany<br><br>Seizures<br><br>Confusion<br><br>Paresthesia<br><br>Irritability | Ionized serum calcium greater than 5.1 mg/L or total serum calcium greater than 10.2 mg/dL (2.5 mmol/L)(total serum calcium levels used)<br><br>Sedative effect on central and peripheral nervous system<br><br>Muscle weakness, lack of coordination, constipation, abdominal pain, and distension<br><br>Confusion<br><br>Depressed or absent tendon reflexes<br><br>Dysrhythmias |
| **Diagnose** | Calcium—needed for blood clotting, skeletal muscle contraction<br><br>Ionized serum calcium less than 4.5 mg/dL or total serum calcium less than 8.6 mg/dL (2.2 mmol/L)<br><br>Regulated by parathyroid hormone and vitamin D, which facilitates reabsorption of calcium from bone and enhances absorption from the GI tract<br><br>Causes—hypoparathyroidism, pancreatitis, renal failure, steroids and loop diuretics, inadequate intake, post-thyroid surgery | Causes—malignant neoplastic diseases, hyperparathyroidism, excessive intake, immobility, excessive intake of calcium carbonate antacids |
| **Plan/ Implementation** | Orally—calcium gluconate (less concentrated) or calcium chloride; administer with orange juice to maximize absorption<br><br>Parenterally—calcium gluconate<br><br>Effect is transitory and additional doses may be necessary<br><br>Use caution with digitalized clients because both are cardiac depressants<br><br>Calcium may cause vessel irritation and should be administered through a long, stable intravenous line<br><br>Avoid infiltration since tissue can become necrotic and slough<br><br>Administer at a slow rate to avoid high serum concentrations and cardiac depression<br><br>Seizure precautions<br><br>Maintain airway because laryngeal stridor can occur<br><br>Maintain safety needs since confusion is often present<br><br>Increase dietary intake of calcium, calcium supplements<br><br>Regular exercise<br><br>Administer phosphate-binding antacids, calcitriol, vitamin D | IV administration of 0.45% NaCl or 0.9% NaCl<br><br>Encourage fluids<br><br>furosemide<br><br>Calcitonin—decreases calcium level<br><br>Mobilize the client<br><br>Restrict dietary calcium<br><br>Prevent development of renal calculi<br><br>Increase fluid intake<br><br>Maintain acidic urine<br><br>Prevent UTI<br><br>Surgical intervention may be indicated in hyperparathyroidism<br><br>Injury prevention<br><br>Limit intake of calcium carbonate antacids |

▶ **MAGNESIUM IMBALANCES**

**A.** Assessment (see Table 6)

**B.** Analysis (see Table 6)

**C.** Plan/Implementation (see Table 6)

**D.** Evaluation

1. Has client's fluid and electrolyte balance been re-established?

2. Have complications been prevented?

| Table 6  MAGNESIUM IMBALANCES | | |
|---|---|---|
| | HYPOMAGNESEMIA | HYPERMAGNESEMIA |
| Assessment | less than 1.3 mEq/L (0.53 mmol/L)<br>Magnesium acts as a depressant<br>Increased neuromuscular irritability<br>Tremors, tetany, seizures<br>Dysrhythmias<br>Depression, confusion<br>Dysphagia | greater than 2.3 mEq/L (0.95 mmol/L)<br>Depresses the CNS<br>Depresses cardiac impulse transmission<br>Hypotension<br>Facial flushing, muscle weakness<br>Absent deep tendon reflexes, paralysis<br>Shallow respirations |
| Diagnose | Normal−1.3–2.3 mEq/L (0.53–0.95 mmol/L)<br>Causes−alcoholism, GI suction, diarrhea, intestinal fistulas, abuse of diuretics or laxatives<br>Usually seen with other electrolyte deficits | Causes−renal failure, excessive magnesium administration (antacids, cathartics) |
| Plan/Implementation | Increased intake of dietary Mg−green vegetables, nuts, bananas, oranges, peanut butter, chocolate<br>Parenteral administration of supplements−magnesium sulfate<br>Monitor cardiac rhythm and reflexes to detect depressive effects of magnesium<br>Keep self-inflating breathing bag, Monitor respiratory status airway and oxygen at bedside, in case of respiratory emergency<br>Calcium preparations may be given to counteract the potential danger of myocardial dysfunction that may result from magnesium intoxication secondary to rapid infusions<br>Oral−long-term maintenance with oral magnesium<br>IV administration−assess renal function<br>Monitor for digitalis toxicity<br>Maintain seizure precautions<br>Provide safety measures because confusion is often present<br>Test ability to swallow before PO fluids/ food because of dysphagia | Discontinue oral and IV Mg<br>Emergency<br>Support ventilation<br>IV calcium gluconate<br>Hemodialysis<br>Monitor reflexes<br>Teach about OTC drugs containing Mg<br>Monitor cardiac rhythm; have calcium preparations available to antagonize cardiac depression |

# ▶ BURNS

**A.** Assessment

    1. "Rule of Nines" (see Figure 1)

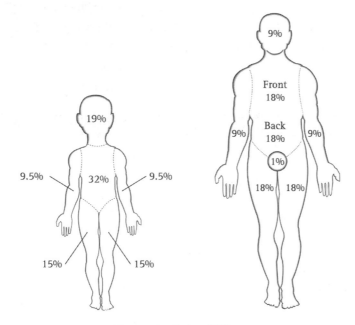

**Figure 1  Rule of Nines**

    2. Determination of intensity (see Table 7)

| Table 7  CLASSIFICATION OF BURNS | | | | |
|---|---|---|---|---|
| **SUPERFICIAL** | **SUPERFICIAL PARTIAL-THICKNESS** | **DEEP PARTIAL-THICKNESS** | **FULL-THICKNESS** | **DEEP FULL-THICKNESS** |
| Similar to first-degree | Similar to second-degree | Similar to second-degree | Similar to third-degree | Similar to third-degree |
| Skin pink to red<br>Painful | Skin pink to red<br>Painful | Skin red to white<br>Painful | Skin red, white, brown, black<br>Pain possible | Skin black<br>No pain |
| Epidermis<br>Sunburn | Epidermis and dermis<br>Scalds, flames | Epidermis and dermis<br>Scalds, flames, tar, grease | All skin layers<br>  Prolonged contact<br>  with hot objects | All skin layers, possibly muscles and tendon<br>Flames, electricity |
| Heals in 3 to 5 days | Heals in 2 weeks | Heals in 1 month<br>Possible grafting | Heals in weeks to months | Heals in weeks to months<br>Escharotomy<br>Grafting |

**B.** Analysis (see Table 8)

    1. At risk

        a. Young children

        b. Elderly

2. Prevention
   a. Keep all matches and lighters away from children
   b. Do not leave children alone around fires
   c. Install and maintain smoke detectors
   d. Set water-heater temperature no higher than 120°F (48.9°C)
   e. Do not smoke in bed or fall asleep while smoking
   f. Use caution when cooking
   g. Keep a working fire extinguisher in the home
3. Thermal—contact with hot substance (solids/liquids/gases)

| Table 8  NURSING CARE FOR BURN CLIENT | |
|---|---|
| **GOAL** | **NURSING CONSIDERATIONS** |
| Correct fluid and electrolyte imbalance | First 24–48 h (emergent/resuscitative phase): <br>     IV fluids balanced salt solution (Lactated Ringers), plasma <br>     Rapid for first 8 h, more slowly over remaining 16 h <br> 2–5 d after burn (intermediate phase): <br>     Packed RBCs <br>     Indwelling catheter to monitor hourly output; should be at least 30 ml/h <br>     Careful administration of IV fluids; check for signs of fluid overload versus dehydration <br>     Monitor blood pressure, TPR, wt, serum electrolytes |
| Promote healing | Cap, gown, mask, and gloves worn by nurse <br> Wound care at least once a day <br> Debridement (removal of nonviable tissue)—hydrotherapy is used to loosen dead tissue, 30 min maximum <br> Escharotomy (incising of leathery covering of dead tissue conducive to bacterial growth)—used to alleviate constriction, minimize infection <br> Dressing: careful sterile technique, avoid breaking blisters, wound may be covered or left exposed <br> Application of topical antibacterial medications: silver sulfadiazine—closed method; monitor for hypersensitivity, rash, itching, burning sensation in areas other than burn, decreased WBC; mafenide—open method; monitor acid/base balance and renal function; remove previously applied cream; Silver nitrate—keep dressings wet with solution to avoid over concentrations; handle carefully; can leave a gray/black stain <br> Grafting: biological (human amniotic membrane, cadaver, allograft); autografting when granulation bed is clean and well vascularized <br> Tetanus prophylaxis <br> Avoid hypothermia and add humidity |
| Support nutrition | High-caloric, high-carbohydrate, high-protein diet; may require PN or tube feeding; oral nutrient supplements; vitamins B, C, and iron; H2 histamine blockers and antacids to prevent stress ulcer (Curling's ulcer) <br> NG tube to prevent gastric distention, early acute gastric dilation, and paralytic ileus associated with burn shock; monitor bowel sounds |
| Control pain | Pain medication (morphine)—given IV at first due to impaired circulation and poor absorption <br>     Monitor VS frequently; analgesic 30 min before wound care |

| **Table 8  NURSING CARE FOR BURN CLIENT** *(CONTINUED)* | |
|---|---|
| **GOAL** | **NURSING CONSIDERATIONS** |
| Prevent complications of immobility | Prevent contractures—maintain joints in neutral position of extension; shoes to prevent foot drop; splints; active and passive ROM exercises at each dressing change; turn side to side frequently; skin care to prevent breakdown |
| | Stryker frame or Circ-O-Lectric bed may facilitate change of position |
| | Facial exercises and position that hyperextends neck for burns of face and neck |
| | Consult with physical therapist |
| Support client | Counsel client regarding change in body image |
| | Encourage expression of feelings and demonstrate acceptance of client |
| | Evaluate client's readiness to see scarred areas, especially facial area |
| | Assist client's family to adjust to changed appearance |
| | Consider recommending client for ongoing counseling |
| | Support developmental needs of children, e.g., sick children need limits on behavior |
| | Assist client in coping with immobilization, pain, and isolation |
| | Prepare client for discharge—anticipate readmission for release of contractures/cosmetic surgery; proper use of any correctional orthopedic appliances, pressure garments (used to decrease scarring); how to change dressings |

4. Chemical—contact with strong acids or strong bases; prolonged contact with most chemicals

5. Electrical—contact with live current; internal damage may be more severe than expected from external injury

6. Radiation—exposure to high doses of radioactive material

**C.** Plan/Implementation

1. Emergency care—on the scene

   a. Stop the burning process

   b. Thermal—smother; stop, drop, and roll

   c. Chemical—remove clothing and flush/irrigate skin/eyes

   d. Electrical—shut off electrical current or separate person from source with a nonconducting implement

   e. Ensure airway, breathing, and circulation

   f. Immediate wound care—keep person warm and dry; wrap in clean, dry sheet/blanket

2. Nursing care (see Table 8)

3. Stages following severe burns (see Table 9)

| Table 9  PHASES FOLLOWING SEVERE BURNS | |
|---|---|
| **EMERGENT/RESUSCITATIVE** | **INTERMEDIATE/ACUTE** |
| First 24–48 hours | Begins 36–48 hours after burn |
| Fluid loss through open wound or extravasation into deeper tissues | Decrease in peripheral edema |
| Hypovolemia | Blood volume restored |
| Renal complications possible | Diuresis if renal system unimpaired |
| $K^+$ (hyperkalemia) | $K^+$ (hypokalemia) |
| ↓ BP, ↑ Pulse | ↑ BP |

**D.** Evaluation

1. Have client's physical needs been met?

2. Have complications from the burn been prevented?

# ▶ ADRENAL DISORDERS

**A.** Assessment (see Table 10)

**B.** Analysis (see Table 10)

1. Adrenal cortex

   a. Glucocorticoids

   b. Mineralocorticoids

   c. Androgen and estrogen

2. Adrenal medulla

   a. Norepinephrine

   b. Epinephrine

**C.** Plan/Implementation

1. Addison's disease

   a. High-protein, high-carbohydrate, high-sodium, low-potassium diet

   b. Wear Medic-Alert bracelet

   c. Protect from infection

   d. Monitor for hypoglycemia, hyponatremia

   e. Assist with 24-hour urine collection for 17-hydroxycorticosteroids (refrigerate urine during collection)

   f. Administer hormonal replacement—may be lifelong

   g. Avoid factors that precipitate Addisonian crisis

      1) Physical stress

      2) Psychological stress

      3) Inadequate steroid replacement

_thin,
weak,
dehydrated_ →

_Buffalo hump_
_hairy_

| Table 10  ADRENAL DISORDERS | | |
|---|---|---|
| | **ADDISON'S DISEASE** | **CUSHING'S SYNDROME** |
| **Assessment** | Fatigue, weakness, dehydration, ↓ BP, hyperpigmentation, ↓ resistance to stress, alopecia<br><br>Weight loss, pathological fractures<br><br>Depression, lethargy, emotional lability<br><br>_low BS  high potassium_ | Fatigue, weakness, osteoporosis, muscle wasting, cramps, edema, ↑ BP, purple skin striations, hirsutism, emaciation, depression, decreased resistance to infection, moon face, buffalo hump, obesity (trunk), mood swings, masculinization in females, blood sugar imbalance |
| **Diagnose** | Hyposecretion of adrenal hormones (mineralocorticoids, glucocorticoids, androgens)<br><br>Pathophysiology: _low sodium_<br>  ↓ Na⁺ dehydration<br><br>  ↓ Blood volume + shock<br><br>  ↑ K⁺ metabolic acidosis + arrhythmias _high K+_<br><br>  ↓ Blood sugar + insulin shock<br><br>Diagnostic tests:<br>  CT and MRI<br><br>  Hyperkalemia and hyponatremia<br><br>  ↓ Plasma cortisol<br><br>  ↓ Urinary 17-hydroxycorticosteroids and 17-ketosteroids<br><br>ACTH stimulation test<br><br>Treatment: hormone replacement | Hypersecretion of adrenal hormones (mineralocorticoids, glucocorticoids, androgens)<br><br>Pathophysiology:<br>  ↑ Na⁺ ↑ blood volume + ↑ BP<br><br>  ↓ K⁺ metabolic alkalosis + shock<br><br>  ↑ Blood sugar + ketoacidosis<br><br>Diagnostic tests:<br>  Skull films<br><br>  Blood sugar analysis<br><br>  Hypokalemia and hypernatremia<br><br>  Plasma cortisol level<br><br>  Urinary 17-hydroxycorticosteroids and 17-ketosteroids<br><br>Treatment: hypophysectomy, adrenalectomy |

h.  Observe for clinical manifestations of Addisonian crisis (precipitatedby physical or emotional stress, sudden withdrawal of hormones)

1)  Nausea and vomiting

2)  Abdominal pain

3)  Fever

4)  Extreme weakness

5)  Severe hypoglycemia, hyperkalemia, and dehydration develop rapidly

6)  Blood pressure falls, leading to shock and coma; death results if not promptly treated

      i. Treatment of Addisonian crisis

        1) Administer and assess hydrocortisone therapy

        2) Carefully monitor IV infusion of 0.9% NaCl or $D_5$W/NaCl

        3) Administer IV glucose, glucagon

        4) Administer insulin with dextrose in normal saline; administer potassium-binding and excreting resin (e.g., sodium polystyrene sulfonate)

        5) Monitor vital signs

  2. Cushing's syndrome

    a. Assure the client that most physical changes are reversible with treatment

    b. High-protein, low-carbohydrate, high-potassium, low-sodium, low-calorie diet; fluid restriction

    c. Use careful technique to prevent infection

    d. Eliminate environmental hazards for pathological fractures

    e. Observe for hyperactivity, GI bleeding, fluid volume overload

    f. Administer aminoglutethimide or metyrapone to decrease cortisolproduction

    g. Provide postadrenalectomy care

      1) Flank incision—painful to breathe, so encourage coughing and deep breathing

      2) Ensure client safety to decrease risk of fractures

      3) Monitor for shock

      4) Monitor for hypertension

      5) Administer cortisone and mineralocorticoids as ordered

    h. Anticipate slow recovery from anesthesia in obese client

    i. Anticipate slow wound healing

    j. Monitor glucose level, monitor urine output

**D.** Evaluation

  1. Has the client's fluid and electrolyte balance been maintained?

## ▶ PHEOCHROMOCYTOMA

**A.** Assessment

  1. Intermittent hypertension

  2. Increased heart rate, palpitations during hypertensive episodes

  3. Nausea and vomiting, weight loss

  4. Hyperglycemia, glucosuria, polyuria

  5. Diaphoresis, pallor, tremor, nervousness during hypertensive episodes

  6. Pounding headache, weakness, visual disturbances during hypertensive episodes

  7. Pain

8. Urinary vanillylmandelic acid (VMA) test

   a. 24-hour urine for VMA—breakdown product of catecholamine metabolism

   b. Normal results: 1–5 mg, positive for tumor if significantly higher

   c. Foods affecting VMA excretion excluded 3 days before test

      1) Coffee

      2) Tea

      3) Bananas

      4) Vanilla

      5) Chocolate

   d. All drugs discontinued during test

   e. Urine collected on ice or refrigerated with preservative

9. Clonidine suppression test—conidine levels not decreased

**B.** Diagnose

1. Definition—hypersecretion of catecholamines (epinephrine and norepinephrine) activate fight-or-flight response due to secreting tumors of the adrenal medulla; tumor can also occur anywhere, from neck to pelvis, along course of sympathetic nerve chain

2. Potential nursing diagnoses

   a. Deficient knowledge

   b. Decreased cardiac output/ineffective tissue perfusion

**C.** Plan/Implementation

1. Avoid physical and emotional stress

2. Monitor blood pressure in lying and sitting positions

3. Frequent bathing, but avoid chilling

4. Administer analgesics for pain, sedatives and tranquilizers for rest and relaxation

5. Increase caloric, vitamin, and mineral intake due to increased metabolic demand

6. Avoid coffee, tea, cola, and foods containing tyramine

7. Limit activity

8. Administer adrenergic-blocking medications

9. Administer apresoline for hypertensive crisis

10. Allow time to verbalize concerns to decrease nervousness and tremors

11. Provide postsurgical care—adrenalectomy or medullectomy

**D.** Evaluation

1. Has the client's fluid and electrolyte balance been maintained?

2. Have complications been prevented?

## ▶ CHRONIC OBSTRUCTIVE PULMONARY DISEASE (COPD)

**A.** Assessment

1. Change in skin color—cyanosis or reddish color

2. Weakness, weight loss

3. Risk factors

   a. Smoking tobacco

   b. Passive tobacco smoke

   c. Occupational exposure

   d. Air pollution, coal, gas, asbestos exposure

   e. Genetic abnormalities—alpha 1antitrypsin deficiency

4. Use of accessory muscles of breathing, dyspnea

5. Changes in posture—day and hs

6. Cough, changes in color, consistency of sputum

7. Abnormal ABGs—$PaO_2$, and $PaCO_2$

8. Adventitious breath sounds

9. Changes in sensorium, memory impairment

**B.** Diagnose

1. Most common cause of lung disease in United States

2. Group of conditions associated with obstruction of air flow entering or leaving the lungs; genetic and environmental causes—smoking and air pollution

   a. Asthma—chronic disease with episodic attacks of breathlessness

   b. Emphysema—overinflation of alveoli resulting in destruction of alveolar walls; predisposing factors: smoking, chronic infections,and environmental pollution

   c. Chronic bronchitis—inflammation of bronchi with productive cough

   d. Cystic fibrosis—hereditary dysfunction of exocrine glands causing obstruction because of flow of thick mucus

      1) Causes—sweat gland dysfunction, respiratory dysfunction, GI dysfunction

      2) Diagnostic tests

         a) Sweat chloride analysis test—elevated levels of sodium and chloride

         b) GI enzyme evaluation—pancreatic enzyme deficiency

3. Potential nursing diagnoses

   a. Ineffective airway clearance

   b. Imbalanced nutrition: less than body requirements

   c. Anxiety

   d. Compromised family coping

   e. Activity intolerance

      f. Deficient knowledge

      g. Social interaction, impaired

      h. Risk for infection

      i. Impaired gas exchange

**C.** Plan/Implementation

    1. Assess airway clearance

    2. Listen to breath sounds

    3. Administer low-flow oxygen to prevent $CO_2$ narcosis for emphysema

    4. Encourage fluids (6–8 glasses, 3000 ml/24 hours), provide small, frequent feedings

    5. Administer medications: bronchodilators, mucolytics, corticosteroids, anticholinergics, leukotriene inhibitors, influenza and pneumococcal vaccines

    6. Metered dose inhalers (MDI)

      a. May be used with or without spacers

      b. Delivers medication directly to lungs

      c. Medications used with inhalers

        1) Beta-2 adrenergic drugs: albuterol, metaproterenol, terbutaline, salmeterol

        2) Corticosteriods: fluticasone, prednisone

        3) Cromolyn sodium and nedocromil

        4) Anticholinergics: ipratropium, tiotropium

      d. Medications should be administered so that bronchodilators are given first to open the airways, and then other medications are given

      e. Spacers attach to the MDI to hold medication in the chamber long enough for the client to inhale medication directly to the airways

      f. Teach proper use of MDI and spacers

      g. Caution against overuse

      h. Teach client to report decreasing effectiveness of medication and adverse effects

      i. Teach client to clean equipment thoroughly

      j. Teach client to rinse mouth thoroughly with water after steriod treatment to minimize risk of infection from oral candidiasis

    7. Client teaching

      a. Breathing exercises

      b. Stop smoking

      c. Avoid hot/cold air or allergens

      d. Instructions regarding medications

      e. Avoid close contact with persons who have respiratory infections or "flu"

      f. Avoid crowds during times of the year when respiratory infections most commonly occur

      g. Maintain a high resistance with adequate rest, nourishing diet, avoidance of stress, and avoidance of exposure to temperature extremes, dampness, and drafts

    h. Practice frequent, thorough oral hygiene and handwashing

    i. Advise about prophylactic influenza vaccines

    j. Instruct to observe sputum for indications of infection

**D.** Evaluation

    1. Are client's ABGs stable?

    2. Has client stopped smoking?

    3. Has airway clearance been maintained?

    4. Does client perform self-care?

    5. Are breathing patterns improved?

    6. Does client cope with chronic disease?

# ▶ PNEUMONIA

**A.** Assessment

    1. Fever, chills

    2. Cough productive of rust-colored, green, whitish-yellow sputum (depending on organism)

    3. Dyspnea, pleuritic pain, accessory muscle use, upright position

    4. Tachycardia, crackles, sonorous wheezes, bronchial breath sounds

    5. Elevated WBC count, sputum culture and sensitivity, blood culture and sensitivity

**B.** Diagnose

    1. Causes include bacteria, fungus, virus, parasite, chemical

    2. Inflammatory process that results in edema of lung tissues and extravasation of fluid into alveoli, causing hypoxia

    3. Risk factors

        a. Community-acquired pneumonia

            1) Older adult

            2) Has not received pneumococcal vaccination

            3) Has not received yearly flu vaccine

            4) Chronic illness

            5) Exposed to viral infection or flu

            6) Smokes or drinks alcohol

        b. Hospital-acquired pneumonia

            1) Older adult

            2) Chronic lung disease

            3) Aspiration

            4) Presence of endotracheal, tracheostomy, or nasogastric tube

            5) Mechanical ventilation

            6) Decreased levels of consciousness

            7) Immunosuppression (disease or pharmacologic etiology)

    4. Potential nursing diagnoses

       a. Ineffective airway clearance

       b. Activity intolerance

       c. Deficient knowledge

       d. Deficient fluid volume

**C.** Plan/Implementation

    1. Assess vital signs every 4 hours

    2. Cough and breathe deeply every 2 hours

    3. Assess breath sounds, and oxygen saturation

    4. Incentive spirometer—5–10 breaths per hour while awake

    5. Chest physiotherapy

    6. Encourage fluids to 3,000 ml/24 h

    7. Suction as needed

    8. Oxygen therapy

    9. Semi-Fowler's position/bedrest

    10. Teach about fluid intake and smoking cessation

    11. Medications

       a. Mucolytics

       b. Expectorants

       c. Bronchodilators (e.g., beta-2 agonists)—nebulizer or MDI

       d. Antibiotics

**D.** Evaluation

    1. Is there improved airway clearance?

    2. Is there a reduction in symptoms?

    3. Are the client's vital signs stable?

# ▶ CONGENITAL HEART ANOMALIES

**A.** Assessment (see Table 1)

**B.** Diagnose

    1. History-predisposing factors

       a. Maternal rubella during pregnancy

       b. Maternal alcoholism

       c. Maternal age over 40 years

       d. Maternal insulin-dependent diabetes (IDDM)

       e. Sibling(s) with heart disease

       f. Parent with congenital heart disease

       g. Other congenital anomalies

| Table 1  CONGENITAL HEART ANOMALIES | |
| --- | --- |
| **ACYANOTIC TYPE** | **CYANOTIC TYPE** |
| Normal color | Cyanosis usually from birth; clubbing of fingers |
| Normal CNS function | May have seizures due to hypoxia; fainting; confusion |
| Possible exercise intolerance | Marked exercise intolerance; may have hypoxic spells following exercise; squats to decrease respiratory distress |
| Possible weight loss or gain (with fluid retention) | Difficulty eating because of inability to breathe at the same time, with subsequent weight loss |
| Small stature; failure to thrive | Small stature; failure to thrive |
| Characteristic murmur; increased frequency of respiratory infections | Characteristic murmur; frequent and severe respiratory infections |

2. General effects of heart malformation

    a. Increased workload—overloading of chambers results in hypertrophy and tachycardia

    b. Pulmonary hypertension (increased vascular resistance) results in dyspnea, tachypnea, and recurrent respiratory infections

    c. Inadequate systemic cardiac output results in exercise intolerance and growth failure

    d. Arterial desaturation from shunting of deoxygenated blood directly into the systemic circulation results in polycythemia, cyanosis, cerebral changes, clubbing, squatting

    e. Murmurs due to abnormal shunting of blood between two heart chambers or between vessels

3. Types of defects (see Figure 1)

    a. Increased pulmonary blood flow (acyanotic)

        1) Ventricular septal defect (VSD)—abnormal opening between right and left ventricles; may vary in size from pinhole to absence of septum

            a) Characterized by loud, harsh murmur

            b) May close spontaneously by age 3—surgery may be indicated (purse-string closure of defect or pulmonary artery banding)

2) Atrial septal defect (ASD)—abnormal opening between the two atria; severity depends on the size and location

**Figure 1. Congenital Heart Defects**

a) Small defects high on the septum may not cause clinical symptoms

b) Murmur audible and distinct for defect

c) Unless defect is severe, prophylactic closure is done in later childhood

3) Patent ductus arteriosus (PDA)—failure of that fetal structure to close after birth (in fetus, ductus arteriosis connects the pulmonary artery to the aorta to shunt oxygenated blood from placenta directly into systemic circulation, bypassing the lungs)

a) PDA allows blood to be shunted from aorta (high pressure) to pulmonary artery (low pressure), causing additional blood to be reoxygenated in the lungs; result is increased pulmonary vascular congestion and right ventricular hypertrophy

b) Characteristic murmur, widened pulse pressure, bounding pulse, and tachycardia

c) Treatment is surgical intervention to divide or ligate the patent vessel

b. Obstruction to blood flow from ventricles (acyanotic)

1) Coarctation of the aorta—narrowing of the aorta

a) High blood pressure and bounding pulses in areas receiving blood from vessels proximal to the defect; weak or absent pulses distal to the defect, cool extremities, and muscle cramps

b) Murmur may or may not be present

c) Surgical treatment involves resection of the coarcted portion and end-to-end anastomosis or replacement of the constricted section using a graft

d) High incidence of complications if left untreated

2) Pulmonic stenosis—narrowing at the entrance to the pulmonary artery

a) Resistance to blood flow causes right ventricular hypertrophy

b) Commonly seen with PDA

c) Severity depends on degree of defect

d) Surgery recommended for severe defect (pulmonary valvotomy)

    3) Aortic stenosis—narrowing of aortic valve causes decreased cardiac output

        a) Murmur usually heard

        b) Surgery recommended

  c. Decreased pulmonary blood flow (cyanotic)

    1) Tetralogy of Fallot—four defects: ventricular septal defect, pulmonic stenosis, overriding aorta, right ventricular hypertrophy (first three are congenital, fourth is acquired due to increased pressure within the right ventricle)

        a) Cyanosis, clubbing of fingers, delayed physical growth and development

        b) Child often squats or assumes knee-chest position

        c) Treatment is surgical correction

  d. Mixed blood flow (cyanotic)

    1) Transposition of the great vessels—pulmonary artery leaves from the left ventricle and the aorta leaves from the right ventricle

        a) Unless there is an associated defect to compensate, this condition is incompatible with life

        b) Depending on severity of condition—severe cyanosis to mild HF

        c) Treatment is surgical correction

    2) Truncus arteriosus—failure of normal septation and embryonic division of pulmonary artery and aorta, resulting in a single vessel that overrides both ventricles, giving rise directly to the pulmonary and systemic circulations

        a) Blood from both ventricles enters the common artery and flows either to the lungs or the aortic arch and body

        b) Cyanosis, left ventricular hypertrophy, dyspnea, marked activity intolerance, and growth retardation

        c) Harsh murmur audible; congestive heart failure usually develops

        d) Palliative treatment—banding both pulmonary arteries to decrease the amount of blood going to lungs

        e) Corrective treatment—closing ventricular septal defect so truncus originates from left ventricle, and creating pathway from right ventricle

    3) Total anomalous venous return—absence of direct communication between pulmonary veins and left atrium; pulmonary veins attach directly to the right atrium or to various veins draining toward the right atrium

        a) Cyanosis, pulmonary congestion, and heart failure

        b) Audible murmur

        c) Surgical correction involves restoring the normal pulmonary venous circulation

4. Compensatory mechanisms observed in cyanotic heart disease
   a. Tachycardia
   b. Polycythemia
   c. Posturing—squatting, knee-chest position
5. Potential nursing diagnoses
   a. Decreased cardiac output
   b. Excess fluid volume
   c. Risk for impaired gas exchange
   d. Activity intolerance
   e. Deficient knowledge
   f. Disabled family coping

C. Plan/Implementation
   1. Prevent congenital heart disease
      a. Optimal maternal nutrition, prenatal care, and avoidance of drugs and alcohol
      b. Immunization against rubella in females
   2. Recognize early symptoms—cyanosis, poor weight gain, poor feeding habits, exercise intolerance, unusual posturing; carefully evaluate heart murmurs
   3. Monitor vital signs and heart rhythm
   4. Provide support for client as well as restful environment
   5. Prepare client for invasive procedures
   6. Monitor intake and output
   7. Provide calm environment and promote rest
   8. Medications
      a. Digoxin
      b. Iron preparations
      c. Diuretics
      d. Potassium
   9. Change feeding pattern for infant
      a. Small amounts every 2 hours
      b. Enlarged nipple hole
      c. Diet—low sodium, high potassium

D. Evaluation
   1. Does child demonstrate good growth and development patterns?
   2. Do family and child cope with alterations caused by congenital defect?

## ▶ HEART FAILURE (HF)

A. Assessment (see Table 2)
B. Diagnose
   1. Failure of the cardiac muscle to pump sufficient blood to meet the body's metabolic needs
   2. Ventricles cannot empty completely, which causes backup of circulation

3. Causes of heart failure (see Table 3)

| Table 2 HEART FAILURE | |
|---|---|
| **LEFT-SIDED FAILURE** | **RIGHT-SIDED FAILURE** |
| Dyspnea, paroxysmal nocturnal dyspnea | Dependent edema (ankle, lower extremities) |
| Orthopnea | Liver enlargement and abdominal pain |
| Pleural effusion | Anorexia, nausea, bloating |
| Cheyne-Stokes respirations | Coolness of extremities secondary to venous congestion in major organs |
| Pulmonary edema, rales (crackles) | Anxiety, fear, depression |
| Cough with frothy, blood-tinged sputum | Weight gain |
| Decreased renal function—elevated BUN, albuminuria | |
| Edema, weight gain | |
| Changes in mental status (cerebral anoxia) | |
| Fatigue, muscle weakness | |
| S3 gallop | |

4. Potential nursing diagnoses
   a. Decreased cardiac output
   b. Activity intolerance
   c. Anxiety
   d. Deficient knowledge
   e. Impaired gas exchange
   f. Ineffective tissue perfusion (cerebral)

**C.** Plan/Implementation
   1. Administer cardiac glycosides
      a. Digoxin—fundamental drug in the treatment of heart failure, especially when associated with low cardiac output
      b. Two categories of dosages
         1) Rapid digitalization—aimed at administering the drug rapidly to achieve detectable effect
         2) Gradual digitalization—client placed on smaller amounts, designed to replace the digoxin lost by excretion while maintaining "optimal" cardiac functioning
   2. Administer angiotensin-converting enzyme (ACE) inhibitors or angiotensin-receptor blockers (ARBs)—decrease afterload and improve myocardial contractility
   3. Administer diuretics—thiazide diuretics, carbonic anhydrase inhibitors, aldosterone antagonists, loop diuretics
   4. Administer vasodilators—decrease afterload and improve contractility
   5. Administer morphine—decrease afterload
   6. Administer inotropic medications—improve cardiac contractility
   7. Administer Human B-type natriuretic peptides—vasodilates
   8. Administer beta-adrenergic blockers—decrease myocardial oxygen demand

9. Diet
   a. Restricted sodium diet
      1) Normal intake: 6–15 g/day
      2) No table salt: 1.6–2.8 g/day
      3) No salt: 1.2–1.4 g/day
      4) Strict low-sodium diet: 0.2–1 g/day
   b. Low calorie, supplemented with vitamins—promotes weight loss, thereby reducing the workload of the heart
   c. Bland, low residue—avoids discomfort from gastric distention and heartburn
   d. Small, frequent feedings to avoid gastric distention, flatulence, and heartburn

| Table 3  CAUSES OF HEART FAILURE | | |
|---|---|---|
| **DISEASE** | **PATHOLOGY** | **RESULT** |
| Hypertensive disease | Vessels become narrowed; peripheral resistance increases | Cardiac muscle enlarges beyond its oxygen supply |
| Arteriosclerosis | Degenerative changes in arterial walls cause permanent narrowing of coronary arteries | Cardiac muscle enlarges beyond its oxygen supply |
| Valvular heart disease | Stenosed valves do not open freely; scarring and retraction of valve leaflets result in incomplete closure | Workload increases until heart fails |
| Rheumatic heart disease | Infection causes damage to heart valves, making them incompetent or narrowed | Incompetent valves cause blood to regurgitate backward; workload increases until heart fails |
| Ischemic heart disease | Coronary arteries are sclerosed or thrombosed | Blood supply is insufficient to nourish heart |
| Constrictive pericarditis | Inflamed pericardial sac becomes scarred and constricted, causing obstruction in blood flow | Low cardiac output and increased venous pressure<br>Decreases filling of heart |
| Circulatory overload (IV fluid over-load; sodium retention; renal shutdown) | Excessive fluid in circulatory system | Overwhelms heart's ability to pump |
| Pulmonary disease | Damage to arterioles of lungs causes vascular constriction; this increases workload of heart | Right ventricular enlargement and failure |
| Tachydysrhythmias | Decreases ventricular filling time | Decreased cardiac output |

10. Record I and O
11. Weigh daily
12. Oxygen therapy and continuous positive airway pressure (CPAP)
13. Teach about disease process, medications and energy management

**D.** Evaluation

1. Is client able to perform activities of daily living without difficulty?

2. Is client knowledgeable about dietary restrictions?

# ► ANGINA PECTORIS

**A.** Assessment

1. Pain—may radiate down left arm; arm pain associated with stress, exertion, or anxiety

2. Relieved with rest and nitroglycerin

**B.** Diagnose

1. Cause—coronary atherosclerosis

2. Risk factors for coronary artery disease

   a. Nonmodifiable (client has no control)

      1) Increasing age

      2) Family history of coronary heart disease

      3) Men more likely to develop heart disease than premenopausal women

      4) Race

   b. Modifiable risk factors (client can exercise control)

      1) Elevated serum cholesterol

      2) Cigarette smoking and/or secondhand exposure

      3) Hypertension

      4) Diabetes mellitus

      5) Physical inactivity

      6) Obesity

      7) Depression or chronic stress

      8) Oral contraceptive use or hormone replacement therapy

      9) Substance abuse-methamphetamines or cocaine

3. Significance—warning sign of ischemia

**C.** Plan/Implementation

1. Health promotion

   a. No smoking

   b. Follow balanced diet that limits intake of fat and sodium

   c. Check blood pressure and cholesterol regularly

   d. Engage in regular physical activity—goal is reduction of blood pressure and pulse rate upon exertion

2. Administer vasodilators, aspirin, glycoprotein, IIb/IIIa inhibitors, beta blockers, angiotensin receptor blockers, calcium channel blockers

3. Exercise program—goal is reduction of blood pressure and pulse rate upon exertion

4. Percutaneous transluminal coronary angioplasty (PTCA) and stent placement

   a. Balloon-tipped catheter inserted under fluoroscopy to the occluded coronary artery

b. Plaque is compressed against wall to open lumen of vessel

c. IV heparin by continuous infusion is used to prevent thrombus formation

d. IV or intracoronary nitroglycerin or sublingual nifedipine is given to prevent coronary vasospasm

e. Monitor for complications (closure of vessel, bleeding, reaction to the dye, hypotension, hypokalemia, dysrhythmias)

f. Health care provider will prescribe long-term nitrate, calcium channel blocker, and aspirin therapy

5. Coronary artery bypass graft surgery (CABG)

   a. Indications—to increase blood flow to heart muscle in clients with severe angina

   b. Saphenous vein or internal mammary artery used for graft; as many as five arteries may be bypassed

   c. Preoperative

      1) Educational and psychological preparation

      2) Medications discontinued—digitalis 12 hours preop, diuretics 2–3 days preop, aspirin and anitcoagulants 1 week preop

      3) Medications administered—potassium chloride to maintain normal potassium level, beta blockers, calcium-channel blockers, antiarrhythmics, antihypertensives, prophylactic antibiotics 20–30 minutes before surgery

   d. Postoperative

      1) Receives mechanical ventilation for 6–24 hours

      2) Connect chest tubes to water-seal drainage system

      3) Ground epicardial pacer wire and tape to client

      4) Assess pulmonary artery and arterial pressures and heart rate and rhythm

      5) Pain relief

      6) Monitor for complications—fluid and electrolyte imbalance, hypotension or hypertension, hypothermia, bleeding, cardiac tamponade, altered cerebral perfusion

      7) Be alert to psychological state, disorientation, or depression

      8) Provide activity as tolerated with progress as ordered, from feet dangling over side of bed, to sitting in chair, to walking in room by third day

   e. Provide guidance concerning long-term care and follow-up

**D.** Evaluation

  1. Does client experience relief of pain and reduction of anxiety?

  2. Does client institute lifestyle changes to decrease stress?

  3. Does client comply with medication, diet, and activity recommendations?

# ▶ PERIPHERAL VASCULAR DISEASE

A. Assessment (see Table 4)

B. Diagnose

   1. Predisposing factors (see Table 4)

C. Plan/Implementation (see Table 4)

D. Evaluation

   1. Has adequate tissue perfusion been re-established?

   2. Does the client have stable vital signs, good color, and adequate peripheral pulses?

   3. Is client free from infection?

   4. Is client free from pain?

   5. Do client and significant others understand and comply with activity restrictions?

| Table 4  PERIPHERAL VASCULAR DISEASE | | | |
|---|---|---|---|
| TYPE | ASSESSMENT | PREDISPOSING FACTORS | TREATMENT/NURSING CONSIDERATIONS |
| Arterial (Arteriosclerosis, Raynaud's disease, Buerger's disease) | Dependent rubor<br>Cool, shiny skin<br>Cyanosis<br>Ulcers, gangrene<br>Impaired sensation<br>Intermittent claudication<br>Decreased peripheral pulses<br>Pallor with extremity elevation<br>Rest pain | Smoking<br>Exposure to cold<br>Emotional stress<br>Diabetes mellitus<br>High-fat diet<br>Hypertension<br>Obesity | Monitor peripheral pulses<br>Good foot care<br>Do not cross legs<br>Regular exercise<br>Stop smoking<br>Transluminal angioplasty<br>Arterial bypass<br>Endarterectomy Amputation<br>Vasodilators<br>Anticoagulants<br>Antiplatelet medications |
| Venous (Varicose veins, Thrombophlebitis) | Cool, brown skin<br>Edema, ulcers, pain<br>Normal or decreased pulses | Immobility<br>Pregnancy<br>Hereditary<br>Obesity<br>Surgery<br>CHF<br>Injury to vein wall<br>Hypercoagulability | Monitor peripheral pulses<br>Thrombectomy<br>Avoid extremes of temperature<br>Elastic stockings, TED hose, intermittent pneumatic compression devices (IPC)<br>Anticoagulants<br>Activity as ordered<br>Encourage early ambulation<br>Elevate legs<br>Warm moist packs |

# ▶ HYPERTENSION

A. Assessment

   1. May be no symptoms

   2. Headache, dizziness, facial flushing

   3. Anginal pain

4. Intermittent claudication

5. Retinal hemorrhages and exudates

6. Severe occipital headaches associated with nausea, vomiting, drowsiness, giddiness, anxiety, and mental impairment

7. Polyuria, nocturia, protein and RBCs in urine, diminished ability of kidneys to concentrate urine

8. Dyspnea upon exertion—left-sided heart failure

9. Edema of the extremities—right-sided heart failure

**B.** Diagnose

1. Persistent elevation of the systolic blood pressure above 140 mm Hg and diastolic blood pressure above 90 mm Hg

2. Causes

   a. Risk factors

      1) Family history of hypertension

      2) Excessive sodium intake

      3) Excessive intake of calories

      4) Physical inactivity

      5) Excessive alcohol intake

      6) Contributing factors—history of renal and/or cardiovascular disease

      7) Low potassium intake

      8) Stressful lifestyle

      9) Age

   b. Primary (essential or idiopathic)—constitutes 90% of all cases; may be benign (gradual onset and prolonged course) or malignant(abrupt onset and short dramatic course, which is rapidly fatal unless treated)

   c. Secondary—develops as a result of another primary disease of the cardiovascular system, renal system, adrenal glands, or neurological system, medications

3. Complications

   a. Renal failure

   b. Stroke

   c. Transient ischemic attacks (TIAs)

   d. Retinal hemorrhages

4. Potential nursing diagnoses

   a. Knowledge deficit

   b. Management of therapeutic regimen: individual, ineffective

   c. Noncompliance related to medications

**C.** Plan/Implementation

1. Administer antihypertensive medications—diuretics, calcium-channel blockers, ACE inhibitors, angiotensin receptor blocker, beta blockers, aldosterone blockers, central alpha antagonists

2. Teaching

   a. Medication adverse effects and compliance with medication

   b. Dietary restriction of sodium and fat

    c. Weight control

    d. Moderate alcohol intake

    e. Increase physical activity

    f. Stop smoking

    g. Health care follow-up

    h. Change positions slowly because of possible orthostatic hypotension

**D.** Evaluation

    1. Is client's blood pressure within normal limits?

    2. Is client compliant with therapeutic regime?

## ▶ ANEMIA

**A.** Assessment

    1. Mild

        a. Hemoglobin 13–18 g/dL male (130–180 g/L): usually asymptomatic

        b. Symptoms usually follow strenuous exertion: palpitations, dyspnea, diaphoresis

    2. Moderate

        a. Dyspnea, palpitations

        b. Diaphoresis

        c. Chronic fatigue

    3. Severe

        a. Pale, exhausted all the time

        b. Severe palpitations

        c. Sensitivity to cold

        d. Loss of appetite

        e. Profound weakness

        f. Dizziness, syncope

        g. Headache

        h. Cardiac complications—CHF, angina pectoris

**B.** Diagnose

    1. A decrease in the number of erythrocytes or a reduction in hemoglobin

**C.** Plan/Implementation

    1. Identify cause

    2. Frequent rest periods

    3. Frequent turning and positioning

    4. Diet high in protein, iron, vitamins

    5. Small, easily digestible meals

    6. Good oral hygiene

    7. Monitor blood transfusions

    8. Protect from sources of infection

**D.** Evaluation

    1. Does client maintain normal hemoglobin and erythrocyte levels?

    2. Does client maintain adequate tissue perfusion and gas exchange?

# ▶ IRON DEFICIENCY ANEMIA

A. Assessment

1. Fatigue

2. Decreased serum albumin, gamma globulin, and transferrin

3. Glossitis (inflammation of tongue)

4. "Spoon" fingernails (koilonychia)

5. Impaired cognition

B. Diagnose

1. Most common type

2. Causes: decreased dietary intake; malabsorption after gastric resection; blood loss due to ulcers, gastritis, GI tumors, menorrhagia (excessive menstrual bleeding); poor absorption due to high-fiber diet

C. Plan/Implementation

1. Dietary addition of iron-rich foods

2. Iron supplements IM or IV iron dextran (IV route is preferred), IM route causes pain, skin staining, and higher incidence of anaphylaxis; take oral supplements with meals if experience GI upset, then resume between meals for maximum absorption, take with ascorbic acid; use straw if liquids are used

3. Iron Preparations

D. Evaluation

1. Serum values within normal limits.

2. Client experiences a reduction of symptoms.

# ▶ VITAMIN $B_{12}$ ANEMIA AND PERNICIOUS ANEMIA

A. Assessment

1. Pallor

2. Fatigue

3. Weight loss

4. Sore, red tongue

5. Balance and gait disturbances

6. Paresthesias in hands and feet

B. Diagnose

1. Pernicious anemia: gastric mucosa fails to secrete sufficient intrinsic factor required for absorption of vitamin $B_{12}$; diagnosed by Schilling test (fast for 12 hours; given small dose of radioactive $B_{12}$ in water to drink, followed by large, nonradioactive dose IM, 24-hour urine specimen collected, measured for radioactivity)

2. Inadequate dietary intake (can occur with vegans who eat no meat or meat products)

3. Bone marrow produces fewer, larger (macrocytic) red blood cells

C. Plan/Implementation

1. Initial IM administration of 25 to 100 micrograms of vitamin $B_{12}$, followed by 500 to 1,000 micrograms every 1 to 2 months or cyanocobalamin nasal spray

2. Vegetarians prevent or treat by taking vitamins or fortified soy milk

D. Evaluation

1. Serum values remain within normal limits

2. Client experiences a reduction of symptoms

# ► SICKLE CELL DISEASE

A. Assessment

1. Pain (may be severe)

2. Swelling of joints during crisis

3. Fever

4. Jaundice (especially of sclerae)

5. Tachycardia, cardiac murmurs

6. Hemoglobin 7–10 g/dL (70–100 g/L); sickled cells on peripheral blood smear

B. Diagnose

1. Severe hemolytic anemia resulting from defective hemoglobin, hemoglobin becomes sickle-shaped in presence of low oxygenation

2. Symptoms are caused by hemolysis and thrombosis

C. Plan/Implementation

1. Check joint areas for pain and swelling

2. Check for signs of infection (osteomyelitis and pneumonia common)

3. Promptly treat infection (to prevent crisis)

4. Avoid high altitudes and exposure to extreme temperature

5. Encourage fluid intake (dehydration promotes crisis)

6. Administer folic acid daily

7. During crisis provide analgesics (PCA with morphine sulfate or hydromorphone) and hydration (3–5 L of IV fluids/day for adults; 1600 ml/m2/day for child)

8. Administer hydroxyurea; risk of leukemia and bone marrow suppression

D. Evaluation

1. Has client comfort been maintained?

2. Are parents knowledgeable about ways to prevent sickle cell crisis?

# ► HEMOPHILIA

A. Assessment

1. Spontaneous easy bruising

2. Joint pain with bleeding

3. Prolonged internal or external bleeding from mild trauma, gingival bleeding, GI bleeding, hematuria

4. Pallor

**B.** Diagnose

    1. Causes

        a. Sex-linked, transmitted to male by female carrier, recessive trait

        b. Factor VIII deficiency—hemophilia A—most common

    2. Treatment

        a. Plasma or factor VIII cryoprecipitate

        b. Bedrest

        c. Analgesics (aspirin contraindicated)

**C.** Plan/Implementation

    1. Assess for internal bleeding

    2. Analgesics for joint pain—not aspirin

    3. Avoid IM injections

    4. Bedrest during bleeding episodes

    5. Assist with coping with chronic disease and altered lifestyle

    6. Teach to avoid contact sports; engage in activities such as golf, swimming

    7. Teach about replacement of clotting factor

**D.** Evaluation

    1. Is normal blood volume maintained?

    2. Is client aware of restrictions on use of analgesics?

## ▶ PITUITARY DISORDERS

**A.** Assessment (see Table 5)

**B.** Diagnose (see Table 5)

    1. Anterior hormones—Growth, TSH, ACTH, LH, FSH

    2. Posterior hormones—oxytocin, vasopressin, ADH

**C.** Plan/Implementation (see Table 5)

| Table 5  PITUITARY DISORDERS | | |
|---|---|---|
| | DWARFISM (HYPOPITUITARISM) | ACROMEGALY |
| Assessment | Height below normal, body proportions normal, bone/tooth development retarded, sexual maturity delayed, skin fine, features delicate | Body size enlarged, coordination poor, flat bones enlarged, sexual abnormalities, deep voice, skin thick and soft, visual field changes |
| Diagnose | Hyposecretion of growth hormone; occurs before maturity<br><br>Etiology unclear; predisposition–pituitary tumors, idiopathic hyperplasia<br><br>Treatment: hormone replacement (human growth hormone, thyroid growth hormone, testosterone)<br><br>Complication: diabetes | Hypersecretion of growth hormone occurs after maturity<br><br>Etiology: unclear<br><br>Diagnosis: growth hormone measured in blood plasma<br><br>Treatment: external irradiation of tumor, atrium-90 implant transnasally, hypophysectomy (removal of pituitary or portion of it with hormone replacement) |
| Potential nursing diagnosis | Self-esteem disturbance<br><br>Risk for sexual dysfunction | Body image disturbance Nutrition, altered<br><br>Chronic pain<br><br>Risk for sexual dysfunction |
| Plan/Implementation | Monitor growth and development<br><br>Provide emotional support<br><br>Assess body image<br><br>Refer for psychological counseling as needed<br><br>Monitor medications<br><br>Hormone replacement therapy<br><br>Thyroid hormone replacement<br><br>Testosterone therapy<br><br>Human chorionic gonadotropin (hCG) injections | Monitor blood sugar level<br><br>Provide emotional support<br><br>Provide safety due to poor coordination and vision<br><br>Administer dopamine agonists; somatostatin analogs; growth hormone receptor blockers<br><br>Provide care during radiation therapy<br><br>Provide posthypophysectomy care:<br><br>    Elevate head<br><br>    Check neurological status and nasal drainage<br><br>    Monitor BP frequently<br><br>    Observe for hormonal deficiencies (thyroid, glucocorticoid)<br><br>    Observe for hypoglycemia<br><br>    Monitor intake and output<br><br>    Provide cortisone replacement before and after surgery<br><br>Avoid coughing<br><br>Avoid tooth brushing for 2 weeks |

**D.** Evaluation

1. Have the child's growth and developmental needs been met?

2. Have the parents adjusted to child's condition?

# ▶ CANCER

**A.** Assessment

  1. American Cancer Society Warning Signs

    a. Change in bowel, bladder habits

    b. A sore that does not heal

    c. Unusual bleeding or discharge

    d. Thickening or a lump in the breast or elsewhere

    e. Indigestion or difficulty in swallowing

    f. Obvious change in a wart or mole

    g. Nagging cough or hoarseness

**B.** Diagnose

  1. Risk factors

    a. Immunosuppression

    b. Advancing age

    c. Genetic predisposition

  2. Causative factors

    a. Physical

      1) Radiation—excessive exposure to sunlight and radiation

      2) Chronic irritation

    b. Chemical

      1) Food additives—e.g., nitrites

      2) Industry—e.g., asbestos

      3) Pharmaceutical—e.g., stilbesterol

      4) Smoking

      5) Alcohol

    c. Genetic

    d. Viral—incorporated into cell genesis: Epstein-Barr virus, Burkitt's lymphoma

    e. Stress—co-causative factor

  3. Common cancer types

    a. Caucasian

      1) Lung

      2) Breast

      3) Colorectal

      4) Prostate

    b. African American

      1) Lung

      2) Prostate

      3) Breast

            4) Colorectal

            5) Uterine

        c. Asian

            1) Breast

            2) Colorectal

            3) Prostate

            4) Lung

            5) Stomach

        d. Hispanic

            1) Prostate

            2) Breast

            3) Colorectal

            4) Lung

    4. Classifications

        a. Carcinoma—epithelial tissue

        b. Sarcoma—connective tissue

        c. Lymphoma—lymphoid tissue

        d. Leukemia—blood-forming tissue (WBCs and platelets)

    5. Potential nursing diagnoses

        a. Skin integrity, impaired

        b. Risk for infection

        c. Fear/death anxiety

        d. Grieving

        e. Acute/chronic pain

        f. Fatigue

**C.** Plan/Implementation

    1. Cancer prevention

        a. Avoid known carcinogens

            1) Don't smoke

            2) Wear sunscreen

            3) Eliminate asbestos in buildings

        b. Modify dietary habits

            1) Avoid excessive intake of animal fat

            2) Avoid nitrates found in prepared lunch meats, sausage, and bacon

            3) Decrease intake of red meat

            4) Limit alcohol intake to one or two drinks per day

            5) Increase intake of bran, broccoli, cauliflower, brussels sprouts, cabbage, and foods high in vitamin A and C

    2. Chemotherapy

    3. Teletherapy (radiotherapy)

        a. External radiation (e.g., cobalt)

            1) Leave radiology markings intact on skin

            2) Avoid creams, lotions, deodorants, and/or perfumes, unless prescribed

3) Use lukewarm water to cleanse area

4) Assess skin for redness, cracking

5) Administer antiemetics for nausea, analgesics for pain

6) Observe skin, mucous membranes, and hair follicles for adverse effects

7) No hot water bottle, tape; don't expose area to cold or sunlight

8) Wear cotton clothing

b. Brachytherapy (internal radiation) (e.g., cesium, radium, gold)

1) Sealed source (cesium)—mechanically positioned source of radioactive material placed in body cavity or tumor

a) Lead container and long-handled forceps in room in event of dislodged source

b) Save all dressings, bed linens until source is removed; then discard dressings and linens as usual

c) Urine, feces not radioactive

d) Do not stand close or in line with radioactive source

e) Client on bedrest while implant in place

f) Position of source verified by radiography

2) Unsealed source of radiation—unsealed liquid given orally, or instilled in body cavity (e.g., $^{131}$I)

a) All body fluids contaminated

b) Greatest danger from body fluids during first 24–96 hours

3) Nursing care for internal radiation

a) Assign client to private room

b) Place "Caution: Radioactive Material" sign on door

c) Wear dosimeter film badge at all times when interacting with client (offers no protection but measures amount of exposure; each nurse has individual badge)

d) Do not assign pregnant nurse to client

e) Rotate staff caring for client; limit close contact to 30 minutes per 8 hour shift

f) Organize tasks so limited time is spent in client's room

g) Limit visitors

h) Encourage client to do own care

i) Provide shield in room

j) Use antiemetics for nausea

k) Consider body image (e.g., alopecia)

l) Provide comfort measures, analgesic for pain

m) Provide good nutrition

4. Skin care

a. Avoid use of soaps and powders

b. Wear cotton, loose-fitting clothing

5. Mouth care

a. Stomatitis—develops 5–14 days after chemotherapy begins

b. Symptoms—erythema, ulcers, bleeding

    c. Rinse with saline or chlorhexidine; avoid hard-bristled toothbrush, dental floss, lemon glycerin swabs

    d. Avoid hot (temperature) or spicy foods

    e. Topical antifungals and anesthetics

6. Hair care

    a. Alopecia commonly seen, alters body image

    b. Assist with wig or hair piece

    c. Scarves, hats

7. Nutritional changes

    a. Anorexia, nausea, and vomiting commonly seen with chemotherapy

    b. Malabsorption and cachexia (wasting) common

    c. Make meals appealing to senses

    d. Conform diet to client preferences and nutritional needs

    e. Small, frequent meals with additional supplements between meals (high-calorie, high-protein diet)

    f. Encourage fluids but limit at meal times

    g. Perform oral hygiene and provide relief of pain before meal time

    h. PN as needed

8. Neutropenia precautions—prevent infection among clients with immunosuppression; absolute neutrophil count less than or equal to 1000 cells x $10^3$/mm$^3$

    a. Assess skin integrity every 8 hours; auscultate breath sounds, presence of cough, sore throat; check temperature every 4 hours, report if higher than 101° F (38°C); monitor CBC and differential daily

    b. Private room when possible

    c. Thorough hand hygiene before entering client's room

    d. Allow no staff with cold or sore throat to care for client

    e. No fresh flowers or standing water

    f. Clean room daily

    g. Low microbial diet; no fresh salads, unpeeled fresh fruits and vegetables

    h. Deep breathe every 4 hours

    i. Meticulous body hygiene

    j. Inspect IV site, meticulous IV site care

9. Pain relief—three-step ladder approach

    a. For mild pain—nonnarcotic medication used(acetaminophen) along with antiemetics, antidepressants, glucocorticoids

    b. For moderate pain—weak narcotics (codeine) and nonnarcotics are used

    c. For severe pain—strong narcotics are used (morphine)

    d. Give pain medications on regularly scheduled basis (preventative approach), additional analgesics given for breakthrough pain

10. Activity level

    a. Alternate rest and activity

    b. Maintain normal lifestyle

11. Psychosocial issues

    a. Encourage participation in self-care and decision-making

    b. Provide referral to support groups, organizations

    c. Hospice care

**D.** Evaluation

    1. Has client been assisted through stages of grief?

    2. Has client's comfort been maintained?

## ▶ LEUKEMIA

**A.** Assessment

    1. Ulcerations of mouth and throat

    2. Pneumonia, septicemia

    3. Altered leukocyte count ($15,000-500,000 \times 10^3/mm^3$)

    4. Anemia, fatigue, lethargy, bone and joint pain, hypoxia

    5. Bleeding gums, ecchymosis, petechiae, retinal hemorrhages

    6. Weakness, pallor, weight loss, hepatomegaly, splenomegaly

    7. Headache, disorientation, convulsions

**B.** Diagnose

    1. Neoplastic disease that involves the blood-forming tissues of the bone marrow, spleen, and lymph nodes; abnormal, uncontrolled, and destructive proliferation of one type of white cell and its precursors

    2. Diagnostic tests

        a. Bone marrow aspiration

            1) Informed consent required

            2) Done at iliac crest and sternum

            3) Local anesthetic used

            4) Apply sterile dressing to area after procedure; apply pressure to site if bleeding

            5) Complications

                a) Osteomyelitis

                b) Bleeding

                c) Puncture of vital organs

    3. Classification of the leukemias

        a. Acute leukemia—rapid onset and progresses to a fatal termination within days to months; more common among children and young adults

        b. Chronic leukemia—gradual onset with a slower, more protracted course; more common between ages 25 and 60

    4. Factors associated with development

        a. Viruses

        b. Ionizing radiation

        c. Genetic predisposition

        d. Absorption of certain chemicals, e.g., benzene, pyridine, and aniline dyes

C. Plan/Implementation

1. Assess for signs of bleeding, e.g., petechiae, bruising, bleeding, thrombocytopenia; follow bleeding precautions

2. Monitor for signs of infection, e.g., changes in vital signs, chills, neutropenia

3. Good mouth care

4. High-calorie, high-vitamin diet

5. Frequent feedings of soft, easy-to-eat food

6. Antiemetics

7. Neutropenia precautions, if necessary

8. Strict handwashing

9. Prevent skin breakdown, e.g., turning, positioning

10. Administer and monitor blood transfusions (whole blood, platelets)

11. Administer medications, treatments as ordered, and observe for adverse effects

   a. Chemotherapy

      1) Nausea, vomiting, diarrhea

      2) Stomatitis, alopecia, skin reactions

      3) Bone marrow depression

   b. Radiation or radioisotope therapy

   c. Bone marrow transplants

D. Evaluation

1. Is client in remission?

2. Does client exhibit minimal complications of the disease?

## ▶ SKIN CANCER

A. Assessment

1. Basal cell carcinoma—small, waxy nodule on sun-exposed areas of body (e.g., face); may ulcerate and crust

2. Squamous cell carcinoma—rough, thick, scaly tumor seen on arms or face

3. Malignant melanoma—variegated color (brown, black mixed with gray or white) circular lesion with irregular edges seen on trunk or legs

B. Diagnose

1. Major risk factor—overexposure to sun

2. Basal cell carcinoma—most common type of skin cancer; rarely metastasize but commonly reoccurs

3. Squamous cell carcinoma—may metastasize to blood or lymph

4. Malignant melanoma—most lethal of skin cancers; frequently seen 20–45 years old; highest risk persons with fair complexions, blue eyes, red or blond hair, and freckles; metastases to bone, liver, spleen, CNS, lungs, lymph

5. Diagnosed by skin lesion biopsy

C. Plan/Implementation

   1. Postop care following surgical excision

   2. Teach prevention

      a. Avoid exposure to sun 10 a.m. to 3 p.m.

      b. Use sunscreen with SPF (solar protection factor) to block harmful rays (especially important for children)

      c. Reapply sunscreen after swimming or prolonged time in sun

      d. Use lip balm with sunscreen protection

      e. Wear hat when outdoors

      f. Do not use lamps or tanning booths

      g. Teach client to examine skin surfaces monthly

   3. Teach how to identify danger signs of melanoma—change in size, color, shape of mole or surrounding skin

   4. Chemotherapy for metastases

D. Evaluation

   1. Is client knowledgeable about ways to prevent skin cancer?

   2. Is client knowledgeable about danger signs of malignant melanoma?

# ▶ INTRACRANIAL TUMORS

A. Assessment—signs and symptoms vary depending on location

   1. Motor deficits

   2. Language disturbances

   3. Hearing difficulties, visual disturbances (occipital lobe)

   4. Dizziness, paresthesia (cerebellum), coordination problems

   5. Seizures (motor cortex)

   6. Personality disturbances (frontal lobe)

   7. Papilledema

   8. Nausea and vomiting

   9. Drowsiness, changes in level of consciousness

B. Diagnose

   1. Types—classified according to location

      a. Supratentorial—incision usually behind hairline, surgery within the cerebral hemisphere

      b. Infratentorial—incision made at nape of neck around occipital lobe; surgery within brain stem and cerebellum

   2. Causes—unknown

   3. Medical/surgical management—intracranial surgery (burr holes, craniotomy, cranioplasty),and radiation

C. Plan/Implementation

   1. Preoperative care

      a. Detailed neurological assessment for baseline data

      b. Head shave—prep site

      c. Psychological support

      d. Prepare client for postoperative course

2. Postoperative care

    a. Maintain patent airway

    b. Elevate head of bed 30–45° after supratentorial surgery

    c. Position client flat and lateral on either side after infratentorial surgery

    d. Monitor vital and neurological signs

    e. Observe for complications—respiratory difficulties, increased intracranial pressure, hyperthermia, meningitis, wound infection

    f. Administer medications—corticosteroids, osmotic diurectics, mild analgesics, anticonvulsants, antibiotics, antipyretics, antiemetics, hormone replacement as needed; no narcotics postoperatively (masks changes in LOC), use acetaminophen

**D.** Evaluation

    1. Have postoperative complications been avoided?

    2. Has client adjusted to the change in body image?

## ▶ PANCREATIC TUMORS

**A.** Assessment

    1. Weight loss

    2. Vague upper or mid-abdominal discomfort

    3. Abnormal glucose tolerance test (hyperglycemia)

    4. Jaundice, clay-colored stools, dark urine

**B.** Diagnose

    1. Tumors may arise from any portion of the pancreas (head or tail); each has unique clinical manifestations

    2. Diagnostic tests—CT, CT-guided needle biopsy, MRI

    3. Risk factor—smoking, pancreatitis, exposure to environmental toxins

**C.** Plan/Implementation

    1. Medical

        a. High-calorie, bland, low-fat diet; small, frequent feedings

        b. Avoid alcohol

        c. Anticholinergics

        d. Chemotherapy, radiation therapy, stent placement

    2. Surgery (Whipple procedure)—removal of head of pancreas, distal portion of common bile duct, the duodenum, and part of the stomach

    3. Postop care

        a. Monitor for peritonitis and intestinal obstruction

        b. Monitor for hypotension

        c. Monitor for steatorrhea

        d. Administer pancreatic enzymes

        e. Monitor for diabetes mellitus

**D.** Evaluation

    1. Has client's comfort been maintained?

    2. Have postoperative complications been avoided?

# ► CARCINOMA OF THE LARYNX

**A.** Assessment

1. Pain radiating to the ears
2. Hoarseness, dysphagia, foul breath
3. Dyspnea
4. Enlarged cervical nodes
5. Hemoptysis

**B.** Diagnose

1. Diagnostic tests
   a. Laryngoscopy, Bronchoscopy
   b. Biopsy
   c. CT, MRI
   d. X-rays
2. Causes
   a. Industrial chemicals
   b. Cigarette smoking and alcohol use
   c. Straining of the vocal cords
   d. Chronic laryngitis
   e. Family predisposition

**C.** Plan/Implementation

1. Caring for the client with a laryngectomy
   a. Preoperative care
      1) Explain compensatory methods of communication
      2) Referral to speech therapy
   b. Postoperative care
      1) Laryngectomy care—stoma care, suction
      2) Place in semi-Fowler's position
      3) Turn, cough, and deep breathe
      4) Provide humidified oxygen
      5) Suction oral secretions
      6) Assess condition of skin flap
      7) Nasogastric, gastrostomy, or jejunostomy feeding tube
2. Observe for postoperative complications after laryngectomy
   a. Respiratory difficulties
   b. Fistula formation and wound breakdown
   c. Rupture of carotid artery
   d. Stenosis of trachea
3. Monitor weight, food intake, and fluid intake and output
4. Communication for total laryngectomy clients
   a. Esophageal speech
   b. Artificial larynx—commonly used mechanical device for speech
5. Radiation therapy—small, localized cancers; sore throat, increased hoarseness, dysphagia

**D.** Evaluation
1. Is client knowledgeable about compensatory methods of artificial speech?
2. Has client adjusted to altered body image?

Chapter 6

# PHYSIOLOGICAL INTEGRITY: BASIC CARE AND COMFORT

| Sections | Concepts Covered |
|---|---|
| 1. Mobility and Immobility | Mobility, Client Education: Providing |
| 2. Conditions Limiting Mobility | Mobility, Skin Integrity, Client Education: Providing |
| 3. Interventions to Promote Comfort | Comfort, Client Education: Providing |
| 4. Musculoskeletal Trauma | Mobility, Client Education: Providing |
| 5. Rest and Sleep Disturbances | Rest/Sleep, Client Education: Providing |
| 6. Nutrition | Nutrition, client Education: Providing |
| 7. Elimination | Elimination |

# MOBILITY AND IMMOBILITY

▶ **MOBILITY**

**A.** Assessment

1. Body build, height, weight–proportioned within normal limits
2. Posture, body alignment–erect
   a. Lumbar lordosis–exaggerated concavity in the lumbar region
   b. Kyphosis–exaggerated convexity in the thoracic region
   c. Scoliosis–lateral curvature of a portion of the vertebral column
3. Gait, ambulation–smooth
4. Joints–freely movable (see Table 1)
5. Skin integrity–intact
6. Muscle tone, elasticity, strength–adequate
7. Exercise level–appropriate
8. Rest and sleep patterns–adequate
9. Sexual activity–appropriate
10. Job-related activity–acceptable
11. Developmental mobility–within normal limits

| Table 1  JOINT MOVEMENTS | |
|---|---|
| **MOVEMENT** | **ACTION** |
| Flexion | Decrease angle of joint, e.g., bending elbow |
| Extension | Increase angle of joint, e.g., straightening elbow |
| Hyperextension | Excessively increase angle of joint, e.g., bending the head backward |
| Abduction | Moving bone away from midline of body |
| Adduction | Moving bone toward midline of body ("add" to body) |
| Rotation | Moving bone around its central axis |
| Dorsiflexion | Flexion of the foot toward the trunk of the body ("toes toward the nose") |
| Plantar flexion | Flexion of the foot away from the trunk of the body ("pointing the toes") |
| Inversion | Turning the foot inward at the ankle |
| Eversion | Turning the foot outward at the ankle |
| Pronation | Rotation of the forearm so that the palm of the hand turns downward |
| Supination | Rotation of the forearm so that the palm of the hand turns upward |

**B.** Diagnose

1. Activity

   a. Maintains muscle tone and posture

   b. Serves as an outlet for tension and anxiety

2. Exercise

   a. Maintains joint mobility and function

   b. Promotes muscle strength

   c. Stimulates circulation

   d. Promotes optimum ventilation

   e. Stimulates appetite

   f. Promotes elimination

   g. Enhances metabolic rate

3. Potential nursing diagnoses

   a. Impaired walking

   b. Activity intolerance

   c. Risk for falls

   d. Risk for injury

**C.** Plan/Implementation

1. Avoid injury

   a. Prevent motor vehicle accidents, use seat belts and helmets

   b. Avoid job-related accidents, follow safety procedures

   c. When engaging in contact sports, perform proper body conditioningand use protective devices

   d. For aged persons, rugs should be secure, stairways lit and clear of debris

   e. During pregnancy use bathtub grips, low-heeled shoes

   f. Assist client to sit on side of bed

      1) Place hand under knees and shoulders of client

      2) Instruct client to push elbow into bed; at the same time the nurse should lift the client's shoulders with one arm and swing the client's legs over edge of bed with the other arm

   g. Assist client to stand

      1) Face client with hands firmly grasping each side of his/her rib cage

      2) Push nurse's knee against one knee of the client

      3) Rock client forward as he/she comes to a standing position

      4) Pivot client to position him/her to sit in chair (placed on client's stronger side)

   h. Assist client out of bed

      1) If client has a weaker side, move the client toward the stronger side (easier for client to pull the weak side)

      2) Use the larger muscles of the legs to accomplish a move rather than the smaller muscles of the back

3) Drawsheets are a better method of moving a client than sliding a client across a surface

4) Always have an assistant standing by if there is any possibility of problems in completing a transfer

   i. Teach client ADLs

1) Observe what client can do and allow him/her to do it

2) Encourage client to exercise muscles used for activity

3) Start with gross functional movement before going to finer motions

4) Extend period of activity as much and as fast as the client can tolerate

5) Give positive feedback immediately after every accomplishment

**D.** Evaluation

1. Is the client's mobility within normal limits?

2. Has a safe transfer been accomplished?

# ▶ IMMOBILITY

**A.** Assessment

1. Gait, ambulation

2. Joint movement

3. Muscle tone

4. Skin integrity

| Table 2  THERAPEUTIC EXERCISES | | |
|---|---|---|
| EXERCISE | DESCRIPTION | RATIONALE |
| Passive range of motion | Performed by nurse without assistance from client | Retention of joint range of motion; maintenance of circulation |
| Active assistive range of motion | Performed by client with assistance of nurse | Increases motion in the joint |
| Active range of motion | Performed by client without assistance | Maintains mobility of joints and increases muscle strength |
| Active resistive range of motion | Performed by client against manual or mechanical resistance | Provision of resistance to increase muscle strength; 5-pound bags/ weights may be used |
| Isometric exercises | Performed by client; alternate contraction and relaxation of muscle without moving joint | Maintenance of muscle strength when joint immobilized |

**B.** Diagnose

1. Activity intolerance

2. Impaired walking

3. Risk for Disuse syndrome

4. Fatigue

**C.** Plan/Implementation

    1.  Therapeutic exercises (see Table 2)

    2.  Prevent complication of immobility (see Table 3)

    3.  Maintain specific therapeutic positions (see Table 4)

**D.** Evaluation

    1.  Have complications of immobility been prevented?

    2.  Has client resumed normal functioning?

| Table 3 COMPLICATIONS OF IMMOBILITY | | |
|---|---|---|
| **COMPLICATION** | **SEQUELAE** | **NURSING CONSIDERATIONS** |
| Decubitus ulcer | Osteomyelitis<br>Tissue maceration<br>Infection | Frequently turn, provide skin care<br>Ambulate as appropriate<br>Use draw sheet when turning to avoid shearing force<br>Provide balanced diet with adequate protein, vitamins, and minerals<br>Use air mattress, flotation pads, elbow and heel pads, sheepskin<br>Assist with use of Stryker frame or Circ-O-Lectric bed |
| Sensory input changes | Confusion, disorientation | Orient frequently<br>Place clock, calendar within sight |
| Osteoporosis | Pathological fractures<br>Renal calculi | Encourage weight-bearing on long bones<br>Provide balanced diet<br>Monitor estrogen therapy, if ordered |
| Negative nitrogen balance | Anorexia, debilitation, weight loss | Give high-protein diet and small, frequent feedings |
| Hypercalcemia | Impaired bone growth | Reduce calcium in diet, encourage fluids |
| Increased cardiac workload | Tachycardia | Use trapeze to decrease Valsalva maneuver when moving in bed<br>Teach client how to move without holding breath |
| Contractures | Deformities | Frequent change of position<br>Use pillows, trochanter rolls, foot board to promote proper body alignment<br>Exercise as appropriate |

| Table 3 COMPLICATIONS OF IMMOBILITY *(CONTINUED)* | | |
|---|---|---|
| **COMPLICATION** | **SEQUELAE** | **NURSING CONSIDERATIONS** |
| Thrombus formation | Pulmonary emboli | Leg exercises—flexion, extension of toes for 5 minutes every hour |
| | | Ambulate as appropriate |
| | | Frequent change of position |
| | | Avoid using knee gatch on bed or pillows to support knee flexion |
| | | Use TED or elastic hose |
| | | Assess edema, warmth and pain |
| Orthostatic hypotension | Weakness, faintness, dizziness | Teach client to rise from bed slowly |
| | | Increase activity gradually |
| Stasis of respiratory secretions | Hypostatic pneumonia | Teach client the importance of turning, coughing, and deep breathing |
| | | Administer postural drainage as appropriate |
| Constipation | Fecal impaction | Ambulate as appropriate |
| | | Increase fluid intake and fiber in diet |
| | | Ensure privacy for use of bed pan or commode |
| | | Administer stool softeners, e.g., Colace |
| Urinary stasis | Urinary retention<br>Renal calculi | Have client void in normal position, if possible |
| | | Increase fluid intake |
| | | Low-calcium diet, increase acid ash residue to acidify urine and prevent formation of calcium stones |
| Boredom | Restlessness | Allow visitors, use of radio, television |
| | | Schedule occupational therapy |
| Depression | Insomnia<br>Restlessness | Encourage self-care |
| | | Start with simple, gross activity before advancing to finer motor movements |
| | | Increase period of activity as rapidly as client can tolerate |
| | | Support client with positive feedback for effort/ accomplishment |

| Table 4 SPECIFIC THERAPEUTIC POSITIONS | |
|---|---|
| POSITION | FUNCTION |
| Supine | Avoids hip flexion, which can compress arterial flow |
| Dorsal recumbent | Supine with knees flexed, more comfortable |
| Prone | Promotes extension of the hip joint<br>Not well tolerated by persons with respiratory or cardiovascular difficulties |
| Side lateral or side-lying | Allows drainage of oral secretions |
| Knee-chest | Provides maximal visualization of rectal area |
| Side with upper leg bent (Sim's) | Allows drainage of oral secretions<br>Decreases abdominal tension |
| Head elevated (Fowler's) | Increases venous return<br>Allows maximal lung expansion<br>High-Fowler's: 60–90°<br>Fowler's: 45–60°<br>Semi-Fowler's: 30–45°<br>Low-Fowler's: 15–30° |
| Modified Trendelenburg (feet elevated 20°, knees straight, trunk flat, and head slightly elevated) | Increases blood return to heart<br>Used for shock |
| Head elevated and knees elevated | Increases blood return to heart<br>Relieves pressure on lumbosacral area |
| Elevation of extremity | Increases venous return<br>Decreases blood volume to extremity |
| Lithotomy (Flat on back, thighs flexed, legs abducted) | Increases vaginal opening for examination |

## ▶ ASSISTIVE DEVICES

A. Tilt table
   1. Used for weight-bearing on long bones to prevent decalcification of bones and resulting bone weakness, renal calculi
   2. Stimulates circulation to lower extremities
   3. Use elastic stockings to prevent postural hypotension
   4. Should be done gradually; board can be tilted in 5–10° increments
   5. Blood pressure should be checked during the procedure
   6. If blood pressure goes down and dizziness, pallor, diaphoresis, tachycardia, or nausea occur, stop procedure

B. Crutches (see Table 5)
   1. Guideline for crutch height—measure two fingers below axilla
   2. Client should support weight on handpiece, not on axilla—brachialas plexus may be damaged, producing "crutch palsy"

3. Crutches should be kept 8 to 10 inches out to side

4. Elbows should be flexed at 20–30° angle for correct placement of hand grips

5. Stop and rest if diaphoretic or short of breath

| Table 5 CRUTCH WALKING GAITS | | |
|---|---|---|
| GAIT | DESCRIPTION | USES |
| Four-point | Slow, safe; right crutch, left foot, left crutch, right foot | Use when weight-bearing is allowed for both legs |
| Two-point | Faster, safe; right crutch and left foot advance together; left crutch and right foot advance together | Use when weight-bearing is allowed for both legs |
| Three-point | Faster gait, safe; advance weaker leg and both crutches simultaneously; then advance good leg | Use when weight-bearing is allowed on one leg |
| Swing-to-swing-through | Fast gait but requires more strength and balance; advance both crutches followed by both legs (or one leg is held up) | Use when partial weight-bearing is allowed on both legs |
| NOTE: To go up stairs: advance good leg first, followed by crutches and affected leg. To go down stairs: advance crutches with affected leg first, followed by good leg. ("Up with the good, down with the bad.") | | |

C. Walker

1. Definition—metal frame with handgrips, four legs and an open side; used for clients who need greater stability than that provided by other ambulatory aids

2. Guidelines for use

a. Elbows should be flexed at 20–30° angle when standing withhands on grips

b. Lift and move walker forward 8–10 inches

c. With partial or nonweight-bearing put weight on wrists and arms and step forward with affected leg, supporting self on arms, andfollow with good leg

d. Nurse should stand behind client, hold onto gait belt at waist asneeded for balance

e. Sit down by grasping armrest on affected side, shift weight to goodleg and hand, lower self into chair

f. Client should wear sturdy shoes

D. Cane

1. Types

a. Straight cane—least stable type

b. Quad cane—has four legs, provides more stability

2. Guideline for use

a. Tip should have concentric rubber rings as shock absorber and to provide optimal stability

b. Flex elbow 30° angle and hold handle; tip of cane should be 15 cm lateral to the base of the fifth toe

c. Hold cane in hand opposite affected extremity

d. Advance cane and affected leg

e. Lean on cane when moving good leg

f. To go up and down stairs, step up on good extremity, then place cane and affected extremity on step; reverse when going down ("up with the good, down with the bad")

E. Lift (Hoyer)

1. Used for clients who cannot help themselves and/or are too heavy for safe lifting by others

2. Mechanically operated metal frame with a sling usually made of canvas straps

3. Lock the bed; raise the bed to promote the use of good body mechanics by the nurse

4. Center canvas straps under client by rolling client side to side, one under the shoulders and one under the knees

5. Widen base-adjusting lever and lock

6. Position lift base under bed and center lift arm over the canvas sling; lock lift wheels

7. While holding onto arm, release valve to lower arm enough to attach sling

8. Attach sling to overhead arm using hook facing away from client

9. The shorter arm of the sling goes under the client's back; client should be centered in sling

10. Instruct client to cross arms over chest and lock lift wheels

11. Close release valve and pump using long, slow, even strokes; then unlock lift wheels

12. One person guides lift, second person lifts legs off the bed and steadies the sling

13. Position wheelchair between lift base legs; lock legs and lift wheels

14. One person slowly releases valve to lower arm while second person guides client into wheelchair

F. Sliding board

1. Place wheelchair close to bed, lock wheels, lock the bed

2. Remove arm rest from wheelchair

3. Powder the sliding board

4. Place one end of sliding board under client's buttocks; the other end on the surface of the wheelchair

5. Instruct client to push up with hands to shift buttocks, and then slide across board to wheelchair

6. Assist client to slide gently off the bed

**G.** Adaptive devices

1. Buttonhook—threaded through buttonhole to assist with buttoning shirts
2. Extended shoe horn—can also be used to turn light switches on and off from wheelchair
3. Gel pad—placed under plate or items to prevent shifting during use
4. Foam build-ups—applied to eating utensils, pen and pencils, buttonhook
5. Velcro straps—applied to utensils, pen, and pencil to stabilize in hand
6. Long-handled reacher—assists to obtain objects from high or low location

▶ **HERNIATED INTERVERTEBRAL DISK**

**A.** Assessment

1. Low back pain (knife-like)
2. Lack of muscle tone
3. Poor posture or body mechanics
4. Sensory changes

**B.** Diagnose

1. Diagnostic procedures
   a. Computerized tomography
   b. Magnetic resonance imaging
   c. Myelography—encourage fluids, keep head of bed elevated 30° to reduce risk of seizures
   d. Diskogram

2. Surgical procedures
   a. Laminectomy—excision of a portion of the lamina to expose the affected disk for removal
   b. Laminectomy with fusion—involves several disks; operation includes use of bone graft to strengthen the weakened vertebral column
   c. Minimally invasive surgery; microdiskectomy
   d. Interbody cage fusion

**C.** Plan/Implementation

1. Preoperative
   a. Apply moist heat
   b. Put client in Fowler's position with moderate hip and knee flexion
   c. Use firm mattress, bedboard, or floor for back support
   d. Isometric exercises for abdominal muscles
   e. Daily exercise program
   f. Assist with exercises initiated in physical therapy
   g. Medications—muscle relaxants, NSAIDs, analgesics
   h. Traction—separates vertebrae to relieve pressure on nerve
   i. TENS (transcutaneous electrical nerve stimulation)

2. Postoperative
   a. Maintain body alignment
   b. Log-roll every two hours with pillow between legs
   c. Calf exercises
   d. Assess for sensation and circulatory status, especially of lower extremities
   e. Monitor elimination
   f. Assist with ambulation

g. Support neck after cervical laminectomy

h. Straight back during ambulation

3. Client teaching

a. Exercise daily but avoid strenuous exercises

b. Correct posture at all times

c. Avoid prolonged sitting, standing, walking, driving

d. Rest at intervals

e. Use hardboard or firm mattress for bed

f. Avoid prone position

g. Avoid straining or lifting heavy objects

**D.** Evaluation

1. Have complications been prevented?

2. Does client understand teaching?

## ▶ DEVELOPMENTAL DYSPLASIA OF THE HIP (DDH)

**A.** Assessment

1. Uneven gluteal folds and thigh creases (deeper on affected side) (see Figure 1)

**Figure 1.  Congenital Hip Dislocation**

2. Limited abduction of hip with pain, unequal knee height with thigh flexion

3. Ortolani's sign (seen in infants less than 4 weeks old) (see Figure 1)

a. Place infant on back, leg flexed

b. Click sound heard when affected hip is moved to abduction

4. Shortened limb on affected side in older infant and child

5. Delays in walking; limp, lordosis, and waddling gait with older child

**B.** Diagnose

1. Predisposition

a. Intrauterine position (breech)

b. Gender (female)

c. Hormonal imbalance (estrogen)

    d. Cultural and environmental influences—some cultures carry their children straddled against the hip joint, causing a decreased incidence (Far Eastern and African); cultures that wrap infants tightly in blankets or strap to boards have high incidence (Navajo Indian)

2. Definition—acetabulum unable to hold head of femur

3. Confirmed by x-ray

4. Potential nursing diagnoses

    a. Physical mobility, impaired

    b. Body image disturbance

    c. Injury, risk for

**C.** Plan/Implementation

1. Newborn to 6 months (intervention varies with age and extent)

    a. Reduced by manipulation

    b. Splinted with proximal femur centered in the acetabulum in position of flexion

    c. Pavlik harness—worn full-time for 3–6 months until hip stable for infants less than 3 months age (see Figure 2)

**Figure 2. Pavlik Harness**

    d. Encourage normal growth and development by allowing child to perform appropriate activities

    e. Teach parents: reapply harness and rationale for maintaining abduction

    f. Tell parents to move child from one room to another for environmental change

    g. Discuss modification in bathing, dressing, and diapering with parents

        1) Since harness is not to be removed, sponge bath is recommended

        2) Put undershirt under chest straps and knee sox under foot and leg pieces to prevent skin irritation

        3) Check skin areas 2–3 times a day

        4) Gently massage skin under straps daily to stimulate circulation

        5) Avoid use of lotions and powders

        6) Place diapers under straps

        7) Pad shoulder straps as needed

      h.  Tell parents to touch and hold child to express affection and reinforce security

2.  16–18 months

      a.  Gradual reduction by traction (bilateral Bryant's traction)

      b.  Cast for immobilization (see Figure 3)

3.  Older Child

      a.  Preliminary traction

      b.  Open reduction

      c.  Hip spica cast (see Figure 3)

**Figure 3.  Hip Spica Cast**

**D.**  Evaluation

    1.  Has hip joint alignment been re-established?

    2.  Have child's growth and developmental needs been met?

## ▶ SCOLIOSIS

**A.**  Assessment (see Figure 4)

    1.  Poor posture

    2.  Uneven hips or scapulae

    3.  Kyphosis lump on back

    4.  Uneven waistline

    5.  Visualization of deformity—bend at waist 90°

**Figure 4. Scoliosis**

**B.** Diagnose

1. Definition—lateral deviation of one or more vertebrae commonly accompanied by rotary motion

2. Types

   a. Functional—flexible deviation that corrects by bending

   b. Structural—permanent, hereditary deviation

3. Potential nursing diagnoses

   a. Disturbed body image

   b. Deficient knowledge

   c. Ineffective therapeutic regimen management

   d. Impaired physical mobility

**C.** Plan/Implementation

1. Exercise for functional type—teach isometric exercises to strengthen the abdominal muscles

   a. Sit-ups

   b. Pelvic tilt

   c. Push-ups with pelvic tilt

2. Electrostimulation

3. Surgery—spinal fusion with Harrington rod insertion; Dwyer instrumentation with anterior spinal fusion; screw and wire (Luque) instrumentation

4. Thoracolumbosacral orthotic (TLSO) brace

   a. Types effective for 30–40 degree curves not associated with extreme deformity

      1) Thoracolumbosacral orthotic (TSLO) brace

      2) Boston brace (TSLO) brace

      3) Milwaukee brace (cerico-throraco-lumbo-sacral orthotic)

  b. Nursing care: Underarm orthosis made of plastic custom molded to the body and shaped to correct or hold the deformity

   1) Skin care to pressure areas

   2) Wear t-shirt under brace to minimize skin irritation

   3) Teach isometric exercises to strengthen abdominal muscles

   4) Provide activities consistent with limitations, yet allow positive peer relationships to promote healthy self-concept

  c. Wear for 23 hours—removed 1 hour for personal hygiene

**D.** Evaluation

 1. Has child's lateral deviation of the spine been corrected?

 2. Have the child's growth and developmental needs been met?

## ▶ CLUB FOOT (TALIPES EQUINOVARUS)

**A.** Assessment

 1. Plantar flexion or dorsiflexion

 2. Inversion/adduction of forepart of foot

**B.** Diagnose

 1. Rigid abnormality of talus bone at birth

 2. Does not involve muscles, nerves, or blood vessels

**C.** Plan/Implementation

 1. Foot exercises—manipulation of foot to correct position every 4 hours regularly

 2. Casts and splints correct the deformity in most cases if applied early (see Figure 5); changed every few days for 1–2 weeks, then at 1–2-week intervals to accommodate infant's rapid growth

 3. Surgery is usually required for older child

 4. Denis-Browne—horizontal abduction bar with footplates

**Figure 5. Casting of Talipes Equinovarus**

**D.** Evaluation

 1. Has mobility of foot been maintained?

 2. Has structure of foot been corrected?

# ▶ JOINT DISORDERS

**A.** Assessment (see Table 1)

**B.** Diagnose (see Table 1)

1. Risk factors

    a. Osteoarthritis

    1) Increased age

    2) Obesity

    3) Trauma to joints due to repetitive use

    a) Carpet installer

    b) Construction worker

    c) Farmer

    d) Sports injuries

    b. Rheumatoid arthritis

    1) Positive family history

    c. Gout

    1) Obesity

    2) Diuretics

    3) Family history

2. Diagnostic tests

    a. Arthrocentesis—needle puncture of a joint space to remove accumulated fluid

    1) Strict asepsis is essential to avoid infection

    2) Usually elastic bandage wrap and joint rest for 24 hours to prevent hemorrhage

    b. Arthroscopy—direct visualization of a joint by use of arthroscope

    1) Local anesthesia given

    2) Teach breathing exercises to reduce discomfort

    3) Post-test bulky pressure dressing applied

3. Potential nursing diagnoses

    a. Acute/chronic Pain

    b. Impaired physical mobility

    c. Self-care deficit

    d. Disturbed body image

    e. Ineffective role performance

**C.** Plan/Implementation

1. Nursing care (see Table 1)

2. Medications: analgesics, anti-inflammatory medication

**D.** Evaluation

1. Has joint mobility been maintained?

2. Has client comfort been maintained?

| Table 1 JOINT DISORDERS | | | | |
|---|---|---|---|---|
| TYPE | ASSESSMENT | DIAGNOSE | DIAGNOSTIC TESTS | NURSING CONSIDERATIONS |
| Rheumatoid arthritis<br><br>Juvenile rheumatoid arthritis (JRA) | Joint pain, swelling, and limitation of movement<br>Contracture deformities<br>Nodules over bony prominences<br>Ulnar deviation<br>High fever and rheumatoid rash, particularly seen in JRA<br>Salmon-pink macular rash on chest, thighs, and upper arms | Systemic; pannus formation<br>Bony ankylosis<br>Progressive<br>Remissions and exacerbations | Rheumatoid factor (may be negative)<br>C-reactive protein<br>ESR, ANA<br>Aspiration of synovial fluid<br>X-rays | Pain management, rest, activity, exercise<br>Weight control if obese<br>Heat (e.g., warm tub baths; warm, moist compresses; paraffin dips)<br>Splints for joints<br>Analgesics, anti-inflammatory drugs<br>Disease-modifying antirheumatic drugs<br>Immunosuppressive drugs<br>Antitumor necrosis drugs |
| Osteoarthritis | Joint pain, swelling, and limitation of movement<br>Contracture deformities<br>Joint stiffness after rest<br>Heberden's and Bouchard's nodes of the fingers | Nonsystemic; spur formation; closure of joint spaces<br>Degenerative<br>No remissions | X-rays of joints show narrowing of joint spaces | Pain management, rest, activity, exercise<br>Weight control if obese<br>Analgesics, anti-inflammatory drugs<br>Heat application |
| Gout | Joint pain, swelling, limitation of movement<br>Contracture deformities<br>Tophi | Nonsystemic<br>Disturbed purine metabolism<br>Elevated uric acid in blood<br>Tophi formation (deposits of urates in joints)<br>Exacerbations | X-rays<br>Blood tests—WBC, ESR, uric acid level<br>Synovial aspiration | Pain management<br>Diet: avoid meats rich in purines (e.g., organ meats, sardines, fish), alcohol, ketoacidosis, dehydration<br>Analgesics—aspirin<br>Medications for gout |

# ▶ PAGET'S DISEASE

**A.** Assessment

1. Pain

2. Bowed legs, decreased height

3. Shortened trunk with long-appearing arms

4. Enlarged skull

5. Long bone, spine, and rib pain

6. Labored, waddling gait

7. Kyphosis

8. Pathologic fractures

**B.** Diagnose

1. Unknown etiology

2. Excessive bone resorption (loss)

3. Occurs more often in older adults

C. Plan/Implementation

   1. Administer analgesics

   2. Encourage rest

   3. Prevent pathological fractures by using safety precautions

   4. Administer medications: calcitonin, biphosphonates, e,g., alendronate; pamidronate.

D. Evaluation

   1. Has client comfort been maintained?

   2. Have complications been prevented?

# ▶ BURSITIS

A. Assessment

   1. Pain due to inflammation

   2. Decreased mobility, especially on abduction

B. Diagnose

   1. Definition—inflammation of connective tissue sac between muscles, tendons, and bones, particularly affecting shoulder, elbow, and knee

   2. Potential nursing diagnoses

      a. Acute/chronic pain

      b. Impaired physical mobility

      c. Self-care deficit

C. Plan/Implementation

   1. Rest

   2. Immobilize affected joint with pillows, splints, slings

   3. Administer pain medication, muscle relaxants (diazepam), steroids

   4. Apply heat/cold packs to decrease swelling

   5. Promote exercise (ROM)

   6. Assist in performance of ADL by modifying activities relative to limitations

   7. Assist with cortisone injection, draining of bursae

D. Evaluation

   1. Has client's pain been minimized?

   2. Has client's mobility been maintained?

# ▶ OSTEOPOROSIS

A. Assessment

   1. Decreased height

   2. Low back pain, especially hips and spine

   3. Kyphosis

B. Diagnose

   1. Reduction in bone mass with no changes in mineral composition

   2. Degenerative disease characterized by generalized loss of bone density and tensile strength

3. Diagnosed by bone mineral density (BMD) T-scores—BMD T-score less than or equal to 2.5 indicates osteoporosis

4. Risk factors

   a. Age greater than 60 years

   b. Small-framed and lean body build

   c. Caucasian or Asian race

   d. Inadequate intake of calcium or vitamin D

   e. Postmenopausal

   f. Immobility and sedentary lifestyle

   g. History of smoking

   h. High alcohol intake

   i. Prolonged use of steroids

5. Potential nursing diagnoses

   a. Acute/chronic pain

   b. Self-care deficit

   c. Risk for trauma

**C.** Plan/Implementation

1. Diet high in calcium, protein, and vitamin D

2. Teach about medications

3. Encourage weight-bearing on the long bones (walking)

4. Fall prevention

5. ROM exercises

6. Physiotherapy

7. Safety precautions to prevent pathological fractures

   a. Use back brace or splint for support

   b. Use bedboards or hard mattress

8. Administer medications: calcitonin; biphosphonates, e.g., alendronate; selective receptor modulators, e.g., raloxifene; estrogen replacement therapy

**D.** Evaluation

1. Has client's mobility been maintained?

2. Is client knowledgeable about dietary requirements?

## ▶ OSTEOMYELITIS

**A.** Assessment

1. Pain

2. Swelling, redness, warmth on affected area

3. Fever, leukocytosis

4. Elevated sedimentation rate

5. Positive culture and sensitivity

6. X-ray of affected part

**B.** Diagnose

1. Infection of the bone, usually caused by *Staphylococcus aureus*, carried by the blood from a primary site of infection or from direct invasion, e.g., orthopedic surgical procedures or fractures

2. Risk factors

   a. Poorly nourished

   b. Elderly

   c. Obesity

   d. Impaired immune system

   e. Long-term corticosteroid therapy

3. Potential nursing diagnoses

   a. Acute pain

   b. Ineffective bone tissue perfusion

   c. Risk for injury

   d. Deficient knowledge

**C.** Plan/Implementation

1. Teach about risk factors for osteomyelitis, e.g., joint prosthesis

2. Medications: analgesics, antibiotics, antipyretics

3. Support affected extremity with pillows, splints to maintain proper body alignment

4. Provide cool environment and lightweight clothing

5. Avoid exercise and heat application to the affected area

6. Encourage fluid intake, monitor intake and output

7. Asepsis with wound care

8. Provide diversionary activities

9. High-protein diet with sufficient carbohydrates, vitamins, and minerals

10. Instruct about home wound care and antibiotic administration

**D.** Evaluation

1. Has client comfort been maintained?

2. Have complications been prevented?

# ▶ OSTEOMALACIA

**A.** Assessment

1. Bone pain and tenderness

2. Muscle weakness

3. Bowed legs, kyphosis

4. X-ray (porous bones)

**B.** Diagnose

1. Decalcification of bones due to inadequate intake of vitamin D, absence of exposure to sunlight, or intestinal malabsorption, chronic kidney disease

2. Potential nursing diagnoses
   a. Injury, risk for
   b. Delayed growth and development
   c. Body image disturbance

**C.** Plan/Implementation

1. Administration of analgesics
2. Increase sun exposure
3. Instruct about high vitamin D foods (milk, eggs, vitamin D enriched cereals and bread products)
4. Administer vitamin D, calcium, and expose to sunlight and/or ultraviolet irradiation
5. Assist with performance of ADL to prevent pathological fractures

**D.** Evaluation

1. Has client mobility been maintained?
2. Has client's pain been minimized?

## ▶ SPINA BIFIDA/NEURAL TUBE DEFECTS

**A.** Assessment (see Figure 6)

1. Dimpling at the site (spina bifida occulta)
2. Bulging, saclike lesion filled with spinal fluid and covered with a thin, atrophic, bluish, ulcerated skin (meningocele)
3. Bulging, saclike lesion filled with spinal fluid and spinal cord element (myelomeningocele)
4. Hydrocephalus increases risk
5. Paralysis of lower extremities
6. Musculoskeletal deformities—club feet, dislocated hips, kyphosis, scoliosis
7. Neurogenic bladder and bowel, prolapsed rectum

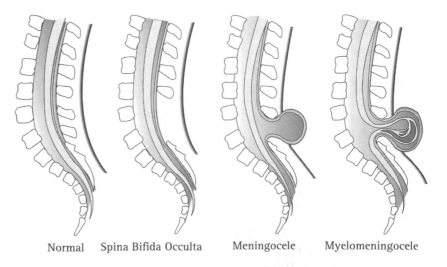

Normal    Spina Bifida Occulta    Meningocele    Myelomeningocele

**Figure 6.  Types of Spina Bifida**

**B.** Diagnose

1. Congenital anomaly of the spinal cord characterized by nonunion between the laminae of the vertebrae

2. Risk factors

   a. Maternal folic-acid deficiency

   b. Previous pregnancy affected by neural tube defect

3. Etiology

   a. Combination of unknown genetic/environmental factors

   b. Advanced maternal age

   c. High levels of alpha-fetoprotein at amniocentesis

**C.** Plan/Implementation

1. Occulta: no treatment

2. Meningocele/myelomeningocele: surgical repair at 24–48 hours

3. Observe for irritation, CSF leakage, and signs of infection

4. Maintain optimum asepsis; cover lesion with moist sterile dressings

5. Position client on abdomen or semiprone with sandbags

6. Provide optimum skin care, especially to perineal area

7. Check for abnormal movement of extremities, absent or abnormal reflexes, incontinence, fecal impaction, flaccid paralysis of lower extremities

8. Observe for increased intracranial pressure (headache, changes in LOC, motor functions, and vital signs)

9. Observe for symptoms of meningeal irritation or meningitis

10. Provide frequent sources of stimulation appropriate for child's age level

11. Provide postoperative care—vertebral fusion or surgical repair

12. Focus postoperative observation on detecting signs of meningitis, shock, increased intracranial pressure, and respiratory difficulty

13. Foster parental bonding

14. Perform family teaching on how to care for child at home

15. Discuss with family referrals for PT, orthopedic procedures, bladder and bowel management

**D.** Evaluation

1. Have complications been prevented?

2. Have infant's physical needs been met?

# ▶ HYDROCEPHALUS

**A.** Assessment

1. Fronto-occipital circumference increases at abnormally fast rate (see Figure 7)

2. Split sutures and widened, distended, tense fontanelles

3. Prominent forehead, dilated scalp veins

4. Sunset eyes, nystagmus

5. Irritability, vomiting

6. Unusual somnolence

7. Convulsions
8. High-pitched cry

**Figure 7. Ventriculoperitoneal Shunt for Hydrocephalus**

**B.** Diagnose

1. Congenital or acquired condition characterized by an increase in the accumulation of CSF within the ventricular system and subsequent increase in ventricular pressure

2. Causes

    a. Neoplasm

    b. Aqueductal stenosis—stenosis/obstructions in ventricular system

    c. Spina bifida

    d. Congenital cysts/vascular malformations

3. Types

    a. Communicating—due to increased production of CSF or impaired absorption of CSF

    b. Noncommunicating—due to obstruction/blockage of CSF circulation between ventricles and subarachnoid space

**C.** Plan/Implementation

1. Operative management

    a. Ventriculoperitoneal shunt—connection between ventricles and peritoneal cavity (see Figure 7)

    b. Ventricular atrial shunt—connection between ventricles and right atrium

    c. Ventricular drainage—provides external drainage of fluid

2. Observation of shunt functioning

3. Observe for increased intracranial pressure and for signs of shunt infection (irritability, high pitched cry, lethargy)

4. Postoperative positioning—on unoperated side in flat position; do not hold infant with head elevated

5. Shunt needs to be modified as child grows

6. Continual testing for developmental abnormalities/intellectual delay

7. Discharge planning/community referral

8. Teach parents about increased risk for allergies if myelomeningocele present

**D.** Evaluation

1. Has child attained optimal growth and development?

# ▶ NEUROMUSCULAR DISORDERS

**A.** Assessment (see Table 2)

**B.** Diagnose (see Table 2)

| Table 2 NEUROMUSCULAR DISORDERS | | |
|---|---|---|
| | **CEREBRAL PALSY** | **MUSCULAR DYSTROPHY** |
| Assessment | Athetosis, spasticity, rigidity, ataxia, atonicity; repetitive, involuntary, slow, gross movements<br><br>Neonate: cannot hold head up, feeble cry, inability to feed, body noticeably arched or limp<br><br>Infant: failure-to-thrive syndrome<br><br>Toddler/preschooler: intellectual delay, delayed physical development | Muscle weakness, lordosis/ scoliosis, waddling gait, joint contractures<br><br>Stumbling and falling |
| Analysis | Voluntary muscles poorly controlled due to brain damage<br><br>Etiology: unclear<br><br>Predisposition: prematurity, existing prenatal brain abnormalities, trauma, anoxia, or infection at time of birth<br><br>Treatment: ambulation devices, surgical lengthening of heel cord to promote stability and function<br><br>Medications: muscle relaxants, tranquilizers, anticonvulsants, baclofen, intrathecal pump | Progressive muscular weakness, atrophy of voluntary muscles, no nerve effect<br><br>Etiology: genetic<br><br>Diagnostic tests: CPK (creatinine phosphokinase), abnormal electromyogram, abnormal muscle biopsy<br><br>Predisposition: heredity Progressive/terminal<br><br>Treatment: intensive physical therapy, active and passive stretching and ROM<br><br>Light spinal braces or long leg braces may help ambulation |
| Potential nursing diagnosis | Nutrition: less than body requirements<br><br>Compromised family coping<br><br>Self-care deficit<br><br>Impaired physical mobility<br><br>Delayed growth and development | Self-care deficit<br><br>Compromised family coping<br><br>Body image disturbance<br><br>Impaired physical mobility<br><br>Ineffective breathing pattern<br><br>Impaired swallowing<br><br>Delayed growth and development |

C. Plan/Implementation

1. Cerebral palsy

   a. Assist with early diagnosis

   b. Assist with physical and occupational therapy

   c. Give referrals to appropriate agencies

   d. Provide emotional support to parents and client

   e. Assist with feeding, place food at back of mouth or on either side of tongue toward cheek, apply slight downward pressure with the spoon

   f. Never tilt head backward when feeding (leads to choking)

   g. High-calorie diet

2. Muscular dystrophy

   a. Promote safety to avoid slips and falls due to gait and movement disturbances; use braces or wheelchair

   b. Assist with diagnostic tests

   c. Client/parent education on nature of the disease

   d. Provide emotional support to child and family

   e. Discuss balance between activity and rest for the child

   f. Prevent contractures

   g. Referrals to appropriate agencies

D. Evaluation

1. Has child's mobility been maintained?

2. Have the child's nutritional needs been met?

## ▶ DISTURBED TRANSMISSION OF NERVE IMPULSES

A. Assessment (see Table 3)

B. Diagnose (see Table 3)

| Table 3 | DISORDERS OF NERVE IMPULSE TRANSMISSION | | |
|---|---|---|---|
| | **PARKINSON'S DISEASE** | **MYASTHENIA GRAVIS** | **MULTIPLE SCLEROSIS** |
| **Assessment** | Tremors (pill-rolling motion), akinesia (loss of automation), rigidity, weakness<br><br>"Motorized" propulsive gait, slurred monotonous speech, dysphagia<br><br>Salivation, masklike expression, drooling<br><br>Constipation<br><br>Depression<br><br>Dementia | Muscular weakness produced by repeated movements soon disappears following rest<br><br>Diplopia, ptosis, impaired speech, dysphagia<br><br>Respiratory distress<br><br>Periods of remissions and exacerbations | Early—vision, motor sensation changes<br><br>Late—cognitive and bowel changes<br><br>Muscular incoordination, ataxia, spasticity, intention tremors, nystagmus, chewing and swallowing difficulties, impaired speech<br><br>Incontinence, emotional instability, sexual dysfunction |
| **Analysis** | Deficiency of dopamine; increased acetylcholine levels<br><br>Etiology unclear; chronic and progressive; intellect intact<br><br>Does not lead to paralysis | Deficiency of acetylcholine at myoneural junction<br><br>Etiology unclear; chronic and progressive; intellect intact<br><br>Diagnosis—based on administration of anticholinesterase; positive result evidenced by a striking increase in muscular strength 5–10 minutes after administration<br><br>No muscular atrophy<br><br>No loss of sensation | Demyelination of white matter throughout brain and spinal cord<br><br>Etiology unclear; chronic and progressive; intellect intact<br><br>Leads to paraplegia or complete paralysis |
| **Nursing diagnosis** | Self-care deficit<br><br>Nutrition, altered<br><br>Body image disturbance<br><br>Caregiver rule strain<br><br>Communication, impaired verbal<br><br>Impaired walking<br><br>Impaired swallowing | Self-care deficit<br><br>Airway clearance, ineffective<br><br>Physical mobility, impaired<br><br>Impaired swallowing<br><br>Anxiety/fear | Self-care deficit<br><br>Nutrition, altered<br><br>Urinary elimination, altered<br><br>Physical mobility, impaired<br><br>Fatigue<br><br>Disturbed visual, Kinesthetic,<br><br>Tactile,<br><br>Sensory perception<br><br>Powerlessness<br><br>Compromised/Disabled Family coping |

**C.** Plan/Implementation

1. Parkinson's disease

    a. Encourage finger exercises, e.g., typing, piano-playing

    b. ROM as appropriate

    c. Teach client ambulation modification, refer to physical therapy

        1) Goose-stepping walk

        2) Walk with wider base

        3) Concentrate on swinging arms while walking

        4) Turn around slowly using small steps

    d. Promote family understanding of the disease

        1) Client's intellect is not impaired

        2) Sight and hearing are intact

        3) Disease is progressive but slow

        4) Does not lead to paralysis

    e. Refer for speech therapy, potential stereotactic surgery

    f. Administer dopaminergics, e.g., levodopa–carbidopa; dopamineagonists, e.g., pramipexole; anticholinergics, e.g., benztropine, trihexyphenidyl; antivirals, e.g., amantadine

2. Myasthenia gravis

    a. Promote family understanding of the disease

        1) It is neither a central nervous system nor a peripheral nervous system disease

        2) There is no muscular atrophy or loss of sensation

        3) It is not hereditary

    b. Administer medications before eating

        1) Anticholinesterases

        2) Corticosteroids

        3) Immunosuppressants

    c. Good eye care (artificial tears, eye patch for diplopia)

    d. Maintain optimal mobility

    e. Provide environment that is restful and free of stress

    f. Client teaching

        1) Importance of taking medications on time; dosage depends on physiological needs and living patterns

        2) Wear Medic-Alert band

        3) Avoid factors that may precipitate myasthenia crisis, e.g., infections, emotional upsets, use of streptomycin or neomycin (they produce muscular weakness), surgery

        4) Be alert for myasthenia crisis—sudden inability to swallow, speak, or maintain a patent airway

3. Multiple sclerosis (MS)

    a. Teach relaxation and coordination exercises

    b. Teach progressive resistance exercises, ROM

    c. Encourage fluid intake 2000 mL/day

    d. Warm baths and packs

    e. Administer medications–immunosuppressants; corticosteroids;antispasmodics; interferon beta-1a; monoclonal antibodies

    f. Wide-based walk, use of cane or walker

    g. Use weighted bracelets and cuffs to stabilize upper extremities

    h. Bladder and bowel training (care of Foley catheter if appropriate)

    i. Self-help devices

    j. Eye patch for diplopia

    k. No tetracycline or neomycin because they increase muscle weakness with MS

    l. Occupational therapy

    m. Provide emotional support

    n. Referrals–National Multiple Sclerosis Society

**D.** Evaluation

1. Is client able to maintain independent functioning?

2. Have client's physical needs been met?

# AMYOTROPHIC LATERAL SCLEROSIS (LOU GEHRIG'S DISEASE)

**A.** Assessment

1. Tongue fatigue, atrophy with fasciculations (brief muscle twitching)

2. Nasal quality to speech, dysarthria

3. Dysphagia, aspiration

4. Progressive muscular weakness, muscular wasting, atrophy, spasticity

   a. Usually begins in upper extremities

   b. Distal portion affected first

   c. Fasciculations

5. Emotional lability, cognitive dysfunction

6. Respiratory insufficiency (usual cause of death)

7. No alteration in autonomic, sensory, or mental function

**B.** Diagnose

1. Progressive, degenerative disease involving the lower motor neurons of the spinal cord and cerebral cortex; the voluntary motor system is particularly involved with progressive degeneration of the corticospinal tract, leads to a mixture of spastic and atrophic changes in cranial and spinal musculature

2. No specific pattern exists—involvement may vary in different parts of the same area

3. Possible etiologies

   a. Genetic, familial

   b. Chronic (slow) viral infection

   c. Autoimmune disease

   d. Environmental factors (toxic, metabolic)

**C.** Plan/Implementation

1. Apply principles of care of client with progressive, terminal disease

2. Treat self-care deficits symptomatically

3. Maintain adequate nutrition

4. Physical therapy/speech therapy

5. Adaptive home equipment

6. Provide psychosocial support

**D.** Evaluation

1. Is client able to maintain optimal physical functioning for as long as possible?

2. Has client comfort been maintained?

# INTERVENTIONS TO PROMOTE COMFORT

## ▶ PAIN

**A.** Assessment

1. The fifth vital sign
2. History
   a. P–precipitating factors
   b. Q–quality
   c. R–region/radiation
   d. S–severity
   e. T–timing
3. Potential responses to pain (see Table 1)

| Table 1 POTENTIAL RESPONSES TO PAIN | |
|---|---|
| ASSESSMENT | RESULT |
| Increased BP and heart rate leads to increased blood flow to brain and muscles<br><br>Rapid, irregular respirations leads to increased $O_2$ supply to brain and muscles | Enhanced alertness to threats<br><br>Preoccupation with painful stimulus |
| Increased pupillary diameter leads to increased eye accommodation to light | Increased visual perception of threats |
| Increased perspiration | Removal of excess body heat |
| Increased muscle tension leads to increased neuromuscular activity | Musculoskeletal system ready for rapid motor activity and responsiveness |
| Altered GI motility leads to nausea and vomiting | Altered metabolic processes |
| Apprehension, irritability, and anxiety<br>Verbalizes pain | Enhanced mental alertness to threats<br>Communication of suffering and pleas for help |

**B.** Diagnose

1. Definition–"Whatever the person says it is, and it exists whenever the person says it does"
2. Types
   a. Acute–an episode of pain that lasts from a split second to about 6 months; causes decreased healing, vital sign changes, diaphoresis
   b. Chronic–an episode of pain that lasts for 6 months or longer; causes fatigue, depression, weight gain, immobility
3. Factors influencing pain experiences
   a. Individual's responses or reactions to pain are generally dependent on what is expected and accepted in his/her culture
   b. Past experiences with pain generally make the individual more sensitive to the pain experience

4.  Potential nursing diagnoses
    a.  Acute/chronic pain
    b.  Activity intolerance
    c.  Ineffective therapeutic regimen management
    d.  Social isolation
    e.  Readiness for enhanced comfort
    f.  Imbalanced nutrition: less than body requirements

**C.** Plan/Implementation

1.  Establish a therapeutic relationship
    a.  Tell client you believe what he/she says about his/her pain experience
    b.  Listen and allow client to verbalize
    c.  Allow client to use own words in describing pain experience

2.  Establish a 24-hour pain profile
    a.  Location
        1)  External
        2)  Internal
        3)  Both external and internal
        4)  Area of body affected
    b.  Character and intensity
        1)  Acute/chronic
        2)  Mild/severe
    c.  Onset
        1)  Sudden
        2)  Insidious
    d.  Duration
    e.  Precipitating factors
    f.  Identify associated manifestations, as well as alleviating or aggravating factors

3.  Teach client about pain and pain relief
    a.  Explain quality and location of impending pain, (e.g., before uncomfortable procedure)
    b.  Help client learn to use slow, rhythmic breathing to promote relaxation
    c.  Explain effects of analgesics and benefits of preventative approach
    d.  Demonstrate splinting techniques that help reduce pain

4.  Reduce anxiety and fears
    a.  Give reassurance
    b.  Offer distraction
    c.  Spend time with client

5.  Provide comfort measures
    a.  Proper positioning
    b.  Cool, well ventilated, quiet room
    c.  Back rub
    d.  Allow for rest

6. Administer pain medications

   a. Use preventive approach

      1) If pain is expected to occur throughout most of a 24-hour period, a regular schedule is better than prn

      2) Usually takes a smaller dose to alleviate mild pain or prevent occurrence of pain

      3) Pain relief is more complete and client spends fewer hours in pain

      4) Helps prevent addiction

   b. PCA (client-controlled analgesia) pumps—a portable device that delivers predetermined dosage of intravenous narcotic (e.g., dose of 1 mg morphine with a lock-out interval of 5–15 minutes for a total possible dose of 5 mg per hour)

   c. Non-opioid analgesics

   d. Nonsteroidal anti-inflammatory drugs (NSAIDs)

   e. Opioids

   f. Anticonvulsants

   g. Alpha-2 adrenergics

7. Other methods of pain relief

   a. Neurectomy/sympathectomy

   b. TENS (transcutaneous electric nerve stimulation)—produces tingling, buzzing sensation in area of pain; used for chronic and acute pain

8. Complementary and alternative methods of pain control

   a. Relaxation techniques

   b. Meditation

   c. Progressive relaxation

   d. Yoga/exercise

   e. Distraction

   f. Guided imagery

   g. Herbal remedies

   h. Biofeedback

   i. Acupuncture

   j. Heat/cold application

   k. Therapeutic touch; consider cultural factors

   l. Massage

   m. Hypnosis

**D.** Evaluation

   1. Has client comfort been maintained?

   2. Is client able to demonstrate splinting techniques to reduce pain?

# CONTUSIONS, SPRAINS, JOINT DISLOCATIONS

**A.** Assessment

1. Contusions

   a. Ecchymosis

   b. Hematoma

2. Strains/sprains

   a. Pain

   b. Swelling

3. Joint dislocations

   a. Pain

   b. Deformity

**B.** Diagnose

1. Contusions—injury of soft tissue

2. Strains—muscle and/or tendon pull or tear

3. Sprains—torn ligament or stretched ligament

4. Dislocation—displacement of joint bones so their articulating surfaces lose all contact

**C.** Plan/Implementation

1. Contusions—treated with cold application for 24 hours followed by moist heat; apply elastic bandage

2. Strains/sprains—treated with rest and elevation of affected part; intermittent ice compresses for 24 hours, followed by heat application; apply elastic pressure bandage; minimize use

3. Dislocations—considered an orthopedic emergency; treated with immobilization and reduction, e.g., the dislocated bone is brought back to its normal position, usually under anesthesia; bandages and splints are used to keep affected part immobile until healing occurs

**D.** Evaluation

1. Is client comfort restored?

2. Have complications been prevented?

# FRACTURES

**A.** Assessment

1. Swelling, pallor, ecchymosis of surrounding subcutaneous tissue

2. Loss of sensation to body parts

3. Deformity

4. Pain and/or acute tenderness

5. Muscle spasms

6. Loss of function, abnormal mobility

7. Crepitus (grating sound on movement of ends of broken bone)

8. Shortening of affected limb

9. Decreased or absent pulses distal to injury

10. Affected extremity colder than contralateral part

B. Diagnose

1. Fractures—break in continuity of bone

2. Types (see Figure 1, panels A–D)

3. Complications of fractures

a. Fat emboli—caused after fracture of long bones when fat globules move into bloodstream; may occlude major vessels

b. Hemorrhage

c. Delayed union—healing of fracture is slowed; caused by infection or distraction of fractured fragments; will see increase in bone pain

d. Malunion—improper alignment of fracture fragments; may develop with premature weight-bearing

e. Nonunion—healing has not occurred 4–6 months after fracture; insufficient blood supply, repetitive stress on fracture site, infection, inadequate internal fixation; treated by bone grafting, internal fixation, electric bone stimulation

f. Sepsis

g. Compartment syndrome—high pressure within a muscle compartment of an extremity compromises circulation; pressure may be internal (bleeding) or external (casts); if left untreated neuromuscular damage occurs within 4–6 hours; limb can become permanently useless within 24–48 hours; will see unrelenting pain out of proportion to injury and unrelieved by pain medication, decreased pulse strength, numbness and tingling of extremity, possible cyanosis, and pale cool extremity

h. Peripheral nerve damage

A. Complete: break across entire cross-section of bone

B. Incomplete: break through portion of bone

C. Closed: no external communication

D. Open: extends through skin

**Figure 1 Types of Fractures**

**C.** Plan/Implementation

1. Provide emergency care

   a. Immobilization before client is moved by use of splints; immobilize joint below and above fracture

   b. In an open fracture, cover the wound with sterile dressings or cleanest material available; control bleeding by direct pressure

   c. Check temperature, color, sensation, capillary refill distal to fracture

   d. Emergency room—give narcotic adequate to relieve pain (except in presence of head injury)

2. Treatment

   a. Splinting—immobilization of the affected part to prevent soft tissue from being damaged by bony fragments

   b. Internal fixation—use of metal screws, plates, nails, and pins to stabilize reduced fracture

   c. Open reduction—surgical dissection and exposure of the fracture for reduction and alignment

   d. Closed reduction—manual manipulation or of fracture

3. Traction (see Figures 2–6)
   a. Purposes
      1) Reduce the fracture
      2) Alleviate pain and muscle spasm
      3) Prevent or correct deformities
      4) Promote healing
   b. Types of traction
      1) Skin (Buck's extension, Russell's, pelvic traction)—pulling force applied to skin
      2) Skeletal (halo, Crutchfield tongs)—pulling force applied to bone
   c. Care
      1) Maintain straight alignment of ropes and pulleys
      2) Assure that weights hang free
      3) Frequently inspect skin for breakdown areas
      4) Maintain position for countertraction
      5) Encourage movement of unaffected areas
      6) Investigate every report of discomfort/difficulty immediately and thoroughly
      7) Maintain continuous pull
      8) Clean pins with half-strength peroxide or saline and sterile swabs 1–2 times a day, if ordered

**Figure 2  Buck's Traction**

> Relieves muscular spasm of legs and back; if no fracture, may turn to either side; with fracture, turn to unaffected side. 8–20 lb used; 40 lb for scoliosis. Elevate foot of bed for countertraction. Use trapeze for moving. Place pillow beneath lower legs, not heel. Don't elevate knee gatch.

**Figure 3   Russell's Traction**

"Pulls" contracted muscles; elevate foot of bed with shock blocks to provide countertraction; sling can be loosened for skin care; check popliteal pulse. Place pillows under lower leg. Make sure heel is off the bed. Must not turn from waist down. Lift client, not leg, to provide assistance.

**Figure 4   Cervical (skull tongs)**

Realigns fracture of cervical vertebrae and relieves pressure on cervical nerves; never lift weights—traction must be continuous. No pillow under the head during feeding; hard to swallow, may need suctioning.

**Figure 5  Balanced Suspension**

Realigns fractures of the femur; uses pulley to create balanced suspension by countertraction to the top of the thigh splint. Thomas splint (positioned under anterior thigh) with Pearson attachment (supports leg from knee down) frequently used.

**Figure 6  Halo Fixation Device (vest)**

Provides immobilization of cervical spine; pins are used to maintain traction; care of insertion site includes cleansing area around pins using sterile technique. If prescribed by health care provider, clean with half-strength peroxide or saline and sterile swabs 1–2 times/day.

4.  Casting—provides rigid immobilization of affected body part for support and stability, may be plaster or fiberglass (lighter, stronger, water-resistant, porous; diminishes skin problems, does not soften when wet, thus allowing for hydrotherapy)

    a.  Immediate care

        1)  Avoid covering cast until dry (48 hours or longer); handle with palms, not fingertips (plaster cast)

        2)  Avoid resting cast on hard surfaces or sharp edges

        3)  Keep affected limb elevated above heart on soft surface until dry; don't use heat lamp or cover with heavy blankets

      4) Watch for danger signs, e.g., blueness or paleness, pain, numbness, or tingling sensations on affected area; if present, elevate casted area; if it persists, contact health care provider

      5) Elevate arm cast above level of heart

    b. Intermediate care

      1) When cast is dry, client should be mobilized

      2) Encourage prescribed exercises (isometrics and active ROM of joints above and below cast)

      3) Report to health care provider any break in cast or foul odor from cast

      4) Tell client not to scratch skin underneath cast, skin may break and infection can set in; don't put anything underneath cast

      5) If fiberglass cast gets wet, dry with hair dryer on cool setting

    c. After-cast care

      1) Wash skin gently

      2) Apply baby powder, cornstarch, or baby oil

      3) Have client gradually adjust to movement without support of cast

      4) Inform client that swelling is common

      5) Elevate limb and apply elastic bandage

    d. Complications

      1) Impaired circulation

      2) Peripheral nerve damage

      3) Pressure necrosis

**D.** Evaluation

    1. Has fracture healed without complications?

    2. Has client mobility been restored?

# ▶ FRACTURED HIP

**A.** Assessment

    1. Leg shortened, adducted, externally rotated

    2. Pain

    3. Hematoma, ecchymosis

    4. Confirmed by x-rays

**B.** Diagnose

    1. Commonly seen with elderly women with osteoporosis

    2. Potential nursing diagnoses

      a. Impaired physical mobility

      b. Risk for peripheral neurovascular dysfunction

      c. Risk for impaired gas exchange

      d. Acute pain

**C.** Plan/Implementation

1. Total hip replacement—acetabulum, cartilage, and head of femur replaced with artificial joint (see Figure 7)
2. Abduction of affected extremity (use splints, wedge pillow, or 2 or 3 pillows between legs)
3. Turn client as ordered; keep heels off bed
4. Ice to operative site
5. Over bed trapeze to lift self onto fracture bedpan
6. Prevention of thromboembolism—low molecular weight heparin (LMWH) and warfarin; do not sit for prolonged periods
7. Initial ambulation with walker
8. Crutch walking—three-point gait
9. Chair with arms, wheelchair, semireclining toilet seat
10. Medications—anticoagulants to prevent pulmonary embolism, antibiotics to prevent infection
11. Don't sleep on operated side
12. Don't flex hip more than 90°
13. Continuous passive motion device—used after knee replacement to prevent development of scar tissue; extends and flexes knee
14. Use adaptive devices for dressing—extended handles, shoe horns
15. Report increased hip pain to health care provider immediately
16. Cleanse incision daily with mild soap and water; dry thoroughly
17. Teach client to inspect hip daily for redness, heat, drainage; if present, call health care provider immediately
18. Complications
    a. Dislocation of prosthesis
    b. Excessive wound drainage
    c. Thromboembolism
    d. Infection
19. Postoperative discharge teaching
    a. Maintain abduction
    b. Avoid stooping
    c. Do not sleep on operated side until directed to do so
    d. Flex hip only to 90°
    e. Never cross legs
    f. Avoid position of flexion during sexual activity
    g. Walking is excellent exercise; avoid overexertion
    h. In 3 months, will be able to resume ADLs, except strenuous sports

Acetabular (Pelvic) Component

Femoral (Proximal) Component

Femoral (Distal) Component

Tibial Component

**Figure 7  Total Hip and Knee Replacement**

**D.** Evaluation

1. Is client knowledgeable about restrictions of activity?

2. Have complications of total hip replacement been prevented?

## ▶ AMPUTATION

**A.** Assessment

1. Trauma

2. Peripheral vascular disease

3. Osteogenic sarcoma

**B.** Diagnose

1. Disarticulation—resection of an extremity through a joint

2. Above-knee amputation (AKA)

3. Below-knee amputation (BKA)

4. Guillotine or open surface

5. Closed or flap

**C.** Plan/Implementation (see Table 1)

1. Delayed prosthesis fitting—residual limb covered with removable cast or residual limb sock; note if penrose drain is inserted follow orders for dressing changes

2. Immediate prosthesis fitting—residual limb covered with dressing and rigid plastic dressing; Penrose drain usually not inserted; rigid dressing helps prevent bleeding by compressing residual limb

3. Phantom limb pain—experienced immediately postop up to 2–3 months postop; occurs more frequently in AK amputations; feeling that extremity is crushed, cramped, or twisted into abnormal position; may be intense burning or cramping

   a. Acknowledge feelings

   b. Early intensive rehabilitation

   c. Residual limb desensitization with kneading massage

   d. Distraction and activity

   e. TENS (transcutaneous electrical nerve stimulation), ultrasound, local anesthetic

   f. Beta blockers used for dull, burning sensations

   g. Anticonvulsants used for stabbing and cramping sensations

   h. Antidepressants used to improve mood and coping ability

   i. Antispasmodics for muscle spasms or cramping

   j. Complementary and alternative therapies—biofeedback and hypnosis

4. Promotion of mobility—ROM exercises; trapeze with overhead frame; firm mattress; prone position every 3 hours for 20 to 30 minutes

| Table 1  POST-OPERATIVE AMPUTATION CARE | | |
|---|---|---|
| **TYPE OF CARE** | **DELAYED PROSTHESIS FITTING** | **IMMEDIATE PROSTHESIS FITTING** |
| Residual limb care | Observe dressings for signs of excessive bleeding; keep large tourniquet on hand to apply around residual limb in event of hemorrhage; dressings changed daily until sutures removed; wrap with elastic bandage to shape, reduce edema, and keep dressing in place; figure-eight because it prevents restriction of blood flow | Observe rigid dressing for signs of oozing; if blood stain appears, mark area and observe every 10 minutes for increase; report excessive oozing immediately to health care provider; provide cast care; guard against cast slipping off |
| Positioning | If ordered by health care provider, elevate residual limb by elevating foot of bed to hasten venous return and prevent edema. | Elevation of residual limb for 24 hours usually sufficient; rigid cast acts to control swelling |
| Turning | Turn client to prone position for short time first postop day, then 30 min 3 times daily to prevent hip contracture; have client roll from side to side | Same; rigid cast, however, acts to prevent both hip and joint contractures |
| Exercises | Have client start exercises to prevent contractures 1st or 2nd day postop, including: active range of motion, especially of remaining leg, strengthening exercises for upper extremities, hyperextension of residual limb | Exercises not as essential because rigid dressing prevents contractures; early ambulation prevents immobilization disabilities |

| Table 1 POST-OPERATIVE AMPUTATION CARE *(CONTINUED)* | | |
|---|---|---|
| TYPE OF CARE | DELAYED PROSTHESIS FITTING | IMMEDIATE PROSTHESIS FITTING |
| Ambulation | Dangle and transfer client to wheelchair and back within 1st or 2nd day postop; crutch walking started as soon as client feels sufficiently strong | Dangle and assist client to ambulate with walker for short period 1st day; increase length of ambulation each day; in physical therapy client uses parallel bars, then crutches, then cane |
| Psychological support | Observe for signs of depression or despondency; remind depressed client that he/she will receive prosthesis when wound heals | Observe for signs of depression; clients usually less depressed if they awaken with prosthesis attached |
| Discharge | Teach residual limb care—inspect daily for abrasions, wash, expose to air, do not apply lotions, use only cotton or wool residual limb socks | Same |

**D.** Evaluation

1. Has client's mobility been maintained?

2. Have complications been prevented?

# REST AND SLEEP DISTURBANCES

## ▶ HOSPITALIZED CLIENTS

**A.** Assessment

1. Restlessness
2. Fatigue
3. Inability to concentrate
4. Irritability
5. Depression
6. Hallucinations after extended periods of sleeplessness

**B.** Diagnose

1. Rest—basic physiological need
   a. Allows body to repair its own damaged cells
   b. Enhances removal of waste products from the body
   c. Restores tissue to maximum functional ability before another activity is begun
2. Sleep—basic physiological need, although the purpose and reason for it is unclear; possible theories include:
   a. To restore balance among different parts of the central nervous system
   b. To mediate stress, anxiety, and tension
   c. To help a person cope with daily activities
3. Causes of disturbances
   a. Stress
   b. Drugs, e.g., hypnotics, barbiturates
   c. Unfamiliar environment
4. Potential nursing diagnoses
   a. Sleep pattern disturbance
   b. Activity intolerance
   c. Injury, risk for

**C.** Plan/Implementation

1. Establish database on client's pattern of rest and sleep
2. Give care in blocks of time to allow uninterrupted periods of rest and sleep
3. Remove unpleasant odors
4. Avoid unnecessary light and noises
5. Avoid excessively warm or cool temperatures
6. Reposition client as appropriate
7. Spend time with client
8. Give unhurried backrub
9. Straighten and replace wrinkled or soiled linens

10. Give warm, nonstimulating beverages
11. Give pain medication—preferable to sleep medications, which interfere with REM stage of sleep
12. Provide diversionary and occupational activities during the day to relieve boredom and utilize nighttime for sleep
13. Listen actively to client's concerns
14. Explain treatments ahead of time
15. Give a thorough orientation to the hospital setting

**D.** Evaluation
1. Is client able to fall asleep and stay asleep?
2. Has client's comfort been maintained?

## ▶ ELDERLY CLIENTS

**A.** Assessment
1. Difficulty getting to sleep
2. Waking early in the morning
3. Brief periods of wakefulness during the night

**B.** Diagnose
1. Sleep patterns change with advancing age
2. Levels of deep sleep occur less frequently

**C.** Plan/Implementation
1. Establish regular schedule for sleeping, go to bed at same time and wake up at same time
2. Avoid caffeinated beverages late in the evening
3. Establish bedtime ritual
   a. Warm bath
   b. Warm milk
4. Exercise regularly
5. If unable to sleep, perform quiet activity or read
6. Bedroom should be well ventilated and humidified
7. Reduce daytime napping and inactivity
8. Evaluate for sleep apnea
9. Evaluate for nocturia

**D.** Evaluation
1. Is client able to wake refreshed?
2. Is client able to perform ADLs?

## ▶ SLEEP APNEA SYNDROME

**A.** Assessment
1. Client snores loudly, stops breathing for 10 seconds or more, then awakens abruptly with loud snort; multiple nighttime awakenings
2. Excessive daytime sleepiness and fatigue
3. Morning headache
4. Sore throat

5. Personality and behavioral changes

6. Dysrhythmias, hypertension, increased risk of stroke, myocardial infarction and heart failure

**B.** Diagnose

1. Occurs in older, overweight men, elderly, people with thick necks, smokers

2. Polysomnography (PSG)—EEG, EMG, ECG, oxygen saturation levels; diaphragmatic movement monitored during sleep

3. Types

   a. Obstructive—lack of airflow due to occlusion of pharynx

   b. Central—cessation of airflow and respiratory movements

   c. Mixed—combination of central and obstructive apnea within an episode

**C.** Plan/Implementation

1. Avoid alcohol and medications that depress upper airway

2. Weight-reduction diet and activity

3. For severe cases, if client is hypoxic and hypercapnic, will use continuous positive airway pressure (CPAP) or bilevel positive airway pressure (BIPAP) with additional oxygen

4. Position-fixing devices used to prevent tongue obstruction and subluxation of neck

5. Surgery to correct obstruction

6. Low-flow oxygen

7. Tracheostomy if life-threatening dysrhythmias are present; unplugged only during sleep

**D.** Evaluation

1. Has client's sleeping pattern been restored?

2. Is client knowledgeable about how to use home equipment?

# ▶ ALZHEIMER'S DISEASE

**A.** Assessment

1. Forgetfulness progressing to inability to recognize familiar faces, places, objects

2. Depression, paranoia, combativeness

3. Unable to formulate concepts and think abstractly

4. Impulsive behavior

5. Short attention span

6. Agitation and increase in physical activity

7. Night wandering

8. Inability to perform ADLs (unkempt appearance)

9. Dysphasia

10. Incontinence

**B.** Diagnose

1. Progressive, irreversible, degenerative neurological disease characterized by loss of cognitive function and disturbance in behavior

2. Risk factors

   a. Age

   b. Family history

3. Potential nursing diagnoses

   a. Self-care deficit

   b. Communication, impaired verbal

   c. Incontinence, total

4. Death occurs due to complications

   a. Pneumonia

   b. Malnutrition

   c. Dehydration

**C.** Plan/Implementation

1. Support cognitive function

   a. Provide calm, predictable environment and present change gradually

   b. Establish regular routine

   c. Give clear and simple explanations and repeat information

   d. Display clock and calendar

   e. Color-code objects and areas

2. Provide for safety

   a. Use night light, call light, and low bed with half-bed rails

   b. Allow smoking only with supervision

   c. Monitor medications and food intake

   d. Secure doors leading from house

   e. Gently distract and redirect during wandering behavior

   f. Avoid restraints (increases combativeness)

   g. Client should wear identification bracelet or neck chain

   h. Frequent reorientation

3. Reduce anxiety and agitation

   a. Reinforce positive self-image

   b. Encourage to enjoy simple activities (e.g., walking, exercising, socializing)

   c. Keep environment simple, familiar, noise-free

   d. If client experiences catastrophic reaction (overreaction to excessive stimulation), remain calm and stay with client; provide distraction such as listening to music, rocking, or therapeutic touch to quiet client

4. Improve communication

   a. Reduce noise and distractions

   b. Use clear, easy-to-understand sentences

   c. Provide lists and simple written instructions

5. Promote independence in ADLs

   a. Organize daily activities into short, achievable steps

   b. Allow client to make choices when appropriate

   c. Encourage to participate in self-care activities

6. Provide for socialization

   a. Encourage letters, visits (one or two persons at a time), phone calls

   b. Provide a pet

7. Promote good nutrition

   a. Simple, calm environment

   b. Offer one dish at a time to prevent playing with food

   c. Cut food into small pieces to prevent choking

   d. Check temperature of foods to prevent burns

   e. Use adaptive equipment as needed for feeding self

   f. Provide apron or smock instead of bib to respect dignity

8. Promote balance of activity and rest

   a. Allow client to walk in protected environment

   b. Provide music, warm milk, back rub to encourage sleep

   c. Discourage long naps during the day

9. Provide teaching and support to caregivers

   a. Refer to Alzheimer's Association, family support groups, respite care, adult day care

10. Complementary/alternative therapy

    a. Ginkgo biloba

    b. Fish high in omega-3 fatty acids

    c. 1000 international units vitamin E twice daily

11. Administer medications—cholinesterase inhibitors; NMDA-receptor antagonists antidepressants

**D.** Evaluation

   1. Has client's independence been maintained as much as possible?

   2. Are caretakers knowledgeable about how to care for client at home?

## ▶ THYROID DISORDERS

**A.** Assessment (see Table 1)

**B.** Diagnose (see Table 1)

| | Table 1 THYROID DISORDERS | |
|---|---|---|
| | MYXEDEMA/HYPOTHYROIDISM | GRAVES' DISEASE/HYPERTHYROIDISM |
| Assessment | Diagnostic tests:<br>  ↓ BMR (basal metabolic rate)<br>  ↓ T3<br>  ↓ T4<br>  ↑ TSH<br>Decreased activity level<br>Sensitivity to cold<br>Potential alteration in skin integrity<br>Decreased perception of stimuli<br>Obesity, weight gain<br>Potential for respiratory difficulty<br>Constipation<br>Alopecia<br>Bradycardia<br>Dry skin and hair<br>Decreased ability to perspire<br>Reproductive problems | Diagnostic tests:<br>  ↑ BMR<br>  ↑ T3<br>  ↑ T4<br>  High titer anti-thyroid antibodies<br>Hyperactivity<br>Sensitivity to heat<br>Rest and sleep deprivation<br>Increased perception of stimuli<br>Weight loss<br>Potential for respiratory difficulty<br>Diarrhea<br>Tachycardia<br>Exophthalmus<br>Frequent mood swings<br>Nervous, jittery<br>Fine, soft hair |
| Analysis | Hyposecretion of thyroid hormone<br>Slowed physical and mental functions | Hypersecretion of thyroid hormone<br>Accelerated physical and mental functions |
| Predisposing factors | Inflammation of thyroid<br>Iatrogenic—thyroidectomy, irradiation, overtreatment with antithyroids<br>Pituitary deficiencies<br>Iodine deficiency<br>Idiopathic | Thyroid-secreting tumors<br>Iatrogenic–overtreatment for hypothyroid<br>Pituitary hyperactivity<br>Severe stress, e.g., pregnancy |
| Treatment and management | Hormone replacement (levothyroxine sodium) | Antithyroid drugs (SSKI methimazole, propylthiouracil)<br>Irradiation ($^{131}$I)<br>Surgery |
| Potential nursing diagnosis | Disturbed body image<br>Imbalanced nutrition: more than body requirements<br>Activity intolerance<br>Constipation<br>Hypothermia<br>Deficient knowledge<br>Decreased cardiac output | Activity intolerance<br>Altered body temperature<br>Social interaction, impaired<br>Imbalanced nutrition: less than body requirements<br>Hyperthermia<br>Fatigue<br>Risk for impaired tissue integrity |

C. Plan/Implementation

1. Myxedema/hypothyroidism

   a. Pace activities

   b. Allow client extra time to think, speak, act

   c. Teaching should be done slowly and in simple terms

   d. Frequent rest periods between activities

   e. Maintain room temperature at approximately 75°F

   f. Provide client with extra clothing and bedding

   g. Restrict use of soaps and apply lanolin or creams to skin

   h. High-protein, low-calorie diet

   i. Small, frequent feedings

   j. Prevent constipation—high-fiber, high-cellulose foods

   k. Increase fluid intake

   l. Cathartics or stool softeners as ordered

   m. Explain to client that symptoms are reversible with treatment

   n. Explain to family that client's behavior is part of the condition andwill change when treatment begins

   o. Administer drug replacement therapy (e.g., levothyroxine;dose gradually increased and adjusted.)

   p. Administer sedatives carefully—risk of respiratory depression

   q. Instruct about causes of myxedema coma (acute illness, surgery, chemotherapy, discontinuation of medication)

2. Graves' disease/hyperthyroidism

   a. Limit activities to quiet ones (e.g., reading, knitting)

   b. Provide for frequent rest periods

   c. Restrict visitors and control choice of roommates

   d. Keep room cool; advise light, cool clothing

   e. Avoid stimulants, (e.g., coffee)

   f. Accept behavior

   g. Use calm, unhurried manner when caring for client

   h. Interpret behavior to family

   i. Administer antithyroid medication, irradiation with $^{131}$I PO (short-term)

   j. Provide post-thyroidectomy care

      1) Low or semi-Fowler's position

      2) Support head, neck, and shoulders to prevent flexion or hyperextension of suture line; elevate head of bed 30°

      3) Tracheostomy set and suction supplies at bedside

      4) Give fluids as tolerated

5) Observe for complications

    a) Laryngeal nerve injury—detected by hoarseness

    b) Thyroidtoxicosis—increased temperature, increased pulse, hypertension, abdominal pain, diarrhea, confusion, agitation, seizures; treatment—hypothermia blanket, $O_2$, potassium iodine, propylthiouracil (PTU), propranolol, hydrocortisone, acetaminophen; also caused by trauma, infection, palpation, RAI therapy

    c) Hemorrhage; check back of neck and upper chest for bleeding

    d) Respiratory obstruction

    e) Tetany (decreased calcium from parathyroid involvement—check Chvostek's and Trousseau's signs

    f) Have IV calcium gluconate or IV calcium chloride available

6) Analgesics, cold steam inhalations for sore throat

7) Adjust diet to new metabolic needs

  k. Antithyroid medications—methimazole; propylthiouracil; potassium iodide (SSKI); radioactive iodine

**D.** Evaluation

  1. Is client knowledgeable about the dietary considerations?

  2. Have complications been prevented?

## ▶ PARATHYROID DISORDERS

**A.** Assessment (see Table 2)

**B.** Diagnose (see Table 2)

**C.** Plan/Implementation (see Table 2)

**D.** Evaluation

  1. Has client's mobility been maintained?

  2. Have complications been prevented?

| Table 2  PARATHYROID DISORDERS | | |
|---|---|---|
| | **HYPOPARATHYROIDISM** | **HYPERPARATHYROIDISM** |
| **Assessment** | Tetany<br>Muscular irritability (cramps, spasms)<br>Carpopedal spasm, clonic convulsions<br>Dysphagia<br>Paresthesia, laryngeal spasm<br>Anxiety, depression, irritability<br>Tachycardia<br>    + Chvostek's sign<br>    + Trousseau's sign | Fatigue, muscle weakness<br>Cardiac dysrhythmias<br>Emotional irritability<br>Renal calculi<br>Back and joint pain, pathological fractures<br>Pancreatitis, peptic ulcer |
| **Diagnose** | Decreased secretion of parathyroid hormone<br>Introgenic–post thyroidectomy<br>Hypomagnesemia<br>Diagnostic tests:<br>    Serum calcium ↓<br>    Serum phosphorus ↑<br>    ↓ parathyroid hormone (PTH)<br>    X-ray–bones appear dense | Oversecretion of parathyroid hormone<br>Benign parathyroid tumor<br>Parathyroid carcinoma<br>Neck trauma<br>Neck radiation<br>Diagnostic tests:<br>    ↑ Serum calcium<br>    ↓ Serum phosphorus<br>    X-ray–bones appear porous<br>    ↑ serum parathyroid hormone |
| **Potential nursing diagnosis** | Risk for injury<br>Deficient knowledge | Risk for injury<br>Impaired urinary elimination<br>Nutrition: less than body requirements<br>Constipation |
| **Plan/Implementation** | Emergency treatment–calcium chloride or gluconate over 10–15 minutes<br>Calcitriol 0.5–2 mg daily for acute hypocalcemia<br>Ergocalciferol 50,000–400,000 units daily<br>Observe for tetany<br>Low-phosphorus, high-calcium diet | Relieve pain<br>Prevent formation of renal calculi increase fluid intake<br>Offer acid-ash juices (improves solubility of calcium)<br>Administer appropriate diet<br>Prevent fractures<br>Safety precautions<br>Monitor potassium levels (counteracts effect of calcium on cardiac muscles)<br>Provide postparathyroidectomy care (essentially same as for thyroidectomy)<br>IV Furosemide and saline promote calcium excretion<br>IV phosphorus is used only for rapid lowering of calcium level<br>Surgery–parathyroidectomy |

# ▶ NUTRITION

**A.** Assessment

1. Physical signs (see Table 1)
2. Laboratory values: hemoglobin, hematocrit, serum albumin

| Table 1 PHYSICAL SIGNS OF ADEQUATE NUTRITIONAL STATUS | |
|---|---|
| **BODY AREA** | **NORMAL APPEARANCE** |
| Hair | Shiny, firm, intact scalp without areas of pigmentation |
| Teeth | Evenly spaced, straight, no cavities, shiny |
| Tongue | Deep red in color |
| Gums | Firm, without redness, even-colored |
| Skin | Smooth, moist, even shading |
| Nails | Firm, without ridges |
| Extremities | Full range of motion |
| Abdomen | Flat, non-tender |
| Legs | Good color |
| Skeleton | No malformations |
| Weight | Normal for height |
| Posture | Erect |
| Muscles | Firm |
| GI | Good appetite and digestion |
| Vitality | Good endurance, good sleep patterns |

3. Health history
   a. Chronic diseases—dietary alteration may be necessary because of disease entity, e.g., low-sodium diet for heart disease
   b. Therapies—treatment modalities may alter food intake, e.g., adverse effects of chemotherapy and radiation therapy, such as nausea and vomiting, may cause a decrease in intake
   c. Surgeries—some surgeries may alter actual intake, e.g., head and neck surgery, and/or absorption concurrent with digestion, e.g., GI surgery
   d. Usual eating habits (takes 1–2 weeks for malnutrition to develop)
   e. Recent changes in appetite or food history
   f. Level of growth and development (increased needs)

**B.** Diagnose

1. Caloric requirement—a calorie is a measurement unit of energy; person's height and weight, as well as level of activity, determine energy need; average adult requires anywhere from 1,500 kcal to 3,000 kcal a day

2. Fluid requirement—average fluid requirement for normal healthy adult is approximately 1,800–2,500 ml/day

3. Nutrient requirements

    a. Carbohydrates—first substance used for energy production in starvation; only source of energy production for the brain

    b. Fats—second source of energy production used by the body in starvation; waste products are ketone bodies, which can create an acidic environment in the blood

    c. Proteins—last energy source used in starvation; depletion of protein leads to muscle wasting as well as loss of oncotic pressure in the vascular space; low albumin level in the blood indicates protein malnutrition

    d. Vitamins—organic substances found in foods; essential in small quantities for growth and for transformation of food substances into tissue

        1) Fat-soluble vitamins (see Table 2)

        2) Water-soluble vitamins (see Table 3)

        3) Minerals (see Table 4)

| Table 2 FAT-SOLUBLE VITAMINS | | | |
|---|---|---|---|
| **VITAMINS** | **FUNCTION(S)** | **PRIMARY SOURCE(S)** | **CLINICAL MANIFESTATION(S)** |
| A | Visual acuity<br><br>Adaptation to light and dark | Beta-carotene<br><br>Liver<br><br>Egg yolk<br><br>Cream, milk, margarine<br><br>Yellow fruits, and orange and green leafy vegetables (carrots, squash, peaches)<br><br>Butter, cheese | D: Night blindness, skin infection, xerophthalmia, corneal ulceration<br><br>T: CNS changes (lethargy, headache)<br><br>GI (portal hypertension) |
| D | Calcification of bones<br><br>Absorption of Ca, phosphorus | Fish oils<br><br>Fortified milk/dairy products, egg yolks<br><br>Sunlight's irradiation of body cholesterol | D: Rickets, poor bone growth<br><br>T: Hypercalcemia, renal calculi |
| E | Antioxidant<br><br>Growth | Green leaf vegetables<br><br>Fats, oils<br><br>Liver<br><br>Grains, nuts | D: Breakdown of red blood cells<br><br>Hemolytic anemia<br><br>T: Fatigue, headache, blurred vision, diarrhea |
| K | Blood clotting | Leafy vegetables<br><br>Eggs, cheese<br><br>Synthesized by intestinal bacteria | D: Bleeding, bruises<br><br>T: Anemia, liver/renal damage, and intestinal bacterial infection |
| **D: DEFICIENCY T: TOXICITY** | | | |

| Table 3 WATER–SOLUBLE VITAMINS | | | |
|---|---|---|---|
| VITAMINS | FUNCTION(S) | PRIMARY SOURCES | CLINICAL MANIFESTATION(S) |
| Thiamine (B$_1$) | Normal growth<br>Carbohydrate metabolism | Legumes, meat<br>Enriched grains<br>Eggs, fish | D: Beriberi (numbness, decreased reflexes fatigue)<br>    Wernicke-Korsakoff syndrome<br>T: Shock |
| Riboflavin (B$_2$) | Coenzyme in protein and energy metabolism | Milk<br>Liver (organ meats) | D: Ariboflavinosis<br>    Tissue inflammation |
| Niacin (nicotinic acid) | Normal growth | Meat<br>Grains | D: Pellagra (rough, scaly skin, glossitis, decreased weight)<br>T: Vasodilation, flushing |
| Pyridoxine (B$_6$) | Amino acid metabolism | Corn and soy<br>Meat and liver<br>Yeast, egg yolk, sunflowers | D: Anemia, CNS changes (seizures)<br>    Peripheral neuropathy<br>T: Diminished proprioceptive sensory function |
| Folic acid | RBC formation | Liver<br>Oranges<br>Broccoli | D: Anemia<br>T: Diminished proprioceptive and sensory function |
| Cyanocobalamin (B$_{12}$) | Nerve function<br>RBC formation | Meat<br>Milk, eggs | D: Pernicious anemia |
| Ascorbic acid (C) | Collagen synthesis | Fruits, esp. citrus<br>Vegetables<br>Tomatoes | D: Scurvy (joint pain and weakness)<br>    Anemia (in infants)<br>T: Oxalate hypersensitivity |
| **D: DEFICIENCY T: TOXICITY** | | | |

| Table 4 MINERALS | | | |
|---|---|---|---|
| MINERAL | PRIMARY FUNCTION(S) | PRIMARY SOURCE(S) | DEFICIENCY SYMPTOM(S) |
| Calcium | Bone formation<br>Muscle contraction<br>Thrombus formation | Milk products<br>Green leafy vegetables<br>Eggs | Rickets<br>Porous bones<br>Tetany |
| Phosphorus | Bone formation<br>Cell permeability | Milk, eggs<br>Nuts | Rickets |
| Fluoride | Dental health | Water supply | Dental caries |
| Iodine | Thyroid hormone synthesis | Seafood<br>Iodized salt | Goiter |
| Sodium | Osmotic pressure<br>Acid-base balance<br>Nerve irritability | Table salt<br>Canned vegetables<br>Milk, cured meats<br>Processed foods | Fluid and electrolyte imbalance |

| Table 4  MINERALS *(CONTINUED)* | | | |
|---|---|---|---|
| MINERAL | PRIMARY FUNCTION(S) | PRIMARY SOURCE(S) | DEFICIENCY SYMPTOM(S) |
| Potassium | Water balance in cells<br>Protein synthesis<br>Heart contractility | Grains, meats<br>Vegetables | Arrhythmias<br>Fluid and electrolyte imbalance |
| Iron | Hemoglobin synthesis | Liver, oysters<br>Leafy vegetables<br>Apricots | Anemia<br>Lethargy |

| Table 5  FOOD GUIDELINES | | |
|---|---|---|
| GROUP | FOOD EXAMPLES | RECOMMENDED DAILY INTAKE |
| Grains | Bread, cereals, cooked cereals, popcorn, pasta, rice, tortillas<br>Half of all grains should be whole grains | Children—3–5 ounce equivalents<br>Teens—5–7 ounce equivalents<br>Young adults—6–8 ounce equivalents<br>Adults—6–7 ounce equivalents<br>Older adults—5–6 ounce equivalents |
| Vegetables | Dark green vegetables (broccoli, spinach, greens, leafy vegetables), orange vegetables (carrots, pumpkin, sweet potatoes), dried beans and peas (split peas, pinto, kidney, black, soy [tofu]), starchy vegetables (corn, peas, white potatoes) | Children—1–1½ cups<br>Teens—2–3 cups<br>Young adults—2½–3 cups<br>Adults—2½–3 cups<br>Older adults—2–2½ cups |
| Fruits | Apple, bananas, strawberries, blueberries, orange, melons, dried fruits, fruit juices | Children—1–1½ cups<br>Teens—1½–2 cups<br>Young adults—2 cups<br>Adults—1½–2 cups<br>Older adults—1½–2 cups |
| Oils | Nuts, butter, margarine, cooking oils, salad dressings | Children—3–4 teaspoons<br>Teens—5–6 teaspoons<br>Young adults—6–7 teaspoons<br>Adults—5–6 teaspoons<br>Older adults—5–6 teaspoons |
| Milk | Milk, yogurt, cheese, puddings | Children—2 cups<br>Teens—3 cups<br>Young adults—3 cups<br>Adults—3 cups<br>Older adults—3 cups |
| Meat and beans | Meat, poultry, fish, dry beans, eggs, peanut butter, nuts, seeds | Children—2–4 ounce equivalents<br>Teens—5–6 ounce equivalents<br>Young adults—5½–6½ ounce equivalents<br>Adults—5–6 ounce equivalents<br>Older adults—5–5½ ounce equivalents |

**C.** Plan/Implementation

   1. General diet—eat a variety of foods (see Table 5)

   2. Vegetarian diet

      a. Types

         1) Vegan diet includes fruits, vegetables, nuts, beans, and seeds; excludes all sources of animal protein, fortified foods, and nutritional supplements of animal origin; risk of vitamin $B_{12}$ deficiency

         2) Lacto-vegetarian diet includes all foods on a vegan diet, along with milk, cheese, yogurt, and other milk products as the only source of animal protein; avoids meat, fish, poultry and eggs

         3) Ovo-vegetarian diet includes all foods on a vegan diet, along with eggs as the only source of animal protein

         4) Lacto–ovo-vegetarian diet includes all foods on a vegan diet, along with milk, cheese, yogurt, other milk products, and eggs as only sources of animal protein

         5) "Red-meat abstainers" consider themselves vegetarians and eat animal products with the exception of red meat

      b. Analysis

         1) Become vegetarians due to religion (Seventh Day Adventists), ecology, economic reasons, health reasons

         2) Risk deficiency of vitamin $B_{12}$ associated with megaloblastic anemia; vitamin $B_{12}$ is found only in animal products

         3) Risk toxic levels of vitamin A causing anorexia, irritability, dry skin, hair loss

      c. Plan/Implementation

         1) Increase intake of legumes, beans, nuts, seeds, tofu, dark green leafy vegetable

         2) Eat fortified cereals, soy beverages, and meat analogs

         3) Must eat adequate amounts of protein, calcium, zinc, vitamin D, and vitamin $B_{12}$

         4) During pregnancy should take supplements to meet increased nutritional needs

         5) Children may experience mild anemia due to the poor availability of iron from grains and legumes; should include source of vitamin C with meals; diet should include nonmeat animal proteins such as milk, cheese, and eggs; vegan diet is unable to sustain growth needs of children

         6) Vegetarian diet often causes weight loss due to elimination of meat which is a major source of fat; fat has twice the number of kilocalories per gram than carbohydrates or proteins

3. Choose My Plate—recommendations by the U.S. Department of Agriculture; includes diet choices for vegetarians and members of ethnic/cultural groups (see Figure 1)

**Figure 1  ChooseMyPlate.gov**

4. Common therapeutic diets (see Table 6)

5. Complementary/Alternative therapies

   a. General guidelines for herbal and dietary supplements

      1) Supplements do not compensate for an inadequate diet

      2) Recommended daily amounts (RDA) should not be exceeded due to the potential for toxicity

      3) Multivitamin-mineral products recommended for certain age or gender groups contain different amounts of some minerals

      4) Iron supplements beyond those contained in multivitamin-mineral combinations are intended for short-term or special-need (e.g., pregnancy) use and should not be taken for longer periods of time because of potential for toxicity

      5) Most adolescent and adult females should consume calcium 1,000 to 1,300 mg daily

      6) Supplementing with selenium as an antioxidant and zinc to prevent colds and promote wound healing is not proven

6. Herbals used to lower cholesterol:

   a. Flax or flaxseed

      1) Decreases the absorption of other medications

      2) Nausea, vomiting, increased flatulence

      3) May decrease absorption of other medications

   b. Garlic

      1) Increases the effects of anticoagulants and antiplatelets

      2) Increases the hypoglycemic effects of insulin

      3) May stimulate labor

    c.  Green tea

        1)  Produces a stimulant effect when the tea contains caffeine

        2)  Multiple drug interactions—anticoagulants, antiplatelets, beta blockers

    d.  Soy

        1)  Multiple drug interactions—estrogens, tamoxifen

**D.** Evaluation

    1.  Have client's nutritional needs been met?

    2.  Have any nutritional deficiencies been corrected?

| Table 6  COMMON THERAPEUTIC DIETS | | |
|---|---|---|
| **CLEAR LIQUID DIET** | **FULL LIQUID DIET** | **LOW–FAT, CHOLESTEROL–RESTRICTED DIET** |
| Sample meal items: Gelatin dessert, popsicle, tea with lemon, ginger ale, bouillon, fruit juice without pulp | Sample meal items: Milkshakes, soups, custard; all clear liquids | Sample meal items: Fruit, vegetables, cereals, lean meat |
| Common medical diagnoses: Postoperative; acute vomiting or diarrhea | Common medical diagnoses: GI upset (diet progression after surgery) | Common medical diagnoses: Atherosclerosis, cystic fibrosis (CF) |
| Purpose: To maintain fluid balance | Purpose: Nutrition without chewing | Purpose: To reduce calories from fat and minimize cholesterol intake |
| Not allowed: Fruit juices with pulp, milk | Not allowed: Jam, fruit, solid foods, nuts | Not allowed: Marbled meats, avocados, milk, bacon, egg yolks, butter |
| **SODIUM-RESTRICTED DIET** | **HIGH-ROUGHAGE, HIGH-FIBER DIET** | **LOW-RESIDUE DIET** |
| Sample meal items: Cold baked chicken, lettuce with sliced tomatoes, applesauce | Sample meal items: Cracked wheat bread, minestrone soup, apple, brussel sprouts | Sample meal items: Roast lamb, buttered rice, sponge cake, "white" processed foods |
| Common medical diagnoses: Heart failure, hypertension, cirrhosis | Common medical diagnoses: Constipation, large bowel disorders | Common medical diagnoses: Temporary GI/elimination problems (e.g., lower bowel surgery) |
| Purpose: To lower body water and promote excretion | Purpose: To maximize bulk in stools | Purpose: To minimize intestinal activity |
| Not allowed: Preserved meats, cheese, fried foods, cottage cheese, canned foods, added salt | Not allowed: White bread, pies and cakes from white flour, "white" processed foods | Not allowed: Whole wheat, corn, bran |

| Table 6  COMMON THERAPEUTIC DIETS *(CONTINUED)* | | |
|---|---|---|
| **HIGH–PROTEIN DIET** | **KIDNEY DIET** | **LOW PHENYLALANINE DIET** |
| Sample meal items:<br>30 grams powdered skim milk and 1 egg in 100 ml water<br>*or*<br>Roast beef sandwich and skim milk | Sample meal items:<br>Unsalted vegetables, white rice, canned fruits, sweets | Sample meal items:<br>Fats, fruits, jams, low-phenylalanine milk |
| Common medical diagnoses:<br>Burns, infection, hyperthyroidism | Common medical diagnoses:<br>Chronic/Acute renal failure | Common medical diagnoses:<br>Phenylketonuria (PKU) |
| Purpose:<br>To re-establish anabolism to raise albumin levels | Purpose:<br>To keep protein, potassium, and sodium low | Purpose:<br>Low-protein diet to prevent brain damage from imbalance of amino acids |
| Not allowed:<br>Soft drinks, "junk" food | Not allowed:<br>Beans, cereals, citrus fruits | Not allowed:<br>Meat, eggs, beans, bread |

## ► CULTURAL FOOD PATTERNS

*Not all members of a culture choose to follow all dietary traditions.*

A. Orthodox Jewish

1. Dietary laws based on Biblical and rabbinical regulations

2. Laws pertain to selection, preparation, and service of food

3. Laws

   a. Milk/milk products never eaten at same meal as meat (milk may not be taken until 6 hours after eating meat)

   b. Two meals contain dairy products and one meal contains meat

   c. Separate utensils are used for meat and milk dishes

   d. Meat must be kosher (drained of blood)

   e. Prohibited foods

      1) Pork

      2) Diseased animals or animals who die a natural death

      3) Birds of prey

      4) Fish without fins or scales (shellfish—oysters, crab, lobster)

B. Muslim

1. Dietary laws based on Islamic teachings in Koran

2. Laws

   a. Fermented fruits and vegetables prohibited

   b. Pork prohibited

   c. Alcohol prohibited

      d. Foods with special value: figs, olives, dates, honey, milk, buttermilk

      e. Meat must be Halal (drained of blood)

      f. Follow humane process of slaughter of animals for meat

   3. 30-day period of daylight fasting required during Ramadan

**C.** Hispanic

   1. Basic foods: dried beans, chili peppers, corn

   2. Use small amounts of meat and eggs

   3. Saturated fat use in food preparation common

**D.** Puerto Rican

   1. Main type of food is viandos—starchy vegetables and fruits (plantain and green bananas)

   2. Diet includes large amounts of rice and beans

   3. Coffee main beverage

**E.** Native American

   1. Food has religious and social significance

   2. Diet includes meat, bread (tortillas, blue corn bread), eggs, vegetables (corn, potatoes, green beans, tomatoes), fruit

   3. Frying common method of food preparation

**F.** African American

   1. Minimal use of milk in diet

   2. Frequent use of leafy greens (turnips, collards, and mustard)

   3. Pork, fat, cholesterol, and sodium common in diet

**G.** French American

   1. Foods are strong-flavored and spicy

   2. Frequently contains seafood (crawfish)

   3. Food preparation starts with a roux made from heated oil and flour, vegetables and seafood added

**H.** Chinese

   1. Uses freshest food available; cooked at a high temperature in a wok using a small amount of fat and liquid

   2. Meat used in small amounts

   3. Eggs and soybean products used for protein

**I.** Japanese

   1. Rice is basic food

   2. Soy sauce is used for seasoning

   3. Tea is main beverage

   4. Seafood frequently used (sometimes raw fish—sushi)

**J.** Southeast Asian

   1. Rice is basic food, eaten in separate rice bowl

   2. Soups frequently used

   3. Fresh fruits and vegetables frequently part of diet

   4. Stir-frying in wok is common method of food preparation

**K.** Italian

1. Bread and pasta are basic foods
2. Cheese frequently used in cooking
3. Food seasoned with spices, wine, garlic, herbs, olive oil

**L.** Greek

1. Bread is served with every meal
2. Cheese (feta) frequently used for cooking
3. Lamb and fish frequently used
4. Eggs used in main dish, but not breakfast food
5. Fruit used for dessert

## ▶ PREMATURE INFANTS

**A.** Assessment

1. Body composition—premature infant has more water, less protein and fat per pound than full-term infant
2. Poor temperature control due to little subcutaneous fat
3. Bones are poorly calcified
4. Sucking reflexes are poor
5. Gastrointestinal and renal function are poor
6. Prone to infection
7. Immature development of lungs

**B.** Diagnose

1. Less than 2,500 g and less than 37 weeks gestation
2. Nutritional requirements
   a. 100–200 cal/kg/day
   b. Higher sodium, calcium, and protein requirements than full-term infant

**C.** Plan/Implementation

1. Feeding
   a. Parenteral nutrition—usually required until oral feedings can be established
   b. Gavage feedings—usually given because of poor sucking coordination
   c. Soft (preemie) nipples are usually effective for very small infants
2. Supplements
   a. Vitamins A, C, D, and iron are usually given orally
   b. Occasionally, vitamin E is needed to prevent oxidation of RBCs
   c. Long-chain fats are not well tolerated; medium-chain triglycerides (MCTs) are often used
   d. Glucose is often substituted for lactose in premature formulas because of its passive absorption in GI tract
   e. Vitamin K prophylaxis to prevent clotting problems

**D.** Evaluation

1. Has infant gained weight?

2. Have complications been prevented?

# ▶ FULL-TERM INFANTS

**A.** Assessment

1. Energy requirements are high; 120 cal/kg/day

2. Rooting and sucking reflexes are well developed

3. Six to eight wet diapers per day and at least 1 stool daily

**B.** Diagnose

1. Weighs more than 2,500 g and greater than 37 weeks gestation

**C.** Plan/Implementation

1. Breastfeeding

   a. Human milk is ideal food; recommended for first 6 to 12 months of life

   b. Colostrum is secreted at first

      1) Clear and colorless

      2) Contains protective antibodies

      3) High in protein and minerals

   c. Milk is secreted after day 2 to 4

      1) Milky white appearance

      2) Contains more fat and lactose than colostrum

2. Formula feeding

   a. Formula is cow's milk modified to resemble human milk more closely; avoid cow's milk first year (deficient in vitamins and iron)

      1) Diluted to reduce protein content

      2) Sugar is added to increase carbohydrate content

      3) Home preparation from evaporated milk is most economical

      4) Formula is necessary for first 12 months of life; then, unmodified cow's milk is acceptable

      5) If problems with diarrhea, change formula to prevent profound dehydration

   b. Feeding technique

      1) Child should be cradled when fed

      2) Child should be regulator of milk volume

3. Introduction to solid foods (see Table 7)

   a. Introduce only one at a time for each two–week period

   b. Least allergenic foods are given in first half of the first year; more allergenic foods (e.g., egg, orange juice) are offered in last half of first year; usual order: cereal, fruit, vegetables, potatoes, meat, egg, orange juice

   c. No honey should be given during first year due to high risk of botulism

| Table 7  INTRODUCTION TO SOLID FOODS ||
| AGE | FOOD |
| --- | --- |
| 1–4 months | Liquid vitamins only—A, D, C, fluoride (if indicated) |
| 4–5 months | Cereal—usually rice is first; strained fruit |
| 5–6 months | Strained vegetables; strained meat |
| 7–9 months | Chopped meat; hard breads and "finger foods"; potato baked, mashed |

## ▶ TODDLERS

**A.** Assessment

1. Six to eight teeth have erupted
2. Begins to use large muscles and bones

**B.** Diagnose

1. 12 to 36 months

**C.** Plan/Implementation

1. Allow choice of foods from food pyramid to prevent struggle over eating; may prefer one type of food over another
2. Needs fewer calories in diet but more protein and calcium than infant
3. Give 32 ounces or less of formula to decrease risk iron-deficiency anemia

**D.** Evaluation

1. Have toddler's nutritional needs been met?

## ▶ PRESCHOOLER AND SCHOOL-AGE

**A.** Assessment

1. Growth rate slows
2. Protein and calcium needs remain high

**B.** Diagnose

1. Growth rate is gradual until adolescence; then spurts occur

**C.** Plan/Implementation

1. Nutritional intake (see Table 8)

| Table 8 NUTRIENT INTAKE FOR CHILDREN | |
|---|---|
| FOOD | SERVINGS |
| Fruits and vegetables | 4–8 |
|     Vitamin C type | 1–2 |
|     Vitamin A type | 1–2 |
|     Fruit type | 1–2 |
|     Other vegetables | 1–2 |
| Cereals (bread, etc.) | 4 |
| Fats and carbohydrates | To meet caloric needs |
| Meats (proteins, peanuts, eggs) | 3 |
| Milk (cheese, yogurt) | 2–3 |

**D.** Evaluation

    1. Have the nutritional needs of the school-age child been maintained?

## ▶ ADOLESCENT NUTRITION

**A.** Assessment

    1. Rapid growth spurts occur

    2. Acne develops

**B.** Diagnose

    1. Caloric, calcium, and protein needs are high

    2. Females experience menstrual losses of iron; require increased intake

    3. Mineral and vitamin needs are high because of rapid tissue growth

**C.** Plan/Implementation

    1. High-calorie, high-protein diet

    2. High intake of iron for menstruating adolescents

    3. High minerals and vitamins in diet

**D.** Evaluation

    1. Have adolescent's nutritional needs been met?

## ▶ ADULT AND ELDERLY POPULATION

**A.** Assessment

    1. Balanced diet continues to be important

    2. Calorie limitation with decreasing physical activity

    3. Declining ability to chew and changing taste perception can cause impaired nutrition in the elderly

**B.** Diagnose

    1. With increased age, reduction in calories needed, improved food quality

    2. Need same level of minerals and vitamins as in early adulthood

**C.** Plan/Implementation
1. Goal is to decrease calories but to ensure food consumed is high in minerals and vitamins
2. Prevent osteoporosis in postmenopausal women
3. Complementary/Alternative Therapy
   a. To reduce all-cause mortality, older adults should consume oral protein and energy supplements

**D.** Evaluation
1. Have the nutritional needs of the elderly been met?
2. Has weight gain been controlled?

## ▶ NUTRITION DURING PREGNANCY AND LACTATION

**A.** Assessment
1. Pre-pregnancy weight
2. Maternal age
3. Labs: hemoglobin and hematocrit
4. Pre-existing health problems

**B.** Diagnose
1. Age and parity of mother varies
2. Preconception nutrition influences overall requirements
3. Individual needs vary; recommended weight gain is 24–28 pounds
4. Folic acid needed to prevent neural tube defects and megaloblastic and macrocytic anemia

**C.** Plan/Implementation
1. Diet plan for pregnancy and lactation (see Table 9)
2. High-risk pregnancies
   a. Adolescence
      1) Must meet own nutritional requirements (high protein and calcium)
      2) Tendency to deliver low-birthweight babies

| Table 9  DIET PLAN FOR PREGNANCY AND LACTATION | | |
|---|---|---|
| **FOOD** | **PREGNANCY** | **LACTATION** |
| Protein (meat, 1 egg, cheese) | 3 servings | 4 servings |
| Vegetable—yellow or green (includes vitamin C foods) | 5 servings | 5–6 servings |
| Bread and cereal (whole grain or enriched) | 5 servings | 5 servings |
| Milk products (cheese, ice cream, milk, cottage cheese) | 4 cups | 5 cups |
| Calories over maintenance | +300/day | +500/day |
| Folic acid | 400 mcg | 280 mcg |

   b. Diabetes

      1) Glucose levels must be monitored closely

      2) Prevent postmature deliveries

      3) C-section may be necessary because mother may not be able to handle the glucose requirements of labor

   c. Sickle cell–stress of labor and pregnancy must be considered in relation to oxygenation capabilities of these mothers; C-section is usually indicated

   d. Cardiac–myocardial stress specifically related to delivery may require decreased activity, as well as C-section, to decrease demand on heart

**D.** Evaluation

   1. Have the nutritional needs of the pregnant woman been met?

   2. Have the nutritional needs of the lactating woman been met?

# ▶ ENTERAL NUTRITION

**A.** Alternative feeding (required because of inability to use gastrointestinal route)

**B.** Liquid food delivered to the stomach, distal duodenum, or proximal jejunum via a nasogastric, percutaneous endoscopic gastrostomy (PEG), or percutaneous endoscopic jejunostomy (PEJ) tube

**C.** Conditions requiring enteral feeding (see Table 10)

| Table 10 CONDITIONS REQUIRING ENTERAL FEEDING ||
|---|---|
| **CONDITION** | **CAUSE** |
| Preoperative need for nutritional support | Inadequate intake preoperatively, resulting in poor nutritional state |
| Gastrointestinal problems | Fistula, short-bowel syndrome, Crohn's disease, ulcerative colitis, nonspecific maldigestion or malabsorption |
| Adverse effects of oncology therapy | Radiation, chemotherapy |
| Alcoholism, chronic depression, eating disorders | Chronic illness, psychiatric, or neurological disorder |
| Head and neck disorders or surgery | Disease or trauma |

**D.** Complications of enteral feeding (see Table 11)

| Table 11 COMPLICATIONS OF ENTERAL FEEDINGS | |
|---|---|
| **COMPLICATION** | **NURSING CONSIDERATIONS** |
| Mechanical<br>Tube displacement | Replace tube |
| Aspiration | Elevate head of bed, check residual before feeding |
| Gastrointestinal<br>Cramping, vomiting,<br>diarrhea | Decrease feeding rate<br>Change formula to more isotonic<br>Administer at room temperature |
| Metabolic<br>Hyperglycemia | Monitor glucose, serum osmolality<br>Monitor glucose, give insulin if needed<br>Reduce infusion rate |
| Dehydration | Flush tube with water according to hospital policy |
| Formula–drug interactions | Check compatibility<br>Flush tubing prior to and after medication |

## ▶ PARENTERAL NUTRITION

**A.** Assessment

  1. Conditions requiring enteral feeding (see Table 10)

**B.** Diagnose

  1. Method of supplying nutrients to the body by the intravenous route (see Figure 2)

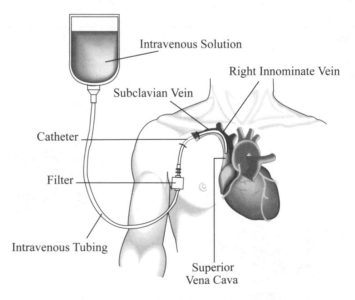

Figure 2  Parenteral Nutrition (PN)

2. Types of solutions
   a. PN—amino acid-dextrose formulas; 2–3 liters of solution given over 24 h; 500 ml of 10% fat emulsions (Intralipid) given with PN over 6 h 1–3 times/week; fine bacterial filter used
   b. TNA (Total Nutrient Admixture)—amino acid-dextrose-lipid, "3-in-1" formula; 1-liter solution given over 24 h; no bacterial filter used
   c. Lipids—provides fatty acids
3. Methods of administration
   a. Peripheral—used to supplement oral intake; should not administer dextrose concentrations above 10% due to irritation of vessel walls; usually used for less than 2 weeks
   b. Central—catheter inserted into subclavian vein
      1) Peripherally inserted catheters (PICC)—catheter threaded through central vein; dextrose solution ≥10% basilic or cephalic vein to superior vena cava; usually ≤4 weeks
      2) Percutaneous central catheters through subclavian vein
      3) Triple lumen central catheter often used; distal lumen (16-gauge) used to infuse or draw blood samples, middle lumen (18-gauge) used for PN infusion, proximal lumen (18-gauge) used to infuse or draw blood and administer medications
      4) If single lumen catheter used, cannot use to administer medications (may be incompatible) or give blood (RBCs coat catheter lumen); medications and blood must be given through peripheral IV line, not piggyback to the PN IV line
   c. Atrial
      1) Right atrial catheters—Hickman/Biovac and Groshong
      2) Subcutaneous port—Huber needle used to access port through skin

**C.** Plan/Implementation
1. Initial rate of infusion 50 ml/h and gradually increased (100–125 ml/h) as client's fluid and electrolyte tolerance permits
2. Infuse solution by pump at constant rate to prevent abrupt change in infusion rate
   a. Increased rate results in hyperosmolar state (headache, nausea, fever, chills, malaise)
   b. Slowed rate results in "rebound" hypoglycemia caused by delayed pancreatic reaction to change in insulin requirements; do not discontinue suddenly
3. Client must be carefully monitored for signs of complications; infection and hyperglycemia are common (see Table 12)

| Table 12  COMPLICATIONS OF PN | |
|---|---|
| COMPLICATION | NURSING CONSIDERATIONS |
| Infection/Sepsis | Maintain closed intravenous systems with filter<br>No blood drawn or medications given through PN line<br>Dry sterile occlusive dressing applied to site |
| Pneumothorax because of line placement | PN to be started only after chest x-ray validates correct placement<br>Monitor breath sounds and for presence of shortness of breath |
| Hyperglycemia<br>Hyperosmolar coma | Monitor glucose level and serum osmolality<br>Administer insulin according to sliding scale insulin |
| Hypoglycemia | Hang 10% dextrose solution if PN discontinued suddenly |
| Fluid overload | Monitor breath sounds, weight and peripheral perfusion<br>Do not "catch up" if PN behind |
| Air embolism | Monitor for respiratory distress<br>Valsalva maneuver during tubing and cap change |

4. Change IV tubing and filter every 24 hours

5. Keep solutions refrigerated until needed; allow to warm to room temperature before use

6. If new solution unavailable, use 10% dextrose and water solution until available

7. Monitor daily weight, glucose, temperatures, intake and output; three times a week check BUN, electrolytes (calcium, magnesium); check CBC, platelets, prothrombin time, liver function studies (AST, ALT), prealbumin, serum albumin once a week

8. Do not increase flow rate if PN behind scheduled administration time

9. Discontinuation

   a. Gradually tapered to allow client to adjust to decreased levels of glucose

   b. After discontinued, isotonic glucose solution administered to prevent rebound hypoglycemia (weakness, faintness, diaphoresis, shakiness, confusion, tachycardia)

**D.** Evaluation

   1. Is the client receiving PN free from infection?

   2. Is the client receiving PN well hydrated?

# ▶ URINARY ELIMINATION

**A.** Assessment

1. Characteristics of urine

   a. Color—yellow

   b. Consistency—clear, transparent

   c. Specific gravity—1.010–1.030

   d. pH—4.5–8.0

   e. 24-hour production—1,000–2,000 mL (approximately 1 mL/Kg/hr)

2. Serum changes

   a. BUN (normal 10–20 mg/dL) (3.6–7.1 mmol/L)

   b. Creatinine (normal 0.7–1.4 mg/dL)(62–124 µmol/L)

**B.** Diagnose

1. Potential nursing diagnoses

   a. Impaired urinary elimination

   b. Readiness for enhanced urinary elimination

   c. Fluid volume deficit

   d. Urinary retention

   e. Urinary incontinence

2. Definitions

   a. Anuria—total urinary output less than 100 mL/24 hours

   b. Oliguria—total urinary output 100–400 mL/24 hours

   c. Polyuria—total urinary output greater than 2000 mL/24 hours

   d. Dysuria—painful or difficult voiding

3. Predisposing factors

   a. Bedrest

   b. Tumors

   c. Prostatic hypertrophy, anticholinergic medications

   d. Decreased bladder tone—previous use of indwelling catheter, childbirth

   e. Cancer

   f. Neurogenic—CVA, spinal injuries

   g. Calculi

   h. Stress

   i. Urinary tract infection

**C.** Plan/Implementation

1. Hydration—adequate intake 1,500–2,000 mL/day

2. Voiding habits

   a. Know client's pattern

   b. Provide time and privacy

3. Teach Kegel exercises—strengthen muscles of pelvic floor; tighten pelvic muscles for count of 3, then relax for count of 3; perform lying down, sitting and standing for total of 45

4. Teach bladder retraining

   a. Triggering techniques—stroking medial aspect of thigh, pinching area above groin, pulling pubic hair, providing digital anal stimulation (used with upper motor neuron problem); Valsava and Credé maneuvers (used with lower motor neuron problem)

   b. Intermittent catheterization every 2–3 hours after attempting to void and Valsalva or Credé maneuver; if volume is less than 150 mL, time interval is increased to 3–4 hours, then 4–6 hours; never more than 8 hours

   c. Toileting schedule—first thing in a.m., before and after meals, before and after physical activity, bedtime

   d. Bladder training—drink a measured amount of fluid every 2 hours, then attempt to void 30 minutes later; time between voiding should be gradually increased

5. Catheterization

6. Respond immediately to call

7. Avoid diuretics such as caffeine

8. Encourage fluid intake to 2,000 mL

9. Clamp indwelling catheters intermittently before removal

10. Toilet training

    a. Never begin before 18th month of life

    b. 2–3 years: bladder reflex control achieved

    c. 3 years: regular voiding habits established

    d. 4 years: independent bathroom activity

    e. 5 years: nighttime control expected

11. Enuresis—bed-wetting in a child at least 5 years old

    a. Usually have small bladder capacity

    b. More common in males

    c. Tend to be deep sleepers

**D.** Evaluation

1. Is client's voiding pattern adequate?

2. Has toilet training been successfully completed?

▶ **BOWEL ELIMINATION**

**A.** Assessment

1. Abdomen nontender and symmetrical

2. High-pitched gurgles indicate normal peristalsis

3. Stool light to dark brown in color

4. Negative guaiac for occult blood

5. Negative for fat, mucus, pus, pathogens

**B.** Diagnose—potential nursing diagnoses

1. Bowel incontinence

2. Constipation

3. Perceived constipation

4. Risk for constipation

5. Diarrhea

**C.** Plan/Implementation

1. Promote normal elimination

   a. Teach client to respond to urge to defecate

   b. Provide facilities, privacy, and allow sufficient time

   c. Fluids—encourage adequate intake; 8 or more glasses of fluid daily; hot liquids and fruit juices

   d. Foods—encourage fiber, fruits, vegetables, grains

   e. Activity—encourage exercise and ambulation to maintain muscle tone

   f. Emotional state—teach client that stress affects autonomic nervous system, which controls peristalsis

   g. Positioning

      1) For ambulatory client—teach that optimal posture is with feet flat on floor, hips and knees flexed

      2) For bedrest client—place in Fowler's position on bedpan

**D.** Evaluation

1. Has the client maintained a normal pattern of bowel elimination?

2. Is client's diet adequate to promote normal bowel elimination?

# ▶ CONGENITAL MALFORMATIONS OF THE URINARY TRACT

**A.** Assessment (see Table 1)

**B.** Diagnose (see Table 1)

**C.** Plan/Implementation (see Table 1)

| Table 1 CONGENITAL MALFORMATIONS OF THE URINARY TRACT | | |
|---|---|---|
| **ASSESSMENT** | **ANALYSIS** | **NURSING CONSIDERATIONS** |
| Epispadias | Urethral opening on dorsal surface of the penis | Surgical correction<br>No circumcision—foreskin used in surgical repair |
| Hypospadias | Male urethral opening on the ventral surface of penis, or female urethral opening in vagina | Surgical reconstruction<br>No circumcision—foreskin used in surgical repair |
| Bladder exstrophy | Posterior and lateral surfaces of the bladder are exposed | Reconstructive surgery to close bladder and abdominal wall |

**D.** Evaluation

1. Have parents adjusted to the altered body image of their infant?

2. Has reconstructive surgery been successful?

# ▶ KIDNEY AND URETERAL CALCULI (UROLITHIASIS)

A. Assessment

1. Pain (renal colic)—depends on location of stone (flank pain with renal calculi, radiating flank pain with ureter or bladder stones); pain often severe

2. Diaphoresis

3. Nausea and vomiting

4. Fever and chills

5. Hematuria, WBCS and bacteria in urine

B. Diagnose

1. Nephrolithiasis—kidney stones; ureterolithiasis—stones in ureter

2. Causes

   a. Obstruction and urinary stasis

   b. Hypercalcemia, dehydration, immobility, gout, increased intake of oxalates (spinach, Swiss chard, wheat germ, peanuts)

3. Diagnostic tests—intravenous pyelogram, renal ultrasound, CT scan, cystoscopy, MRI, x-ray of kidneys, ureter and bladder (KUB)

C. Plan/Implementation

1. Monitor I and O and temperature

2. Avoid overhydration or underhydration to decrease pain when passing stone

3. Strain urine and check pH of urine

4. Monitor temperature

5. Analgesics

6. Diet for prevention of stones—most stones contain calcium, phosphorus, and/or oxalate

   a. Low in calcium if stones are due to excessive dietary calcium—avoid milk, cheeses, dairy products

   b. Low in sodium—sodium increases calcium in urine

   c. Low in oxalates to prevent increased calcium absorption (avoid: spinach, cola, tea, chocolate)

   d. Avoid vitamin D-enriched foods (increases calcium absorption)

   e. Decrease purine sources—organ meats

   f. To make urine alkaline, restrict citrus fruits, milk, potatoes

   g. To acidify urine increase consumption of eggs, fish, cranberries

7. Drug therapy

   a. Antibiotics (broad spectrum)

   b. Thiazide diuretics, orthophosphate, sodium cellulose phosphase—decrease calcium reabsorption

   c. Allopurinol and vitamin B6 (pyridoxine)—decrease oxalic acid levels

   d. Allopurinol—decrease uric acid levels

8. Surgery (see Table 2)

| Table 2  COMMON SURGERIES OF THE URINARY TRACT | | |
|---|---|---|
| NAME | PROCEDURE | NURSING CONSIDERATIONS |
| Stenting | Stent placed in ureter during ureteroscopy | Indwelling catheter may be placed |
| Retrograde ureteroscopy | Ureteroscope used to remove stone | Indwelling catheter may be placed |
| Percutaneous ureterolithotomy or nephrolithotomy | Lithotripter inserted through skin | Ureterostomy tube may be left in place |
| Nephrolithotomy | Incision into kidney to remove stones | Ureteral catheter<br>Incisional drain<br>Don't irrigate nephrostomy tube<br>Indwelling catheter |
| Pyelolithotomy | Flank incision into kidney to remove stones from renal pelvis | Incisional drain<br>Surgical dressing<br>Ureteral catheter |
| Ureterolithotomy | Incision into ureter to remove stones | Do not irrigate ureteral catheter<br>Check incisional drain<br>Check surgical dressing |
| Nephrectomy | Removal of kidney due to tumor, infection, anomalies | Penrose drain<br>Indwelling catheter<br>Surgical dressing<br>Check urine output closely<br>"Last resort" intervention |
| Nephrostomy | Flank incision and insertion of nephrostomy tube into renal pelvis | Penrose drain<br>Surgical dressing |

9. Mechanical intervention (cystoscopy with catheter insertion)
10. Extracorporeal shock-wave lithotripsy (ESWL)
    a. Strain urine following procedure
    b. Voided parts of stones sent to lab for analysis
    c. Encourage to increase fluid intake to facilitate passage of broken stones
    d. Teach to report fever, decreased urinary output, pain
    e. Hematuria expected but should clear in 24 hours
D. Evaluation
    1. Is client knowledgeable about dietary restrictions?
    2. Has client comfort been maintained?

# ▶ CYSTITIS

A. Assessment
    1. Urgency, frequency
    2. Burning on urination, cloudy urine, strong odor to urine

**B.** Diagnose

1. Inflammation of bladder
2. Predisposing factors
   a. Females more prone
   b. Catheterization, instrumentation

**C.** Plan/Implementation

1. Obtain clean-catch midstream urine specimen for urinalysis, urine culture, colony count, and possibly Gram stain
2. Encourage fluids 3,000 mL/day
3. Cranberry juice or other urinary acidifiers
4. Culture and sensitivity (C and S)
5. Medications: antibiotics (e.g., sulfamethoxazole-trimethoprim), urinary tract analgesics (e.g., phenazopyridine)
6. Teach females to void before and after intercourse
7. Clean properly after defecation (wipe front to back)
8. Void every 2–3 hours

**D.** Evaluation

1. Have client's symptoms subsided?
2. Is client knowledgeable about ways to prevent a recurrence of cystitis?

## ▶ PYELONEPHRITIS

**A.** Assessment

1. Chills, fever
2. Malaise
3. Flank pain
4. Urinary frequency, dysuria
5. CVA tenderness

**B.** Diagnose

1. Definition—inflammation of kidney caused by bacterial infection
2. Predisposing factors
   a. Urinary tract infection
   b. Pregnancy
   c. Tumor
   d. Urinary obstruction
   e. Usually caused by *E. coli*
3. Diagnostic tests—urinalysis (RBCs, bacteria, leukocyte casts)

**C.** Plan/Implementation

1. Bedrest during acute phase
2. Antibiotic therapy, antiseptics, analgesics
3. Encourage fluid intake 3000 mL/day

**D.** Evaluation

1. Is client compliant with medication regimen?
2. Have client's symptoms subsided?

# GLOMERULONEPHRITIS

**A.** Assessment

1. Fever, chills

2. Hematuria, red cell casts, proteinuria, urine dark-colored

3. Weakness, pallor

4. Dyspnea, weight gain, lung rales, fluid overload

5. Anorexia, nausea, vomiting (uremia)

6. Generalized and/or facial and periorbital edema

7. Moderate-to-severe hypertension

8. Headache, decreased level of consciousness, confusion

9. Abdominal or flank pain

10. Oliguria with fixed specific gravity (indicates impending renal failure)

11. Antistreptolysin-O titers, decreased serum complement levels, renal biopsy

**B.** Diagnose

1. Damage to glomerulus caused by an immunological reaction that results in proliferative and inflammatory changes within the glomerular structure

2. Acute glomerulonephritis (most common) usually caused by *Group A beta hemolytic streptococcal* infection elsewhere in the body (URI, skin infection); *Chlamydia, pneumococcal, mycoplasma* or *klebsiella* pneumonia; autoimmune diseases, e.g., SLE, *beta-hemolytic streptococcal* infection elsewhere in the body

3. Occurs 10 days after a skin or throat infection

**C.** Plan/Implementation

1. Administer medications to eliminate infection; alter immune balance to alleviate inflammation; treat volume overload and hypertension

   a. Antibiotics

   b. Corticosteroids

   c. Antihypertensives

   d. Immunosuppressive medications

   e. Diuretics

2. Restrict sodium intake; restrict water if oliguric

3. Daily weights

4. Assess I and O and serum potassium

5. Bedrest

6. High-calorie, low-protein diet

7. Dialysis (uremia) or plasma electrophoreses if renal failure develops (antibody removal)

**D.** Evaluation

1. Have complications been prevented?

2. Is client knowledgeable about dietary/fluid restrictions?

## ▶ PROSTATIC HYPERTROPHY (BENIGN PROSTATIC HYPERPLASIA)

**A.** Assessment

1. Hesitancy (dribbling, weak urinary stream)
2. Frequency, urgency, dysuria, nocturia
3. Hematuria before or after voiding
4. Retention

**B.** Diagnose

1. Enlargement of the prostate gland; causes urinary flow obstruction, incontinence, possible infection
2. Benign hypertrophy, increase in size with age (over 50)
3. BUN and creatinine
4. Prostate-specific antigen (PSA)—normal is less than 4 mg/mL; may be increased in prostatitis, prostatic hypertrophy, prostate cancer
5. Trans-abdominal or trans-rectal ultrasound
6. Prostate biopsy

**C.** Plan/Implementation

1. Conservative—urinary antiseptics and follow-up
2. Administer medications
   a. 5-alpha reductive inhibitor
   b. Alpha-blocking medications
3. Suprapubic cystostomy—opening into bladder, drainage via catheter through abdominal wall (temporary measure to divert urine)
   a. Covered with sterile dressing
   b. Connected to sterile closed drainage system
   c. To test ability to void, clamp catheter for 4 hours, have client void, unclamp catheter and measure residual urine; if residual is less than 100 mL on 2 occasions (morning and evening), catheter is removed
   d. After removal of catheter, sterile dressing placed over site
4. Prostatectomy
   a. Transurethral (TURP)
   b. Suprapubic resection (through bladder)
   c. Retropubic resection (through abdomen)
5. Assess for shock and hemorrhage—check dressing and drainage: urine may be reddish-pink initially, monitor continuous bladder irrigation (CBI); monitor vital signs
6. Monitor intake and output after catheter removed; expect dribbling and urinary leakage around wound
7. Avoid long periods of sitting and strenuous activity until danger of bleeding is over
8. Complementary and alternative therapies
   a. Saw palmetto
   b. Lycopene

9. Avoid consumption of large amounts of fluids, caffeine

10. Avoid anticholinergic, antihistamine, decongestant medication

**D.** Evaluation

1. Has normal urinary elimination been restored?

2. Is client knowledgeable about postoperative care?

# ▶ URINARY DIVERSIONS

**A.** Assessment

1. Bladder tumors requiring cystectomy

2. Birth defects

3. Strictures and trauma to ureters and urethra

4. Neurogenic bladder

5. Interstitial cystitis

**B.** Diagnose

1. Types (see Table 3 and Figure 1)

| Table 3   URINARY DIVERSIONS | | |
|---|---|---|
| NAME | PROCEDURE | NURSING CONSIDERATIONS |
| Nephrostomy | Flank incision and insertion of nephrostomy tube into renal pelvis | Penrose drain<br>Surgical dressing |
| Ureterosigmoidostomy | Ureters detached from bladder and anastomosed to sigmoid colon | Urine and stool are evacuated through anus<br>Encourage voiding via rectum every 2–4 h; no enemas or cathartics<br>Monitor complications—fluid and electrolyte imbalance, pyelonephritis, obstruction |
| Cutaneous ureterostomy | Single or double-barreled stoma, formed from ureter(s) excised from bladder and brought out through the skin into the abdominal wall | Stoma usually constructed on right side of abdomen below waist<br>Extensive nursing intervention required for alteration in body image |
| Ileal conduit | Portion of terminal ileum is used as a conduit; ureters are replanted into ileal segment; distal end is brought out through skin and forms a stoma | Most common urinary diversion<br>Check for obstruction (occurs at the anastomosis)<br>Postop mucus threads normal |
| Kock pouch<br>Continent ileal conduit | Ureters are transplanted to an isolated segment of ileum (pouch) with a one-way valve; urine is drained by a catheter | Urine collects in pouch until drained by catheter<br>Valve prevents leakage of urine<br>Drainage of urine by catheter is under control of client<br>Pouch must be drained at regular intervals |

Ureterosigmoidostomy    Cutaneous Ureterostomy    Ileal Conduit

**Figure 1. Types of Urinary Diversions**

**C.** Plan/Implementation (see Table 3)

**D.** Evaluation

1. Is client knowledgeable about how to care for urinary diversion equipment?

2. Has client adjusted to change in body image?

## ▶ ACUTE KIDNEY DISORDERS

**A.** Assessment

1. Oliguric phase of acute kidney injury (AKI)

    a. Urinary output less than 0.5 mL/kg/hr

    b. Nausea, vomiting

    c. Irritability, drowsiness, confusion, coma

    d. Restlessness, twitching, seizures

    e. Increased serum $K^+$, BUN, creatinine

    f. Increased $Ca^+$, $Na^+$, decreased pH

    g. Anemia

    h. Pulmonary edema, CHF

    i. Hypertension

    j. Albuminuria

2. Diuretic or recovery phase of acute kidney injury

    a. Urinary output 4–5 liter/day

    b. Increased serum BUN

    c. $Na^+$ and $K^+$ loss in urine

    d. Increased mental and physical activity

3. Chronic

    a. Anemia

    b. Acidosis

    c. Azotemia

    d. Fluid retention

    e. Urinary output alterations

**B.** Diagnose

1. Causes of acute kidney injury

   a. Prerenal

      1) Circulating volume depletion

      2) Vascular obstruction

      3) Vascular resistance

   b. Acute kidney injury (see Table 4)

      1) Acute tubular necrosis (ATN)

         a) Nephrotoxic drugs

         b) Transfusion reaction

      2) Trauma

      3) Glomerulonephritis

      4) Severe muscle exertion

      5) Genetic conditions—polycystic kidney disease

   c. Postrenal failure

      1) Obstruction—benign prostatic hyperplasia, tumors, renal or urinary calculi

2. Causes of chronic kidney disease

   a. Hypertension

   b. Diabetes mellitus

   c. Lupus erythematosus

   d. Sickle cell disease

   e. Chronic glomerulonephritis

   f. Repeated pyelonephritis

   g. Polycystic kidney disease

   h. Nephrotoxins

| Table 4   ACUTE KIDNEY INJURY | |
| --- | --- |
| **LOW–OUTPUT STAGE** | **HIGH–OUTPUT STAGE** |
| Limit fluids | Fluids as needed to replace output |
| Diet adjustment | Diet adjustment |
| Specific medications as needed, e.g., Kayexalate for high potassium | Replacement for potassium |
| Treatment: dialysis (hemodialysis or peritoneal dialysis) | Treatment: dialysis (hemodialysis or peritoneal dialysis) |

**C.** Plan/Implementation

1. Dialysis (see Tables 5 and 6)

| Table 5 HEMODIALYSIS AND PERITONEAL DIALYSIS | | |
|---|---|---|
| | HEMODIALYSIS | PERITONEAL DIALYSIS |
| Circulatory access | Subclavian catheter<br>AV fistula, AV graft | Catheter in peritoneal cavity (Tenckoff, Gore-Tex) |
| Dialysis bath | Electrolyte solution similar to that of normal plasma | Similar to hemodialysis |
| Dialyzer | Artificial kidney machine with semipermeable membrane | Peritoneum is dialyzing membrane |
| Procedure | Blood shunted through dialyzer for 3–5 h 2 to 3 times/wk | Weigh client before and after dialysis<br>Repeated cycles can be continuous<br>Catheter is cleansed and attached to line leading to peritoneal cavity<br>Dialysate infused into peritoneal cavity to prescribed volume<br>Dialysate is then drained from abdomen after prescribed amount of time |
| Complications | Hemorrhage<br>Hepatitis<br>Nausea and vomiting<br>Disequilibrium syndrome (headache, mental confusion)<br>Muscle cramps<br>Air embolism<br>Sepsis | Protein loss<br>Peritonitis<br>  Cloudy outflow, bleeding<br>  Fever<br>  Abdominal tenderness, lower back problems<br>  Nausea and vomiting<br>  Exit site infection<br>  Hypotension and hypovolemia |
| Nursing considerations | Check "thrill" and bruit every 8 h<br>Don't use extremity for BP or to obtain blood specimens<br>Monitor BP, apical pulse, temperature, respirations, breath sounds, weight<br>Monitor for hemorrhage during dialysis and 1 h after procedure | Constipation may cause problems with infusion and outflow; high-fiber diet, stool softener<br>If problems with outflow, reposition client (supine or low-Fowler's, side to side)<br>Monitor BP, apical pulse, temperature, respirations, breath sounds, weight<br>Clean catheter insertion site and apply sterile dressing |

2. Monitor potassium levels; sodium polystyrene sulfonate (orally or retention enema) for elevated levels

3. Daily weight, I and O

4. Diet

   a. Oliguric phase—limit fluids; restriction of protein, potassium, and sodium

   b. After diuretic phase—high carbohydrate diet; restriction of protein, potassium, and sodium

   c. Chronic failure—regulate protein intake, fluid intake to balance fluid losses, some restriction of sodium and potassium, vitamin supplements; more protein allowed with dialysis

| Table 6   PERITONEAL DIALYSIS | |
|---|---|
| TYPES | NURSING CONSIDERATIONS |
| Continuous ambulatory (CAPD) | Client performs self-dialysis 7 days/wk for 24 h/day<br>Dialysate warmed (use heating pad), infused, dwell time 4–8 h<br>Tubing and bag disconnected or rolled up and worn under clothing<br>After dwell time, fluid drained back into bag and process repeated |
| Automated | Uses machine with warming chamber for dialysate infusion, dwell, and outflow<br>Times and volumes preset; 30-minute exchanges (10 minutes for infusion, 10 min for dwell, 10 min for outflow) for 8–10 h |
| Intermittent | 4 days a week for 10 h/day<br>Can be automated or manual |
| Continuous | Automated machine used at night<br>Final exchange is left in place during the next day and then drained that night |

5. Monitor IV fluids

6. Use of diuretics controversial

7. Aluminum hydroxide used for elevated phosphate levels

8. Bedrest during acute phase

9. Good skin care

10. Monitor for infection; antibiotics if needed

11. Kidney transplant

    a. Donor selection: cadaver, identical twin, tissue match, histocompatible

    b. Preop: client education

       1) Explain surgical procedure and follow-up care to client

       2) Show client where the donated kidney will be located (iliac fossa anterior to iliac crest)

       3) Use of immunosuppressive drugs (e.g., prednisone, imuran, cyclosporine)

       4) Need for infection prevention (gingival disease and cavities)

    c. Postop

       1) Monitor vital signs, intake and output—expect scant urine production for several weeks postop

       2) Daily weight

       3) Vascular access care—may need hemodialysis until transplanted kidney functions well (2–3 weeks for kidney from cadaver)

4) Psychological support for donor and recipient

5) Monitor for complications

   a) Hemorrhage

   b) Shock

   c) Rejection—Acute (days to months; decreased urine output, increased BUN and creatinine, fever, tenderness and swelling over graft site); chronic (months to years; gradual decrease in renal function, proteinuria, gradual increase in BUN and creatinine)

   d) Infection

   e) Pulmonary complications

   f) Adverse effects of immunosuppressive and steroid medications

**D.** Evaluation

1. Has normal kidney function been re-established?

2. Have complications of acute renal failure been avoided?

Chapter 7

# SAFE AND EFFECTIVE CARE ENVIRONMENT

| Sections | Concepts Covered |
|---|---|
| 1. Management of Care | Legal/Ethics, Client Education: Providing |
| 2. Safety and Infection Control | Immunity, Immune Response, Infection, Client Education: Providing |

## ▶ NURSE/CLIENT RELATIONSHIP

**A.** Professionalism

   1. Specific knowledge and skills—foundation of nursing science

   2. Person-centered

   3. Autonomy and accountability—adheres to standards of practice and is responsible for care given

   4. Nurse practice act

   5. Ethical standards

      a. Respect for human dignity—give respectful service regardless of client's personal characteristics

      b. Confidentiality—does not discuss condition with anyone not involved with care

      c. Competence—has knowledge and skills to provide care

      d. Advocacy—protects client from incompetent or unethical practice

      e. Research—participates in process of scientific inquiry

      f. Promotion of public health—committed to local and global goals for health of community

**B.** Therapeutic nature of the nurse/client relationship

   1. Professional

      a. Client-centered

      b. Responsible

      c. Goal-oriented

      d. Ethical

   2. Characterized by genuineness

   3. Nurse acts as a role model

   4. Nurse copes with own feelings

   5. Protected relationship—nurse or client (client) cannot be forced to reveal communication between them unless person who would benefit from relationship agrees to reveal it

## ▶ CLIENT'S BILL OF RIGHTS

**A.** Privacy

   1. Right to be left alone without unwarranted or uninvited publicity

   2. Right to make personal choices without interference (e.g., contraception, abortion, right to refuse treatment)

3. Right to have personal information kept confidential and distributed only to authorized personnel (consider the Health Insurance Portability and Accountability Act—HIPAA)

   a. Violated when confidential information revealed to unauthorized person(s), or unauthorized personnel directly or indirectly observes client without permission

   b. Authorized personnel—people involved in diagnosis and treatment(related to care of client)

   c. Health care team can't use data, photographs, videotapes, research data without explicit permission of client

   d. Be cautious about release of information on the phone (difficult to identify caller accurately)

   e. Necessary to obtain client's permission to release information to family members or close friends

   f. For employees, can only verify employment and comply with a legal investigation

**B.** Respectful care

**C.** Current information

**D.** Informed consent

1. Requirements

   a. Capacity—age (adult), competence (can make choices and understand consequences)

   b. Voluntary—freedom of choice without force, fraud, deceit, duress, coercion

   c. Information must be given in understandable form (lay terminology)

   d. Cannot sign informed consent if client has been drinking alcohol or has been premedicated

   e. Informed consent may not be required in emergency situations

2. Minors who can provide own consent for treatment

   a. Married minors

   b. Over a specific age (e.g., 12) for STIs, HIV testing, AIDS treatment, drug and alcohol treatment

   c. Emancipated and mature minors

   d. Minors seeking birth control services

   e. Minors seeking outpatient psychiatric services or inpatient voluntary admissions to a psychiatric facility

   f. Pregnant minor

      1) Can sign consent for themselves and the fetus

      2) After delivery

         a) The mother retains right to provide consent for infant

         b) Mother cannot give own consent unless she fits into one of other exemptions

3. Includes

   a. Explanation of treatment and expected results

   b. Anticipated risks and discomforts

    c. Potential benefits

    d. Possible alternatives

    e. Answers to questions

    f. Statements that consent can be withdrawn at any time

  4. Legal responsibility

    a. Rests with individual who will perform treatment

    b. When nurse witnesses a signature, it means that there is reason to believe that the client is informed about upcoming treatment

**E.** Confidentiality

  1. Right to privacy of records

  2. Information used only for purpose of diagnosis and treatment

  3. Not released to others without permission; verify identity of persons asking for information

**F.** Refusal of treatment

  1. Self-determination act—federal law requiring health care facilities to provide written information to adult clients about their rights to make health care decisions

  2. Aggressive treatment

    a. Extraordinary support measures used to maintain individual's physiologic processes

    b. May be withheld to avoid prolonging life without dignity

    c. Supportive care is provided to promote comfort and reduce suffering

  3. Advanced directives

    a. Living wills

      1) Legal document signed by competent individual indicates treatment or life-saving measures (e.g., surgery, CPR, antibiotics, dialysis, respirator, tube feedings) to be used if individual's ability to make decisions is lost due to terminal illness or a permanently unconscious state

      2) Indicates who is authorized to make health care decisions if individual becomes incapacitated

      3) Legally binding in most states

    b. Durable power of attorney for health care

      1) Permits a competent adult to appoint surrogate or proxy in the event that the adult becomes incompetent

      2) Health care provider must follow decisions stated in documents

      3) In most states proxy can perform all legal actions needed to fulfill adult's wishes

**G.** Reasonable response to a request for services

**H.** Right to know hospital/clinic regulations

# ▶ RESTRAINTS

**A.** Restraints

1. Omnibus Budget Reconciliation Act provides clients with the right to be free from physical and chemical restraints imposed for the purpose of discipline or convenience and not required to treat medical symptoms

2. Mechanical restraint

   a. Needed to meet the client's therapeutic needs or ensure safety

   b. Least restrictive type of restraint to meet needs

   c. Accurate and thorough documentation needed

3. Chemical restraint

   a. Psychotropic drugs cannot be used to control behavior

   b. Can be used only for diagnoses-related conditions

   c. Inappropriate use causes deep sedation, agitation, combativeness

4. Informed consent is needed to use restraints

5. If client is unable to consent to use of restraints, then consent of proxy must be obtained after full disclosure of risks and benefits

6. Restraint of client without informed consent or sufficient justification is false imprisonment

**B.** Nursing considerations

1. Assess and document need for restraints (risk for falls, risk of injury to others, potential for removal of IV lines or other equipment)

2. Consider and document use of alternative measures

3. Health care provider's order is required specifying duration and circumstances under which restraints should be used

4. Cannot order restraints to be used PRN

5. Monitor client closely, periodically reassess for continued need for restraints, document

6. Remove for skin care and range of motion exercises

7. Use alternative measures prior to use of restraints (reorientation, family involvement, frequent assistance with toileting)

# ▶ ADVOCACY

**A.** Nurse as client advocate should

1. Actively support clients' rights

2. Defend clients' participation in decisions affecting them

3. Communicate clients' needs to interdisciplinary team (health care provider, RN, PT, dietitian, social worker, psychologist)

4. Safeguard clients' autonomy and independence

5. Provide clients with information about needs and available options so that clients can make informed decisions about health care

# ▶ LEGAL ISSUES

A. Negligence—unintentional failure of individual to perform an act that a reasonable person would or would not perform in similar circumstances; can be act of omission or commission

B. Malpractice—professional negligence involving misconduct or lack of skill in carrying out professional responsibilities

   1. Required elements

      a. Duty—relationship between nurse and client

      b. Breach of duty

      c. Causation—nurse conduct causes injury

      d. Injury

C. Invasion of privacy—release of information to an unauthorized person without the client's consent

D. Assault—intentional threat to cause harm or offensive unwanted contact; battery—intentional touching without consent

E. False imprisonment

   1. Client is denied discharge from a health care facility

   2. Client is denied discharge after signing an against medical advice (AMA) document

   3. Client is placed in restraints without appropriate medical need

F. Laws

   1. Rules of conduct established and enforced by authority

   2. Reflect public policy

   3. Indicates what society views as good and bad, right and wrong behavior

G. Accountability

   1. Nurse is responsible for using reasonable care in practicing nursing

   2. To remain competent, nurse needs to participate in lifelong learning programs

H. State laws

   1. Nurse practice acts—define "reasonable care" in each state; scope of nursing practice, roles, rules, educational requirements

   2. Licensure requirements—differ slightly in requirements among states

   3. Good Samaritan laws—limit the liability of professionals in emergency situations

   4. Tarasoff Act—duty to warn of threatened suicide or harm to others

I. Need to assess health care provider's orders—must be safe and correct

J. Notify supervisor if more nurses are needed for safe client care

# ▶ ORGAN/TISSUE DONATION/TRANSPLANT

1. Clients have a right to decide to become an organ donor

2. Clients have a right to decide to refuse organ donation or transplant

3. Clients 18 years or older may choose to donate organs

4. Requests to the family are usually completed by the health care provider or a specially trained nurse

5. Religious beliefs should be taken into consideration when approaching the family

## ▶ MANAGED CARE

A. Health care focuses on individual client needs along the health continuum (wellness to illness)

B. Managed care
1. Goal is reduced health care costs
2. Focuses on client outcomes and maintenance of quality
3. Uses an interdisciplinary approach
4. Emphasizes costs; approval needed for diagnostic tests
5. Critical pathways (care maps) used as foundations for activities and guide services that clients receive for specific health conditions

C. Continuous quality improvement (CQI; previously called quality assurance)
1. Quality improvement is essential for all providers of client health care
2. Prevention-focused approach provides basis for managing risk
3. Involves organized incident reporting
4. Focused team: group of 5–10 people
5. Process
    a. Senior management establishes policy
    b. Coordinator provides for process and management health care team training
    c. Team, headed by a team leader, evaluates and improves the process

D. Risk management
1. Planned program of loss prevention and liability control
2. Problem-focused
3. Identifies, evaluates, develops plan, and takes corrective action against potential risks that would injure clients, staff, visitors
4. Focuses on noncompliance, informed consent, right to refuse treatment

E. Collaborative practice team
1. Consists of clinical experts: nursing, medicine, physical therapy, social work
2. Determines expected outcomes
3. Determines appropriate interventions with a specified time frame
4. Involves specific client diagnoses that are high-volume (frequently seen), high-cost, high-risk (frequently develop complications)

F. For managed care to be successful, need
1. Support from health care providers, nurses, administrators
2. Qualified nurse managers
3. Collaborative practice teams
4. Quality management system
5. All professionals are equal members of the team (one discipline doesn't determine interventions for another discipline)

6. Members agree on final draft of critical pathways, take ownership of client outcomes, accept responsibility and accountability for interventions and client outcomes

**G.** Critical pathways

1. Reduce complications

2. Reduce cost

3. Increase collaboration

4. Improve quality of care

5. Provide direction for care

6. Orient staff to expected outcomes for each day

7. If outcomes not achieved, case manager is notified and situation is analyzed to determine how to modify critical path

8. Alteration in time frame or interventions is a "variance"

9. All variances are tracked to note trends

10. Variance—change in established plan that includes more, different, or fewer services to client to achieve desired outcome

11. Interventions presented in modality groups (medications, nursing activities)

12. Include

    a. Specific medical diagnoses

    b. Expected length of stay

    c. Client identification data

    d. Appropriate time frames (days, hours, minutes, visits) for interventions

    e. Clinical outcomes

    f. Client outcomes

**H.** Variances

1. Deviations from specific plans (individual receives more, less, or different services)

2. Information is included in a database and is used to evaluate services provided

3. Continuous quality improvement (CQI) strategies are used to monitor variances

**I.** Case manager—usually has advanced degree and considerable experience

1. Doesn't provide direct client care

2. Supervises care provided by licensed and unlicensed personnel

3. Coordinates, communicates, collaborates, solves problems

4. Facilitates client care for a group of clients (10–15)

5. Follows client through the system from admission to discharge

6. Notes "variances" from expected progress

**J.** Case management

1. Identifies, coordinates, monitors implementation of services needed to achieve desired outcomes within specified period of time

2. Involves principles of CQI

3. Promotes professional practice

▶ **ASSIGNMENT VERSUS DELEGATION**

**A.** Assignment—allocating to health care team members work required to care for groups of individuals

1. Process

   a. Determine nursing care required to meet clients' needs (take into account time required, complexity of activities, acuity of clients, and infection control)

   b. Consider knowledge and abilities of staff members

   c. Decide which staff person is best able to provide care

   d. Take into account continuity of care

   e. Determine assignments to increase efficiency

   f. Describe assignments in measurable terms

   g. Be specific about expected results

   h. Give assignments to staff members (assign total responsibility for total client care, avoid assigning only procedures)

   i. Provide additional help as needed

**B.** Delegation

1. Responsibility and authority for performing a task (function, activity, decision) is transferred to another individual who accepts that responsibility and authority

2. Depending on state Nurse Practice Acts, LPN/PNs may delegate tasks to nursing assistive personnel (NAP), (NAP includes the nursing providers excluding RNs, such as UAP, NAs, CNAs, etc.)

3. Delegator remains accountable for task

4. Delegatee is accountable to delegator for responsibilities assumed

5. Can only delegate tasks for which that nursing care level is responsible

6. Definitions

   a. Responsibility—obligation to accomplish a task

   b. Accountability—accept ownership for results or lack of results

7. In delegation, responsibility is transferred; in accountability, it is shared

8. Guidelines

   a. Can delegate only those tasks for which you are responsible

   b. Responsibility is determined by

      1) Nurse practice acts (defines scope of nursing practice)

      2) Standards of care (established by organization)

      3) Job description (defined by organization)

      4) Policy statement (from organization)

   c. Must transfer authority (the right to act) along with the responsibility to act

   d. Empowers delegatee to accomplish task

9. Steps for delegation

   a. Define task to be delegated

      1) Can delegate only work for which you have responsibility and authority

       2) Delegate what you know best so you can provide guidance and feedback

         a) Routine tasks

         b) Tasks you don't have time to accomplish

         c) Tasks with lower priority

   b. Determine who should receive delegated task

   c. Identify what the task involves, determine its complexity

   d. Match task to individual by assessing individual skills and abilities

       1) Evaluate capacity of individual to perform task

       2) Consider availability, willingness to assume responsibility

   e. Provide clear communication about your expectations regarding the task, answer questions

10. To delegate

   a. Assume face-to-face position

   b. Establish eye contact

   c. Describe task using "I" statements

   d. Provide what, when, where, how of the task to be delegated

   e. State if delegatee needs to provide written or verbal report after the task is completed

   f. If written report is needed, inform delegatee where to put the report (e.g., table, chart, form)

   g. Identify what changes or incidents need to be brought to delegator's attention (e.g., "If client's BP is greater than 140/90, let me know immediately.")

   h. Provide reason for task, give incentive for accepting responsibility and authority

   i. Tell delegatee how and how often task will be evaluated

   j. Describe expected outcome and timeline for completion of task

11. Identify constraints for completing task and risks

12. Identify variables that would change authority and responsibility (e.g., "Feed client if coherent and awake; if client is confused, do not feed and notify me immediately.")

13. Obtain feedback from delegatee to make sure he/she understands task to be performed and your expectations; ask for questions, give additional information

14. Reach mutual agreement on task

15. Monitor performance and results according to established goals

16. Give constructive feedback to delegatee

17. Confirm that delegated tasks are performed as agreed

18. Delegator must remain accessible during performance of task

19. Don't delegate

   a. Total control

   b. Discipline issues

   c. Confidential tasks

   d. Technical tasks

  e. Controversial tasks

  f. During a crisis

20. Levels of delegation (in ascending order)

  a. Gather information for delegatee so you can decide what needs to be done

  b. List alternate courses of action and allow delegatee to choose course of action

  c. Have delegatee perform part of task and obtain approval before proceeding with the rest of the task

  d. Have delegatee outline entire course of action for the task and approve it before proceeding

  e. Allow delegatee to perform entire task using any preferred method, and report only results

21. Rule for determining delegatee—delegate to lowest person on hierarchy who has the required skills and abilities and who is allowed to do the task legally and according to the organization

22. Obstacles to delegation

  a. Nonsupportive environment—rigid organizational culture, lack of resources (limited personnel)

  b. Insecure delegator

  c. Fear of competition

  d. Fear of liability

  e. Fear of loss of control

  f. Fear of overburdening others

  g. Fear of decreased personal job satisfaction

  h. Unwilling delegatee

  i. Fear of failure

  j. Inexperience or incompetence

23. Ineffective delegation

  a. Under delegation

    1) Doesn't transfer full authority

    2) Takes back responsibility

    3) Fails to equip or direct delegatee

    4) Questions competence of delegatee

  b. Reverse delegation—lower person on hierarchy delegates to person higher on hierarchy

  c. Over delegation—delegator loses control of the situation by delegating too much authority and responsibility to delegatee

24. Rights of delegation

  a. Right task

  b. Right person (knowledge, skills, ability

  c. Right time (not in a crisis)

  d. Right information

  e. Right supervision (is task being performed correctly?)

  f. Right follow-up

25. Delegation empowers others, builds trust, enhances communication and leadership skills, develops teamwork, increases productivity

26. Failure to delegate and supervise properly can result in liability; need to consider delegatee's competence and qualifications

27. Nurses have a legal responsibility to make sure persons under their supervision perform consistently with established standards of nursing practice

# ▶ CRITICAL THINKING

**A.** Involves creativity, problem-solving, decision-making

**B.** Nursing responsibilities

1. Observe

2. Decide what data are important

3. Validate and organize data

4. Look for patterns and relationships

5. State problem

6. Transfer knowledge from one situation to another

7. Decide on criteria for evaluation

8. Apply knowledge

9. Evaluate according to criteria established

# ▶ DECISION MAKING

**A.** Purposeful and goal-directed; nurse identifies and selects options and alternatives

**B.** Types of decision making

1. Prescriptive

   a. Involves routine decisions with objective information

   b. Options are known and predictable

   c. Decisions made according to standard procedures or analytical tools

2. Behavioral

   a. Involves the nonroutine and unstructured information

   b. Options are unknown or unpredictable

   c. Decisions made by obtaining more data, using past experiences, using creative approach

3. Satisficing

   a. Solution minimally meets objectives

   b. Expedient; use when time is an issue

4. Optimizing

   a. Goal is to select ideal solution

   b. Best decision comes from this process but is the most time consuming

**C.** Phases

1. Define objectives

2. Generate options

3. Analyze options

a. Identify advantages and disadvantages

b. Rank options

4. Select option that will successfully meet the defined objective

5. Implement the selected option

6. Evaluate the outcome

## ▶ PROBLEM SOLVING

**A.** Focus is trying to solve immediate problems; includes decision making

**B.** Methods

1. Trial and error

a. Repeated attempts at different solutions until it is identified that one solution works best

b. Used by inexperienced staff

2. Experimentation

a. Study problem using trial periods or pilot projects to determine best outcome

b. Will have greater probability of achieving best outcome if sufficient time devoted to the process

3. Purposeful inaction

a. Do-nothing approach

b. Use when problem is judged to be insignificant or outside a person's control

**C.** Steps

1. Define the problem

2. Gather data

3. Analyze data

4. Develop solutions

5. Select and implement a solution

6. Evaluate the results

## ▶ DISTRIBUTION OF RESOURCES

**A.** Distributive justice

1. Gives an individual what he/she deserves regardless of race, color, creed, gender, or socioeconomic status

2. Provides equal access to care for all

3. Designed to manage health care according to need rather than provide care for everyone

**B.** Resources—staff, time, equipment, supplies, knowledge

**C.** Allocation of resources

1. Decision regarding how resources will be distributed

2. There is a finite number of resources in health care that must be used wisely and efficiently

3. Primary principle is to provide the greatest good for the greatest number of people

    a. Approval for inpatient admissions or emergency room visits required by insurance companies

    b. Early discharge from inpatient settings

    c. Stimulus for managed care—model of service delivery that focuses on client outcomes

    d. Is interdisciplinary and emphasizes cost

**D.** Rationing—decision about how limited resources (e.g., transplants) will be used

**E.** Nursing management

    1. Judiciously use resources to achieve identified client goals

    2. Coordinate the services received by a group of clients over a specific time period

    3. Identify client needs

    4. Identify resources available to meet needs

    5. Organize and direct use of available resources

    6. Evaluate the extent to which desired client outcomes are met controlling the process of client care

**F.** Standard of care and practice

    1. Guide nursing activities

    2. Used to evaluate quality of care

**G.** Resolution of conflict

    1. Determine the facts

    2. Identify the problem

    3. Ask for suggestions for resolution from those involved

    4. Determine solutions

    5. Evaluate results

    6. Evaluate conflict resolution

# ▶ DOCUMENTATION

**A.** Purpose

    1. Promotes communication

    2. Maintains a legal record

    3. Meets requirements of regulatory agencies

    4. Required for third-party reimbursement

**B.** Characteristics of good documentation

    1. Legible

    2. Accurate, factual, no summarizing data

    3. Timely

    4. Thorough

    5. Well organized and concise (follow chronological order of events)

    6. Confidential

    7. Proper grammar and spelling

    8. Authorized abbreviations

**C.** Documenting changes in client conditions

1. Assess
   a. Client's vital signs, symptoms, behaviors, reports from client, responses to treatments (PRN medications, dietary changes, I and O)
   b. Interdisciplinary team information
   c. Information from family members or significant other
2. Notify health care provider if client's physiological status and functional abilities change significantly
3. Notify interdisciplinary team of changes in medical plan (RN is responsible for coordinating interdisciplinary team for client)
4. Notify family or significant other about changes in client's condition and plan of care
   a. Nature of change
   b. Why changes were made
   c. Actions undertaken to provide needed care for client
   d. List of revisions on medical plan of care
   e. Help family to take active part in client's care and management
   f. Follow policy for privacy and confidentiality
5. Document in timely manner
   a. Date and time
   b. Nursing assessment
   c. Name of health care provider informed
   d. Date, time, method (e.g., telephone)
   e. Information provided about client
   f. Actions taken (revisions in plan of care)
   g. Information given and to whom (client, name of family, significant other)
   h. Responses by client and family members or significant other
6. Considerations
   a. If an error is made in charting, use a single line through the error and doc your initials, date, and time—do not erase, white out, or scratch out an error
   b. Do not chart for anyone else
   c. Keep your electronic access private
   d. Do not leave your electronic chart open when you are not in attendance

## ▶ INCIDENT REPORTS

A. Definition
   1. Agency record of unusual occurrence or accident and physical response
   2. Accurate and comprehensive report on any unexpected or unplanned occurrence that affects or could potentially affect a client, family member, or staff person
B. Purpose
   1. Documentation and follow-up of all incidents
   2. Used to analyze the severity, frequency, and cause of occurrences

3. Analysis is the basis for intervention

C. Charting

   1. Don't include a reference to the incident report

   2. Don't use words such as "error" or "inappropriate"

   3. Don't include inflammatory words or judgmental statements

   4. If there are adverse reactions to incident, chart follow-up note updating client's status

   5. Documentation of client's reactions should be included as status changes and should be continued until client returns to original status

D. Sequence

   1. Person discovers and reports actual or potential risk

   2. Risk manager receives report within 24 hours

   3. Investigation of incident is conducted

   4. Referring health care provider and risk management committee consult together

E. Risk manager

   1. Clarifies misinformation for client and family

   2. Explains what happened to client and family

   3. Client is referred to appropriate resources

   4. Care is provided free of charge

   5. All records, incident reports, follow-up actions taken are filed in a central location

F. Common situations that require an incident report

   1. Medication errors—omitted medication, wrong medication, wrong dosage, wrong route

   2. Complications from diagnostic or treatment procedures (e.g., blood sample stick, biopsy, x-ray, LP, invasive procedure, bronchoscopy, thoracentesis)

   3. Incorrect sponge count in surgery

   4. Failure to report change in client's condition

   5. Falls

   6. Client is burned

   7. Break in aseptic technique

   8. Medical–legal incident

      a. Client or family refuses treatment as ordered and refuses to sign consent

      b. Client or family voices dissatisfaction with care and situation cannot be or has not been resolved

▶ **CHANGE OF SHIFT REPORT**

**A.** Regularly scheduled, structured exchange of information

**B.** Focuses on anticipated needs of individual clients in next 24 hours

**C.** Enables health care workers to

    1. Organize work for specified time period

    2. Communicate concerns

    3. Provide continuity of care or consistent follow-through

**D.** Included

    1. Client's status

    2. Current care plan

    3. Responses to current care

    4. Things needing further attention

**E.** Reporting nurse describes

    1. Actual or potential client needs

    2. How these needs were addressed during previous shift by nursing and interdisciplinary team

    3. Information about laboratory studies, diagnostic tests, treatments, and nursing activities anticipated during next shift

    4. Reporting nurse must legally communicate all facts relevant to continuity of care of assigned clients

    5. Information must be pertinent, current, and accurate

**F.** Change-of-shift reports should not contain

    1. Information already known by the oncoming shift

    2. Descriptions of routines (am or pm care)

    3. Rumors or gossip

    4. Opinions or value judgments (about client's lifestyle)

    5. Client information that does not relate to health condition, needs, or treatments (e.g., idiosyncrasies)

**G.** To give change-of-shift report

    1. Gather data to be discussed (flow sheets, work sheets, Kardex, progress notes, chart)

    2. Avoid copying data in order to prevent errors and reduce time required

    3. Use outline to organize report

    4. Provide in logical, uniform manner

**H.** To deliver change-of-shift report, include

    1. Client information

        a. Name, room, and bed number

        b. Note if off the unit (recovery room, diagnostic test, etc.)

    2. Medical plan

        a. Admitting diagnosis

        b. Attending health care provider

        c. Major diagnostic or surgical procedures with dates

    d. Health care provider's orders that have been discontinued or affect next shift

    e. IV solutions, flow rates, when current bag is scheduled to be completed, amount of solution remaining to be infused

    f. Medications

    g. Response to treatment (expected and untoward effects)

    h. Client's emotional response to condition

    i. Use of and response to PRN medications

    j. Completion of special procedures

3. Nursing plan

    a. Personalized nursing approaches

    b. Special equipment, supplies, or pacing of activities

    c. Response to diet

    d. Behavioral response to treatment and health status (e.g., denial, frustration)

    e. Nursing assessments (e.g., vital signs, I and O, activity level)

    f. New concerns

    g. Changing client needs

    h. Client outcomes

    i. Interdisciplinary plans

    j. Referrals

    k. Teaching plans

    l. Discharge plans

**I.** Nurse receiving report should learn

1. Individual client's symptoms

2. Discomforts

3. What has been done

4. What remains to be done

5. How client has responded to treatments and activities so changes can be made to meet client needs

**J.** To receive change-of-shift report

1. Determine

    a. Number of clients

    b. Number of staff available for client care

    c. Anticipated admissions, transfers, discharges

    d. Clients in critical condition

    e. Clients with specific needs (e.g., blood transfusions, returning from surgery)

2. Complete assignment sheets for staff under your supervision

3. Write assignment on client care worksheets

4. Make a "to do" list identifying tasks to be performed during shift (helps to organize activities)

**K.** During change-of-shift report

1. Determine appropriateness of client care assignments

2. Note key information about client condition, progress, response to treatments

**L.** Types of change-of-shift reports

1. Face-to-face

   a. Reporting nurse answers questions from oncoming staff

   b. Provides flexibility to report to a number of different oncoming staff

   c. Provides flexibility in pacing and sequencing of report

   d. Nurses listen to report only on their clients

2. Taped

   a. Less time-consuming because of lack of interruptions

   b. Nurse is frequently more systematic and thorough

   c. Gives nurse more sense of control over the process

   d. Reporting nurse can perform nursing activities while next shift is listening to report

   e. Reporting nurse returns to clarify information, answer questions, update information that changed since report was recorded

**M.** Organization of change-of-shift report

1. Computerized client care summary or Kardex—current summary of client's needs, status, goals or desired outcomes, care plans, nursing interventions, medications, medical treatments; updated during change-of-shift report

2. Assignment work sheet—uses chart for detailed information about individual clients

3. Progress notes or flow sheets provide detailed information about symptoms and effectiveness of treatments

**N.** Method of service delivery and change-of-shift reports

1. Functional method

   a. RN of previous shift reports to RN of oncoming shift

   b. Other staff may attend report or be given report according to assignments from RN

2. Team nursing method

   a. All members of oncoming shift attend report

   b. Reduces amount of time and communication needed to make changes in nursing care for client

3. Primary nursing method

   a. RN assigned to direct care of individual clients reports to RN assigned to direct care of same individual clients

4. Case management method

   a. Scheduled structured discussions with nursing team and interdisciplinary team in addition to change-of-shift reports

# CULTURAL NORMS

A. Cultural norms—group of individuals' values and beliefs that strongly influence individual's actions and behaviors

B. Values—personal preferences, commitments, motivations, patterns of using resources, objects, people, or events that have special meaning and influence individual's choices, behaviors, actions

C. Beliefs
1. Basic assumptions or personal convictions that the individual thinks are factual or takes for granted
2. Used to determine values
3. Handed down from generation to generation
4. Include cultural traditions

# ETHICS

A. Definition
1. Principles of right and wrong, good and bad
2. Governs our relationship with others
3. Used to identify solutions to problems arising from conflicts
4. Based on personal beliefs and cultural values that guide decision- making and determine conduct
5. As cultural diversity increases, need to understand ethical principles increases

B. ANA Code of Ethics—decision-making framework for solving ethical problems
1. Nurse provides care with respect for human dignity and uniqueness of individual without consideration of social or economic status, personal attributes, or nature of health problems
2. Nurse safeguards the client's right to privacy
3. Nurse acts to safeguard client and public when health care and safety are at risk from incompetent, unethical, or illegal practice of an individual
4. Nurse assumes responsibility and accountability for own individual actions and judgments
5. Nurse maintains competence in nursing
6. Nurse uses informed judgment, competence, and qualifications in accepting responsibilities and delegating nursing activities to others
7. Nurse participates in activities contributing to the development of the profession's body of knowledge
8. Nurse participates in profession's efforts to implement and improve standards of care
9. Nurse participates in profession's efforts to establish and maintain conditions of employment conducive to high-quality nursing care
10. Nurse participates in profession's efforts to protect the public from misinformation and misrepresentation and to maintain the integrity of nursing

11. Nurse collaborates with members of the health professions and others to promote community and national efforts to meet the health care needs of the public

C. Ethical principles of nursing

1. Autonomy—support of client's independence to make decisions and take action for themselves

2. Beneficence—duty to help others by doing what is best for them; client advocacy for refusal of care, autonomy overrides beneficence

3. Nonmaleficence—"do no harm"; act with empathy toward client and staff without resentment or malice; violated by acts performed in bad faith or with ill will, or when making false accusations about client or employee

4. Justice—use available resources fairly and reasonably

5. Veracity—communicate truthfully and accurately

6. Confidentiality—safeguard the client's privacy

7. Fidelity—following through on what the nurse says will be done; carefully attending to the details of the client's care

D. Ethical reasoning process

1. Recognize a moral issue

2. Analyze facts and identify the dilemma

3. Decide on possible alternative actions

4. Select specific action

5. Evaluate the effectiveness of the action

E. Behaviors for handling reports of dissatisfaction

1. Use active listening without interrupting or arguing

2. Don't get defensive

3. Ask person what is expected for solution to problem

4. Explain what you can and cannot do to solve the problem

5. Agree on specific steps that will be taken and determine a timeline

## ▶ CLIENT EDUCATION

A. Assessment

1. Definition—process of learning

2. Type of information needed

   a. Specific knowledge

   b. Type of learning

      1) Cognitive

      2) Psychomotor

      3) Affective

3. Client's motivation

   a. Client may need help to see need for learning

   b. Important to remove barriers to learning readiness, if possible

4. Client's needs

   a. Health behavior desired

   b. Current level of knowledge/understanding

     c. Skill level

     d. Client's attitudes and beliefs

     e. Social, cultural, and environmental factors influence health behavior

**B.** Diagnose

   1. Client education process requires skilled communication

     a. Mutual goals set

     b. Client feedback critical

   2. Factors influencing compliance with health regimen

     a. Duration—shorter duration increases compliance

     b. Complexity—greater complexity causes greater noncompliance

     c. Adverse effects—the greater the adverse effects, the greater the noncompliance

**C.** Plan/Implementation

   1. Set priorities

   2. Set realistic goals

   3. Consider involving family and significant other

   4. Use nonjudgmental, empathetic approach

   5. Use demonstration and return-demonstration for teaching skills

   6. Allow for practice periods

   7. Ensure, by observation, that knowledge has been incorporated

   8. Point out any success/benefits

   9. Recognize the difficulty of changing behavior

**D.** Evaluation

   1. Is the client able to verbalize an understanding of the health plan?

   2. Can the client demonstrate the required skills?

   3. Have identified health outcomes been reached?

# DISCHARGE PLANNING/HOME CARE

**A.** Assessment

   1. Begins with first encounter

   2. Potential effects of health problems identified

   3. Family and other social supports identified

   4. Client's functional level assessed

   5. Environmental factors identified

   6. Community agencies identified

   7. Client's preferences are always considered

   8. Mutually agreeable and appropriate plan is the goal of thorough assessment

**B.** Diagnose

   1. Goal is as much independence for client as safely possible

   2. Client's strengths as well as limitations are considered

   3. Community care between hospital and home maintained through appropriate referrals

   4. Appropriate level of care is determined

**C.** Plan/Implementation

1. Collaborate with interdisciplinary team and client to identify feasible, safe, humane plan

2. Make referrals to appropriate community services

3. Plan ways to adapt the home environment to client's current functional ability

4. Implement client education plan

5. Home care nurse continues this process

   a. Monitors health status

   b. Assesses client's needs in home environment

   c. Facilitates implementation of services

   d. Coordinates care

   e. Continues client education

**D.** Evaluation

1. Is the client's health status relatively stable at home?

2. Is the client safe at home?

3. Have services been implemented in a timely fashion and are they consistent with client's needs?

4. Is the client making the expected progress in terms of rehabilitation?

5. Have the client's and family's psychosocial needs been recognized and addressed?

# ▶ INFECTIONS AND INFECTION CONTROL

**A.** Assessment

1. Local (focal point)—heat, redness, pain/tenderness, swelling, possible drainage (bloody, serous, purulent), abscess (localized collection of pus), cellulitis (involving cellular and connective tissue)

2. Systemic (generalized)—fever, malaise, weakness

3. White blood cell count (WBC)—normally 4,500–11,000 x $10^3$/mm3 (4.5 11 x $10^9$/L); increase indicates the presence of disease or injury; differential of 30–40% lymphocytes; increased number immature neutrophils ("shift to left")

4. Erythrocyte sedimentation rate (ESR)—elevations greater than 15–20 mm/h indicate the presence of inflammation

5. Cultures and antibiotic sensitivity of suspected infectious site

   a. Should be obtained before onset of antibiotic therapy

   b. Specimens must be carefully collected and identified

   c. Preliminary results in 24 hours; final results in 72 hours

6. Highly sensitive C-reactive protein (hsCRP)—marker of inflammation

**B.** Diagnose

1. Inflammation—immediate, short-term, nonspecific response to the adverse effects of injury, i.e., physical irritants (trauma/foreign body) or chemical irritants (strong acids/alkalies) or invasion by microorganisms

2. Communicable diseases—caused by pathogenic microorganisms and transmitted by direct contact, droplet spread, contaminated articles, or through carriers (see Table 1)

3. Hospital-Acquired Infections (HAI)—nearly 2 million (5%) hospital clients acquire an infection in the hospital; most often caused by *Staphylococcus aureus*

**C.** Plan/Implementation

1. Treatment of infection or infectious disease with appropriate antibiotic medication

2. Standard Precautions (barrier)—used with all clients

   a. Primary strategy for infection control in all settings

   b. Most important way to reduce transmission of pathogens

| Table 1  COMMON COMMUNICABLE DISEASES OF CHILDHOOD | | |
|---|---|---|
| **NAME/INCUBATION** | **TRANSMISSION/CLINICAL PICTURE** | **NURSING CONSIDERATIONS** |
| Chickenpox (Varicella) 13–17 days | Prodromal: slight fever, malaise, anorexia<br><br>Rash is pruritic, begins as macule, then papule, and then vesicle with successive crops of all three stages present at any one time; lymphadenopathy; elevated temperature<br><br>Transmission: spread by direct contact, airborne, contaminated object | Isolation until all vesicles are crusted; communicable from 1 day before rash<br><br>Avoid use of aspirin due to association with Reye's syndrome; use Acetaminophen<br><br>Topical application of calamine lotion or baking soda baths<br><br>Airborne and contact precautions in hospital |
| Diphtheria 2–5 days | Prodromal: resembles common cold<br><br>Low-grade fever, hoarseness, malaise, pharyngeal lymphadenitis; characteristic white/gray pharyngeal membrane<br><br>Transmission: direct contact with a carrier, infected client contaminated articles | Contact and droplet precautions until two successive negative nose and throat cultures are obtained<br><br>Complete bedrest; watch for signs of respiratory distress and obstruction; provide for humidification, suctioning, and tracheostomy as needed; severe cases can lead to sepsis and death<br><br>Administer antitoxin therapy |
| Pertussis (Whooping Cough) 5–21 days, usually 10 | Prodromal: upper respiratory infection for 1–2 weeks<br><br>Severe cough with high-pitched "whooping" sound, especially at night, lasts 4–6 weeks; vomiting<br><br>Transmission: direct contact, droplet, contaminated articles | Hospitalization for infants; bedrest and hydration<br><br>Complications: pneumonia, weight loss, dehydration, hemorrhage, hernia, airway obstruction<br><br>Maintain high humidity and restful environment; suction; oxygen<br><br>Administer erthromycin and pertussis immune globulin |
| Rubella (German Measles) 14–21 days | Prodromal: none in children, low fever and sore throat in adolescent<br><br>Maculopapular rash appears first on face and then on rest of the body<br><br>Symptoms subside first day after rash<br><br>Transmission: droplet spread and contaminated articles | Contact precautions<br><br>Isolate child from potentially pregnant women<br><br>Comfort measures; antipyretics and analgesics<br><br>Rare complications include arthritis and encephalitis<br><br>Droplet precautions<br><br>Risk of fetal deformity |
| Rubeola 10–20 days | Prodromal: fever and malaise followed by cough and Koplik's spots on buccal mucosa<br><br>Erythematous maculopapular rash with face first affected; turns brown after 3 days when symptoms subside<br><br>Transmission: direct contact with droplets | Isolate until 5th day; maintain bedrest during first 3–4 days<br><br>Institute airborne and seizure precautions<br><br>Antipyretics, dim lights; humidifier for room<br><br>Keep skin clean and maintain hydration |
| Scarlet fever 2–4 days | Prodromal: high fever with vomiting, chills, malaise, followed by enlarged tonsils covered with exudate, strawberry tongue<br><br>Rash: red tiny lesions that become generalized and then desquamate; rash appears within 24 hours<br><br>Transmission: droplet spread or contaminated articles<br><br>Group A beta-hemolytic streptococci | Droplet precautions for 24 hours after start of antibiotics<br><br>Ensure compliance with oral antibiotic therapy<br><br>Bedrest during febrile phase<br><br>Analgesics for sore throat<br><br>Encourage fluids, soft diet<br><br>Administer penicillin or erythromycin |

| Table 1 COMMON COMMUNICABLE DISEASES OF CHILDHOOD *(CONTINUED)* | | |
|---|---|---|
| **NAME/INCUBATION** | **TRANSMISSION/CLINICAL PICTURE** | **NURSING CONSIDERATIONS** |
| Mononucleosis 4–6 weeks | Malaise, fever, enlarged lymph nodes, sore throat, flulike aches, low-grade temperature<br><br>Highest incidence 15–30 years old<br><br>Transmission: direct contact with oral secretions, unknown | Advise family members to avoid contact with saliva (cups, silverware) for about 3 months<br><br>Treatment is rest and good nutrition; strenuous exercise is to be avoided to prevent spleen rupture<br><br>Complications include encephalitis and spleen rupture |
| Tonsillitis (streptococcal) | Fever, white exudate on tonsils<br><br>Positive culture GpA strep | Antibiotics<br><br>Teach parents serious potential complications: rheumatic fever, glomerulonephritis |
| Mumps 14–21 days | Malaise, headache, fever, parotid gland swelling<br><br>Transmission: direct contact with saliva, droplet | Isolation before and after appearance of swelling<br><br>Soft, bland diet<br><br>Complications: deafness, meningitis, encephalitis, sterility |

   c. Standard precautions apply to contact with blood, body fluids, non intact skin, and mucous membranes from all clients

   d. Handwashing

      1) Done immediately on contact with blood or bodily fluids

      2) Wash hands before putting on or taking off gloves, between client contacts, between procedures or tasks with same client, immediately after exposure to blood or bodily fluids

   e. Gloves

      1) Use clean, non-sterile when touching blood, body fluids, secretions, excretions, contaminated articles

      2) Put on clean gloves just before touching mucous membranes or non intact skin, for touching blood, body fluids, secretions, contaminated items or if gloves torn or heavily soiled

      3) Change gloves between tasks/procedures

      4) Remove gloves promptly after use, before touching items and environmental surfaces

   f. Masks, eye protection, face shield (Personal Protective Equipment)

      1) Used to protect mucous membranes of eyes, nose, mouth during procedures and client care activities likely to generate splashes or sprays of blood, bodily fluids, or excretions

   g. Gowns (Personal Protective Equipment)

      1) Use clean, non-sterile gowns to protect skin and prevent soiling of clothing during procedures and client care activities likely to generate splashes and sprays of blood, bodily fluids, or excretions

      2) Should remove promptly, and wash hands after leaving client's environment

h. Environmental control

1) Do not need to use special dishes, glasses, eating utensils; can use either reusable or disposable

2) Don't recap used sharps, or bend, break, or remove used needles

3) Don't manipulate used needle with two hands; use a one-handed scoop technique. Place used sharps in a puncture-resistant container

4) Use mouthpieces, resuscitation bags, or other devices for mouth-to-mouth resuscitation

i. Client placement

1) Private room if client has poor hygiene habits, contaminates the environment, or can't assist in maintaining infection control precautions (e.g., infants, children, altered mental status client)

2) When cohorting (sharing room) consider the epidemiology and mode of transmission of the infecting organism

j. Transport

1) Use barriers (e.g., mask, impervious dressings)

2) Notify personnel of impending arrival and precautions needed

3) Inform client of ways to assist in prevention of transmission

3. Transmission-based precautions apply to clients with documented or suspected infections with highly transmissible or epidemiologically important pathogens; prevent spread of pathogenic microorganisms

a. Airborne precautions

1) Used with pathogens smaller than 5 microns that are transmitted by airborne route; droplets or dust particles that remain suspended in the air

2) Private room with monitored negative air pressure with 6–12 air changes per hour (airborne infection isolation room)

3) Keep door closed and client in room; susceptible persons should not enter room or wear N-95 HEPA filter

4) Can cohort or place client with another client with the same organism, but no other organism

5) Private room is the best situation

6) Place mask on client if being transported

7) Tuberculosis—wear fit-test respirator mask

8) Example of disease in category: measles (rubeola), *M. tuberculosis*, varicella (chicken pox), disseminated zoster (shingles)

b. Droplet precautions

1) Used with pathogens transmitted by infectious droplets; droplets larger than 5 microns

2) Involves contact of conjunctiva or mucous membranes of nose or mouth; happens during coughing, sneezing, talking, or during procedures such as suctioning or bronchoscopy

3) Private room or with client with same infection but no other infection; wear mask if in close contact

    4) Maintain spatial separation of three feet between infected client and visitors or other clients; visitors wear mask if less than three feet

    5) Door may remain open

    6) Place mask on client if being transported

    7) Examples of disease in category: diphtheria, Group A streptococcus pneumonia, pneumonia or meningitis caused by *N. meningitidis* or H. influenzae Type B, Rubella, mumps, pertussis

  c. Contact precautions

    1) Needed with client care activities that require physical skin-to-skin contact (e.g., turn clients, bathe clients), or occurs between two clients (e.g., hand contact), or occurs by contact with contaminated inanimate objects in client's environment

    2) Private room or with client with same infection but no other infection

    3) Clean, non-sterile gloves for client contact or contact with potentially contaminated areas

    4) Change gloves after client contact with fecal material or wound drainage

    5) Remove gloves before leaving client's environment and wash hands with antimicrobial agent

    6) Wear gown when entering room if clothing will have contact with client, environment surfaces, or if client is incontinent, has diarrhea, an ileostomy, colostomy, or wound drainage

    7) Remove PPE (gown) before leaving room

    8) Use dedicated equipment or clean and disinfect between clients

    9) Example of diseases in category: infection caused by multidrug-resistant organisms (e.g., MRSA and vancomycin-resistant organisms), herpes simplex, herpes zoster, *clostridium difficile*, respiratory syncytial virus, pediculosis, scabies, rotavirus, hepatitis type A

# ▶ TUBERCULOSIS

**A.** Assessment

  1. Progressive fatigue, nausea, anorexia, weight loss

  2. Irregular menses

  3. Low-grade fevers over a period of time

  4. Night sweats

  5. Irritability

  6. Cough with mucopurulent sputum, occasionally streaked with blood; chest tightness and a dull aching chest; dyspnea

  7. Diagnostic procedures

    a. Skin testing (see Table 2)

    b. Sputum smear for acid-fast bacilli, induce by respiratory therapy in am and pm; not specific for TB

    c. Chest x-ray routinely performed on all persons with positive PPD to detect old and new lesions; tubercles may be seen in lungs

    d. QuantiFERON-TB Gold test; results within 24 hours

**B.** Diagnose

    1. *Mycobacterium tuberculosis* (acid-fast gram-positive bacillus) transmitted by airborne droplets; bacillus multiplies in bronchi or alveoli, resulting in pneumonitis; may lie dormant for many years and be reactivated in periods of stress; may spread to other parts of body

    2. Risk factors

        a. Close contact with someone who has active tuberculosis

        b. Immunocompromised

        c. IV drug abuser

        d. Persons who live in institutions

        e. Lower socioeconomic group

        f. Immigrants from countries with a high prevalence of tuberculosis (Latin American, Southeast Asia, Africa)

    3. Incidence increasing in immigrant populations, poverty areas, elderly, alcoholics, drug abusers, and persons with AIDS

| Table 2  TB SKIN TESTING | |
| --- | --- |
| **TEST** | **NURSING CONSIDERATIONS** |
| Mantoux Test<br>  Purified Protein<br>    Derivative (PPD) | Given intradermally in the forearm<br><br>Read in 48–72 hours; measure induration across the forearm (palpable, hardened palpation, not the erythema)<br><br>Results:<br>  1. 15-mm or greater induration (hard area under the skin) = significant (positive) reaction for clients without certain risk factors. Does not mean that active disease is present, but indicates exposure to TB or the presence of inactive (dormant) disease<br><br>  2. 10 mm–14.9 mm induration for clients at risk (ex: recent immigrants, injection drug users, children less than 4 years old)<br><br>  3. 5 mm–9.9 mm for clients with AIDS, on immunosurpressant therapy, transplant clients. |
| Multiple Puncture Test (Tine) | Read test in 48–72 hours<br>Vesicle formation = positive reaction<br>Screening test only<br>Questionable or positive reactions verified by Mantoux Test |

**C.** Plan/Implementation

  1. Notification of state health department; evaluation of contacts

  2. Isoniazid prophylaxis—not recommended for those individuals greater than 35 years old who are at low risk because of increased risk of associated toxic hepatitis; persons less than 35 get 6–9 months therapy with isoniazid

    a. Household contacts

    b. Recent converters

    c. Persons under age 20 with positive reaction and inactive TB

    d. Susceptible health care workers

    e. Newly infected persons

    f. Significant skin test reactors with abnormal x-ray studies

    g. Significant skin test reactors up to age 35

  3. Chemotherapy—to prevent development of resistant strains, two or three medications are usually administered concurrently; frequently a 6– or 9–month regimen of isoniazid and rifampin; ethambutol and streptomycin may be used initially

  4. Isolation for 2–4 weeks (or three negative sputum cultures) after drug therapy is initiated; sent home before this (family already exposed)

  5. Teaching

    a. Cover mouth and nose with tissue when coughing, sneezing, laughing; place tissues in plastic bag

    b. wear mask in crowds

    c. Avoid excessive exposure to dust and silicone

    d. Handwashing

    e. Must take full course of medications

    f. Encourage to return to clinic for sputum smears

    g. Good nutrition (increased iron, protein, vitamins B and C)

**D.** Evaluation

  1. Has the spread of TB been prevented?

  2. Is the client compliant with the medication regimen?

# ▶ HEPATITIS

**A.** Assessment

  1. Fatigue

  2. Jaundice (icterus), yellow sclera

  3. Anorexia, RUQ pain and tenderness, malaise

  4. Clay-colored stools, tea-colored urine

  5. Pruritus: accumulation of bile salts under the skin

  6. Liver function studies: elevated ALT, AST, alkaline phosphatase (ALP), bilirubin

  7. Prolonged PT

  8. Percutaneous liver biopsy

  9. Antibodies to specific virus; e.g., anti-HAV

| Table 3  CLASSIFICATIONS OF HEPATITIS | | | | |
|---|---|---|---|---|
| TYPE | HIGH RISK GROUP | INCUBATION | TRANSMISSION | NURSING CONSIDERATIONS |
| Hepatitis A (HAV) | Young children<br><br>Institutions for custodial care<br><br>International travelers to developing countries | 15–50 days | Common in fall, early winter<br><br>Fecal–oral<br><br>Shellfish from contaminated water<br><br>Poor sanitation<br><br>Contaminated food handlers<br><br>Oral–anal sexual activity | Survives on hands<br><br>Diagnostic tests—<br>    Cultured in stool and detected in serum before onset of disease<br><br>Prevention–improved sanitation;<br>    Hepatitis A vaccine<br><br>Treated with gamma globulin early postexposure<br>    No preparation of food |
| Hepatitis B (HBV) | Immigrants from areas of HBV endemicity<br><br>Drug addicts<br><br>Fetuses from infected mothers<br><br>Homosexually active men<br><br>Clients on dialysis<br><br>Male prisoners<br><br>Transfusion recipients<br><br>Health care workers | 48–180 days | Blood and body fluids<br><br>Parenteral drug abuse<br><br>Sexual contact<br><br>Hemodialysis<br><br>Accidental contaminated needle exposure<br><br>Maternal–fetal route | Diagnostic tests—<br>    Hepatitis B surface antigen, anti-HBc, anti-HBe<br><br>    Treatment–Hepatitis B vaccine (Heptavax-B, Recombivax HB),<br><br>    Hepatitis B immune globulin (HBIg) postexposure; interferon alpha-2b; lamivudir<br><br>Chronic carriers—frequent; potential for chronicity 5–10%<br><br>Complications: cirrhosis; liver cancer |
| Hepatitis C (HCV) | Persons receiving frequent blood transfusions<br><br>International travelers<br><br>Hemophilia clients | 14–180 days | Contact with blood and body fluids<br><br>IV drug users | May be asymptomatic<br><br>Complications: cirrhosis; liver cancer<br><br>Great potential for chronicity |
| Delta or Hepatitis D (HDV) | Drug addicts<br><br>Concurrent HBV infection | 14–56 days | Co-infects with Hepatitis B<br><br>Close personal contact<br><br>Parenteral transmission | Diagnostic test–HD Ag in serum |

| Table 3 CLASSIFICATIONS OF HEPATITIS *(CONTINUED)* | | | | |
|---|---|---|---|---|
| TYPE | HIGH RISK GROUP | INCUBATION | TRANSMISSION | NURSING CONSIDERATIONS |
| Hepatitis E | Persons living in under-developed countries | 15–64 days | Oral-fecal Contaminated water | Resembles Hepatitis A<br><br>Does not become chronic<br><br>Usually seen in young adults<br><br>Seen in travelers from Asia, Africa,<br><br>Mexico |
| Toxic Hepatitis | Elderly<br><br>Drug-induced (INH, diuretics,<br><br>Tetracycline, carbon tetachloride, Tylenol, ETOH)<br><br>Alcohol | | Noninfectious inflam-mation of liver | Removal of causative substance<br><br>Check level of consciousness<br><br>Encourage fluids |

**B.** Diagnose

1. Acute inflammatory disease of the liver resulting in cell damage from liver cell degeneration and necrosis

2. Potential nursing diagnoses

   a. Fatigue

   b. Physical mobility, impaired

   c. Impaired liver function

   d. Acute pain

   e. Deficient knowledge

3. Classifications (see Table 3)

**C.** Plan/Implementation

1. Frequent rest periods

2. If clients diagnosed with hepatitis A are diapered or incontinent, contact precautions in addition to standard precautions

3. Contact precautions in addition to standard precautions for clients diagnosed with hepatitis A

4. Diet low in fat, high in calories, carbohydrates and protein; no alcoholic beverages

5. For pruritus—calamine, short clean nails, antihistamines

6. Medications

   a. Vitamin K

   b. Antiviral drugs: interferon and lamivudine

   c. Post-exposure Hepatitis B vaccine

7. Teach client and family

   a. Avoid alcohol and potentially hepatotoxic prescription/OTC medications (particularly aspirin and sedatives)

   b. Balance rest and activity periods

   c. Techniques to prevent spread

   d. Cannot donate blood

   e. Note and report recurrence of signs and symptoms

 **D.** Evaluation

  1. Has permanent liver damage been avoided?

  2. Has client comfort been maintained?

## ▶ LYME DISEASE

**A.** Assessment

 1. Stage 1

  a. Rash (erythematous papule that develops into lesion with a clear center) develops at site of tick bite within 2–30 days; concentric rings develop, suggesting a bull's-eye; lesion enlarges quickly

  b. Regional lymphadenopathy

  c. Development of flulike symptoms (malaise, fever, headache, myalgia, stiff neck, arthralgia, conjunctivitis) within one to several months, lasts 7–10 days and may reoccur

 2. Stage 2

  a. Develops within 1–6 months if untreated

  b. Cardiac conduction defects

  c. Neurologic disorders: facial paralysis; paralysis that is not permanent

 3. Stage 3

  a. Arthralgias, enlarged or inflamed joints occur within one to several months after the initial infection, chronic fatigue, cognitive disorders

  b. May persist for several years

**B.** Diagnose

 1. Multisystem infection transmitted to humans by tick bite

 2. Most common in summer months

**C.** Plan/Implementation

 1. Prevention

  a. Cover exposed areas when in wooded areas

  b. Check exposed areas for presence of ticks

 2. Nursing care

  a. Administer antibiotics for 3–4 weeks: doxycycline, ceftriaxone, azithromycin during stage 1

  b. Administer IV penicillin G during later stages

**D.** Evaluation

 1. Has infection been prevented by wearing proper clothing in wooded areas?

 2. If infected, has treatment been initiated early to prevent complications?

## ▶ SEXUALLY TRANSMITTED INFECTIONS (STI)

A. Assessment (see Table 4)

B. Diagnose—potential nursing diagnoses

   1. Health maintenance, altered

   2. Sexual patterns, altered

C. Plan/Implementation (see Table 4)

D. Evaluation

   1. Is client knowledgeable about treatment for STD?

   2. Have sexual contacts been notified and evaluated?

## ▶ AIDS

A. Assessment

   1. HIV positive—presence of HIV in the blood

   2. AIDS—syndrome with CD4/TC counts below 200

   3. Opportunistic infections

      a. *P. jiroveci(P. carinii)* pneumonia

         1) Gradually worsening chest tightness and shortness of breath

         2) Persistent, dry, nonproductive cough, rales

         3) Dyspnea and tachypnea

         4) Low-grade/high fever

         5) Progressive hypoxemia and cyanosis

      b. *C. albicans* stomatitis or esophagitis

         1) Changes in taste sensation

         2) Difficulty swallowing

         3) Retrosternal pain

         4) White exudate and inflammation of mouth and back of throat

| Table 4  SEXUALLY TRANSMITTED INFECTIONS | | | | |
|---|---|---|---|---|
| TYPE | SYMPTOMS | DIAGNOSTIC TESTS | TRANSMISSION AND INCUBATION | NURSING CONSIDERATIONS |
| Syphilis | Stage 1: painless chancre disappears within 4 weeks<br><br>Stage 2: copper-colored rash on palms and soles; low-grade fever<br><br>Stage 3: cardiac and CNS dysfunction | VDRL, RPR, FTA-ABS, MHA-TP (to confirm syphilis when VDRL and RPR are positive)<br><br>Dark Field Microscopic examination | Mucous membrane or skin; congenital; kissing, sexual contact<br><br>10–90 days | Prevention—condoms<br><br>Treat with penicillin G IM<br><br>For PCN allergy—erythromycin for 10–15 days<br><br>Ceftriaxone and tetracyclines (nonpregnant females)<br><br>Retest for cure<br><br>Abstinence from sexual activity until treatment complete<br><br>Reportable disease |
| Gonorrhea | Thick discharge from vagina or urethra<br><br>Frequently asymptomatic in females<br><br>If female has symptoms, usually has purulent discharge, dysuria, and dyspareunia (painful intercourse)<br><br>Symptoms in male include painful urination and a yellow-green discharge | Culture of discharge from cervix or urethra<br><br>Positive results for other STD diagnostic tests | Mucous membrane or skin; congenital; vaginal, orogenital, anogenital sexual activity<br><br>2–7 days | IM ceftriaxone 1 time and PO doxycyline BID for 1 week; azithromycin<br><br>IM aqueous penicillin with PO probenecid (to delay penicillin urinary excretion) PO azithromycin or doxycycline is used to treat chlamydia, which coexists in 45% of cases<br><br>Spectinomycin if allergy to ceftriaxone<br><br>Monitor for complications, pelvic inflammatory disease |
| Genital Herpes (HSV-2) | Painful vesicular genital lesions<br><br>Difficulty voiding<br><br>Recurrence in times of stress, infection, menses | Direct examination of cells<br><br>HSV antibodies | Mucous membrane or skin; congenital<br><br>Virus can survive on objects such as towels<br><br>3–14 days | Acyclovir (not cure)<br><br>Emotional support<br><br>Sitz baths<br><br>Local medication<br><br>Client must notify sexual contacts<br><br>Monitor Pap smears on regular basis—increased incidence of cancer of cervix<br><br>Precautions about vaginal delivery |

| Table 4  SEXUALLY TRANSMITTED INFECTIONS *(CONTINUED)* | | | | |
|---|---|---|---|---|
| TYPE | SYMPTOMS | DIAGNOSTIC TESTS | TRANSMISSION AND INCUBATION | NURSING CONSIDERATIONS |
| Chlamydia | Men—dysuria, frequent urination, watery discharge<br><br>Women—may be asymptomatic, thick discharge with acrid odor, pelvic pain, yellow-colored discharge; painful menses | Direct examination of cells<br><br>Enzyme-linked ELISA | Mucous membrane; sexual contact<br><br>1–3 weeks | Notification of contacts<br><br>May cause sterility<br><br>Treat with azithromycin, doxycycline, erythromycin |
| Condylomata acuminata (genital warts) | Initially single, small papillary lesion spreads into large cauliflowerlike cluster on perineum and/ or vagina or penis; may be itching/burning | Direct exam<br><br>Biopsy<br><br>HPV | Majority due to human papilloma virus (HPV)<br><br>Mucous membrane; sexual contact; congenital<br><br>1–3 months | Curettage, cryotherapy with liquid nitrogen or podophyllin resin<br><br>Kerotolytic medications<br><br>Avoid intimate sexual contact until lesions are healed<br><br>Strong association with incidence of genital dysplasia and cervical carcinoma<br><br>Atypical, pigmented, or persistent warts should be biopsied<br><br>Notify contacts |

c.  *C. neoformans*—severe debilitating meningitis

   1)  Fever, headache, blurred version

   2)  Nausea and vomiting

   3)  Stiff neck, mental status changes, seizures

d.  Cytomegalovirus (CMV)—significant factor in morbidity and mortality

   1)  Fever, malaise

   2)  Weight loss, fatigue

   3)  Lymphadenopathy

   4)  Retinochoroiditis characterized by inflammation and hemorrhage

   5)  Visual impairment

   6)  Colitis, encephalitis, pneumonitis

   7)  Adrenalitis, hepatitis, disseminated infection

e.  Kaposi's sarcoma—most common malignancy

   1)  Varied size, purplish-brown, nonpainful, nonpruritic palpable lesions occurring on any part of the body

   2)  Most commonly seen on the skin

   3)  Diagnosed by biopsy

4. Diagnostic tests

    a. Positive HIV antibody on enzyme-linked immunosorbent assay (ELISA) and confirmed by Western blot assay or indirect immunoflourescence assay (IFA)

    b. Viral load testing, CD4 to CD8 ratio, antigen assays

    c. Radioimmunoprecipitation assay (RIPA)

    d. CBC reveals leukopenia with serious lymphopenia, anemia, thrombocytopenia

**B.** Diagnose

1. AIDS (acquired immunodeficiency syndrome)—a syndrome distinguished by serious deficits in cellular immune function associated with positive human immunodeficiency virus (HIV); evidenced clinically by development of opportunistic infections (e.g. *Pneumocystis jiroveci pneumonia*, Candida albicans, cytomegalovirus), enteric pathogens, and malignancies (most commonly Kaposi's sarcoma)

    a. High-risk groups

        1) Homosexual/bisexual men, especially with multiple partners

        2) Intravenous drug abusers

        3) Hemophiliacs via contaminated blood products

        4) Blood transfusion recipients prior to 1985

        5) Heterosexual partners of infected persons

        6) Children of infected women/in utero or at birth

    b. Transmission—contaminated blood or body fluids, sharing IV drug needles, sexual contact, transplacental and possibly through breast milk

    c. Time from exposure to symptom manifestation may be prolonged (10–12 years)

| Table 5  NURSING CARE OF A CLIENT WITH ACQUIRED IMMUNE DEFICIENCY SYNDROME ||
| PROBLEM | NURSING CONSIDERATIONS |
| --- | --- |
| Fatigue | Provide restful environment<br>Assist with personal care<br>Monitor tolerance for visitors |
| Pain | Give meds as appropriate<br>Assess level of pain |
| Disease susceptibility | Implement infection control precautions<br>Handwashing on entering and leaving room<br>Monitor for oral infections and meningitis<br>Give antibiotics as ordered |
| Respiratory distress | Monitor vital signs, breath sounds<br>Give bronchodilators and antibiotics as ordered<br>Suction and maintain $O_2$ as ordered<br>Monitor for symptoms of secondary infections |

| Table 5  NURSING CARE OF A CLIENT WITH ACQUIRED IMMUNE DEFICIENCY SYNDROME *(CONTINUED)* | |
|---|---|
| PROBLEM | NURSING CONSIDERATIONS |
| Anxiety, depression | Use tact, sensitivity in gathering personal data |
| | Encourage expression of feelings |
| | Respect client's own limits in ability to discuss problems |
| Anorexia, diarrhea | Monitor weight |
| | Encourage nutritional supplements |
| | Assess hydration |

**C.** Plan/Implementation

1. Preventive measures

   a. Avoidance of IV drug use (needle-sharing)

   b. Precautions regarding sexual patterns—sex education, condoms, avoid multiple partners

   c. Use standard precautions

2. Nursing care (see Table 5)

   a. No effective cure; antiviral medications (e.g., Zidovudine, Aciclovir) are being used to slow progression of symptoms

   b. Treatment specific to the presenting condition

      1) Kaposi's sarcoma—local radiation (palliative), single agent/ combination chemotherapy

      2) Fungal infections—nystatin swish and swallow, clotrimazole oral solution, amphotericin B with/without flucytosine

      3) Viral infections—Acyclovir, Ganciclovir

   c. Contact precautions in addition to standard precautions

   d. Nutrition—high protein and calories

   e. Symptomatic relief—comfort measures

   f. Maintain confidentiality

   g. Provide support

      1) Client and family coping—identify support systems

      2) Minimize social isolation—no isolation precautions are needed to enter room to talk to client, take VS, administer PO medications

      3) Encourage verbalization of feelings

   h. Client client/family discharge teaching

      1) Behaviors to prevent transmission—safe sex, not sharing toothbrushes, razors, and other potentially blood- contaminated objects

      2) Measures to prevent infections—good nutrition, hygiene, rest, skin and mouth care, avoid crowds

**D.** Evaluation

1. Has client comfort been maintained?

2. Is client knowledgeable about medication regimen?

## ▶ POISON CONTROL

A. Assessment

1. Airway, breathing, circulation (ABC)—treat the client first, then the poison

2. Identify poison—amount ingested, time of ingestion; save vomitus

3. Diagnostics

   a. Urine and serum analysis

   b. Long-bone x-rays if lead deposits suspected

   c. CAT scan, EEG

| Table 6 TEACHING PREVENTION OF ACCIDENTAL POISONING IN CHILDREN ||
|---|---|
| ACTION | RATIONALE |
| Proper storage—locked cabinets | Once child can crawl, can investigate cabinets and ingest contents of bottles |
| Never take medicine in front of children | Children are interested in anything their parents take and will mimic taking medicine |
| Never leave medication in purse, on table, or on kitchen counter | Children will investigate area and ingest bottle contents |
| Never refer to medicine as candy | Increases interest in taking medicine when unsupervised |
| Leave medicines, cleaning supplies in original containers | Pill boxes, soda bottles increase attractiveness and inhibit identification of substance should poisoning occur |
| Provide activities and play materials for children | Encourages child's interest without endangering him/her |
| Teach need for supervision of small children | Small children cannot foresee potential harm and need protection |

B. Diagnose—potential nursing diagnoses

1. Injury, risk for

2. Health maintenance, altered

C. Plan/Implementation

1. Prevention—most toxic ingestions are acute (see Table 6)

   a. Child-proofing—store all potentially poisonous substances in locked out-of-reach area

   b. Increased awareness of precipitating factors

      1) Growth and development characteristics—under/overestimating the capabilities of the child

      2) Changes in household routine

      3) Conditions that increase emotional tension of family members

2. Instructions for caretaker in case of suspected poison ingestion

   a. Recognize signs and symptoms of accidental poisoning—change in child's appearance/behavior; presence of unusual substances in child's mouth, hands, play area; burns, blisters and/or suspicious odor around child's mouth; open/empty containers in child's possession

   b. Initiate steps to stop exposure

    c. Call Poison Control Center—be prepared to provide information

        1) Substance—name, time, amount, route

        2) Child—condition, age, weight

    d. Poison Control Center (PCC) will advise to begin treatment at home or to bring child to an emergency facility

    e. Syrup of Ipecac is no longer recommended for treatment at home; Any Ipecac in the home should be disposed of safely

    f. No emetic or other substance should be given at home without consultation with the PCC or health care provider

    g. Save any substance, vomitus, stool, urine

    h. Induce vomiting only if indicated by Poison Control Center or health care provider

    i. Contraindications to inducing vomiting

        1) When child is in danger of aspiration—decreased level of consciousness, severe shock, seizure(s), diminished gag reflex

        2) When substance is petroleum distillate (lighter fluid, kerosene, paint remover) because of increased risk of aspiration pneumonia, or strong corrosive (acid/alkali drain cleaner), which may redamage esophagus and pharynx

    j. General considerations

        1) Water may be used to dilute the toxin; avoid giving large amounts of fluids when medication has been ingested because this may accelerate gastric emptying and speed drug absorption

        2) Milk may delay vomiting

        3) Do not attempt to neutralize a strong acid/alkali because this may cause a heat-producing reaction that can burn tissue

        4) There are only a few specific antidotes (physiologic antagonist reversing effect); there is no universal antidote

3. Emergency care in a health care facility

    a. Basic life support

        1) Respiratory—intubate if comatose, seizing, or no gag reflex; frequent blood gases

        2) Circulation

            a) IV fluids; maintain fluid and electrolyte balance

            b) Cardiac monitor—essential for comatose child and with tricyclic antidepressant or phenothiazine ingestion

    b. Gastric lavage and aspiration—client is intubated and positioned head down and on left side; large oro/nasogastrictube inserted and repeated irrigations of normal saline instilleduntil clear; not more than 10 ml/ kg; must be done within 60 minutes

    c. Activated charcoal—absorbs compounds, forming a non-absorbable complex; 5–10 g for each g of toxin

        1) Give within 30 minutes of ingestion and after emetic

        2) Mix with water to make a syrup; given PO or via gastric tube

4. Hasten elimination

   a. Diuretics—for substances eliminated by kidneys

   b. Chelation—heavy metals (e.g., mercury, lead, and arsenic) are not readily eliminated from body; progressive buildup leads to toxicity; a chelating agent binds with the heavy metal, forming a complex that can be eliminated by kidneys, peritoneal hemodialysis (e.g. deferoxamine, dimercaprol, calcium EDTA)

5. Prevent recurrence—crisis intervention with nonjudgmental approach; acknowledge difficulty in maintaining constant supervision; explore contributory factors; discuss and educate about growth and development influences as well as passive (child restraint closures) and active safety measures

**D.** Evaluation

1. Has child's safety been maintained?

2. Are parents knowledgeable about ways to prevent accidental poisoning?

## ▶ ASPIRIN (SALICYLATE) POISONING

**A.** Assessment

1. Tinnitus, nausea, sweating, dizziness, headache

2. Change in mental status

3. Increased temperature, hyperventilation (respiratory alkalosis)

4. Later, metabolic acidosis, and respiratory acidosis, bleeding, and hypovolemia

**B.** Diagnose

1. Toxicity begins at doses of 150–200 mg/kg; 4 grams may be fatal to child

   a. Altered acid–base balance (respiratory alkalosis) due to increased respiratory rate

   b. Increased metabolism causes greater $O_2$ consumption, $CO_2$ and heat production

   c. Metabolic acidosis results in hypokalemia, dehydration, and kidney failure

   d. May result in decreased prothrombin formation and decreased platelet aggregation, causing bleeding

**C.** Plan/Implementation

1. Induce vomiting; initiate gastric lavage with activated charcoal

2. Monitor vital signs and laboratory values

3. Maintain IV hydration and electrolyte replacement; monitor I and O, skin turgor, fontanels, urinary specific gravity

4. Reduce temperature—tepid water baths or hypothermia blankets; prone to seizures

5. Vitamin K, if needed, for bleeding disorder; guaiac of vomitus/stools

6. IV sodium bicarbonate enhances excretion

**D.** Evaluation

1. Are the client's vital signs stable?

2. Is the client's acid–base balance restored?

# ► ACETAMINOPHEN POISONING

**A.** Assessment

1. First 2 hours, nausea and vomiting, sweating, pallor, hypothermia, slow-weak pulse

2. Followed by latent period (1–1.5 days) when symptoms abate

3. If no treatment, hepatic involvement occurs (may last up to 1 week) with RUQ pain, jaundice, confusion, stupor, coagulation abnormalities

4. Diagnostic tests—serum acetaminophen levels at least 4 hours after ingestion; liver function tests AST, ALT, and kidney function tests (creatinine, BUN)—change in renal and liver function is a late sign

**B.** Diagnose

1. Toxicity begins at 150 mg/kg

2. Major risk is hepatic necrosis

**C.** Plan/Implementation

1. Induce vomiting

2. *N*-Acetylcysteine–specific antidote; most effective in 8–10 hours; must be given within 24 hours; given PO every 4 hours × 72 hours or IV × 3 doses

3. Maintain hydration; monitor output

4. Monitor liver and kidney function

**D.** Evaluation

1. Have liver and kidney damage been prevented?

2. Has the client's hydration been maintained?

# ► LEAD TOXICITY (PLUMBISM)

**A.** Assessment

1. Physical symptoms

    a. Irritability

    b. Sleepiness

    c. Nausea, vomiting, abdominal pain, poor appetite

    d. Constipation

    e. Decreased activity

    f. Increased intracranial pressure (e.g., seizures and motor dysfunction)

2. Environmental sources

    a. Flaking, lead-based paint (primary source)

    b. Crumbling plaster

    c. Odor of lead-based gasoline

    d. Pottery with lead glaze

    e. Lead solder in pipes

3. Diagnostic tests

    a. Blood lead level less than or equal to 9 micrograms per deciliter is normal

    b. Erythrocyte protoporphyrin (EP) level

    c. CBC—anemia

    d.  X-rays (long bone/GI)—may show radiopaque material, "lead lines"

**B.**  Diagnose

    1.  Child—practice of pica (habitual and compulsive ingestion of nonfood substances); children absorb more lead than adults; paint chips taste sweet

    2.  Pathology—lead is slowly excreted by kidneys and GI tract; stored in inert form in long bones; chronic ingestion affects many body systems

        a.  Hematological—blocks formation of hemoglobin, leading to microcytic anemia (initial sign) and increased erythrocyte protoporphyrin (EP)

        b.  Renal—toxic to kidney tubules, allowing an abnormal excretion of protein, glucose, amino acids, phosphates

        c.  CNS—increases membrane permeability, resulting in fluid shifts into brain tissue, cell ischemia, and destruction causing neurological and intellectual deficiencies with low-dose exposure; with high-dose exposure, intellectual delay, convulsions, and death (lead encephalopathy)

**C.**  Plan/Implementation

    1.  Chelating agent—promotes lead excretion in urine and stool (dimercaprol, calcium disodium, EDTA); succimer, deferoxamine

        a.  Maintain hydration

        b.  Identify sources of lead and institute deleading procedures; involve local housing authorities as needed

        c.  Instruct parents about supervision for pica and ways to encourage other activities for the child

**D.**  Evaluation

    1.  Is a referral to social service/public health agency needed?

    2.  Is assistance with obtaining child care necessary?

## ▶ HAZARDS AND HAZARDOUS WASTE

**A.**  Types of hazards

    1.  Chemical hazards—dusts, gases, fumes, mists

    2.  Psychophysiologic hazards—stress associated with job demands (e.g., rotating shifts, overtime, violence in the workplace)

    3.  Biologic hazards—exposure to infectious agents (e.g., TB, hepatitis B)

    4.  Ergonomic hazards—imbalance between individual and equipment, such as repetitive actions leading to carpal tunnel syndrome (ergonomics: study of interaction of human body with use of mechanical and electrical machines)

    5.  Safety hazards—precautions with equipment, fire safety, electrical systems

    6.  Hazardous materials (e.g., explosion from stored chlorine used for private swimming pool, radioisotope accident in nuclear medicine)

        a.  Exposure—presence of hazardous waste in environment

        b.  OSHA (Federal Occupational Safety and Health Administration) mandates acceptable levels of exposure to chemicals

        c.  Dose—amount of substance inhaled, ingested, absorbed through skin or eyes

    d. When there is a problem during transportation of chemical materials, information is provided from a central source; advises rescue and health care workers about the substance, its effect, and how to treat exposure

**B.** Hazardous materials causing immediate threat to life; client treated and then decontaminated

    1. Chlorine

    2. Cyanide

    3. Ammonia

    4. Phosgene

    5. Hydrogen sulfide

    6. Organophosphate insecticides

    7. Nitrogen dioxide

**C.** Hazardous materials with cancer-causing potential; client decontaminated and then treated

    1. Polychlorinated biphenyls

**D.** Ethical issues

    1. Autonomy

        a. Workers have right to know about hazardous chemicals and materials in the workplace and community so that they can take appropriate action to protect themselves

        b. Workers have right to know critical health and safety information

        c. Information must be presented so that it is tailored to meet the needs of the work force, taking into account language and literacy

    2. Beneficence (doing good)

        a. Involvement of worker groups in planning hazard communication training and designing written hazardous awareness materials;should integrate adult learning theory principles

**E.** Nursing care

    1. Before treatment, determine

        a. Does chemical pose threat to caregivers?

        b. If yes, has client been decontaminated?

        c. If chemical poses no threat or decontamination has been completed,client can be treated

        d. If chemical poses threat and client has not been decontaminated but has immediate life-threatening condition, health care workers put on protective garments and provide care to stabilize client; environment is sealed to prevent spread of chemical

    2. Goals

        a. Decontaminate individual

        b. Prevent spread of contamination

        c. Clean and remove contaminated water and waste

        d. Monitor personnel exposed

    3. Preparation

        a. Cover floor from entrance to treatment room

    b.  Seal off air vents

    c.  Rope off designated area

    d.  Security keeps nonessential personnel away from area

    e.  Place needed equipment in treatment room

    f.  Place equipment that may be needed outside treatment room

    g.  Remove extraneous supplies from treatment room

4.  Decontamination procedure

    a.  Client walks, is wheeled, or is placed on a clean stretcher covered in plastic

    b.  Client is transported over protected floor to treatment room

    c.  Client is taken to decontamination shower accompanied by health care worker wearing protective clothing and a respirator (if needed)

    d.  Client's clothing removed and placed in hazard bag (clothing contains 95% of contamination)

    e.  Valuables placed in separate bag for later decontamination

    f.  Client washes with soap and water, paying particular attention to body orifices (especially nostrils) and hairy areas

    g.  Client shampoos hair

    h.  Client's wounds are irrigated

    i.  Waste water collected in container if there is no containment unit for shower

    j.  If client was exposed to radiation, is then scanned with radiation detector meter with special attention to body orifices and hairy areas

    k.  Floor covering is removed and placed in hazard bag

    l.  Health care workers remove and bag protective clothing

    m.  After shower, client puts on clean clothes, and steps onto clean floor

    n.  Medical evaluation is then started

5.  Decontamination procedure for client requiring care before decontamination

    a.  Treatment room is considered to be contaminated

    b.  Designated health care worker stands at door to transcribe documentation (medical records not taken into room) and get necessary equipment

    c.  Health care workers may not enter or leave room without performing special procedures

## ▶ ACCIDENT PREVENTION

**A.** Newborn infant

1.  Don't smoke around infants, increases risk of upper respiratory tract infections

2.  Don't leave infant unattended in a high place or unstrapped in a safety seat

3.  Use rear-facing car safety seat

4.  Make sure furniture is free of lead-based paint

5.  Crib slats should be no further apart than 2 3/8"; the mattress should be tight-fitting

6.  Place infant flat on back after eating and for sleeping

**B.**  2 months old

1.  Don't hold infant while smoking or drinking hot liquid

2.  Set water heater at 120–130°F; test bath water temperature with inner aspect of the wrist before immersing infant

**C.**  4 months old

1.  Keep small objects and small pieces of food out of infant's reach

2.  Don't use teething biscuits—they become small and can obstruct airway

3.  Teach older siblings/children not to give infant small things

**D.**  6 months old

1.  Child-proof the home, especially the kitchen and bathroom; remove all dangerous items or place out of reach

2.  Use safety gates at bottom/top of stairs; use drawer safety latches, plug fillers

3.  Keep poison control number on phone; use as needed

**E.**  9 months old

1.  Use nonskid rugs, socks with nonskid strips, nonskid strips in bathtub

2.  Keep wastebaskets covered or out of reach

3.  Pad sharp edges of furniture

4.  Never leave child unattended near water or in bathtub

5.  Don't use electrical appliances near water

**F.**  1 to 3 years old

1.  Don't use toys with small pieces or give food with small pieces (peanuts, hard candy and a responsible adult present when near water

2.  Hold child's hand when walking near the street

3.  Encourage the child to sit down while eating

4.  Secure all medications in locked area; have Poison Control number available

5.  Turn pot handles toward the back of the stove and cover all electrical outlets

6.  Use rear-facing car seat until child reaches height and weight allowed by car safety seat manufacturers; after age 2 years or has outgrown a rear-facing car seat, use forward-facing car seat with harness as long as possible

**G.**  3 to 6 years old

1.  Use bicycle helmet; ride bicycle on right-hand side of the road or on sidewalk; make sure the bicycle is the correct size, feet should touch the ground when sitting on the bicycle seat

2.  Teach child not to eat things from outside (e.g., mushrooms) until checked by parents

3.  Look both ways before crossing street

4.  If weight or height above forward-facing limit, use belt-positioning booster seat until seat belt fits properly

**H.** 6 to 11 years old

1. Obey traffic signals while on bike; use reflectors on bike; wear light clothing

2. When playing group sports look for teams divided by size and maturation, not by age; use protective equipment; helmet while bike riding, skateboarding or rollerblading

**I.** Adolescent

1. Teach appropriate ways to deal with anger and threats

2. Teach safety for swimming and diving

3. Use car safety restraint; lap and seat belts

4. Teach hazards of drinking and driving

**J.** Adult

1. Use car safety restraint

2. Teach responsible behavior to reduce sexually transmitted diseases and alcohol-related accidents

3. Suicide prevention

4. Handgun control and safety

5. Motorcycle helmet use

6. Smoke and carbon monoxide detector use; fire extinguisher use

**K.** Elderly

1. At risk for injuries

   a. Muscle weakness

   b. Changes in balance

   c. Gait abnormalities

   d. Slowed reaction time

   e. Use of medications

   f. Chronic medical conditions (e.g., Parkinson's disease)

   g. Changes in vision, hearing, smell

2. Remove throws rugs, door thresholds; make sure floors are smooth and nonslip

3. Clear pathways of furniture

4. Use solid chairs with arm rests

5. Provide good lighting with accessible switches; use night light

6. Adapt kitchen and bathroom; use raised toilet seat, grab bars

7. Use cordless phone

8. Teach correct way to go up and down stairs; use hand rail, don't limit vision by carrying large load

9. Don't wear long gowns or robes or pants with flowing material

10. Wear sturdy, comfortable, nonskid shoes; don't wear flimsy slippers

11. Keep pet feeding dishes out of main walkway

12. Maintain mobility through exercise and assistive devices

# ▶ DISASTER PLANNING

**A.** Assessment—greatest good for the greatest number of people

1. Resources used for clients with strongest probability of survival

2. Nurses make tough decisions about which order clients will be seen

3. Decisions are based on assessment of injuries and knowledge of probable outcomes

4. Use Airway, Breathing, Circulation, neurologic Dysfunction (ABCDs) to prioritize

**B.** Planning

1. Triage under usual conditions

   a. Emergent—immediate threat to life

   b. Urgent—major injuries requiring immediate treatment

   c. Nonurgent—minor injuries that do not require immediate treatment

2. Triage with mass casualties

   a. Red—unstable clients who require immediate care to save life (e.g., occluded airway, active hemorrhaging); first category seen

   b. Yellow—stable clients who can wait 30–60 minutes for treatment (e.g., moderate burn, eye injury); second category to be seen

   c. Green—stable clients who can wait longer to be treated (e.g., "walking wounded"); third category to be seen

   d. Black—unstable clients having massive injuries that will probably prove fatal (e.g., massive body trauma); last category to be treated; supportive and comfort measures provided (e.g., pain control)

   e. DOA (dead on arrival)

**C.** Implementation

1. Care standardized according to standing orders

   a. IV fluids

   b. Lab tests

   c. Diagnostic procedures

   d. Medications (e.g., analgesics, tetanus prophylaxis, antibiotics)

2. Specialists become "generalists"

3. Nurses may have expanded responsibilities (e.g., suturing, surgical airway)

4. Use of diagnostic procedures may be limited (e.g., CT scans) with multiple trauma

5. Use of hospital resources determined by designated disaster medical officer

6. Areas of hospital are used as needed for treatment

7. Resources are obtained to provide emotional and spiritual care to clients and families

8. Person is designated to deal with media and traffic control

9. Measures are implemented to track unidentified clients

10. Procedures for handling evidence from disaster may be implemented

11. Hospitals practice disaster drills several times a year

**D.** Evaluation

1. Have the clients been cared for in an orderly fashion?

2. Have clients' physical needs been met?

▶ **BIOTERRORISM**

| Table 7  BIOTERRORISM | | | |
|---|---|---|---|
| TYPE | SYMPTOMS | TRANSMISSION AND INCUBATION | NURSING CONSIDERATIONS |
| Anthrax Cutaneous | 1–7 days after exposure: itching with small papule or vesicle<br><br>2 days after lesion formation: enlarged painless lesion with necrotic center<br><br>7–10 days after lesion formation: black eschar forms; sloughs after 12th day | Skin contact 1–7 days<br><br>No person-to-person transmission<br><br>High risk: exposure to contaminated animal hides, veterinarians, personnel who handle contaminated materials, military | Standard precautions<br>Decontamination<br>• Bag clothes in labeled, plastic bags<br>• Do not agitate clothes<br>• Instruct client to shower thoroughly with soap and water and shampoo hair<br>• Wear gloves, gown, and respiratory protection<br>• Decontaminate surfaces with bleach solution (one-part household bleach to nine-parts water)<br>• Administer oral fluoroquinolones for post-exposure prophylaxis<br>• Administer doxycycline, erythromycin, ciprofloxacin |
| Anthrax Inhalation | Initial: sore throat, mild fever, muscles aches, malaise followed by possible brief improvement<br><br>2–3 days later: abrupt onset of respiratory failure and shock, fever, hemorrhagic meningitis | Aerosolized spores<br>1–7 days up to 60 days<br>No person-to-person transmission | Standard precautions<br>Ventilator support for respiratory therapy<br>IV and PO ciprofloxacin and doxycycline |
| Botulism | Drooping eyelids, weakened jaw clench, dysphasia, blurred vision, symmetric descending weakness, 12–72 hours after exposure respiratory dysfunction; may cause death | Contaminated food 12–36 hours<br>Aerosol inhalation 24–72 hours<br>No person-to-person transmission | Standard precautions<br>Contact health department and Centers for Disease Control and Prevention (CDC) if suspicion of single case<br>Supportive care |
| Plague Bubonic | Fever, headache, general illness, painful, swollen regional lymph nodes (bubo); develops into septicemia and plague pneumonia | Infected rodent to man by infected fleas<br>2–8 days | Standard precautions for treatment of bubo;<br>    Droplet precautions for plague pneumonia<br>Administer antibiotics<br>Apply insecticides to kill fleas, control rat population |

| Table 7 BIOTERRORISM *(CONTINUED)* | | | |
|---|---|---|---|
| **TYPE** | **SYMPTOMS** | **TRANSMISSION AND INCUBATION** | **NURSING CONSIDERATIONS** |
| Pneumonic Plague | 2–4 days after exposure, fever, productive cough containing infectious particles, chest pain, hemoptysis, bronchopneumonia, rapid shock, and death | Aerosolized inhalation<br>1–3 days<br>Person-to-person transmission occurs through large aerosol droplets | Droplet precautions until 72 hours of antibiotic therapy<br>Place in private room or cohort with clients with same diagnosis<br>Administer antibiotics: Streptomycin, ciprofloxacin, doxycycline<br>Decontamination<br>• Bag clothes in labeled, plastic bags<br>• Do not agitate clothes<br>• Instruct client to shower thoroughly with soap and water and shampoo hair<br>• Wear gloves, gown, and respiratory protection<br>• Decontaminate surfaces with bleach solution (one-part household bleach to nine-parts water) |
| Smallpox | Occur in 10–17 days; fever, myalgia synchronous onset of rash that is most prominent on face and extremities (palms and soles included), rash scabs over in 1–2 weeks | Airborne and droplet exposure, contact with skin lesions<br>Client infectious until scabs separate (about 3 weeks) | Airborne, contact, and standard precautions place in private room with door closed, monitored negative air pressure, 6–12 air exchanges per hour<br>Decontaminate items contaminated by infectious lesions using contact precautions; single case is considered a public health emergency<br>If exposed, administer vaccination within 3 days of contact; vaccination does not give lifelong immunity |

*Note*: The plagues (bubonic and pneumonic) are included together.

Chapter 8

# HEALTH PROMOTION AND MAINTENANCE

| **Sections** | **Concepts Covered** |
|---|---|
| 1. Growth and Development | Development |
| 2. Childbearing—Normal | Reproductive, Client Education: Providing |
| 3. Childbearing—Maternal Complications | Fluid Volume, Coagulation, Metabolism, Perfusion, Client Education: Providing |
| 4. Childbearing—Neonatal Normal | Fluid and Electrolyte Balance, Gas Exchange |
| 5. Neonatal Complications | Gas Exchange, Immunity |
| 6. Reproduction | Reproduction, Sexuality, Client Education: Providing |
| 7. Prevention and Early Detection of Disease | Health Promotion, Client Education: Providing |

# GROWTH AND DEVELOPMENT

## ➤ HEALTH MAINTENANCE

**A.** Assessment

1.  Factors influencing growth and development

    a.  Genetic, hereditary, prenatal

    b.  Environmental

        1)  Family, cultural

        2)  Socioeconomic and culture

        3)  Living environment

    c.  Gender

    d.  Parental

    e.  Stress

    f.  Relationships and attachments

    g.  Physical, nutrition and emotional health (see Table 1)

2.  Expected stages of play development

    a.  Age characteristics

        1)  Exploratory–(holding toys: age 0–1 yr)

        2)  Toys as adult tools–(imitation: age 1–7 yr)

        3)  Games and hobbies (age 8–12 yr)

    b.  Social characteristics

        1)  Solitary play–alone, but enjoys presence of others, interest centered on own activity (infancy)

        2)  Parallel play–plays alongside, not with, another; characteristic of toddlers, but can occur in other age groups (toddler)

        3)  Associative play–no group goal; often follows a leader (preschool)

        4)  Cooperative play–organized, rules, leader/follower relationship established (school-age)

3.  Physical measurements compared with expected norms

    a.  Height

    b.  Weight

    c.  Head circumference

    d.  Chest circumference

4.  Screening tests

    a.  Denver II–evaluates children from birth to 6 years in 4 skill areas: personal–social, fine motor, language, gross motor

        1)  Age adjusted for prematurity by subtracting the number of months preterm

        2)  Questionable value in testing children of minority/ethnic groups

    b.  Stanford-Binet

    c.  I.Q. related to genetic potentialities and environment; intelligence tests used to determine I.Q.; mental age × 100 = I.Q./chronological age

| Table 1 OVERVIEW OF ERIKSON'S DEVELOPMENTAL TASKS THROUGHOUT THE LIFE SPAN | | | | |
|---|---|---|---|---|
| AGE | STAGE | ERIKSON'S TASK | POSITIVE OUTCOME | NEGATIVE OUTCOME |
| Birth to 1 year | Infancy | Trust vs. mistrust | Trusts self and others | Demonstrates an inability to trust; withdrawal, isolation |
| 1 year to 3 yrs | Toddler | Autonomy vs. shame and doubt | Exercises self-control and influences the environment directly | Demonstrates defiance and negativism |
| 3 to 6 yrs | Preschool | Initiative vs. guilt | Begins to evaluate own behavior; learns limits on influence in the environment | Demonstrates fearful, pessimistic behaviors; lacks self-confidence |
| 6 to 12 yrs | School-age | Industry vs. inferiority | Develops a sense of confidence; uses creative energies to influence the environment | Demonstrates feelings of inadequacy, mediocrity, and self-doubt |
| 12 to 20 yrs | Adolescence | Identity vs. role diffusion | Develops a coherent sense of self; plans for a future of work/education | Demonstrates inability to develop personal and vocational identity |
| 20 to 40 yrs | Young adulthood | Intimacy vs. isolation | Develops connections to work and intimate relationships | Demonstrates an avoidance of intimacy and vocational career commitments |
| 40 to 65 yrs | Middle adulthood | Generativity vs. stagnation | Involved with established family; expands personal creativity and productivity | Demonstrates lack of interests, commitments Preoccupation with self-centered concerns |
| 65+ yrs | Late adulthood | Integrity vs. despair | Identification of life as meaningful | Demonstrates fear of death; life lacks meaning |

B. Diagnose

1. Potential nursing diagnoses

   a. Knowledge deficit

   b. Decreased growth

   c. Decreased development

   d. Changes in growth and development pattern

2. Process—sequence is orderly and predictable; rate tends to be variable within (more quickly/slowly) and between (earlier/later) individuals

3. Growth—increase in size (height and weight); tends to be cyclical, more rapid *in utero*, during infancy, and adolescence

4. Development—maturation of physiological and psychosocial systems to more complex state

   a. Developmental tasks—skills and competencies associated with each developmental stage that have an effect on subsequent stages of development

   b. Developmental milestone—standard of reference to compare the child's behavior at specific ages

   c. Developmental delay(s)—variable of development that lags behind the range at a given age

5. Muscular coordination and control—proceeds in head-to-toe (cephalocaudal), trunk-to-periphery (proximodistal), gross-to-fine developmental pattern

**C.** Plan/Implementation

1. Establish a therapeutic relationship

2. Identify age-appropriate behavioral milestones

3. Educate caregivers on proper health care for children

   a. Health care provider visits, immunization schedules, childhood diseases

   b. Review diet and exercise patterns

4. Observe for alterations of parenting

   a. Behavior patterns of parents and child

   b. Identify healthy relationships and unhealthy relationships, e.g., failure to thrive, indications of child abuse

5. Observe and document screening

6. Promote socialization, activity, play

   a. Promote improved social skills and decreased social isolation

   b. Provide simple activities or tasks to promote self-esteem

7. Meet basic health and safety needs (hygienic, nutritional, rest and exercise)

8. Recognize spans and ranges of normalcy

**D.** Evaluation

1. Are all aspects of child's growth and development within normal limits for individual child?

2. Do parents have an understanding of child's developmental needs?

3. Have factors negatively impacting child's growth and development been eliminated or lessened?

# ▶ INFANCY—BIRTH TO 12 MONTHS

A. Assessment (see Table 2)

1. Physical growth and development (see Table 2)
2. Developmental milestones (see Table 2)
3. Attachment established during first year

B. Diagnose

1. Potential nursing diagnoses

   a. Injury, risk for
   b. Parenting, risk for altered

2. Potential problems in infancy

   a. Injury
   b. Failure to thrive
   c. Development delay

C. Plan/Implementation

1. Screen infants routinely for growth and development
2. Evaluate infant/parent relationships during feeding activities
3. Begin anticipatory guidance activities with parents
4. Select age-appropriate toys (see Table 2)
5. Introduce complementary foods

   a. Introduce only one food at a time for each two-week period
   b. Least allergenic foods are usually given in first half of the first year (iron-fortified rice cereal); more allergenic foods, (e.g., egg, orange juice) are offered in last half of first year; usual order: cereal, fruits, vegetables, potatoes, meat, egg, orange juice

6. Document age-appropriate social skills, social attachments, reaction to separation

   a. Phases of separation anxiety

      1) Protest—cries/screams for parents; inconsolable by others
      2) Despair—crying ends; less active; disinterested in food/play; clutches "security" object if available
      3) Denial—appears adjusted; evidences interest in environment; ignores parent when he/she returns; resigned, not contented

| Table 2 INFANT GROWTH AND DEVELOPMENT | |
|---|---|
| **1 MONTH** | **7 MONTH** |
| Head sags<br>Early crawling movements | Sits for short periods using hands for support<br>Grasps toy with hand (partially successful)<br>Fear of strangers begins to appear<br>Lability of mood (abrupt mood shifts) |
| **2 MONTH** | **8 MONTH** |
| Closing of posterior fontanelle<br>Diminished tonic neck and Moro reflexes<br>Able to turn from side to back<br>Eyes begin to follow a moving object<br>Social smile first appears | Anxiety with strangers |
| **3 MONTH** | **9 MONTH** |
| Can bring objects to mouth at will<br>Head held erect, steady<br>Binocular vision<br>Smiles in mother's presence Laughs audibly | Elevates self to sitting position<br>Rudimentary imitative expression<br>Responds to parental anger<br>Expressions like "dada" may be heard |
| **4 MONTH** | **10 MONTH** |
| Appearance of thumb apposition<br>Absent tonic neck reflex<br>Evidence of pleasure in social contact<br>Drooling<br>Moro reflex absent after 3–4 mo | Crawls well<br>Pulls self to standing position with support<br>Brings hands together<br>Vocalizes one or two words |
| **5 MONTH** | **11 MONTH** |
| Birth weight usually doubled<br>Takes objects presented to him/her | Erect standing posture with support |
| **6 MONTH** | **12 MONTH** |
| Average weight gain of 4 oz per week during second 6 mo<br>Teething may begin (lower central incisors)<br>Can turn from back to stomach<br>Early ability to distinguish and recognize strangers | Birth weight usually tripled<br>Needs help while walking<br>Sits from standing position without assistance<br>Eats with fingers<br>Usually says two words in addition to "mama" and "dada" |
| **AGE–APPROPRIATE TOYS** | |
| Birth to 2 months | Mobiles 8–10 inches from face |
| 2–4 mo | Rattles, cradle gym |
| 4–6 mo | Brightly colored toys (small enough to grasp, large enough for safety) |
| 6–9 mo | Large toys with bright colors, movable parts, and noisemakers |
| 9–12 mo | Books with large pictures, large push-pull toys, teddy bears |

**D.** Evaluation

1. Has infant's growth and development progressed within normal limits?

2. Is parent/infant relationship secure?

3. Do parents demonstrate increased knowledge about injury prevention?

## ▶ TODDLER—12 TO 36 MONTHS

**A.** Assessment (see Table 3)

1. Growth and development (see Table 3)

2. Begins to establish independence

**B.** Diagnose

1. Potential nursing diagnoses

   a. Injury, risk for

   b. Poisoning, risk for

   c. Nutrition: less than body requirements, altered

2. Potential problems in toddlerhood

   a. Negativism

   b. Safety, abuse

**C.** Plan/Implementation

1. Routine screening of toddler growth and development

2. Evaluate toddler, parent reactions to separation

3. Continue anticipatory guidance activities with parents

4. Reinforce the desirability of stable daily routines for play, feeding and rest

5. Select age-appropriate toys (see Table 3)

**D.** Evaluation

1. Has growth and development progressed within normal limits?

2. Do parents demonstrate knowledge of household hazards?

3. Have parents learned to cope with temperament?

| Table 3   TODDLER GROWTH AND DEVELOPMENT | |
|---|---|
| **15 MONTH** | **24 MONTH** |
| Walks alone | Early efforts at jumping |
| Builds 2-block tower | Builds 5- to 6-block tower |
| Throws objects | 300-word vocabulary |
| Grasps spoon | Obeys easy commands |
| Names commonplace objects | |
| **18 MONTH** | **30 MONTH** |
| Anterior fontanelle usually closed | Walks on tiptoe |
| Walks backward | Builds 7- to 8-block tower |
| Climbs stairs | Stands on one foot |
| Scribbles | Has sphincter control for toilet training |
| Builds 3-block tower | |
| Oral vocabulary—10 words | |
| Thumb sucking | |
| **AGE-APPROPRIATE TOYS** | |
| Push-pull toys | Dolls |
| Low rocking horses | Stuffed animals |

# PRESCHOOL—36 MONTHS TO 6 YEARS

**A.** Assessment (see Table 4)

1. Growth and development (see Table 4)

2. Psychosexual development begins

**B.** Diagnose

1. Potential nursing diagnoses

    a. Injury, risk for

    b. Grieving, dysfunctional

    c. Difficulty in group situations

2. Potential problems in preschool years

    a. Fear of injury, mutilation, and punishment

    b. Safety

**C.** Plan/Implementation

1. Screen school-aged children routinely for growth and development

2. Evaluate parent/child relationships

3. Continue anticipatory guidance activities with parents

4. Reinforce the desirability of stable daily routines for play, feeding, and rest

5. Reinforce the idea of parents as role models who allow their children to make age-appropriate decisions

6. Select age-appropriate toys (see Table 4)

| Table 4  PRESCHOOL GROWTH AND DEVELOPMENT | |
|---|---|
| **3 YEARS** | **5 YEARS** |
| Copies a circle | Runs well |
| Builds bridge with 3 cubes | Jumps rope |
| Less negativistic than toddler, decreased tantrums | Dresses without help |
| Learns from experience | 2,100-word vocabulary |
| Rides tricycle | Tolerates increasing periods of separation from parents |
| Walks backward and downstairs without assistance | Beginnings of cooperative play |
| Undresses without help | Gender-specific behavior |
| 900-word vocabulary, uses sentences | Skips on alternate feet |
| May invent "imaginary" friend | Ties shoes |
| **4 YEARS** | |
| Climbs and jumps well | |
| Laces shoes | |
| Brushes teeth | |
| 1,500-word vocabulary | |
| Skips and hops on one foot | |
| Throws overhead | |
| **AGE-APPROPRIATE TOYS AND ACTIVITIES** | |
| Child imitative of adult patterns and roles. Offer playground materials, housekeeping toys, coloring books, tricycles with helmet. | |

D. Evaluation

1. Have parents established the child's routines of play, feeding, and sleep?

2. Has child demonstrated coping skills regarding separations from parents?

3. Has child demonstrated day and night continence?

4. Does child have firm basis for development of positive body image?

# ▶ SCHOOL AGE—6 TO 12 YEARS

A. Assessment (see Table 5)

1. Growth and development (see Table 5)

2. Intense period of industry and productivity

3. Begins logical patterns of thought

4. Peer relationships important

5. Likes and dislikes established

| Table 5 SCHOOL-AGE GROWTH AND DEVELOPMENT | |
|---|---|
| **6 YEARS** | **9 YEARS** |
| Self-centered, show-off, rude | Skillful manual work possible |
| Extreme sensitivity to criticism | Conflicts between adult authorities and peer group |
| Begins losing temporary teeth | Better behaved |
| Appearance of first permanent teeth | Conflict between needs for independence and dependence |
| Ties knots | Likes school |
| **7 YEARS** | **10–12 YEARS** |
| Temporal perception improving | Remainder of teeth (except wisdom) erupt |
| Increased self-reliance for basic activities | Uses telephone |
| Team games/sports/organizations | Capable of helping |
| Develops concept of time | Increasingly responsible |
| Boys prefer playing with boys and girls with girls | More selective when choosing friends |
|  | Develops beginning of interest in opposite sex |
| **8 YEARS** | Loves conversation |
| Friends sought out actively | Raises pets |
| Eye development generally complete | |
| Movements more graceful | |
| Writing replaces printing | |
| **AGE-APPROPRIATE TOYS, GAMES, AND ACTIVITIES** | |
| Construction toys | Participation in repair, building, and mechanical activities, household chores |
| Use of tools, household and sewing tools, table games, sports | |

**B.** Diagnose

1. Potential nursing diagnoses

   a. Injury, risk for

   b. Grieving, dysfunctional

   c. Difficulty with social relationships, school

   d. Difficulty with body image, self-esteem, self-concept

2. Potential problems in school-age years

   a. Enuresis: bed-wetting

   b. Encopresis: incontinence of feces

   c. Safety: injuries, head lice are common

**C.** Plan/Implementation

1. Screen school-aged children routinely for growth and development

2. Evaluate parent/child relationships

3. Continue anticipatory guidance activities with parents

4. Reinforce the desirability of stable daily routines for play, feeding, and rest

5. Reinforce the idea of parents as role models who allow their children to make age-appropriate decisions

6. Select age-appropriate toys (see Table 5)

7. Encourage physical activity

**D.** Evaluation

1. Have parents and child coped with problems with urinary or bowel elimination?

2. Has child adjusted to challenges of school?

3. Have parents been educated regarding pubescent changes?

4. Has child successfully avoided injury?

## ▶ ADOLESCENCE—12 TO 20 YEARS

**A.** Assessment (see Table 6)

1. Growth and development (see Table 6)

2. Body image very important

3. Peer and social relationships very important

4. Identity/autonomy important

**B.** Diagnose

1. Potential nursing diagnoses

a. Injury, risk for

b. Self-esteem disturbance

c. Health maintenance, altered

2. Potential problems in adolescence

a. Adolescent pregnancy

b. Poor self-image

c. Safety

d. Drug and alcohol misuse/abuse

e. AIDS

f. High school dropout

g. Violence

| Table 6 ADOLESCENT GROWTH AND DEVELOPMENT | |
|---|---|
| **PHYSICAL DEVELOPMENT—PUBERTY** | **FEMALE CHANGES** |
| Attainment of sexual maturity | Increase in pelvic diameter |
| Rapid alterations in height and weight | Breast development |
| Girls develop more rapidly than boys | Altered nature of vaginal secretions |
| Onset may be related to hypothalmic activity, which influences pituitary gland to secrete hormones affecting testes and ovaries | Appearance of axillary and pubic hair |
| | Menarche—first menstrual period |
| Testes and ovaries produce hormones (androgens and estrogens) that determine development of secondary sexual characteristics | **PHYSICAL DEVELOPMENT—ADOLESCENT** |
| | More complete development of secondary sexual characteristics |
| Pimples or acne related to increased sebaceous gland activity | Improved motor coordination |
| | Wisdom teeth appear (ages 17–21) |
| Increased sweat production | **PSYCHOSEXUAL DEVELOPMENT** |
| Weight gain proportionally greater than height gain during early stages | Masturbation as expression of sexual tension |
| | Sexual fantasies |
| Initial problems in coordination—appearance of clumsiness related to rapid, unsynchronized growth of many systems | Experimental sexual intercourse |
| | **PSYCHOSOCIAL DEVELOPMENT** |
| Rapid growth may cause easy fatigue | Preoccupied with rapid body changes, what is "normal" |
| Preoccupation with physical appearance | Conformity to peer pressure |
| **MALE CHANGES** | Moody |
| Increase in genital size | Increased daydreaming |
| Breast swelling | Increased independence |
| Appearance of pubic, facial, axillary, and chest hair | Moving toward a mature sexual identity |
| Deepening voice | |
| Production of functional sperm | |
| Nocturnal emissions | |

**C.** Plan/Implementation

1. Screen the adolescent routinely for growth and development

2. Evaluate parent/child/peer relationships

3. Continue anticipatory guidance activities with parents and adolescents

4. Reinforce the desirability of stable daily routines for work and rest

5. Continue to reinforce the idea of parents and significant others as role models who allow their children to make age-appropriate decisions

6. Counsel adolescent to delay impulsive actions with long-term consequences (e.g., adolescent pregnancy, drug and alcohol misuse, AIDS, high school dropout), and the use of problem-solving skills

7. Encourage the development of educational/vocational options

8. Promote appropriate, safe approaches to resolve conflicts with peers and adults

**D.** Evaluation

1. Has parents' understanding/perception of adolescent's developmental needs increased?

2. Does adolescent have a larger repertoire of adaptive coping mechanisms?

3. Does adolescent/parent identify and use coping mechanisms?

4. Is adolescent comfortable with body image?

5. Do adolescent and parents recognize risks involved with motor vehicles, alcohol, etc.?

6. Does adolescent have social peer groups?

## ▶ 20 TO 40 YEARS

A. Assessment (see Table 7)

1. Growth and development (see Table 7)

2. Work, career important

3. Establishes intimacy

B. Diagnose—potential nursing diagnoses

1. Altered health maintenance

2. Altered self-esteem

3. Difficulty with relationships

4. Potential for increased stress

C. Plan/Implementation

1. Meet physical and mental health needs

2. Evaluate relationships, especially with chosen partner

3. Observe responses to stress

4. Anticipatory guidance

D. Evaluation

1. Have client's physical and emotional needs been met?

2. Has client coped, adapted to stressors?

3. Is client committed to relationships and career?

4. Is client knowledgeable about aging process?

5. Is client satisfied with life at this point?

| Table 7 ADULTHOOD GROWTH AND DEVELOPMENT | | |
|---|---|---|
| **20 TO 33 YEARS** | **33 TO 40 YEARS** | **35 TO 40 YEARS** |
| Decreased hero worship | Period of discovery, rediscovery of interests and goals | (There in some overlap in years) |
| Increased reality | Increased sense of urgency | Self-questioning |
| Independent from parents | Life more serious | Fear of middle age and aging |
| Possible marriage, partnership | Major goals to accomplish | Reappraises the past |
| Realization that everything is not black or white, some "gray" areas | Plateaus at work and marriage, partnership | Discards unrealistic goals |
| Looks towards future, hopes for success | Sense of satisfaction | Potential changes of work, marriage, partnership "Sandwich" generation—concerned with children and aging parents |
| Peak intelligence, memory | | Increased awareness of mortality |
| Maximum problem-solving ability | | Potential loss of significant others |

## 40 TO 65 YEARS

**A.** Assessment (see Table 8)

   1. Physical functioning (see Table 8)

   2. Cognitive functioning (see Table 8)

   3. Relationships change

   4. Work, career important

**B.** Diagnose—potential nursing diagnoses

   1. Decreased cognitive and physical functioning

   2. Altered family

   3. Self-care deficit

   4. Altered body image

**C.** Plan/Implementation

   1. Help client adjust to changes of aging

   2. Help client adjust to changing roles

   3. Anticipatory guidance

**D.** Evaluation

   1. Does client have realistic self-expectations?

   2. Is client adapting and accepting limits?

   3. Have the client's physical and psychosocial needs been met?

| Table 8   MIDDLE ADULTHOOD GROWTH AND DEVELOPMENT | | |
| --- | --- | --- |
| **40 TO 55 YEARS** | **48 TO 60 YEARS** | **50 TO 65 YEARS** |
| Graying hair, wrinkling skin | Evaluates past | Increasing physical decline |
| Pains and muscle aches | Sets new goals | Increasingly forgetful |
| Realization—future shorter time span than past | Defines value of life, self | Accepts limitations |
| Menopause | Assesss legacies—professional, personal | Modification of lifestyle |
| Decreased sensory acuity | Serenity and fulfillment | Decreased power Retirement |
| Powerful, policy makers, leaders | Balance between old and young | Less restricted time, able to choose different activities |
| Relates to older and younger generations | Accepts changes of aging | |

## 65 AND ABOVE

**A.** Assessment (see Table 9)

   1. Physical and cognitive functioning (see Table 9)

   2. Significant relationships change

   3. Activities may be limited

   4. Decreased sense of taste and smell

   5. Financial constraints

**B.** Diagnose

   1. Self-care deficit

   2. Isolation

   3. Altered relationships

4. Decreased independence

5. Family processes, altered

C. Plan/Implementation

1. Assist clients with adjusting to lifestyle changes

2. Allow client to verbalize concerns

3. Prevent isolation

4. Provide assistance as required

D. Evaluation

1. Has client successfully adjusted to decreased abilities and increased dependence?

2. Is client involved in activities for physical and mental stimulation?

3. Is the client in a safe environment?

4. Does client see life as meaningful?

| Table 9  ADULTHOOD GROWTH AND DEVELOPMENT ||
| --- | --- |
| **65 TO 80 YEARS** | **GREATER THAN 80 YEARS** |
| Physical decline | Signs of aging very evident |
| Loss of significant others | Few significant relationships |
| Appraisal of life | Withdrawal, risk of isolation |
| Appearance of chronic diseases | Self-concern |
| Reconciliation of goals and achievements | Accepting of death, face mortality |
| Changing social roles | Increased losses |
|  | Decreased abilities |

## ▶ INTELLECTUAL DELAY

A. Assessment

1. Sensory deficits (see Table 10)

2. Physical anomalies

3. Delayed growth and development

B. Diagnose: Sub-average intellectual function (I.Q. less than 70) with concurrent impairment in adaptive functioning; onset under the age of 18

1. Characteristics

a. Lack of, or destruction of, brain cells

2. Causes

a. Heredity

b. Infection

c. Fetal anoxia

d. Cranial or chromosomal abnormalities

e. Intracranial hemorrhage

C. Plan/Implementation

1. Assist parents with adjustment

2. Provide sensory stimulation

| | Table 10 INTELLECTUAL DELAY | | | |
|---|---|---|---|---|
| CLASSIFICATION | I.Q. RANGE | PRESCHOOL GROWTH AND DEVELOPMENT | SCHOOL TRAINING AND EDUCATION | ADULT SOCIAL/ VOCATIONAL LEVEL |
| I. Mild | 55–70 | Slow to walk, feed self, and talk compared with other children | With special education, can learn reading and math skills for third-to-sixth grade level | Can achieve social/ vocational self-maintenance<br><br>May need occasional psychosocial support |
| II. Moderate | 40–55 | Delays in motor development<br><br>Can do some self-help activities | Responds to training<br><br>Does not progress with reading or math skills<br><br>Poor communication skills | Sheltered, usually incapable of self-maintenance |
| III. Severe | 25–40 | Marked delay in development<br><br>May be able to help self minimally | Can profit from habit training<br><br>Has some understanding of speech | Dependent on others for care<br><br>Can conform to routine |
| IV. Profound | Under 25 | Significant delay, minimal-capacity functioning | May respond to skill training<br><br>Shows basic emotional responses | Incapable of self-maintenance, needs nursing care |

   3. Encourage socially acceptable behavior

   4. Provide emotional support

**D.** Evaluation

   1. Have parents adjusted to disabilities of child?

   2. Has child obtained optimal functioning?

# ▶ FETAL ALCOHOL SYNDROME

**A.** Assessment

   1. Thin upper lip, epicanthal folds, maxillary hypoplasia

   2. Intellectual deficiencies, motor deficiencies, microcephaly, and hearing disorders

   3. Irritability during infancy and hyperactivity during childhood

   4. Small for gestational age

**B.** Diagnose

   1. Leading cause of intellectual delay

   2. Caused by excessive alcohol ingestion during pregnancy

   3. Preventable if mother avoids alcohol during pregnancy

**C.** Plan/Implementation

   1. Prevention

      a. Instruct women to stop consuming alcohol 3 months before conception

      b. There is no safe level of alcohol consumption during pregnancy

2. At birth

    a. Swaddle infant and decrease environmental stimuli

    b. Administer sedatives to decrease symptoms of withdrawal

3. Monitor infant's weight gain

4. Promote nutritional intake

**D.** Evaluation

1. Has the mother stopped drinking?

2. Has child achieved optimal functioning?

## ▶ DOWN SYNDROME

**A.** Assessment

1. Intellectual delay—I.Q. range from 20 to 70

2. Marked hypotonia; short stature

3. Altered physical development—epicanthal folds, low-set ears, protruding tongue, low nasal bridge

**B.** Diagnose

1. Characteristics

    a. Chromosomal abnormality involving an extra chromosome (number 21)

2. Causes

    a. Unknown

    b. Associated with maternal age greater than 35

**C.** Plan/Implementation

1. Provide stimulation—OT, PT, special education

2. Observe for signs of common physical problems: 30–40% have heart diseases; 80% have hearing loss; respiratory infections are common

3. Establish and maintain adequate nutrition, parental education, and support

**D.** Evaluation

1. Has child achieved optimal functioning?

2. Have parents adjusted to child's disability?

## ▶ LEARNING DISABILITIES

**A.** Assessment

1. Hyperkinesis (sometimes absent)

2. Decreased attention span, i.e., attention deficit disorder (ADD)

3. Perceptual deficits

4. Aggression/depression

**B.** Diagnose

    1. Characteristics

        a. Learning and behavioral disorders that occur because of CNS malfunctioning

        b. Neuropsychological testing—reveals individual differences

        c. Average to high I.Q.

**C.** Plan/Implementation

    1. Reduce frustration

    2. Special educational intervention; small class size

    3. Provide safety and security

    4. Administer medications, e.g., Ritalin, Dexedrine

    5. Refer to appropriate resources—special education, parent support groups

**D.** Evaluation

    1. Is child developing to his/her greatest potential?

    2. Have referrals been made to appropriate resources?

     c. Fundal height—measurement of fundal height from the top of symphysis pubis to the top of the fundus with a flexible, nonstretchable tape measure, used as a gross estimate of dates

       1) Above the level of symphysis—between 12 and 14 weeks

       2) At the umbilicus or 20 cm—about 20 weeks

       3) Rises about 1 cm/week until 36 weeks, after which it varies

2. Obstetric classification

     a. Gravida—the total number of pregnancies regardless of duration (includes present pregnancy); nulligravida—woman who has never been pregnant

     b. Para—number of past pregnancies that have gone beyond the period of viability (capability of the fetus to survive outside of the uterus—after 20 weeks gestation or greater than 500 g) regardless of the number of fetuses (eg twins) or whether the infant was born alive or dead

     c. Term—born from beginning of 38 to end of 42 week

     d. Abortion—any pregnancy that terminates before the period of viability

3. Characteristic findings

     a. Uterus—increases in size, at 12–14 weeks, above symphysis pubis

     b. Cervix—softens, mucus plug in canal, bluish color (Chadwick's sign)

     c. Abdomen—stretches, striae

     d. Breasts—enlarged, tender

     e. Blood volume—increases 30% and peaks at 28 weeks

     f. Cardiac output—increased by 750 ml/min

     g. Ventilation—decreased tidal volume in third trimester

     h. Digestion—decreased peristalsis and increased pressure

     i. Skin

       1) Pink or reddish streaks (striae gravidarum) on breasts, abdomen, buttocks, and/or thighs; result of fat deposits causing stretching of the skin

       2) Increased pigmentation on the face; blotchy brown areas on the forehead and cheeks (chloasma or "mask of pregnancy"); on the abdomen, dark line from the umbilicus to the symphysis pubis (linea nigra)

       3) Minute vascular spiders

       4) Umbilicus is pushed outward and by the seventh month, depression disappears, becomes a darkened area on the abdominal wall

       5) Sweat and sebaceous glands more active

     j. Urinary—frequency and stasis result from pressure

     k. Endocrine

       1) Placenta—produces estrogen, progesterone, human chorionic gonadotrophin (hCG), human placental lactogen (hPL)

       2) Pituitary—elevated estrogen and progesterone, suppressed LH, FSH, and oxytocin

3) Weight gain—steady, consistent is ideal; based on pre-pregnancy BMI

   a) BMI less than 18.5; total weight gain range 28–40 lb

   b) BMI 18.5–24.9; total weight gain range 25–35 lb

   c) BMI 25–29.9; total weight gain 15–25 lb

   d) BMI greater than 30; weight gain total 11–20 lb

4. Diagnostic test—hCG is measured by radioimmunoassay in blood and urine; serum more sensitive, so results are more accurate and available earlier

5. Verifying pregnancy

   a. Presumptive—changes felt by woman: amenorrhea, nausea/vomiting ("morning sickness"), breast sensitivity, fatigue, quickening (maternal perception of fetal movement occurring between 16 and 20 weeks of gestation), urinary frequency

   b. Probable—changes observed by examiner: uterine enlargement, soufflé and contractions, positive urine pregnancy tests, Hegar's sign (softening and compressibility of isthmus of uterus), Chadwick's sign (bluish color of cervix)

   c. Positive—definite signs of pregnancy: fetal heartbeat (8–12 weeks by Doptone and by 18–20 weeks auscultation), palpation of fetal movement, visualization of fetus by ultrasound

6. Fetal assessment

   a. Fetal heart rate (FHR)—a significant predictor of fetal well-being; at term 120–160 beats/min

   b. Fetal movement (FM)—a regular pattern of 10 movements in one hour twice a day is a good indicator of fetal well-being; fewer than three movements in a one-hour period should be reported

**B.** Diagnose

1. Potential nursing diagnoses

   a. Deficient knowledge

   b. Risk for ineffective role performance

   c. Risk for imbalanced nutrition: less than body requirements

   d. Risk for fetal injury

2. Fertilization—union of ovum and spermatozoa, occurs about 24 hours after ovulation; usually outer third of fallopian tube

3. Implantation

   a. Upper part of uterus

   b. About one week after fertilization

4. Early placental development

   a. Combination of endometrium and fetal chorionic layer (maternal and embryonic parts)

   b. Chorion produces human chorionic gonadotrophin (hCG)

   c. Transmits nutrients from maternal bloodstream by a number of mechanisms

    d. Transfer of oxygen from mother to fetus by diffusion

    e. Removes waste products of fetal metabolism into mother's bloodstream from which they will be excreted

**C.** Plan/Implementation

    1. Encourage prenatal care

    2. Manage discomforts of pregnancy (see Table 1)

**D.** Evaluation

    1. Have woman's physical needs been met?

    2. Is client knowledgeable about her pregnancy?

| Table 1  DISCOMFORTS OF PREGNANCY | |
| --- | --- |
| **ASSESSMENT** | **NURSING CONSIDERATIONS** |
| Nausea and vomiting (morning sickness) | May occur any time of day<br>Dry crackers on arising<br>Eat small, frequent meals<br>Avoid strong odors and greasy foods |
| Constipation, hemorrhoids | Bulk foods, fiber, stool softeners<br>Generous fluid intake<br>Encourage regularity, routine |
| Leg cramps | Increase calcium intake<br>Dorsiflex feet, local heat |
| Breast soreness | Well-fitting bra<br>Bra may be worn at night |
| Backache | Emphasize posture and good body mechanics<br>Careful lifting<br>Good shoes<br>Pelvic tilt exercises |
| Heartburn | Small frequent meals<br>Antacids—avoid those containing phosphorus<br>Decrease fatty and fried foods<br>Avoid supine position after meals |
| Dizziness | Slow, deliberate movements<br>Support stockings<br>Monitor intake |
| Vertigo, lightheadedness | Vena cava or maternal hypotensive syndrome<br>Turn on left side |
| Urinary frequency | Kegel exercises<br>Decrease fluids before bed<br>Report signs of infection |

# FETAL DEVELOPMENT

**A.** Assessment

1. Maternal considerations

   a. High-risk group

   b. Environment

   c. Medications, drugs, alcohol

   d. Nutrition–should be no attempt at weight reduction

   e. Age

2. Genetic considerations

   a. African Americans for sickle-cell disease, Northern European descendants of Ashkenazi Jews for Tay-Sachs disease,Mediterranean ancestry for thalassemia; couples with a history of a child with a defect; family history of a structural abnormality orsystemic disease that may be hereditary; closely related parents; women over 40

   b. Chromosomal alteration—may be numeric or structural

      1) Down's syndrome (trisomy 21)—increased in women over 35 years; characterized by a small, round head with flattened occiput, low-set ears, large fat pads at the nape of a short neck, protruding tongue, small mouth and high palate, epicanthal folds with slanted eyes, hypotonic muscles with hypermobility of joints, short, broad hands with inward curved little finger, transverse simian palmar crease, mental deficiencies

      2) Turner's syndrome (female with only one X)—characterized by stunted growth, fibrous streaks in ovaries, usually infertile, no intellectual impairment, occasionally perceptual problems

      3) Klinefelter's syndrome (male with extra X)—normal intelligence to mild intellectual delay, usually infertile

   c. Autosomal defects—defects occurring in any chromosome pair other than the sex chromosomes

      1) Autosomal dominant—union of normal parent with affected parent gene; the affected parent has a 50% chance of passing on the abnormal gene in each pregnancy; BRCA-1 and BRCA-2 breast cancer, Type 2 diabetes, Marfan syndrome, polycystic kidney disease

      2) Autosomal recessive—requires transmission of abnormal gene from both parents for expression of condition; cystic fibrosis, sickle cell disease

      3) Sex-linked transmission traits—trait carried on a sex chromosome (usually the X chromosome); may be dominant or recessive, but recessive is more prevalent; e.g., hemophilia, color blindness

d. Inborn errors of metabolism—disorders of protein, fat, or carbohydrate metabolism due to absent or defective enzymes that generally follow a recessive pattern of inheritance

1) Phenylketonuria (PKU)—disorder due to autosomal recessive gene creating a deficiency in the liver enzyme phenylalanine hydroxylase, which metabolizes the amino acid phenylalanine; results in metabolites accumulation in the blood; toxic to brain cells

2) Tay-Sachs disease—autosomal recessive trait resulting from a deficiency of hexosaminidase A, resulting in apathy and regression in motor and social development and decreased vision

3) Cystic fibrosis (mucoviscidosis or fibrocystic disease of the pancreas)—an autosomal recessive trait characterized by generalized involvement of exocrine glands, resulting in altered viscosity of mucus-secreting glands throughout the body

3. Diagnostic tests

a. Alpha-fetal protein (AFP) test—fetal serum protein to predict neural tube defects, threatened abortion, fetal distress; decreased AFP levels suggest possible Down syndrome

1) Done between 16 and 18 weeks

2) High incidence of false-positive results (delivered normal neonates)

3) Usual concurrent test for presence of acetylcholinesterase

b. Chorionic villus sampling (CVS)—early antepartal test to diagnose fetal karyotype, sickle-cell anemia, PKU, Down syndrome, Duchenne muscular dystrophy

1) Done between 8 and 12 weeks

2) Complications include bleeding, spontaneous abortion, rupture of membranes

3) Rh-negative mother should receive Rho(D) immune globulin (IGIM) after test to prevent Rh isoimmunization

4) Ultrasound used to guide; sample of fetal placental tissue

5) Full bladder required

c. Amniocentesis—amniotic fluid is aspirated by a needle inserted through the abdominal and uterine walls

1) Done at 16 weeks to detect genetic disorder; possible after 14 weeks gestation

2) Done at 30 weeks to assess L/S ratio (lecithin/sphingomyelin) to determine lung maturity

3) Prior to the procedure, the client's bladder should be emptied if greater than 20 weeks gestation; ultrasonography (x-ray only if necessary) is used to avoid trauma from the needle to the placenta, fetus

4) Test results take 2 to 4 weeks

     5) Complications include premature labor, infection, Rh isoimmunization, abruptio placentae, amniotic embolism; Rh-negative mother should receive Rho(D) immune globulin (IGIM) after procedure

     6) Monitor fetus electronically after procedure, monitor for uterine contractions

     7) Teach client to report decreased fetal movement, contractions, abdominal discomfort, fluid loss, or fever after procedure

  d. Ultrasound—transducer on abdomen transmits sound waves that show fetal image on screen

     1) As early as five weeks to confirm pregnancy, gestational age

     2) Multiple purposes—to determine position, number, measurement of fetus(es) and other structures (placenta)

     3) Client must drink fluid prior to test to have full bladder to assist in clarity of image

     4) No known harmful effects for fetus or mother

     5) Noninvasive

  e. Non-stress test (NST)—ultrasound transducer records fetal movements, and Doppler ultrasound measures fetal heart rate to assess fetal well-being after 28 weeks

     1) Client should eat snacks

     2) A reactive non-stress test (good finding) is two or more FHR accelerations of 15 bpm lasting 15 seconds over a 20-minute interval, and return of FHR to normal baseline

  f. Contraction stress test (CST), either nipple stimulation or oxytocin stimulation—evaluates fetal response to stress of labor

     1) Performed after 28 weeks

     2) Woman in semi-Fowler's or side-lying position

     3) Positive contraction-stress; decelerations with at least 50% of contractions; potential risk to fetus, cesarean may be necessary

     4) Negative contraction stress test—no late decelerations with a minimum of three contractions lasting 40–60 seconds in 10-minute period

     5) Monitor for post-test labor onset

  g. Estriol levels—serial 24-hour maternal urine samples or serum specimens to determine fetoplacental status; decreasing levels usually indicate deterioration

**B.** Diagnose—potential nursing diagnoses

  1. Knowledge deficits

  2. Lack of prenatal care

**C.** Plan/Implementation

1. Teach optimal nutrition and exercise

2. Advise avoidance of hazards

   a. Urinary tract infections (UTI)—lower tract characterized by urinary frequency and urgency, dysuria, and sometimes hematuria; manifested in upper tract by fever, malaise, anorexia, nausea, abdominal/back pain; confirmed by greater than 100,000/ml bacterial colony count by clean catch urine; sometimes asymptomatic; treated with sulfa-based medications and ampicillin

   b. TORCH test series—group of maternal systemic infections that can be transmitted across the placenta or by ascending infection (after rupture of membranes [ROM]) to the fetus; infection early in pregnancy may produce significant and devastating fetal deformities, whereas later infection may result in overwhelming active systemic disease and/or CNS involvement causing severe neurological impairment or death of newborn

      1) Toxoplasmosis (protozoa; transplacental to fetus)—discourage eating undercooked meat and handling cat litter box

      2) Other

         a) Syphilis

         b) Varicella/shingles (transplacental to fetus or droplet to newborn)—caution susceptible woman about contact with the disease and zoster immune globulin for exposure

         c) Group B beta-hemolytic streptococcus (direct or indirect to fetus during labor and delivery)—treated with penicillin

         d) Hepatitis B (transplacental and contact with secretions during delivery)—screen and immunize maternal carriers; treat newborn with HBIg

         e) Hepatitis A—need to encourage good handwashing techniques

         f) AIDS (as with hepatitis)—titers in newborn may be passive transfer of maternal antibodies or active antibody formation

      3) Rubella (transplacental)—prenatal testing required by law; caution susceptible woman about contact; vaccine is not given during pregnancy

      4) Cytomegalovirus (CMV)—transmitted in body fluids; detected by antibody/serological testing

      5) Herpes 2 (transplacental, ascending infection within 4–6 hours after ROM or contact during delivery if active lesions)—cesarean delivery if active lesions

3. Teach/prepare for procedures

4. Teach danger signs of pregnancy

   a. Gush of fluid or bleeding from vagina

   b. Regular uterine contractions

   c. Severe headaches, visual disturbances, abdominal pain, or persistent vomiting

   d. Fever or chills

e. Swelling in face and fingers

f. Decrease in fetal movement

5. Teach client to report decrease in fetal movement

**D.** Evaluation

1. Has client remained free of complications and is fetus in stable condition?

2. Does client have sufficient knowledge of pregnancy and childbirth?

# LABOR AND DELIVERY

**A.** Assessment

1. Characteristic findings

a. Onset

1) Lightening—subjective sensation as fetus descends into pelvic inlet

a) Primipara (occurs up to two weeks prior to delivery)

b) Multipara (may not occur until labor begins)

2) Softening of cervix

3) Expulsion of mucus plug (show)

4) Uterine contractions that are progressive and regular

b. Cervical changes

1) Effacement—progressive thinning and shortening of cervix (0–100%)

2) Dilation—opening of cervix os during labor (0–10 cm)

c. Rupture of membranes—rupture of amniotic sac (ROM)

1) Check fetal heart tones to assess for fetal distress

2) Prolapsed cord

a) Symptoms—premature rupture of membranes, presenting part not engaged, fetal distress, protruding cord

b) Nursing care—call for help, push against presenting part to relieve pressure on cord, place in Trendelenburg or knee- chest position

c) Treatment successful—fetal heart tones remain unchanged

2. Fetal monitoring

a. Intermittent auscultation

b. Electronic monitoring

1) External—ultrasound over fetal back monitors, FHR and a pressure transducer monitors uterine tone

a) Transabdominal, noninvasive

b) Client needs to decrease extra-abdominal movements

2) Internal—fetal scalp probe provides FHR, and an internal transducer provides intra-uterine pressure readings

a) Membranes must be ruptured, cervix sufficiently dilated, and presenting part low

b) Invasive procedure

    c. Results of monitoring

       1) Normal FHR 120–160; must obtain a baseline

3. Tachycardia (greater than 160 bpm lasting longer than 10 minutes)—early sign of fetal hypoxia, associated with maternal fever, fetal anemia, fetal or maternal infection, drugs (atropine, vistaril), maternal hyperthyroidism, fetal heart failure; nonreassuring sign when associated with late decelerations, severe variable decelerations, or absence of variability

4. Bradycardia (less than 110 bpm lasting longer than 10 minutes)—late sign of fetal hypoxia, associated with maternal drugs (anesthetics), prolonged cord compression, fetal congenital heart block, maternal supine hypotensive syndrome; nonreassuring sign when associated with loss of variability and late decelerations

5. Variability—beat to beat fluctuation; measured by EFM only

    a. Normal (6–25 bpm)–indicator of fetal well-being

    b. Absent (0–2 bpm) or decreased (3–5 bpm) may be associated with fetal sleep state, fetal prematurity, reaction to drugs (narcotics, barbiturates, tranquilizers, anesthetics), congenital anomalies, hypoxia, acidosis; if persists for more than 30 minutes, may indicate fetal distress

    c. Increased (greater than 25 bpm)–significance unknown

6. Accelerations—15 bpm rise above baseline followed by a return; usually in response to fetal movement or contractions; indicates fetal well-being

7. Decelerations—fall below baseline lasting 15 seconds or more, followed by a return to baseline

    a. Early: onset close to the beginning or before peak of contraction; most often uniform mirror image of contraction on tracing; associated with head compression, in second stage with pushing; reassuring pattern

    b. Late: onset after contraction is established; usually begins at the peak of the contraction, with slow return to baseline after the contraction is complete; indicative of fetal hypoxia because of deficient placental perfusion; caused by PIH, maternal diabetes, placenta previa, abruption placentae; nonreasurring sign

    c. Variable decelerations—transient U/V-shaped reduction occurring at any time during uterine contracting phase; decrease usually more than 15 bpm, lasting 15 seconds, return to baseline in less than 2 minutes from onset, indicative of cord compression, which may be relieved by change in mother's position; ominous if repetitive, prolonged, severe, or slow return to baseline, administer $O_2$, discontinue oxytocin

    d. Nursing interventions for abnormal results

       1) None for early decelerations

       2) For late decelerations (at the first sign of abnormal tracing)—position mother left side-lying (if no change, move to other side, Trendelenburg or knee-chest position); administer oxygen by mask, start IV or increase flow rate, stop oxytocin if appropriate, prepare for C-section

     3) For variable decelerations—reposition mother to relieve pressure on the umbilical cord

8. Factors affecting labor and delivery

   a. Lie—relationship of spine of fetus to spine of mother; longitudinal (parallel), transverse (right angles), oblique (slight angle off a true transverse lie)

   b. Presentation—part of fetus that presents to (enters) maternal pelvic inlet

     1) Cephalic/vertex—head (95% of labors)

     2) Breech/buttocks (3–4%)

        a) Frank (most common)—flexion of hips and extension of knees

        b) Complete—flexion of hips and knees

        c) Footing/incomplete—extension of hips and knees

     3) Shoulder (transverse lie)—rare

   c. Attitude—relationship of fetal parts to each other; usually flexion of head and extremities on chest and abdomen to accommodate to shape of uterine cavity

   d. Position—relationship of fetal reference point to maternal pelvis (see Figure 1); to find best location for FHR assessment, determine the location of the fetal back; weeks of gestation may alter the location, as well

     1) Fetal reference point

        a) Vertex presentation—dependent upon degree of flexion of fetal head on chest; full flexion—occiput (O); full extension—chin (M); moderate extension (military)—brow (B)

        b) Breech presentation—sacrum (S)

        c) Shoulder presentation—scapula (SC)

     2) Maternal pelvis is designated per her right/left and anterior/posterior

     3) Expressed as standard three-letter abbreviation; e.g., LOA = left occiput anterior, indicating vertex presentation with fetal occiput on mother's left side toward the front of her pelvis (see Figure 1). To find best location for FHR assessment, determine the location of the fetal back. Weeks of gestation may alter the location, as well

        a) LOA—left occiput anterior, most common; FHR best heard below umbilicus on mother's left side

        b) LOP—left occiput posterior

        c) ROA—right occiput anterior

        d) ROP—right occiput posterior

        e) LSA—left sacrum anterior

        f) RSA—right sacrum anterior

     4) Configuration and diameter of pelvis

     5) Distensibility of uterus

**Figure 1  Determining Position**

e.  Station—level of presenting part of fetus in relation to imaginary line between ischial spines (zero station) in midpelvis of mother (see Figure 2)

1)  −5 to −1 indicates a presenting part above zero station (floating); +1 to +5, a presenting part below zero station

2)  Engagement—when the presenting part is at station zero or below

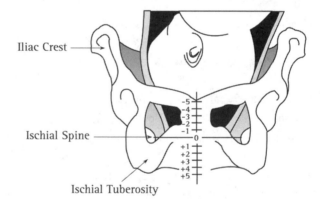

**Figure 2  Station of Presenting Part**

f.  Contractions

1)  Three phases

a)  Increment—steep crescent slope from beginning of the contraction until its peak

b)  Acme/peak—strongest intensity

c)  Decrement—diminishing intensity

    2) Characteristics of contractions

        a) Frequency: time frame in minutes from the beginning of one contraction to the beginning of the next one or the peak of one contraction to the peak of the next; frequency less than every two minutes should be reported

        b) Duration: time frame in seconds from the beginning of a contraction to its completion; more than 90 seconds should be reported because of potential risk of uterine rupture or fetal distress

        c) Intensity: the strength of a contraction at acme; may be assessed by subjective description from the woman, palpation (mild contraction—slightly tense uterus easy to indent with fingertips; moderate—firm fundus difficult to indent with fingertips; strong—rigid, board-like fundus)

  g. True vs. false labor (see Table 2)

| Table 2  TRUE VS. FALSE LABOR | |
| --- | --- |
| **TRUE** | **FALSE** |
| Cervix progressively effaced and dilated | Cervical changes do not occur |
| Contractions—regular with increasing frequency (shortened intervals), duration, and intensity | Contractions—irregular with usually no change in frequency, duration, or intensity |
| Discomfort radiates from back around the abdomen | Discomfort is usually abdominal |
| Contractions do not decrease with rest | Contractions may lessen with activity or rest |

  h. Stages of labor

    1) Stage 1—beginning to complete cervical dilation (0–10 cm)

    2) Stage 2—complete dilation to birth of baby

    3) Stage 3—birth to delivery of placenta

    4) Stage 4—first 4 hours after delivery of placenta

  i. Cultural influences

  j. *Not all members of a culture will choose actions below.*

    1) Japan—natural childbirth, may labor silently

    2) China—stoic response to pain, side-lying position for labor and birth

    3) India—female relatives present

    4) Laos—may use squatting position for birth

  k. Participation in childbirth preparation classes

**B.** Diagnose—potential nursing diagnoses

  1. Potential knowledge deficits

  2. Difficulty adapting and coping with stress

  3. Risk of complications

  4. Need for pain management

  5. Labor may not progress

**C.** Plan/Implementation

1. Monitor progress—maternal

   a. First stage of labor: beginning of labor to complete cervical dilation

      1) Phase one (latent): 0–3 cm; contractions 10–30 sec long, 5–30 min apart; mild to moderate

      2) Phase two (active): 4–7 cm; contractions 40–60 sec long, 3–5 min apart; moderate to strong

      3) Phase three (transition): 8–10 cm; contractions 45–90 sec long, 1½–2 min apart; strong

   b. Second stage of labor: complete cervical dilation to delivery of fetus

      1) Phase 1: 0 to +2 station; contractions 2–3 min apart

      2) Phase 2: +2 to +4 station; contractions 2–2.5 min apart; increase in dark red bloody show; increased urgency to bear down

      3) Phase 3: +4 to birth; contractions 1–2 min apart; fetal head visible; increased urgency to bear down

   c. Third stage of labor: birth and delivery of placenta

      1) Placental delivery—slight gush of blood and lengthening of umbilical cord; check for remaining fragments

   d. Fourth stage of labor: first 4 hours after delivery

2. Monitor progress—fetal

   a. During labor check FHR

   b. Manage fetal distress (see Table 3)

| Table 3   MANAGEMENT OF FETAL DISTRESS | |
| --- | --- |
| ASSESSMENT | NURSING CONSIDERATIONS |
| Irregular fetal heartbeat | Turn client onto left side<br>Give supplemental oxygen<br>Check for cord prolapse<br>Start intravenous line |
| Umbilical cord prolapse | Elevate presenting part off the cord<br>Call for help<br>Place client in Trendelenburg or knee-chest position<br>Give supplemental oxygen<br>Start intravenous line |

3. Monitor discomfort/exhaustion/pain control—support client in choice of pain control

   a. Relaxation techniques taught during pregnancy where breathing is taught as a relaxed response to contraction

   b. Low back pain—advise massage of sacral area

   c. Use different breathing techniques during different phases of labor

   d. Encourage rest between contractions

4. Keep couple informed of progress

5. Administer analgesic (consider: orders, client request, stage of labor, and fetal well-being)

   a. May prolong labor

   b. Local/block/general

6. Educate client about anesthetics

   a. Systemic analgesics

      1) Opioid agonists—morphine; risk of maternal and fetal respiratory depression and sedation

      2) Opioid agonist-antagonist analgesics—butophanol, nalbuphine—less risk of respiratory depression

   b. Nerve block analgesia and anesthesia

      1) Local—for episiotomy; lidocaine, chloroprocaine; may be given with epinephrine

      2) Pudendal nerve block—for episiotomy or when forceps or vacuum extractor used

   c. Spinal anesthesia (block)—used for Cesarean birth; local anesthetic with fentanyl injected into subarachnoid space at level or 3rd to 5th lumbar vertebrae; risk of maternal hypotension and respiratory depression, fetal distress; postdural puncture headache

   d. Epidural anesthesia or analgesia (block)—most popular

      1) Lumbar—injected into epidural space between 4th and 5th lumbar vertebrae; bupivacaine, ropivacaine, fentanyl, sufentanil; may be client-controlled epidural analgesia

   e. Combined spinal-epidural analgesia—opioid injected into epidural space followed by local anesthetic

7. Prepare for delivery

   a. Normal spontaneous

   b. Vaginal birth after cesarean (VBAC)

8. Newborn care at delivery—immediate actions

   a. Establish airway

   b. Observe for Apgar score at 1 and 5 minutes

   c. Clamp umbilical cord

   d. Maintain warmth

   e. Place identification band on baby and mother

**D.** Evaluation

1. Can mother participate effectively in delivery process?

2. Is mother able to rest between contractions?

3. Has mother established eye contact with neonate after birth?

4. Have complications with mother been avoided?

▶ **POSTPARTUM**

A.  Assessment (see Table 4)

1.  Physical

2.  Cultural influences

| Table 4  FOURTH STAGE OF LABOR | | |
|---|---|---|
| **FIRST 1–2 HOURS** | | **NURSING CONSIDERATIONS** |
| Vital signs (BP, pulse) | q 15 min | Follow protocol until stable |
| Fundus | q 15 min | Position—at the level of the umbilicus for the first 12 hours, then descends by one finger breadth each succeeding day, pelvic organ usually by day 10 |
| Lochia (color, volume) | q 15 min | Lochia (endometrial sloughing)—day 1–3 rubra (bloody with fleshy odor; may be clots); day 4–9 serosa (pink/brown with fleshy odor); day 10+ alba (yellow–white); at no time should there be a foul odor (indicates infection) |
| Urinary | Measure first void | May have urethral edema, urine retention |
| Bonding | Encourage interaction | Emphasize touch, eye contact |

B.  Diagnose—potential nursing diagnoses

1.  Physical mobility, impaired

2.  Parenting, risk for altered

3.  Self-care deficit

C.  Plan/Implementation

1.  If ordered, Rho(D) immune globulin (IGIM) to mother—Rho(D) immune globulin (IGIM) promotes lysis of fetal Rh-positive RBCs circulating in maternal bloodstream before Rh-negative mother develops her own antibodies to them

2.  Assess lochia color and volume

3.  Check episiotomy and perineum for signs and symptoms of infection

4.  Assess for attachment/bonding—influenced by maternal psychosocial-cultural factors, infant health status, temperament, and behaviors, circumstances of the prenatal, intrapartal, postpartal, and neonatal course; evidenced initially by touching and cuddling, naming, "en face" positioning for direct eye contact, later by reciprocity and rhythmicity in maternal–infant interaction

5.  Promote successful feeding

6.  Nonnursing woman—suppress lactation

    a.  Mechanical methods—tight-fitting bra for 72 hours, ice packs, minimize breast stimulation

7. Nursing woman—successful lactation is dependent on infant sucking and maternal production and delivery of milk (letdown/milk ejection reflex); monitor and teach preventive measures for potential problems (see Table 5)

   a. Nipple irritation/cracking

      1) Nipple care—clean with warm water, no soap, and dry thoroughly; absorbent breast pads if leaking occurs; apply breast milk to nipples and areola after each feeding and air dry; apply warm compresses after each feeding and air dry

      2) Position nipple so that infant's mouth covers a large portion of the areola and release infant's mouth from nipple by inserting finger to break suction

      3) Rotate breastfeeding positions

| Table 5  LACTATION PRINCIPLES | |
| --- | --- |
| **BREAST CARE—ANTEPARTUM AND POSTPARTUM** | **INITIATING BREAST FEEDING** |
| Soap on nipples should be avoided during bathing to prevent dryness<br><br>Redness or swelling can indicate infection and should always be investigated | Relaxed position of mother is essential—support dependent arm with pillow<br><br>Alternate which breast is offered first<br><br>Five minutes on each breast is sufficient at first—teach proper way to break suction<br><br>Most of the areola should be in infant's mouth to ensure proper sucking |

   b. Engorgement—nurse frequently (every 30 minutes to 3 hours) and long enough to empty breasts completely (evidenced by sucking without swallowing); warm shower or compresses to stimulate letdown; alternate starting breast at each feeding; mild analgesic 20 minutes before feeding and ice packs between feedings for pronounced discomfort

   c. Plugged ducts—area of tenderness and lumpiness often associated with engorgement; may be relieved by heat and massage before feeding

   d. Expression of breast milk—to collect milk for supplemental feedings, to relieve breast fullness or to build milk supply; may be manually expressed or pumped by a device and refrigerated for no more than 48 hours or frozen in plastic bottles (to maintain stability of all elements) in refrigerator freezer for 2 weeks and deep freezer for 2 months (do not thaw in microwave or on stove)

   e. Medications—most drugs cross into breast milk; check with health care provider before taking any medication

8. "Postpartum blues" (day 3–7)—normal occurrence of "roller coaster" emotions, weeping, "letdown feeling"; usually relieved with emotional support and rest/sleep; report if prolonged or later onset

9. Urinary incontinence

    a. Kegel exercises—tighten pubococcygeal muscles, hold for count of 3, then relax; do 10 times tid

    b. Avoid diuretics such as caffeine

10. Sexual activities—abstain from intercourse until episiotomy is healed and lochia has ceased (usually 3–4 weeks); may be affected by fatigue, fear of discomfort, leakage of breast milk, concern about another pregnancy; assess and discuss couple's desire for and understanding about contraceptive methods; breastfeeding does not give adequate protection; oral contraceptives should not be used during breastfeeding

**D.** Evaluation

1. Has bonding been initiated?

2. Are feeding techniques established?

3. Is uterine involution progressing normally?

4. Has client received anticipatory guidance?

## ▶ PARENTING

**A.** Assessment

1. Knowledge of growth and development

2. Family composition

3. Family dynamics

4. Cultural influences

5. Resources available to parents

6. Support mechanisms

7. Previous experiences, age of parents

8. Attachments, interpersonal relationships

9. Communication between parents and with child

10. Expectations of parents

11. Motivation and commitment of parents

**B.** Diagnose—potential nursing diagnoses

1. Risk for impaired parenting

2. Readiness for enhanced knowledge

3. Readiness for enhanced family processes

4. Readiness for enhanced parenting

**C.** Plan/Implementation

1. Promote realistic age-appropriate expectations (social, motor, language)

2. Provide anticipatory guidance

3. Educate regarding routine health care

4. Observe response to stress

5. Encourage active participation

6. Support as needed

**D.** Evaluation

1. Is there an understanding of development needs? Are age-appropriate decisions made?

2. Are there signs of adaptive coping?

3. Is there participation in screening?

4. Has normal bonding occurred?

5. Does the child respond appropriately to the parent and to others?

6. Can the parent interpret the needs of the child?

7. Has acceptable behavior been defined and are limits being set? Is there an acceptable means of discipline?

8. Has successful teaching occurred?

9. Do the parents experience a sense of satisfaction?

10. Are there sufficient data or is there a need for further assessment?

# SPONTANEOUS ABORTION (UNPLANNED TERMINATION OF A PREGNANCY)

**A.** Assessment

1. Persistent uterine bleeding and cramp-like pain

2. Laboratory finding–negative or weakly positive urine pregnancy test

3. Obtain history, including last menstrual period

4. Types (see Table 1)

| Table 1 CLINICAL CLASSIFICATION OF SPONTANEOUS ABORTION | | |
| --- | --- | --- |
| TYPE | ASSESSMENT | NURSING CONSIDERATIONS |
| Threatened | Vaginal bleeding and cramping<br><br>Soft uterus, cervix closed | Ultrasound for intrauterine sac, quantitative hCG<br><br>Decrease activity for 24–48 hours, avoid stress, no sexual intercourse for 2 weeks after bleeding stops<br><br>Monitor amount and character of bleeding; report clots, tissue, foul odor |
| Inevitable, if cervical dilation cannot be prevented | Persistent symptoms, hemorrhage, moderate to severe cramping<br><br>Cervical dilation and effacement | Monitor for hemorrhage (save and count pads) and infection; if persistent or increased symptoms, D and C<br><br>Emotional support for grief and loss |
| Incomplete | Persistent symptoms, expulsion of part of products of conception | Administer IV/blood, oxytocin D and C or suction evacuation |
| Complete | As above, except no retained tissue | Possible methylergonovine; no other treatment if no evidence of hemorrhage or infection |
| Missed–fetus dies *in utero* but is not expelled | May be none/some abating of above symptoms<br><br>Cervix is closed<br><br>If retained greater than 6 weeks, increased risk of infection, DIC, and emotional distress | D and C evacuation within 4–6 weeks<br><br>After 12 weeks, dilate cervix with several applications of prostaglandin gel or suppositories of laminaria (dried sterilized seaweed that expands with cervical secretions) |
| Habitual–3 or more | May be incompetent cervix, infertility | Cerclage (encircling cervix with suture) |

**B.** Diagnose

1. Causes

  a. Chromosomal abnormalities

  b. Teratogenic drugs

  c. Abnormalities of female reproductive tract

2. Potential nursing diagnosis

  a. Anxiety, fear

  b. Deficient knowledge

  c. Deficient fluid volume

  d. Grieving

3. Termination of pregnancy spontaneously at any time before the fetus has attained viability

**C.** Plan/Implementation

1. Monitor vital signs

2. Monitor for bleeding, cramping, pain

3. Monitor hydration status and electrolyte balance

4. Administer Rho(D) immune globulin (IGIM) as needed

5. Save all tissues

6. Teach purpose of bedrest

7. Prepare client for surgical procedure if indicated (D and C, therapeutic abortion)

8. Provide emotional support for grief and loss

**D.** Evaluation

1. Has the woman adjusted to the loss of the pregnancy?

2. Have complications been prevented?

## ▶ ECTOPIC PREGNANCY

**A.** Assessment

1. Missed period

2. Unilateral lower quadrant pain after 4–6 weeks of normal pregnancy

3. Rigid, tender abdomen

4. Referred shoulder pain can occur

5. Low hematocrit, low hCG levels in urine and blood

6. Bleeding—gradual oozing to frank bleeding

**B.** Diagnose

1. Pain due to implantation of egg outside of uterus

2. Potential for anxiety and grieving

3. Potentially life-threatening to mother due to hemorrhage

4. Causes

  a. Pelvic inflammatory disease (PID)

  b. Previous tubal surgery

  c. Congenital anomalies of the fallopian tubes

C. Plan/Implementation

1. Prepare for surgery

2. Monitor for shock preoperatively and postoperatively

3. Provide emotional support and expression of grief

4. Administer Rho(D) immune globulin (IGIM) to Rh-negative women

5. Discharge teaching

D. Evaluation

1. Has the woman adjusted to the loss of the pregnancy?

2. Have complications been prevented?

# HYPERTENSION/PREECLAMPSIA/ECLAMPSIA

A. Preexisting hypertension (HTN)—diagnosed and treated before the 20th week of pregnancy; requires strict medical and obstetrical management

B. Gestational Hypertension—characterized by hypertension (systolic pressure greater than 140 mm Hg and/or diastolic pressure greater than 90 mm Hg) without proteinuria after 20 weeks gestation and resolving by 12 weeks postpartum; treated with frequent evaluation of BP and protein in urine

C. Preeclampsia and Eclampsia

1. Assessment—increased risk in African Americans, primigravida older than 35 years or younger than 17 years, multiple fetuses or history of and renal disease, family history of hypertension in previous pregnancy; prenatal screening at each visit for symptomatology

| Table 2  CHARACTERISTICS OF PREECLAMPSIA AND ECLAMPSIA | | | | | |
|---|---|---|---|---|---|
| CONDITION | BP | PROTEINURIA | SEIZURES | HYPERREFLEXIA | OTHER |
| Mild preeclampsia | Greater than 140/90 mm Hg after 20 weeks gestation | 300 mg/L per 24 h<br><br>Greater than 1+ random sample | No | No | Mild facial edema<br><br>Weight gain (greater than 4.5 lb/wk) |
| Severe preeclampsia | Greater than 160/110 mm Hg | Greater than 500 mg/L per 24 h<br><br>Greater than 3+ random sample | No | Yes | Headache<br><br>Oliguria<br><br>Blurred vision<br><br>RUQ pain<br><br>Thrombocytopenia<br><br>HELLP (hemolysis, elevated liver enzymes, low platelet count) |
| Eclampsia | Greater than 160/110 mm Hg | Marked proteinuria | Yes | No | Same as severe preeclampsia<br><br>Severe headache<br><br>Renal failure<br><br>Cerebral hemorrhage |

| Table 3  PREECLAMPSIA AND ECLAMPSIA TREATMENT | |
|---|---|
| **CONDITION** | **TREATMENT** |
| Mild preeclampsia | Bed rest in left lateral position<br>Monitor BP daily<br>6–8 8 oz drinks/day<br>Frequent follow up |
| Severe preeclampsia | Depends on fetal age<br>Only cure is delivery of fetus (induction of labor)<br>Control BP (hydralyzine), prevent seizures (magnesium sulfate)<br>Prevent long term morbidity and maternal mortality<br>Emotional support if delivery prior to age of viability |
| Eclampsia (Medical Emergency) | Support through seizures and potential coma<br>Ensure patent airway, $O_2$ support<br>DIC management<br>Delivery of fetus<br>Emotional support if delivery prior to age of viability<br>In cases of severe hypertension, seizures may still occur 24–48 h postpartum; monitor magnesium sulfate or hydralazine if continued postpartum |

**D.** Evaluation

1. Has the infant been delivered safely?

2. Have complications been prevented?

3. Is the family coping effectively?

## ▶ PLACENTA PREVIA

**A.** Assessment

1. First- and second-trimester spotting

2. Third trimester bleeding that is sudden, bright-red, potentially profuse, *painless*

3. Ultrasonography—classified by degree of obstruction

**B.** Diagnose

1. The placenta is implanted in the lower uterine segment, usually near or over the cervical opening; placenta may partially or totally cover cervical os

2. Potential nursing diagnoses

   a. Impaired fetal gas exchange

   b. Risk for deficient fluid volume

   c. Deficient knowledge

   d. Risk for maternal injury

   e. Anxiety and fear

**C.** Plan/Implementation

1. Hospitalization initially

   a. Bedrest side-lying or Trendelenburg position for at least 72 hours

    b. Ultrasound to locate placenta

    c. No vaginal, rectal exam (if becomes necessary, must be done in OR under sterile conditions)

    d. Amniocentesis for lung maturity; monitor for changes in bleeding and fetal status

    e. Assess Daily Hgb and Hct

    f. Weigh peripads (1 gram = 1 mL blood loss)

    g. Two units of cross-matched blood available

    h. Assess amount of blood loss

  2. Send home if bleeding ceases and pregnancy to be maintained

    a. Limit activity

    b. No douching, enemas, coitus

    c. Assess fetal movement

    d. Non stress test at least every 1–2 weeks

    e. Assess complications

  3. Delivery by cesarean if evidence of fetal maturity, excessive bleeding, active labor, other complications

**D.** Evaluation

  1. Was the infant delivered safely?

  2. Were complications prevented?

# ABRUPTIO PLACENTAE—(PREMATURE SEPARATION OF PLACENTA)

**A.** Assessment

  1. *Painful,* dark red vaginal bleeding; bleeding may be scant to profuse

  2. Abdomen (uterus) is tender, painful, tense

  3. Possible fetal distress, maternal shock

  4. Contractions

**B.** Diagnose

  1. Premature separation of the placenta

  2. Occurrence increased with maternal hypertension and cocaine abuse

  3. Potential nursing diagnoses

    a. Deficient fluid volume

    b. Impaired fetal gas exchange

    c. Acute pain

    d. Anxiety and fear

**C.** Plan/Implementation

  1. Monitor for maternal shock and fetal distress

    a. Blood loss seen may not match symptoms

    b. Could have rapid fetal distress

  2. Prepare for immediate delivery

3. Monitor for postpartal complications

  a. Disseminated intravascular coagulation (DIC)—bleeding gums, bleeding around IV insertion sites

  b. Pulmonary emboli

  c. Infection

  d. Renal failure

**D.** Evaluation

  1. Has the woman's fluid and electrolyte balance been maintained?

  2. Have complications been prevented?

## ▶ DIABETES

**A.** Assessment

  1. Urine screening for ketones

  2. Blood sugar levels; oral glucose tolerance test

  3. Glucose tolerance test (1-h test at 24–28 weeks) for women at average risk

  a. Age 25 or older

  b. Obesity

  c. Family history of diabetes in first-degree relative

  d. Hispanic, African American, Native American, or Asian American

  e. History of abnormal glucose tolerance

  4. Glycosylated hemoglobin ($HbA_{1C}$)—(indicates past serum glucose levels over previous 3 months); normal is 3.5–6%

**B.** Diagnose

  1. Potential nursing diagnoses

  a. Deficient knowledge

  b. Risk for risk-prone health behaviors

  c. Risk for unstable blood glucose

  d. Imbalanced nutrition: less than body requirements

  2. Classification

  a. Type 1—complications more common

  b. Type 2

  c. Gestational diabetes (GDM)—increased demand for insulin during pregnancy

  d. Impaired fasting glucose tolerance

  3. Diabetes increases risk for

  a. Maternal infections—UTIs and vaginal yeast infections

  b. Hypertensive states of pregnancy

  c. Hydramnios (greater than 2,000 ml amniotic fluid) and consequent preterm labor

  d. Macrosomia (large for gestational age but may have immature organ systems)

  e. Congenital anomalies (neural tube defects)

  f. Prematurity and stillbirth

     g. Respiratory distress syndrome (RDS)

     h. Untreated ketoacidosis can cause coma and death of mother and fetus

  4. Gestational diabetes

     a. Hyperglycemia after 20 weeks when insulin need accelerates

     b. Usually controlled by diet

     c. Oral hypoglycemics not used—teratogenic and increase risk of neonatal hypoglycemia

     d. Risk factors

       1) Obesity

       2) Family history of diabetes

       3) History of gestational diabetes

       4) Hypertension, preeclampsia/eclampsia, recurrent UTIs, monilial vaginitis, polyhydramnios; previously large infant (9-lb, 4,000 g or more)

       5) Previously unexplained death/anomaly or stillbirths

       6) Glycosuria, proteinuria on two or more occasions

  5. Testing for diabetes—at 24–28 weeks for all gravidas

     a. Screen blood glucose level 1 hour after 50 g concentrated glucose solution

     b. Three-hour glucose tolerance test; normal findings:
       FBS—less than 92 mg/dL (5.1 mmol/L)

       1 hour—less than 180 mg/dL (10 mmol/L)

       2 hours—less than 153 mg/dL(8.5 mmol/L)

       3 hours—less than 140 mg/dL (7.8 mmol/L)

     c. If two or more abnormal findings, significant for diabetes

     d. Glycosylated hemoglobin (HbA1c)—measures control past three months; elevations (greater than 6%) in first trimester associated with increased risk of congenital anomalies and spontaneous abortion; in the last trimester, elevations with macrosomia

**C.** Plan/Implementation

  1. Reinforce need for careful monitoring throughout pregnancy, including frequent medical/nursing evaluations

  2. Evaluate understanding of modifications in diet/insulin coverage

  3. Teach client and at least one significant other

     a. Diet—eat prescribed amount of food daily at same times; daily exercise

     b. Home glucose monitoring

     c. Insulin—purpose, dosage, administration, action, adverse effects, potential change in amount needed during pregnancy as fetus grows and immediately after delivery, no oral hypoglycemics (teratogenic)

  4. Assist with stress reduction

  5. Fetal surveillance

**D.** Evaluation

1.  Does client remain free of hypoglycemia and hyperglycemia?

2.  Are the mother and infant free from complications?

3.  Does the client demonstrate compliance?

4.  Do the woman and family show effective coping?

## ► CARDIAC DISEASE

**A.** Assessment

1.  Chest pain

2.  Dyspnea on exertion; dyspnea at rest; edema

3.  Monitor vital signs and do EKG as heart lesion (especially with mitral valve involvement) may become aggravated by pregnancy

**B.** Diagnose

1.  Potential nursing diagnoses

    a.  Acute pain

    b.  Decreased cardiac output

    c.  Impaired fetal gas exchange

    d.  Anxiety/fear

    e.  Deficient knowledge

    f.  Activity intolerance

    g.  Maternal injury

2.  Treatment of heart disease in pregnancy is determined by the functional capacity of the heart, and type of delivery will be influenced by the mother's status and the condition of fetus

**C.** Plan/Implementation

1.  Encourage rest and adequate nutrition during pregnancy

2.  Assess maternal vital signs and fetal heart rate

3.  Encourage moderation in physical activity

4.  Teach importance of avoidance and early treatment of upper respiratory infections

5.  Be alert for signs of heart failure: increase of dyspnea; tachycardia; weight gain

6.  Assess activity level during labor

    a.  Assess vital signs frequently

    b.  Place client on cardiac monitor and on external fetal monitor.

    c.  Maintain bedrest with mother in side-lying or semi-recumbent position

    d.  Administer oxygen as prescribed

    e.  Assess for signs of pulmonary edema and heart failure

    f.  Provide emotional support

**D.** Evaluation

1.  Was the infant delivered safely?

2.  Were cardiac complications in the mother prevented?

# SYPHILIS

**A.** Assessment

1. Blood tests (VDRL)

2. Primary lesion (chancre) located on internal or external genitalia

   a. Secondary stage may be unnoticeable

3. Previous obstetrical history of spontaneous abortion, premature births, or full-term stillbirth

4. Method of infection

   a. Congenital

   b. Acquired—sexually

**B.** Diagnose—potential nursing diagnoses

1. Delayed growth and development

2. Deficient knowledge

**C.** Plan/Implementation

1. Administer penicillin, which crosses placenta, thereby additionally treating fetus

**D.** Evaluation

1. Has the infection been successfully treated?

2. Have complications in the infant been prevented?

# GONORRHEA

**A.** Assessment

1. Positive culture of vaginal secretions

2. Purulent discharge or asymptomatic

**B.** Diagnose

1. Potential nursing diagnoses

   a. Risk for infection

   b. Deficient knowledge

2. May complicate pregnancy and cause sterility

**C.** Plan/Implementation

1. Teach about antibiotic as ordered

2. Instill prophylactic medication into baby's eyes after delivery

**D.** Evaluation

1. Have complications in the infant been avoided?

# PRE-EXISTING INFECTIONS

**A.** Assessment

1. History

2. Exposure—especially rubella, syphilis, herpes, HIV, CMV

3. Screening

**B.** Diagnose

   1.  Risk for infection

   2.  Deficient knowledge

**C.** Plan/Implementation

   1.  Assist with cultures; antibody levels

   2.  Teach administration of medications as ordered

   3.  Prepare for possible cesarean section, surgical procedure

**D.** Evaluation

   1.  Have complications in the infant been avoided?

   2.  Does mother have knowledge about pre-existing infection?

## ▶ GESTATIONAL TROPHOBLASTIC DISEASE (HYDATIDIFORM MOLE)

**A.** Assessment

   1.  Elevated hCG levels

   2.  Uterine size greater than expected for dates

   3.  No FHR

   4.  Minimal dark red/brown vaginal bleeding with passage of grapelike clusters

   5.  No fetus by ultrasound

   6.  Increased nausea and vomiting and associated gestational hypertension

**B.** Diagnose

   1.  Degenerative anomaly of chorionic villi

**C.** Plan/Implementation

   1.  Curettage to completely remove all molar tissue that can become malignant

   2.  Pregnancy is discouraged for 1 year

   3.  hCG levels are monitored for 1 year (if continue to be elevated, may require hysterectomy and chemotherapy)

   4.  Contraception discussed; IUD not used

   5.  Administer Rho(D) immune globulin (IGIM) to Rh-negative women

**D.** Evaluation

   1.  Has the woman adjusted to the lack of a viable pregnancy?

   2.  Has the Rh-negative woman received Rho(D) immune globulin (IGIM)?

## ▶ PRETERM LABOR

**A.** Assessment

   1.  Occurs between 20 and 37 weeks gestation, uterine contractions and cervical changes

   2.  Risk factors

     a.  African American

     b.  Older than 35 or younger than 17

     c.  Low socioeconomic status

    d. Previous preterm labor or birth

    e. Medical disease

    f. Smoking or substance abuse

    g. Problems with pregnancy

**B.** Diagnose—potential nursing diagnoses

    1. Acute pain

    2. Risk for fetal injury

    3. Deficient knowledge

**C.** Plan/Implementation

    1. Bedrest, side-lying

    2. Uterine monitoring, daily weights

    3. Maintain good nutrition

    4. Relaxation techniques

    5. Administration of medication (e.g., terbutaline)

**D.** Evaluation

    1. Has client complied with treatment?

    2. Has client given birth at or near term to a healthy mature infant?

# ▶ INDUCTION OF LABOR

**A.** Assessment

    1. Mother cannot have CPD

    2. Fetus must have mature vertex presentation

    3. Fetus must have engaged head

    4. Mother has "ripened" cervix, or it is induced to "ripen"

    5. Indications

        a. Diabetes

        b. Postmaturity

        c. Gestational hypertension

        d. Fetal jeopardy

        e. Logistical factors—(rate of rapid birth, distance from hospital)

**B.** Diagnose—potential nursing diagnoses

    1. Risk for maternal and fetal injury

    2. Deficient knowledge

**C.** Plan/Implementation

    1. Assess fetus continuously by external monitor

    2. Monitor BP, pulse, progress of labor of mother

    3. Prepare for amniotomy (rupture of membranes)

    4. Begin oxytocin administration

        a. Begin at 0.5–1 milliunits/min; increase dose 1–2 milliunits/min at intervals of 30–60 minutes until desired contractions; can administer up to 20 mU/min (follow unit/health care provider policy/order)

        b. Piggyback to principal intravenous line

        c. Administer via infusion pump

        d. Usual contraction pattern: q 2–3 minutes, lasting for 90 seconds or less

        e. Stop infusion if fetal distress or hypertonic contractions begin (contractions that last more than 90 seconds or occur more frequently than every 2 minutes)

**D.** Evaluation

   1. Has the woman delivered safely?

   2. Have complications been prevented?

## ▶ CESAREAN DELIVERY

**A.** Assessment

   1. Dystocia (abnormal or difficult labor)

   2. Previous Cesarean birth

   3. Breech presentation or CPD

   4. Fetal distress

   5. Active maternal gonorrhea or herpes type 2 infections

   6. Prolapsed umbilical cord

   7. Hypertensive states of pregnancy

   8. Placenta previa, abruptio placentae

   9. Fetal anomalies (e.g., hydrocephaly)

**B.** Diagnose

   1. Potential nursing diagnoses

        a. Anxiety

        b. Powerlessness

        c. Deficient knowledge

   2. Classification

        a. Vertical incision

           1) More blood loss

           2) Rapid delivery

        b. Low-segment transverse incision

           1) Less blood loss

           2) Vaginal birth after cesarean (VBAC) a possibility

**C.** Plan/Implementation

   1. Obtain lab tests—type and crossmatch, urinalysis, CBC

   2. Provide routine preop care; IV fluid

   3. Insert indwelling bladder catheter

   4. Provide emotional support; as a new mother first, surgical client second

   5. Administer preop medication—usually lower narcotic dose than routine preop medication

   6. Monitor for hemorrhage

        a. Assess fundus for firmness and location; massage if boggy

        b. Assess skin incision and dressing for signs of for excessive bleeding

        c. Assess vital signs for evidence of shock

   7. Routine postop care

8. Provide comfort measures and medications to control pain

9. Splint the incision site while the client does deep breathing exercises

10. Give the mother her infant as soon as possible to promote parent/child bonding

11. Encourage ambulation

**D.** Evaluation

1. Has the infant been delivered safely?

2. Have complications been prevented?

# PRECIPITOUS DELIVERY OUTSIDE HOSPITAL SETTING

**A.** Assessment

1. Determine that transport to hospital/birthing center is not possible

2. Evaluate mother's cognitive status and explain actions

**B.** Diagnose—potential nursing diagnoses

1. Risk for maternal and fetal injury

2. Deficient knowledge

**C.** Plan/Implementation

1. Remain with client

2. Prepare sterile or clean environment

3. Support infant's head; apply slight pressure to control delivery

4. Slip a nuchal cord, if present, over head

5. Rotate infant externally as head emerges

6. Deliver shoulders, trunk

7. Dry baby and place on mother's abdomen

8. Hold placenta as delivered

9. Wrap baby in blanket and put to breast

10. Check for bleeding and fundal tone

11. Arrange transport to hospital

12. Support mother and family

**D.** Evaluation

1. Has the infant been delivered safely?

2. Have complications been prevented?

# POSTPARTUM HEMORRHAGE

Definition: blood loss greater than 500 mL after a vaginal birth or 1000mL after a Cesarean birth

**A.** Assessment

1. Uterine tone and location

2. Blood loss amount:

    a. Accurate measurement of blood loss is accomplished by weighing peri pads.

    b. Large: Blood loss greater than 6 inches (15 cm) to saturated on a peri pad in 1 hour (50–80 mL)

    c. Moderate amount: Blood loss greater than 4 inches (10 cm) but less than 6 inches (15 cm) on peri pad in 1 hour (25–50 mL)

3. Lochia regressing to a previous stage

4. History

    a. Multiparity

    b. Retained placental fragments

    c. Overdistended uterus

    d. Prolonged labor or delivery of large infant

**B.** Diagnose—potential nursing diagnoses

1. Deficient fluid volume

2. Risk for infection

3. Risk for maternal injury

4. Impaired parenting

**C.** Plan/Implementation

1. Massage uterus post delivery if not firm

2. Assess involution for early identification of problems

3. Administer oxytocin, ergonovine or methylcryonovine maleate, prostaglandin as ordered

    a. Produces contractions of uterus

    b. Controls postpartum hemorrhage

    c. Potential adverse effects are hypertension, nausea, and vomiting

4. Monitor for signs of shock

**D.** Evaluation

1. Has the woman's fluid balance been maintained?

2. Have complications been prevented?

## ▶ POSTPARTUM INFECTION

**A.** Assessment

1. Temperature 100.4°F or higher on any two consecutive postpartum days exclusive of the first 24 hours; chills, tachycardia

2. Abdominal pain or severe afterpains, perineal discomfort

3. Lochia—foul odor, prolonged rubra phase, decreased or increased amount

4. Localized tenderness

5. Diagnostic tests

    a. Blood cultures, culture of lochia, urine cultures, increased erythrocyte sedimentation rate (ESR)

    b. White blood cell count–significant increase over a 6-hour time period

**B.** Diagnose—potential nursing diagnoses

  1. Risk for infection

  2. Deficient knowledge

**C.** Plan/Implementation

  1. Encourage early ambulation

  2. Change peripads frequently

  3. Provide adequate nutrition, fluid intake, and sleep

  4. Monitor for signs of infection

  5. Administer antibiotics if ordered

**D.** Evaluation

  1. Have complications been prevented?

  2. Does client have adequate understanding of good hygiene techniques?

# POSTPARTUM DEPRESSION

**A.** Assessment

  1. Decrease in estrogen and progesterone may precipitate "baby blues"

  2. Occurs during first year, often by fourth week

  3. Possibly associated with changing hormone levels

  4. Sadness and crying

  5. Difficulty concentrating

  6. Fatigue

  7. Appetite and sleep disturbances

**B.** Diagnose—potential nursing diagnoses

  1. Insomnia

  2. Risk for self-directed violence

  3. Interrupted family processes

  4. Anxiety disturbed thought processes

**C.** Plan/Implementation

  1. Encourage verbalization of feelings and identification of concerns

  2. Assess potential for suicide

  3. Consult with medical and psychiatric staff

  4. Support groups

  5. Administer medication

  6. Assist with care of baby

**D.** Evaluation

  1. Is the woman able to cope with the stress of a newborn?

  2. Is the woman able to verbalize her feelings?

# CHILDBEARING—NEONATAL NORMAL *Section 4*

## NORMAL NEWBORN

| Table 1   NEWBORN ASSESSMENT | | |
|---|---|---|
| SYSTEM | ASSESSMENT | NURSING CONSIDERATIONS |
| Respiration/perfusion | Rate—quiet vs. active<br>Labored—retractions, grunting<br>Color, heart rate, heart murmurs<br>Nose breather | Keep airway patent<br>Limit activities—decreases $O_2$ consumption<br>Monitor blood gases/blood pressure<br>Keep supplemental $O_2$ use limited to that required<br>Monitor for respiratory distress (increased respiratory rate, grunting, nasal flaring, intercostals retractions)<br>Prepare for possible intubation |
| Nutrition | Weight and length<br>Head circumference<br>Bottle feeding<br>Chest circumference<br>Situations that increase demand:<br>Sepsis<br>Ventilatory distress<br>Stress | Monitor volume of fluid intake<br>Dipstick and specific gravity on urine<br>Caloric value of intake<br>Monitor output volume in first 24 hours |
| Heat regulation | Ability to maintain normal body temperature<br>Acidosis may develop if poor temperature regulation | Provide regular monitoring<br>Adjust environmental temperature appropriately:<br>Body covering<br>Warmer or isolette |

| Table 1 NEWBORN ASSESSMENT *(CONTINUED)* | | |
|---|---|---|
| **SYSTEM** | **ASSESSMENT** | **NURSING CONSIDERATIONS** |
| CNS | Reflexes:<br> Tonic neck<br> Babinski<br> Moro<br> Autonomics—sucking, rooting, swallowing<br>Fontanelles—bulging or flat<br>Severe hypo- or hyperactivity<br>Activity/sleep/cry:<br> Hyperirritable<br> Depressed<br>Anatomical anomalies:<br> Cranial—hydrocephalus, microcephaly<br> Spinal<br>Paralysis/paresis:<br> Erb's palsy<br> Bell's palsy<br> Lower extremities | Respond to life-threatening problems immediately:<br> Absence of swallow reflex<br> Bulging fontanelle<br> Cranial nerve injuries |
| Parenting | Infant—behavior, individual differences<br>Mother/father:<br> Pattern of touching<br> Reciprocity of interaction<br> Age and development level<br> Guilt, anxiety, grief reactions<br> Ability to interact | Report any deviations |
| Circumcision | Observe for infection, bleeding | Record first voiding after procedure Apply dressing |

**A.** Assessment (see Table 1)

1. Airway—bulb suctioning—mouth first, then nose
2. Apgar score (performed at 1 and 5 minutes of age)
   a. Scoring (see Table 2)
   b. Interpretations
      1) 0–3: poor
      2) 4–6: fair
      3) 7–10: excellent

| Table 2  APGAR SCORE | | | |
|---|---|---|---|
| | **0** | **1** | **2** |
| Heart rate | Absent | Slow (less than 100 bpm) | Normal (greater than 100 bpm) |
| Respiratory effort | Absent | Slow, irregular | Good cry |
| Muscle tone | Flaccid | Some flexion | Active |
| Reflexes | No response | Weak cry | Vigorous cry |
| Color | Blue, pale | Body pink, extremities blue | Completely pink |
| **TOTAL _____** | | | |

3.  Measurements at term

   a.  Weight—6–9 lb (2,700–4,000 g); normal five to ten percent weight loss in first few days should be regained in 1–2 weeks

   b.  Length—19–21 inches (48–53 cm)

   c.  Head circumference—13–14 inches (33–35 cm); 1/4 body length

   d.  Chest—1 inch less than head circumference, 12–13 inches (30.5–33 cm)

4.  Vital signs

   a.  Temperature

      1)  Rectal—not recommended as routine because of potential for rectal mucosa irritation and increased risk of perforation

      2)  Axillary—97.7–99.7°F (36.5–37.6°C); thermometer should remain in place at least 3 minutes unless an electronic thermometer is used

   b.  Apical rate—100 bpm (sleep); 120–140 bpm (awake); up to 180 bpm (crying); assessed by auscultation for 1 full minute when infant not crying

   c.  Respirations—30–60 breaths/min; primarily diaphragmatic and abdominal, synchronous with chest movements; may be short (less than 15 sec) periods of apnea; since neonate is an obligatory nose breather, it is important to keep nose and mouth clear

   d.  Blood pressure—65/41 mm Hg in arm and calf

5.  Posture

   a.  Maintains fetal position for several days

   b.  Resistance to extension of extremities

6.  Skin—sensitive to drying

   a.  Erythematous (beefy red) color for a few hours after birth; then pink or as expected for racial background; acrocyanosis (bluish discoloration of hands and feet) is normal for 24 hours

   b.  Vernix caseosa—protective gray-white fatty substance of cheesy consistency covering the fetal/newborn skin; do not attempt vigorous removal

c. Lanugo—light distribution of downy, fine hair may be over the shoulder, forehead, and cheeks; extensive amount is indicative of prematurity

d. Milia—distended sebaceous glands appearing as tiny, white, pinpoint papules on forehead, nose, cheeks, and chin of neonate that disappear spontaneously in a few days or weeks

e. Pigmentation

1) Mongolian spots—bluish gray or dark nonelevated pigmentation area over the lower back and buttocks present at birth in some infants (African American, Hispanic, Asian)

2) Birthmarks

a) Telangiectatic nevi ("stork bites")—cluster of small, flat, red localized areas of capillary dilatation usually on eyelids, nose, nape of neck; can be blanched by the pressure of the finger; usually fade during infancy

b) Nevus vasculosus (strawberry mark)—raised, demarcated, dark red, rough-surfaced capillary hemangioma in dermal and subdural layers; grow rapidly for several months and then begin to fade; usually disappear by 7 years of age

c) Nevus flammeus (port wine stain)—reddish, usually flat, discoloration commonly on the face or neck; does not grow and does not fade

7. Head—may appear asymmetrical because of overriding of cranial bones during labor and delivery (molding)

a. Fontanelles—"soft spots" at junction of cranial bones

1) Anterior fontanel—diamond shaped 2.5–4 cm, easily felt, usually open and flat (may be moderate bulging with crying/stooling); sustained bulging occurs with increased intracranial pressure, depression with dehydration; may be slight pulsation; closes by 18 months of age

2) Posterior—triangular 0.5–1 cm, not easily palpated; closes between 8 and 12 weeks of life

b. Cephalhematoma—collection of blood under the periosteum of a cranial bone appearing on first and second day; does not cross suture line; disappears in weeks to months

c. Caput succedaneum—localized soft swelling of the scalp often associated with a long and difficult birth; present at birth; overrides the suture line; fluid is reabsorbed within hours to days after delivery

d. Face—symmetrical distribution and movement of all features; asymmetry may signify paralysis of facial cranial nerve (Bell's palsy)

e. Eyes—eyelids may be edematous; pupils equal and react to light; absence of tears, corneal reflex, blink reflex, areas of subconjunctival hemorrhage

f. Mouth—sucks well when stimulated; hard and soft palate intact when examined with clean-gloved finger, gag reflex, rooting reflex

g. Ears—tops (pinnae) should be parallel with the inner and outer canthus of eyes; low-set ears are associated with chromosomal abnormalities, intellectual delay and/or internal organ abnormalities; hearing is evaluated by an arousal response to loud or moderately loud noise unaccompanied by vibration, startle reflex

8. Chest—breast enlargement lasting up to 2 weeks may occur in both males and females

9. Abdomen

    a. Cylindrical and slightly protuberant

    b. Umbilical cord—initially white and gelatinous with 2 arteries and 1 vein, shriveled and black by 2–3 days, falls off within 1–2 weeks; foul-smelling discharge is indicative of infection requiring immediate treatment to prevent septicemia

    c. First stool is black and tarry (meconium) passed within 12–24 hours; followed by thin green-brown transitional stools the third day; then 1–2 formed pale yellow to light brown stools/day with formula feeding or loose golden yellow stools with sour milk odor with every breast feeding

10. Genitourinary—urine is present in bladder at birth, but neonate may not void for 12–24 hours (may be brick-red spots on diaper from passage of uric acid crystals); thereafter usually voids pale yellow urine 6–10 times/day

    a. Female—labia relatively large and approximated; may have normal thick white discharge; a white cheese-like substance (smegma) and/or blood tinge (pseudomenstruation)

    b. Male—testes can be felt in scrotum

11. Trunk and extremities

    a. Arms and legs symmetric in shape and function

    b. Hips abduct to > 60°; symmetric inguinal and buttocks creases indicating no hip dislocation

    c. Foot in straight line

12. Reflexes

    a. Rooting and sucking—turns toward any object touching/stroking cheek/mouth, opens mouth, and sucks rhythmically when finger/nipple is inserted into mouth (usually disappears by 4–7 months)

    b. Pupillary—constriction on exposure of light

    c. Palmar grasp—pressure on palm elicits grasp (fades by 3–4 months)

    d. Plantar grasp—pressure on sole behind toes elicits flexion (lessens by 8 months)

    e. Tonic neck—fencing position; lying on back with head turned to one side, arm and leg on that side of body will be in extension while extremities on opposite side will be flexed (disappears by 3–4 months)

    f. Moro—elicited by sudden disturbance in the infant's immediate environment, body will stiffen, arms in tense extension followed by embrace gesture with thumb and index finger in a "c" formation (disappears after 3–4 months)

    g. Positive-supporting—infant will stiffen legs and appear to stand when held upright

    h. Stepping reflex—when held upright with one foot touching a flat surface, will step alternatingly (fades 4–5 months)

    i. Babinski's sign—stroking the sole of the foot from heel upward across ball of foot will cause all toes to fan (reverts to usual adult response by 12 months)

**B.** Diagnose—potential nursing diagnoses

    1. Airway clearance, ineffective

    2. Thermoregulation, ineffective

    3. Growth and development, altered

**C.** Plan/Implementation

    1. Establish airway and maintain

    2. Observe for Apgar score at 1 and 5 minutes

    3. Clamp umbilical cord

    4. Maintain warmth and keep exposure to environment minimal

    5. Place identification band on baby and mother

    6. Administer prophylactic medications

       a. Eye prophylaxis

       b. Administer intramuscular vitamin K—for first 3–4 days of life (the neonate is unable to synthesize vitamin K)

    7. Record first stool and urine

    8. Weigh and measure baby

    9. Observe and support mother–infant bond

   10. Begin and monitor feeding schedule

       a. Before initiating first formula feeding, check for readiness (active bowel sounds, absence of abdominal distention, and lusty cry) and for absence of gagging, choking, regurgitating associated with tracheoesophageal fistula or esophageal atresia by giving a small amount of sterile water (glucose is irritating to lungs)

       b. Since colostrum is readily absorbed by the gastrointestinal and respiratory system, breastfeeding may be started immediately after birth

   11. Umbilical cord care—clean cord and surrounding skin; no tub baths until cord falls off; fold diapers below to maintain dry area; report redness, drainage, foul odor

   12. Care of penis

       a. Uncircumcised—do not force retraction of foreskin (complete separation of foreskin and glans penis takes from 3–5 years); parents should be told to gently test for retraction occasionally during the bath, and when it has occurred, gently clean glans with soap and water

b. Circumcised (surgical removal of prepuce/foreskin)

1) Ensure signed permission before procedure; provide comfort measures during and after procedure

2) Postprocedure monitor for bleeding and voiding, apply A and D ointment or petroleum jelly (except when Plastibell is used)

3) Teach parents to clean area with warm water squeezed over penis and dry gently; a whitish yellow exudate is normal and should not be removed; if Plastibell is used, report to pediatrician if it has not fallen off in about 8 days

**D.** Evaluation

1. Did the infant make an optimal transition to extrauterine life?

2. Have complications been prevented?

# NEONATAL COMPLICATIONS

▶ **RESPIRATORY DISTRESS SYNDROME (RDS)**

**A.** Assessment

1. Labored respiration after several minutes or hours of normal respiration initially

2. Cyanosis, expiratory grunting, nasal flaring, intercostal and subcostal retractions, tachypnea (greater than 60 breath/min)

3. Unresponsiveness, apneic episodes

4. Diagnostic tests

   a. Ultrasound—biparietal diameter

   b. Amniocentesis

      1) Lipid level

      2) Creatinine level

      3) L/S ratio

   c. $PO_2$ less than 50 mm Hg; $CO_2$ greater than 60 mm Hg

**B.** Diagnose

1. Causes

   a. Prematurity

   b. Surfactant deficiency disease

2. Potential nursing diagnosis

   a. Impaired gas exchange

   b. Impaired spontaneous ventilation

   c. Risk for infection

   d. Risk for impaired parent infant attachment

**C.** Plan/Implementation

1. Maintain body temperature

2. Maintain neutral thermal environment

3. Parenteral nutrition during acute phase (nipple and gavage feeding contraindicated)

4. IV fluids

5. Maintain patent airway

6. Positioning—side-lying with head supported by small folded blanket or on back with neck slightly extended

7. Suctioning as needed

8. PEEP or CPAP—keep nasal prongs in place; high frequency ventilation

9. Oxygen hood or mechanical ventilation

10. Medications—antibiotics, diuretics, vitamin E, surfactant

**D.** Evaluation

1. Is the newborn able to maintain respirations?

2. Is the newborn able to maintain a patent airway?

▶ **PERINATAL ASPHYXIA**

**A.** Assessment

1. Meconium staining (nonbreech)

2. Signs of intracranial damage, increased pressure, altered fontanelles, seizures, bradycardia

3. Abnormal respirations with cyanosis and decreased respiratory rate

**B.** Diagnose

1. Potential nursing diagnoses

   a. Impaired gas exchange

   b. Ineffective tissue perfusion

2. Predisposing conditions

   a. Small for gestational age

   b. Maternal history of heavy cigarette smoking; preeclampsia/eclampsia; multiple gestations

**C.** Plan/Implementation

1. Prepare for aggressive ventilatory assistance

2. Keep airway open

**D.** Evaluation

1. Is tissue perfusion adequate?

2. Is neurological status normal?

▶ **HYPERBILIRUBINEMIA**

**A.** Assessment

1. Physiologic jaundice—caused by immature hepatic function, resolving cephalohematoma; jaundice after 24 hours, peaks at 72 hours, lasts 5–7 days; no treatment necessary

2. Breast-feeding jaundice (early onset)—caused by poor milk intake; onset 2–3 days, 72 hours peak; treated by frequent breastfeeding, caloric supplements

3. Breastmilk jaundice (late onset)—caused by factor in breast milk; onset 4–5 days, peak 10–15 days; treated by discontinuing breast feeding for 24 hours

4. Pathologic jaundice (Hemolytic anemia)—caused by blood antigen incompatibility; onset first 24 hours; peak variable; treated by phototherapy, exchange transfusions

**B.** Diagnose—potential nursing diagnoses

1. Risk for injury (CNS involvement)

2. Risk for injury (effects of treatment)

**C.** Plan/Implementation

1. Assess serum bilirubin levels (term 2–5 d less than 12 mg/dL (less than 205 μ mol/L))

2. Observe depth and extent for jaundice

3. Observe behavior of infant

4. Phototherapy
    a. Increase fluid intake
    b. Observe for adverse effects
    c. Patch eyes; uncover eyes every 2 hours
    d. Expose as much skin as possible; cover genitals
    e. Provide sensory stimulation
    f. Provide opportunities for bonding
5. Exchange transfusion if necessary to remove excess bilirubin

**D.** Evaluation
1. Have complications been prevented?
2. Has bonding taken place?

# HEMOLYTIC DISEASE OF NEWBORN (PATHOLOGIC JAUNDICE)

**A.** Assessment
1. Jaundice within 24 hours of birth
2. Serum bilirubin level elevates rapidly
3. Hematocrit decreased, anemia due to hemolysis of large number of erythrocytes
4. Coombs Test—detects antibodies attached to circulating erythrocytes, performed on cord blood sample

**B.** Diagnose
1. Destruction of RBCs from antigen–antibody reaction
2. Baby's Rh antigens enter mother; mother produces antibody; antibodies re-enter baby and causes hemolysis and jaundice
3. Rare during first pregnancy

**C.** Plan/Implementation
1. Assist in early identification
2. Phototherapy with fluorescent lighting—alters nature of bilirubin to aid excretion; infant's eyes and genitals must be covered
3. Exchange transfusion, if indicated—removes bilirubin and maternal hemolytic antibodies

**D.** Evaluation
1. Has child been protected from eye irritation and dehydration during phototherapy?
2. Has parent/child relationship been maintained during treatments?

# NECROTIZING ENTEROCOLITIS

**A.** Assessment
1. Feeding intolerance, bile-colored vomiting, abdominal distension
2. Blood in stool
3. Temperature instability
4. Hypothermia
5. Lethargy

6.  Onset 4–10 days after feeding started

7.  Diagnostics

a.  Hematest—positive stools

b.  Abdominal radiograph shows air in bowel wall

**B.** Diagnose—potential nursing diagnoses

1.  Nutrition; less than body requirements, imbalanced

2.  Deficient fluid volume

**C.** Plan/Implementation

1.  Stop oral feedings; NPO; insert nasogastric tube; observe for 24–48 hours

2.  Administer antibiotics and intravenous fluids as ordered

3.  Handle infant carefully; avoid tight diapering

4.  Provide caloric needs via PN or small oral feedings

5.  Careful handwashing

**D.** Evaluation

1.  Have the infant's nutritional needs been met?

▶ **HYPOGLYCEMIA**

**A.** Assessment

1.  Blood sugar less than 35 mg/dL(1.9 mmol/L)(normal 40–80 mg/dL)(2.2–4.4 mmol/L)

2.  Jitteriness

3.  Irregular respiratory effort

4.  Cyanosis

5.  Weak, high-pitched cry

6.  Lethargy

7.  Twitching

8.  Eye-rolling

9.  Seizures

**B.** Diagnose—potential nursing diagnoses

1.  Deficient knowledge

2.  Risk for unstable blood glucose

**C.** Plan/Implementation

1.  Monitor glucose level soon after birth and repeat in 4 hours

2.  Administer glucose carefully to avoid rebound hypoglycemia

3.  Initiate feedings if infant not lethargic; reassess glucose levels immediately before feeding

**D.** Evaluation

1.  Have the infant's glucose levels returned to normal?

# NARCOTIC-ADDICTED INFANTS/NEONATAL ABSTINENCE SYNDROME (NAS)

**A.** Assessment

1. High-pitched cry, hyperreflexivity, decreased sleep

2. Diaphoresis, tachypnea (greater than 60/min), restlessness

3. Tremors, uncoordinated sucking, frequent sneezing and yawning, nonnutritive sucking

4. Drug withdrawal from narcotics, barbiturates, or cocaine; may manifest as early as 12–24 hours after birth, up to 7–10 days after delivery

**B.** Diagnose—potential nursing diagnoses

1. Risk for injury

2. Nutrition, less than body requirements, imbalanced

3. Risk for impaired parent/child attachment

**C.** Plan/Implementation

1. Assess muscle tone, irritability, vital signs

2. Administer phenobarbital, chlorpromazine, diazepam, paregoric, methadone as ordered

3. Report symptoms of respiratory distress

4. Reduce environmental stimulation (e.g., dim lights, decrease noise level)

5. Provide adequate nutrition/fluids; provide pacifier for nonnutritive sucking

6. Monitor mother–child interactions

7. Wrap infant snugly, rock, and hold tightly

**D.** Evaluation

1. Are environmental stresses decreased?

2. Have further complications been prevented?

3. Has adequate hydration been maintained?

# COLD STRESS

**A.** Assessment

1. Mottling of skin or cyanosis

2. Abnormal blood gases (metabolic acidosis), hypoxia, hypoglycemia

**B.** Diagnose

1. Infant unable to increase activity and lacks a shivering response to cold

2. Heat is produced through metabolic process

3. Oxygen consumption and energy are diverted from maintaining normal brain cell, cardiac function, and growth to thermogenesis

4. Causes

   a. Hypoxemia ($PO_2$ less than 50 torr)

   b. Intracranial hemorrhage or any CNS abnormality

   c. Hypoglycemia (less than 40 mg/dL)(less than 2.2 mmol/L)

C. Plan/Implementation

1. Place in heated environment immediately after birth; dry infant immediately

2. Maintain neutral thermal environment

   a. Double-walled or servocontrolled incubator

   b. Radiant warming panel

   c. Open bassinet with cotton blankets and head covered

   d. Place infant on mother's abdomen

3. Monitor temperature

4. Fabric-insulated cap for head

D. Evaluation

1. Have complications been prevented?

## ▶ NEONATAL SEPSIS

A. Assessment

1. Temperature instability, especially hypothermia

2. Poor sucking, vomiting, diarrhea, feeding intolerances

3. Lethargy, convulsive activity

4. Episodes of apnea

5. Lack of weight gain, dehydration

B. Diagnose—predisposing factors

1. Prematurity

2. Maternal signs and symptoms of infection (beta-hemolytic streptococcal vaginosis)

3. Invasive procedures and resuscitation

4. Premature rupture of membranes; prolonged rupture of membranes

5. Prolonged labor or delivery by cesarean section or forceps

6. Aspiration of meconium fluid

C. Plan/Implementation

1. Administration of prophylactic antibiotics for 7–10 days

2. Administer oxygen

3. Temporarily discontinue oral feedings

4. Transfusion with fresh, irradiated granulocytes or polymorphonuclear leukocytes

5. IV gammaglobulin to prevent nosocomial infection

D. Evaluation

1. Have the infant's nutritional needs been met?

# CLEFT LIP AND PALATE

**A.** Assessment

   1. Cleft lip—small or large fissure in facial process of upper lip or up to nasal septum, including anterior maxilla

   2. Cleft palate—midline, bilateral, or unilateral fissures in hard and soft palate

**B.** Diagnose

   1. Definition—congenital malformation

   2. Lip is usually repaired during 1 to 3 months of age

   3. Palate is usually repaired before child develops altered speech patterns; between 12–18 months

**C.** Plan/Implementation

   1. Parents will have strong reaction to birth of defective infant—provide support and information

   2. Assess infant's ability to suck

   3. Surgical repair

      a. Preoperative

         1) Maintain adequate nutrition

         2) Feed with soft nipple, special lamb's nipple, Brechet feeder (syringe with rubber tubing), or cup; feed slowly and burp often

      b. Postoperative

         1) Maintain airway

            a) Observe for respiratory distress, aspiration, or blockage from edema, check ability to swallow

            b) Provide suction equipment and endotracheal tube at bedside

         2) Guard suture line

            a) Keep suture line clean and dry

            b) Use lip-protective devices, i.e., Logan bow or tape (see Figure 1)

            c) Maintain side-lying position on unaffected side

            d) Clean suture line with cotton-tipped swab dipped in saline, then apply thin coat of antibiotic ointment

            e) Minimize crying with comfort measures—rocking, cuddling

            f) Use elbow restraints as needed

**Figure 1  Logan Bow**

  3) Provide nutrition

    a) Use feeding techniques to minimize trauma—usually very slow to feed

    b) Burp baby frequently during feedings

  4) Facilitate parents' positive response to child

  5) Provide referrals to speech therapy and orthodontists as needed

**D.** Evaluation

 1. Has defect been repaired?

 2. Have infant's nutritional needs been met?

# NORMAL REPRODUCTION

**A.** Assessment

1. Knowledge of normal sexual function

2. Prevention of illness through self-care

3. Promotion of health through control of fertility

4. Cultural influences

**B.** Diagnose

1. Potential nursing diagnoses

   a. Health-seeking behaviors (reproduction)

   b. Readiness for enhanced knowledge

   c. Anxiety related to reproductive health

2. Diagnostic tests and procedures (e.g., culdoscopy, laparoscopy)

**C.** Plan/Implementation

1. Provide privacy

2. Assess knowledge

3. Teach about breast self-exam (BSE), Pap test, mammogram, testicular self-exam

4. Instruct client in breast self-examination

   a. Examine monthly

      1) Menstruating women—1 week after onset of menstrual period

      2) Nonmenstruating women—American Cancer Society suggests a routine, such as the first day of each month

   b. Procedure

      1) Inspect breasts in mirror

      2) Examine breasts first with arms at sides, second with arms above head, and third with hands on hips

      3) Use finger pads of 3 middle fingers to palpate breasts to detect unusual growths while lying down

      4) Look for dimpling or retractions

      5) Examine nipples for discharge, changes, swelling

5. Provide information about mammography

   a. Assess knowledge of procedure

   b. Schedule after menstrual period (less breast sensitivity)

   c. Inform client that test may cause discomfort: compresses breast between 2 sheets of x-ray film

6. Provide health teaching about testicular self-exam
   a. Procedure
      1) Support testes in palm of one hand and palpate between thumb and forefinger
      2) Best performed in shower when cremaster muscles are relaxed and testes are pendulous
   b. Schedule once monthly
7. Assess knowledge of birth control
   a. Factors
      1) Impact of age, developmental level
      2) Desires of both partners
      3) Capability of use
      4) Permanent or temporary
   b. Plan—teach methods of contraception (see Table 1)
8. Assess knowledge of menopause, climacteric
   a. Menstruation ceases
   b. Symptoms related to hormone changes—vasomotor instability, emotional disturbances, atrophy of genitalia, uterine prolapse
   c. Estrogen replacement therapy (ERT)—contraindicated if family history of breast or uterine cancer, hypertension, or thrombophlebitis
   d. Kegel exercises—for strengthening pubococcygeal muscles
   e. Supplemental calcium—(1 gram HS) to slow osteoporosis
   f. Regular exercise and good nutrition

**D.** Evaluation
1. Has the client developed a plan for control of fertility?
2. Does the client understand self-care techniques?

## ▶ REPRODUCTIVE DISORDERS

**A.** Assessment (see Table 2)
**B.** Diagnose—potential nursing diagnoses
1. Sexuality patterns, ineffective
2. Sexual Dysfunction
3. Readiness for enhanced knowledge

**C.** Plan/Implementation (see Table 2)
**D.** Evaluation
1. Have complications been avoided?
2. Is the client knowledgeable about prevention of infection?

| Table 1 METHODS OF CONTRACEPTION | |
|---|---|
| **METHOD** | **NURSING CONSIDERATIONS** |
| Oral contraceptives—"the pill" | • Action—inhibits the release of FSH, resulting in anovulatory menstrual cycles; close to 100% effective<br><br>• Adverse effects—nausea and vomiting (usually occurring the first 3 months), increased susceptibility to vaginal infections<br><br>• Contraindications—hypertension, thromboembolic disease, and history of circulatory disease, varicosities, or diabetes mellitus<br><br>• Teaching—swallow whole at the same time each day; one missed pill should be taken as soon as remembered that day or two taken the next day; more than one missed pill requires use of another method of birth control for the rest of the cycle; consume adequate amounts of vitamin B; report severe/persistent chest pain, cough and/or shortness of breath, severe abdominal pain, dizziness, weakness and/or numbness, eye or speech problems, severe leg pain |
| Hormone injections—methoxyprogesterone | • Injectable progestin that prevents ovulation for 12 weeks.<br><br>• Convenient because it is unrelated to coitus (requires no action at the time of intercourse) and is 99.7% effective.<br><br>• Injections must be given every 12 weeks. The site should not be massaged after the injection because this accelerates the absorption and decreases the effectiveness time.<br><br>• Menstrual irregularity, spotting, and breakthrough bleeding are common.<br><br>• Return to fertility is 6 to 12 months |
| MPA and estradiol | • A monthly injectable contraceptive. Similar to oral contraceptives in chemical formulation, but has the advantage of monthly rather than daily dosing.<br><br>• Provides effective, immediate contraception within 5 days of the last normal menstrual period (LNMP).<br><br>• Menstrual periods less painful and with less blood loss than medroxyprogesterone acetate<br><br>• Return to fertility is 2 to 4 months |
| Intrauterine device (IUD) | • Action—presumed either to cause degeneration of the fertilized egg or render the uterine wall impervious to implantation; nearly 100% effective<br><br>• Inserted by health care provider during the client's menstrual period, when the cervix is dilated<br><br>• Adverse effects—cramping or excessive menstrual flow (for 2–3 months), infection<br><br>• Teaching—check for presence of the IUD string routinely, especially after each menstrual period; report unusual cramping, late period, abnormal spotting/bleeding, abdominal pain or pain with intercourse, exposure to STI's, infection, missing/shorter/longer IUD string |
| Condom—rubber sheath applied over the penis | • Action—prevents the ejaculate and sperm from entering the vagina; helps prevent sexually transmitted disease; effective if properly used; OTC<br><br>• Teaching—apply to erect penis with room at the tip every time before vaginal penetration; use water-based lubricant, e.g., K-Y jelly, never petroleum-based lubricant; hold rim when withdrawing the penis from the vagina; if condom breaks, partner should use contraceptive foam or cream immediately |
| Female (vaginal) condom | • Allows the woman some protection from disease without relying on the male condom.<br><br>• The device is a polyurethane pouch inserted into the vagina, with flexible rings at both ends. The closed end with its ring functions as a diaphragm. The open end with its ring partially covers the perineum.<br><br>• The female condom should not be used at the same time that the male partner is using a condom.<br><br>• Failure rates are high with the female condom, at about 21%.<br><br>• Increased risk of infections. |

| Table 1 METHODS OF CONTRACEPTION *(CONTINUED)* ||
|---|---|
| **METHOD** | **NURSING CONSIDERATIONS** |
| Diaphragm—flexible rubber ring with a latex-covered dome inserted into the vagina, tucked behind the pubic bone, and released to cover the cervix | • Action—prevents the sperm from entering the cervix; highly effective if used correctly<br>• Must be fitted by health care provider and method of inserting practiced by the client before use<br>• Risk—urinary tract infection (UTI) and toxic shock syndrome (TSS)<br>• Teaching—diaphragm should not be inserted more than 6 hours prior to coitus; best used in conjunction with a spermicidal gel applied to rim and inside the dome before inserting; additional spermicide is necessary if coitus is repeated; remove at least once in 24 hours to decrease risk of toxic shock syndrome; report symptoms of UTI and TSS |
| Vaginal spermicides (vaginal cream, foam, jellies) | • Action—interferes with the viability of sperm and prevents their entry into the cervix; OTC<br>• Teaching—must be inserted before each act of intercourse; report symptoms of allergic reaction to the chemical |
| Subdermal implant | • Action—effective for 5 years; requires surgical insertion and removal<br>• Adverse effects—irregular bleeding, nausea, skin changes |
| Natural family planning (rhythm method, basal body temperature, cervical mucus method) | • Action—periodic abstinence from intercourse during fertile period; based on the regularity of ovulation; variable effectiveness<br>• Teaching—fertile period may be determined by a drop in basal body temperature before and a slight rise after ovulation and/or by a change in cervical mucus from thick, cloudy, and sticky during nonfertile period to more abundant, clear, thin, stretchy, and slippery as ovulation occurs |
| Coitus interruptus | • Action—man withdraws his penis before ejaculation to avoid depositing sperm into vagina; variable effectiveness |
| Sterilization | • Vasectomy (male)—terminates the passage of sperm through the vas deferens<br>  • Usually done in health care provider's office under local anesthesia; permanent and 100% effective<br>  • Teaching—postprocedure discomfort and swelling may be relieved by mild analgesic, ice packs, and scrotal support; sterility not complete until the proximal vas deferens is free of sperm (about 3 months), another method of birth control must be used until two sperm-free semen analysis; success of reversal by vasovasostomy varies from 30 to 85%.<br>• Tubal ligation (female)—fallopian tubes are tied and/or cauterized through an abdominal incision, laparoscopy, or minilaparotomy<br>  • Teaching—usual postop care and instructions; intercourse may be resumed after bleeding ceases<br>  • Success of reversal by reconstruction of the fallopian tubes is 40–75% |

| Table 2 PROBLEMS OF THE REPRODUCTIVE TRACT |||
|---|---|---|
| **DISORDER** | **ASSESSMENT** | **NURSING CONSIDERATIONS** |
| Infertility | Inability to conceive after a year of unprotected intercourse<br>Tests include check of tubal patency, sperm analysis<br>Affects approximately 10–15% of all couples | Support and assist clients through tests<br>Allow expression of feelings and refer to support groups as needed<br>Alternatives include artificial insemination, *in vitro* fertilization, adoption |
| Simple vaginitis | Yellow discharge, itching, burning | Douche, antibiotics, sitz baths |
| Atrophic vaginitis | Occurs after menopause<br>Pale, thin, dry mucosa, itching, dyspareunia | Treated with topical estrogen cream, water-soluble vaginal lubricants, antibiotic vaginal suppositories and ointments |
| Candida albicans | Odorless, cheesy white discharge<br>Itching, inflamed vagina and perineum | Topical clotrimazole<br>Nystatin |

| Table 2   PROBLEMS OF THE REPRODUCTIVE TRACT *(CONTINUED)* | | |
|---|---|---|
| **DISORDER** | **ASSESSMENT** | **NURSING CONSIDERATIONS** |
| Toxic shock syndrome (TSS) | Sudden-onset fever, vomiting, diarrhea, drop in systolic blood pressure, and erythematous rash on palms and soles | Early diagnosis critical to avoid involvement with other organ systems<br><br>Managed with antibiotics, fluid and electrolyte replacement<br><br>Educate about use of tampons |
| Pelvic inflammatory disease (PID) | Local infection spreads to the fallopian tubes, ovaries, and other organs<br><br>Malaise, fever, abdominal pain, leukocytosis, and vaginal discharge<br><br>Risk factors—20 years old or younger, multiple sex partners, IUD, vaginal douching, smoking, history of STIs, history of PID | Managed with antibiotics, fluid and electrolyte replacement, warm douches to increase circulation, rest<br><br>Can cause adhesions that produce sterility |
| Mastitis | Reddened, inflamed breast<br><br>Exudate from nipple<br><br>Fever, fatigue, leukocytosis, pain | Systemic antibiotics, warm packs to promote drainage, rest, breast support |
| Fibrocystic changes | Multiple cyst development<br><br>Free-moving, tender, enlarged during menstrual period and about 1 week before | Review importance and technique of breast self-exam<br><br>Provide frequent monitoring for changes<br><br>Prepare for possibility of aspiration, biopsy, or surgery<br><br>Diet changes and vitamin supplements<br><br>Benign, but associated with increased risk of breast cancer |
| Cancer of the cervix | Early—asymptomatic<br><br>Later—abnormal bleeding, especially postcoital<br><br>Risk factors—low socioeconomic status, began sexual activity or had pregnancy at a young age, multiple sexual partners | Preparation for tests, biopsy<br><br>Internal radiation therapy<br><br>Pap smear |
| Breast cancer | Small, fixed, painless lump<br><br>Rash, or in more advanced cases, change in color, puckering or dimpling of skin, pain and/or tenderness, nipple retraction or discharge<br><br>Axillary adenopathy<br><br>Risk factors—family history of mother, sister, or daughter developing premenopausal breast cancer, age greater than 50, menses begins before age 12, no children or first pregnancy occurs after age 30, menopause after age 55 | Mammography screening<br><br>Prepare for surgery and/or radiation, chemotherapy |
| Uterine fibroids (myomas) | Low back pain, fertility problems,<br><br>Menorrhagia | Benign tumors of myometrium<br><br>Size and symptoms determine action<br><br>Prepare for possible hysterectomy (removal of uterus) or myomectomy (partial resection of uterus) |

| Table 2  PROBLEMS OF THE REPRODUCTIVE TRACT (CONTINUED) | | |
|---|---|---|
| DISORDER | ASSESSMENT | NURSING CONSIDERATIONS |
| Uterine displacement/prolapse | Weak pelvic support, sometimes after menopause<br><br>Pain, menstrual interruption, fertility problems<br><br>Urinary incontinence | Kegel exercises—isometric exercises of the muscle that controls urine flow (pubococcygeus, or PC muscle) can improve pelvic musculature support<br><br>Pessary—device inserted into vagina that gives support to uterus in cases of retroversion or prolapse; must be inserted and rechecked by health professional<br><br>Hormone replacement therapy—improves pelvic muscle tone<br><br>Surgical intervention—colporrhaphy (suturing fascia and musculature to support prolapsed structures) |
| Endometriosis | Found in colon, ovaries, supporting ligaments, causes inflammation and pain<br><br>Causes dysmenorrhea and infertility, backache<br><br>Most common in young nulliparous women | Advise client that oral contraceptives suppress endometrial buildup or that surgical removal of tissue is possible<br><br>Inform client that symptoms abate after childbirth and lactation |
| Endometrial cancer | Watery discharge, irregular menstrual bleeding, menorrhagia<br><br>Diagnosed by endometrial biopsy or curettage<br><br>Risk factors—age greater than 55, postmenopausal bleeding, obesity, diabetes mellitus, hypertension, unopposed estrogen replacement therapy | Internal radiation implants:<br>   Must restrict movements; bedrest with air mattress<br>   Enema, douche, low-residue diet, ample fluids<br>   Indwelling catheter and fracture pan for elimination<br>   Visitors and professionals wear protective garments and limit exposure time<br>   Dislodged implant must be handled with special tongs and placed in lead-lined container for removal; call hospital radiation therapy specialist first<br>Hysterectomy:<br>   Subtotal—removal of fundus only<br>   Total—removal of the uterus (vagina remains intact)<br>   Total abdominal hysterectomy with bilateral salpingooophorectomy (TAH-BSO)—removal of uterus, fallopian tubes, and ovaries<br>   Radical—removal of lymph nodes as well as TAH-BSO<br>   Assess for hemorrhage, infection, thrombophlebitis<br>   If ovaries removed, estrogen replacement therapy (ERT) may be needed |
| Ovarian cyst | Pelvic discomfort<br><br>Palpable during routine exam | May do biopsy or removal to prevent necrosis<br><br>Monitor by sonography |
| Ovarian cancer | Family history of ovarian cancer, client history of breast, bowel, endometrial cancer, nulliparity, infertility, heavy menses, palpation of abdominal mass (late sign), diagnosis by ultrasound, CT, x-ray, IVP | Surgical removal, chemotherapy, staging of tumor after removal<br><br>Foster verbalization of feelings, ensure continuity of care, encourage support systems |

| Table 2 PROBLEMS OF THE REPRODUCTIVE TRACT *(CONTINUED)* | | |
|---|---|---|
| **DISORDER** | **ASSESSMENT** | **NURSING CONSIDERATIONS** |
| Orchitis | Complication of mumps, virus, STI may cause sterility, pain, and swelling | Prophylactic gammaglobulin if exposed to mumps virus<br><br>Administration of drugs specific for organism<br><br>Ice packs to reduce swelling, bedrest, scrotal support |
| Prostatitis | May be complication of lower UTIs<br><br>Acute—fever, chills, dysuria, purulent penile discharge; elevated WBC and bacteria in urine<br><br>Chronic—backache, urinary frequency, enlarged, firm, slightly tender prostate | Antibiotics, sitz baths<br><br>Increased fluid intake<br><br>Activities to drain the prostate |
| Benign prostatic hypertrophy (BPH) | Enlargement of the glandular and cellular tissue of the prostate, resulting in compression on the urethra and urinary retention; most often in men over 50 years old<br><br>Dysuria, frequency, urgency, decreased urinary stream, hesitancy, and nocturia; later symptoms may be cystitis, hydronephrosis, or urinary calculi<br><br>KUB, x-ray, IVP, and cystoscopy demonstrate prostate enlargement and urinary tract change | Preoperative<br>　Promote urinary drainage<br>　Assure nutrition<br>　Correct fluid and electrolyte balance<br>　Antibiotics<br>　Acid-ash diet to treat infection<br>Postoperative<br>　Assure patency of three-way Foley catheter; may have continuous irrigation with normal saline to remove clots (CBI)<br>　If traction on catheter (pulled taut and taped to abdomen or leg to prevent bleeding), keep client's leg straight<br>　Monitor drainage (reddish-pink and progress to clear)<br>　Discourage attempts to void around catheter; control/treat bladder spasms<br>　Teach bladder retraining by contracting and relaxing sphincter; instruct to avoid heavy lifting, straining at bowel movement, prolonged travel; inform about potential for impotence and discuss alternative ways of expressing sexuality |
| Prostate cancer | Urinary urgency, frequency, retention<br><br>Back pain or pain radiating down leg<br><br>Risk factors—increasing age | Hormonal and chemotherapy; surgical removal |

# PREVENTION AND EARLY DETECTION OF DISEASE

## HEALTH AND WELLNESS

**A.** Wellness—person functions at highest potential for well-being

**B.** Health promotion

1. Activities that assist person to develop resources that improve quality of life

2. Alteration of personal habits, lifestyle, environment to reduce risks and enhance health and well-being

**C.** Concepts

1. Self-responsibility

   a. Individual has control over life

   b. Individual can make choices that promote health

2. Nutritional awareness—properly balanced diet

3. Stress reduction and management—manages stress appropriately

4. Physical fitness—regular exercise promotes health

   a. Improves cardiovascular functioning

   b. Decreases cholestcrol and LDLs

   c. Reduces weight

   d. Prevents body degeneration and osteoporosis

   e. Improves flexibility, muscle strength, endurance

**D.** Programs

1. General wellness

2. Smoking cessation

3. Exercise/physical conditioning

4. Weight control

5. Stress management

6. Nutritional awareness

7. Work safety

## HEALTH SCREENING

**A.** Newborn

1. PKU (phenylketonuria)—absence of enzyme needed to metabolize essential amino acid phenylalanine; Guthrie blood test

2. Hypothyroidism—deficiency of thyroid hormones; heel-stick blood sample

3. Galactosemia—error of carbohydrate metabolism

4. Sickle-cell disease—abnormally shaped hemoglobin

5. HIV (human immunodeficiency virus)

**B.** Infant/child

1. Developmental screening—Denver-II

2. Carrier screening for siblings and family members of a child with cystic fibrosis

3. Cholesterol screening for children with family history of hyperlipidemia, xanthomas, sudden death, early angina, or MI (less than 50 yr men, less than 60 yr women) in siblings, parents, uncles, aunts, grandparents

4. Lead poisoning—children (6–72 months) at highest risk

   a. Live in deteriorated housing

   b. Siblings or close peer with lead poisoning

   c. Household member with hobbies (e.g., stained glass) or lead-related occupations

5. Neuroblastoma—measure VMA and HVA (catecholamine metabolities)

**C.** School-age

1. Hearing and vision tests at 4 yr, 5 yr, then yearly during school

2. Height, weight

3. Dental exam

4. Medical assessment

5. Psychological exams

**D.** Adolescent

1. Developmental screening

2. PD

3. Sexuality

   a. Menstrual history

   b. Extent of sexual activity

   c. Contraceptive knowledge

4. Affect—symptoms of depression

5. Breast self-exam or testicular exam

6. Pelvic with pap smear—if sexually active or 18 years old, performed annually

**E.** Adult/elderly

1. Breast self-exam or testicular exam (see Table 1)

2. Cancer screenings

   a. Sigmoidoscopy—greater than 50 years old, performed every 10 years

   b. Fecal occult blood test—greater than 50 years old, performed yearly

   c. Digital rectal exam—greater than 40 years old, performed yearly

   d. Colonoscopy—beginning at age 50, every 10 years

   e. Pelvic exam for women—18–40 years old, performed every 3 years with Pap test

   f. Endometrial tissue sample for women who are at risk at menopause

   g. Mammography for women 35–39 years old once as baseline, after 40 yearly

   h. Health counseling and cancer check-ups—greater than 40 years old, performed yearly

3.  Hypertension screening (see Tables 2 and 3)
4.  Diabetes screening
5.  Hearing and vision screening

| Table 1  SELF-CARE: REPRODUCTIVE SYSTEM | | |
|---|---|---|
| **TEST** | **AGE TO BEGIN (YRS)** | **REPEAT** |
| Breast self-exam | 18–20 | Monthly |
| Papanicolaou test (Pap smear) | 18, or at least start of sexual activity | Yearly |
| Mammogram | 35–39<br>40 and older | Once as baseline<br>Annually |
| Testicular self-exam | onset of puberty | Monthly |

| Table 2  BLOOD PRESSURE SCREENING (MM HG)* | | |
|---|---|---|
| **SYSTOLIC** | **DIASTOLIC** | **FOLLOW-UP RECOMMENDED** |
| less than 120 | less than 80 | Recheck in 2 years |
| 120–139 | 80–89 | Recheck in 1 year |
| 140–159 | 90–99 | Confirm within 2 months |
| 160–179 | 100–109 | Evaluate or refer to source of care within 1 month |
| 180–209 | 110–119 | Evaluate or refer to source of care within 1 week |
| ≥210 | ≥120 | Evaluate or refer to source of care immediately |

*Recommendations are for adults age 18 and older.*

| Table 3  ERRORS IN BLOOD PRESSURE MEASUREMENT | |
|---|---|
| Inaccurately high | Cuff is too short or too narrow (e.g., using a regular blood pressure cuff on an obese arm), or the brachial artery may be positioned below the heart |
| High diastolic | Unrecognized auscultatory gap (a silent interval between systolic and diastolic pressures that may occur in hypertensive clients or because you deflated the blood pressure cuff too rapidly); immediate reinflation of the blood pressure cuff for multiple blood pressure readings (resultant venous congestion makes the Korotkoff sounds less audible); if the client supports his or her own arm, then sustained muscular contraction can raise the diastolic blood pressure by 10% |
| Inaccurately low | Cuff is too long or too wide; the brachial artery is above the heart |
| Low systolic | Unrecognized auscultatory gap (a rapid deflation of the cuff or immediate reinflation of the cuff for multiple readings can result in venous congestion, thus making the Korotkoff sounds less audible and the pressure appear lower) |

▶ **IMMUNITY**

A. Assessment

1. Antigen/antibody response

a. Antigen—a foreign protein that stimulates antibody formation response

b. Antibody—protective protein that acts as a defense mechanism

2. Active immunity

a. Permanent

b. Antigenic substance stimulates the individual's own antibody formations (e.g., tetanus)

3. Passive immunity

a. Temporary

b. Resistance acquired by introduction of antibodies from a source other than the individual (e.g., gamma globulin, breast feeding)

B. Diagnose

1. Antigen/antibody response—functions to neutralize, eliminate, or destroy substances recognized as foreign (nonself) by the body before the occurrence of potential harm to body tissues

C. Plan/Implementation

1. Recommended immunization schedule for infants and children (see Table 4) and adults (see Tables 5 and 6)

2. Contraindications to immunization

a. Severe febrile illness

b. Live viruses should not be given to anyone with altered immune system, e.g., undergoing chemotherapy, radiation, or with immunological deficiency

c. Previous allergic response to a vaccine

d. Recently acquired passive immunity, e.g., blood transfusion, immunoglobulin

3. Interrupted schedule or uncertain immunity status

a. Not necessary to repeat immunizations when the schedule is interrupted; continue schedule at next visit or when immunization is again appropriate

b. If there is no evidence of immunizations and the child is less than 7 years old give: DTaP, IPV, Tine; 4–6 weeks later MMR; 1 month after second immunization give DTaP and IPV; repeated in another month and again in 10–16 months

c. Can give DTaP, IPV, MMR

4. Nursing care (see Table 6)

D. Evaluation

1. Do the parents know what adverse effects of the immunization their child may experience?

2. Did the child receive the immunizations as scheduled?

## Table 4  CHILDHOOD IMMUNIZATION

**Figure 1. Recommended Immunization Schedule for Children and Adolescents Aged 18 Years or Younger—United States, 2017.**
**(FOR THOSE WHO FALL BEHIND OR START LATE, SEE THE CATCH-UP SCHEDULE [FIGURE 2]).**
These recommendations must be read with the footnotes that follow. For those who fall behind or start late, provide catch-up vaccination at the earliest opportunity as indicated by the green bars in Figure 1. To determine minimum intervals between doses, see the catch-up schedule (Figure 2). School entry and adolescent vaccine age groups are shaded in gray.

| Vaccine | Birth | 1 mo | 2 mos | 4 mos | 6 mos | 9 mos | 12 mos | 15 mos | 18 mos | 19-23 mos | 2-3 yrs | 4-6 yrs | 7-10 yrs | 11-12 yrs | 13-15 yrs | 16 yrs | 17-18 yrs |
|---|---|---|---|---|---|---|---|---|---|---|---|---|---|---|---|---|---|
| Hepatitis B[1] (HepB) | 1ˢᵗ dose | ◀— 2ⁿᵈ dose —▶ | | | ◀————————— 3ʳᵈ dose —————————▶ | | | | | | | | | | | | |
| Rotavirus[2] (RV) RV1 (2-dose series); RV5 (3-dose series) | | | 1ˢᵗ dose | 2ⁿᵈ dose | See footnote 2 | | | | | | | | | | | | |
| Diphtheria, tetanus, & acellular pertussis[3] (DTaP: <7 yrs) | | | 1ˢᵗ dose | 2ⁿᵈ dose | 3ʳᵈ dose | | ◀——— 4ᵗʰ dose ———▶ | | | | | 5ᵗʰ dose | | | | | |
| *Haemophilus influenzae* type b[4] (Hib) | | | 1ˢᵗ dose | 2ⁿᵈ dose | See footnote 4 | | ◀— 3ʳᵈ or 4ᵗʰ dose, See footnote 4 —▶ | | | | | | | | | | |
| Pneumococcal conjugate[5] (PCV13) | | | 1ˢᵗ dose | 2ⁿᵈ dose | 3ʳᵈ dose | | ◀——— 4ᵗʰ dose ———▶ | | | | | | | | | | |
| Inactivated poliovirus[6] (IPV: <18 yrs) | | | 1ˢᵗ dose | 2ⁿᵈ dose | ◀————————— 3ʳᵈ dose —————————▶ | | | | | | | 4ᵗʰ dose | | | | | |
| Influenza[7] (IIV) | | | | | Annual vaccination (IIV) 1 or 2 doses | | | | | | | | Annual vaccination (IIV) 1 dose only | | | | |
| Measles, mumps, rubella[8] (MMR) | | | | | See footnote 8 | | ◀——— 1ˢᵗ dose ———▶ | | | | | 2ⁿᵈ dose | | | | | |
| Varicella[9] (VAR) | | | | | | | ◀——— 1ˢᵗ dose ———▶ | | | | | 2ⁿᵈ dose | | | | | |
| Hepatitis A[10] (HepA) | | | | | | | ◀—— 2-dose series, See footnote 10 ——▶ | | | | | | | | | | |
| Meningococcal[11] (Hib-MenCY ≥6 weeks; MenACWY-D ≥9 mos; MenACWY-CRM ≥2 mos) | | | | See footnote 11 | | | | | | | | | | 1ˢᵗ dose | | 2ⁿᵈ dose | |
| Tetanus, diphtheria, & acellular pertussis[12] (Tdap: ≥7 yrs) | | | | | | | | | | | | | | Tdap | | | |
| Human papillomavirus[13] (HPV) | | | | | | | | | | | | | | See footnote 13 | | | |
| Meningococcal B[11] | | | | | | | | | | | | | | See footnote 11 | | | |
| Pneumococcal polysaccharide[5] (PPSV23) | | | | | | | | | | | | See footnote 5 | | | | | |

| ■ Range of recommended ages for all children | ■ Range of recommended ages for catch-up immunization | ■ Range of recommended ages for certain high-risk groups | ■ Range of recommended ages for non-high-risk groups that may receive vaccine, subject to individual clinical decision making | □ No recommendation |
|---|---|---|---|---|

**NOTE: The above recommendations must be read along with the footnotes of this schedule.**

**FIGURE 2. Catch-up immunization schedule for persons aged 4 months through 18 years who start late or who are more than 1 month behind—United States, 2017.**

The figure below provides catch-up schedules and minimum intervals between doses for children whose vaccinations have been delayed. A vaccine series does not need to be restarted, regardless of the time that has elapsed between doses. Use the section appropriate for the child's age. Always use this table in conjunction with Figure 1 and the footnotes that follow.

| Vaccine | Minimum Age for Dose 1 | Minimum Interval Between Doses | | | |
|---|---|---|---|---|---|
| | | Dose 1 to Dose 2 | Dose 2 to Dose 3 | Dose 3 to Dose 4 | Dose 4 to Dose 5 |
| **Children age 4 months through 6 years** | | | | | |
| Hepatitis B[1] | Birth | 4 weeks | 8 weeks *and* at least 16 weeks after first dose. Minimum age for the final dose is 24 weeks. | | |
| Rotavirus[2] | 6 weeks | 4 weeks | 4 weeks[2] | | |
| Diphtheria, tetanus, and acellular pertussis[3] | 6 weeks | 4 weeks | 4 weeks | 6 months | 6 months[3] |
| *Haemophilus influenzae* type b[4] | 6 weeks | 4 weeks if first dose administered before the 1st birthday. 8 weeks (as final dose) if first dose was administered at age 12 through 14 months. No further doses needed if first dose was administered at age 15 months or older. | 4 weeks[4] if current age is younger than 12 months **and** first dose was administered at younger than age 7 months, **and** at least 1 previous dose was PRP-T (ActHib, Pentacel, Hiberix) or unknown. 8 weeks *and* age 12 through 59 months (as final dose)[4] • if current age is younger than 12 months **and** first dose was administered at age 7 through 11 months; OR • if current age is 12 through 59 months **and** first dose was administered before the 1st birthday, **and** second dose administered at younger than 15 months; OR • if both doses were PRP-OMP (PedvaxHIB; Comvax) **and** were administered before the 1st birthday. No further doses needed if previous dose was administered at age 15 months or older. | 8 weeks (as final dose) This dose only necessary for children age 12 through 59 months who received 3 doses before the 1st birthday. | |
| Pneumococcal[5] | 6 weeks | 4 weeks if first dose administered before the 1st birthday. 8 weeks (as final dose for healthy children) if first dose was administered at the 1st birthday or after. No further doses needed for healthy children if first dose was administered at age 24 months or older. | 4 weeks if current age is younger than 12 months and previous dose given at <7 months old. 8 weeks (as final dose for healthy children) if previous dose given between 7-11 months (wait until at least 12 months old); OR if current age is 12 months or older and at least 1 dose was given before age 12 months. No further doses needed for healthy children if previous dose administered at age 24 months or older. | 8 weeks (as final dose) This dose only necessary for children aged 12 through 59 months who received 3 doses before age 12 months or for children at high risk who received 3 doses at any age. | |
| Inactivated poliovirus[6] | 6 weeks | 4 weeks[6] | 4 weeks[6] | 6 months[6] (minimum age 4 years for final dose). | |
| Measles, mumps, rubella[8] | 12 months | 4 weeks | | | |
| Varicella[9] | 12 months | 3 months | | | |
| Hepatitis A[10] | 12 months | 6 months | | | |
| Meningococcal[11] (Hib-MenCY ≥6 weeks; MenACWY-D ≥9 mos; MenACWY-CRM ≥2 mos) | 6 weeks | 8 weeks[11] | See footnote 11 | See footnote 11 | |
| **Children and adolescents age 7 through 18 years** | | | | | |
| Meningococcal[11] (MenACWY-D ≥9 mos; MenACWY-CRM ≥2 mos) | Not Applicable (N/A) | 8 weeks[11] | | | |
| Tetanus, diphtheria; tetanus, diphtheria, and acellular pertussis[12] | 7 years[12] | 4 weeks | 4 weeks If first dose of DTaP/DT was administered before the 1st birthday. 6 months (as final dose) if first dose of DTaP/DT or Tdap/Td was administered at or after the 1st birthday. | 6 months if first dose of DTaP/DT was administered before the 1st birthday. | |
| Human papillomavirus[13] | 9 years | Routine dosing intervals are recommended.[13] | | | |
| Hepatitis A[10] | N/A | 6 months | | | |
| Hepatitis B[1] | N/A | 4 weeks | 8 weeks **and** at least 16 weeks after first dose. | | |
| Inactivated poliovirus[6] | N/A | 4 weeks | 4 weeks[6] | 6 months[6] | |
| Measles, mumps, rubella[8] | N/A | 4 weeks | | | |
| Varicella[9] | N/A | 3 months if younger than age 13 years. 4 weeks if age 13 years or older. | | | |

**NOTE: The above recommendations must be read along with the footnotes of this schedule.**

**Figure 3. Vaccines that might be indicated for children and adolescents aged 18 years or younger based on medical indications**

| VACCINE ▼ INDICATION ► | Pregnancy | Immunocompromised status (excluding HIV infection) | HIV infection CD4+ count (cells/μL) | | Kidney failure, end-stage renal disease, on hemodialysis | Heart disease, chronic lung disease | CSF leaks/ cochlear implants | Asplenia and persistent complement component deficiencies | Chronic liver disease | Diabetes |
| | | | <15% of total CD4 cell count | ≥15% of total CD4 cell count | | | | | | |
|---|---|---|---|---|---|---|---|---|---|---|
| Hepatitis B[1] | | | | | | | | | | |
| Rotavirus[2] | | SCID* | | | | | | | | |
| Diphtheria, tetanus, & acellular pertussis[3] (DTaP) | | | | | | | | | | |
| *Haemophilus influenzae* type b[4] | | | | | | | | | | |
| Pneumococcal conjugate[5] | | | | | | | | | | |
| Inactivated poliovirus[6] | | | | | | | | | | |
| Influenza[7] | | | | | | | | | | |
| Measles, mumps, rubella[8] | | | | | | | | | | |
| Varicella[9] | | | | | | | | | | |
| Hepatitis A[10] | | | | | | | | | | |
| Meningococcal ACWY[11] | | | | | | | | | | |
| Tetanus, diphtheria, & acellular pertussis[12] (Tdap) | | | | | | | | | | |
| Human papillomavirus[13] | | | | | | | | | | |
| Meningococcal B[11] | | | | | | | | | | |
| Pneumococcal polysaccharide[5] | | | | | | | | | | |

| | | |
|---|---|---|
| ■ Vaccination according to the routine schedule recommended | ▣ Recommended for persons with an additional risk factor for which the vaccine would be indicated | ▦ Vaccination is recommended, and additional doses may be necessary based on medical condition. See footnotes. |
| □ No recommendation | ■ Contraindicated | ▨ Precaution for vaccination |

*Severe Combined Immunodeficiency

NOTE: The above recommendations must be read along with the footnotes of this schedule.

Footnotes can be found at www.cdc.gov/vaccines/hcp/acip-recs/index.html

## Table 5   ADULT IMMUNIZATION

Figures 1 and 2 should be read with the footnotes that contain important general information and considerations for special populations.

Figure 1. Recommended immunization schedule for adults aged 19 years or older by age group, United States, 2017

| Vaccine | 19–21 years | 22–26 years | 27–59 years | 60–64 years | ≥ 65 years |
|---|---|---|---|---|---|
| Influenza[1] | 1 dose annually | | | | |
| Td/Tdap[2] | Substitute Tdap for Td once, then Td booster every 10 yrs | | | | |
| MMR[3] | 1 or 2 doses depending on indication | | | | |
| VAR[4] | 2 doses | | | | |
| HZV[5] | | | | 1 dose | |
| HPV–Female[6] | 3 doses | | | | |
| HPV–Male[6] | 3 doses | | | | |
| PCV13[7] | | | | | 1 dose |
| PPSV23[7] | 1 or 2 doses depending on indication | | | | 1 dose |
| HepA[8] | 2 or 3 doses depending on vaccine | | | | |
| HepB[9] | 3 doses | | | | |
| MenACWY or MPSV4[10] | 1 or more doses depending on indication | | | | |
| MenB[10] | 2 or 3 doses depending on vaccine | | | | |
| Hib[11] | 1 or 3 doses depending on indication | | | | |

 Recommended for adults who meet the age requirement, lack documentation of vaccination, or lack evidence of past infection

Recommended for adults with additional medical conditions or other indications

No recommendation

**Figure 2. Recommended immunization schedule for adults aged 19 years or older by medical condition and other indications, United States, 2017**

| Vaccine | Pregnancy[1-6,9] | Immuno-compromised (excluding HIV infection)[3-7,11] | HIV infection CD4+ count (cells/µL)[3-7,9-11] < 200 | ≥ 200 | Asplenia, persistent complement deficiencies[7,10,11] | Kidney failure, end-stage renal disease, on hemodialysis[7,9] | Heart or lung disease, chronic alcoholism[7] | Chronic liver disease[7-9] | Diabetes[7,9] | Healthcare personnel[3,4,9] | Men who have sex with men[6,8,9] |
|---|---|---|---|---|---|---|---|---|---|---|---|
| Influenza[1] | 1 dose annually | | | | | | | | | | |
| Td/Tdap[2] | 1 dose Tdap each pregnancy | Substitute Tdap for Td once, then Td booster every 10 yrs | | | | | | | | | |
| MMR[3] | contraindicated | | | 1 or 2 doses depending on indication | | | | | | | |
| VAR[4] | contraindicated | | | 2 doses | | | | | | | |
| HZV[5] | contraindicated | | | 1 dose | | | | | | | |
| HPV–Female[6] | | 3 doses through age 26 yrs | | | | | | | | | |
| HPV–Male[6] | | 3 doses through age 26 yrs | | | 3 doses through age 21 yrs | | | | | | 3 doses through age 26 yrs |
| PCV13[7] | | 1 dose | | | | | | | | | |
| PPSV23[7] | | 1, 2, or 3 doses depending on indication | | | | | | | | | |
| HepA[8] | | 2 or 3 doses depending on vaccine | | | | | | | | | |
| HepB[9] | | 3 doses | | | | | | | | | |
| MenACWY or MPSV4[10] | | 1 or more doses depending on indication | | | | | | | | | |
| MenB[10] | | 2 or 3 doses depending on vaccine | | | | | | | | | |
| Hib[11] | | 3 doses post-HSCT recipients only | | | 1 dose | | | | | | |

Recommended for adults who meet the age requirement, lack documentation of vaccination, or lack evidence of past infection

Recommended for adults with additional medical conditions or other indications

Contraindicated

No recommendation

**Footnotes. Recommended immunization schedule for adults aged 19 years or older, United States, 2017**

## 1. Influenza vaccination

### General information

- All persons aged 6 months or older who do not have a contraindication should receive annual influenza vaccination with an age-appropriate formulation of inactivated influenza vaccine (IIV) or recombinant influenza vaccine (RIV).
- In addition to standard-dose IIV, available options for adults in specific age groups include: high-dose or adjuvanted IIV for adults aged 65 years or older, intradermal IIV for adults aged 18 through 64 years, and RIV for adults aged 18 years or older.
- Notes: Live attenuated influenza vaccine (LAIV) should not be used during the 2016–2017 influenza season. A list of currently available influenza vaccines is available at www.cdc.gov/flu/protect/vaccine/vaccines.htm.

### Special populations

- Adults with a history of egg allergy who have only hives after exposure to egg should receive age-appropriate IIV or RIV.
- Adults with a history of egg allergy other than hives, e.g., angioedema, respiratory distress, lightheadedness, or recurrent emesis, or who required epinephrine or another emergency medical intervention, may receive age-appropriate IIV or RIV. The selected vaccine should be administered in an inpatient or outpatient medical setting and under the supervision of a healthcare provider who is able to recognize and manage severe allergic conditions.
- Pregnant women and women who might become pregnant in the upcoming influenza season should receive IIV.

## 2. Tetanus, diphtheria, and acellular pertussis vaccination

### General information

- Adults who have not received tetanus and diphtheria toxoids and acellular pertussis vaccine (Tdap) or for whom pertussis vaccination status is unknown should receive 1 dose of Tdap followed by a tetanus and diphtheria toxoids (Td) booster every 10 years. Tdap should be administered regardless of when a tetanus or diphtheria toxoid-containing vaccine was last received.
- Adults with an unknown or incomplete history of a 3-dose primary series with tetanus and diphtheria toxoid-containing vaccines should complete the primary series that includes 1 dose of Tdap. Unvaccinated adults should receive the first 2 doses at least 4 weeks apart and the third dose 6–12 months after the second dose.
- Notes: Information on the use of Td or Tdap as tetanus prophylaxis in wound management is available at www.cdc.gov/mmwr/preview/mmwrhtml/rr5517a1.htm.

### Special populations

- Pregnant women should receive 1 dose of Tdap during each pregnancy, preferably during the early part of gestational weeks 27–36, regardless of prior history of receiving Tdap.

## 3. Measles, mumps, and rubella vaccination

### General information

- Adults born in 1957 or later without acceptable evidence of immunity to measles, mumps, or rubella (defined below) should receive 1 dose of measles, mumps, and rubella vaccine (MMR) unless they have a medical contraindication to the vaccine, e.g., pregnancy or severe immunodeficiency.
- Notes: Acceptable evidence of immunity to measles, mumps, or rubella in adults is: born before 1957, documentation of receipt of MMR, or laboratory evidence of immunity or disease. Documentation of healthcare provider-diagnosed disease without laboratory confirmation is not acceptable evidence of immunity.

### Special populations

- Pregnant women who do not have evidence of immunity to rubella should receive 1 dose of MMR upon completion or termination of pregnancy and before discharge from the healthcare facility; nonpregnant women of childbearing age without evidence of rubella immunity should receive 1 dose of MMR.
- Adults with primary or acquired immunodeficiency including malignant conditions affecting the bone marrow or lymphatic system, systemic immunosuppressive therapy, or cellular immunodeficiency should not receive MMR.
- Adults with human immunodeficiency virus (HIV) infection and CD4+ T-lymphocyte count ≥200 cells/μl for at least 6 months who do not have evidence of measles, mumps, or rubella immunity should receive 2 doses of MMR at least 28 days apart. Adults with HIV infection and CD4+ T-lymphocyte count <200 cells/μl should not receive MMR.
- Adults who work in healthcare facilities should receive 2 doses of MMR at least 28 days apart; healthcare personnel born before 1957 who are unvaccinated or lack laboratory evidence of measles, mumps, or rubella immunity, or laboratory confirmation of disease should be considered for vaccination with 2 doses of MMR at least 28 days apart for measles or mumps, or 1 dose of MMR for rubella.
- Adults who are students in postsecondary educational institutions or plan to travel internationally should receive 2 doses of MMR at least 28 days apart.
- Adults who received inactivated (killed) measles vaccine or measles vaccine of unknown type during years 1963–1967 should be revaccinated with 1 or 2 doses of MMR.
- Adults who were vaccinated before 1979 with either inactivated mumps vaccine or mumps vaccine of unknown type who are at high risk for mumps infection, e.g., work in a healthcare facility, should be considered for revaccination with 2 doses of MMR at least 28 days apart.

## 4. Varicella vaccination

### General information

- Adults without evidence of immunity to varicella (defined below) should receive 2 doses of single-antigen varicella vaccine (VAR) 4–8 weeks apart, or a second dose if they have received only 1 dose.
- Persons without evidence of immunity for whom VAR should be emphasized are: adults who have close contact with persons at high risk for serious complications, e.g., healthcare personnel and household contacts of immunocompromised persons; adults who live or work in an environment in which transmission of varicella zoster virus is likely, e.g., teachers, childcare workers, and residents and staff in institutional settings; adults who live or work in environments in which varicella transmission has been reported, e.g., college students, residents and staff members of correctional institutions, and military personnel; nonpregnant women of childbearing age; adolescents and adults living in households with children; and international travelers.
- Notes: Evidence of immunity to varicella in adults is: U.S.-born before 1980 (for pregnant women and healthcare personnel, U.S.-born before 1980 is not considered evidence of immunity); documentation of 2 doses of VAR at least 4 weeks apart; history of varicella or herpes zoster diagnosis or verification of varicella or herpes zoster disease by a healthcare provider; or laboratory evidence of immunity or disease.

### Special populations

- Pregnant women should be assessed for evidence of varicella immunity. Pregnant women who do not have evidence of immunity should receive the first dose of VAR upon completion or termination of pregnancy and before discharge from the healthcare facility, and the second dose 4–8 weeks after the first dose.
- Healthcare institutions should assess and ensure that all healthcare personnel have evidence of immunity to varicella.
- Adults with malignant conditions, including those that affect the bone marrow or lymphatic system or who receive systemic immunosuppressive therapy, should not receive VAR.
- Adults with human immunodeficiency virus (HIV) infection and CD4+ T-lymphocyte count ≥200 cells/μl may receive 2 doses of VAR 3 months apart. Adults with HIV infection and CD4+ T-lymphocyte count <200 cells/μl should not receive VAR.

## 5. Herpes zoster vaccination

### General information

- Adults aged 60 years or older should receive 1 dose of herpes zoster vaccine (HZV), regardless of whether they had a prior episode of herpes zoster.

### Special populations

- Adults aged 60 years or older with chronic medical conditions may receive HZV unless they have a medical contraindication, e.g., pregnancy or severe immunodeficiency.
- Adults with malignant conditions, including those that affect the bone marrow or lymphatic system or who receive systemic immunosuppressive therapy, should not receive HZV.
- Adults with human immunodeficiency virus (HIV) infection and CD4+ T-lymphocyte count <200 cells/μl should not receive HZV.

## 6. Human papillomavirus vaccination

### General information

- Adult females through age 26 years and adult males through age 21 years who have not received any human papillomavirus (HPV) vaccine should receive a 3-dose series of HPV vaccine at 0, 1-2, and 6 months. Males aged 22 through 26 years may be vaccinated with a 3-dose series of HPV vaccine at 0, 1–2, and 6 months.
- Adult females through age 26 years and adult males through age 21 years (and males aged 22 through 26 years who may receive HPV vaccination) who initiated the HPV vaccination series before age 15 years and received 2 doses at least 5 months apart are considered adequately vaccinated and do not need an additional dose of HPV vaccine.
- Adult females through age 26 years and adult males through age 21 years (and males aged 22 through 26 years who may receive HPV vaccination) who initiated the HPV vaccination series before age 15 years and received only 1 dose, or 2 doses less than 5 months apart, are not considered adequately vaccinated and should receive 1 additional dose of HPV vaccine.
- Notes: HPV vaccination is routinely recommended for children at age 11 or 12 years. For adults who had initiated but did not complete the HPV vaccination series, consider their age at first HPV vaccination (described above) and other factors (described below) to determine if they have been adequately vaccinated.

### Special populations

- Men who have sex with men through age 26 years who have not received any HPV vaccine should receive a 3-dose series of HPV vaccine at 0, 1-2, and 6 months.
- Adult females and males through age 26 years with immunocompromising conditions (described below), including those with human immunodeficiency virus (HIV) infection, should receive a 3-dose series of HPV vaccine at 0, 1-2, and 6 months.
- Pregnant women are not recommended to receive HPV vaccine, although there is no evidence that the vaccine poses harm. If a woman is found to be pregnant after initiating the HPV vaccination series, delay the remaining doses until after the pregnancy. No other intervention is needed. Pregnancy testing is not needed before administering HPV vaccine.
- Notes: Immunocompromising conditions for which a 3-dose series of HPV vaccine is indicated are primary or secondary immunocompromising conditions that might reduce cell-mediated or humoral immunity, e.g., B-lymphocyte antibody deficiencies, complete or partial T-lymphocyte defects, HIV infection, malignant neoplasm, transplantation, autoimmune disease, and immunosuppressive therapy.

## 7. Pneumococcal vaccination

### General information

- Adults who are immunocompetent and aged 65 years or older should receive 13-valent pneumococcal conjugate vaccine (PCV13) followed by 23-valent pneumococcal polysaccharide vaccine (PPSV23) at least 1 year after PCV13.
- Notes: Adults are recommended to receive 1 dose of PCV13 and 1, 2, or 3 doses of PPSV23 depending on indication. When both PCV13 and PPSV23 are indicated, PCV13 should be administered first; PCV13 and PPSV23 should not be administered during the same visit. If PPSV23 has previously been administered, PCV13 should be administered at least 1 year after PPSV23. When two or more doses of PPSV23 are indicated, the interval between PPSV23 doses should be at least 5 years. Supplemental information on pneumococcal vaccine timing for adults aged 65 years or older and adults aged 19 years or older at high risk for pneumococcal disease (described below) is available at www.cdc.gov/vaccines/vpd-vac/ pneumo/downloads/adult-vax-clinician-aid.pdf. No additional doses of PPSV23 are indicated for adults who received PPSV23 at age 65 years or older. When indicated, PCV13 and PPSV23 should be administered to adults whose pneumococcal vaccination history is incomplete or unknown.

### Special populations

- Adults aged 19 through 64 years with chronic heart disease including congestive heart failure and cardiomyopathies (excluding hypertension); chronic lung disease including chronic obstructive lung disease, emphysema, and asthma; chronic liver disease including cirrhosis; alcoholism; or diabetes mellitus; or who smoke cigarettes should receive PPSV23. At age 65 years or older, they should receive PCV13 and another dose of PPSV23 at least 1 year after PCV13 and at least 5 years after the most recent dose of PPSV23.
- Adults aged 19 years or older with immunocompromising conditions or anatomical or functional asplenia (described below) should receive PCV13 and a dose of PPSV23 at least 8 weeks after PCV13, followed by a second dose of PPSV23 at least 5 years after the first dose of PPSV23. If the most recent dose of PPSV23 was administered before age 65 years, at age 65 years or older, administer another dose of PPSV23 at least 8 weeks after PCV13 and at least 5 years after the most recent dose of PPSV23.
- Adults aged 19 years or older with cerebrospinal fluid leak or cochlear implant should receive PCV13 followed by PPSV23 at least 8 weeks after PCV13. If the most recent dose of PPSV23 was administered before age 65 years, at age 65 years or older, administer another dose of PPSV23 at least 8 weeks after PCV13 and at least 5 years after the most recent dose of PPSV23.
- Notes: Immunocompromising conditions that are indications for pneumococcal vaccination are congenital or acquired immunodeficiency including B- or T-lymphocyte deficiency, complement deficiencies, and phagocytic disorders excluding chronic granulomatous disease; human immunodeficiency virus (HIV) infection; chronic renal failure and nephrotic syndrome; leukemia, lymphoma, Hodgkin disease, generalized malignancy, and multiple myeloma; solid organ transplant; and iatrogenic immunosuppression including long-term systemic corticosteroid and radiation therapy. Anatomical or functional asplenia that are indications for pneumococcal vaccination are sickle cell disease and other hemoglobinopathies, congenital or acquired asplenia, splenic dysfunction, and splenectomy. Pneumococcal vaccines should be given at least 2 weeks before immunosuppressive therapy or an elective splenectomy, and as soon as possible to adults who are diagnosed with HIV infection.

## 8. Hepatitis A vaccination

### General information

- Adults who seek protection from hepatitis A virus infection may receive a 2-dose series of single antigen hepatitis A vaccine (HepA) at either 0 and 6–12 months (Havrix) or 0 and 6–18 months (Vaqta). Adults may also receive a combined hepatitis A and hepatitis B vaccine (HepA-HepB) (Twinrix) as a 3-dose series at 0, 1, and 6 months. Acknowledgment of a specific risk factor by those who seek protection is not needed.

### Special populations

- Adults with any of the following indications should receive a HepA series: have chronic liver disease, receive clotting factor concentrates, men who have sex with men, use injection or non-injection drugs, or work with hepatitis A virus-infected primates or in a hepatitis A research laboratory setting.
- Adults who travel in countries with high or intermediate levels of endemic hepatitis A infection or anticipate close personal contact with an international adoptee, e.g., reside in the same household or regularly babysit, from a country with high or intermediate level of endemic hepatitis A infection within the first 60 days of arrival in the United States should receive a HepA series.

## 9. Hepatitis B vaccination

### General information

- Adults who seek protection from hepatitis B virus infection may receive a 3-dose series of single-antigen hepatitis B vaccine (HepB) (Engerix-B, Recombivax HB) at 0, 1, and 6 months. Adults may also receive a combined hepatitis A and hepatitis B vaccine (HepA-HepB) (Twinrix) at 0, 1, and 6 months. Acknowledgment of a specific risk factor by those who seek protection is not needed.

### Special populations

- Adults at risk for hepatitis B virus infection by sexual exposure should receive a HepB series, including sex partners of hepatitis B surface antigen (HBsAg)-positive persons, sexually active persons who are not in a mutually monogamous relationship, persons seeking evaluation or treatment for a sexually transmitted infection, and men who have sex with men (MSM).
- Adults at risk for hepatitis B virus infection by percutaneous or mucosal exposure to blood should receive a HepB series, including adults who are recent or current users of injection drugs, household contacts of HBsAg-positive persons, residents and staff of facilities for developmentally disabled persons, incarcerated, healthcare and public safety workers at risk for exposure to blood or blood-contaminated body fluids, younger than age 60 years with diabetes mellitus, and age 60 years or older with diabetes mellitus at the discretion of the treating clinician.
- Adults with chronic liver disease including, but not limited to, hepatitis C virus infection, cirrhosis, fatty liver disease, alcoholic liver disease, autoimmune hepatitis, and an alanine aminotransferase (ALT) or aspartate aminotransferase (AST) level greater than twice the upper limit of normal should receive a HepB series.
- Adults with end-stage renal disease including those on pre-dialysis care, hemodialysis, peritoneal dialysis, and home dialysis should receive a HepB series. Adults on hemodialysis should receive a 3-dose series of 40 µg Recombivax HB at 0, 1, and 6 months or a 4-dose series of 40 µg Engerix-B at 0, 1, 2, and 6 months.
- Adults with human immunodeficiency virus (HIV) infection should receive a HepB series.
- Pregnant women who are at risk for hepatitis B virus infection during pregnancy, e.g., having more than one sex partner during the previous six months, been evaluated or treated for a sexually transmitted infection, recent or current injection drug use, or had an HBsAg-positive sex partner, should receive a HepB series.
- International travelers to regions with high or intermediate levels of endemic hepatitis B virus infection should receive a HepB series.
- Adults in the following settings are assumed to be at risk for hepatitis B virus infection and should receive a HepB series: sexually transmitted disease treatment facilities, HIV testing and treatment facilities, facilities providing drug-abuse treatment and prevention services, healthcare settings targeting services to persons who inject drugs, correctional facilities, healthcare settings targeting services to MSM, hemodialysis facilities and end-stage renal disease programs, and institutions and nonresidential day care facilities for developmentally disabled persons.

## 10. Meningococcal vaccination

### Special populations

- Adults with anatomical or functional asplenia or persistent complement component deficiencies should receive a 2-dose primary series of serogroups A, C, W, and Y meningococcal conjugate vaccine (MenACWY) at least 2 months apart and revaccinate every 5 years. They should also receive a series of serogroup B meningococcal vaccine (MenB) with either a 2-dose series of MenB-4C (Bexsero) at least 1 month apart or a 3-dose series of MenB-FHbp (Trumenba) at 0, 1–2, and 6 months.
- Adults with human immunodeficiency virus (HIV) infection who have not been previously vaccinated should receive a 2-dose primary series of MenACWY at least 2 months apart and revaccinate every 5 years. Those who previously received 1 dose of MenACWY should receive a second dose at least 2 months after the first dose. Adults with HIV infection are not routinely recommended to receive MenB because meningococcal disease in this population is caused primarily by serogroups C, W, and Y.
- Microbiologists who are routinely exposed to isolates of *Neisseria meningitidis* should receive 1 dose of MenACWY and revaccinate every 5 years if the risk for infection remains, and either a 2-dose series of MenB-4C at least 1 month apart or a 3-dose series of MenB-FHbp at 0, 1–2, and 6 months.
- Adults at risk because of a meningococcal disease outbreak should receive 1 dose of MenACWY if the outbreak is attributable to serogroup A, C, W, or Y, or either a 2-dose series of MenB-4C at least 1 month apart or a 3-dose series of MenB-FHbp at 0, 1–2, and 6 months if the outbreak is attributable to serogroup B.
- Adults who travel to or live in countries with hyperendemic or epidemic meningococcal disease should receive 1 dose of MenACWY and revaccinate every 5 years if the risk for infection remains. MenB is not routinely indicated because meningococcal disease in these countries is generally not caused by serogroup B.
- Military recruits should receive 1 dose of MenACWY and revaccinate every 5 years if the increased risk for infection remains.
- First-year college students aged 21 years or younger who live in residence halls should receive 1 dose of MenACWY if they have not received MenACWY at age 16 years or older.
- Young adults aged 16 through 23 years (preferred age range is 16 through 18 years) who are healthy and not at increased risk for serogroup B meningococcal disease (described above) may receive either a 2-dose series of MenB-4C at least 1 month apart or a 2-dose series of MenB-FHbp at 0 and 6 months for short-term protection against most strains of serogroup B meningococcal disease.
- For adults aged 56 years or older who have not previously received serogroups A, C, W, and Y meningococcal vaccine and need only 1 dose, meningococcal polysaccharide serogroups A, C, W, and Y vaccine (MPSV4) is preferred. For adults who previously received MenACWY or anticipate receiving multiple doses of serogroups A, C, W, and Y meningococcal vaccine, MenACWY is preferred.
- Notes: MenB-4C and MenB-FHbp are not interchangeable, i.e., the same vaccine should be used for all doses to complete the series. There is no recommendation for MenB revaccination at this time. MenB may be administered at the same time as MenACWY but at a different anatomic site, if feasible.

## 11. *Haemophilus influenzae* type b vaccination

### Special populations

- Adults who have anatomical or functional asplenia or sickle cell disease, or are undergoing elective splenectomy should receive 1 dose of *Haemophilus influenzae* type b conjugate vaccine (Hib) if they have not previously received Hib. Hib should be administered at 14 days before splenectomy.
- Adults with a hematopoietic stem cell transplant (HSCT) should receive 3 doses of Hib in at least 4 week intervals 6–12 months after transplant regardless of their Hib history.
- Notes: Hib is not routinely recommended for adults with human immunodeficiency virus infection because their risk for *Haemophilus influenzae* type b infection is low.

**Table. Contraindications and precautions for vaccines recommended for adults aged 19 years or older***

The Advisory Committee on Immunization Practices (ACIP) recommendations and package inserts for vaccines provide information on contraindications and precautions related to vaccines. Contraindications are conditions that increase chances of a serious adverse reaction in vaccine recipients and the vaccine should not be administered when a contraindication is present. Precautions should be reviewed for potential risks and benefits for vaccine recipient. For a person with a severe allergy to latex, e.g., anaphylaxis, vaccines supplied in vials or syringes that contain natural rubber latex should not be administered unless the benefit of vaccination clearly outweighs the risk for a potential allergic reaction. For latex allergies other than anaphylaxis, vaccines supplied in vials or syringes that contain dry, natural rubber or natural rubber latex may be administered.

**Contraindications and precautions for vaccines routinely recommended for adults**

| Vaccine | Contraindications | Precautions |
|---|---|---|
| All vaccines routinely recommended for adults | • Severe reaction, e.g., anaphylaxis, after a previous dose or to a vaccine component | • Moderate or severe acute illness with or without fever |

**Additional contraindications and precautions for vaccines routinely recommended for adults**

| Vaccine | Additional Contraindications | Additional Precautions |
|---|---|---|
| IIV[1] | | • History of Guillain-Barré Syndrome within 6 weeks after previous influenza vaccination<br>• Egg allergy other than hives, e.g., angioedema, respiratory distress, lightheadedness, or recurrent emesis; or required epinephrine or another emergency medical intervention (IIV may be administered in an inpatient or outpatient medical setting and under the supervision of a healthcare provider who is able to recognize and manage severe allergic conditions) |
| RIV[1] | | • History of Guillain-Barré Syndrome within 6 weeks after previous influenza vaccination |
| LAIV[1] | • LAIV should not be used during 2016–2017 influenza season | • LAIV should not be used during 2016–2017 influenza season |
| Tdap/Td | • For pertussis-containing vaccines: encephalopathy, e.g., coma, decreased level of consciousness, or prolonged seizures, not attributable to another identifiable cause within 7 days of administration of a previous dose of a vaccine containing tetanus or diphtheria toxoid or acellular pertussis | • Guillain-Barré Syndrome within 6 weeks after a previous dose of tetanus toxoid-containing vaccine<br>• History of Arthus-type hypersensitivity reactions after a previous dose of tetanus or diphtheria toxoid-containing vaccine. Defer vaccination until at least 10 years have elapsed since the last tetanus toxoid-containing vaccine<br>• For pertussis-containing vaccine, progressive or unstable neurologic disorder, uncontrolled seizures, or progressive encephalopathy (until a treatment regimen has been established and the condition has stabilized) |
| MMR[2] | • Severe immunodeficiency, e.g., hematologic and solid tumors, chemotherapy, congenital immunodeficiency or long-term immunosuppressive therapy[3], human immunodeficiency virus (HIV) infection with severe immunocompromise<br>• Pregnancy | • Recent (within 11 months) receipt of antibody-containing blood product (specific interval depends on product)[4]<br>• History of thrombocytopenia or thrombocytopenic purpura<br>• Need for tuberculin skin testing[5] |
| VAR[2] | • Severe immunodeficiency, e.g., hematologic and solid tumors, chemotherapy, congenital immunodeficiency or long-term immunosuppressive therapy[3], HIV infection with severe immunocompromise<br>• Pregnancy | • Recent (within 11 months) receipt of antibody-containing blood product (specific interval depends on product)[4]<br>• Receipt of specific antiviral drugs (acyclovir, famciclovir, or valacyclovir) 24 hours before vaccination (avoid use of these antiviral drugs for 14 days after vaccination) |
| HZV[2] | • Severe immunodeficiency, e.g., hematologic and solid tumors, chemotherapy, congenital immunodeficiency or long-term immunosuppressive therapy[3], HIV infection with severe immunocompromise<br>• Pregnancy | • Receipt of specific antiviral drugs (acyclovir, famciclovir, or valacyclovir) 24 hours before vaccination (avoid use of these antiviral drugs for 14 days after vaccination) |
| HPV vaccine | | • Pregnancy |
| PCV13 | • Severe allergic reaction to any vaccine containing diphtheria toxoid | |

1. For additional information on use of influenza vaccines among persons with egg allergy, see: CDC. Prevention and control of seasonal influenza with vaccines: recommendations of the Advisory Committee on Immunization Practices—United States, 2016–17 influenza season. MMWR 2016;65(RR-5):1–54. Available at www.cdc.gov/mmwr/volumes/65/rr/rr6505a1.htm.

2. MMR may be administered together with VAR or HZV on the same day. If not administered on the same day, separate live vaccines by at least 28 days.

3. Immunosuppressive steroid dose is considered to be daily receipt of 20 mg or more prednisone or equivalent for two or more weeks. Vaccination should be deferred for at least 1 month after discontinuation of immunosuppressive steroid therapy. Providers should consult ACIP recommendations for complete information on the use of specific live vaccines among persons on immune-suppressing medications or with immune suppression because of other reasons.

4. Vaccine should be deferred for the appropriate interval if replacement immune globulin products are being administered. See: CDC. General recommendations on immunization: recommendations of the Advisory Committee on Immunization Practices (ACIP). MMWR 2011;60(No. RR-2). Available at www.cdc.gov/mmwr/preview/mmwrhtml/rr6002a1.htm.

5. Measles vaccination may temporarily suppress tuberculin reactivity. Measles-containing vaccine may be administered on the same day as tuberculin skin testing, or should be postponed for at least 4 weeks after vaccination.

* Adapted from: CDC. Table 6. Contraindications and precautions to commonly used vaccines. General recommendations on immunization: recommendations of the Advisory Committee on Immunization Practices. MMWR 2011;60(No. RR-2):40–41 and from: Hamborsky J, Kroger A, Wolfe S, eds. Appendix A. Epidemiology and prevention of vaccine preventable diseases. 13th ed. Washington, DC: Public Health Foundation, 2015. Available at www.cdc.gov/vaccines/pubs/pinkbook/index.html.

**Acronyms of vaccines recommended for adults**

| | | | | | |
|---|---|---|---|---|---|
| HepA | hepatitis A vaccine | LAIV | live attenuated influenza vaccine | PCV13 | 13-valent pneumococcal conjugate vaccine |
| HepA-HepB | hepatitis A and hepatitis B vaccines | MenACWY | serogroups A, C, W, and Y meningococcal conjugate vaccine | PPSV23 | 23-valent pneumococcal polysaccharide vaccine |
| HepB | hepatitis B vaccine | | | RIV | recombinant influenza vaccine |
| Hib | *Haemophilus influenzae* type b conjugate vaccine | MenB | serogroup B meningococcal vaccine | Td | tetanus and diphtheria toxoids |
| HPV vaccine | human papillomavirus vaccine | MMR | measles, mumps, and rubella vaccine | Tdap | tetanus toxoid, reduced diphtheria toxoid, and acellular pertussis vaccine |
| HZV | herpes zoster vaccine | MPSV4 | serogroups A, C, W, and Y meningococcal polysaccharide vaccine | VAR | varicella vaccine |
| IIV | inactivated influenza vaccine | | | | |

CS270457-A

| Table 6  SUMMARY OF ADOLESCENT/ADULT IMMUNIZATION RECOMMENDATIONS | | | | | |
|---|---|---|---|---|---|
| | TETANUS, DIPTHERIA AND ACELLULAR PERTUSSIS (TD/TDAP) | INFLUENZA | PNEUMOCOCCAL POLYSACCHARIDE (PPSV) | MEASLES AND MUMPS | SMALL POX |
| Indications | All adults<br>Tdap should replace a single dose of Td for adults aged less than 65 years who have not previously received a Tdap dose. | Ages 19–49 for persons with medical/exposure indications<br>Adults 50 y and older<br>Clients with chronic conditions<br>During influenza season for women in 2nd and 3rd trimester of pregnancy<br>Persons traveling to foreign countries<br>Residents of nursing homes, long-term care, assisted-living facilities | Ages 19–64 for persons with medical/exposure indications<br>Adults 65 y and older<br>Alaskan Natives and some Native Americans<br>Residents of nursing homes, long-term care, assisted-living facilities | Adults born after 1957 without proof of vaccine on or after first birthday<br>HIV-infected persons without severe immunosuppression<br>Travelers to foreign countries<br>Persons entering college | First responders |
| Schedule | Two doses 4–8 wk apart<br>Third dose 6–12 mo<br>Booster at 10 y intervals for life<br>Tdap or Td vaccine used as indicated | Annually each fall | One dose Should receive at age 65 if received at least 5 y previously<br>Administered if vaccination status unknown | One dose<br>Two doses if in college, in health care profession, or traveling to foreign country with 2nd dose one month after 1st | One dose |
| Contra-indications | Severe allergic reaction to previous dose<br>Encephalopathy not due to another cause within 7 days of DTaP | Allergy to eggs | | Severe allergic reaction<br>Known severe immunodeficiency | History of eczema or other skin conditions that disrupt epidermis, pregnancy or breast feeding, or women who wish to conceive<br>28 days after vaccination Immunosuppression, allergy to small pox vaccine receiving topical ocular steroid medication, moderate-to-severe recurrent illness, being under the age of 18, household contacts with history of eczema |
| Comments | Precautions:<br>Moderate or severe illness with or without fever | | | Check pregnancy status of women<br>Should avoid pregnancy for 30 d after vaccination<br>Elevated temperature may be seen for 1–2 weeks<br>Precautions:<br>Recent receipt of antibody-containing blood product<br>Moderate or severe illness with or without fever | Vaccinia can be transmitted from an unhealed vaccination site to other persons by close contact. Wash hands with soapy water immediately after changing bandage; place bandages in sealed plastic bag; cover site with gauze and wear long-sleeved clothing. When performing client care, keep site covered with gauze and a semiper-meable dressing. |

| | RUBELLA | HEPATITIS B | POLIOVIRUS: IPV | VARICELLA | HEPATITIS A | HUMAN PAPILLOMAVIRUS VACCINE (HPV) |
|---|---|---|---|---|---|---|
| **Indications** | Persons (especially women) without proof of vaccine on or after first birthday<br>Health-care personnel at risk of exposure to rubella and who have contact with pregnant clients | Persons at risk to exposure to blood or blood-containing body fluids<br>Clients and staff at institutions for develop-mentally disabled<br>Hemodialysis clients<br>Recipients of clotting-factor concentrates<br>Household contacts and sex partners of clients with HBV<br>Some international travelers<br>Injecting drug users<br>Men who have sex with men<br>Heterosexuals with multiple sex partners or recent STD<br>Inmates of longterm correc-tional facilities<br>All unvaccinated adolescents | Travelers to countries where it is epidemic<br>Unvaccinated adults whose children receive IPV | Persons without proof of disease or vaccination or who are seronegative<br>Susceptible adolescents/adults living in house holds with children<br>Susceptible healthcare workers<br>Susceptible family contacts of immunocompromised persons<br>Nonpregnant women of childbearing age<br>International travelers<br>High risk persons: teachers of young children, day care employees, residents and staff in institutional settings, college students, inmates and staff of correctional institutions, military personnel | Travelers to countries with high incidence<br>Men who have sex with men<br>Injecting and illegal drug users<br>Persons with chronic liver disease<br>Persons with clotting factor disorders<br>Food handlers | All females age 11/12 to 25 |
| **Schedule** | One dose | Three doses<br>Second dose 1–2 mo after 1st<br>Third 4–6 mo after 1st | IPV recommended<br>Two doses at 4–8 wk intervals<br>Third dose 2–12 mo after second<br>OPV no longer recommended in U.S. | Two doses separated by 4–8 wk | Two doses separated by 6–12 mo | Three doses<br>Second dose 2 mo after 1st<br>Third dose 6 mo after 2nd |
| **Contra-indications** | Allergy to neomycin<br>Pregnancy<br>Receipt of immune globulin or blood/ blood products in previous 3–11 mo | Severe allergic reaction to vaccine | Severe allergic reaction after previous dose | Severe allergic reaction to vaccine<br>Immunosuppressive therapy or immunodeficiency (including HIV infection)<br>Pregnancy | Severe allergic reaction to vaccine | |
| **Comments** | Check pregnancy status of women<br>Should avoid pregnancy for 3 mo after vaccination | Precautions:<br>Low birth weight infant<br>Moderate or severe illness with or without fever | Temperature elevation may be seen for 1–2 weeks<br>Precautions:<br>Pregnancy moderate or severe illness with or without fever | Check pregnancy status of women<br>Should avoid pregnancy for 1 mo after vaccination<br>Immune globulin or blood/ blood product in previous 11 mo<br>Moderate or severe illness with or without fever | Swelling and redness at injection site common<br>Precaution: pregnancy | |

**Table 6  SUMMARY OF ADOLESCENT/ADULT IMMUNIZATION RECOMMENDATIONS (CONTINUED)**

| Table 7 NURSING CONSIDERATIONS FOR THE CHILD RECEIVING IMMUNIZATION | | |
|---|---|---|
| NAME | ROUTE | NURSING CONSIDERATIONS |
| DTaP (diphtheria, tetanus, pertussis) | IM anterior or lateral thigh (No IMs in gluteal muscle until after child is walking) | Potential adverse effects include fever within 24–48 hours, swelling, redness, soreness at injection site<br>More serious adverse effects–continuous screaming, convulsions, high fever, loss of consciousness<br>Do not administer if there is past history of serious reaction |
| MMR (measles, mumps, rubella) | SC anterior or lateral thigh | Potential adverse effects include rash, fever, and arthritis; may occur 10 days to 2 weeks after vaccination<br>May give DTaP, MMR, and IPV at same time if family has history of not keeping appointments for vaccinations |
| IPV (inactivated polio) | IM | Reactions very rare |
| HB (hepatitis B) | IM vastus lateralis or deltoid | Should not be given into dorsogluteal site<br>Mild local tenderness at injection site |
| Tuberculosis test | Intradermal | May be given 4–6 year and 11–16 years if in high prevalence areas<br>Evaluated in 48–72 hours<br>PPD (purified protein derivative) 0.1 ml<br>Tine test (multiple puncture) less accurate |
| TD (tetanus/ diphtheria booster) | IM anterior or lateral thigh | Repeat every 10 years |
| Live attenuated rubella | SC anterior or lateral thigh | Give once only to women who are antibody-negative for rubella, and if pregnancy can be prevented for 3 months postvaccination |
| Live attenuated mumps | SC | Give once<br>Prevention of orchitis (and therefore sterility) in susceptible males |

# ALLERGEN RESPONSE

A. Assessment

  1. Prodromal—reports weakness, apprehension, impending doom, dry/scratchy throat (feeling of "lump in throat"); nausea and vomiting

  2. Cutaneous—generalized intense pruritus and urticaria (hives), angioedema (swelling) of lips and eyelids

  3. Bronchial—increasing respiratory distress with audible wheezing, rales; diminished breath sounds heard on auscultation

  4. Circulatory—hypotension and a rapid, weak, irregular pulse, dysrhythmias, shock, cardiac arrest can occur within minutes

B. Diagnose

  1. Hypersensitivity—exaggerated or inappropriate reaction of a previously sensitized immune system resulting in a typical pathological process and tissue damage

  2. Anaphylaxis—serious multiple system response (vasogenic shock) to an antigen-antibody reaction upon subsequent exposure (rarely upon first contact) to a substance (allergen) for which the person has developed a severe hypersensitivity

  3. Immense amounts of histamine are rapidly dispersed throughout the circulatory system resulting in extensive vasodilation and increased capillary permeability leading to acute hypovolemia and vascular

collapse; there is also severe edema of bronchial tissue resulting in pulmonary obstruction; without treatment, severe hypoxemia and ultimately death will occur

4. Common allergens—drug/chemicals (penicillin, radiopaque dyes, aspirin, bisulfates, vaccines, blood components), toxins (snake, bee, wasp, hornet), and food (berries, chocolate, eggs, shellfish, seafood, nuts)

5. Potential nursing diagnoses

    a. Skin integrity, impaired

    b. Airway clearance, ineffective

**C.** Plan/Implementation

1. Establish airway (ABC)

2. Administer aqueous epinephrine (adrenaline) 1:1,000—0.1 ml up to 0.5 ml (0.1 mg/kg body weight) SC in arm opposite to side of injection/sting; same dose may be repeated every 15–20 minutes PRN (three times with children)

3. Start IV with large-bore needle for rapid infusion of fluids, if needed; monitor I and O

4. Tourniquet may be applied on extremity proximal to injection of allergen to prevent further absorption

5. Oxygen, suction, and life support as needed

6. Other medications may be used—diphenhydramine as antihistamine, aminophylline for severe bronchospasm, vasopressors for severe shock, corticosteroids for persistent/recurrent symptoms

7. Assess all clients about possible allergic reactions to foods, medications, insects

8. Ensure that clients remain in health setting at least 20–30 minutes after receiving injection

9. Teach client and family how to avoid the identified allergen; ensure/reinforce wearing Medic-Alert items

10. For sensitivity to insect venom, instruct the client and/or family members in the use of the emergency anaphylaxis kit (either epinephrine and syringes or automatic injector), to be kept with the person at all times

11. Hyposensitization/desensitization/immunotherapy—SC administration of gradually increasing dosages of the offending allergen

**D.** Evaluation

1. Was the reaction to the allergen controlled?

2. Does the family/client know how to provide emergency care?

▶ **LATEX ALLERGY**

**A.** Assessment

1. Contact urticaria; lip, mouth

2. Upper airway edema

3. Flushing and generalized edema

4. Rhinitis, conjunctivitis

5. Bronchospasms

6. Anaphylactic shock

**B.** Diagnose

1. Caused by repeated exposure to natural latex rubber protein products
2. High risk populations
   a. Children with neural tube defects
   b. Clients with urogenital abnormalities
   c. Clients with spinal cord injuries
   d. History of multiple surgeries
   e. Health care workers, hairdressers, cleaning staff
   f. Allergies to banana, avocado, chestnut, kiwi, papaya, peaches

**C.** Plan/Implementation

1. Screen for latex sensitivity
2. Provide latex-safe environment
3. Instruct client to avoid latex products
   a. Gloves
   b. Catheters
   c. Brown ace bandages
   d. Band-Aid dressing
   e. Elastic pressure stocking
   f. Balloons
   g. Condoms
   h. Feminine hygiene pad
4. Wear Medic-Alert identification

**D.** Evaluation

1. Is the client knowledgeable about how to avoid latex?

# ATOPIC ALLERGY

**A.** Assessment

1. History of offending allergen, pollens (trees, grass, weeds), or environmental substances (dust, animals, feathers)
2. Upper respiratory symptoms—rhinorrhea (runny nose), sneezing, mucosal edema, and congestion, pharyngeal and conjunctival itching and tearing
3. Etiology and severity may be determined by skin testing

**B.** Diagnose

1. Airway clearance, ineffective
2. Includes hay fever, rhinitis, asthma

**C.** Plan/Implementation

1. Provide symptomatic relief
2. Teach client how to avoid allergies

**D.** Evaluation

1. Is client knowledgeable about how to avoid offending allergen?
2. Is client able to control symptoms of allergic response?

## ▶ PHYSICAL ASSESSMENT

**A.** Purpose

1. Assess client's current health status

2. Interpret physical data

3. Decide on interventions based on data obtained

**B.** Preparation

1. Gather equipment

   a. Ophthalmoscope

   b. Tuning fork

   c. Cotton swabs

   d. Snellen eye chart

   e. Thermometer

   f. Penlight

   g. Tongue depressor

   h. Ruler/tape measure

   i. Safety pin

   j. Balance scale

   k. Gloves

   l. Nasal speculum

   m. Vaginal speculum

2. Provide for privacy (drape) in quiet, well-lit environment

3. Explain procedure to client

4. Ask client to empty bladder

5. Drape client for privacy

6. Compare findings on one side of body with other side and compare with normal

7. Make use of teaching opportunities (dental care, eye exams, self-exams of breast or testicle)

8. Use piece of equipment for entire assessment, then return to equipment tray

**C.** Techniques used in order performed, except for abdominal assessment

1. Inspection (visually examined)

   a. Starts with first interaction

   b. Provide good lighting

   c. Determine

      1) Size

      2) Shape

      3) Color

      4) Texture

      5) Symmetry

      6) Position

2. Palpation (touch)

   a. Warm hands

   b. Approach slowly and proceed systematically

   c. Use fingertips for fine touch (pulses, nodes)

   d. Use dorsum of fingers for temperatures

   e. Use palm or ulnar edge of hand for vibration

   f. Start with light palpation, then do deep palpation

   g. Use bimanual palpation (both hands) for deep palpation and to assess movable structure (kidney)–place sensing hand lightly on skin surface, place active hand over sensing hand and apply pressure

   h. Ballottement–push fluid-filled tissue toward palpating hand so object floats against fingertips

   i. Determines

      1) Masses

      2) Pulsation

      3) Organ size

      4) Tenderness or pain

      5) Swelling

      6) Tissue fullness and elasticity

      7) Vibration

      8) Crepitus

      9) Temperature

      10) Texture

      11) Moisture

3. Percussion (tap to produce sound and vibration)

   a. Types

      1) Direct–strike body surface with 1 or 2 fingers

      2) Indirect–strike finger or hand placed over body surface

      3) Blunt–use reflex hammer to check deep tendon reflexes; Use blunt percussion with fist to assess costovertebral angle (CVA) tenderness

   b. Sounds

      1) Resonance–moderate-to-loud, low-pitched (clear, hollow) sound of moderate duration; found with air-filled tissue (normal lung)

      2) Hyperresonance–loud, booming, low-pitched sound of longer duration found with overinflated air-filled tissue (pulmonary emphysema); normal in child due to thin chest wall

      3) Tympany–loud, drumlike, high-pitched or musical sound of moderately long duration found with enclosed, air-filled structures (bowel)

      4) Dull–soft, muffled, moderate-to-high-pitched sound of short duration; found with dense, fluid-filled tissue (liver)

      5) Flat–very soft, high-pitched sound of short duration; found with very dense tissue (bone, muscle)

    c. Determines

      1) Location, size, density of masses

      2) Pain in areas up to depth of 3–5 cm (1–2 inches)

    d. Performed after inspection and palpation, except for abdominal assessment; for abdomen perform inspection, auscultation, percussion, palpation

  4. Auscultation

    a. Equipment

      1) Use diaphragm of stethoscope to listen to high-pitched sounds (lung, bowel, heart); place firmly against skin surface to form tight seal (leave ring)

      2) Use bell to listen to soft, low-pitched sounds (heart murmurs); place lightly on skin surface

    b. Listen over bare skin (not through clothing); moisten body hair to prevent crackling sounds

| Table 8 NORMAL VITAL SIGNS | | | |
|---|---|---|---|
| AGE | NORMAL RESPIRATORY RATE | NORMAL PULSE RATE | NORMAL BLOOD PRESSURE (BP) |
| Newborn | 30–60 per minute | 120–140 beats per minute (bpm)<br><br>May go to 180 when crying | 65/41 mm Hg |
| 1–4 years | 20–40 per minute | 70–110 beats per minute (bpm) | 90/60 mm Hg |
| 5–12 years | 16–22 per minute | 60–95 beats per minute (bpm) | 100/60 mm Hg |
| Adult | 12–20 per minute | 60–100 beats per minute (bpm) | less than 120/80 mm Hg |
| Factors influencing respiration: fever, anxiety, drugs, disease | | | |
| Factors influencing BP: disease, drugs, anxiety, cardiac output, peripheral resistance, arterial elasticity, blood volume, blood viscosity, age, weight, exercise | | | |
| Factors influencing pulse rate and rhythm: drug, pathology, exercise, age, gender, temperature, BP, serum electrolytes | | | |

**D.** Findings

  1. General survey

    a. General appearance

      1) Apparent age

      2) Sex

      3) Racial and ethnic group

      4) Apparent state of health

      5) Proportionate height and weight

      6) Posture

      7) Gait, movements, range of motion

      8) Suitable clothing

9) Hygiene

10) Body and breath odor

11) Skin color, condition

12) Presence of assistive device, hearing aid, glasses

b. General behavior

1) Signs of distress

2) Level of consciousness, oriented ×3, mood, speech, thought process appropriate

3) Level of cooperation, eye contact (culture must be considered)

2. Vital signs (see Table 8)

a. Temperature (see Table 9)

1) Infants—performed axillary

2) Intra-auricular probe allows rapid, noninvasive reading when appropriate

3) Tympanic membrane sensors—positioning is crucial, ear canal must be straightened

b. Pulse (rate, rhythm)

c. Respirations (rate, pattern, depth)

1) Adult—costal (chest moves), regular, expiration slower than inspiration, rate 12–20 respirations/minute

2) Neonates—diaphragmatic (abdomen moves), irregular, 30–60 respirations/minute

3) Breathing patterns

a) Abdominal respirations—breathing accomplished by abdominal muscles and diaphragm; may be used to increase effectiveness of ventilatory process in certain conditions

b) Apnea—temporary cessation of breathing

c) Cheyne-Stokes respiration—periodic breathing characterized by rhythmic waxing and waning of the depth of respirations

d) Dyspnea—difficult, labored, or painful breathing (considered "normal" at certain times, e.g., after extreme physical exertion)

e) Hyperpnea—abnormally deep breathing

f) Hyperventilation—abnormally rapid, deep, and prolonged breathing

i) Caused by central nervous system disorders, drugs that increase sensitivity of respiratory center or acute anxiety

ii) Produces respiratory alkalosis due to reduction in $CO_2$

g) Hypoventilation—reduced ventilatory efficiency; produces respiratory acidosis due to elevation in $CO_2$

h) Kussmaul's respirations (air hunger)—marked increase in depth and rate

i) Orthopnea—inability to breathe except when trunk is in an upright position

j) Paradoxical respirations—breathing pattern in which a lung (or portion of a lung) deflates during inspiration (acts opposite to normal)

| Table 9 NORMAL BODY TEMPERATURE | | |
|---|---|---|
| METHOD USED | FAHRENHEIT | CELSIUS |
| Oral | 98.6° | 37.0° |
| Rectal | 99.6° | 37.6° |
| Axillary | 97.6° | 36.5° |
| Factors influencing reading: elderly client, faulty thermometer, dehydration, environment, infections | | |

   k) Periodic breathing—rate, depth, or tidal volume changes markedly from one interval to the next; pattern of change is periodically reproduced

  4) Cyanosis—skin appears blue because of an excessive accumulation of unoxygenated hemoglobin in the blood

  5) Stridor—harsh, high-pitched sound associated with airway obstruction near larynx

  6) Cough

   a) Normal reflex to remove foreign material from the lungs

   b) Normally absent in newborns

 d. Blood pressure

  1) Check both arms and compare results (difference 5–10 mm Hg normal)

  2) Pulse pressure (normal 30–40 mm Hg)

  3) Cover 50% of limb from shoulder to olecranon with cuff; too narrow: abnormally high reading; too wide: abnormally low reading

3. Nutrition status

 a. Height, weight; ideal body weight, men—106 lbs for first 5 feet, then add 6 lbs/inch; women—100 for first 5 feet, then add 5 lbs/inch; add 10% for client with larger frame; subtract 10% for client with small frame

4. Skin

 a. Check for pallor on buccal mucosa or conjunctivae, cyanosis on nail beds or oral mucosa, jaundice on sclera

 b. Scars, bruises, lesions

 c. Edema (eyes, sacrum), moisture, hydration

 d. Temperature, texture, turgor (pinch skin, tented 3 seconds or less is normal), check over sternum for elderly

5. Hair

 a. Hirsutism—excess

 b. Alopecia—loss or thinning

6. Nails (indicate respiratory and nutritional status)

 a. Color

    b.  Shape, contour (normal angle of nail bed less than or equal to 160°, clubbing: nail bed angle greater than or equal to 180° due to prolonged decreased oxygenation)

    c.  Texture, thickness

    d.  Capillary refill (normal ≤3-second return of color)

7.  Head

    a.  Size, shape, symmetry

    b.  Temporal arteries

    c.  Cranial nerve function (see Table 10)

8.  Eyes

    a.  Ptosis—drooping of upper eyelid

    b.  Color of sclerae, conjunctiva

    c.  Pupils

        1)  Size, shape, equality, reactivity to light and accommodation (PERRLA)

    d.  Photophobia—light intolerance

    e.  Nystagmus—abnormal, involuntary, rapid eye movements

    f.  Strabismus—involuntary drifting of one eye out of alignment with the other eye; "lazy eye"

    g.  Corneal reflex

    h.  Visual fields (peripheral vision)

    i.  Visual acuity—Snellen chart, normal 20/20

    j.  Ophthalmoscope exam

        1)  Red reflex—red glow from light reflected from retina

        2)  Fundus

        3)  Optic disk

        4)  Macula

    k.  Corneal light reflection—same position on each cornea; asymmetrical reflection—strabismus

9.  Ears

    a.  Pull pinna up and back to examine children's (3 years of age and older) and adult's ears

    b.  Pull pinna down and back to examine infants' and young childrens' (younger than 3 years of age) ears

    c.  Tympanic membrane—cone of light at 5 o'clock position right ear, 7 o'clock position left ear

    d.  Weber test—assesses bone conduction; vibrating tuning fork placed in middle of forehead; normal—hear sound equally in ears

    e.  Rinne test—compares bone conduction with air conduction; vibrating tuning fork placed on mastoid process, when client no longer hears sound, positioned in front of ear canal; normal—should still be able to hear sound; air conduction greater than bone conduction by 2:1 ratio (positive Rinne test)

10. Nose and sinuses

    a. Septum midline

    b. Alignment, color, discharge

    c. Palpate and percuss sinuses

11. Mouth and pharynx

    a. Oral mucosa

    b. Teeth (normal 32)

    c. Tongue

    d. Hard and soft palate

    e. Uvula, midline

    f. Tonsils

    g. Gag reflex

    h. Swallow

    i. Taste

12. Neck

    a. Range of motion of cervical spine

    b. Cervical lymph nodes (normal less than or equal to 1 cm round, soft, mobile) nontender

    c. Trachea position

    d. Thyroid gland

    e. Carotid arteries—check for bruit and thrill

    f. Jugular veins

13. Thorax and lungs

    a. Alignment of spine

    b. Anteroposterior to transverse diameter (normal adult 1:2 to 5:7); 1:1 barrel chest

| Table 10  CRANIAL NERVE ASSESSMENT | | | |
|---|---|---|---|
| **#/NERVE** | **FUNCTION** | **NORMAL FINDINGS** | **NURSING CONSIDERATIONS** |
| (I) Olfactory | Sense of smell | Able to detect various odors in each nostril | Have client smell a nonirritating substance such as coffee or tobacco with eyes closed<br><br>Test each nostril separately |
| (II) Optic | Sense of vision | Clear (acute) vision near and distant | Snellen eye chart for far vision<br><br>Read newspaper for near vision<br><br>Ophthalmoscopic exam |
| (III) Oculomotor | Pupil constriction, raising of eyelids | Pupils equal in size and equally reactive to light | Instruct client to look up, down, inward<br><br>Observe for symmetry and eye opening<br><br>Shine penlight into eye as client stares straight ahead<br><br>Ask client to watch your finger as you move it toward face |

| | Table 10 CRANIAL NERVE ASSESSMENT *(CONTINUED)* | | |
|---|---|---|---|
| **#/NERVE** | **FUNCTION** | **NORMAL FINDINGS** | **NURSING CONSIDERATIONS** |
| (IV) Trochlear | Downward and inward movement of eyes | Able to move eyes down and inward | (See Oculomotor) |
| (V) Trigeminal | Motor—jaw movement<br>Sensory—sensation on the face and neck | Able to clench and relax jaw<br>Able to differentiate between various stimuli touched to the face and neck | Test with pin and wisp of cotton over each division on both sides of face<br>Ask client to open jaw, bite down, move jaw laterally against pressure<br>Stroke cornea with wisp of cotton |
| (VI) Abducens | Lateral movement of the eyes | Able to move eyes in all directions | (See Oculomotor) |
| (VII) Facial | Motor—facial muscle movement<br>Sensory—taste on the anterior two-thirds of the tongue (sweet and salty) | Able to smile, whistle, wrinkle forehead<br>Able to differentiate tastes among various agents | Observe for facial symmetry after asking client to frown, smile, raise eyebrows, close eyelids against resistance, whistle, blow<br>Place sweet, sour, bitter, and salty substances on tongue |
| (VIII) Acoustic | Sense of hearing and balance | Hearing intact<br>Balance maintained while walking | Test with watch ticking into ear, rubbing fingers together, Rinne and Weber tests<br>Test posture, standing with eyes closed<br>Otoscopic exam |
| (IX) Glossopharyngeal | Motor—pharyngeal movement and swallowing<br>Sensory—taste on posterior one-third of tongue (sour and bitter) | Gag reflex intact, able to swallow<br>Able to taste | Place sweet, sour, bitter, and salty substances on tongue<br>Note ability to swallow and handle secretions<br>Stimulate pharyngeal wall to elicit gag reflex |
| (X) Vagus | Swallowing and speaking | Able to swallow and speak with a smooth voice | Inspect soft palate—instruct to say "ah"<br>Observe uvula for midline position<br>Rate quality of voice |
| (XI)<br>Spinal accessory | Motor—flexion and rotation of head; shrugging of shoulders | Able to flex and rotate head; able to shrug shoulders | Inspect and palpate sternocleido-mastoid and trapezius muscles for size, contour, tone<br>Ask client to move head side to side against resistance and shrug shoulders against resistance |
| (XII) Hypoglossal | Motor—tongue movements | Can move tongue side to side and stick it out symmetrically and in midline | Inspect tongue in mouth<br>Ask client to stick out tongue and move it quickly side to side<br>Observe midline, symmetry, and rhythmic movement |

   c. Respiratory excursion

   d. Respirations

   e. Tactile fremitus—(vibration produced when client makes sound of "99")

    f.  Diaphragmatic excursion—assesses degree and symmetry of diaphragm movement; percuss from areas of resonance to dullness

    g.  Breath sounds—bilaterally equal

      1)  Normal

        a)  Vesicular—soft and low-pitched breezy sounds heard over most of peripheral lung fields

        b)  Bronchovesicular—medium pitched, moderately loud sounds heard over the mainstem bronchi

        c)  Bronchial—loud, coarse, blowing sound heard over the trachea

      2)  Adventitious (abnormal); caused by fluid or inflammation

        a)  Rales—crackling or gurgling sounds (also known as crackles) commonly heard on inspiration

        b)  Rhonchi—musical sounds or vibrations commonly heard on expiration

        c)  Wheezes—squeaky sounds heard during inspiration and expiration associated with narrow airways

        d)  Pleural friction rub—grating sound or vibration heard during inspiration and expiration

    h.  Vocal resonance

      1)  Bronchophony—say "99" and hear more clearly than normal; loud transmission of voice sounds caused by consolidation of lung

      2)  Egophony—say "E" and hear "A" due to distortion caused by consolidation of lung

      3)  Whispered pectoriloquy—hear whispered sounds clearly due to dense consolidation of lung

    i.  Costovertebral angle percussion—kidneys

14.  Heart Sounds (corresponds with Figure 1)

    a.  Angle of Louis—manubrial sternal junction at second rib

    b.  Aortic and pulmonic areas—right and left second intercostal spaces alongside sternum

    c.  Erbs' point—third intercostal space just to the left of the sternum

    d.  Tricuspid area—fourth or fifth intercostal space to the left

    e.  Mitral area—fifth intercostal space at left midclavicular line (apex of heart)

    f.  Point of maximal impulse (PMI)

      1)  Impulse of the left ventricle felt most strongly

      2)  Adult—left fifth intercostal space in the midclavicular line (8–10 cm to the left of the midsternal line)

      3)  Infant—lateral to left nipple

    g.  S1 and S2

      1)  S1 "lubb"—closure of tricuspid and mitral valves; dull quality and low pitch; onset of ventricular systole (contraction)

      2)  S2 "dubb"—closure of aortic and pulmonic valves; snapping quality; onset of diastole (relaxation of atria, then ventricles)

h. Murmurs—abnormal sounds caused by turbulence within the heart valve; turbulence within a blood vessel is called a bruit; three basic factors result in murmurs

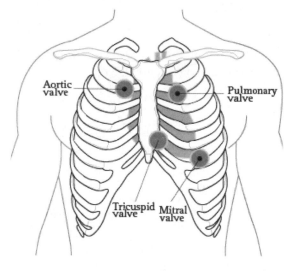

**Figure 1  Heart Sounds (intercostal spaces)**

1) High rate of blood flow through either a normal or abnormal valve

2) Blood flow through a sclerosed or abnormal valve, or into a dilated heart chamber or vessel

3) Blood flow regurgitated backward through an incompetent valve or septal defect

i. Pulse deficit—difference between apical and radial rate

j. Jugular veins—normally distend when the client lies flat, but are not visible when the client's head is raised 30 to 45°

15. Peripheral vascular system

a. Pulses

1) Radial—passes medially across the wrist; felt on radial (or thumb) side of the forearm

2) Ulnar—passes laterally across the wrist; felt on the ulnar (little finger) side of the wrist

3) Femoral—passes beneath the inguinal ligament (groin area) into the thigh; felt in groin area

4) Carotid—pulsations can be felt over medial edge of sternocleidomastoid muscle in neck

5) Pedal (dorsalis pedis: dorsal artery of the foot)—passes laterally over the foot; felt along top of foot

6) Posterior tibial—felt on inner side of ankle below medial malleous

7) Popliteal—felt in popliteal fossa, the region at the back of the knee

8) Temporal—felt lateral to eyes

9) Apical—left at fifth intercostal space at midclavicular line

16. Breasts and axillae

    a. Size, shape, symmetry

    b. Gynecomastia—breast enlargement in males

    c. Nodes—normal nonpalpable

17. Abdomen

    a. Knees flexed to relax muscles and provide for comfort

    b. Inspect and auscultate, then percuss and palpate

    c. Symmetry, contour

    d. Umbilicus

    e. Bowel sounds; normal high-pitched gurgles heard with the diaphragm of the stethoscope at 5–20-second intervals

        1) Hypoactive—less than 3/minute

        2) Hyperactive—loud, frequent

    f. Aorta, renal, iliac, femoral arteries auscultated with the bell of the stethoscope

    g. Peritoneal friction rub—grating sound varies with respirations; inflammation of liver

    h. Liver and spleen size

    i. Inguinal lymph nodes

    j. Rebound tenderness—inflammation of peritoneum

    k. Kidneys

    l. Abdominal reflexes

18. Neurological system

    a. Deep tendon reflexes (DTRs)—assesses sensory and motor pathways; compare bilaterally; 0 (absent) through 4+ (hyperactive) scale

    b. Cerebellar function—coordination; point-to-point touching, rapid, alternating movements, gait

    c. Mental status (cerebral function)

    d. Cranial nerve function

    e. Motor function

        1) Strength

        2) Tone

    f. Sensory function

        1) Touch, tactile localization

        2) Pain

        3) Pressure

        4) Temperature

        5) Vibration

        6) Proprioception (position sense)

        7) Vision

        8) Hearing

        9) Smell

        10) Taste

19. Musculoskeletal system
    a. Muscle tone and strength
    b. Joint movements; crepitus-grating sound abnormal
20. Genitalia
    a. Provide privacy
    b. Inspect outer structures (labia, urethral meatus, vaginal introitus, anus, penis, scrotum)
    c. Use firm, deliberate touch
    d. Note any abnormalities
       1) Hypospadias—urethral meatus located on the underside of the penile shaft
       2) Epispadias—urethral meatus located on the upper side of the penile shaft
       3) Hemorrhoids—dilated veins in the anal area
    e. Male
       1) Penis—foreskin, glans
       2) Hypospadias—meatus located on underside of penile shaft
       3) Epispadias—meatus located on upper side of penile shaft
       4) Scrotum
       5) Inguinal area
    f. Female
       1) Lithotomy position
       2) Cervix
21. Anus and rectum
    a. Rectal prolapse—protrusion of rectal mucous membrane through anus
    b. Hemorrhoids—dilated veins
    c. Anal sphincter
    d. Male—prostate gland
    e. Female—cervix
    f. Stool—normal color brown; assess for presence of blood

# Chapter 9

# PSYCHOSOCIAL INTEGRITY

| Sections | Concepts Covered |
|---|---|
| 1. Coping and Adaptation | Cognition, Emotional Processes |
| 2. Psychosocial Adaptation | Emotional Processes, Behavior |
| 3. Psychopathology | Intracranial Regulation |
| 4. Chemical Dependency | Cognition, Ego Integrity/Self Concept, Behavior |
| 5. Abuse and Neglect | Interpersonal Relationships |

# COPING AND ADAPTATION

## ▶ MENTAL HEALTH CONCEPTS

**A.** Assessment

    1. Appearance, behavior, or mood

        a. Well groomed, relaxed

        b. Self-confident, self-accepting

    2. Speech, thought content, and thought process

        a. Clear, coherent

        b. Reality-based

    3. Sensorium

        a. Oriented to person, place, and time

        b. Good memory

        c. Ability to abstract

    4. Insight and judgment—accurate self-perception and awareness

    5. Family relationships and work habits

        a. Satisfying interpersonal relationships

        b. Ability to trust

        c. Ability to cope effectively with stress

        d. Environmental mastery

    6. Level of growth and development

**B.** Diagnose

    1. Potential support systems or stressors

        a. Religious organizations or community support

        b. Family

        c. Socioeconomic resources

        d. Education

        e. Cultural norms

    2. Potential risk factors

        a. Family history of mental illness

        b. Medical history—imbalances can cause symptoms resembling emotional illness

    3. Satisfaction of basic human needs in order of importance (Maslow) (see Figure 1)

        a. Physical—oxygen, water, food, sleep, sex

        b. Safety—physical, security, order

        c. Love and belonging—affection, companionship, identification

        d. Esteem and recognition—status, success, prestige

        e. Self-actualization—self-fulfillment, creativity

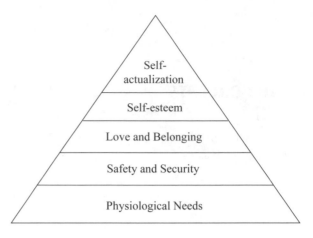

**Figure 1  Maslow Hierarchy of Needs**

4. Potential nursing diagnoses

    a. Social interaction, impaired

    b. Anxiety

    c. Individual coping, ineffective

    d. Self-esteem disturbance

| Table 1  THERAPEUTIC RESPONSES | | |
|---|---|---|
| **RESPONSE** | **GOAL/PURPOSE** | **EXAMPLES** |
| Using silence (nonverbal) | Allows client time to think and reflect; conveys acceptance<br><br>Allows client to take lead in conversation | Use proper nonverbal communication, remain seated, maintain eye contact, sit quietly and wait |
| Using general leads or broad openings | Encourages client to talk<br><br>Indicates interest in client<br><br>Allows client to choose subject<br><br>Sets tone for depressed client | "What would you like to talk about? Then what? Go on..."<br><br>"What brought you to the hospital?"<br><br>"What can you tell me about your family?" |
| Clarification | Encourages recall and details of particular experience<br><br>Encourages description of feelings<br><br>Seeks clarification, pinpoints specifics<br><br>Makes sure nurse understands client | "Give me an example."<br><br>"Tell me more."<br><br>"And how do you feel when you're angry?"<br><br>"Who are 'they'?" |
| Reflecting | Paraphrases what client says<br><br>Reflects what client says, especially feelings conveyed | "It sounds like you're feeling angry."<br><br>"In other words, you really felt abandoned."<br><br>"I hear you saying it was hard to come to the hospital." |

**C.** Plan/Implementation

1. Therapeutic communication—listening to and understanding client while promoting clarification and insight (see Tables 1, 2, and 3)

   a. Goals

   1) To understand client's message (verbal and nonverbal)

   2) To facilitate verbalization of feelings

   3) To communicate understanding and acceptance

   4) To identify problems, goals, and objectives

   b. Guidelines

   1) Nonverbal communication constitutes two-thirds of all communication and gives the most accurate reflection of attitude; key point of psychiatric interventions is say nothing, listen

      a) Physical appearance, body movement, posture, gesture, facial expression

      b) Contact—eye contact, physical distance maintained, ability to touch and be touched

   2) The person's feelings and what is verbalized may be incongruent, e.g., client denies feeling sad but appears morose

   3) Implied messages are as important to understand as overt behavior, e.g., continual interruptions may represent loneliness or fear

| Table 2  RESPONSES TO AVOID IN THERAPEUTIC COMMUNICATION | |
|---|---|
| **RESPONSE** | **EXAMPLES** |
| Closed-ended questions that can be answered by a "yes" or "no" or other monosyllabic responses; prevents sharing; puts pressure on client | "How many children do you have?"<br>"Who do you live with?"<br>"Are you feeling better today?" |
| Advice-giving—encourages dependency, may not be right for a particular client | "Why don't you... ?"<br>"You really should cut your hair and wear makeup." |
| Responding to questions that are related to one's qualifications or personal life in an embarrassed or concrete way; keep conversation client-centered | "Yes, I am highly qualified."<br>"You know nurses are not permitted to go out with their clients." |
| Arguing or responding in a hostile way | "If you do not take your medication, there is really nothing we can do to help you." |
| Reassuring—client benefits more by exploring own ideas and feelings | "You will start feeling much better any day."<br>"Don't worry, your doctors will do everything necessary for your care." |
| "Why" questions—can imply disapproval and client may become defensive | "Why didn't you take your medication?" |
| Judgmental responses—evaluate client from nurse's values | "You were wrong to do that. "<br>"Don't you think your being unfaithful has destroyed your marriage?" |

| Table 3 TREATMENT MODALITIES FOR MENTAL ILLNESS | | |
|---|---|---|
| TYPE | ASSUMPTIONS | FOCUS OF TREATMENT |
| Biological | Emotional problem is an illness<br><br>Cause may be inherited or chemical in origin | Medications, ECT |
| Psychoanalytical (individual) | Anxiety results when there is conflict between the id, ego, and superego parts of the personality<br><br>Defense mechanisms form to ward off anxiety | The therapist helps the client to become aware of unconscious thoughts and feelings; understand anxiety and defenses |
| Milieu therapy | Providing a therapeutic environment will help increase client's awareness of feelings, increase sense of responsibility, and help him/her return to his/her community | Positive physical and social environment<br><br>Structured groups and activities<br><br>One-on-one intervention<br><br>May be token program, open wards, self-medication |
| Group therapy | Relationship with others will be recreated among group members and can be worked through; members can also directly help one another | Members meet regularly with a leader to form a stable group<br><br>Members learn new ways to cope with stress and develop insight into their behavior with others |
| Family therapy | The problem is a family problem, not an individual one<br><br>Sick families lack a sense of "I" in each member<br><br>The tendency is to focus on sick member's behavior as the source of trouble<br><br>The sick member's symptom serves a function in the family | Therapist treats the whole family<br><br>Helps members to each develop their own sense of identity<br><br>Points out function of sick member to the rest of the family |
| Activity therapy | Important group interactions occur when group members work on a task together or share in recreation | Organized group activities created to promote socialization, increase self-esteem |
| Play therapy | Children express themselves more easily in play than in verbal communication<br><br>Choice of colors, toys, and interaction with toys is revealing as reflection of child's situation in the family | Provide materials and toys to facilitate interaction with child, observe play, and help child to resolve problems through play |
| Behavioral therapy and behavior modification | Psychological problems are the result of learning<br><br>Deficiencies can be corrected through learning | Operant conditioning—use of rewards to reinforce positive behavior; becomes more important than external reinforcement<br><br>Desensitization—used to treat phobias; client slowly adjusts to threatening objects |

**D.** Evaluation

1. Is there increased self-knowledge and insight?

2. Has client's self-esteem increased?

3. Has client's interpersonal relationships and work habits improved?

4. Does client demonstrate new and improved coping skills?

5. Does client have an enhanced enjoyment of life?

# ANXIETY

**A.** Assessment

1. Cardiovascular

   a. Increased pulse, blood pressure, and respiration

   b. Palpitations, chest discomfort/pain

   c. Perspiration, flushing, and heat sensations

   d. Cold hands and feet

   e. Headache

2. Gastrointestinal

   a. Nausea, vomiting, and diarrhea

   b. Belching, heartburn, cramps

3. Musculoskeletal

   a. Increased muscle tension and tendon reflexes

   b. Increased generalized fatigue

   c. Tremors, jerking of limbs

   d. Unsteady voice

4. Intellectual

   a. Poor comprehension—may be unable to follow directions

   b. Poor concentration, selective inattention

   c. Focus on detail

   d. Impaired problem solving

   e. Unable to communicate

      1) Thoughts may become random, distorted, disconnected with impaired logic

      2) Rapid, high-pitched speech

5. Social and emotional

   a. Feelings of helplessness and hopelessness

   b. Feelings of increased threat, dread, horror, anger, and rage

   c. Use of defense mechanisms and more primitive coping behaviors

      1) Shouting, arguing, hitting, kicking

      2) Crying, rocking, curling up, and withdrawal

**B.** Diagnose

1. Definition—feeling of dread or fear in the absence of an external threat or disproportionate to the nature of the threat

2. Predisposing conditions
   a. Prolonged unmet needs of dependency, security, love, and attention
   b. Stress threatening security or self-esteem
   c. Unacceptable thoughts or feelings surfacing to consciousness, e.g., rage, erotic impulses, flashbacks

3. Levels of anxiety
   a. Mild—high degree of alertness, mild uneasiness
   b. Moderate—heart pounds, skin cold and clammy, poor comprehension
   c. Severe—symptoms of moderate anxiety plus hallucinations, delusions
   d. Panic—symptoms of severe anxiety plus inability to see and hear, inability to function; may regress to less appropriate behaviors

4. Ego defense mechanisms—methods, usually unconscious, of managing anxiety by keeping it from awareness; may be adaptive or maladaptive
   a. Denial—failure to acknowledge an intolerable thought, feeling, experience, or reality, e.g., an alcoholic who says he does not have a drinking problem
   b. Displacement—redirection of emotions or feelings to a subject that is more acceptable or less threatening, e.g., yelling at the dog when angry with the boss
   c. Projection—attributing to others one's unacceptable feelings, impulses, thoughts, or wishes, e.g., saying someone you are angry with dislikes you
   d. Undoing—an attempt to erase an unacceptable act, thought, feeling, or desire, e.g., apologizing excessively; obsessive compulsive behavior
   e. Compensation—an attempt to overcome a real or imagined shortcoming, e.g., a small person excels in sports
   f. Substitution—replacing desired, impractical, or unobtainable object with one that is acceptable or attainable, e.g., marrying someone who looks like previous significant other

| Table 4  NURSING INTERVENTIONS IN ANXIETY | |
|---|---|
| **GENERAL PRINCIPLES** | **NURSING CONSIDERATIONS** |
| Assess level of anxiety | Use standardized tool for consistency |
| | Look at body language, speech patterns, facial expressions, defense mechanisms, and behavior used |
| | Distinguish levels of anxiety |
| Keep environmental stresses/ stimulation low when anxiety is high | First action |
| | Need to intervene with severe or panic level |
| | Brief orientation to unit or procedures |
| | Written information to read later, when anxiety is lower |
| | Pleasant, attractive, uncluttered environment |
| | Provide privacy if presence of other clients is overstimulating |
| | Provide physical care if necessary |
| | Avoid offering several alternatives or decisions when anxiety is high |

| Table 4  NURSING INTERVENTIONS IN ANXIETY *(CONTINUED)* | |
|---|---|
| **GENERAL PRINCIPLES** | **NURSING CONSIDERATIONS** |
| Assist client to cope with anxiety more effectively | Acknowledge anxious behavior; reflect and clarify |
| | Always remain with client who is moderately or severely anxious |
| | Assist client to clarify own thoughts and feelings |
| | Encourage measures to reduce anxiety, e.g., exercise, activities, talking with friends, hobbies |
| | Assist client to recognize his/her strengths and capabilities realistically |
| | Provide therapy to develop more effective coping and interpersonal skills, e.g., individual, group |
| | May need to administer antianxiety medications |
| Maintain accepting and helpful attitude toward client | Use an unhurried approach |
| | Acknowledge client's distress and concerns about problem |
| | Encourage clarification of feelings and thoughts |
| | Evaluate and manage own anxiety while working with client |
| | Recognize the value of defense mechanisms and realize that client is attempting to make the anxiety tolerable in the best way possible |
| | Acknowledge defense but provide reality, e.g., "You do not see that you have a problem with alcohol but your blood level is high." |
| | Do not attempt to remove a defense mechanism at any time |

  g. Introjection—a form of identification in which there is a symbolic taking into oneself the characteristics of another, e.g., blaming oneself when angry with another

  h. Repression—unacceptable thoughts kept from awareness, e.g., inability to remember a traumatic event

  i. Reaction formation—expressing attitude directly opposite to unconscious wish or fear, e.g., being excessively kind to a person who is actually disliked

  j. Regression—return to an earlier developmental phase in the face of stress, e.g., bedwetting, baby-talk

  k. Dissociation—detachment of painful emotional experience from consciousness, e.g., sleepwalking

  l. Suppression—consciously putting a disturbing thought or incident out of awareness, e.g., deciding not to deal with something unpleasant until next day

  m. Sublimation—substituting constructive activity for strong impulses that are not acceptable

 5. Potential nursing diagnoses

  a. Individual coping, ineffective

  b. Anxiety

| Table 5  ANXIETY DISORDERS | | |
| --- | --- | --- |
| TYPE | ASSESSMENT | NURSING CONSIDERATIONS |
| Phobia | Apprehension, anxiety, helplessness when confronted with phobic situation or feared object<br><br>Examples of specific fears:<br><br>Acrophobia—heights<br><br>Claustrophobia—closed areas<br><br>Agoraphobia—open spaces | Avoid confrontation and humiliation<br><br>Do not focus on getting client to stop being afraid<br><br>Systematic desensitization<br><br>Relaxation techniques<br><br>General anxiety measures (see Table 4)<br><br>May be managed with antidepressants |
| Obsessive-compulsive disorder (OCD) | Obsession—repetitive, uncontrollable thoughts<br><br>Compulsion—repetitive, uncontrollable acts, e.g., rituals, rigidity, inflexibility | Accept ritualistic behavior<br><br>Structure environment<br><br>Provide for physical needs<br><br>Offer alternative activities, especially ones using hands<br><br>Guide decisions, minimize choices<br><br>Encourage socialization<br><br>Group therapy<br><br>Managed with clomipramine, SSRIs<br><br>Stimulus–response prevention |
| Functional neurologic disorder | Physical symptoms with no organic basis, unconscious behavior—could include blindness, paralysis, convulsions without loss of consciousness, stocking and glove anesthesia, "la belle indifference" | Diagnostic evaluation<br><br>Discuss feelings rather than symptoms<br><br>Promote therapeutic relationship with client<br><br>Avoid secondary gain |

**C.** Plan/Implementation

1. Goals

   a. Decrease anxiety

   b. Recognize anxiety, e.g., restlessness

   c. Identify precipitants of anxiety

   d. Establish more effective coping mechanisms

   e. Increase self-esteem

2. Institute measures to decrease anxiety (see Table 4)

3. Provide nursing care for anxiety disorders (see Table 5)

4. Administer antianxiety medications as ordered

5. Use realistic, measurable objectives to evaluate effectiveness

6. Medications—benzodiazepines, buspirone, zolpidem, zaleplon, propranolol

**D.** Evaluation

1. Can client recognize symptoms of anxiety and anxiety-provoking situations?

2. Are client's daily activities less restricted as a result of decreased symptomatic behavior?

3. Are episodes of anxiety decreased as a result of new behaviors?

4. Is the client able to ask for help?

5. Is the client able to talk about feelings?

# ▶ SITUATIONAL CRISIS

**A.** Assessment (see Table 6)

1. Stages of crisis

   a. Denial

   b. Increased tension, anxiety

   c. Disorganization, inability to function

   d. Attempts to escape the problem, pretends problem doesn't exist, blames others

   e. Attempts to reorganize

   f. General reorganization

2. Precipitating factors

   a. Developmental stages

      1) Birth, adolescence

      2) Midlife, retirement

   b. Situational factors

      1) Natural disasters

      2) Financial loss

   c. Threats to self-concept

      1) Loss of job

      2) Failure at school

      3) Onset of serious illness

**B.** Diagnose (see Table 6)

1. Characteristics

   a. Temporary state of disequilibrium precipitated by an event

   b. Self-limiting—usually 4–6 weeks

   c. Crisis can promote growth and new behaviors

2. Potential nursing diagnoses

   a. Individual coping, ineffective

   b. Powerlessness

   c. Complicated grieving

**C.** Plan/Implementation (see Table 6)

1. Goal-directed, focus on the here and now

2. Focus on client's immediate problems

| | GRIEVING CLIENT | DYING CLIENT | RAPE TRAUMA |
|---|---|---|---|
| | Table 6 SITUATIONAL/TRAUMATIC CRISES | | |
| Assessment | Stages of grief<br>  a. Shock and disbelief<br>  b. Awareness of the pain of loss<br>  c. Restitution<br>Acute grief period 4–8 wks<br>Usual resolution within 1 yr<br>Long-term resolution over time | Stages of dying<br>  a. Denial<br>  b. Anger<br>  c. Bargaining<br>  d. Depression<br>  e. Acceptance | Stages of crisis<br>  a. Acute reaction lasts 3–4 wk<br>  b. Reorganization is long-term<br>Common responses to rape<br>  a. Self-blame, embarrassment<br>  b. Phobias, fear of violence, death, injury<br>  c. Anxiety, insomnia<br>  d. Wish to escape, move, relocate<br>  e. Psychosomatic disturbances |
| Diagnose | Potential problems<br>  a. Family of deceased or separated<br>    – Guilt<br>    – Anger<br>    – Anxiety<br>  b. Client undergoing surgery or loss of body part<br>    – Anger<br>    – Withdrawal<br>    – Guilt<br>    – Anxiety<br>    – Loss of role | Potential problems<br>  a. Avoidance behavior<br>  b. Inability to express feelings when in denial<br>  c. Feelings of guilt<br>  d. Withdrawal<br>  e. Lonely, frightened<br>  f. Anxiety of client and family | Potential problems<br>  a. Fears, panic reactions, generalized anxiety<br>  b. Guilt<br>  c. Inability to cope<br>Current crisis may reactivate old unresolved trauma<br>Follow emergency room protocol: may include clothing, hair samples, NPO<br>Be alert for potential internal injuries, e.g., hemorrhage |
| Intervention | Apply crisis theory<br>Focus on the here and now<br>Provide support to family when loved one dies<br>Provide family privacy<br>Encourage verbalization of feelings<br>Facilitate expressions of anger and rage<br>Emphasize strengths<br>Increase ability to cope<br>Support adjustment to illness, loss of body part | Apply crisis theory<br>Support staff having feelings of loss<br>Keep communication open<br>Allow expression of feelings<br>Focus on the here and now<br>Let client know he/she is not alone<br>Provide comforting environment<br>Be attentive to need for privacy<br>Provide physically comforting care, e.g., back rubs<br>Give sense of control and dignity<br>Respect client's wishes | Apply crisis theory<br>Focus on the here and now<br>Write out treatments and appointments for client, as anxiety causes forgetfulness<br>Record all information in chart<br>Give client referrals for legal assistance, supportive psychotherapy, and rape crisis center<br>Follow up regularly until client is improved |
| Evaluation | Does client express feelings of disbelief, anger, and hurt?<br>Are anxiety and helplessness gradually replaced by a sense of competence?<br>Does client work positively with physical and emotional challenges?<br>Have the bereaved resumed their social activities? | Has an open, honest approach to dying helped all concerned grieve together with less fear and avoidance?<br>Did the client feel less isolated and alone because of openness, daily support, and diligence in spite of prognosis?<br>Were the stages of dying accepted and understood by those around the client? | Is client at precrisis level of functioning?<br>Are there any unresolved emotional responses to the rape trauma experience?<br>Did the client utilize referral services? |

3. Explore nurse's and client's understanding of the problem
   a. Define the event (client may truly not know what has precipitated the crisis)
   b. Confirm nurse's perception by reviewing with client
   c. Identify the factors that are affecting problem-solving
   d. Evaluate how realistically client sees the problems or concerns
4. Help client become aware of feelings and validate them
   a. Acknowledge feelings, (e.g., "This must be a painful situation for you.")
   b. Avoid blaming client for problems and concerns
   c. Avoid blaming others, as this prevents insight
   d. Encourage ventilation with nurse to relieve anxiety
   e. Tell client he will feel better, but it may take 1 or 2 months
5. Develop a plan
   a. Encourage client to make as many arrangements as possible (avoid dependence)
   b. Write out information, since comprehension is impaired, (e.g., referrals)
   c. Maximize client's situational supports
6. Find new coping skills and manage feelings
   a. Focus on strengths and present coping skills
   b. Encourage client to form new coping skills and social outlets, reaching out to others
   c. Facilitate future planning
      1) Ask client "What would you like to do?", "Where would you like to go from here?"
      2) Give referrals when needed, family counseling, vocational counseling

**D.** Evaluation
1. Has stress decreased?
2. Is client at precrisis level of functioning?
3. Does client have a larger repertoire of adaptive coping mechanisms?
4. Is client able to identify cause and significance of disruption?
5. Faulty resolution of crisis may occur when individual's behavior compounds the crisis, e.g., breakup of the family in response to a child's problems
6. Faulty resolution may occur when conflicts re-emerge because new coping skills have not been learned to handle both the old and the new crises at the same time

# ACUTE/POST-TRAUMATIC STRESS DISORDER

**A.** Assessment
1. Develops after (immediate or delayed) a perceived traumatic event
2. Timing of exposure to a traumatic event (e.g., combat, rape, murder, fire, other catastrophe)

3. Response to trauma causes intense fear or horror

4. Recurrent or distressing recollections of event (images, thoughts, feelings)

5. Distressing dreams or nightmares

6. Acting or feeling like the trauma is recurring (flashbacks)

7. Hypervigilance and exaggerated startle response

8. Irritability or outbursts of anger

9. Avoidance or numbing

**B.** Diagnose

1. 9 or more symptoms from the 5 following categories: Intrusion, Negative mood, Dissociative symptoms, Avoidance and Arousal

2. Duration of symptoms is at least one month

3. Syndrome can emerge months to years after traumatizing event

4. Biological changes due to impact of stressor and excessive arousal of sympathetic nervous system

**C.** Plan/Implementation

1. Help client integrate the traumatic experience

   a. Encourage client to talk about painful stored memories

      1) Have client recall images of traumatic event with as much detail as possible (called flooding); will be done by staff with high level of expertise

      2) Use empathetic responses to the expressed distress (e.g., "That must have been hard for you.")

      3) Remain nonjudgmental about client's shameful or horrific experience

      4) Allow client to grieve over losses

   b. Assist client to challenge existing ideas about event and substitute more realistic thoughts and expectations

      1) Point out irrational thinking to the client

      2) Help client recognize the limits of his/her control over the stressful event

2. Assist client with emotional regulation

   a. Help client label his/her feelings and find ways to express them safely

   b. Teach stress management techniques

   c. Involve client in anger management program

      1) Recognize anger as normal feeling

      2) Teach time-out or other ways of walking away from problematic situations involving anger

      3) Teach nonintrusive communication techniques

         a) Speak in first person

         b) Move away from object (person) of anger

         c) Cognitive restructuring (e.g., using thoughts like "This person cannot make me lose control")

   d. Develop a schedule of regular physical activity with client (e.g., walking, running, weightlifting)

    e. Use empowering strategies such as keeping a journal of disturbed thoughts and feelings in response to flashbacks, nightmares, or other problems

    f. Teach methods to reduce sleep disturbances

       1) Regular bedtime

       2) Use bed for sleeping and lovemaking exclusively; no TV or reading

       3) Do not lie in bed sleepless for more than half an hour; get up and move around and then come back to bed

  3. Enhance the client's support systems

    a. Refer to self-help group

    b. Include family and friends in psycho-educational activities

    c. Explore opportunities for socialization

  4. Educate client regarding the recovery process

    a. Assess for and treat substance abuse

    b. Administer antidepressants

**D.** Evaluation

  1. Is client performing relaxation techniques?

  2. Is client participating in social situations with family and friends?

  3. Has the client's amount of undisturbed sleep increased?

# DEPRESSIVE DISORDERS

**A.** Assessment

  1. Possible changes in self-esteem/self-confidence

    a. Low self-esteem

    b. Self-deprecation

    c. Feelings of helplessness/hopelessness

    d. Obsessive thoughts and fears

    e. Ruminations and worries

    f. Sense of doom, failure

    g. Regressed behavior—immature, demanding, whines for help

  2. Possible changes in self-care

    a. Unkempt, depressed appearance

    b. Multiple reports of physical discomfort

    c. Prone to injury, accidents, and infections

    d. Lack of energy

    e. Changes in usual sleep pattern

       1) Insomnia

       2) Feels unrested after night's sleep

    f. Weight loss, poor appetite, weight gain

    g. Constipation

    h. Amenorrhea

    i. Lack of sexual desire

3. Possible changes in cognitive/mental functioning

   a. Decreased attention span and concentration

   b. Slowed speech, thought processes, and motor activity

   c. Impaired reality testing (psychotic depression)

   d. Withdrawn

   e. Ambivalent and indecisive behavior

   f. Agitation and psychomotor restlessness

   g. Suicidal ideation

4. Suicide/homicide potential

   a. Has plan and means to carry out plan; actual date established (anniversary, birthdate, etc.)

   b. Identifies others who may become involved in the plan

**B.** Diagnose

1. Psychodynamics

   a. Depression—response to real or imagined loss

   b. Anger and aggression toward self results from feelings of guilt about negative or ambivalent feelings

   c. Introjection occurs (incorporation of a loved or hated object or person into one's own ego)

2. Types of depression—determined by onset and severity of symptoms

   a. Major depression

   b. Dysthymic disorder

   c. Depression Not Otherwise Specified (NOS)

3. Potential nursing diagnoses

   a. Self-care deficit

   b. Self-esteem disturbance

   c. Individual coping, ineffective

   d. Social interaction, impaired

   e. Violence: self-directed, risk for

   f. Powerlessness

   g. Interrupted family processes

**C.** Plan/Implementation

1. Be alert for signs of self-destructive behavior

   a. Report all behavior changes to the team, especially increased energy or agitation

   b. In psychotic depression, observe for any signs that voices are commanding client to harm self (e.g., question the client, "What are the voices saying to you?")

2. Meet physical needs

   a. Promote nutrition

      1) Provide pleasant surroundings and companionship during meals

      2) Give more frequent feedings, favorite foods because of decreased appetite, high carbohydrate foods, nutritious drinks

   b. Medicate for constipation PRN and encourage fluids

    c. Promote rest

       1) Medicate for insomnia PRN and watch while client swallows pill

       2) Provide a quiet sleeping arrangement; stay with client if necessary; check on client periodically

    d. Promote self-care as much as possible

3. Decrease anxiety and indecisiveness

    a. Administer antianxiety medications

    b. Listen to and explore feelings

       1) Avoid pep talks; don't disagree with self-deprecation because client will not believe it

       2) Avoid excessive cheeriness and promise of a bright future

       3) Keep encouragement brief; client cannot incorporate compliments

    c. Avoid presenting choices, as client feels too inadequate to make decisions

    d. Be brief and simple, avoid long explanations because of decreased attentiveness and poor concentration

       1) Give a brief orientation

       2) Use simple language and repeat when necessary

    e. Provide a structured, written schedule

4. Support self-esteem

    a. Provide a warm, supportive environment

    b. Be client while client is slowed down and cannot think quickly; demonstrate acceptance to promote client self-acceptance

    c. Provide consistent daily care

       1) One-to-one nursing coverage is ideal

       2) Be consistent and predictable—keep all appointments and make few staff changes (they may be seen as a rejection)

       3) Anticipate staff feelings of ineffectiveness as part of caring for depressed clients and continue a positive approach

    d. Give tasks to relieve guilt and increase self-esteem

       1) Avoid tasks at which the client will fail

       2) Give simple tasks that require minimal concentration

5. Help decrease social withdrawal

    a. Pursue the client who avoids contact because of fear of rejection

       1) Sit with client during long quiet times

       2) Point out when client stays alone excessively

       3) Touch to promote acceptance (note: do *not* touch the psychotic client, as this may be seen as intrusion); be aware of cultural acceptance of touch

    b. Introduce to others when ready

    c. Use other treatment modalities

       1) Group therapy to communicate acceptance and increase self-esteem

       2) Family therapy to prevent scapegoating and explore feelings

       3) Individual therapy to decrease fear of rejection

6. Help with anger and fear of losing control

   a. Channel anger into acceptable outlets, e.g., sports, carpentry

   b. Encourage expressions of anger—small expressions initially; client may become suicidal if anger is expressed before able to do so safely

7. Encourage coping

   a. Imply confidence in client's capabilities

      1) Don't make client dependent

      2) Discuss excessive demands

   b. Give assistance when needed, but work together

8. Administer antidepressant medications

   a. Caution client about adverse effects and time required for medication to become effective

   b. Observe for suicidal tendency as depression lifts, usually at 10 days to 2 weeks after start of medication

9. Assist with electroconvulsive therapy (ECT)—convulsions similar to tonic-clonic seizures are induced to treat depression

   a. Preparation of client (see Table 7)

   b. Procedure

      1) Anesthetist gives short-acting intravenous anesthesia and muscle-relaxing drug, e.g., succinylcholine

      2) Keep oxygen and suction on hand

      3) Position client in supine position with arms at sides during convulsion

   c. Adverse effects and complications

      1) Confusion and memory loss for recent events

      2) Transient headaches, muscle soreness, drowsiness

   d. Post-procedure care

      1) Orient client; client will not remember treatment

      2) Take blood pressure, respirations

      3) Stay with client during period of confusion

      4) Signs of diminished depression appear after 6–12 treatments

10. Alternative/Complementary therapies

    a. Phototherapy

       1) First-line treatment for seasonal affective disorder (SAD)

       2) Minimum 2500 lux of light 30 minutes a day

    b. St. John's wort

       1) Herbal medication

       2) Do not take if major depression, pregnancy, or in children younger than 2 years

       3) Do not take with amphetamines, MAOIs, SSRIs, levodopa, and 5-HT

       4) Avoid tyramine-containing foods, excessive sunlight

       5) Contraindicated in pregnancy and during lactation

    c. Exercise

       1) 30 minutes at least 5 times per week

| Table 7  NURSING CONSIDERATIONS FOR ELECTROCONVULSIVE THERAPY (ECT) |
| --- |
| 1. Prepare client by explaining procedure and telling client about potential temporary memory loss and confusion |
| 2. Informed consent, physical exam, labwork |
| 3. NPO after midnight for an early morning procedure |
| 4. Have client void before ECT |
| 5. Remove dentures, glasses, jewelry |
| 6. Give muscle relaxant and short-acting barbiturate anesthetic to induce brief general anesthesia |
| 7. Given Atropine 30 min before treatment to decrease secretions |
| 8. Have oxygen and suction on hand |
| 9. After procedure, take vital signs, orient client |
| 10. Observe client's reaction and stay with him |
| 11. Observe for sudden improvement and indications of suicidal threats after ECT treatment |

**D.** Evaluation

1. Does the client feel accepted?
2. Is client able to express views without fear of retaliation?
3. Is client able to cope in spite of negative self-view?
4. Are new behaviors evident?
5. Is there an increase in self-esteem?
6. Have potential problems associated with ECT treatments been prevented?

# SUICIDE

**A.** Assessment

1. Symptoms same as in depression
2. Behavioral clues of impending suicide (see Table 8)

| Table 8  BEHAVIORAL CLUES OF IMPENDING SUICIDE |
| --- |
| 1. Any sudden change in client's behavior |
| 2. Becomes energetic after period of severe depression |
| 3. Improved mood 10–14 days after taking antidepressant may mean suicidal plans made |
| 4. Finalizes business or personal affairs |
| 5. Gives away valuable possessions or pets |
| 6. Withdraws from social activities and plans |
| 7. Appears emotionally upset |
| 8. Presence of weapons, razors, pills (means) |
| 9. Has death plan |
| 10. Leaves a note |
| 11. Makes direct or indirect statements (e.g., "I may not be around then.") |

**B.** Diagnose

1. Predisposing factors

   a. Male over 50 years old

   b. Age range 15–19 years old

   c. Clients with poor social attachments; isolation

   d. Clients with previous attempts

   e. Clients with personality disorders

   f. Psychotic individuals with command hallucinations to kill themselves

   g. Overwhelming precipitating events

      1) Terminal or degenerative disease, e.g., cancer, kidney disease

      2) Death or loss of loved one through divorce or separation

      3) Financial loss, job loss, school failure

2. Understanding self-destructive behavior

   a. Attempts to cope fail, leaving the client with low self-esteem and feelings of hopelessness and helplessness

   b. Client feels guilty and overwhelmed in response to precipitating event and may see suicide as relief

   c. Ambivalence about suicide may lead to cry for help or attention

   d. Aggression and rage turned toward self (introjection) or into an attempt to punish others

   e. Most common as depression is lifting

      1) 10–14 days after antidepressant medication begun

      2) New signs of energy or improvement

3. Potential nursing diagnoses

   a. Violence: self-directed, risk for

   b. Risk for suicide

**C.** Plan/Implementation

1. Implement measures for depression

2. Be alert for signs of self-destructive behavior (suicide/homicide assessment) (see Table 8)

3. Remove all potentially dangerous items

4. Provide strong therapeutic relationship to increase client self-worth

   a. Establish authoritative and credible matter-of-fact manner to increase confidence

   b. Place on one-to-one observation and stay with client to help control self-destructive impulses

   c. Let the client know that the nurse will assist in seeking every possible resource to ease troubles

   d. Relieve client's feelings of embarrassment, e.g., "I see you are upset. You are wise to seek help."

5. Discuss all behavior with team members
   a. Note indirect clues as cry for help, e.g., presence of pills
   b. Observe for sudden increased energy level as indication of possible impending suicide attempt
   c. Note increase in anxiety, insomnia
6. Give client a sense of control other than through suicide
   a. Assist with problem-solving and decision-making
   b. Develop and use a suicidal contract
   c. Avoid excess support, as this encourages dependency and eventual feelings of abandonment
7. Provide family therapy where indicated
   a. Avoid taking client's side as family is not direct cause of suicidal urge
   b. Look for scapegoating or acting out of family destructiveness
8. Intervene quickly and calmly during actual attempts
   a. Remove the harmful objects from the client (e.g., razor, ropes) without inflicting harm on self and/or client
   b. Stay by the client's side and reassure the client that you are there to help
   c. Avoid judgmental remarks or interpretations, e.g., "Why did you do this?"
9. Contract with client
   a. "No suicide," "no harm," or "no self-injury" contracts are made between psychiatric health care professionals and clients who are admitted to a psychiatric unit with depression and/or suicide ideation or self-injurious acting-out
   b. Clients agree to contact staff if they have an impulse to be self-destructive
   c. Client is asked to abide by the signed contract
   d. Client is periodically reminded of the contract
   e. Limit-setting lets client know that self-destructive acts are not permitted
   f. Staff members do anything within power to prevent client self-destruction

D. Evaluation
   1. Has self-inflicted injury been avoided?
   2. Have self-destructive tendencies decreased?

# SITUATIONAL ROLE CHANGES

A. Assessment
   1. Death of spouse/significant other
   2. Divorce/separation
   3. Personal illness/injury
   4. Marriage
   5. Job loss
   6. Retirement

7. Pregnancy/new baby

8. Job change/relocation

9. "Empty nest"/child leaving home

10. Graduation from high school/college/tech school

11. Spouse beginning or ending full-time employment

**B.** Diagnose

1. Coping strategies—specific skills or actions consciously used to manage effects of stress

2. Reactions to change can be positive, negative, neutral

3. Reactions determined by

   a. Client's learned behaviors to cope with change

   b. Significance of event

   c. Client's physical and emotional state at time of change

   d. Client's control over change

   e. Number of changes over lifetime

   f. Positive or negative resolution to previous changes

**C.** Plan/Implementation

1. Place changes in time line; rank from least to most severe

2. Discuss resolution to previous changes; determine what was helpful in the past

3. Use learned coping strategies

   a. Establish and maintain a routine

   b. Limit or avoid changes

   c. Designate time to focus on adaptation to change

   d. Use time efficiently

   e. Change environment to reduce stress

   f. Regular exercise

   g. Humor

   h. Good nutrition

   i. Rest/sleep

   j. Relaxation techniques

   k. Utilize support system

   l. Work on increasing self-esteem

   m. Pray/meditate

   n. Some cultures use rituals

**D.** Evaluation

1. Has client coped with role change effectively?

2. Have new coping strategies been learned?

# STRESS

**A.** Assessment

1. Headache

2. Sleep problems, fatigue, irritability

3. Restlessness, rapid speech and movement

4. GI upset

5. Tachycardia, palpitations, hot flashes

6. Frequent urination, dry mouth

7. Crying

8. Use of alcohol or drugs

9. Withdrawal from friends and family

**B.** Diagnose

1. Stressors

   a. Family

   b. Job

   c. Environment

   d. Lifestyle

   e. Body image changes

   f. Situational role change

**C.** Plan/Implementation

1. Determine what client sees as stressful

2. Identify how stressful these items are to client

3. Determine how client has coped with stressors in the past

4. Provide support—encourage family visits, listen to client's concerns, involve pastoral and social services

5. Provide control—maintain client independence; allow client to make choice concerning timing and sequencing of activities

6. Provide information—answer questions, provide information about procedures, events

7. Recognize client feelings—acknowledge anger

8. Support client's own coping strategies

9. Interventions

   a. Biofeedback—use of electrical instruments to identify somatic changes (e.g., muscle activity, skin surface activity)

   b. Progressive muscle relaxation—tensing then relaxing major muscle groups in sequential steps

   c. Meditation—conscious removal of thoughts filling mind, or filling mind with only one thought

   d. Guided imagery—thinking about peaceful scene involving total relaxation

**D.** Evaluation

1. Is client able to identify stressors?

2. Has client used appropriate coping strategies to deal with stress?

## ▶ BURNOUT

**A.** Assessment

1. Emotional or physical exhaustion
2. Depersonalization, inability to become involved with others
3. Decreased effectiveness
4. Stress-related behavior becomes persistent problem
5. Usual coping strategies ineffective
6. Person feels overwhelmed, helpless
7. At risk for physical or mental illness

**B.** Diagnose

1. Process in which the person disengages from work in response to excessive or prolonged stress
2. Sources of stress may be in environment, self, or in interactions
3. Determined by the person's ability to adapt

**C.** Plan/Implementation

1. Provide social support
2. Begin counseling
3. Utilize employee assistance programs

**D.** Evaluation

1. Is the person demonstrating increased ability to handle day-to-day issues?
2. Is the person re-engaging with persons and the environment?

## ▶ SUPPORT SYSTEMS

**A.** Assessment

1. Family—role of each member (authority figure, peacemaker)
2. Spouse/significant other
3. Friends
4. Coworkers
5. Groups, clubs, organizations
6. Pet or inanimate object (security blanket)

**B.** Diagnose

1. Culture and socioeconomic status influence support systems
2. Social network defines client's self-image and sense of belonging

**C.** Plan/Implementation

1. Assess developmental stage (adolescence, early adulthood, late adulthood) to plan utilization of support systems
2. Enlist support persons who have been effective in previous, similar, stressful situations

**D.** Evaluation

1. Has client used support system effectively to deal with change/stressors?
2. Has client maintained a positive self-image?

# SUDDEN INFANT DEATH SYNDROME (SIDS)

**A.** Assessment

   1. Occurs during first year of life, peaks at two to four months

   2. Occurs between midnight and 9 AM

   3. Increased incidence in winter, peaks in January

**B.** Diagnose

   1. Thought to be brainstem abnormality in neurologic regulation of cardiorespiratory control

   2. Third leading cause of death in children from one week to one year of age

   3. Higher incidence of SIDS

      a. Infants with documented apparent life-threatening events (ALTEs)

      b. Siblings of infant with SIDS

      c. Preterm infants who have pathological apnea

      d. Preterm infants, especially with low birth weight

      e. African decent infants

      f. Multiple births

      g. Infants of addicted mothers

      h. Infants who sleep on abdomen

**C.** Plan/Implementation

   1. Home apnea monitor

   2. Place all healthy infants in supine position to sleep

   3. Support parents, family

   4. Referral to Sudden Infant Death Foundation

**D.** Evaluation

   1. Has the infant reached one year of age without incident?

   2. Does the family cope with the loss of their child?

# PSYCHOSOCIAL ADAPTATION

## COUNSELING TECHNIQUES

**A.** Techniques

1. Confrontation—call attention to discrepancies between what the client says (verbal communication) and what the client does (nonverbal communication)

2. Contracting—establish expected behaviors and goals as well as rules and consequences with client that structure nurse/client interactions

3. Focusing—create order, guidelines, and priorities by assisting the client in identifying problems and establishing their relative importance

4. Interpreting—explore with the client possible explanations for feelings

5. Making connections—help the client connect seemingly isolated phenomena by filling in blanks and establishing relationships

6. Modeling—exemplify through actions and verbalizations the behaviors that the client is working toward

7. Providing feedback—give the client constructive information about how the nurse perceives and hears him/her

8. Reframing—look at the issue through a different perspective by using different examples and descriptions

9. Stating observations—describe what is happening in the nurse/client relationship that might have relevance to other things happening in client's life

10. Summarizing—give feedback to client about the general substance of the interview or interpersonal exchange before ending

**B.** Implementation

1. These techniques aid the nurse in promoting change and growth in clients

2. Nurse should demonstrate behaviors of

    a. Congruence or genuineness

    b. Empathy (the ability to see things from the client's perspective)

    c. Positive regard or respect

## RELIGIOUS AND SPIRITUAL INFLUENCES ON HEALTH

*Not all members of a religion or spiritual path will choose to follow all the traditions.*

**A.** Assessment

1. Wears amulets, charms, clothing, jewelry

2. Carries a talisman (object that has supernatural powers)

3. Makes noise to scare off evil entities

4. Drinks/ingests potions, tonics, or foods

5. Performs or refrains from performing activity at certain times

6. Method of disposal of objects that come into contact with person

7. Performs religious ceremony (e.g., baptism)

8. Avoids doing actions that are harmful to others

9. Avoids behaviors that are not socially sanctioned

10. Emotional investment related to aspects of mind or soul, distinct from body

11. Reflects individual values, beliefs, ethical choices

**B.** Diagnose

1. Religion provides explanation for illness and misfortune

2. Religion can prevent illness and misfortune

3. Client's spiritual beliefs affect all aspects of life, relationships, sense of right and wrong

4. Religion is the basis for health care behaviors and decisions

5. Religion is a basic human need that must be satisfied for individual's well-being

**C.** Plan/Implementation

1. Seek assistance from persons knowledgeable about client's religious practices

2. Be aware of your own spirituality and beliefs

3. Be respectful and sensitive to client's religious beliefs

4. Do not impose your own religious beliefs on client or believe that if client finds religion, this will spiritually enrich client

5. Observe client's verbal and nonverbal behavior; may indicate spiritual distress

6. Examples

   a. Roman Catholic—sacrament of the sick

   b. Buddhist—believe in healing through faith

   c. Christian Science—practice spiritual healing

   d. Church of Jesus Christ of Latter Day Saints—anoint with oil, pray, lay on hands

   e. Hinduism—faith healing

   f. Islam—use herbal remedies and faith healing

   g. Jehovah's Witness—mental and spiritual healing

   h. Judaism—prays for sick

   i. Mennonite—prayer and anointing with oil

   j. Seventh-Day Adventist—anointing with oil and prayer

   k. Unitarian/Universalist—use of science to facilitate healing

**D.** Evaluation

1. Have client's spiritual beliefs been preserved and accommodated?

2. Has client felt free to express spiritual beliefs?

# BIPOLAR DISORDER

**A.** Assessment

1. Disoriented, incoherent

2. Delusions of grandeur, cheerful, euphoria

3. Flight of ideas, easily distractable

4. Inappropriate dress; excessive makeup and jewelry

5. Lacks inhibitions

6. Uses sarcastic, profane, and abusive language

7. Quick-tempered, agitated

8. Talks excessively, jokes, dances, sings; hyperactive

9. Can't stop moving to eat, easily stimulated by environment

10. Decreased appetite

11. Weight loss

12. Insomnia

13. Regressed behavior

14. Sexually indiscreet, hypersexual

**B.** Diagnose

1. Classifications

   a. Bipolar I: at least one manic episode and one depressive episode or mixed episodes

   b. Bipolar II: lifetime experience of at least one episode of major depression or at leas hone hypomanic episode

   c. Cyclothymic disorder: adults at least 2 years (children 1 year) of both hypomanic and depression periods without fulfilling criteria for and episode of mania, hypo mania or major depression

2. Psychodynamics

   a. Bipolar disorder is an affective disorder

   b. Reality contact is less disturbed than in schizophrenia

   c. Elation or grandiosity can be a defense against underlying depression or feelings of low self-esteem

   d. Testing, manipulative behavior results from poor self-esteem

3. Predisposing factors

   a. Hereditary—genetic

   b. Biochemical

4. Problems

   a. Easily stimulated by surroundings

      1) Hyperactive and anxious

      2) Unable to meet physical needs

   b. Aggressive and hostile due to poor self-esteem

    c. Denial

    d. Testing, manipulative, demanding, disruptive, intrusive behavior

    e. Superficial social relationships

  5. Potential nursing diagnoses

    a. Disturbed thought processes

    b. Self-care deficit

    c. Violence: self-directed or directed at others, risk for

    d. Social interaction, impaired

    e. Interrupted family processes

    f. Self-esteem disturbance

**C.** Plan/Implementation

  1. Institute measures to deal with hyperactivity/agitation

    a. Simplify the environment and decrease environmental stimuli

      1) Assign to a single room away from activity

      2) Keep noise level low

      3) Soft lighting

    b. Limit people

      1) Anticipate situations that will provoke or overstimulate client, e.g., activities, competitive situations

      2) Remove to quiet areas

    c. Distract and redirect energy

      1) Choose activities for brief attention span, e.g., chores, walks

      2) Choose physical activities using large movements until acute mania subsides, e.g., dance

      3) Provide writing materials for busy work when acute mania subsides, e.g., political suggestions, plans

  2. Provide external controls

    a. Assign one staff person to provide controls

    b. Do not encourage client when telling jokes or performing, e.g., avoid laughing

    c. Accompany client to room when hyperactivity is escalating

    d. Guard vigilantly against suicide as elation subsides and mood evens out

  3. Institute measures to deal with manipulativeness

    a. Set limits, e.g., limit phone calls when excessive

      1) Set firm consistent times for meetings—client often late and unaware of time

      2) Refuse unreasonable demands, e.g., asks for date with the nurse

      3) Explain restrictions on behavior and reasons so client does not feel rejected

    b. Communicate using a firm, unambivalent consistent approach

      1) Use staff consistency in enforcing rules

      2) Remain nonjudgmental, e.g., when client disrobes say, "I cannot allow you to undress here."

3) Never threaten or make comparisons to others, as it increases hostility and poor coping

c. Avoid long, complicated discussions

1) Use short sentences with specific straightforward responses

2) Avoid giving advice when solicited, e.g., "I notice you want me to take responsibility for your life."

4. Meet physical needs

a. Meet nutritional needs

1) Encourage fluids; offer water every hour because client will not take the time to drink

2) Give high-calorie finger foods and drinks to be carried while moving, e.g., cupcakes, sandwiches

3) Serve meals on tray in client's room when too stimulated

b. Encourage rest

1) Sedate PRN

2) Encourage short naps

c. Supervise bathing routines when client plays with water or is too distracted to clean self

5. Administer medications—mood-stabilizing medications (lithium, valproic acid, carbamazepine)

6. Help decrease denial and increase client's awareness of feelings

a. Encourage expression of real feelings through reflecting

b. Help client acknowledge the need for help when denying it, e.g., "You say you don't need love, but most people need love. It's okay to feel that."

c. Function as a role model for client by communicating feelings openly

d. Help client recognize demanding behavior, e.g., "You seem to want others to notice you."

e. Encourage client to recognize needs of others

f. Have client verbalize needs directly, e.g., wishes for attention

**D.** Evaluation

1. Are client's needs met?

2. Does client observe feelings of others as well as self?

3. Does client realistically see areas of competence?

4. Is client able to limit destructive and/or impulsive behavior?

5. Is client able to work cooperatively and honestly with staff?

# SCHIZOPHRENIA

**A.** Assessment

1. Withdrawal from relationships and from the world

a. Neologisms, rhyming so that others can't understand communication

b. Concrete thinking

c. Social ineptitude—aloof and fails to encourage interpersonal relationships, ambivalence toward others

2. Inappropriate or flat affect

3. Hypochondriasis and/or depersonalization

4. Suspiciousness—sees world as a hostile, threatening place

5. Poor reality testing—delusions, hallucinations, neurologisms

    a. Hallucinations—false sensory perceptions in the absence of an external stimulus; may be auditory, visual, olfactory, or tactile

    b. Delusions—persistent false beliefs, e.g., client may believe stomach is missing

        1) Grandeur—belief that one is special, e.g., a monarch

        2) Persecutory—belief that one is victim of a plot

        3) Ideas of reference—belief that environmental events are directed toward the self, e.g., client sees people talking and believes they are discussing the client

6. Loose associations

7. Short attention span, decreased ability to comprehend stimuli

8. Regression

9. Inability to meet basic survival needs

    a. Unable to feed oneself (poor nutritional habits)

    b. Poor personal hygiene

    c. Inappropriate dress for the weather/environment

**B.** Diagnose

1. Specific types of schizophrenia (see Table 1)

| Table 1  SCHIZOPHRENIA | |
|---|---|
| **SUB-TYPE** | **PRESENTING SYMPTOMS** |
| Disorganized | Inappropriate behavior such as silly laughing and regression, transient hallucinations; disorganized behavior and speech |
| Catatonic | Sudden-onset mutism, bizarre mannerisms, remains in stereotyped position with waxy flexibility; may have dangerous periods of agitation and explosive behavior |
| Paranoid | Late onset in life, characterized by suspicion and ideas of persecution and delusions and hallucinations; may be angry or hostile |
| Undifferentiated | General symptoms of schizophrenia<br><br>Symptoms of more than one type of schizophrenia |
| Residual | No longer exhibits overt psychotic symptoms; difficulty with social relationships |

2. Potential nursing diagnoses

    a. Disturbed thought processes

    b. Disturbed sensory perception

    c. Self-care deficit

    d. Violence: directed toward self or others, risk for

    e. Social isolation

**C.** Plan/Implementation (see Tables 2 and 3)

   1.  Maintain client safety

      a.  Protect from altered thought processes

         1)  Decrease sensory stimuli, remove from areas of tension

         2)  Validate reality

         3)  Recognize that client is experiencing hallucination

         4)  Do not argue with client

         5)  Respond to feeling or tone of hallucination or delusion

         6)  Be alert to hallucinations that command client to harm self or others

| Table 2  NURSING CARE OF CLIENT WHO ACTS WITHDRAWN | |
|---|---|
| **PROBLEM** | **INTERVENTIONS** |
| Lack of trust and feeling of safety and security | Keep interactions brief, especially orientation |
| | Structure environment |
| | Be consistent and reliable; notify client of anticipated schedule changes |
| | Decrease physical contact |
| | Eye contact during greeting |
| | Maintain attentiveness with head slightly leaning toward client and nonintrusive attitude |
| | Allow physical distance |
| | Accept client's behavior, e.g., silence; maintain matter-of-fact attitude toward behavior |
| Hallucinations | Maintain accepting attitude |
| | Do not argue with client about reality of hallucinations |
| | Comment on feeling, tone of hallucination, e.g., "That must be frightening to you." |
| | Encourage diversional activities, e.g., playing cards, especially activities in which client can gain a sense of mastery, e.g., artwork |
| | Encourage discussions of reality-based interests |
| Lack of attention to personal needs, e.g., nutrition, hygiene | Assess adequacy of hydration, nutrition |
| | Structure routine for bathing, mealtime |
| | Offer encouragement or assistance if necessary, e.g., sit with client or feed client if appropriate |
| | Decrease environmental stimuli at mealtime, e.g., suggest early dinner before dining room crowds |
| | Positioning and skin care for catatonic client |

      b.  Protect from erratic and inappropriate behavior

         1)  Communicate in calm, authoritative tone

         2)  Address client by name

         3)  Observe client for early signs of escalating behavior

      c.  Administer antipsychotic medications

2. Meet physical needs of severely regressed clients

   a. Poor basic hygiene—may have to be washed initially

   b. Poor nutritional habits—may have to be fed

      1) Ask client to pick up fork; if unable to make decision, then feeding is necessary

      2) When ready, encourage client to eat in dining room with others

   c. May be nonverbal initially; do not force into groups

3. Establish a therapeutic relationship—engage in individual therapy

   a. Institute measures to promote trust

      1) Same as general withdrawal from reality (see Table 2)

      2) Be consistent and reliable in keeping all scheduled appointments

      3) Avoid direct questions (client may feel threatened)

      4) Accept client's indifference, e.g., failure to smile or greet nurse, and avoidance behavior, e.g., hostility or sarcasm

      5) Discuss all staff changes, especially vacations and absences

   b. Encourage client's affect by verbalizing what you observe, e.g., "You seem to think that I don't want to stay." Use client's name in a calm, authoritative tone

   c. Tolerate silences—may have to sit through long silences with client who is too anxious to speak (catatonic)

   d. Accept regression as a normal part of treatment when new stresses are encountered

      1) With delusional regression, respond to associated feeling, not to the delusion, e.g., client claims he has no heart, nursing response: "You must feel empty."

      2) Help pinpoint source of regression, e.g., anxiety about discharge

| Table 3  NURSING CARE OF A CLIENT WHO ACTS SUSPICIOUS | |
|---|---|
| **PROBLEM** | **INTERVENTIONS** |
| Mistrust and feeling of rejection | Keep appointments with clients |
| | Clear, consistent communication |
| | Allow client physical distance and keep door open when interviewing |
| | Genuineness and honesty in interactions |
| | Recognize testing behavior and show persistence of interest in client |
| Delusions | Allow client to verbalize the delusion in a limited way |
| | Do not argue with client or try to convince that delusions are not real |
| | Point out feeling tone of delusion |
| | Provide activities to divert attention from delusions |
| | Solitary activities best at first and then may progress to noncompetitive games or activities |
| | Do not reinforce delusions by validating them |
| | Focus on potential real concerns of client |

4. Engage in family therapy—especially when client is returning to family; understand the problem involves the family; establish a "family client" in need of support

5. Engage in socialization or activity group therapy according to client's ability

    a. Accept nonverbal behavior initially

    b. If client cannot tolerate group, do not force or embarrass

    c. Act as a social role model for client

6. Provide simple activities or tasks to promote positive self-esteem and success

    a. Finger painting and clay are good choices for regressed catatonic client

    b. Encourage attendance at occupational, vocational, and art therapy sessions

    c. Avoid competitive situations with paranoid—solitary activities are better

**D.** Evaluation

1. Is there increased self-knowledge and insight?

2. Has client's self-esteem increased?

3. Have client's interpersonal relationships and work habits improved?

4. Does the client have new and improved coping skills?

5. Does the client have enhanced enjoyment of life?

# PERSONALITY DISORDERS

**A.** Assessment (see Table 4)

**B.** Diagnose (see Table 4)

**C.** Plan/Implementation (see Table 4)

**D.** Evaluation

1. Is the client able to verbally communicate and express feelings with staff members?

2. Is the client able to establish a trusting relationship with key therapeutic staff members?

| Table 4 PERSONALITY DISORDERS | | | |
|---|---|---|---|
| **TYPES** | **ASSESSMENT** | **DIAGNOSE** | **NURSING CONSIDERATIONS** |
| Paranoid | Suspiciousness<br><br>Hypersensitive, humorless, serious<br><br>Ideas of reference<br><br>Cold, blunted affect<br><br>Quick response with anger or rage | Interprets actions of others as personal threat<br><br>Uses projection: externalizes own feelings by projecting own desires and traits to others<br><br>Holds grudges | Establish trust<br><br>Be honest and nonintrusive<br><br>Low doses of phenothiazines to manage anxiety<br><br>Structured social situations<br><br>Be calm, authoritative, matter of fact |
| Schizoid | Shy and introverted; rarely has close friends<br><br>Little verbal interaction<br><br>Cold and detached | Uses intellectualization: describes emotional experiences in matter-of-fact way<br><br>Daydreaming may be more gratifying than real life | Same as paranoid |
| Schizotypal | Seems eccentric and odd<br><br>Sensitive to rejection and anger<br><br>Vague, stereotypical, overelaborate speech<br><br>Suspicious of others<br><br>Blunted or inappropriate affect | Similar to schizophrenia, fewer and milder psychotic episodes<br><br>Problems in thinking, perceiving, communicating<br><br>Common disorder among biological relatives of schizophrenics | Same as paranoid<br><br>Low-dose neuroleptics may decrease transient psychotic symptoms |
| Antisocial | Disregard for rights of others<br><br>Lying, cheating, stealing, promiscuous behaviors<br><br>Appears charming and intellectual, smooth-talking<br><br>Unlawful, aggressive and reckless behaviors<br><br>Lack of guilt, remorse, and conscience<br><br>Immature and irresponsible, especially in finances | Genetic predisposition<br><br>Correlates with substance abuse and dependency problems<br><br>More common in males<br><br>Rationalizes and denies own behaviors | Firm limit-setting<br><br>Confront behaviors consistently<br><br>Enforce consequences<br><br>Group therapy |
| Borderline | Seeks brief and intense relationships<br><br>Blames others for own problems<br><br>Depression, intense anger, labile mood, posttraumatic symptoms<br><br>Temper tantrums, physical fights<br><br>Impulsiveness, manipulative<br><br>Repetitive self-destructiveness, self-mutilation, suicidal<br><br>Overspending, promiscuity, compulsive overeating | 75% are women and have been sexually abused<br><br>Problems with identity, self image, thinking, and mood<br><br>Uses splitting to avoid pain and to protect self<br><br>Projective identification used to protect the self<br><br>Biological, environmental, and stress-related factors, including traumatic home environment<br><br>Abnormalities in serotonin systems<br><br>Suicidal behaviors occur when blocked, frustrated, or stressed | Help person identify and verbalize feelings and control negative behaviors<br><br>Use empathy<br><br>Behavioral contracts to decrease self-mutilation<br><br>Journal-writing<br><br>Consistent limit-setting needed<br><br>Supportive confrontation<br><br>Enforce unit rules<br><br>Psychopharmacology used sparingly for anxiety, psychotic states, suicidal ideation, mood swings<br><br>Group therapy |

| Table 4  PERSONALITY DISORDERS *(CONTINUED)* | | | |
| --- | --- | --- | --- |
| TYPES | ASSESSMENT | DIAGNOSE | NURSING CONSIDERATIONS |
| Narcissistic | Arrogant, appears indifferent to criticism while hiding anger, rage, or emptiness<br><br>Lacks ability to feel or demonstrate empathy<br><br>Sense of entitlement<br><br>Use others to meet their own needs<br><br>Displays grandiosity | Views others as superior or inferior to self<br><br>Shallow relationships with others<br><br>Feelings of others not understood or considered<br><br>Uses rationalization to blame others<br><br>Expects special treatment<br><br>Needs to be admired | Mirror what person sounds like, especially contradictions<br><br>Supportive confrontation to increase sense of self-responsibility<br><br>Limit-setting and consistency<br><br>Focus on the here and now<br><br>Teach that mistakes are acceptable, imperfections do not decrease worth |
| Histrionic | Draws attention to self, thrives on being the center of attention<br><br>Silly, colorful, frivolous, seductive<br><br>Hurried, restless<br><br>Temper tantrums and outbursts of anger<br><br>Overreacts<br><br>Dissociation used to avoid feelings<br><br>Somatic reports to avoid responsibility and support dependency | Cannot deal with feelings<br><br>Shallow, rapidly shifting emotions<br><br>Easily influenced by others | Positive reinforcement for unselfish or other-centered behaviors<br><br>Help clarify feelings and facilitate appropriate expression |
| Dependent | Dependent on others for everyday decisions<br><br>Passive<br><br>Problem initiating projects or working independently<br><br>Anxious or helpless when alone<br><br>Preoccupied with fear of being alone to care for self | Fears loss of support and approval<br><br>Lacks self-confidence | Emphasize decision-making to increase self-responsibility<br><br>Teach assertiveness<br><br>Assist to clarify feelings, needs, and desires |
| Anxious–Avoidant | Timid, socially uncomfortable, withdrawn<br><br>Hypersensitive to criticism<br><br>Avoids situations where rejection is a possibility<br><br>Lacks self-confidence | Fears intimate relationships due to fear of ridicule<br><br>Believes self to be socially inept, unappealing, or inferior | Gradually confront fears<br><br>Discuss feelings before and after accomplishing a goal<br><br>Teach assertiveness<br><br>Increase exposure to small groups |
| Obsessive-compulsive | Sets high personal standards for self and others<br><br>Preoccupied with rules, lists, organization, details<br><br>Overconscientious and inflexible<br><br>Rigid and stubborn<br><br>Cold affect, may speak in monotone<br><br>Indecisive until all facts accumulated<br><br>Repetitive thoughts and actions | Difficulty expressing warmth<br><br>Rigid and controlling with others<br><br>Perfectionism interferes with task fulfillment | Explore feelings<br><br>Help with decision-making<br><br>Confront procrastination and intellectualization<br><br>Teach that mistakes are acceptable |

▶ ## MANIPULATIVE BEHAVIOR

**A.** Assessment

1. Makes unreasonable requests for time, attention, and favors

2. Divides staff against each other—attempts to undermine nurse's role

3. Intimidates others

   a. Uses others' faults to own advantage, e.g., naiveté

   b. Makes others feel guilty

4. Uses seductive and disingenuous approach

   a. Makes personal approach with staff, e.g., acts more like friend than client

   b. Frequently lies and rationalizes

   c. Takes advantage of others for own gain

5. Frequently lies and rationalizes

6. May malinger or behave in helpless manner, e.g., feigns illness to avoid task

**B.** Diagnose

1. Predisposing conditions

   a. Bipolar disorder

   b. Substance abuse, alcoholism

   c. Antisocial disorders

   d. Adolescent adjustment reactions

2. Potential nursing diagnoses

   a. Impaired social interaction

   b. Social isolation

   c. Violence: self-directed, risk for

   d. Violence: directed at others, risk for

**C.** Plan/Implementation

1. Goals

   a. Help client set limits on his behavior

   b. Help client learn to see the consequences of his behavior

   c. Help family members understand and deal with client

   d. Promote staff cooperation and consistency in caring for client

2. Use consistent undivided staff approach

   a. Clearly define expectations for client

   b. Adhere to hospital regulations

   c. Hold frequent staff conferences to avoid conflicts and increase staff communication

3. Set limits

   a. Do not allow behaviors that endanger or interfere with the rights or safety of others

   b. Carry out limit-setting, avoid threats and promises

   c. Give alternatives when possible

   d. Remain nonjudgmental

e. Avoid arguing or allowing client to rationalize behavior

f. Be brief in discussions

4. Be constantly alert for potential manipulation

a. Favors, compliments

b. Attempts to be personal

c. Malingering, helplessness

5. Be alert for signs of destructive behavior

a. Suicide

b. Homicide

D. Evaluation

1. Is staff cohesiveness maintained?

2. Do the client's actions interfere with the rights of others?

3. Does client set limits on own behavior?

4. Has self-injury been avoided?

5. Has injury to others been avoided?

# VIOLENT/AGGRESSIVE BEHAVIOR

A. Assessment

1. Physical or verbal abuse of staff and/or other clients

2. Overt anger and passive-aggressive behaviors

3. Increased anxiety levels, physical signs of tension, change in pace or intensity of speech

B. Diagnose

1. Assault cycle—triggering phase, escalation phase, verbal aggression phase, crisis phase, recovery phase, postcrisis depression phase

2. Caused by intrapersonal, familial, interpersonal, and environmental stressors

C. Plan/Implementation (see Table 5)

1. Consider the source and the target of the anger

2. Consider displacement of anger in delusions and hallucinations

3. Assessanger at a safe distance, remain calm, assure that safe escape route is present

4. Allow client to ventilate without violence, assist client to identify source of anger

5. Ask client to assess his/her own potential for violence

6. Contract with the client to use nonviolent methods to control anger

7. Be prepared to use seclusion if escalation with potential for violence exists

| Table 5 NURSING CARE OF A CLIENT WHO ACTS VIOLENT ||
| PROBLEM | INTERVENTIONS |
| --- | --- |
| Increased agitation/anxiety | Recognize signs of impending violence, e.g., increased motor activity, pacing, or sudden stop—"calm before the storm" |
| | Identify self, speak calmly but firmly, and in normal tone of voice |
| | Help verbalize feelings |
| | Use nonthreatening body language, e.g., arms to side, palm outward, keep distance, avoid blocking exit, avoid body contact |
| | Avoid disagreeing with client or threatening client |
| | Decrease stimuli—remove threatening objects or people |
| Violence | Intercede early |
| | Continue nonthreatening behavior |
| | If client needs to be restrained to protect self or others, get help (at least four people) |
| | Move in organized, calm manner, stating that nurse wants to help and that you will not permit client to harm self or others |
| | Use restraints correctly, e.g., never tie to bedside rail, check circulation frequently |

D. Evaluation

  1. Client approaches staff and discusses angry impulses without acting-out

  2. Violent episodes are minor and controlled

  3. Unit safety is maintained

## ▶ EATING DISORDERS

A. Assessment (see Table 6)

B. Diagnose (see Table 6)

C. Plan/Implementation (see Table 6)

D. Evaluation

  1. Have client's physical needs been met?

  2. Does client have insight into eating disorder?

| Table 6  EATING DISORDERS | | |
| --- | --- | --- |
| **DISORDER** | **ASSESSMENT/DIAGNOSE** | **NURSING CONSIDERATIONS** |
| Anorexia nervosa | Most common in females 12–18 years old<br><br>Characterized by fear of obesity, dramatic weight loss, distorted body image, very structured food intake<br><br>Anemia, amenorrhea<br><br>Cathartics, diuretics, and enemas may be used for purging<br><br>Excessive exercise<br><br>Induced vomiting used for purging<br><br>May have cardiotoxicity secondary to use of ipecac<br><br>May have electrolyte imbalance | Monitor clinical status (e.g., weight, intake, vital signs)<br><br>Monitor hydration and electrolytes, especially potassium<br><br>Behavior modification may help in acute phase<br><br>Family therapy<br><br>Support efforts to take responsibility for self<br><br>Explore issues regarding sexuality<br><br>Contract with client |
| Bulimia | Characterized by all of the characteristics of anorexia and binge eating (eating increased amounts of high calorie food in a short period of time)<br><br>May be of normal weight or overweight<br><br>Tooth erosion and decay<br><br>GI bleeding (upper and/or lower)<br><br>May use vomiting, laxatives, enemas, diuretics or weight-loss medications | May be managed with antidepressants (e.g., SSRI)<br><br>Nutritional assessment and counseling |

# CHEMICAL DEPENDENCY *Section 4*

## ACUTE ALCOHOL INTOXICATION

**A.** Assessment (see Table 1)

**B.** Diagnose (see Table 1)

**C.** Plan/Implementation (see Table 1)

| Table 1  POTENTIAL ALCOHOL INTOXICATION | | |
| --- | --- | --- |
| ASSESSMENT | POTENTIAL NURSING DIAGNOSIS | NURSING CONSIDERATIONS |
| Drowsiness | Acute confusion | Monitor vital signs frequently |
| Slurred speech | Risk for injury | Allow client to "sleep it off" |
| Tremors | Risk for ineffective breathing pattern | Protect airway from aspiration |
| Impaired thinking/memory loss | Risk for aspiration | Assess need for IV glucose |
| Nystagmus | | Assess for injuries |
| Diminished reflexes | | Assess for signs of withdrawal and chronic alcohol dependence |
| Nausea/vomiting | | |
| Possible hypoglycemia | | Counsel about alcohol use |
| Increased respiration | | Potential problems of alcohol poisoning and CNS depression |
| Belligerence/grandiosity | | |
| Loss of inhibitions | | |
| Depression | | |

**D.** Evaluation

   1. Short-term: Has injury been prevented and CNS status maintained?

   2. Long-term: Have chronic intoxication and CNS damage been avoided?

## ALCOHOL WITHDRAWAL

**A.** Assessment (see Table 2)

**B.** Diagnose—potential nursing diagnoses

   1. Anxiety

   2. Injury, risk for

   3. Self-care deficit

   4. Thought process, altered

C. Plan/Implementation (see Table 2)

| Table 2   ALCOHOL WITHDRAWAL | | |
|---|---|---|
| WITHDRAWAL | DELIRIUM TREMENS | NURSING CONSIDERATIONS |
| Tremors | Tremors | Administer (benzodiazepines, chlordiazepoxide, diazepam) sedation as needed |
| Easily startled | Anxiety | |
| Insomnia | Panic | |
| Anxiety | Disorientation, confusion | Monitor vital signs, particularly pulse, BP, temperature |
| Anorexia | Hallucination | Seizure precautions |
| Alcoholic hallucinations | Vomiting | Provide quiet, well-lit environment |
| | Diarrhea | |
| | Paranoia | Orient client frequently |
| | Delusional symptoms | Don't leave hallucinating, confused client alone |
| | Ideas of reference | |
| | Suicide attempts | Administer anticonvulsants as needed |
| | Grand mal convulsions (especially first 48 hours after drinking stopped) | Administer thiamine IV or IM as needed |
| | Potential coma/death | Administer IV glucose as needed 10% mortality rate |

D. Evaluation

1. Has injury been avoided (head trauma, aspiration of vomitus)?

2. Have normal serum glucose levels been maintained?

3. Have nutritional deficiencies been treated?

# ▶ CHRONIC ALCOHOL DEPENDENCE

A. Assessment

1. Persistent incapacitation

2. Cyclic drinking or "binges"

3. Daily drinking with increase in amount

4. Potential chronic central nervous system disorder (see Table 3)

5. Sexual relationships may be disturbed

| Table 3 CHRONIC CNS DISORDERS ASSOCIATED WITH ALCOHOLISM | | | |
|---|---|---|---|
| | ALCOHOLIC CHRONIC BRAIN SYNDROME (DEMENTIA) | WERNICKE'S SYNDROME | KORSAKOFF'S PSYCHOSIS |
| Symptoms | Fatigue, anxiety, personality changes, depression, confusion<br><br>Loss of memory of recent events<br><br>Can progress to dependent, bedridden state | Confusion, diplopia, nystagmus, ataxia<br><br>Disorientation, apathy | Memory disturbance with confabulation, loss of memory of recent events, learning problem<br><br>Possible problem with taste and smell, loss of reality testing |
| Nursing considerations | Balanced diet, abstinence from alcohol | IV or IM thiamine, abstinence from alcohol | Balanced diet, thiamine, abstinence from alcohol |

6. Others in family may take over alcoholic's role, e.g., children may take parent's role, resulting in loss of childhood opportunities

7. Children often feel shame and embarrassment

8. High percentage of children develop problems with alcohol themselves

9. Incidence of family violence is increased with alcohol use

B. Diagnose—potential nursing diagnoses

1. Imbalanced nutrition: less than body requirements

2. Chronic low self esteem

3. Social isolation

4. Dysfunctional family processes: alcoholism

C. Plan/Implementation

1. Counseling the alcoholic

   a. Identify problems related to drinking—in family relationships, work, medical, and other areas of life

   b. Help client to see/admit problem

      1) Confront denial with slow persistence

      2) Maintain relationship with client

2. Establish control of problem drinking

   a. Concrete support to identify potentially troublesome settings that trigger drinking behavior

   b. Alcoholics Anonymous—valuable mutual support group

      1) Peers share experiences

      2) Learn to substitute contact with humans for alcohol

      3) Stresses living in the present; stop drinking one day at a time

      c. Disulfiram—drug used to maintain sobriety; based on behavioral therapy

        1) Once sufficient blood level is reached, disulfiram interacts with alcohol to provide severe reaction

        2) Symptoms of disulfiram-alcohol reaction include flushing, coughing, difficulty breathing, nausea, vomiting, pallor, anxiety

        3) Contraindicated in diabetes mellitus, atherosclerotic heart disease, cirrhosis, kidney disease, psychosis

  3. Counsel the spouse of the alcoholic

      a. Initial goal is to help spouse focus on self

      b. Explore life problems from spouse's point of view

      c. Spouse can attempt to help alcoholic once strong enough

      d. Al-Anon: self-help group of spouses and relatives

        1) Learn "loving detachment" from alcoholic

        2) Goal is to try to make one's own life better and not to blame the alcoholic

        3) Provides safe, helpful environment

  4. Counsel children of alcoholic parents

      a. Overcome denial of problem

      b. Establish trusting relationship

      c. Work with parents as well; avoid negative reactions to parents

      d. Referral to Alateen: organization for teenagers of alcoholic parent; self-help, similar to Al-Anon

**D.** Evaluation

  1. Has client abstained from alcohol?

  2. Has client maintained nutritional status?

  3. Has client reduced his/her social isolation?

## ▶ NONALCOHOL SUBSTANCE ABUSE

**A.** Assessment (see Table 4)

**B.** Diagnose

  1. Drug addiction—a physiological and psychological dependence; increasing doses needed to maintain "high" (tolerance)

  2. Substance abusers have a low frustration tolerance and need for immediate gratification to escape anxiety

  3. Addiction may result from prolonged use of medication for physical or psychological pain

  4. Becomes a problem with some nurses

  5. Potential nursing diagnoses

      a. Ineffective denial/coping

      b. Dysfunctional family processes: substance abuse

      c. Violence: directed toward self or others, risk for

**C.** Plan/Implementation

1. Observe for signs and symptoms of intoxication or drug use

   a. Examine skin for cuts, needle-marks, abscesses, or bruises

   b. Recognize symptoms of individual drug overdose

   1) Hypotension, decreased respirations with narcotics and sedatives

   2) Agitation with amphetamines and hallucinogens

2. Treat symptoms of overdose

   a. Maintain respiration—airway when needed

   b. IV therapy as necessary

   c. Administer naloxone

   1) Antagonist to narcotics—induces withdrawal, stimulates respirations

   2) Short-acting—symptoms of respiratory depression may return; additional doses may be necessary

   d. Gastric lavage for overdose of sedatives taken orally

   e. Dialysis to eliminate barbiturates from system

3. Observe for signs of withdrawal, e.g., sweating, agitation, panic, hallucinations

   a. Identify drug type

   b. Seizure precautions

   c. Keep airway on hand

   d. Detoxify gradually

   1) Methadone or naltrexone used for long-term maintenance and acute withdrawal (narcotic)

   2) Decreasing doses of drug substitute

4. Treat panic from acute withdrawal and/or marked depression

   a. Hospitalize temporarily for psychotic response

   b. Decrease stimuli, provide calm environment

   c. Protect client from self-destructive behavior

| Table 4   NONALCOHOL SUBSTANCE ABUSE | | | |
|---|---|---|---|
| **MEDICATION/DRUG** | **SYMPTOMS OF ABUSE** | **SYMPTOMS OF WITHDRAWAL** | **NURSING CONSIDERATIONS** |
| **Barbiturates** (downers, barbs, pink ladies, rainbows, yellow jackets)<br>Phenobarbital<br>Nembutal | Respiratory depression<br>Decreased BP and pulse<br>Coma, ataxia, seizures<br>Increasing nystagmus<br>Poor muscle coordination<br>Decreased mental alertness | Anxiety, insomnia<br>Tremors, delirium<br>Convulsions | Maintain airway (intubate, suction)<br>Check LOC and vital signs<br>Start IV with large-gauge needle<br>Give sodium bicarbonate to promote excretion<br>Give activated charcoal, use gastric lavage<br>Hemodialysis |
| **Narcotics**<br>Morphine<br>Heroin (horse, junk, smack)<br>Codeine<br>Dilaudid<br>Methadone–for detoxification and maintenance | Marked respiratory depression<br>Hyperpyrexia<br>Seizures, ventricular dysrhythmias<br>Euphoria, then anxiety, sadness, insomnia, sexual indifference<br>Overdose–severe respiratory depression, pinpoint pupils, coma<br>Stupor leading to coma | Watery eyes, runny nose<br>Loss of appetite<br>Irritability, tremors, panic<br>Cramps, nausea<br>Chills and sweating<br>Elevated BP<br>Hallucinations, delusions | Maintain airway (intubate, suction)<br>Control seizures<br>Check LOC and vital signs<br>Start IV, may be given bolus of glucose<br>Have lidocaine and defibrillator available<br>Treat for hyperthermia<br>Give naloxone to reverse respiratory depression<br>Hemodialysis |
| **Stimulants** (uppers, pep pills, speed, crystal meth)<br>Cocaine (crack)<br>Amphetamine<br>Benzedrine<br>Dexedrine | Tachycardia, increased BP, tachypnea, anxiety<br>Irritability, insomnia, agitation<br>Seizures, coma, hyperpyrexia, euphoria<br>Nausea, vomiting<br>Hyperactivity, rapid speech<br>Hallucinations<br>Nasal septum perforation (cocaine) | Apathy<br>Long periods of sleep<br>Irritability<br>Depression, disorientation | Maintain airway (intubate, suction)<br>Start IV<br>Use cardiac monitoring<br>Check LOC and vital signs<br>Give activated charcoal, use gastric lavage<br>Monitor for suicidal ideation<br>Keep in calm, quiet environment |
| **Cannabis derivatives** (pot, weed, grass, reefer, joint, mary jane)<br>Marijuana<br>Hashish | Fatigue<br>Paranoia, psychosis<br>Euphoria, relaxed inhibitions<br>Increased appetite<br>Disoriented behavior | Insomnia, hyperactivity<br>Decreased appetite | Most effects disappear in 5–8 hr as drug wears off<br>May cause psychosis |
| **Hallucinogens**<br>LSD (acid)<br>PCP (angel dust, rocket fuel)<br>Mescaline (buttons, cactus) | Nystagmus, marked confusion, hyperactivity<br>Incoherence, hallucinations, distorted body image<br>Delirium, mania, self-injury<br>Hypertension, hyperthermia<br>Flashbacks, convulsions, coma | None | Maintain airway (intubate, suction)<br>Control seizures<br>Check LOC and vital signs<br>Reduce sensory stimuli<br>Small doses of diazepam<br>Check for trauma, protect from self-injury |

      d. Stay with client to reduce anxiety, panic, and confusion

      e. Assure client that hallucinations are from drugs and will subside

      f. Administer medications as indicated to manage symptoms of withdrawal and panic

      g. Monitor vital signs

  5. Promote physical health

      a. Identify physical health needs

         1) Rest

         2) Nutrition

         3) Shelter

      b. Complete physical work-up

         1) Heroin addicts need to be followed for liver and cardiac complications, sexually transmitted disease, AIDS

         2) Dental care

  6. Administer methadone for maintenance when indicated

      a. Synthetic narcotic—blocks euphoric effects of narcotics

      b. Eliminates craving and withdrawal symptoms

      c. Daily urine collected to monitor for other drug abuse while on methadone

  7. Implement measures for antisocial personality disorders/manipulative behaviors

      a. Structured, nonpermissive environment

      b. Milieu therapy—peer pressure to conform

      c. Set limits but remain nonjudgmental

      d. Refer to drug-free programs (Synanon, Phoenix House, Odyssey House) for confrontation and support to remain drug-free

  8. Treat underlying emotional problems

      a. Individual therapy—give support and acceptance

      b. Group therapy—to learn new ways of interacting

      c. Promote use of self-help groups

  9. Assist client with rehabilitation, e.g., work programs, vocational counseling, family counseling, completion of schooling

**D.** Evaluation

  1. Is client able to abstain from drugs or to be maintained on methadone?

  2. Has client's independent functioning resumed?

  3. Is treatment ongoing for underlying emotional problems?

  4. Has client stopped committing crime to support drug habit (if this was an issue)?

# CHILD ABUSE

**A.** Assessment

1. Inconsistency between type/location of injury (bruises, burns, fractures, especially chip/spiral) with the history of the incident(s)

2. Unexplained physical or thermal injuries

3. Withdraws or is fearful of parents

4. Sexual abuse—genital lacerations, sexually transmitted diseases

5. Emotional neglect, failure to thrive, disturbed sleep, change in behavior at school

**B.** Diagnose

1. Intentional physical, emotional, and/or sexual misuse/trauma or intentional omission of basic needs (neglect); usually related to diminished/limited ability of parent(s) to cope with, provide for, and/or relate to child

2. Those at high risk include children born prematurely and/or of low birth weight, children under 3 years of age, and children with physical and/or mental disabilities

3. Potential nursing diagnoses

   a. Risk for trauma

   b. Interrupted family processes/impaired parenting

**C.** Plan/Implementation

1. Provide for physical needs first

2. Mandatory reporting of identified/suspected cases to appropriate agency

3. Nonjudgmental treatment of parents; encourage expression of feelings

4. Provide role modeling and encourage parents to be involved in care

5. Teach growth and development concepts, especially safety, discipline, age-appropriate activities, and human nutrition

6. Provide emotional support for child; play therapy (dolls, drawings, making up stories) may be more appropriate way for child to express feelings

7. Initiate protective placement and/or appropriate referrals for long-term follow-up

8. Documentation should reflect only what nurse saw or was told, not nurse's interpretation or opinion

**D.** Evaluation

1. Have parents learned appropriate ways to discipline their child?

2. Have the child's physical needs been met?

## ▶ ELDER ABUSE

**A.** Assessment

1. Battering, fractures, bruises
2. Over/undermedicated
3. Absence of needed dentures, glasses
4. Poor nutritional status, dehydration
5. Physical evidence of sexual abuse
6. Urine burns, excoriated skin, pressure ulcers
7. Fear, apprehension, withdrawal from usual activities

**B.** Diagnose

1. Elderly with chronic illness and depletion of financial resources who are dependent on children and grandchildren
2. Population trends of today contribute to decline in amount of people available to care for elderly
3. Potential nursing diagnoses
   a. Compromised family coping
   b. Risk for trauma
   c. Nutrition, less than body requirements

**C.** Plan/Implementation

1. Provide for safety
2. Provide for physical needs first
3. Report to appropriate agencies (state laws vary)
4. Initiate protective placement and/or appropriate referrals
5. Consider client's rights of self-determination

**D.** Evaluation

1. Is client safe?
2. Have the client's physical needs been met?
3. Have appropriate referrals been made?

## ▶ SEXUAL ABUSE

**A.** Assessment

1. Sexually abused child
   a. Disturbed growth and development
   b. Child becomes protective (parent) of others
   c. Uses defense mechanisms (e.g., denial, dissociation)
   d. Sleep and eating disturbances
   e. Depression and aggression, emotional deadening, amnesia
   f. Poor impulse control
   g. Somatic symptoms (e.g., chronic pain, GI disturbances)
   h. Truancy and running away
   i. Self-destructiveness

2. Adult victims of childhood sexual abuse

    a. Response is similar to delayed postraumatic stress disorder (PTSD)

    b. Nightmares

    c. Unwanted, intrusive memories

    d. Kinesthetic sensations

    e. Flashbacks

    f. Relationship issues, fears of intimacy and abandonment

3. Sexually abused adult

    a. Uses defense mechanisms (e.g., denial, dissociation)

    b. Relationship issues, abusive relationships, fears of intimacy and abandonment

    c. Somatic reports

    d. Homicidal thoughts, violence

    e. Hypervigilance, panic attacks, phobias/agoraphobia

    f. Suicidal thoughts/attempts

    g. Self-mutilation

    h. Compulsive eating/dieting, binging/purging

**B.** Diagnose

1. Victims from every sociocultural, ethnic, and economic group

2. Within the family (incest) and outside the family

3. Usually involves younger, weaker victim

4. Victim is usually urged and coerced, manipulated through fear

5. Difficult to expose abuse; common for child not to be believed

**C.** Plan/Implementation

1. Establish trusting relationship

2. Use empathy, active support, compassion, warmth

3. Nonjudgmental approach

4. Group and individual therapy; appropriate referrals

5. Medications as needed (e.g., antianxiety)

6. Report to appropriate agencies

**D.** Evaluation

1. Does the client demonstrate improved self-esteem?

2. Does the client express self-acceptance and forgiveness of self?

3. Does the client demonstrate adaptive coping to stress?

4. Is the client able to sustain capacity for intimate relationships?

5. Does the client demonstrate reduced anxiety and fear?

# ▶ DOMESTIC VIOLENCE

**A.** Assessment

1. Frequent visits to health care provider's office or emergency room for unexplained trauma

2. Client being cued, silenced, or threatened by an accompanying family member

3. Evidence of multiple old injuries, scars, healed fractures seen on x-ray

4. Fearful, evasive, or inconsistent replies and nonverbal behaviors such as flinching when approached or touched

**B.** Diagnose

1. Family violence is usually accompanied by brainwashing (e.g., victims blame themselves, feel unworthy, and fear that they won't be believed)

2. Long-term results of family violence are depression, suicidal ideation, low self-esteem, and impaired relationships outside the family

3. Women and children are the most common victims, but others include adolescents, men, and parents

**C.** Plan/Implementation

1. Provide privacy during initial interview to insure that the perpetrator of violence does not remain with client; make a statement, e.g., "This part of the exam is always done in private."

2. Carefully document all injuries using body maps or photographs (with consent)

3. Determine the safety of client by specific questions about weapons in the home, substance abuse, extreme jealousy

4. Develop with client a safety or escape plan

5. Refer the client to community resources such as shelters, hotlines, and support groups

**D.** Evaluation

1. Is the client focusing on own needs?

2. Is the client developing concrete plan for shelter or legal aid?

# INDEX